Edward Warren

Also by Win Blevins

Fitz

Rendezvous: Volume One

Rendezvous: Volume Two

Rendezvous: Volume Three

Rivers of the West

The Yellowstone

The High Missouri

The Snake River

The Powder River

Classics of the Fur Trade

The River of the West, The Mountain Years: The Adventures of Joe Meek Part One

The River of the West, The Oregon Years: The Adventures of Joe Meek Part Two

The Long Rifle

The Personal Narrative of James O. Pattie

Edward Warren

Mountain Men Eyewitness Accounts

Classics of the Fur Trade
Book 5

Win Blevins

Edward Warren: Mountain Men Eyewitness Accounts
Paperback Edition
Copyright © 2024 (As Revised) Win Blevins

Wolfpack Publishing
1707 E. Diana Street
Tampa, FL 33610

wolfpackpublishing.com

All rights reserved. No part of this publication may be reproduced in whole or in part, or stored in a retrieval system, transmitted in any form by any means, electronic, mechanical, photocopying, recording, or otherwise, or used to train generative artificial intelligence (AI) technologies, without the express written permission of the Publisher and the Author, other than for brief quotes and reviews.

Paperback ISBN 978-1-63977-556-9
eBook ISBN 978-1-63977-555-2

Contents

Preface xi
Biographical Sketch xv
Introduction xix

Part One

Chapter 1 3
Chapter 2 8
Chapter 3 16
Chapter 4 26
Chapter 5 37

Part Two

Chapter 6 45
Chapter 7 50
Chapter 8 57
Chapter 9 63
Chapter 10 71
Chapter 11 77
Chapter 12 84
Chapter 13 89
Chapter 14 94
Chapter 15 103
Chapter 16 108
Chapter 17 111
Chapter 18 118
Chapter 19 125
Chapter 20 129
Chapter 21 136
Chapter 22 142
Chapter 23 148
Chapter 24 153
Chapter 25 161
Chapter 26 167
Chapter 27 170
Chapter 28 177
Chapter 29 185
Chapter 30 190
Chapter 31 195
Chapter 32 200
Chapter 33 204
Chapter 34 209
Chapter 35 213

Chapter 36	217
Chapter 37	220
Chapter 38	224
Chapter 39	227
Chapter 40	232
Chapter 41	237
Chapter 42	241
Chapter 43	245
Chapter 44	251
Chapter 45	256

Part Three

Chapter 46	263
Chapter 47	268
Chapter 48	273
Chapter 49	280
Chapter 50	285
Chapter 51	291
Chapter 52	295
Chapter 53	299
Chapter 54	304
Chapter 55	310
Chapter 56	315
Chapter 57	319
Chapter 58	325
Chapter 59	332
Chapter 60	339
Chapter 61	344

Part Four

Chapter 62	351
Chapter 63	354
Chapter 64	358
Chapter 65	366
Chapter 66	371
Chapter 67	378
Chapter 68	385
Chapter 69	390
Chapter 70	396
Chapter 71	401
Chapter 72	406
Chapter 73	411
Chapter 74	416
Chapter 75	420
Chapter 76	426
Chapter 77	432
Chapter 78	440

Chapter 79	445
Chapter 80	451
Chapter 81	457
Chapter 82	464
Chapter 83	468
Chapter 84	473
Chapter 85	476
Chapter 86	483
Chapter 87	491
Chapter 88	499
Chapter 89	505
A Look at Book Six:	509
About the Author	511
Notes	513
Bibliography	525

It is somewhere written,

"There is something not unsimilar in point of freedom, between the chimneysweep who clings to the walls of his prison, and the sailor who clings to the mast."

Preface

Edward Warren is an intriguing, frustrating, romantic, odd, and fascinating tale of the Rocky Mountain fur trade.

Originally, its author, William Drummond Stewart, Lord of Grandtully and Baronet of Murthly, offered *Edward Warren* as a novel. The British adventurer wanted to publish some record of his experiences in the American West when that region was truly wild. But he was reluctant to put it forward as his own—so he wrote this book—and another, *Altowan*—and offered it as a novel by an anonymous traveler. Then he appended a curious notice calling the book a *fictitious Autobiography* (sic).

Modern scholarship can show that it was indeed autobiography. That is its value to modern readers—the reason for bringing *Edward Warren* back into print after 130 years of obscurity. Stewart's hero is a psychological self-portrait. The pictures he paints of his companions, the mountain men, and their trade, the fabled beaver trade of the Rocky Mountains, are drawn from life.

So *Edward Warren* is an invaluable eye-witness account. We need not hold it against Stewart's book that it masquerades as a novel—so does another of the classic mountain-man books, George Frederick Ruxton's *Life in the Far West*.

Stewart had the advantage of a more intimate acquaintance than Ruxton. He went west more than a decade earlier, in 1833, while the beaver trade was still in its heyday. He traveled with the fur men, fought Indians with them, took Indian women as they did, and endured the hardships of the camp and trail alongside them. He attended every rendezvous from 1833 to 1838, bridging from the high years to the low ones, when the beaver market plummeted. After going home to assume his titles and estates, Stewart came back to the West for a farewell journey in 1843. He found the mountain men poor, dispersed, giving up—so Stewart provided the means for one more rendezvous, a last hurrah. In that very summer, emblematically, came the first great wave of emigration that would destroy the nomadic life Stewart treasured.

During his decade in and out of the mountains, Stewart came to know the men of the trade. He hobnobbed in St. Louis with movers and shakers, like Kenneth McKenzie, the King of the Missouri, and William Clark, of Lewis & Clark repute. Stewart traveled to the mountains first with Robert Campbell. He rode with Tom Fitzpatrick, Jim Bridger, Bill Williams, and Antoine Clement, and knew Kit Carson, Lucien Fontenelle, Doc Newell, Joe Meek, Andrew Drips, and Joe Walker: a who's who of the mountain trade. On at least one occasion, Stewart was left in command of a brigade. He brought a suit of armor to one rendezvous as a gift for Bridger, Stewart's idea of a suitable gesture.

Stewart's Western experiences made a profound impression on him. He had a romantic spirit—we can see how fervently he loved the free mountain life in the opening pages *of Edward Warren*, and how he mourned the passing of the Indians and the great herds of buffalo. His trapping years forged strong bonds. Campbell and Bill Sublette, owners of Sublette & Campbell, rendezvous suppliers, became lifelong friends, and later shipped bison and antelope to Murthly for Stewart's pleasure. McKenzie felt close enough to Stewart to write to Scotland for the loan of thirty thousand dollars. Clement lived with Stewart at Murthly Castle.

So his sketches of these men and their lives have the weight of authority. Bill Williams in blackened buckskins with his red hair sticking out of his black beaver hat. Joe Meek was always the cut-up, making his horse curvet to show off. Fontenelle the drinker. Carson the protector. Clement the hunter without peer.

Much of the material in *Edward Warren* confirms, expands, and illuminates other reports. We get an account of how the Crows stole Fitzpatrick's horses and furs while Stewart was in charge, and another view of the rendezvous of 1833, at Horse Creek. A full version of the rabid wolf that wrought havoc at rendezvous and killed George Holmes is here, with Stewart's unfortunate part in it.

Such confirmation is worth having: Joe Meek, for instance, tells about that wolf in *The River of the West*: Captain Stewart warned Joe about sleeping it off outside, because *the wolf might easily have bitten him*. Joe's view was the impact would have been on the wolf, not the inebriated man:

"It would have killed him, sure, if it hadn't *cured* him!" Joe describes himself as answering, and Stewart's independent telling of the same tale increases our confidence in Joe's veracity.

When Stewart reports a known event, he jibes well enough with other first-hand accounts to be believed. Sometimes, there are no other accounts. So why should we not regard Stewart as reliable in those instances?

The other truth of *Edward Warren*, the hero, as a self-portrait of the author, is also clear. In their exterior circumstances the two shared some things and not others: Stewart was a mature man of thirty-eight when he went to the mountains, Ned Warren half that. Stewart felt pinched for money—Warren was pinched. Warren had no family or station in life, and Stewart felt alienated from his. Both the author and his creation came from the same British upper class and education and ways of looking at the world.

There is a rough but unmistakable similarity in the fates of the author and hero: Both are called away from their American adventures, back to England. The fictional Warren discovers the secret of his birth and comes into marriage and fortune. Stewart inherited his brother's titles, estates, and income.

It would be fascinating to know how many of the adventures Stewart attributes to Warren actually took place. Some are unmistakable—made clear by Stewart's own footnotes, or by modern scholarship. The two stayed in the same hotels, took the same route to the same rendezvous, even camped in the same spots. Many of Warren's companions go under their actual historical names, and were Stewart's companions as well.

We do not know, though, whether some of the key characters and episodes were wholly invented, modeled on some reality, or even simply transcribed from life. Was there an original of the lovely Rose? Her father, Diego? For Bernard, Warren's nemesis? The old mystic? The Shoshone lad Hi-Hi? Were the author's attitudes as romantic, even naively romantic, as his hero's?

Probably, we will never know most of the answers. That does not diminish the value of what Stewart has given us—one of the few accounts of the mountain-man's life from a participant.

Biographical Sketch

William George Drummond Stewart was born on December 26, 1795, at his ancestral estate, Murthly Castle, in Perthshire, Scotland. His parents, Sir George and Catherine, had five children, of which William was the second eldest son. His father died in 1827, and Catherine followed in 1833, when William was thirty-eight years old. When William was seventeen, his father purchased him a cornetcy in the Sixth Dragoon Guards, and Stewart was only nineteen when he fought at Waterloo, the military high-water mark of the nineteenth century for the British. By the age of twenty-four Stewart was retired at half-pay from the Fifteenth King's Hussars. He followed the sporting life for nearly a decade before an indiscretion prompted his marriage to a young and lovely laundress, Christina, to whom a son, George, had been born in 1830. Soon thereafter, Stewart made a decision to travel to America to see St. Louis and the West.

In part, Stewart was compelled to leave Scotland by the nagging problems that attended his difficult position as the second son in a wealthy family. In England, the inflexible code of primogeniture—the law that provided for inheritance to be passed to the eldest living son—reduced William to the necessity of living on pittances doled out by his father, George, and later by his elder brother, John. The veteran's retirement was by no means adequate for his needs, and a solution was offered to remove himself from a distasteful situation by a visit to the untamed West of the United States.

Stewart arrived at New York with letters of introduction that enabled him to arrange for a place in the Sublette & Campbell caravan of 1833, bound for the Rockies. He paid $500.00 for the privilege of *roughing it* with the trappers on this first jaunt, but as the years passed, and particularly after he gained the family title and control of the purse-strings, his mode of travel grew increasingly sumptuous and extravagant. On his later junkets he would sleep in a multicolored marquee tent and entertain the mountain men with canned sardines and fine liquors, yet he continued to run buffalo and delighted in risk-taking.

Stewart departed from St. Louis on his first venture to the Rockies on April 13, 1833, and did not return until November of 1835, having spent over two and one-half years among the mountain men and Indians.

It was during the 1833 rendezvous on Green River that Stewart witnessed a tragic episode in which a rabid wolf entered the trappers' camp and bit several persons, one of whom was Stewart's tent-mate, George Holmes. Soon after leaving the rendezvous with Tom Fitzpatrick's outfit, William was again involved in a legendary event. He was left in charge of the camp on September 5, 1833, when a band of surly Crows came in and robbed most of the brigade's equipment, horses and some furs.

It is quite possible that Stewart wintered at Taos, New Mexico, with Jim Bridger in 1833-34, for he rode into the 1834 rendezvous at Ham's Fork with Bridger. Stewart joined Nathaniel J. Wyeth's outfit, which wintered at Fort Vancouver in 1834-35, and returned to the 1835 rendezvous on Horse Creek near Green River with a Hudson's Bay Company brigade, following the Snake River—Lewis's Fork—toward Teton Pass and on to Green River. At the 1835 rendezvous Stewart may have seen Marcus Whitman remove two iron arrowheads from Jim Bridger's back, a surgical operation that became part of the lore of the mountain men. It is also probable that he watched the famous duel in which Kit Carson humbled a French braggart named Shunar, presumed to have been employed by Andrew S. Drips.

While Stewart wintered at New Orleans in 1835-36, he developed an interest in cotton speculation with an E. B. Nichols, which buttressed his sagging financial condition. By spring of 1836, he was waiting with a German named Mr. Sillem at Bellevue—near present Omaha, Nebraska—for Tom Fitzpatrick's caravan, again bound for the Rockies. Stewart had two wagons this time, loaded with luxurious comestibles, fine alcohol and a first-rate hunting outfit that included two excellent rifles made at London by Joseph Manton. Also along were three servants, two hunting dogs and two blooded racehorses. After seeing his familiar cronies and some exotic newcomers—Narcissa Whitman and Mr. and Mrs. Henry Spalding, all missionaries destined for Oregon)—Stewart left the 1836 rendezvous on Horse Creek and once again set off to winter at New Orleans. It was at this time—April 1837—that Stewart met and hired a little-known artist, Alfred Jacob Miller, to accompany his entourage of 1837 as the expeditionary artist.

Stewart's third trip to the Rockies and the Green River rendezvous lasted about seven months. When he returned to winter for a third time at New Orleans, Miller came along with well over one hundred field sketches, some eighteen of which would later grace the walls of Murthly Castle as oil paintings. In the spring of 1838, Stewart again went West, this time to a rendezvous at Wind River. By this time, the glory days of the fur trade were drawing to a close, and with a drop-off in business the rollicking good times diminished also.

Upon his return to St. Louis in October or November of 1838, William found notice that his brother John had died on May 20, 1838. This meant that he was now Sir William, nineteenth Lord of Grandtully and seventh Baronet of Murthly. Thus, in April 1839, Sir William returned to Scotland to take up his role as a lord, and with him went Antoine Clement, his favorite hunting companion, perhaps in an effort to enliven the scene at Murthly Castle. The artist Miller also went to Murthly late in 1840 to complete some commissioned work for his patron.

Stewart was not quite ready to settle into a staid and unexciting life, so he made a farewell tour of the West in 1843. This expedition was outfitted in a style consistent with the status of a laird, and at least three men kept some record of the trek—William Sublette, Matt Field and William Clark Kennedy. Sublette and Kennedy hailed from St. Louis, and Field was a correspondent for the New Orleans *Picayune*, whose stories have been made available as *Prairie and Mountain Sketches*. The company was replete with well-to-do sons of the first families of St. Louis, such as Menard, Chouteau and Clark.

During the trip, Stewart's party stopped at many of the landmarks that would be associated with the Oregon Trail, including Independence Rock, where Matt Field noted a hidden spring that Stewart mentioned in *Edward Warren*. The outfit then moved through South Pass and along the Wind River Mountains to Stewart Lake—present Fremont Lake—and on to part of today's Yellowstone National Park, the Norris Geyser Basin. Interpersonal friction grew troublesome as the journey progressed, and on the homeward route, the party split into two groups—Clark Kennerly was in the splinter group, but he bore Stewart no enmity, for he later wrote: *Sir William was a mighty hunter and a prince among sportsmen*. Kennerly also wrote about the unsuccessful pursuit of an albino buffalo bull, which may well have been the source for a similar event written into *Edward Warren*.

In the spring of 1844, Sir William left his beloved Rockies behind and sailed to Scotland and Murthly Castle, never again to visit the scenes of past pleasures.

Publishing History

In New York, Stewart made the acquaintance of J. Watson Webb, a wealthy newspaper publisher, and Webb encouraged the British sportsman to publish something about his adventures in the mountains. Eastern interest in the heroic happenings in the Wild Wild West was high, though not yet what it would become with the likes of Buffalo Bill Cody as publicists. Webb apparently offered editorial help as well, and with this impetus, Stewart wrote his two novels of the Rocky Mountain fur trade, *Altowan* and *Edward Warren*.

Altowan was published—with an introduction by Webb—in 1846 in New York by Harper & *Bros.*, *Edward Warren* in 1854 in London by G. Walker. Of the two, *Edward Warren* is superior, being more clearly written, less given to romantic vagueness, and more specific about the historical personages and events of the West and the fur trade. Neither book evidently had a large printing or significant sale.

The text in this book is a resetting of the first edition, as it appeared, language left uncorrected.

The author's notes are intact at the back of the book, and the reader will find them invaluable for specifying the history behind Stewart's fiction. Win Blevins has added notes at the ends of the chapters.

Introduction

As the east is the region of religion and knowledge, where the history of man is lost in antiquity, and whence came the type of those races in which the development of long-forgotten science and art is exhibited, whence a system of theology revealed on its holy land has been sent forth over the earth, and where the vastest evidences of human power have as yet but partially revealed their extent, where the active mind must seek for the direction in its research after knowledge. So the western hemisphere, richer than Asia in soil, far more favored by the diffusion of abundant rivers, and the clothing of rich forests, contains a people who, though the noblest physically, of the most dignified morality and lofty command over the senses, yet exemplifying how deficient are these qualities to raise the human mind into the higher walks of science, or the loftier flights of imagination. I should feel some hesitation in saying, that a life of animal enjoyment in the hunting grounds of the Red man, should suffice for a well-educated Caucasian, but I have never yet seen one who enjoyed life so well, had so few cares, or bore what he had to endure, with the grandeur of the western savage.

I have endeavored to recall, in a fictitious Autobiography, events in the west which I myself have seen happen, or known to have occurred. The record of which is now a sad, though pleasing memory, from the change which has directed the tide of emigration across the chain of the northern Andes. I shall endeavour to prevent these pages falling into the hands of any but such as may be ready to accept every apology I can offer for intruding on them upon their notice.

Edward Warren

Part One

Chapter One
Of the great changes in the Far West and the disappearance of the Red Man, Bridger's men hunt buffalo, find gold, and neglect and despise it.

The forests of the valley of the Mississippi are fading and falling under the axe, and the blossom of spring, the foliage of summer, and the sear of autumn, are mirrored but at intervals on the bosom of its waters, which are destined one day to run their course far from the song of the bird, or the murmur of waving woods. There were, still however, to be found, at the time of which I write, vast masses of sylvan solitudes on its shores, and on the banks of its tributaries. There remained in their recesses, the bear, the cougar, the wapate[1], and the deer, of the larger animals which had not fled the fatal neighborhood of man, while the watchful lynx, feigning opossum, with the wolf and racoon, were yet to be found in the upper parts of the Missouri. If the Indians of the mountains and plain have been driven from the shelter of the forest, with the bison and the beaver, we know not—they that were there are gone, and most of the animal race which belonged to the land will follow. The only real compensation to the free man for all this change is the horse, and he who has breathed a good steed on the boundless plains, can content himself with what is left.

It was the glorious evening to the peaceful days, when the herd of the wild horse supplied the tribe of the wild man with food, spared his labour, ennobled his habits, and made him free as the winds. It was, indeed, the evening of the roving life of the Far West. In 1833, there was but one man, in all that region of the hunter, who was not there for gain, but the love of sport, and in

---

1. Wapate: Stewart's spelling for *wapiti*, the American elk, which is not the same genus as the European elk.

that year was held the last great rendezvous of the mountain traders. The American Fur Company[2], Sublette and Campbell[3], Bonneville[4], a large camp of Snakes and some Utaws, were there, and that glorious race, the Free Trappers joined them, all on the upper plain of the Susquadee[5], where it issues from the snows of the mountains of the Winds. The plains around were black with bison then, and the tyro, who packed along the camp kettles of the caravan of goods, killed a bull, as he passed with his herd within shot of camp. There are a few bones bleaching there now, but no living thing, unless a few stray antelopes, but there are marks of many a trail to the south and west, and broken wagons and horse bones, ox bones, and the graves of men. The scene of desolation, improvidence, and famine, has marked its course where noble herds of the wild horse had careered in the darkling throng of the bison.

The change began the following year, as the country was invaded by the pedlar and the idler of the east, and the missionary, the system of exploring, and the desire of moving on, has done its work, and the hunter may still, if he dares, roam in the country of the Crows and the Blackfeet, but the great running ground of the Platte and the Susquadee, and the upper waters of the Big Horn, and Sweet Water, and the Black Hills, are comparatively lifeless wastes. Where there had been timber on the course of the human tide, which has set since to the west, it has disappeared. There was a noble poplar, which bore the name of the *Lone Tree*, near Scott's Bluffs, on the north Platte, it had

---

2. American Fur Company: Organized by John Jacob Astor in 1808, this powerful company dominated the Missouri River trade from 1822, but faced serious competition in the mountains from *General* William H. Ashley and his successors. Often challenged but never defeated, the Company used political connections and massive capital to nearly monopolize the American fur trade. According to Hiram Martin Chittenden, the Company was *throughout its career...an object of popular execration, as all grasping monopolies are* (Chittenden, *History of the American Fur Trade of the Far West,* two volumes, Stanford, 1954, I, 344-45).
3. Sublette & Campbell: The company whose principals were William L. Sublette (1799-1845) and Robert Campbell (1804-1879). Both were Ashley men during the mid-1820s, and both fought at the Battle of Pierre's Hole in 1832, during which Campbell carried the wounded Sublette to safety. Incorporated at the end of 1832, the firm Sublette & Campbell became suppliers and carriers for the Rocky Mountain Fur Company. The firm also built Fort William on the Laramie River, later known as Fort Laramie and an important Oregon Trail post. Sublette and Campbell became warm friends of William Drummond Stewart, and helped him collect *exotic* American animals for his estate in Scotland.
4. Bonnville: Benjamin Louis Eulalie de Bonneville (1796-1878), born in France, was the son of an anti-Napoleon family who moved to the United States in 1803. A West Point graduate of 1815, Bonneville began a long military career that was interrupted from 1832-35 while he tried unsuccessfully to break into the Rocky Mountain fur trade. This story is told in Washington Irving's *The Adventures of Captain Bonneville* (1837). Bonneville was the first to take laden wagons over South Pass, and his employee Joseph Reddeford Walker pioneered a new and viable trail to California in 1833-34.
5. Susquadee: Stewart's spelling of the mountain-man name, derived from the Crow Indians, of the modern Green River. It was more often spelled Siskadee, Seedskeeder, or the like. Its headwaters are identified on John C. Frémont's map of 1845 as the New Forks, an area in which much of the action of *Edward Warren* takes place.

been respected alike by the caravan and the hunter, but fell under the knife of one of the first Yankee invasions.

The Missourian French Creole of St. Louis, and the Canadian, had for many years roamed after the beaver, and never quitted its regions for any other enterprise of gain, but cupidity itself rarely tempted them far out of the range of the Bison. It was an inhabitant of New England,[i] whose admirable energy, and mistaken enterprise, first opened the Columbia and the Oregon to the curiosity of his country, as a goal even to the everlasting wagon, and where the course of the steed is stayed.

It was the year following (1834), that the first missionary[6], with his staff, passed through this country, under the protection of different caravans of traders to settle on the Pacific shore, two years afterward followed others, with their wives[7]. Ten years after the first missionary appeared, a single messenger —a *greenhorn*—brought on an express from Snake River, with an order on Boston for a wife, to be sent to the mouth of the Columbia[ii], to replace one who had died. The Indians had already been astonished by the passage through their country of white women, *hung on the sides of their horses*, and a few years after that, through a vast portion of this region, no Red Men were to be found.

Such had been the gradual steps of alteration, preparatory to the wholesale immigration which has partly peopled and partly desolated—but everywhere changed—these western plains.

About that period, I well remember, upon some of the minor feeders of the Platte (it was the spring following the night of the falling stars[8]), somewhere southwest of the Medicine Bow Creek[9], the camp of Jim Bridger[10], that cele-

---

6. First missionary: The missionary party of 1834, headed by Jason Lee (1803-1845), was sent by the American Board of Commissioners for Foreign Missions. A combined Flathead-Nez Percé delegation of four men had arrived in St. Louis late in 1831 in order to request that an emissary of the white man's God be sent to preach to them. Lee and four others went past the Flatheads to Oregon, where Lee became a tireless promoter of American settlement in Oregon. In 1843, Lee was recalled from his mission on charges of speculation and over-secularization.

7. Others, and their wives: The missionary party of 1836 was led by Dr. Marcus Whitman, accompanied by his wife Narcissa, who was much admired by the mountain men. Other members of the party were Henry Hart Spalding, his wife Eliza, and William H. Gray. The latter three failed to adapt to the trail or to the mountain men, and criticized the Whitmans for doing so willingly. Captain Stewart had met Whitman in 1835, and was later acquainted with Mrs. Whitman. Odessa Davenport has suggested that Stewart may have advised Whitman to establish his mission at Waiilatpu, the site he chose. See Odessa Davenport and Mae Reed Porter, *Scotsman in Buckskin: Sir William Drummond Stewart and the Rocky Mountain Fur Trade*, New York, 1963, p. 123.

8. Night of the falling stars: A spectacular meteor display on the night of November 12, 1833, noticed all over America.

9. Medicine Bow Creek: Situated on the west side of the Laramie Plains, this creek is a tributary of the North Fork of the Platte River in present Wyoming.

10. Bridger: Born in Virginia, raised near St. Louis, James Bridger (1804-1881) became one of the most famous mountain men. He ascended the Missouri River with the Ashley party of 1822. *Old Gabe*, as he was known, became associated with Stewart during the Scotsman's initial adventures

leader of the Free Trappers of the mountain wilds, had stopped to make meat[iii]. The ground was not bad for running, and there were vast herds of bison within range. At the evening fires, the song and the tales went round, and the anticipation of the morrow's feast gave spirit to both, rifles and running guns[iv] had been washed, and Antoine Clement[11,v], then the best hunter of the west, had been out to change the piquet of his horse and of that famous mule, who, carrying fourteen stone, could catch a cow, there was movement and hope, and the jollity of temperance, that powerful agent, the stomach, spoke, the French boys in my lodge had washed their shirts as for a holy day, and carolled round the blazing fire like naked savages, while the clothes they had taken off hung above to dry[vi], the horse guard was on the alert, and the wolf, who well knew that the conjunction of the camp and the herd would be fruitful in blood, challenged occasionally with an impatient howl. It was a pleasure to keep late awake, sleep in those days was too sound to dream, and the startling cry[vii] of the grey dawn came upon men who leaped from the earth as if into a new life, to whom all previous existence had been a blank. The palfrey and the mule were ridden out to save the courser, Meek[12], and Newell[13], and Doty[14], and Tom Forsyth, a host of French, and Antoine, before the sun was a half-hour high, were gone, and like the eve of a battle, their morning was quiet and resolved. Many went out after them, to pick up

---

in the West, and probably was the recipient of a suit of English Life Guards armor which Stewart carried to the rendezvous of 1837. See J. Cecil Alter's biography *Jim Bridger,* Norman, Oklahoma, 1962.

11. Antoine Clement: Stewart's guide, companion, and hunter *extraordinaire,* Clement (?-?) was included in all of Stewart's jaunts to the West. He also lived with the Scot at Murthly Castle in Perthshire from 1839 to 1842. Then they returned to America for Stewart's final and most extravagant excursion in the West. During this trip, Clement's younger brother Franqois (age 15) killed himself accidentally while removing a double-barreled gun from a tent. (See Matt Field, *Prairie and Mountain Sketches,* eds. Kate L. Gregg and John Francis McDermott, Norman, Oklahoma, 1959, pp. 111-12.) After the journey of 1843, Clement and Stewart parted company. Clement fought in the Mexican War in Battery A of a light artillery battalion of the Missouri Volunteers. For more on Clement see Marvin C. Ross, Ed., *The West of Alfred Jacob Miller,* Norman, Oklahoma, 1968.

12. Meek: Joseph L. Meek (1810-1875) was a celebrated mountain man and Oregon pioneer. His exploits are fully chronicled in Frances Fuller Victor's, *The River of the West,* reprinted in this series.

13. Newell: Robert *Doctor* Newell (1807-1869), born in Ohio, was hired as a trapper by Smith, Jackson and Sublette in 1829, and became a friend and companion of Joe Meek. He worked for Bent, St. Vrain & Company in 1836-37 as a sub-trader. Newell moved—with Meek—to Oregon in 1840 and took an active hand in the early provisional government in that area. See Dorothy O. Johansen, ed., *Robert Newell's Memoranda,* Portland, 1959.

14. Doty: Probably William M. Doughty (1812-1872), a companion of Meek and Newell. He moved to Oregon in 1839, settling next to Ewing Young. He took part in the provisional government of Oregon in 1843, and his Shoshone wife, Pigeon, bore him two daughters. He figures in Victor's *The River of the West* (pp. 138-40) in some bear-baiting hijinks during 1832 or 1833. See also Harvey E. Tobie, *William Doughty,* in LeRoy R. Hafen, ed., *The Mountain Men and the Fur Trade of the Far West,* ten volumes, Glendale, California, 1965-72, III: 81-88.

what chance might throw in their way, the rest remained inert, John de Velder, a Belgian, amongst them, to take care of the squaws, and some Mexicans to guard the horses. It was noon, and one of these returned exulting into camp, with an air as if he had found a cache of beaver, and proclaimed a mine of gold, he had actually washed, from a basinful of soil, the value of twenty-five cents, but even among the drudges, the idea of digging and washing was unpopular, and there was a hesitation.[viii]

Evening came, and load after load of meat and tired hunters were coming in, and the fires glared to put out the sun, the hump rib was presiding at every blaze, and the fat pudding and the marrow gut were seething in every pan, the tongues, the trophies of they who kill, were yet hung to their saddles, and the pack mules were rolling their blood-smeared coats in the dust. Stretched on his smoothed couch, the hunter smoked in Eastern ease, the mouth of the messenger even is shut till the pipe is done—that supreme mystifier of care, and prompter of dreamy joy.

But the finding of gold is on everyone's tongue, and the sample has been produced. On the greatest part of the followers, there was little doubt but that to coin gold was the great object of life, those to whom they looked up to for food and for defense, who, by habit, swayed their thoughts and regulated their actions, had not yet spoken, the sun was down, and they sat round the steaming bowl, in which every part of the meat was mixed and cut, and all the art of mountain cooking displayed. As the appetite was satiated, the history of the day, the vast concourse of the bison toward the Black Hills, the signs of beaver that had been seen in distant forks,[ix] and the Kenyons,[x] which promised more, the falls, the perils, the feats, and the rewards of the chace, the barren cows[xi] and the fine oxen, which had been seen in the herds, became animating themes, and no one cared to question what was to be done about the gold.

Morn, and with it came the bright sun. Was it to shine upon sordid diggers, or free men of the wilds?

Not, as the day before, had the horses to be used been kept up, when the others were to be turned out Breakfast was over, and Jim cried, "Catch up!" I had mounted and away amongst the first. What was gold to me in that day![xii] But the peddler and the *mover* came, and Antoine, after visiting Paris, Constantinople, and Cairo, has gone to the Blackfoot village. Most of my American comrades are digging roots on the Columbia, and I have lived to be almost tempted to grudge cheap grain to the poor of my native land, for the sake of that gold we then neglected and despised.

Having thus hurriedly noted the gradual revolution which has been operating on the hunting grounds of the Rocky Mountains, to show the difference in the picture of former days and that which the present period would display, I shall allow the hero of my story to tell his own tale.

Chapter Two
Master Edward's family life—incidents at school—the Swiss, Bernard

From my infancy, I know less than infants usually learn. Of the place of my birth, I had been told nothing more than that it was in Yorkshire. My early history, probably from not having been thought of sufficient interest or importance, was forgotten, if ever known, to those with whom I had a connection in boyhood, and therefore, I shall date my memoir from my own recollections.

From my first place of instruction, I was removed to a sort of seminary, at about ten years old. It was a large old-fashioned house near Chester, and I was about the youngest inmate. Without friends or support, I had, during four years, fought my way through the preparatory school, and by good chance, having some popular qualities, I was not much behind in instruction, and some trouble had been taken to lead a disposition which it was difficult to drive.

I remember, when I suppose I was about six years old, going from I knew not where, with I remember not whom, to an old house in the neighborhood of Knutsford, the time was not at a regular vacation, but as I afterward learned, to suit the peculiar habits of my father. The first impression he made upon me has never been effaced. I arrived full of the traditions of other children for their fathersI was told my mother died when I was an infant—and prepared to love him—in short, to have a scene.

I arrived, and after my hands had been inspected by an old servant of forbidding aspect, and also my shoes, I was considered presentable, I suppose, for nothing further was done to either, and I awaited in the old-paneled room into which I first was shown, until the door was opened, and a tall old man entered with an air which did not in the least invite me to rush into his arms, or to consider him of that *genus Father*, of which, from the revolution I felt in my thoughts, I suppose I must have formed some indistinct, but very different idea. As it was, I observed the shorts, the white thread stockings, and what rivetted my attention, pieces of white paper appearing from under the shoes and covering the insteps. There was a cold finger laid upon my head, and I was asked how far I had come. My father, however, answering that, and some other question himself. I still remember the revolution I felt, and which chilled me to the inmost core of my heart.

"We will dine at three," said my father, and with a sort of calm indifference, left me.

I, by some means, got into the yard and made acquaintance with a watchdog—was duly taken to my room to dress for dinner—my clothes were overhauled by a fat housekeeper, to see if they wanted repair, and I got into the dining room by one door as my father appeared by another.

He seemed rather pleased than otherwise at my appearance, though I do not know from what I made the inference, and the dinner ended, I again sallied out and got as far as a small walled garden, with statues and terraces, it was not yet fruit-time, so my walk was one of a character in which there was nothing of the sprightly boy.

I was not yet recovered of my reception, but the sedate deportment seemed to suit the master as well as the servants, and I gradually donned it as that which fitted best. My intercourse with my father, was confined to mealtimes. I know not how he spent the intermediate hours, but if by any chance I ever saw through the rarely open doorway of what was called the study, I perceived a vast folio account book, with numerous papers, which appeared to engross his attention. Visits of this character went on yearly, during my stay at school, and generally at untoward times, consequently, I was left, while my companions were at home during the holydays, which was a circumstance sufficiently irksome on the one hand, but which had the good effect of enabling me to acquire a proficiency in French and German, which I should not otherwise have so readily attained, from an old French master, who, like myself, had nowhere to go. I was his companion during the day, and he really had, I believe, a great fund of general information, and his own early associations had been such, as to render him, in other respects, a valuable Mentor. He was born a noble, had been compromised in some attempt to restore legitimacy in France, and was proscribed and ruined, he had the most remarkable love of truth, and principles of honor bordering upon romance, he always treated the idea of an untruth as unnecessary and mean, and took every means of showing how well we might avoid it.

To my father, I must also render this justice, that during the whole intercourse I had with him, he never once seemed to think it possible that I could mean to deceive him on any point. When I removed to the neighborhood of Chester, I had to take leave of the good old Marquis, unlike most of his sentimental countrymen, he did not weep, so I did not either, but he told me not to forget him, and I never have.

I have said that I was amongst the youngest of those amongst whom I was now thrown, for I came in among them while they were in full career, and was plunged into their studies, and into their fellowship, without the least introduction or preparation. By feeling a perfect indifference, I succeeded in establishing myself pretty well in regard to both. I had no great desire to learn, but neither had I any love of absolute idleness, with my schoolfellows, I was always ready to aid, and never cared to refuse the most unequal combat. I must, however, note one circumstance regarding the principles I acquired from my ancient friend, which was, that the new teacher of modern languages was a young Swiss, without principle, and who hated trouble, the opposite in everything to the loyal Marquis, he was so mean in his mind, so without reverence for everything in heaven and earth, that I at once took my stand against him, and hated him with a cordiality, of which its object was little worthy, he had found out my love for my former instructor, and singled me out, perhaps, as also speaking his language best of my class for his conversation, ordering me to write themes, to give him an opportunity of turning into ridicule all the good principles I had learned to value.

At that early age, for I was not yet eleven, from peculiar circumstances, I had acquired many of the feelings, and much of the reserve of maturer years, and as my hatred grew for the young Swiss, I felt with it the desire of being able to requite the sneers and the obloquy he heaped upon me.

I ought to have stated, that I was always furnished with a more than sufficient share of pocket money, and that I was to a certain degree, indebted to an accident—in being able, by its means, to save a companion from disgrace—for the knowledge of its power and influence.

To take personal vengeance was out of the question, but I found that vanity and profusion rendered my enemy always in want of funds, I discovered that he was a good swordsman, and one day the idea came into my head to make him teach me the use of that weapon, which would put me on a footing with my stronger antagonist, and I proposed to him that I should give him a certain sum for lessons in fencing.

I mention this as an incident, which led to ulterior results.

Suffice it for me to say, that years rolled on in schoolboy-life with hardly any change, and my visits to my father took place yearly, but at no fixed times. I grew to a certain degree rapidly, that is, as much so as to take proportionate thickness along with increasing height.

Never having had the care of a mother, nor that I remember of anyone else, to teach me to dread pain, I never experienced more than physical suffering, which was never heightened by nervous susceptibility, and a corresponding indifference to the accidents which are usually dreaded in life, became a natural characteristic.

At fourteen, I was a good and extremely quick fencer, but strange to say, I had lost the desire of revenge which had first prompted me to be taught. I could see in the eye of my master, however, something I did not like, when the assault became in any degree animated, this, however, did not produce in me other effect than checking any nascent liking I might have felt for him.

I was sixteen, many changes had taken place, some of those school fellows I first remember had entered the army, some the church, I had formed boyish attachments, which had been broken by cruel parents, I had formed dislikes, for which I would at the time have set the world in a blaze, but I had no object of ambition, and no desire to trace any line for my future life. As I had been accustomed to see others leave school at stated periods, exulting in the prospect of home, I remained, evidently a nuisance to the establishment, I also got used to seeing those who were about to enter some career in life depart, without any thought of what was to be my own destiny.

Thus, never being interfered with by my father, I became the more absolutely ready to be disposed of by him without opposition.

I must here relate an accident, not apparently of much importance, but which had important effects on my future life.

The headmaster had one unmarried daughter, who was not unconscious of the claims she possessed for admiration, and my residence alone at the school, had thrown me upon the pity and goodwill, as well as the care of the family at these periods, and I became more intimate with all its members than the usual run of my companions, and though I cannot say that I felt the influence of the tender and romantic love, which may fill the imagination even of a boy, I certainly entertained for this young lady, whose name was Miranda, a very honest and sincere affection, and I felt both proud and happy to be with her whenever I could.

There was a canal near the house, with a walk along its bank, and a row of trees, under whose shade I have often mused and awaited the appearance of Miranda for her evening walk, and where I used to join her, when no one else had been more fortunate before me, perhaps one of the ushers, sometimes the Swiss, but I thought she preferred me to them, and as I have learned since, there was no love in the case, she probably liked my unembarrassed bearing and unconcealed affection, better than the suppressed protestations of admiration, which characterized the manners of her other gallants.

I do not exactly remember how it happened, for there were often little maneuvers between the rivals for her favor, to partake in her walk, and generally no third party intruded, when the ground had been previously secured, but one sultry evening, I had sat down at the root of a tree, and did not perceive the approach of any one with Miranda, and started up from my concealment to give her a little surprise, when I found that she was already accompanied by one of the ushers, who of an interested disposition, was also the most pertinacious, and I believe, the most disagreeable of her admirers, she was indeed startled at my sudden apparition, but recovering herself, ran at me to box my ears, as she said, for my mischief, I ran for it, and she followed. I let her catch me, and we continued together in a wordy strife, the usher came up, and she again attempted to inflict the punishment she had threatened, and he, to gratify his mistress, attempted to aid her, and to hold me, but a trip, accompanied by a push, threw him at her feet, which I told him was the place he ought to have taken of his own accord, and I ran off laughing.

Next evening, I had a book, in which I was interested, and did not perceive Miranda until I was close upon her, she was seated on a bench I myself had made, and with her, this time, was the Swiss. I was so close upon them that I had not time to remark that they were in deep conversation, which was stopped at my coming near, and I sat down beside them. I thought she seemed pleased at my joining them, and we all rose to resume our walk—the Swiss out of humor, and his companion rallying me about my escape from her hands the night before. There was a good deal of familiarity between us, and she threatened to consummate the vengeance which I had then escaped, and the Swiss asked to come to her aid, saying he would be of more use than the usher. I know not whether it was the love of mischief which prompted Miranda to encourage his interference, but there came a scuffle, and by a jerk, I threw my new adversary, not at the feet of the lady fair, but headforemost into the canal. Though the first feeling, as it always is on such occasions, was to laugh, I immediately after rushed into the water to drag out my victim, but though the plunge was not long, I was alarmed to find that he did not at once show symptoms of recovery, and was still further shocked to find that he had received a severe contusion on his head, probably from a stone, of which there were several at the place he had fallen, under the surface of the water. In two or three minutes, however, he recovered, but it was evident that though I had, without intending it, thrown him into the canal, he would have been drowned had I not pulled him out. Miranda told him this, on his coming to his senses, and I showed a real concern for the accident, and attended him to his lodging, which was near, before he was entirely restored to himself.

I had undressed him and rolled him in a warm blanket, and had examined him all over, to see if there was any other injury, but was relieved to find there was none, I had only remarked that there were some letters tattooed on his back, and as I examined his muscular frame, felt grateful, for the first time, to the groom at my father's, a sturdy youth from Lancashire, who used to throw me about every day for an hour during my latter years' visits. The patient's head was a little swelled, and the skin had been broken near the templar artery, so that more care was requisite than for an ordinary wound, and he was forbidden by the doctor, who had now arrived, to permit anything to cause any quickened circulation, in case of an accident. A jug of weak barley-water was the beverage, in case of thirst, and when I returned from reporting progress at the Grange, as our old mansion was called, to watch by his bedside, I found him perfectly collected, and had to interdict his gratitude, which he would have poured forth, for my having saved his life. For my own part, I could not quite understand that a French master, who could make none or little use of his best qualities, which were physical, had much to be thankful for. I do not know why, but I undervalued the life of such a man. However, this did not prevent my feeling every desire to repair the disaster I had occasioned, and I felt grieved at the thought of his being disfigured. To soothe him, I over-colored the interest his accident excited, and brought a number of messages, delivered in the whispering tones of a sick chamber, and losing nothing by my caressing manner. In short, my feelings were much touched, and I hung over him as if he had been an infant, and did not retire to a mattress the people of the house had brought me, until I had soothed him to sleep.

The night was hot, I threw off my clothes, and then, gathering a blanket round me, disposed myself to rest. I soon sank into sleep, but it was not sound, and I had that feeling, in my dreams, which it is impossible to describe, that all was not right. The sun was shining through the lattice when I awoke, there were no curtains. I had not, however, moved, so my companion could not perceive that my eyes were open under the shadow of my arm, but I lay as still as a statue. Opposite me lay him whom I now involuntarily watched, his face was alone visible, there was a bandage on his temple, and a slight hectic on his cheek, he was gazing upon me with the full force of his large grey eye. I always, since I can remember, made it a point to look any one down who fixed my eye, and though unseen, I felt relieved when his eyelid, for a moment, faltered. I cannot tell what feeling or fascination that look brought upon me, but it has never been forgotten.

Things soon recovered with me their wonted course I learned, because no one seemed to care whether I did or no. I had no pursuits, because no one opposed my wishes. I had never been limited in the duration of my visits to my father's house, and I left when I was tired.

There was one thing there, where everything was carried on in quiet economy, that was still less attended to by himself than the rest of his establishment, and that was the stable, two horses were allowed—one to take my father to the town of Knutsford in a *one-horse chaise,* and the other carried the lad before mentioned to the post-office, and occasional messages on household matters. It was necessary that the carriage-horse should be sufficiently good-looking to pass without remark, and sufficiently well broke not to be inconvenient. Not so the other, his looks were the only recommendation in his favor, he was both unmanageable and vicious, but the gardener occasionally worked the other, and the old butler, who had bought both, well knew that if the groom was allowed, he would always use the one easiest managed. He was a lazy fellow, Tom, notwithstanding his liking for me.

It was never questioned, anything I did, and as he said, to learn me to ride, he put me on the sedate steed, and I very soon took much of his work in the way of messages. I must do Tom the justice to say, that he never proposed that I should try the other, but it seemed to me as if I was not permitted to do so, and the desire of mastering a difficulty, and the showy paces and high carriage of the iron grey, tempted me, and I proposed to make the attempt. I remember I was told afterward that poor Tom got up at early dawn the day I was first to be lifted on his back, and galloped the animal to bring down his vivacity, if not subdue his temper, and away we went. I had no fear, and was charmed to rush about on a horse whose action was of a new kind, and whose springy bound I had only to enjoy, and never to urge. Suffice it to say, that, from the first day, I always followed up the liking I took for the saddle. I was several times thrown, but as I had not to clean my courser, I always gave him his head, and he soon found that it was useless to oppose me. I could keep him out six hours, if we had a trial of patience, so, in cases of waywardness, he was glad to give in. I could punish him by taking him, when thirsty, to water, and not permitting him to drink. So that, in the end, I was his master.

I mention these incidents to show how much I ought to be thankful for the chances which were put in my way of learning things which, it was evident, my father never dreamt of, and how it came about.

Neither did there remain a magpie or hawk within miles. There was, in reality, not much to shoot, but I went about it with patient economy, and made sure, at least, of the distance—never attempting anything beyond the shortest range. Rooks I seldom meddled with, as there was a rookery near, and if it happened that I was at the Manor-house when the young ones branched, I could then use an old Innsbruck rifle, which was kept in order by the butler because it was ornamented with silver.

I mentioned that I was past sixteen when the immersion of the Swiss took place. It was some months after that, I was surprised one day by a message from Miranda's father, desiring me to attend him immediately in his study. I recalled to my recollection, as I went along the somber passage which led to the family part of the mansion, all my delinquencies—my little familiarities with the daughter—in short, all those things upon which I wished not to be taken by surprise on appearing before a judge, so summoned for the first time during my abode under his roof.

I found the trainer and modeler of youth seated at one of those eternal tables, covered with green baize, from which emanate absolute rules and twaddling tracts, from which letters of credence—rarely current beyond the paternal roof—are issued, and fiats of intellectual bankruptcy decreed.

I was not then to be driven forth with an unlettered brand on my brow, or a stigma on my general habits, nor was I called then to hear that awful advice, which comes in such a disagreeable shape from the seat of power.

The smile of the schoolmaster to the youth on whom it shines, is so pregnant with omens of the future, such a relief from apprehension for the present and the past, that I have since been surprised that it is not counted as one of the most charming expressions which the human visage can assume.

I was ordered to Liverpool like a bale of goods. But the smile—it was this smile which made all go well.

There had never been an unreasonable interference with my wishes, nor the least wanton exercise of power, so I felt only curiosity as to the cause of my removal, and a desire to unravel the mysterious benignity which had hallowed its annunciation.

The arrangements were to be made for a final departure. Among all my leave-takings, that of most pathos was with the Swiss. He had not sought me much since his accident, but when we met, there was more affection in his manner toward me, and always that almost uncomfortable influence of his eye, when I found it fixed upon me.

Tumultuous questions from my school-mates assailed me, and I shook hands until I was covered with ink. Bernard—the Swiss—threw his arms round my neck, and kissed me on either cheek, and with a convulsive pressure of the hand, we parted without a word.

With Miranda, the scene was more tender, and she did not affect to conceal the tears she shed, or the affection she had for me.

I never have seen her since, but I have felt really happy at hearing that a marriage of affection has also turned out to be one of affluence and domestic joy.

As I grew out of my clothes, I threw them away, and indeed the habits of school are not those of conservatives. Thus, my baggage—in attire—was not bulky. I got it transported to Chester, and bade adieu to the Grange.

Chapter Three
**To London—Fernwold—a moment of danger—
a party, with an ominous incident—raven
tresses**

I had been at Liverpool before, but instead of meeting my father there, I found a letter, very kindly worded, directing me to the New Hummums, Covent Garden, where he hoped I would arrive as soon as possible. This letter he sent by Tom.

No one, who has not experienced it, can believe how grateful it is to have evidence of genuine love and sympathy in a strange place, and as Tom took leave of me, with the vice-like squeeze of his honest, hard hand, he only could stammer out, "Don't forget the Grey, Master Edward!"

I watched his flushed face from the coach, till it turned a corner, and the horn and the whip proclaimed that the over-burthened vehicle was well under weigh.

I, of course, never attempted to leave the coach, to take a shorter cut, on our arrival in the metropolis. I knew nothing of London, and stuck to my seat, as to a friend, until I was rejected and thrown upon my own guidance.

I remembered the name of my rendezvous, and got into a hackney coach, of which I had the vast and dirty interior to myself, conducted by an animal of a species I had never before seen, his face, of burning red, was the only part of our Creator's image visible in him, his hat and his boots covered with wet straw, and his coat shining with all that could make a hackney coachman of 1831 shine. I was glad to get off, for four shillings, from the damp atmosphere which hung about my Jehu, and the grave contempt which lurked in the countenances of the waiter.

I inquired for Mr. Warren, and although he had a sitting-room to himself, I afterward learned that his quiet and economical habits did not produce, for me, much advance in their good opinion, though it was evident they felt I would not be troublesome to watch, and that my baggage was not considered fictitious. The great account book, to which I before alluded, pen, ink, and a newspaper, were on the table before him, and my father rose, at my entry, with an urbane and almost graceful welcome. I was not shaken by the hand, but I was asked if I had had a comfortable journey, to which I answered, "Yes."

He then added, "I hope you will forgive the breach of appointment at Liverpool, I had not time for it, as I had been sent for to come to town on a matter of importance, in which I have been somewhat of a gainer." He said this with something of a chuckle, the first I ever perceived in my intercourse with him. He then placed a chair near the fire—it was yet but the month of May—and resumed his own seat.

"We must dine at six today," he said with a sigh. "I have asked someone to meet you who will be fitter to show you the ways of this Babel than I. If you like to go out for an hour or two, you will have time. If you are lost, do as the man did, who met one of the Exeter Change lions in the Strand—*call a coach*."

I got back, however, with considerable difficulty, and at a great loss of reputation, I had been obliged to let so many people into the secret of my ignorance of London.

When I got down from my bedroom, I found my father also dressed—that is, he wore grey silk stockings, and ruffles to his sleeves.

It was not many minutes before the head waiter opened the door with a flourish, and in walked a tall, showy-looking young man of about twenty.

"You are something particular, old gentleman," he began. "I had the greatest difficulty not to be made do ante-chamber, as I did not give name and reference at the bar. However, here I am, and by a miracle, in good time, too."

"And why not do a little ante-chamber in the Hummums, there is nothing a man of birth should not be able to do," said my father, with a quiet welcome smile. He then turned his guest toward the light, and shook his head, as he perceived the haggard indications of debauch already making apparent inroads on his noble countenance.

The dinner came steaming in. We sat down to table, but there was no wine. There never is in England, unless specially ordered, yet are hotel-keepers dreadfully disappointed if it should not be called for. My father perceived the omission, and ordered some claret. I saw him give a look of affectionate regret to the half-empty bottle, which remained of yesterday.

He then seemed to remember me, and introduced me to his guest, whom he called Fernwold, telling him he would be much obliged by any aid he could show me in regard to town, as it was always most necessary to know something of London.

And this was the only paradox I ever heard from my father on this momentous subject of education.

Our companion was cheerful, and my father really agreeable, with a certain terseness which seasoned the general calmness of his manner. There was a good deal said of which I hardly knew the import, and I perceived that several points were made which I did not understand. It is not the language of the spectator which furnishes the key to what may be considered as good conversation, no more was the light and pleasing bandying of words, between these two, like what I had been accustomed to, than would a beautiful chemical lecture be like instructions for making plum-pudding. However, I caught something of the tone, as the hour and a half of dinner glided on, and I had already brought a smile upon me from our companion, by a word put in at the proper moment.

As we were taking coffee, Fernwold said to me, "If you do not mean to get out of your father a full and accurate description of London, you had better put yourself under my charge, and judge for yourself."

There was no objection made, and we sallied out for the first time. I took the arm, and considered myself the equal of a fine gentleman.

"You would never have got over the gulf between this and St. James's Street," he said, "without me, or a Bentham or Balam, or whoever it was who wrote the Pilgrim's Progress, but you will find no allegory equal to the original, so here we are."

It is useless to repeat all the explanations he gave me of the throng we passed through, he left me for a moment to speak to someone, and I was told *not to budge*, that he would be back in a moment, I waited, it was under the Piazza of Covent Garden, and looking rather lost, I suppose, was immediately accosted by a most civil personage, who was sent by my friend to bring me to him, I turned to accompany this gentleman, and we had not gone three steps, when I saw a cane protruded between us, and a slight tap given to my companion on the shoulder, I thought the gentlemanly-looking man was electrified, he started and turned pale.

Fernwold's *be off, sirrah*, was not long of being obeyed, he seemed inclined to apologize, but a gesture made him comprehend that his best course was to disappear, which he did without much difficulty in the crowd.

"There can be nothing so green in the market tomorrow morning as you are, it is most refreshing—early peas, yet in their pod, are stale compared to you. Bravo! This begins the account well to my credit, and you owe me your watch, your money, and your clothes, most probably your life, how much, I wonder are your teeth worth? They would have been dissecting you under the auspices of St. Bartholomew, when your father was yet in his first cup of tea tomorrow," ran on my companion, as he hurried me through the incumbrances of the street, and dug his elbow into my side. He seemed delighted at the adventure, and held me fast, as if he intended me for his own prey.

We had now got to Leicester Square, and down to the left, there was a row. I should have liked to go, but in that miserably ill-lighted place, what could we see—I was over-ruled, and we went on. We turned to the left out of what appeared the broadway, and entered a street much narrower, and then knocking at a door, we were admitted after a scrutiny through a small hole, and mounted a narrow staircase, a person waiting at the landing opened a door, and we entered a room, where about twenty persons were assembled round a long table, on which there were different colors marked off in certain lines, and heaps of gold and silver, and notes at the side of an ill-looking man who presided. There were also small heaps of silver before the persons round the table, where there was yet room for more. We sat down, and my companion threw down his half-crown, which he lost, he staked another with no better success. In answer to a question of mine, he explained that where he put his money, indicated on which color it was staked, he threw his silver piece down, and it sometimes rolled, so that it was a chance whether or not it remained even within reach. This had happened several times, and if he gained, it had been pushed toward him, but at last, this was given up, and the piece having got a little way off, which he last threw down, and it having won, was quietly taken up with the winnings, by a person close to it.

Fernwold, however, called for his money, and the dealer made a pause. "I had five shillings on the black, just at the edge." The man who had taken it up, and who was a respectable-looking elderly man in blue spectacles, smiling, and in the softest voice, said he had seen nothing before him on the table but a crown of his own. The groom porter gave an appealing look.

"It is the only crown piece I had, and it is marked," said Fernwold, "and the person who took it up, has probably only that in his pocket, at all events, there is a Maltese cross on the King's neck, and it will be found in that man's possession if searched."

There was a great murmur round the table, I could perceive that public opinion was much in favor of the venerable martyr to this accusation, and I expected nothing less than a row, the dealer, however, sent with his wooden trowel a half-sovereign toward us, saying, that it was not worthwhile to have any disturbance for such a trifle, and that it was impossible to search the gentleman.

Fernwold, however, got up and said, "Since you have given this ten shillings, I leave it to be scrambled for on your table, you say the *gentleman* cannot be searched, *I* say, that there is not a gentleman but he"—touching me on the shoulder—"and myself in the room."

I bounded to my feet, and expected to see my companion overpowered in a moment, and to have the fists of my nearest neighbors leveling me, from my unenviable distinction, I would have given a crown at least, to ensure my own head not being broken, there were so many ugly faces, and such an uproar of honest indignation. I really felt that it had been at least a hazardous and sweeping attack.

"You had better keep your seats and go on with your game. I do not mean further to disturb you," said my friend.

He moved toward the door. I could not conceive, as I backed out of the room behind him, how they restrained their anger, which I saw was kindled among some of the younger members, but the door closed upon us, and we went down and reached the street in safety[i].

It was now my turn to make a little attempt at shewing my companion, that folly had not been confined to me during the evening, and that we might have both visited St. Bartholomew's Hospital upon this occasion also.

"You are mistaken," he said, laughing. "You never were safer, these men are under the ban of the law, most of them are sought for by the police, and the act in which they were was illegal. Now for my quarters."

We crossed a wide street, entered a narrow one, turned to the right, and were in St. James's Place, he gave a short, and somewhat peculiar knock at a door, which was opened almost immediately by a man of a most stolid aspect, who looked to us as if he did not know his master, but had let him in by some preconcerted agreement, there were several cloaks and hats on a table at the foot of the staircase.

"Ah! I see we have some friends to congratulate us," said he, as he hurried up the steps, a most decorous looking personage opened a door, and we found some four or five youths in various attitudes, who, by their welcome, seemed to have expected a later arrival.

I could gather but little knowledge of my new acquaintances from the rattling confusion of their talk. There were no introductions, but I felt at ease, because occasionally, someone speaking, appeared to appeal to me, in short, I was taken in amongst them, and had played a few bars on the piano, to prompt an air to someone who was making a bad attempt to sing, when the dignified gentleman out of livery, stood with the handle of the open door in his hand, with a look of hospitable decorum. This dumb show was the only means of attracting our attention, and no voice short of a shriek could have made itself distinguished amongst the sounds issuing from eight youths so full of glee, but the moment he found he had been observed, he got away as fast as he thought it proper to retire, in evident dread of the simultaneous movement which followed.

It was a table which exactly held its eight places, and with persons in the jovial mood, a conversation may be general or divided, it was a sort of meal which suited everyone, the light and substantial, hot and cold, sour and sweet, seemed so well combined, that no taste could be at fault.

Fernwold held up a glass, and asked, "Shall it be of the Rhine or the Garonne, the Meuse or the Rhone."

I said at once, "The Rhine." It was a song of the Rhine which I had begun to play when we were summoned to the board.

"Then we are to have a night on the Rhine," he shouted. They were put down as he spoke, bottles to every two.

I remember, I felt relieved, that it was not champagne, as I am sure it must have disconcerted the serious butler, there was something I liked in the idea of choosing the wine, and it's being all one kind, did not allow any confusion of bottles, while its being good, did not allow a difference of opinion. It may be supposed that my knowledge was but slender of any wine, and I did not know one of those of which I had had the choice, unless champagne, by report.

There were two Germans, they were brought out by the second glass, and we had the song of *Koseousco* and *Father Land*, and then came some English songs—every body said everything, and provoked each other in jest and song, the chandeliers vibrated under the invoke of the *Tyrol Mountains*, and more Stein wine was placed upon the board, as Fernwold sang *Meet me by Moonlight*. Then came another wave of wine, and broke in a chorus of some of those grand old songs, which used to dwell in the echoes of Teutonic Halls. There was another lull, and the mellow voice of a beardless youth came gently upon us in the *Captive Knight to his Dove*, that lad was of the blood of Norman Crusaders, and I thought I could trace the pedigree in the pathos of his song. Wine again, and wild welcome as we took each other's hands right and left round the board.

It was time to improve upon the subtle excellences of the great cask, and the refined and exclusive merits of the flask that had been sealed a hundred years, that night to impart its heretofore secret influence, and unknown flavour.

Now the vast bowl, crowned with flame, that emblem of spirit, and life, and power, which burned from the produce of many a distant land, came to throw its mysterious light upon the scene, and spread its odors lavishly around, where but the individual aroma of the cherished goblet, had before to each meted its separate perfume.

It was thus, that the revelry waxed riotous, and there was scarcely method in our madness, at this moment, the flame burnt high, as it was stirred up in a fresh and brimming reinforcement, and Fernwold looked as if of another world, behind its blue and livid glare, but there was another head above his, strongly marked, and on which also told the deadly light, it was a countenance never to be forgotten. I could not see that he had spoken, but Fernwold sunk back in his seat and half closed his eyes, the large cold eye of the stranger was upon me, and I met it, it was long before he withdrew its gaze, but at last he did, and I felt that he was my fate. I knew the head, I knew every feature, I had known them years, I knew not where seen, but they were familiar. It slowly left the room. Some minutes lapsed before our host recovered, but he shook off his lethargy, as if by a physical effort, and with a flashing eye. The wassail went on, and I had forgotten the momentary interruption.

O Father Matthew, hadst thou been there, either you had never sang another *Tea Deum*, or you would have merited the rewards of a martyr!

Never were men so friendly or so happy, there was no Pharisee, and still less a Sadducee, and I shall believe to my dying day, that there was not a malignant, an envious, or an uncharitable thought in the room.

I know not how I got home, but I lunched with my father who merely *supposed I had had a pretty late party, as Fernwold had a fastish set about him.* I cannot say I had a headache, but I had awoke with the eye of that mask fiend upon me, it was the only thing I remembered distinctly of the hours of revel. I afterward met some of the party in the street, it seemed to me, as if I had known them in another world, and we were friends, though ignorant of each other's names.

After our sedate repast at three o'clock, I sauntered out, and took my way on the tour of our last night's course. I knocked at Fernwold's door, and though after something more of delay than there had been the night before, was admitted by the silent porter, and the solemn butler came out of a side door at the top of the stair, to whom I was delivered up by an intermediary, who preceded me that length. There was no one in the room, but I heard voices in that adjoining, soon after the door opened, and the young master of the mansion entered, there was a slight color on his cheek, and as I, feeling my ignorance of the world, was a keen observerI thought I could perceive that he was slightly ruffled, however, he rallied me on the supper scene, and told me the names of some of the choice spirits of the feast. They were most of them persons of some distinction and high fashion. The foreigners were troubled and troublesome spirits in their own country, with that notion of German unity and patriotism, which may be in its vagueness founded on old songs. Thus far I learned of the guests of the previous night.

"We will take a drive, if you like now, as the day is fine, the conveyance at the door, and all things conducing. I can let you have a walk across the Green Park, having a key to the garden, and we may hear the song of the sparrow, and look upon the Nash palace of the day, and compare it with Whitehall of the past, and the carriage shall await us at Hyde Park Corner."

We were by this time at the door, where a cab was drawn up with a horse which in strength, appeared master of his work, and in bearing, to be conscious of power and beauty.

"Ha, ha, Lincoln!" said his master, and the animal turned his head, and seemed to prepare, by a movement of his legs, for a start. "I always speak to my horse, the voice of man has more power over animals than is generally believed, meet us at the top of Constitution Hill, Jim."

"Yes, my Lord," was the tiger's answer.

And I, for the first time, learned that Fernwold was a Lord, I perceived also, though faintly traced on the brown panel, an Earl's coronet. We were not long of being in the Park, the grass was really green, though the trees and sheep were black.

"There is some freshness here, when the wind is west," said the young Earl, as he took my arm, and we crossed the sward with sturdy steps.

We had soon arrived at the corner, and mounted the vehicle, and were trotting at a good pace down toward Knightsbridge.

"I am going to a nursery garden near Hammersmith," said my companion, as we were darting among the stage coaches, that everywhere hung threatening over us. "You can have nowhere to go, so I have brought you along, you will like the garden, as I like your chat, and you are not early enough for your own Covent Garden, I suppose."

I had no idea of its existence.

"Well, I cannot see, since neither your father nor the market benefit by your being there, how you should remain, when I have told you that there is a room for you with me, you lose half your time in threading Cranbourn Alley. Your father takes a great responsibility, pray tell him so tonight, and pack up."

I was glad he again made the proposal, and unless there was some unexpected opposition, it was a thing agreed.

There can be nothing more beautiful than a garden, especially in Spring, while the foreman was occupied in discussing the merits of new plants, and showing off others, I sauntered down a walk which led me toward the boundary wall, where there is such a variety as there is in a nursery garden, you are in a certain degree distracted, it is in the eye of the lover, of the beautiful in plants and flowers, what a dictionary would be in the hands of one who sought amusement in literature, and I had contemplated, with some interest, the different beds and plots, where separate classes and ages of plants, were ranged in seminaries of secular education.

Thus musing, I was startled by the sound of a window opening, there was a house of the villa order close by, and I saw a head half withdrawn from the open casement just as I looked up, it was one of those heads where the strong contrast of white skin and dark hair tell at a distance, and my attention at once captivated. There was but a moment I caught that large dark eye fixed upon me. The distance was not so great, but that I could read anything but repulsion in the glance, I hesitated and trembled, and the window shut up in its mercy that gazelle eye and those raven tresses from my sight.

The scarcely budding seedlings in their trim beds, in that part of the garden had an immediate interest for me. I paced up and down, and from the earth raised my eye to the contemplation of the sky, in that direction, when its view was obstructed by the building, which for the time contained my heaven. The thing was too apparent, although I thought at the time that it was but another proof of Fernwold's quickness of comprehension, when he taxed me with having found something to attract me behind that muslined lattice. I was really too confused to deny well, so my negation amounted to an acknowledgment, but I accompanied him away, as if glad to get back to town. There was something abstracted in my manner, which did not escape my companion, and he ceased to rally me on it.

Six o'clock had brought to the park its wonted throng, and we entered at the Kensington Gate, and drove along what is the most beautiful part, and what is least frequented, but upon getting to Apsley House, I can remember well, that I thought nothing short of the most reckless madness could induce my noble driver to plunge into a mass of carriages twisting and turning like skaters in all directions, and apparently touching. I recollected, on my first arrival, to have thought my coachman was running against houses, and over passengers, but the one-half of the coach windows were boards, and the rest such dim and dingy glass, that I contented myself with a shudder. I firmly believed we had crept under wagons, and over porters, of whom I saw nothing more than the burthens on their backs, but here, under a bright evening sun, without dust or any other medium of visual obstruction, with a high but not fast trot, we were attacking a phalanx. There was no appearance of doubt in either of the living agents in this daring act, and I sat immovable in resignation, the fat old lady, into whose open barouche we were driving, scarcely seemed to look round, as she glided out of our course like a sylph. A cab was coming at us in full trot, and three horsemen, in loud and eager discourse, a coach of bright yellow, and blue and silver servants, horses, harness ribbons, buckles, and blazonry, shook its vast hammer cloth at us, the great coachman nodded his three-cornered hat, the announcement of our fate. Two fair faces passed in smiling recognition, and we had escaped this opportunity of a splendid catastrophe, and while I tried to look back to see how all this danger had been run or avoided, we were in a quiet and regular stream of dissolving equipages. In this course, we were inexorably carried along, if not by a chain of events, or the thread of fate, by a string of carriages.

"We must get out of this. I am afraid of the calves of these footmen's legs before us," said his Lordship, and we broke out at the gate at Grosvenor Street. "I will drop you at the top of the Haymarket, but do not suppose there is any place in London, I should dislike to be seen in under the protection of your wing."

I did not quite comprehend how, but I saw this was a little quiz, as he usually poked me with his finger, or anything he had in his hand, when he did not mean me to take what he said seriously, and indeed, had he not taught me to make the distinction, I should only have caused him more trouble, as he almost always dealt in enigmas.

Chapter Four
Edward changes lodgings—chance meeting with a lady—further acquaintance

My father, though more uneasy in his manner than usual, seemed almost glad at my departure. I never asked any questions, and knew not whether I was to be a clerk in Somerset House or a guardsman, my time and attention were to be occupied by that mighty city into which I had just been cast. "Welcome, cousin mine," said my host, as I came in for a late breakfast next morning.

"I did not know I had the honor," I began, but was interrupted.

"Never mind the speech, your father, who has been much my friend, is a distant relation, ditto you."

I finished, or rather changed my speech. "I may be the cousin of the Emperor of China, for all that I know, it only seems wonderful, that my father knows my name, as to myself, I learned it with other things at school."

He laughed and added, "Now I will be more frank and tell you how you are to be here. Bed and breakfast, you take alone, unless when we agree about the latter by previous arrangement, luncheon also. There is always something sufficient for a bachelor's table ready at eight, unless ordered expressly at any other hour. You can come into my bedroom, which is divided from yours, you know, only by a passage, when the door is not bolted. And if I am asleep, your own good nature will prevent your waking me, if I am occupied or moody, I suppose you will turn and leave. If, however, I am gay, it will not shew the more that I am glad to have you with me, and we can arrange for the day, but you must not think I mean to keep watch over you, there must be perfect liberty. I shall only have you when it suits us both, and like a great master, give the finishing touch. I do not often ride in London, it requires too much attention, but I have some horses, which I hope you will have taste enough to like, and there is a groom boy, a sort of tiger—in fact, Jim can only be called a cheetah—who is perfection in his way. Like other infants, I suppose, he came into the world crying. I know not how long he continued this, though I do not think he would now do for the hero of a French novel in that respect, but I firmly believe he has never laughed, and he cannot smile. My coachman, for I have no stud-groom, calls him Benjymann, he sees everything without looking, and hears everything without listening, and it has never occurred to me to doubt anything, even an opinion given by him. It is even believed in the household, that he has no affections, in short, I have known lads of this sort, very much in the way on certain occasions, there is no danger of him, and he has plenty of what is called pluck, so when you ride, you may ask him questions without the least hesitation. There is no occasion for your asking me about the riding horses, they are yours, and if I want them any time, I will apply to you. I have some calls to make, it is necessary to keep doors ready to open, when one may wish to have an entry, and I am sufficiently methodical in that respect to be well with some of the best of the great dames, so I can have you invited to most of them, should you like."

There could be no rejoinder to all this, but I felt my eyes sparkle with delight, and I clasped him in my arms like a schoolboy.

"Do not be so good and ingenuous, my dear boy, you make me sad," he sighed.

And I remarked the color come to his wan cheek for the second time since I knew him, as he sat—for we were seated—at a table, side by side on a sofa, like Romans. He parted the hair on my forehead, and gazed upon me with a melancholy smile.

"Now for the wizard *Post*, to know where we are, and what we are about, there is the *Chronicle*." He threw me the other paper.

This I was accustomed to, as my father always took a number of papers.

It was natural, when I took my ride, that I should not wish to begin with Mr. Ben, by shewing any dependence upon him, and I therefore took the only one of two courses I knew, the which was most easy and agreeable, and I rode down the gutter of the park side of Piccadilly in becoming quiet, when I had got off the stones, however, I increased my pace, and involuntarily found myself at the entrance of the lane which conducted to the garden of the day before. I did not alight at the gate by which we had entered then, but went round toward that villa which my active imagination had at one time made into an enchanted palace, and at another, an envious prison. I found a door in the garden wall near the house, but it was closed, and after a glance at such of the windows as faced in that direction, and at which I saw nothing, I turned to enter by the ordinary gate at the other side.

"You can take the horses round, and wait for me at the other door, which you saw beyond," I said, as I gave my bridle to the groom.

The only liberal people about gardens, are those who have plants and flowers to sell, and therefore, to whom any damage done by the public, would be most injurious, the gardens and grounds of the gentry of England are closed from the eager and unfortunate public, who are thus taught to desire, and invited to misuse, the access everywhere denied. I entered without question, and my steps were, of course, bent toward that lattice now closed, I called the foreman, and asked a thousand questions, and really obtained information about plants, which would have been useful in rural life, but no delay I could devise brought the desired vision—was it periodical? The house was the same as the day before.

The sun, however, was not out, perhaps that was the cause, but I could no longer contrive any reason for loitering, gave a little present, and proceeded to find myself in the saddle musing on my way to town. This disappointment in no degree cooled my desire, at least to resolve myself, whether my imagination had not been deceived, and that a little distance had lent its aid to the enchantment. It is needless to say, how often I rode there, how I discovered other places from which I could command a view of the window—carried a small spy glass in my pocket, and meditated hiring an apartment within reach.

A week had passed, the assemblies I went to, and where high beauty and fascinating grace were nightly thrown in my way, where no eye was turned away from my admiration, served to beguile my thoughts, and I became almost ashamed of my passion for the unknown, still there was a sort of obstinacy in me not to be defeated, I hoped, by the closing of a miserable window sash.

I was galloping one day along a road in the neighborhood of my now usual resort, there was a space of green sward on the side, with masses of dwarf bushes upon it, like a piece of common. I urged my horse over those which barred my course, with some impatience, but the extent was small, and the gallop short, when I pulled up, I missed my opera-glass, which had fallen from my pocket. Ben came up, and I asked him if he had observed it, he had, however, in his sober composure, kept the road, and it immediately suggested itself to me, that it must have been in one of the leaps I had taken, that it had fallen out, and I wished to examine on foot the places I had come over.

"If it has not fallen into the bushes, it will be easily found, sir," said he and he asked if he should go back and look. I told him, however, to hold the horses, and I could myself more easily recognize the way I had come.

I went back, in a sort of half bird-nesting search. I found the object of my search, and some violets besides, so I came back in radiant satisfaction. It was then I met the intelligent eye of my attendant, and he touched his hat. This was a sign he wished to speak, and I said, "Well?"

"If you would like a little more of a stretch, sir," he said, "there is a fine place at Wimbledon."

I used the word *intelligent*, I do not know that it expresses what I wished to describe in that stolid look, but I immediately felt inclined to adopt the suggestion, and I said, "We will go there, then, tomorrow."

There had been rain all the morning—the roads were watered—the trees were freshened—flowers blowing, and everything felt odoriferous and revived. As soon as I got out of my ken, I sent Ben in front, and when I quickened my pace, he was to be impelled by my approach. I gave these instructions, but they were useless, he never appeared to look back, and was never overtaken. However, at last we arrived, and he then drew up, and let me pass.

It had been a longer ride than I anticipated, and instead of feeling eager to force my horse over the gorse, and give him a stretch where it is more open, I contented myself with sauntering down a path leading to the right on entering the waste. The primrose was almost past, and the wild hyacinth was also giving way, but there was still great variety in the hedges, and something of that compound of balmy perfume which the sun ever brings forth after the summer shower.

I know not why I took that side, I know not why I felt no inclination to dart over the wide space before me, but to glide gently along under the tall elms which clothed its bounds. There were houses almost constantly, and well-kept grounds. There was a flock of sheep, and a few donkeys. Why had I come there? But I went on, and gazed over the fences, and through the opens. I felt really ashamed of myself, and of the prying vein I had unintentionally fallen into, and turning my horse, he immediately felt I was in another mood.

A swinging gallop, broken by some leaps, soon restored me to animation. The spring of a blackbird from his covert startled my horse, and he swerved, just as a lady, with a little girl, came out of a lane between two of the villas. I do not know that I was near enough to warrant the alarm, but the child tumbled over a bush, in trying to escape, and the lady, as ladies generally do, stood still to be run over, and gave a little scream. I, of course, pulled up and dismounted, to make the best excuse I could, and to comfort the little one, who besides could not rise, having nowhere to place her hands but on the thorns, among which she was cast. The first hesitation of her older companion was passed, and she also had made a movement to respond to the cries for aid, which came, not without cause, from the little thicket. Of course, it was impossible to step over the low intervening bushes without holding up her dress, and of course, my eyes were not shut, and the sight of a beautiful ankle, and swelling limb above, though it lent much more interest to the adventure, did not in any degree hasten my movements, and I did not arrive within reach until my aid was useless. Sacs were worn in those days by ladies, and the sac had fallen in the alarm, and I was in time to offer my own pocket handkerchief, fresh from its folds, to wipe the tears and the few drops of blood which the prickles had brought from the young and blooming cheeks. While I was thinking how near these wounds were to the eyes, I was startled by hearing her exclaim, "Dearest child, how thankful we should be that you are not blinded."

I looked round at the reproach, and found her from whom it came also rubbing off a streak of red blood, which had burst through the stocking, how I longed to seize the handkerchief. Her head was down, and a light and small white bonnet did not confine her luxurious hair, I knew the hair immediately, and when she looked up. I knew the eyes, they were almost reproachful, till my evident confusion and contrition in some degree told in my favor, and then their expression I did not like better, for there was a touch of raillery in them, and I turned away in some confusion.

But she had to get out among the bushes, and I was resolved that I should have my revenge. I lifted up the lighter burthen, and waited until the young lady should do me the favor to make way by preceding me. She hesitated a moment—and there was a wicked little smile—and then she leaped back, with a graceful agility. It was evident then, that though she could not have cleared the brambles at first, without lighting upon the sprawling child, who occupied the accessible angle of the clear spot in which we stood, there could be no difficulty in bounding back.

I was defeated, but I had created a little emotion, and engaged her in a little conflict. She made way—still with that look of mischief and pouting smile—it seemed as if I was expected to perform a similar feat, as the young creature in my arms laughed joyously, and clung closer, in the hope. Grace could not quite be expected in the performance, but I landed safely, with the loss of my rider's hat. I had again to enter the little island of short grass and daisies, where, had Providence listened to my desire of the moment, I should have been sentenced to pass the remainder of my life with the fresh and beautiful creature who stood before me—not even bargaining for everlasting youth.

I placed the recovered object, with its ribbons and feathers, most becomingly on the little fair head.

"It is time for us to return, my little Clara," said again that ringing voice. And I could not help saying, "Surely, you did not mean to make so short a walk?"

"Nor have we. I am now balancing whether we are to thank you, or leave you to the justice of your own conscience."

I am sure I must have looked hurt, for she added more gaily, "Nay, I have not yet said, our blood be upon your head!" She took two or three steps toward the lane.

I saw that I was not absolutely dismissed, and begged to accompany them, in case of accident.

Then came again the sting with the smile—"Shall we meet, do you think, with another horseman?"

The land was shady—overgrown hedges and trees on either side, and without being absolutely crooked, its turns and narrowness prevented our seeing far, and in the course of fifty yards, we could neither perceive an outlet in front or from where we had entered. It was getting shady with tender green, and the young birds were taking their short flights in it, and the song of the old ones was sweet to us, though maybe sung with a beating heart.

"We have not far to go now, and perhaps you will leave us. You cannot see the gate on the left, just beyond the turn, but leave us, Clara and I can tell our own tale!"

"But may I not have the happiness of inquiring, tomorrow," I began.

"Oh, do you think we are to venture out on that dangerous common again? No, no, the shady lane is worth twenty commons, and I do not know what took us out."

Again I looked, as the light step retired, and I could see the beautiful figure bent down, as if giving instructions, or impressing something upon her running companion.

It was time to turn, and feeling that it would be ill-bred to look further after their course, I slowly bent my steps toward the end of the lane.

What had become of my horse? It had never given me the slightest thought, and I looked about. At some distance, under the shade of some trees, was my composed attendant, holding the two horses, while a donkey stood looking at the group, with ears pricked, in evident admiration. Faithful to his part, Ben did not seem to notice my approach until it should become necessary, and I was permitted to mount without the least appearance of anything having occurred beyond the usual incidents of a country ride. But something told me the quiet surface was habit, and that he was not without observation and interest as to the incidents of the day.

For my own part, I rode home full of vague plans to accomplish a more intimate acquaintance, and determined to renew my visit.

It is needless to relate the steps of our intimacy—how the next day, I met the object of my constant thoughts, alone—and that I was subject to a good deal of that sharp raillery, of which I had, in our previous interview, seen some symptoms.

I discovered the slightest foreign accent, and that her mother had been Portuguese, that her name was Isabell, and that she lived for the present, in the villa near which we had walked. There was a little more freedom of manner than is usually found in young English women, and while she had the best of the badinage, I had insensibly contrived to get hold of, and keep, her hand—perseverance is everything—and, from abandoning the hand, I succeeded in capturing the arm, and could feel a heartbeat. As this change occurred, so changed her voice, and the light words and little scorn in their tone, gave place to accents less assured, and occasionally a suppressed sigh.

There was so much timidity in my manner, that hers also became suppressed, and we often remained several minutes without uttering a word, and I felt a little weight begin to hang upon my arm. Something interrupted us, and we separated in some confusion, with me, feeling assured that everyone I met was in my secret.

I know not how it came about, but though there had been a careless boldness in this young creature's manner at first, which would, to all appearance, have led on a more enterprising lover, yet I became timid and backward in the same degree, as our intimacy advanced, and she more disconcerted. There seemed always something about to be asked, and something about to be told, and we parted, both as far from bringing the object of their wishes to the lips as before.

One afternoon, we had strolled down the side of the common, and before we had turned to get back into the lane, a cloud, which had been unobserved or unheeded, began to drop, not the most gentle, hints of a heavy shower. We had to hurry our pace almost to a run, but the shower came on us in a pour. With that feeling habitual to civilized life, when it is necessary to invent excuses for exciting interest, I immediately got into a flurry, and convinced myself that a wetting to an object idolized by me must be fatal, I proposed my coat to be hung over her shoulders, and took it off to apply to this purpose. She was out of breath, and held her hand to her heart to restrain its beating.

"Are you really so foolish? What worse shall I be? and we are only detaining ourselves. Do you really think I am one of those fragile things, incapable of bearing hardship, or willing to allow you, for a little vanity, to make yourself look ridiculous? Instead of that, if you do not wish to keep me to be better soaked, you will let me help you to put on your toga."

This she said with a flash of that spirit which could not, apparently, long remain subdued.

Again we sped across the waste, she bounding before me with that light step, and beautiful limb, which is the chief animal beauty of woman. But the heavy cloud had not relaxed its discharge, and the exertion and the pace were too much for one not in regular training. So, when we got to the mouth of the lane, my companion was fain to cling to me for help, and I had almost to carry her along.

We got to the gate however, and then I thought she was to lose her senses, so completely prostrated did she feel.

There was a little path outside the wall, which led to the backcourt, where

I could still continue to assist her on, without being in sight of the windows. As we got near, it was necessary to speak in whispers, and my head was close to her cheek. She clung to me as if her heart would burst. I felt her balmy breath, and sought her rounded cheek. By a strong effort, she rallied, and placed her hand on my mouth, as she disengaged herself from my arms.

For my part, I cared not whether all London came upon us or not—courage, in these cases of extremity, mounts with the occasion. But the movement of that soft little hand restored me—not to my senses, they were sufficiently alive, but—to my reason.

She looked for a moment in my eyes, and seemed to hesitate—then about to lay hold of the bell—let her arm fall, again approached her lips to my ear, and said, in a voice in which I thought there was some roughness, though it trembled, "Half an hour after sunset, in the lane!"

I heard the bell, and she motioned me away with her hand, she was raised in stature, and wore a look of command. I knew not how to obey. The door opened, and I saw her enter, and no one looked out, and I reeled away stunned and dripping, unhinged, with a heart beating like a woman's.

I found Ben with an umbrella, who disappeared to bring out the horses, the putting up of which having been a thought of his own, he felt bound to restore matters to *status quo* on my re-appearance.

The gallop did me good, and I found a jolly party were to meet in the evening.

Lord Fernwold was not insensible to my absences and distractions, and he sometimes hinted that he hoped the catastrophe would come off soon, whatever it might be, and restore me to common life.

I was no ingredient in the joys of the table that night. My voice was called into action by being asked to sing, and music always, since I can remember myself, restored me to a calm and general train. I thought of her, and sung of her. I remember a curious smile on our host's face as I ended, but the others were pleased, I had some voice, and it is to be believed, inspired as I was by a first love, there was no want of expression to the tender lay.

The party, however, broke up at last, and we retired.

Not as usual did I fall into the profound and willing sleep which waits on a day of activity, crowned with an evening feast. There were some ruffled rose-leaves on my couch, the night was hot—I threw off the clothes—a night-lamp burned—and I got up and bathed my temples, and looking at myself in the glass, I thought my eyes of unusual size, and my face of a strange dead white.

I again threw myself on the bed, soon after, the door gently opened, and my opposite neighbor looked in, as if to see whether I was awake. I suppose, seeing my naked figure on the bed, and the clothes tossed about, he came forward to see if anything was the matter. I shut my eyes at the first sound, ashamed at being caught more in the position of a lunatic than a sober guest. He came and sat down by me in his wrapper.

"I do not know how it is, dear Edward, but I feel that some misfortune is hanging over me, and the blow is to be struck through you. You are going to be ill, or something is to happen."

"Not I," answered I, smiling. "I am only restless." And I stretched myself, yawning, as if inclined to sleep. I was not equal to an explanation, and indeed, could not tell in what position I stood myself. All I knew was, what few like to own, and never the tyro, that I was madly in love.

"I am too old," he rejoined, "to wish for any confidence, and I have no doubt that you will get over the love part of the thing, but I fear you are going to be a victim, and you must make me a promise."

He had taken my hand, and I was touched more than I can describe by his melancholy tone and affectionate manner.

"What is it?" I said.

"That you do not pledge your word to marry, until you have spoken on the subject to me."

I did not answer. It appeared to me that he knew all.

"A gentleman never breaks his word, so it should not be lightly given."

I felt the most unbounded surprise. The subject had never occurred to me in that light. I had never thought of marriage. Yet Isabella was a lady, there could be no doubt in that. There was, amid all her levity and the freedom of her manners, the unmistakeable stamp of high breeding, and there came often from her eyes that flash of haughty pride, and there was a scorn even of herself and her own acts, which was the opposite of anything mean. All this came over me at once, in one recollection.

Fernwold's eyes still beseeched me.

"I promise," I at last answered.

"I have no tears to shed," he said, "or I could weep my thanks, for, believe me, I am much moved, and there are few things that might glad or grieve me now."

There was something that thrilled me to the core, in the desponding of one so young, so bright, so beautiful, so beloved, of high rank and lineage, rarely equaled income, into the controul of which he had not yet entered.

We are all, to a certain degree, egotists, and I soon felt that, if I could draw from him the sad tale of unfortunate love which so overpowered him, it would be an introduction which would embolden me to my own recital afterward.

"Oh, but tell me, you may do it so low, that you shall not hear your own words." I drew his head down to my neck.

"Would you really, then, like me to tell you? My dear boy, I know it would give you pain, and you could in no way help me."

"Ah, you do not know, you cannot know what I might not do. Young and determined, should I make a vow to accomplish anything for you, sooner or later, I feel I have the power." And my better nature was strong in me.

Again, that sad eye and gentle smile.

"Have you so little read men's fate in their looks, that you do not guess what I have to say. But I will tell you circumstantially, for I have consulted all the best doctors, one by one, without any good results."

"Is the case, then, desperate?" I said, with really painful interest. "Surely, with youth, there is always some hope."

"You shall hear," he continued. "Many had been consulted to save, none to condemn. I went to Dr. H——.

"'You are called upon, doctor, with no hope that you can cure. But here is a hundred pounds, tell me fairly what you think.'

"He put back the hand with which I offered this, and looked at me attentively.

"'You are serious? Yes! Come again tomorrow, and I will do what you require, should you still desire it.'

"I went at the hour appointed. He felt my pulse.

"'Your mind is made up, and you can bear the shock?'

"'If it was for tonight,' I answered.

"He continued to hold my wrist.

"'I should recommend immediate change of air.'

"I interrupted him with a look.

"'Well, you know that these things depend upon the air and regimen. In some air, and with proper care, a crisis is kept back. I speak of things as they are. You know it is nearly the height of the gay season. My lord,' he at last said, 'I think it requires as much courage in me to speak, as you to hear.'

"'So far, I understand you, and thank you. Now for the period?'

"'I should think,' said the doctor, in a kind, slow voice, 'that you cannot live over two months.'"

It was well I was on the bed. I felt my whole blood in my head, and that I must have fallen else. It was of himself he had been speaking. I may live to advanced years. They say age only blunts the feelings, however, that may be, as I lay there, I had received a shock, the equal to which I shall never feel again.

"What can be the matter, Edward, what can you mean?"

I lay dead and prostrate. I would not believe what I had heard.

"It must be false," I said, as soon as I had recovered sufficiently to speak.

"And why did you ask me to tell you all this. I was sure it would affect your dear heart. But did I not prepare you—did you not see the sentence coming."

"No, no! I thought you alluded all along to the health of another that was dear to you. Until the last word, I believed it was of another that you had spoken, and would know the fate."

"Should I recover, there will be an unnecessary shock to forgive, should I die—but we will not renew a disagreeable subject. I am uneasy about you. I have always believed in presages, and I think, as life wanes, we see things to others unseen. There has been someone hanging about of late, who has ever been of evil omen to me. I saw him when I lost my father, but it was not he brought the news, but he hung about like a raven. I saw him when I had saved a youth, senior to myself at Eaton. He struggled, and I almost thought, wanted to drown me. That was the source of this illness which is insensibly dragging me under. When I recovered my senses, he was there, and I lay and chilled, while they sent for a carriage. But I keep you awake, and indeed, I have need of some rest myself. Think not of this tonight, we will have a chat at breakfast."

He stooped down, and kissed my forehead, and left me.

I do not know how I got into a troubled sleep, but it probably came upon me by mental exhaustion, it lasted till morn. It was one of those strange double sleeps. I dreamed that I was dreaming.

Chapter Five
Strange portents—a declaration of love—a plot revealed

Waking late, I found, upon being ready, that the opposite room was open, and its occupant gone. He was below, on the divan, and they were pushing the table toward it, already loaded with fruit and those various breads which form the ornament as much as the support of the meal.

"Well, have you got over the fright I gave you last night?" were his first words, while the servants were yet in the room, and his fine color and cheerful voice almost made me feel there had been some delusion.

We were left to the newspapers, however, and anecdotes of the Sailor King, when the solemn servant, out of livery, came in with a card. I could not help looking at it, as it lay on a small golden salver.

"Put it down, Johnson," said Fernwold, after he had seen it, and he resumed the papers.

"We shall not dine together today, I fear, as I have to do host for a widow aunt, who is also an invalid. It is a bargain, by which I am absolved from all calls, and what are considered dutiful attentions, provided, upon certain state occasions, when there is a feast, I come and act the part of host, and appear as if all the old plate was mine, and all the quaint dishes were ordered of my own invention. Her cook is of the period before the first revolution, and I have the bill of fare sent here, that I may learn the names of its contents, as I am expected to be able to recommend something to my aunt from the other end of the table, it sounds a little like a proclamation, but she thinks it a proper attention in public, and after I have handed a duchess, who comes without a neveu, to her carriage, which is a great triumph to my aunt, I am allowed to depart, with a well-earned blessing."

Half this was said as he crossed the room to go out, and he nodded gaily at the door, and said, "Good night!"

I little thought that I should never look upon that calm and sunny brow again.

As soon as I thought he was safely in the next room with the doctor, whose name I had seen in my furtive glance, I also left the room, and took my way to the door, in order to waylay the visitor, and learn something, if possible, of his opinion. His carriage was waiting round the corner, and I had not been there long before its owner himself came hurrying to it. I caught him however, and begged to say two words. I was beginning a preface about relationship and interest, when he cut me short.

"I know what you mean, my young friend, you know there is no answering for accidents, but I really hope—I assure you—I hope change of air and a little attention to diet."

"But Dr. H——'s opinion?" I inquired.

"Oh, you know, he has had the gauntlet thrown down to him, to say something strong and the result of that will be, that our noble friend will begin to act as if he did not think he was made of cast steel. Don't be alarmed, and of all things, don't show yourself so."

He was in his carriage, already nodded, and drove off.

I was, on the whole, reassured. The elasticity of youth is apt to reject warning, and I was glad to cling to the hope furnished by the evident serenity of a medical attendant of such eminence.

As I was out, I thought I would go and call at the Hummums, but my father was not at home, and I waited an hour in vain, for his return. I wished to mention Fernwold's illness to him. I was restless, I had my own rendezvous in the evening, and could not resolve myself into any occupation.

Lunchtime came. I told Ben I should not want the horses. Fernwold had gone out, I sat down alone, all was gloomy, and I felt out of appetite. It was strange that he did not come in. I do not know why, but I expected him, his place was there, and it appeared as if I could not get it out of my sight.

I had become almost nervous, as the afternoon advanced. There was a coach, by which I was to go down to Wimbledon, which was to start at six o'clock. I could not tell why I was so uneasy, but I watched for the sharp knock at the hall door, and left that of the library open, that I might hear it. No knock, however, came, and it wanted but a quarter of six. I took my hat from the hall-table, and looked at the hats and cloaks of my friend, with an interest and sadness which I have since thought prophetic.

The sky was cloudy, but the air was warm, the rain of the day before had laid the dust, the gravel ground under the wheels. The coachman, a graduate of Oxford, occasionally tipped the blossoms with his whip, as he passed, and raised his elbow to those he considered worthy of this notice, making the smallest economies of room, and frowning when one of the leaders broke into a canter. They were a chestnut team, and I ventured to remark that it was a fretful color. He gave me a sort of look and a nod. I do not know if our acquaintance would ever have ripened, it was not that he was uncivil, or contemptuous, because I had in no way shown him that I could strike that key, to which all his thoughts were attuned.

We stopped once or twice, and he gave directions, in half words, touching some mysterious minutiae about the harness, which the ready helper had not observed, but rushed to obey, with an air of admiration at the inspired discovery.

I was occupied in ruminating upon the exclusiveness of the race who guided the four-horse coaches of the England of that day, when we stopped so near where I wished to alight, that I took the opportunity. I touched my hat to the coachman and whether he thought it was in the manner of a superior, or that it was wrong to return anything but a cabalistical sign, I could not tell, but my salutation remained unheeded. I paid the guard, however, for both, and the living load, which overhung the hedges, and brushed the windows of the narrow way, moved smoothly on, as if I had never sat on that honored seat, where I had not possessed the genius to remain.

I had two hours to wait, I felt that it would appear strange to loiter about the immediate neighborhood. I had eaten little luncheon, and the fresh air had given me an appetite. It was a blessing, in this case, to escape in any way from the impatience I felt. I ordered a beefsteak, and took up the history of Jonathan Wild. Wild and reckless adventure had always a charm for me, and I remembered my boyish ventures in the same line, in robbing orchards and hen-roosts, and riding about horses out at pasture half the night, with a cord bridle and a bit made of a small piece of the chain of a jack.

Several persons came in and out. A smart girl waited upon me, with eyes as black as jet, and cheeks like peonies, she seemed to take a malicious pleasure to torment me.

It is the universal law of waiters, on leaving a room, always to take something out with them, like what is now called a go and return ticket. Happily for me, there was a sideboard, besides other tables, to supply her red and ready hand, else I might have myself become a victim to her wants.

The sun had set, and the sky was still overcast. I was half a mile from the lane. It was time to sally forth. I called for the bill, patted the pretty maid's cheek with the most paternal air I could assume, and took my leave. She shook her head at me as I went, and seemed to think I was up to some mischief.

"Good night, cherry cheeks," I hollowed, and ran off.

Taking a circuit, not to be watched, and to fill up the time before it should become dark, I went round part of the common to the left. I ran as if too late, yet it was not much more than dusk when I got to the little road I had so often trod with Isabell. My heart beat with a dread that she would not come, and I was beginning to think how I should get back. It would be too much happiness to meet under the favor of that darkness, which was to shroud all further reserve.

Let he who remembers the boiling of his first passion, conceive my feelings, when I almost rushed upon a dark form close to the gate. I had been there often enough to know that we were to meet in silence, but instead of returning with me, and taking our usual course, she laid her hand on my lips, and took the other way, beckoning me as she went, it was not easy to follow her swift and noiseless steps, but we ran a considerable way, she darted over a stile to the right, and we were in a meadow, following the side of a hedge which bounded it on our left, she still ran on, but turned round every now and then and laughed, as if in glee at some escape. I, of course, was in a moment by her side, her hood had fallen back, the dark locks and lustrous eyes were uncovered, and she was in my arms.

Full of rapturous joy, I began to question her on the cause of this little flight, and if we had been seen.

"What if we have, I cannot care much for appearances, or I should not be running about in the dark with a youth of your virtue."

"Well, you may joke me as you like, Isabella, but just let me tell you what I have got to say."

"Well, you must be short, as you are out of wind, so say on."

"It is not much, but it may be something for you to remember someday, that you have one heart devoted to you."

"Aye, to a girl you consider light."

She broke in with a laugh that was low, and to me sounded not natural, and she moved on. I was cut to the quick, for I remembered the promise I had given to Fernwold.

What can I say, I have nothing, I have a father as dark as night, I know not if I may have enough to clothe myself, as he has never opened his lips about the future. I know that he gambles in the funds, and he has told me almost with triumph, that it would not surprise him, to find any day he rose, that he was worse than a beggar.

I am but little more than seventeen, it would be the most selfish madness to talk of marriage and promises are made but to be broken.

"But I tell you again, I love you, Isabell, I love the earth you tread upon, I love that gay and happy mind, I love your waywardness, and your little wickednesses, and when I look into those eyes, I am jealous of the siren tongue, I was looking into those deep dark orbs, the shadow of night gave them a strange unearthly luster."

"Is all this true," she said slowly, and in a low tone, almost as if questioning herself, but breaking off, she shook her head. "It is useless, I am not good, indeed, I have been basely wicked, and I will not accept your young and golden love, to return what"—she turned away her head—"may be as strong, but a day might come, when we may compare."

We were seated upon the bank, a nightingale sung his song, and the air was calm, and there was not even the gentlest sigh of a night breeze. I could not speak, and she had dropt those dark fringes, almost on the pale cheeks, I felt her hand tremble slightly. At last, she said, summoning an energy, which though not uncharacteristic, broke in strangely on my trance-like happiness.

"Listen, your father, that man of mystery, for some reason, wishes you out of the way, that is, not to be able to thwart his plans. I know no details. You were to be seized this very night, and shut up in a private madhouse. It matters not how I came to be mixed up in this plot, and perhaps, when I tell you that I have been employed to lure you into this snare, that I have prolonged the period of working you up to desire for a night scene with me, that you might be caught, until the success of the scheme would be an everlasting punishment, you would disbelieve me, and forget all, but the unworthiness of one who would play such a part, be it so, I have had a few happy hours. You shall hear from me by some channel ere long, did not that clock strike? There is a lane over the stile, follow it to the right, and get back to town, the hour is passed, that you were to be brought into their hands, I will make some excuse for the failure. Tell all to Lord Fernwold, and take care. I thought I heard a footfall, if you would not make me suffer a remorse you cannot understand, go at once." She bounded from me.

Thunderstruck, I knew not what to think, but mechanically took the direction she had pointed out.

To be the victim of my own father, and betrayed by her whom I loved to madness, but I could not collect my thoughts. A vague sense of danger and despondency was gaining such mastery over me, that I know not how I missed losing my reason.

Part Two

Chapter Six
Imprisonment—passage for the New World—impressions of New York City

I had got into the lane, something tripped me, and I fell, two men were upon me, and two more tied my arms and gagged me. If I walked quietly, well—if not, I was to be bound and carried, I made a sign that I should prefer to walk. I have always had considerable command over myself, and have found that in cases of extreme difficulty, it is best to do nothing.

It is useless to relate the reception I met, that I was asked my name, that I threatened he whom I supposed to be the head of the establishment, that all I said or did was considered a confirmation of my unhappy state. That I was taken to a room with the window at the top of the wall, out of reach, that there was a trap door, through which I was fed from a wooden bowl, plenty of bedclothes, and changes of linen. I pined in this place eleven days, by the marks I made on the wall, on the twelfth, an unusual noise awoke me from a fast-growing apathy, the trap was opened, and I was told that I was to be examined by a medical man. I dressed myself in some haste, even to go along the passage would be something, two herculean keepers accompanied me to a room, here there was a mild-looking old gentleman, who felt my pulse, as I thought, a little awkwardly, asked me how I was, and seemed satisfied with the subdued manner I assumed, giving me to understand, he could not say much until he saw me again in the evening, and I returned to my cell, to ponder over the difference of the promised meeting, and that other, from which I had expected so much happiness, and from which I now suffered the first misery of my life.

It is needless to relate how the mild gentleman soothed me, representing that there had been a mistake, that it was to prevent an imprudent marriage, in short, that I ought not to take it to heart, but go down to Cheshire, and all would be made up. And that if I gave him my word, that I should not be violent, he would himself accompany me that night.

What was to be gained by an exposure? I should be on the parish, it was quite according to my father's ways, to put an end to such a connection as he dreaded, by any means short of personal discussion.

I cannot say how ashamed I was, or how deeply stung by the mysterious and delicate touch with which he handled the character of Isabella, but I was left with the conviction, that I had been her dupe.

I was not long, therefore, of determining to give the promise required, a carriage was at the door. In due time we arrived at Chester, and there was a letter waiting for me there from my father. He wrote, that there was nothing but my absence from England which could make his mind easy about the marriage, which he dreaded, he was obliged to go to London, and perhaps abroad, that he wished me to go to Liverpool, and take a passage in one of the New York packets. I should find my clothes at the Waterloo Hotel, he also sent me a credit upon New York for three hundred pounds, and money for my expenses and passage.

The venerable Doctor took leave of me here, as he said, in accompanying me so far, his only object had been to reconcile me to his friend, my worthy parent.

Fernwold had sailed for Lisbon, and I could not but feel hurt, that he had not written, however, all ties seemed to break off whatever might have attached me to England, and with one sore and tender corner in my heart, I took the stagecoach to Liverpool. The docks were then wonderful, but what most interested me, were those ships which eclipsed all other merchantmen in the port, I made my selection more to please myself in a captain, than to pretend to distinguish among these packets.

I found my whole wardrobe, unless a few gold buttons, which were missing, could be called a loss. I found a Manton fowling piece and rifle, a spyglass, and pocket compass. These were all new, and I could not help regretting my old rifle, and feeling that I had yet to gather confidence in these new arms. I found the rifle a strong and a straight-shooting gun of an ounce bore, it was a calm day upon which I tried it, the fowling piece I had had out already twice, and had found out the difference of the going off of a cap and a flintlock, so I felt how much easier it would be to shoot at a mark with the more immediate ignition, and confidently held to the spot, the ball struck within a couple of inches, above the line was perfect, and I shot no more.

That evening, I cleaned both guns, and packed them up more carefully than I did my less important baggage.

The next day, I was to sail in the swift Sesostris. I anticipated the comforts of that table, which has never been equaled in any packets since, the captain's spirits had risen as the hour approached, and he almost joked me in his dry way, the yellow stewards began to grin, as they marked me out a victim of nausea, and their protecting care. My luggage was on board, the *cheerily oh, oh*, of the sailors, as they strained on the hand spikes, for she was anchored in the stream an hour past. She was short, the anchor tripped, the yards were braced, and we were off.

I cannot describe with what feelings I looked forward to that land, in which there were so many wonders of nature to be overcome, or utilised by that mighty race, the fusion together of all the energies of other lands. I was to walk in the untrodden forest, and see the original man, uncontaminated by the schoolmaster. I was to be free to prey upon the beasts of these wilds, as they might be to prey upon me. I was to build my own canoe, and sail her upon inland seas, and no one to say me nay. My horse was to seek where he listed the choice of food, and to browse upon plants, a prize for European shews. I was to cull the choicest fruits, the apple, the peach, and the pear, when I found them in my way, and where I sought the haunts of men, was to find the unvarnished welcome, and the sacred salt. It was yet morning, the breeze was not strong, though we made good way, having with us the tide, and I remember on the eight bells, I was gazing upon that western sun sinking in the wave, which I could picture lighting with its ruddy fires, the shadows of those groves in which my imagination already wandered.

Those wonders of the deep, which are to be seen in skimming its surface, have often been told, the whale and the iceberg, the fog, the calm, and the storm, the shark prophetic of death, hanging ever in our wake, and the triumph of killing that unrelenting destroyer. The calm, with the oily wave, and the drifting storm, the ship mounting up to heaven, and then plunging as if never again to rise, breasting that wave which seems to throw her back forever from her course, and another and another.

Little did I know, that at few feet beneath, where abysses yawned, or the mountain rose, there was ever unalterable calm, and that the rage of waters was but above. That while we, with improved telescopes, and growing science, survey the surface, and weigh the atmosphere of planets, predict the coming comets, prescribe the course of stars, and read future events in that vast vault, which the solemn night opens to the love of learning—there is yet, down in the deep a space vaster than the dry land, of which we know nothing, whether it is delivered up entirely to an order of animals without reason, or whether there also may be found the divine spirit instilled into created beings, who inhabit its coral caves, and forests of eternal gloom.

I know not if I thus embodied my musings, but the time was fitting, the night was clear and dark, the gallant ship held her course, the breeze slightly abaft the beam, the watch took hardly heed, and the mate who paced the deck, looked up in vain at the unwrinkled sails, there was no change, and his thoughts might descend and stray to the home so strangely dear to the wanderer of the wave.

It was long before I went down to bed, I had seen land that evening, the vessel bounded under more sail, and a freshening breeze, the next shore I was to behold was that of another hemisphere.

After a voyage of no unusual incident or duration, the packet arrived at New York, groups of houses on either side at Brooklyn and Jersey city, have taken the place of masses of trees, which then clothed the heights and shores of the bay, there is, however one spot untouched amid the surrounding strife of wealth, that gem of beauty, the terraced walk, and the shady grove on the brink of the bay, and in the heart of the city, though unornamented by art, it has not yet fallen a victim to the love of gain and mercantile convenience.

A Roman Emperor built a theatre for the people of Rome, containing 88,000 spectators, where might be instilled the most sublime sentiments of virtue, heroism, and love of country, of its prosperity and glory, or where also might be fostered examples of the baser passions, and the delight in cruelty, which however disguised, lurks in the heart of man.

The present race of New York have inherited the aversion to the histrionic art of the plodding Dutch, and the sour Puritans, their predecessors. There is no place of amusement open to the people, and but one small part of that busy city, where business and care are not painfully intruded upon your attention, and which is set apart for recreation. That spot happily remains untouched and open to public use, and if the people do not choose to create for themselves a colosseum or a forum, they have at least spared enough from their taste in prisons, to keep with modest care this incomparable grove.

It was near there I landed, and there is much in the first impression, my baggage was taken to the Custom House, and I was alone, I had been recommended to go to the City Hotel, where the barkeeper never had been known to forget. Dante would have placed him elsewhere.

From Whitehall Stairs, it is but a step to the shade, and thither, like a bird, I flew from the glare of the sun and the bustle of ferry boats, there were no idlers in those days, a change, it would take volumes to describe, has taken place in that city and in the manners of its inhabitants, it has become European. In that day the dress, which is the first thing a newcomer observes, was quite different from what it is now. The women, when they did dress, for there were many who adhered still to the quaker-like simplicity of olden times, were always attired with elegance, but the men had then no idea beyond an expensive suit, they rode in the manner of the French of Lafayette's time, with difficulty touching the stirrup with the point of the toe, and their pantaloons aspiring to the knee, with what in a country not governed by a president, one would call an inter-regnum of stocking. They struck me then as being the worst horsemen I had ever seen—the few who rode for pleasure in the city streets. Now the women have still kept their place in advance, and there is no country in Europe, where an assembly would produce so much splendor as well as taste. The men are far more expensively dressed than in any community in Europe, and in plain clothes, really with taste, jewelry was at a very low estimation then, there was scarcely a ring or a watch guard to be seen, armorial bearings were more to be found on the hackney carriages of that period, than even on the dashing equipages of the present moment.

Horses were inferior, and ranged at about an average of fifty dollars, three o'clock was the hour of dinner, and the evening after supper, in the boarding houses, was finished in the happiest of social fashions, in dancing and music, without formality, and with freedom of manner and intercourse controlled by the most universal decorum. I do not remember in my varied life, having enjoyed society more.

The south had contributed from its sultry sun, the darker cheek and the warmer blood, the small specimens from Europe were mercantile, or emigrant Irish, who, however sad their history, or hateful the insults and injuries which had driven them from their green isle, bore no cloud upon their brow, and shed no gloom where they came.

One of the Berkleys lived in New York, the present Lord Derby had penetrated to Ohio, a few travelers of the pen had roamed through most of the long-settled States and rising territories, but still, a wanderer without an object, was a being of almost an unknown kind.

The counting-house, at its hours of work, engulphed the young as well as the old. A dinner was then a dispatch of food, and had they not been reminded afterward of the event, by picking out parts of their meat from their teeth, with a penknife at the desk, this episode in their daily occupation might have passed unnoticed.

Chapter Seven
A sudden departure—pastoral scenes—St. Louis—social engagements

In this happy state of things, the cholera, that scourge, which comes like knowledge and civilization from the east, had begun to seize upon its prey. A doctor and a clergyman first fled from their posts, and left the city, it is but right to record the justice of providence, and they both died. And notwithstanding stupid civic ordinances and the flaring advices of the public press, the mass of the inhabitants met the danger with resolution and resignment, but it was a damper to a certain degree, and a further motive to those who had any call to places yet free from contamination. I assembled my baggage, and set myself a going, to stop where I should find a good account of the first objects of my desire—the deer and the bear of the western States.

I need not say how many localities were recommended, and where I stopped to hear the drumming of what is called the pheasant[1], and catch a distant glimpse of the white tail of the deer, the turkey was still occupied by domestic care, so that it was not at once that I was to be introduced into the scene of action, and I was almost ready to despair, however, I must acknowledge, that I was both soothed and instructed by wandering in these solemn solitudes, where patience is so sublimely taught, and there is ever varying interest.

I shall never forget the first storm, how the shadows of the lurid clouds came over the shade, and the great drops fell distinctly from leaf to leaf, and

---

1. Pheasant: Stewart is probably referring to a grouse, for the bird called pheasant today was not introduced to the United States until 1880-82, when Judge O. N. Denny, former consul general to Shanghai, brought some to Oregon.

their coming was heard long before they reached the earth, and the lightning flashed more broadly in the dark vault, which gave a hundred echoes to the rolling thunder.

I had sufficiently worked my way, to have learned that a heavy bag is not to be found at any moment in the woods, I had begun to hear of the elk, and was disposed to pass over my want of success with the smaller, in looking for the larger animals, and I determined to turn my face to the northwest to cut my way across from Cincinnati, toward the mouth of the Missouri.

I had got letters to some of the most eminent persons of St. Louis[2], and I had been told by my worthy and respectable bankers of New York, that St. Louis was the spot where the best information could be got, and from whence all parties which penetrated into the wilds were equipped. I had procured an excellent horse, who stepped over logs in his walk or his amble, without extra exertion, and threaded his way through the trees with my saddlebags and myself, I had sent on my other goods by water. It now became a matter of consequence to secure a pheasant or a racoon, in order that I might not be a charge on the limited supply of fresh meat I often found in the log huts where I put up, and I began to practice what I considered the most heroic independence, in roasting a squirrel for myself, when I found a spot at twelve o'clock, where my horse could also make his midday meal.

The dwellers of the woods were then principally Americans, but few Germans having gone beyond the cities, and where they had, were clustered together, and to be found with some faded remains of jager[3] uniform, and an enormous pipe, with a gun slung at their backs roaming about the woods, these were to be avoided, there was no game near their ken.

I became enamored of the life I led, I could wash and change until I came where my stock of linen was to be reproduced, and then I chose the spot where there was the widest elbow room, bringing in turtle or squirrels every day, and feasting on them every night. I told tales, of great cities I had seen, or sung, and the children used to hang upon my words, and stare with their great eyes, and their parents equally wondered, though they showed it less. Many of

---

2. Eminent persons of St. Louis: Stewart had gotten letters of introduction from J. Watson Webb, wealthy financier and editor of two New York newspapers, the *Morning Courier* and the *Enquirer*. Stewart had met Webb in 1832 soon after his arrival in New York. The editor, also a former soldier, provided letters to William Clark, William H. Ashley, William Sublette, Robert Campbell, and—according to Webb's introduction to *Altowan*—to General Henry Atkinson. Webb was later (1839) responsible for arranging an exhibition of eighteen oil paintings by Alfred Jacob Miller at the Apollo Gallery in New York City, before they were shipped to Murthly Castle, Stewart's ancestral home in Scotland. Webb also introduced Stewart to the famous painter Henry Inman, who painted a portrait of Stewart as a gift to Webb. Webb prepared an introduction for, and edited, Stewart's other fur trade novel, *Altowan*, published in New York in 1846. See also Matt Field's note on an Indian who resembled the *editor of the Courier and Enquirer* in *Prairie and Mountain Sketches*, p. 184.

3. Jagar: Stewart's spelling of the German *Jäger*, a hunter or gameskeeper.

them had never been at Cincinnati, they were a simple and noble race, they turned out their beasts, and hunted them up again within a range of many miles.

There was no law among them, and in no part of the earth was it less needed. Every man was armed, and you saw a herd of horses headed by a bell mare, and followed by the owner with his rifle, very much with the air of one who would shoot a deserter from his band, his long chestnut or yellow hair, confined by a braid round his brow, and with his free and lofty port.

Out of this band, he would lend me one to relieve my own horse, and the others were, perhaps, put up from the heat and the flies until evening, I was ever welcome to stay, and free to go. Sometimes I paid moderately for my horse, when there happened to be anything wanted in the house which required ready money, I myself having the debate on the ways and means, in the only chamber the dwelling contained.

When the family was large, I partook of the children's bed, or shared it with another guest, when the family was small, I had, if there was one, a bed to myself on the floor.

It was October, two months I had led the life of a wanderer, and I had acquired a ready use of the rifle, with certain instincts and senses which habit brings forth in the woods, I could take a trail, and keep it at some speed, I could follow the line of a bee[4] loaded for his hollow home, and was a tolerable chopper, where to get at his treasure, a mighty sycamore[i] had to fall, I had learned to distinguish men's tracks, and those of horses, their shoeing or the naked foot, blazes had become as legible as finger-posts[5], and on the cloudy days, the mossy side of the tree, or where it bent from the prevailing storm, indicated the points of the compass, I had traversed Ohio and Indiana, making every day tell, drawing experience, as well as happiness, from all around.

Had I much to regret in England, was there any tie, had I an affectionate parent, or happy home? My best friend was the doomed victim of disease, she I had loved had lent herself to acts of violence against me, of which she was also the cause, was there anything to prevent my yielding myself up to the love of true liberty, to go where I listed, and do what I desired, there was not a vestige of gall in my heart. I had not a word to say against madhouses or fathers, I lay in the woods then, at the mid-days rest, when I wished to listen to the voice of the breeze, until the leaf began to fall on my upturned gaze. The weather was still beautiful, and there was beginning that frost, which is the purifier of the season from autumnal agues.

---

4. Follow the line of a bee: For an illustration of this practice, see Ross, *The West of Alfred Jacob Miller*, plate 122, *The Bee Hunter*.
5. Finger-posts: Signs in the shape of a hand.

I was hale and strong, and no one can describe the healthfulness of thought, who has not also enjoyed that freedom of action.

The pau-pau[ii], the parsimmon, and the wild grape, with the scarlet crab-apple, gave variety to the sylvan meal and the neck of the wild turkey was cut on his perch, that he might fall bursting with every grain, in knocking off the squirrel from the bough, with him came the hickory nut he was carrying to his winter store, and the wild goose, who is said first to have introduced maize among the red men, when he drops, bears at this season in his crop the produce of distant climes. All the aquatic tribes are winging their way from the threatening north, and present in their passage their varied plumage, and the most fastidious gourmand might now indulge to satiety in ducks and quails bursting with fat, the water rail[6] and the snipe.

I cannot say that this was not a sensual life, but it was a period of content, and it has left behind a store of such remembrances as never have faded or dimmed. I had traversed Illinois, and was in the beginning of November on the banks of the father of waters, I had to cross over, and to renew acquaintance with my neglected baggage.

St. Louis, of that day, was beginning to lose its character of a French settlement and though still unlighted and badly paved, with the cellar doors intruding like skylights upon the only footpathed street, the new ones were well laid out, but access by them depended upon the weather, curious old houses of wood standing in their gardens, were still the abode of the chief French families of the place, and that one pre-eminent, in which its mistress on receiving Lafayette[7], the national guest, sometime after I saw it, addressed the object of the country's gratitude:

"C'est votre premiere visite en Amerique, M. le Général?"

The steamers were but few, and mean comparatively, there was a marketplace, and an old Catholic Church, the City Hotel[8] was almost in the country, though kept by a worthy Kentuckian, of the name of Town.

The American Fur Company carried on their extensive Indian trade, in a place little better than a barn. And Robert Campbell, since one of the first merchants of the place, was but a young mountain trader.

---

6. Water rail: A waterfowl related to the American coot.
7. Lafayette: The Marquis de Lafayette, French hero of the American Revolution. He made a farewell visit to his adopted country in 1824-25. During his stay in St. Louis, he was the guest of Pierre Chouteau, the eminent fur trader. Lafayette was in St. Louis for only one day, April 29, 1825, so if the story told by Stewart is true, it may have its origin with the Chouteau family.
8. City Hotel: Though Stewart stayed at the City Hotel in New York, he appears to have stayed at the Mansion House in St. Louis. The Mansion House boasted thirty-six comfortable and spacious lodging rooms, one dining room sixty-five feet by twenty-five feet, a bar room, sitting rooms, two kitchens, one spacious smokehouse, etc. Davenport and Porter, *Scotsman in Buckskin*, p. 23.

Of the American residents, the venerable and hospitable General Clark[9] was the principal, and he was also head Indian agent, having with Lewis first crossed the Rocky Mountains from the Missouri, through the Blackfoot and Flathead country, and wintered on the Columbia, bringing back a museum of curiosities, and a collection of arms, with the portraits of those who bore them.

I had never been much of a plan maker, therefore, I lived contented with the vast variety of society, as well as food, that presented itself at the City Hotel, and stumbled my way down to the marketplace, to have an evening glass of egg nog with Mr. Bennet, that worthy compounder of sherry cobblers and hail storms[10].

There was no theatre, and the only public amusement was a fire, I remember the chimney of a newly built house belonging to an old Frenchman taking fire. We expected a conflagration, and there was a vast audience awaiting the coming of the fire engines. The poor Frenchman was gouty, and had a little touch of delirium tremens, he was in a dreadful state of alarm, and bravely had been carried up to an attic to be near the scene of danger. He appeared at the window, and cast up his eyes toward the clouds of smoke, and the starry sparks above, his appearance was received with a roar of applause, which he took for joy at his misfortune, and he attempted to harangue the concourse below, but few of whom knew why he was there, or what he was about, but as the chimney sent forth its volumes, its owner, the only person who had remained in the house, gesticulated with greater force, while his most beautiful rhetorical images were drowned by universal cheers.

There is no knowing whether the window sill could have much longer kept him within bounds, had not a propitious column of water from an engine, been thrown up to saturate the roof, and the orator disappeared almost as quickly and ignobly as a Punch. I shall never forget the scene, most of his best friends and relations were prominent actors, and we broke up to celebrate the recollection of the pantomime, if not to wish for such another. The reckless mountain boys, who had returned from their summer campaign, were the life and the terror of the place, and in the intervals of debauch, told the tales of the wilds with graphic and inspiring enthusiasm.

I have said before that I had no plans. I waited for letters, as I had no wish to act from impulse.

Sleighing, as the Americans call it became, as the snows came on, the chief pleasure of day. I harnessed my horse, covered his head with bells, and joined

---

9. General Clark: William Clark (1770-1838) was co-leader of the Lewis and Clark Expedition, 1804-06, and later governor of Missouri Territory and Superintendent of Indian Affairs.
10. Hail storms: A mountain version of the mint julep. Mint juleps are mentioned later in the text. Sherry cobblers are also alcoholic drinks.

him to that of a newly acquired friend, and we careered in our furs along the well-trodden roads, and over the open prairies, which there came close to the streets, there is no carriage movement so charming as that of the sledge, you feel that you are moving, instead of rolling insensibly on the well-laid rail, or swung in the cushions of the double-springed chariot.

Toward Christmas, the French began their gumbo balls. They were a sober people, and whether they took their idea from the bullion of Masarin, or wished to economize the time required for supper, they sipped this stringy[iii] potion, between the sets, without requiring any stimulant to their buoyant spirits.

Father Mathew and his vocation were useless there, though in the next street, had his pledge prevailed, the whole organization of society would have been dried up, the kindly greeting of the friend, and the hearty welcome to the stranger, who was yet sacred in that land, was symboled in the offered cup, and however the custom might be produced, occasionally to an excess, the clasp of the hand on introduction, and the form of what should be considered the sacred pledge of goodwill, were the becoming features in the intercourse of the stranger with the inhabitants of the hospitable land, which it would be difficult to replace by the habits of men who distrust even themselves.[iv]

I once met with a sensible New Englander, who was only a water drinker when it suited him, such a being, however, was rarely to be met with in those regions then. A German acquaintance and myself were invited by him to dinner for a Sunday eight days[v] at his farm, we accepted, a qualm of conscience, however, came over me with secret misgivings some days after. This country house was about six miles off, I reflected that it was an early dinner, and that the evening would be still to destroy, that it involved the hire of a vehicle on account of a thaw. There were ladies I had heard, so I should have to be in dinner dress, and I came to the resolution of forfeiting the feast, by means of a bad cold, and sending an excuse.

The German remonstrated, expatiating on the promised pleasure of the banquet, and the beauty of one of the daughters, I was, however, inexorable, and begged him to carry with him in his car the excuse, and the vast volume of regrets I was obliged to send in my place.

Just after dark, my friend returned, covered with mud, with a black eye and a bruised hand, his horse, whose fond recollections of the comforts of home, had not been overcome by the hospitality of the treatment he had experienced in the visit, had broken off at a gallop on his return, and flung the broken carriage to one side, and the passenger on the other, and with the shafts as a relic returned to his yard, the German was in despair at the disaster, the more so, as next day the estimate of the loss was brought in at twenty dollars.

It was to comfort him under the circumstances of personal and pecuniary grief, that I begged an account of the dinner, which had caused them, and it was not without evincing a bitterness which at first astonished me, that he related his adventure.

They had been ushered into the dining room, where the feast, which was not of the best order, was spread out upon the board, and the guests were informed in a sententious tone, that they saw their dinner, that the decanters on the table contained water, for on Sundays he confined himself solely to that beverage, he then offered up a short thanksgiving, perhaps, suited to the occasion, in which I could not discover that my Rhenish friend had joined, and they fell to.

While I am about it, I may as well state, that this was the most unlucky man I ever met. Having got together some money, and aspiring to be a Humboldt in the eyes of his family and friends, he resolved to revisit his cherished Hamburg. He was a beautiful singer, and had some assistance from a young nobleman, who knew him in England, and obtained for him the care of some despatches from the Foreign Office, to facilitate, as he said, the landing of his baggage. He proclaimed his important charge, and pushed on shore, the authorities did not seem to recognize the genuineness of his mission, and demanded his name, he blustered a good deal, and the other passengers were waiting in patience, until their more humble claims to notice might be admitted, and the bearer of despatches from the British Government declared his name.

One of the officers then stepped up, and with a look of recognition, asked if he was then the son of that famous widow V——, who was drowned the other day in the canal. The poor fellow had lost his mother, but the affair did not end there, and the officer further to revenge himself upon the airs of the young townsman, related how this melancholy event had taken place.

The garden of the old lady touched upon the canal, and over it hung a small wooden erection, into this, the widow had obtruded herself. Whether the weight it had to bear had, at last, exceeded the strength of its supports, or that age had weakened them, or whether it was a combination of both these causes, I never learned, but the fabric gave way, and the hapless lady, in her wooden case, perished in a combination of mud and water, which a sanitary committee alone could analyze.

Disgusted with his reception in his native city, V—— returned afterward to America, and I was grieved to hear, died of taking a cold bath in the heat of the yellow fever, near New Orleans.

Chapter Eight
Resolution for adventure—an evil omen?— blows that strike home—departure for the Wild West

The winter had passed, I had not received a line, and I began to feel anxious, as there was a limit to my pecuniary resources, although my habits were not expensive. Everyone around me was forming some plan for the season—to purchase land, to set up a store, to join an expedition—a general movement took place in the spirit of all around, the balls, the revels, or the torpor of winter, had disappeared, and I felt as one condemned to a separation from my fellow-men.

I had six hundred dollars remaining, and I resolved to set out for the Rocky Mountains by the Platte route in company with some half-score others, only four of whom had already been in that country. We were each to have two animals, at least, three if we chose. The larger companies did not in anyway encourage these small bands of adventurers, who were not subjected to their controul, and there was to be no parade of our departure[1].

I went to draw my money from John O'Fallon[2], and while the clerk was making out the bills of exchange, I sat down in the director's room of the

---

1. No parade of our departure: Bernard DeVoto notes that Stewart left St. Louis for his first mountain excursion on or about April 13, 1833 (*Across the Wide Missouri*, p. 27). Louise Barry says the Sublette & Campbell caravan left the Liberty-Lexington, Missouri, area on May 7, having gotten a trading license dated April 15, 1833 (Barry, *The Beginning of the West, Annals of the Kansas Gateway to the American West, 1840-1854*, Topeka, 1972, pp. 231-32). Led by Campbell, the caravan included another newcomer to the trade, Charles Larpenteur, whose journals covering this and many other events are in Larpenteur, *Forty Years a Fur Trader on the Upper Missouri*, ed. Elliot Coues, New York, 1898.
2. John O'Fallon: O'Fallon (?-?) was an Indian agent, trader, and investor in the Santa Fe trade. His brother Benjamin O'Fallon (1793-1843) was a well-known Indian agent and trader.

bank. I could not but feel uneasy at this my last draft on New York, the link with England had already been severed, and I felt about to be delivered over to my own resources and energies, instead of having been sedulously kept from all personal care. I felt at this moment an uneasiness I could not account for, like the presage of misfortune creeping upon me, and I changed my position in an effort to throw it off, when, through the half-closed doorway, I saw two eyes fixed upon me—the same two I had but once seen, though they followed me in my uneasy dreams, from the first supper at Fernwold's to the present hour.

I started from my seat, some figures intervened, and the vision was lost. Had I seen really anyone, or was it a disordered fancy? There were several persons at the bank counter, and I rushed among them, but could see no face I could recognize. I would have run into the street, but it appeared impossible that the dreaded masque—for I really felt a supernatural fear of the apparition—could have gone out bodily, as I had almost kept my eyes constantly on the outer door. I was at last restored to myself by the cashier, who called me to give my signature against the notes he offered.

I received the notes like a Spaniard, uncounted, pocketed them, and took my leave, but with an emotion I could not account for. I rushed up and down the streets, in hope of finding the object of my inquietude, as well as some solution of this haunting I believed myself subject to. I was at last saluted by the demand of a lanky countryman from Illinois, if I wanted to hire anyone for the mountains. This brought me, in some degree, to my senses, and I felt that there was something in my manner sufficiently remarkable.

Having answered that I was not in the way of hiring anyone, I took my way to the hotel, and there I met two of the partners of the expedition. I had got in my pocket the wherewithal, and upon that we held our council.

———

It was the fourth of April. One was to go up as far as the Independence[3], landing by steam with the kits, and a certain quantity of the most useful and portable goods to trade, consisting of guns, knives of the best brand, blankets, and beads, these were to be marked by their owners, to be identified, but to be carried along at the common expense by common mules and two men hired for the purpose. He was there to meet the others, who were, after having collected the animals at Jem Hicklin's[4], near Lexington, to join the baggage at

---

3. Independence: Founded in 1827, Independence, Missouri, by 1830 had become a bustling service center for the Santa Fe and Mountain trades, superseding Franklin, Missouri, established in 1817.
4. Jem Hicklin's: Jem Hicklin may have been drawn from Jonathan Hicklin, apparently from Lexington, Missouri. He was a bondsman for a contract for transporting goods made between the

Independence, and encamp on a spot which had been chosen for the temple of the Lord by the Mormons[5]. It was close to the then celebrated store of John Auld[6], kept under the superintendance of Sam Owens[7]. After making up there their last wants, they were to proceed to the banks of the Kanzas river, near its mouth, and while resting the animals and accustoming them to be without corn, were to await my arrival till about the beginning of May, it was stipulated not later than the second, and if later than that, I was to take their trail and follow.

The boat had been announced as to start the next day. I still wanted a horse and my share of the seven or eight mules to be purchased as common stock. Two of our best judges and steadiest hands were to accompany one of the partners with the purse, to scour the country on each side of the river to Arrow Rock Ferry[8], and so on to Lexington, where it was hoped they would arrive, with what they had to start with, as well as what they further required, in the course of a fortnight, and then proceed more slowly to finish the journey to Independence and the Kanzas. There was no West Port[9] then.

I had to make some visits, the officers quartered in the neighborhood had been very kind, and I took some interest in Black Hawk[10] and his sons, who

---

firm of Jones and Russell and the U.S. Army in 1851 (Barry, *Beginning of the West*, p. 980). A second candidate may be James Prewitt Hickman (1814-1893), a merchant in Boonville, Independence, and Fayette. In the late 1840s he was involved in the Santa Fe trade and became a banker in Chihuahua City before retiring to San Antonio, Texas. See Susan Shelby Magoffin, *Down the Santa Fe Trail and into Mexico: The Diary of Susan Shelby Magoffin, 1846-47*, ed., Stella M. Drumm, New Haven, 1926, p. 58, note 20. See also index entries under *Hickman, James P.* in Barry, *Beginning of the West*.

5. Temple of the Lord by the Mormons: According to Stewart, Independence was considered as a potential site for Zion by the Saints, though no mention of a proposed temple at Independence appears in a recent history of the Mormons. The authors note that the Saints occupied Jackson County (Independence), Missouri, only during 1833-34 before popular resentment forced their removal.

6. John Auld: John Aull (1788-1842) was one of three brothers, including James (1804-1847) and Robert (1807-1878), who were successful merchants in western Missouri. John became involved in mercantile trade in 1819, and by 1840, the brothers operated stores at Lexington, Liberty, Richmond, and Independence, Missouri.

7. Sam Owens: Samuel Owens (1800-1847), known as *Major* Owens, is said by Susan Magoffin (*Down the Santa Fe Trail and into Mexico*) to have operated a general store on the southeast corner of the Square at Independence. He was killed in the Mexican War.

8. Arrow Rock Ferry: From the older French designation *Pierre de la Fleche,* the Arrow Rock is in present Saline County, Missouri, and is thought to have been so named because it was a source of materials for projectile points for local Indian tribes. A ferry was established at Arrow Rock in 1817 and operated until at least 1833. See Charles Van Ravenswaay, *Arrow Rock, Missouri, in Bulletin of the Missouri Historical Society,* 15 (April, 1959): 203-23.

9. Westport: This town grew up near the site of Chouteau's Landing and is presently within the bounds of Kansas City, Missouri, a few miles below the mouth of the Kansas River, on the Missouri River. Founded in 1833-34 near the Santa Fe Trail, Westport became the successor to Independence as an outfitting point for Western travelers.

10. Blackhawk: This Sauk warrior (1767-1838) led an unsuccessful attempt to stave off white encroachment on disputed lands in Illinois. Captain Stewart, Prince Maximilian of Wied-

were at Jefferson Barracks, as prisoners, and spent some days among them at that beautiful spot. I went also to other places, to pay visits, but I cannot say that I could conceal from myself that these were but excuses for loitering, that I might still receive some news from England.

The period I was limited to, by the departure of the boat, was nearly expired, and I had given up all hope but of setting my face to the west, and meeting coming events with manly hope.

It was the evening before the final start from St. Louis, I was sitting by the fire, talking over the ways of the people of Missouri, as compared with those of the old country, with an old Virginian, with whom it was a favorite theme, when our host came in with the *St. Louis Republican* in his hand. It contained extracts from English papers, and he pointed out among the deaths one of my name, and handed me the paper. It was not in the list of deaths under that head, but in a paragraph purporting to come from a Cheshire print, and announced the death of my father.

This was a blow from which I could not recoil, it was already given, and struck home. What affection I had for my father was entirely negative. I could not dislike him, and the sole arbitrary act of his life toward me had been forgotten, or might be justified, and could not make a balance against his previous uniform kindness. But what tended to change the nature of my grief, was the neglect with which I had been treated. Formerly, though I was not required to give any account of my doings, it was to be inferred that some report was made, and though there was no active intercourse, there never appeared estrangement with this parent, who it appeared was gone, without any care to let me know whether I was not now a beggar as well as an orphan.

My first desire was to return, for information, to Europe, but to whom apply? I might be four months without an answer, and that could only be from a servant, from whom I could not expect assistance, and scarcely accurate information. To Fernwold? But he, if able to write—and here I felt that I had never written a line to him, though I loved to think of him—was probably gone to Madeira. Was I then to remain watching the post-office? Did anyone interested to write, know my address? No.

I felt that I had but one course—write to the old butler, to desire to know what had been my father's wishes respecting my future destination, and desire the information to be forwarded to me to St. Louis, to the care of my banker, and in the meantime, to proceed with my westward tour.

I executed this resolve, as far as the letter went, without a moment's delay,

---

Neuwied, Karl Bodmer, and William Clark visited Blackhawk and other Indians jailed at Jefferson Barracks, a large military post about ten miles south of St. Louis, on March 26, 1833. See Reuben Gold Thwaites, ed., *Early Western Travels: 1748-1846*, 32 volumes, Cleveland, 1904-1907, XXII: 228.

and returned from putting it in the post to prepare for my departure. There was no one in the room, and the newspaper was still on the table. There was some interest yet to be taken in English news, though I had made up my mind soon to forget all that was left behind, and I again cast my eyes upon it, as I held it between me and the fire. I did not care about the Grey Ministry or the Reform Parliament[11]. It must be a fault, I suppose, in our days, to have a total indifference about politics, but I looked for the few names I knew among those I could find mentioned, and I saw that of Lieut.-General the Earl of Fernwold, from the Cape, having been replaced in his Government by General Ellismore.

It was thus I also learned the death of my poor Fernwold. I had already expected, it was true, to have heard of this, but it gave me a pang I know not how to describe, and in the silence of a grief I had never felt before, I laid myself down forlorn in that distant land, and in the darkness of the night yielded to unavailing tears.

It was long before I fell asleep, but all the thoughts I could bestow upon myself, in the bitter anguish of that hour, confirmed me in the feeling that I was cut off from all former ties, and I awoke with my mind made up to forget forever the land of my birth.

The kit I selected from my baggage was merely half-a-dozen colored shirts, an overcoat of white blanket with a hood, a leather belt, a broad-brimmed un-napped white hat, my ammunition, and a rifle, a tooth-brush, and a mane-comb which I thought the least likely to break, were in my pocket, a butcher knife was in my belt, and an awl was attached to my pouch, which, with a large transparent horn of powder, and a wooden measure hanging to it, completed my equipment. This was full marching order, but a leather shirt over my cotton one, and my leather leggings, reaching halfway up the thigh and tied to an inner sash, was to be the costume of the steam boat deck and the periods of halt.

After what I had advanced for outfit, and which had been, as I said before, sent forward some time previously, there still remained in my pocket two hundred dollars, and with this, I had to buy a horse at or about Independence, and I might carry with me what coin remained, as, when not over weighty, I had an idea that it might always be of some use.

It is bootless to describe the voyage up the Missouri to Independence landing. I made friends with the pilots, and was nearly recruiting one to go with me. There is no race of people so open as these Western men, they took as much pains to instruct me as if I was an apprentice, and I passed my time really quickly on board.

---

11. Grey Ministry or the Reform Parliament: Earl Grey (1764-1845) reached the peak of his political power in 1831-32. His ministry and the Reform Act rocked Parliament and precipitated civil strife in England during the early 1830s.

There was a little swagger, and a few propositions advanced, which I should not have liked to offer my signature to. I had learned never to argue, and I was allowed, generally, to pass with a look of wonder and conviction.

"The English had always been beat in all actions."

"I had not read the history of the American wars."

Ah, it was a disagreeable subject! To which I assented, muttering something about brothers falling out, if it was necessary to speak, and ending with a glass of grog and an offer of service.

Chapter Nine
Quest for a horse, with dark hints

At Mr. Auld's store, in the great square of Independence, I found Samuel Owens, who had seen the rest of the party more than a fortnight before, and who were now, of course, on the Kanzas. He knew of no horse that would suit, but he could give me the loan of one, which I could use in the search, and he indicated one or two farms, where he thought I might find something.

It was the first of May, but I had that evening and the next, and only some fifteen or sixteen miles to overtake my party, so I set out. The roads were not very clear, the blazes not very explicit, and my search was complicated and fruitless. But I had, at night, reached a point where I expected to have some success, and where there were several holdings in the neighborhood of a prairie, where there were known to be several young horses.

I did not like to over-ride a lent horse, and I pulled up about eight o'clock. The farmer was a young man, owning some dozen of slaves, and a pushing character, knowing all the country round, and having been himself a mountain trapper with General Ashley.

They tell an anecdote of him. When some Frenchmen, who lodged a night at his house, asked him if he could speak French, he answered, "Me spek notin' else."

To my demand, if I could be put up, and have something for the horse I rode, he nodded, and called Pompey from grinning through the rails of the garden fence, to take him to the stable. "But," he added, "you may as lief let him go, he knows his way."

I saw he was recognized, and followed into the house, and I propounded my inquiries about a mount. There was no horse that he knew of which would suit in the country, several dealers and a strong company had already picked up everything of an age to stand the work, and if I got a common hack, which I might do from the Shawnees, it would be as much as, at that season, I could expect. He said he had several mules himself, but no horse.

I was not aware that he was the best authority in the neighborhood, and therefore was not quite ready to give up the hope of finding what I wanted.

However disheartened by this news, so often repeated, and everywhere confirmed, I did not despair, and sat down to supper, endeavoring to draw from my host, if possible, some hope for the grand effort I felt I must make on the following day.

"And you only want one horse to complete your outfit?"

"Yes, I want but one, but I have to choose him myself, and he ought to be a good one, as I am not sure that those who have gone on will not have the pick of the lot, and my own horse was sent on, and will be useless until he gets a little rest. I don't expect to find that they have spared him."

"Nor do I," said my host.

"But have you heard of any good horses being bought in this neighborhood by our party?"

"I do not know which party you mean."

"Oh, I thought I had mentioned, there are some half dozen who were together. But Jos. Heald was the partisan, and it was to him I gave the money for my share of the outfit, and he rode my horse."

"What the French call a *cendre*[1]?"

"Yes."

"And Heald has a slight cast outward of one of his eyes?"

"Exactly."

I thought these questions were put with more interest than at first marked the conversation.

"Aye, a fine beast, a little low in the rump, but deep in the chest, strong in the loins, and short in the legs. But it is well that you do not expect that they have spared him, for I do not believe they have."

There was a pause, during which we heard the barking of the dogs, and the sound of a horse's hoof, and a hail.

"I never go out when people make a noise," said my entertainer. "I always do when they come quiet. It is my habit."

I nodded, to signify that I assented, though I was thinking of something else.

There was a good deal of talking without.

"You see, they are taking care of themselves. I know the talking kind are to be trusted for that."

---

1. Cendré: French for grayish or ashen. Probably refers to the color of Warren's horse.

The door now opened, and a tall, good-looking man, of six or seven and thirty, entered.

"Well, Janisse, what news? Are you not gone yet?"

"I want some mules," said the newcomer, "but I won't be long of overtaking the rest."

"They are gone by Fort Leavenworth and Council Bluffs, I hear."

"Can you put me up to anything about here?"

"Yes, there are some half dozen young ones here, unbroke, and there are some more near the Fire island Prairie.[2]"

"What price?"

"Well, they will range thirty-five now, as the article gets scarce."

"Will your boy have them up by daylight?"

"Oh, they are not far off."

"I might, perhaps, see something of them, if they were like to suit, between a lantern and the moon." And he took his hat, and followed by the owner, went out.

I, a purchaser on a smaller scale, was overlooked.

Janisse was a French creole, from St. Charles, and I afterward learned, was employed by one of the mountain companies to purchase animals for the remount of their caravan.

Their conversation was long, as I could see them in debate from the window at which I sat.

When they re-entered, I thought Janisse eyed me with some attention. But we were invited to partake of a tumbler of grog.

"You will find no better peach brandy in the West," said the newcomer to me, "than in this digging."

"Nor maple sugar," said our host, with a laugh.

"But I'll bet a trifle, good as the brandy may be, it will not make you give the price for the mules."

"What will you bet?"

"Twenty dollars."

"Done," said the dealer. "They are mine."

I perceived that he had thus neatly taken off this sum from what was asked for the lot.

"You do not know of a good horse, near abouts?" I hazarded.

A negative shake of the head was all the answer I received.

"Well, stranger," said our entertainer, "I think, if you are to get what you are in want of, you must be early astir. So, perhaps you would like to turn in."

---

2. Fire Island Prairie: Appears to be the same area indicated in a document of 1785 as *Prado del Fuego* (Fire Prairie), as noted by Abraham P. Nasatir, ed., *Before Lewis and Clark: Documents Illustrating the History of the Missouri, 1785-1804,* two volumes, St. Louis, 1952. I: 125.

I followed him, without speaking, to the open gallery round the building, and mounted a trap-stair, where I found two beds in a slenderly floored garret. I was not long in finding my way into one of these.

It is not always that we are ready to fall asleep in a strange bed, and under disagreeable circumstances, and I tossed about like a Richard calling for a horse, in my anxious thoughts. I heard a low conversation between my entertainer and one of his sisters, and though I could not make out very distinctly the subject, some words led me to think it was about myself, as I thought I detected *very young*, in what he said, and also some expression of regret, and then the sister seemed to beg something of him, and the last words I could catch were, *poor young fellow*.

The sun was not yet up when the first movements in the room below gave notice of the hour of rising, and Pompey—the black—was summoned from some dark corner, by the cheerful and ringing voice of his master.

I was not long of being in the open gallery, which surrounded the house, and finding the usual basin, the water barrel, and the gourd as a ladle, my ablutions were completed.

The women were not up, but Janisse had crept out before the dawn, and was already in the saddle, with a lasso at the pummel, and his cavalcade ready, he had in his hand the halter of one who bore the bell, and the rest followed. I saw him go off between the enclosures as quietly as if he had to make his escape.

It was now my turn. One of the good-natured sisters had got a cup of smoking coffee, which was better still than the morning dram of her brother, who came in, and as he bustled about, I thought there was something on his mind.

He, at last, beckoned me to follow him out. I was surprised at his silence, as I had before found him the most voluble American of the West I had yet met with. We went into the stable, and he then showed me, amongst other animals of different kinds, a mare mule.

"Now, if you can find such a one as that," he broke out, "you need not fear what may happen, nor how long the day. I have never crossed such a one, and nothing damps her, she is a willing and a good crittur. I have known her eat meat as if she had joined the church, and that is a property in a beast. For a tough strain—"

He stopped, as if he really had not words to go on further describing the qualities, of which he evidently did not give a fictitious account. She was a long-bodied, short-legged, brown mule, her ears were particularly short and fine, and she carried them always pricked, she had good withers, and broad flat legs—in short, she was a model in appearance.

"She is a pacer," said her master. And he finished by saying, "I shall not replace her, and I may skim every band in the State, and take the best of the cream, and not be half as well mounted."

He seemed to warm himself with the subject.

"Now, I don't mind if I take a turn with you, to see and get you mounted."

I returned to the house, where there was a plentiful breakfast laid out. Neither of the young ladies partook until we had finished, and I was eager to be away.

While their brother was gone to have the favorite saddled, the youngest sister—who was really a handsome girl, with a healthy brown cheek and dark eyebrows, and I had not neglected to admire the eyes, when I could catch a glimpse of them from under their long lashes—said something to the other, and left the room.

"Brother wants a heavy price for his mule," began she that was left.

"He has not said, but I don't much want a mule to ride."

She looked rather in pity at me. "If Janisse had had your chance, he would not have slept till he had her."

The mule was evidently a household goddess.

I heard the merry voice at the window, there was a hearty friendliness in it, that won me into confidence. I took my saddle from the middle gallery, threw it on my horse, tightened the girths, put on the bridle, and hitched him up at the door.

The brother came in, and to my great relief, said, "Girls, I don't know what you charge for your part of the business, but the stranger and I will settle ours on the way."

"A quarter of a dollar will settle our matters," said the eldest, with a good-natured frankness, "and Mr. Owens will not be long of seeing it either."

"That's right, Lizzy, no long reckonings at the store. Goodbye," he added, with almost a whimper. "I may never see you again."

I had deposited my quarter dollar on the table, and shook hands with the sisters, and as I went out into the gallery, the youngest preceded me, but stopped outside the door. She said hurriedly, "I don't care that my brother should sell his mule, a single straw, but do you buy her, if you can, or turn your head back toward St. Louis. I can't tell you more—but buy the mule."

She gave a little gentle return to the pressure of my hand, and I saw the color mount to her cheek, as she turned to leave me, and I determined to buy the animal, because she bid me, and in remembrance of the goodwill, she shewed toward a stranger.

There is nothing more beautiful than a morning of spring in the woods and brakes of that wild land, alive with the winged tribe, with their varied note and plumage—the flocks of perroquets[3] darting, like a cloud of green

---

3. Flocks of parroquets: Probably the Carolina Parakeet, whose range once extended from the

blossoms, through the boughs, and their little cries—the woodpecker, in his brilliant varieties, in possession of every tree—and at the intervals of other sounds, the universal hum of the solemn bee—the fresh incense of the morning drawn up by the early sun, and occasional traces of cultivation, with its rapid growths, varying the sylvan scene, were calculated to make us feel their influence, and repress, even in one used to their effects, the gabble of common converse. There is nothing more false than the wish to give expression to the feelings which come over us in such scenes, and we rode quietly on side by side where the way was wide, and I followed when we had to break into Indian file.

"I suppose you are pretty much in a puzzle," at last said my companion.

I nodded.

"Well, I may as life tell you what to do as another, and perhaps my advice may be as good, for you are but a raw hand in this sort of business. You have no saddle, I will see to that. You have no powder? A little. Only one knife—no blanket—no bed. We will be at the store immediately. I will lay out there what you ought to have with you, in case you may be separated from the rest."

We had quickened our pace, and were approaching the town. There were a few Indians loitering about, two or three strangers at the hotel on the right hand as we entered the square, and a few indifferent-looking steeds hitched to a transverse beam, supported by two posts, seven feet high. This cross-log had, at proper intervals, wooden pegs stuck in it, with an inclination upward of an angle of forty-five degrees, to prevent the bridle slipping off. The reins can never get foul in this way, and the horse, if there is no under barrier, may circulate under the upper one, but never so far as to interfere with the one tied next to him. This thing is erected at or near the door of every house in the western country, where any number of visitors may be expected.

At the opposite angle of the square is Auld's store, and to his horse-rack we hooked our bridles. They never looked at the animal they had lent me, and he remained standing beside the mule.

There were some Indians in the house—some waiting with patience the equivocal blessing of a credit, and some examining with consummate care and deliberation such articles as they had money to purchase.

I was somewhat interested in these people, who had been driven before the cultivation of the east, within the memory of man, to the borders of those wide wastes, where civilization seems to have paused. There was nothing particularly remarkable in them, but a greater reserve and composure than appears in the character of the white—and a greater love of gaudy dress.

In the meantime, Mr. Owens and my companion had retreated, and my observations might be carried to any extent that could be necessary, as far as

---

eastern seaboard to the Great Plains.

ample time and opportunity could aid them, and several dark gipsey eyes told me that it was not difficult to fathom the love they could accord to the white man, nor to deserve it.

A summons to a sort of back shop cut short my speculations, and I there found, laid out on the floor, the tree of a Spanish saddle complete, covered with parafléche, a pack-saddle, with girths, rings, and thongs, a bundle of riding-cords, a bridle, a packet of cases of English powder, some coarser for trading, a few bars of lead tied together, a few knives, two blankets, two pieces of skin with the fur on to put below the saddles and lay on the ground for a bed, a buffalo robe, and some flints and a steel, with three small tin kettles packing into each other, and a something between a bullet-ladle and a frying-pan, a packet of tea, and a bag of coffee, with two hams, and some rice, the whole not very heavy, but appearing, as spread out there, to be rather bulky.

I had yet to learn to pack such articles, so as to be carried on a mule's back, but my companion soon showed me how to stow them, putting the kettles and the robe, with one blanket for a top pack, to go between the two side bales, consisting of the other articles not every night needed, equally balanced and wrapped up from the weather in several folds of thick cotton stuff, called domestic. It was then I began to see that I needed two animals, but I was here anticipated again.

"There is at the door an Indian horse who does not know more of a stable than of a schoolhouse, and that, with my mule, will do for a start, and if you do not misuse them, they will outgo most beasts for a long journey. The grass is but watery yet, so lead the mule, as the baggage is the easiest berth. I guess you weigh a hundred and sixty, at least?"

"I fear I do."

"And you will weigh more yet, if they don't be right smart in taking your hair. Now, Sam Owens knows the mule, and he can tell you there is none such in his ken. The pony he can let you have cheap, the goods reasonable—but the mule is dear."

"Everything is comparative," I suggested, "and I suppose I need her."

"And if you don't, there is no man in Missouri who does," he answered with a laugh I neither understood nor much relished.

He went out while Owens made up the bill—it was sixty-five dollars.

"Now," added he, as he gave it to me, "as far as I know, you cannot do better than give him his price for the mule. He is a strange wild fellow, and has set his heart upon a high price—as much out of love and honor to his beast, as from the love of cash. And if you had told me yesterday, that you were going with a hundred dollars in your pocket to buy her, I would have told you that it was lost labor, and you had no chance. But as you have got on his soft side—or on that of his sister—buy, if you are to go on. That is all I say."

There was always a disagreeable sort of significance in the way they talked of my expedition, which was very irritating, but I was obliged to smother my annoyance from my shallow purse, and the risk of missing my companions already gone on.

I took out my money at the door, and bravely asked what was the price of the mule, that was to carry me safely over so many dangers.

He said, "A hundred dollars."

I was relieved, it was both within my means and within the price I had expected, and he was evidently more gratified by that than the money.

"Well now, if ever we meet again, and no accident happens to her, you will tell me that she has been the best of good beasts. Good luck to you—and that is the best of all things."

I was mounted on a low, square-built, brown horse, with a mealy muzzle, and various mystic marks upon other parts of his body. I wrung the hand of my late host, and let a whip I had bought for the purpose fall heavily on the flank of my Indian steed, who moved with more alacrity than I had expected, though not quite with the bound of the buck. The mule seemed to follow less willingly than I could wish, but an admonition from a bystander started her, and then there was no further hanging back.

Her former master had turned, when halfway across the square, to see us off, and he hollowed to me, "Take a small bag of corn whenever you can get it, and give her a little for some days, to wean her by degrees."

"Aye, aye!" I answered, and waved my hat. I knew he talked about the mule.

Chapter Ten
An accident of the road—intelligence of betrayal—a family relic

Now fairly launched, the intended temple-ground on my left was passed, and I was soon in the forest—tall trees, and an occasional clearing—the road had its three blazes on the trees, and the wagons of Santa Fé had made the tracks deep and clear.

I was fairly away now, and though the price I had paid for the famous mule which bore my fortunes, was not much in comparison to the prices of horses in England, I was sensible that I had stretched a point in giving a sum greater than was usually asked then for the best horse.

I was to meet Heald on the Kanzas, near its mouth, in a bottom where there are several opens for grass, and good shelter, and not very far from Chouteau's landing. So it had been described to me. When I got a little more than what made halfway, there were several trails, but I was to keep to one that led straight onto a ferry, and not follow the more marked one to the left.

I had asked some necessary questions as I met persons on the way, and I considered myself in the right course, when I saw a wagon before me, which I thought must be going in my direction. It was loaded with sacks, and the driver was riding the near shaft-horse, the road was not broad enough to admit of my riding alongside and holding a conversation, and I kept behind until there should be more room.

There were a good many logs lying about, and several hogs were running among them, as if they had been pursued, making that peculiar noise which marks their raised state. It was but momentary the observation I had of them, and they were ahead of the wagon.

I could not see what was the precise cause, but it now suddenly increased its pace, and taking a curve to the left, I could perceive the driver leaning back in his saddle, as if straining to pull in the team, which appeared quite unmanageable, and going at a furious pace. I immediately quickened mine, in order to be near should any catastrophe occur, which was to be expected from the position of matters before me.

I had no time to deliberate, and I rushed on to try and seize one of the leaders of the four which seemed the most frightened, but before I got halfway, the wagon came against the side of the bank on the right of the road, and was completely turned over, the harness entangled in the legs of the wheelers, and the near horse kicked till he was dragged down by a sack falling on the traces. The driver had kept his seat till the horse fell, but unfortunately, he had his leg under him. The leaders had broken their traces, and were off, snorting, with their tails up, the off horse was still on his legs, but only saved from falling by the breaking of the harness.

This was the posture of affairs when I got up to the spot, and of course, my first care was to get the rider extricated.

"Can you get your leg out," I asked.

"I think I can if the beast lies quiet, but there is something in the way that presses right hard, and I cannot bear much more squeezing." Horses always lie completely still, when you have mastered their heads.

This I recollected, and laid all my weight upon this one and kept him down with but little trouble, he got his leg, and then his foot drawn out, leaving a heavy boot behind, and getting off for a few bruises. I really felt glad that the hearty old man was not seriously hurt. And while he was kicking up the horses to get his boot, after freeing them from their trammels, I congratulated him upon his escape.

"Well, lad, everyone has a right to his own opinion, but *I* think I'm in a precious fix here, I am to miss my market, and lose the best of my team, the boat won't wait for me, I'll bet a trifle."

"As to the team, I can perhaps help you," I said, as I turned to look for my horse, who was with the mule busy cropping the young grass where they could find it in the opens, I mounted, and threw the trail rope of the mule within reach of the wagon, and trotted off on the fresh track, luckily for me, there had been a gentle shower, or a heavy dew the night before, and nothing but the two horses and the herd of swine had been along since, I could easily keep the track while out of the thicket, but all of a sudden it was lost, and I had to check my speed, and find it as it entered among the trees. I then found out the real difficulty of my undertaking, and could see no trace of other horses near that they might have joined. Occasionally, I only saw a turned leaf ahead, and after that had to proceed without any sign. I had been out about an hour, without discovering anything, and it was time to think where I was. I had made a circuit toward the Missouri, but at what precise distance from the road, I could only guess. I had seen some old tracks of shod horses, and also of mules, but nothing fresh, those I looked for then were within the circle I had made, or had crossed the wagon trail, I therefore turned more to the right, to find out how near I was to the road, and then faced round to make my inner cast. I had not been long on this before I saw some of the original causes of my search, the wild pigs, and they were not yet quiet, this gave me some hope, and I broke through every underwood, and looked along anything like an open. I felt the assurance that they were before me, and that they must be now quiet, I urged my stout Indian steed across the fallen trunks, which, however, he always stepped over, instead of leaping, and at last I thought I saw something of a horse in gear, I approached cautiously, he was quite quiet but alone, I dismounted and caught him, but how had the pair separated? Tying both horses to branches of trees, I now, on foot, took the back track of the one I had found, it was a tedious operation, a back track is twice over as difficult as a leading one. Almost in despair, I made a small blaze occasionally, and here and there broke a branch, that I might have the less trouble in getting back, having undertaken, not without rashness, to look up these beasts, I did not like, and could not in conscience give up the search while I had a clue, though a faint one, to guide me to complete it. I still went on, with my eyes cast down, and my ears open, the track at some distance began to break off into little circles, and doubled two or three times, and there were fresh signs still, and I began to feel that I was warm on the scent. I had not now far to go, for I could hear the groaning of some animal in distress behind some vines close by, and thus suddenly came upon the unfortunate horse, who had cast himself entangled in his traces, and in his struggles, had so worked himself up with vine branches and harness, that he was completely helpless, and appeared in great pain, my knife was out in a moment, and I cut through the entangled boughs, not without difficulty, and then by loosening the hems from the collar, got the traces unwound from his limbs, but it was not without having made two unavailing efforts, that he, at last, succeeded in getting on his legs, and I found without any injury. He was a fine large young horse, and I felt I had really done a service to a man I had never seen before, and somehow it was a more grateful and satisfactory feeling, than if I had done much more, acting under the feelings of friendship. The space appeared much shorter as I went back on my trail to the animals I had left tied up, hitching them together, I proceeded to lead them toward the road, which in a short time I struck, not very far behind where lay the wagon. When I got to the spot, I found the loading all out, and the wheels on their legs, detached from the body, which lay ready to be mounted into its original position, the old gentleman had been active.

"Well, where did you get them?"

I told him as near as I could.

"Aye, they would have gone home."

"Yes, one of them."

"How?"

"The other had hoppled himself, and what with vines and chains, he was too well tied together to have made a step."

He examined the horse's legs, which were somewhat marked and swollen by his exertions.

"Will you help me up with the box?"

It looked a labor of Hercules, but I readily acquiesced, there were two straight sticks lying ready cut, which he laid upon the hinder axle, and cogged the wheels, they had been moved directly in front. We then began to raise the body up those slopes by means of levers, and in a short time, it was in its place, the tilt was then stretched upon the bows, after having refilled the interior.

The old farmer, for so he appeared, now took off his hat and wiped his forehead, and proceeding to a box attached to the outside, he took from it a bottle, half a loaf of bread, and a lump of cold bacon, and laying them on the trunk of a fallen tree in the shade, by a gesture invited me to sit down and partake of his provisions.

"That's cider," he said, "I suppose you know bacon and bread when you see them, if not, you may soon be out of reach of learning."

I was hesitating, from the recollection that this was my last day allowed by the party who had gone on.

"Come, none of your old country tricks, out knife and fall to, there are no more hotels on this line."

"By the way, your face is set, and your gear, I would give you a little hint, eat when you can, there may always come a time when you can't."

It was excellent homemade bread, and the slice of fat bacon tasted sweeter than the best butter with it, and the cider was pretty good, and tolerably stiff, so that half a bottle, and I had the best half, did very well.

"I suppose," said my new friend, "you would have sent for a coachbuilder to set up our wagon again in the old country."

He rattled on a few more questions, and at last asked me plump where I was going.

"I told him I was on my way to join Heald's party in the Kanzas Bottom, not far ahead, I believed."

"Hum! I thought you were going to join something of that sort, but—Heald you said?"

"Yes, have you any idea whereabouts they were last camped, so that should they have moved this morning, I may take their trail fresh," I enquired, rather uneasy at the way my questioner stopped.

"Oh, as to where he is, I cannot say, but you think he was to start today?"

"He told me he would wait till today for me on the Kanzas."

"The Kanzas is a wide word," he added, musingly.

"Yes, but at the mouth of the Kanzas."

"Well, I am going to a house not far from Chouteau's land, that I may have a chance to ship my corn, I am too late for Leavensworth, and I don't think it is four miles off. Now, if you will take the advice of one who has no cause to advise you wrong, you will come along there tonight, and start fair tomorrow."

"I would willingly, but I cannot break faith, and in the direction you point, every yard is two out of the way."

"Perhaps you may be right. Now, don't suppose I am blind, and do not see the value of the hand you gave me this afternoon. I am quite aware that I should have had to sit by my corn, until I found someone to help me up with the wagon, that then it might have been late, and that I might have expected the runaway beasts to return to the stable at home, and should not have searched, and that my favorite young horse, which I have bred and broke myself, would have been eat by wolves or hogs before morn. You are a kind-hearted lad, and something more, or I mistake. I don't like to tell you bad news, but I believe you have been done, these fellows have got your horses and booty, and are gone eight days ago, so if you will come and stay the summer with me, you are as welcome as the beams of the sun, and you will have the run of the upper counties among the girls, for I think there is nothing left but old men and niggers of the male kind. What say you?"

I was struck by the unaffected cordial manner in which this was said, but I was not to be turned from my intention, and had made up my mind for a chase at any odds, and this I explained, with a demand for leave to call on my return, he shook me cordially by the hand.

"My name is Josiah Brent," he said. "You will not fail, I'm sure."

"I will make it my first call, if I live to return," I said, as I turned away.

"Stop," he called after me. "I have one thing to say, I have an only boy, a year or two older than yourself, who has gone with the rest, now he is something of a chap, though I say it, here is an old tobacco holder, which came from Germany with his mother's people, he has often asked it of me, now take it with you, and when you want a friend, when you are far from old Missouri, and farther still from your own land, give this to Jim, in the name of his old Dad."

He came toward me, and gave me this family relic, which he declared had never been out of his pocket for twenty years, it was a curiously chased tobacco holder of platanised-looking silver, with a coat of arms emblazoned upon it. I put it in my pocket, until I could find an opportunity of stowing it away in my possible sack.

"You will sleep at Joe Parkes's tonight, and he will put you on the road, goodbye, and good luck."

The hearty old Missourian was busied with his wagon, when a turn of the road took him from my sight, here I was, with almost the certainty that I had been tricked, and with no great prospect of making a better of it.

Chapter Eleven
Meetings with Indians—a new partner—
reflections upon a life in the wilds—a painter

Joe Parkes's was to be my first point, and I had sagacity enough to know that he must be near the trail, or Brent would have given me some further direction, and I jogged on. The road held on in the same line, and must lead to something. I passed over the spot where the town of Westport now stands, and a little further on, found a solitary farmhouse, with some fields to the right. I there inquired if Parkes's was near, and was told to take the first wagon track to the left, and I would be within a half mile of his house, and over the Indian line. In a short time, of course, I found the house just out of the forest, and on the broken borders of the great Prairie.

Parkes[1] was a half-bred Shawnee, who owned a good farm and some slaves, he was at his door watching a swarm of bees, and told me I was welcome to stay the night. I was quite ready to pause before I put my foot on that great steppe, and unsaddled at once. I found a good supper of venison and chicken, and I composed myself to sleep for the last time in a bed, until I might return.

There is something in all this preparation, which is like commencing a sea voyage, with no certain destination. I slept the sleep of the innocent, or the sleep of the just, for it was sweet and tranquil, and awoke with the lark to do the honors of the stable for the last time this journey, to my two only compan-

---

1. Parkes: Joseph Parks (1795-1859), a mixed-blood (three-quarters white, one-quarter Shawnee), was a highly respected farmer and interpreter. Stewart must have known Parks by 1837 when Alfred Jacob Miller made a watercolor of a house thought to belong to Parks. Stewart visited Parks in 1843, while en route to his final sojourn in the Rockies. See Ross, *The West of Alfred Jacob Miller*, plate 48, and Field, Prairie *and Mountain Sketches*, pp. 8-9.

Buckwheat cakes and honey, fried ham and eggs, with excellent coffee, awaited my return, and I ruminated upon my powers of frying ham and making coffee, as I laid in a plentiful store. Everything was astir in the morning air, as if the birds were to accompany me on my solitary way, the trail had been easily pointed out which leads to the grove, where there is a good spring—water being in dry weather scarce in the neighborhood, and toward that grove of tall trees in the distance I was to bend my course, and there rest and refresh the horses.

I had not forgotten the advice I had received at Independence, and had accordingly, a little sack of Indian corn, and though the grass had been much dirtied and eat, there were some pickings yet, and the small allowance of grain made it a profitable halt for the cattle, who were to commence the campaign now in earnest.

Just, however, as I was about to pull up, I heard a hail behind me, and a couple of Indians, dressed in leather shirts and blue cloth leggings, with scarlet garters tied in rosettes on each side, appeared pushing their mules and a led horse to overtake me. I halted to find out what they wanted, and one of them said, "If you like to come a little further on, we know a house, and something to eat."

I looked doubtingly.

"Joe Parkes sent us," the other added, and I followed, not sorry to put off the first day of cooking in the Prairie.

I enquired how far it was off the trail, and was answered, "Scarcely at all." With a point to another grove a little to the right, in the distance.

"He is the parson, and also the schoolmaster of the Shawnees,[2]" added my informant. "We will get there about dinner time."

This was said by the tallest and the oldest of the two, who was also the most Indian looking, the other was younger and slighter, not quite so frank, but was of a more intelligent aspect, with a certain slyness in his eye, as well as good nature. This I could easily observe as we took our line toward the promised seat of theology and grammar, for the two red men took the lead, and talked their own tongue, as if I had not been on the same continent.

The barking of sundry lurchers of furious appearance, indicated that behind a gentle swell, which they defended, lay the house we were bound for.

The missionary being a white man, and there being both whites and negroes in his establishment, and all the visitors being red, the dogs had not the same prejudice of race, as those of the Indian village, who rarely get over their antipathies to strangers.

---

2. Schoolmaster of the Shawnees: Shawnee Mission was founded late in 1830 by a Methodist minister, the Reverend Thomas Johnson and his wife, Sarah, in present Wyandotte County, Kansas.

The two Indians called a halt, they had had their talk, and the younger one a Delawar, named Jim Macairy, had made up his mind as well as his wallet, to accompany me, that he might join some of his countrymen, already trapping between the Black Hills and the Ute country.

Jim said he would pack along a half-grown pig, which he expected to get here, for the first few days, in case the camps already gone on had scared off the game, but on the whole, he thought two were better together than one, and if I had no objection to him as a guide, he would go along with me, all this was proposed in a moment, and as quickly accepted, for I began to feel that it would be both dangerous and difficult to go alone, where it would be necessary sometimes to hide all day, by what I had learned, and even to leave the track.

These thoughts had come upon me before, as I contemplated the chance of a long, stern chase.

"Well, now for the pig," said Jim, having thus given his bargain with me its due precedence.

The divine schoolmaster appeared at his door, with a pasteboard alphabet in his hand, with which he had been instructing the young Indians how to read the Bible and the newspapers, and which now shaded the sun from his eyes as he surveyed our party.

"We want dinner," said the elder Indian. "Can we have any."

"You will have what is to be had," said the man of letters, sententiously.

"And can I buy a pig from you," said my future companion.

"If can command one," said the scholar, and he shook the elements of knowledge over his head, at which was conjured up a good-looking grinning mulatto, who was to feed our horses, and let slip the dogs of war[3] among the swinish tribe.

Like most Protestant missionaries in that country, this one had chosen a spot where he had sufficiently plowed, for keeping in winter his large stock of mares and cows, which ran free in summer over the broad Prairies, and a few fat oxen for the barracks. He had his wife and his slaves, and was a good-natured man of sounding periods, equally happy as a despot in his school, and uncontradicted in his parlor, or in his pulpit.

The day was past its prime, and we got ready, the other Indian and I, but Jim had to stay and catch us up at a spot agreed upon where we were to cross the Kanzas.

It was a fresh evening, for there had been some flying showers.

---

3. Let slip the dogs of war: Shakespeare, *Julius Caesar*, III.i.273.

In that day, the usual crossing was some distance below the Kanzas village, and my guide had chosen a spot near a slew, or deserted course of the river, the tall trees which shaded its banks, gave a gloomy look to this still water, forming a considerable bend, and only filled up where it would have joined the stream. Along this pool, when the sun was low, we threaded our way to the end, where it is dammed up against the Kanzas, now somewhat swollen by the melting of the snows.

Although there are these two outlets, my companion considered the animals safe within the slew, and we unsaddled near it, on the edge of a small grassy open. There was a thicket of bushes as a shelter, and festoons of the grapevine hung around and above, whose flowers of the sweetest odor loaded the evening breeze with perfume, I never remember to have breathed such sweet and balmy air. While I piled my pack, in order to cover it from the danger of rain, and threw the apichimoes[4] on the ground to sit upon, and the saddles, the Shawnee lit a fire, and we soon had a flaring blaze, which shone far into the shadows of the evening, darkened beneath the trees. The kettles were unpacked, and introduced into active life, the coffee already simmering on the edge of the fire, and the steaming kettle ready for whatever was to be put into it, when up trotted the led horse of Jim, with his little kit, and the pig equitably divided on either side, and no sooner had he stopped, which he did directly at the fire, than a part of the meat was put into the ready pot, and a racoon was begun to be skinned for the same destination, and soon followed.

Jim said nothing, but seemed happy, and I was contented to observe, that I should not have an idle or sulky neighbor.

A bell was produced, and attached to one of the horses which was to go back next morning, but might act the part of bell mare for the last night in the woods.

It was my first camp, we had a plentiful supper, and laid ourselves down to rest after it.

Jim went a little later to gather the beasts together to the water at a place where there was a convenient slope in the bank, and at his return, they drew their beds so as to have the feet near the fire, as did I mine, and we all lay down side by side, looking up at the young moon and the starry heavens. The Indians sung in their guttural tongue the low, interminable chants, which bring back associations to them, which make their dark eyes flash with a savage glare. Mine were half-closed, and my thoughts were far away.

---

4. Apichimoe: Also spelled apishimore, meaning saddle pad. See also: *Two pieces of skin with the fur on to put below the saddles and lay on the ground for a bed.* In *Altowan* Stewart describes it as *a piece of buffalo fur generally long enough to sleep on, worn folded under the saddle*—[Sir William Drummond Stewart,] *Altowan, Or, Incidents of Life and Adventure in the Rocky Mountains. By an Amateur Traveler,* ed. J. Watson Webb, New York, 1846, p. 36. See also Ross, *The West of Alfred Jacob Miller,* plate 79.

Isabella and Fernwold wandered through them like phantoms. Was I never to taste more than a sip of the joys of life, whenever I approached anything like happiness, was the cup ever to be dashed from my lips?

But the birds of night were singing, everything belonging to the day was still a perfect calm and a perfect solitude, the horse bell tinkled a note now and then, as a link to the earth, but distance soothed it gently down, till it was merged in the murmur of the woods, when left to the dominion of nature.

It must appear strange that I should not have felt oppressed at entering upon a journey with an Indian of whom I knew nothing, with the probability of a deadly dispute, if I safely reached the point I aimed at—an outcast who knew not the name of his own mother, who had every reason to believe himself a beggar. Yet there I lay, subdued by the outward senses of sound and smell, and the influences of a wild new life dawning upon me. I remember well how I started up among my waking dreams, when the thought came over me. Had these misfortunes happened when I was in London or Liverpool, I had indeed been stricken, there would have been no woodland couch for me there, and I should have offended some grave law of public order in that land of liberty, by lying down to rest under a green tree. My heart bounded under the feeling, that I was not beholden to the trashy twaddle of law manufactories for my freedom, but to space, to a fair field on which to win my way.

Above all this, there is an inexpressible charm in the life I was about to begin, there is something in the air, there is something in the rich woodland, and in the silent waste, that is of inexplicable interest. I have since taken many a journey in various ways, on the swift rail, on the mighty deep, in the mountain wilds, on eastern steppes, whose undulating plains I have rolled over drawn by a cloud of Cossack horses, but never have I felt the enjoyment of travel but there, where I could dwell upon its pleasures, and enjoy its troubles and mishaps.

We had fed full—and at last, the inert enjoyment of the scene gave way, and a heavier spell came over me.

Well on in the night I woke, with a sense of cold, the moon was down, the fire was but a few cinders, and all round a deeper shadow, I drew round me the friendly robe, and shrunk under it as a snail. I was thankful to have awoke, as I had the pleasure to fall asleep again, there was no horrible boots to come and call at a neighboring door, divided off by a little paper partition—I could sleep on.

The elder Indian, however, seemed to think that the shorter stretch of his journey, threw the greater duty of cook upon him before he should take his leave. I went out to gather in the band, they were happily not far apart, and I got them together without difficulty. Thus I was launched.

After packing up, we went a few hundred yards up the stream, and then again laid down our loads, we had to seek a few dry trees to cut and lay in a square, tied together at the corners by thongs of lime-tree bark, and that of the slippery elm, our kits and saddles being placed on this raft, the friendly Shawnee stripped and plunged into the river, wading as far as it was fordable, and pushing the raft before him, and then taking the string in his teeth, struck out for the opposite shore, our clothes were already gone on the raft, and we stood shivering on the bank ready to mount and make a similar transit, the mule was the only shy animal to take the water of our cavalcade, but this appeared more from a sense of cold, than fear or want of habit. They were all, however, landed at the foot of the small prairie on the opposite shore, the animals rolled themselves in the sand, and then on the grass, we ran about, in half an hour all were dry, the Indians took leave of each other, and the one who remained shook hands with me, and again took to the water to reach his horse, tied on the opposite bank.

It was now that a system of concealment was necessary, two men, and above all, one an Indian, are always considered fair game by the small thieves of the different tribes, through whose countries we had to pass, and therefore, the usual track and crossings of creeks was to be avoided. I found Jim quite familiar with the country, and we made forced marches, and stopped some hours in the middle of the day, where there was concealment and grass.

It was on the third day after crossing the Kanzas, we had arrived about ten o'clock on the timbered bank of a stream called the Blue, it was partially swollen, and difficult access, so that though we had kept to the right of the trail, we should have to go down to the usual crossing, on account of the swampy nature of the bottom. Having unsaddled and turned out the animals in a grassy hollow on the edge of the wood, and I having taken my station so as to command the access to the spot by the wood and also the open country beyond, the Delaware carefully examined the priming of his rifle, and set out to see what signs there might be at the crossing.

Having remained carefully watching the four animals, who however, themselves, are the more watchful of the two, I took up my rifle, adjusted the cap, and looked with satisfaction at its solidity and comparative lightness, to those small-bored unwieldy barrels in use in the Western States.

The underwood being thick, I got up to change my position, but carefully keeping within it, I had moved about for some little time, looking for nests of turkeys or whatever I might light upon, when I thought I perceived a slight noise, as of the cracking of a dead branch, and then I could observe the bushes move, was it an Indian on the watch? I had already been long enough his mark, and he would have, if his intentions were evil, lain still that he might have powder-burnt me, no, it was a beast of some sort, and of considerable size. While these reflections were passing in my mind, I still kept my eye on the bushes, in the course in which they had been agitated, and caught a glimpse of the dun fur of a cougar, which now seemed to be making away more slowly, but losing it again I stole forward, in the eagerness of one who had never been in contact with this ferocious tribe of animals before, and though afterward I might have had more command over my nerves, I must own that I felt my heart beat, as I expected every moment he would climb a tree, or express himself sufficiently to give me a chance. I was in this eager, but stealthy pursuit, and I thought at last I could see the body of the animal through some branches, I only waited for the mass, which I believed must be the cougar, to give the smallest sign of life to fire, the rifle was already at my cheek when I felt a hand laid softly on my shoulder. It is most thrilling to be touched lightly and unexpectedly in such a moment, and I felt a cold shudder creep through me, though I had a sufficient command of myself not to start or speak. I looked to all appearance coolly round, and found the dark and serious eyes of my companion fixed upon me. I saw there was something the matter and merely articulated *a painter*.[i]

Chapter Twelve
Eavesdropping—discoveries and plans—an ambush and a chase by night

He nodded and said, "Come here."
I uncocked my rifle, and quietly followed.
"A painter is a coup," said Jim," but I have seen two or three strangers at the crossing, and it may be good to avoid them, or perhaps to join them. You can look and hear, for they talk quite open, and we can get close."

He quickened his pace almost to a run, and it was not long before we arrived at a spot where the river had formerly washed away the bank in such a way, as to leave a perpendicular brink of ten feet above, a little deposit of sand, upon which were two or three logs of driftwood. We cautiously neared the brink above, and stopped to listen, I could hear nothing, and Jim shook his head.

"They must be gone," he said. "I will look," and he crawled under the low bushes.

I lay down on his track, to follow him the further with my eyes. When he had got to the edge, he stopped, and made a sign, I retreated, and he was again noiselessly at my side.

"One sits there still, the others are gone, but will, of course, come back to him, we will go close the moment we hear voices, as when they are talking, or best of all, when they are seated with their backs to us, there is less danger of their observing that they are watched."

For more than a quarter of an hour we sat and heard no sound, at last, a low voice spoke, and another answered, "All right." We repeated the word with a smile, as we stole again to the edge of the bank.

I now stretched my head into a thicket of weeds, and through them, saw what made me almost suddenly draw back—it was to be a day of suppressed emotions, but they spoke.

"They must be dodging on one side or other of the trail, but they cannot be far ahead, and we must fall in with them on the Platte, even if they should be there before us, for they must take some time to cross."

"Well," said a voice, "let us catch up and be moving." They all returned together by the trail, apparently to get their horses.

"What do you think," said my companion, as he saw me gaze after them.

"I will tell you bye and bye," I answered. "When they are beyond, on the opposite bank"—pointing toward it—"we will wait here and see them over."

You cannot put a lighter tax upon an Indian, than to try his patience, the Delaware grew into a statue on the spot, and I had but to follow his example.

Twenty minutes or half an hour had elapsed, and we heard the tread of hoofs, there were three persons mounted on horses, and two mules pretty well loaded as far as appearance went, they had a deep step or two, and took a long diagonal course, but accomplished the ford without difficulty, and disappeared in the opposite grove.

I breathed again more freely, and stooping down, we threaded our way back to where we had left our saddles.

"If there are any Caws[i] following, they will be here soon, so we shall know that much also," said Jim, evidently pleased by his discovery.

We sat down by our loads, after a look at the animals, who were eagerly cropping the young grass, which had come up after the burning, which annually takes place in these regions. I lit my pipe as a prelude to a talk, and to collect my thoughts.

"I know two of these men," I began, the Indian nodded, evidently pleased at my reserve. "One is from the old country, and must be just arrived, and with him is a Missourian of the name of Smith, of Heald's party, who you have heard has gone off with my property, the other I know nothing of."

"The old countryman is a greenhorn by your account, the other having left Heald's band, has had some difference with him, and the third, I can say, is not a mountain man, they are looking for us, and I half think we should join them," thus spoke Jim Macarey, and there seemed some reason in what he said. "We will find it easier for the horses in the trail, and we had better take it after them, and think the thing over, I would not join them the first camp, but see how things turn out."

We had had a pretty long rest, the horses were full, and there was now nothing to prevent our proceeding, as we were threading our way down to the crossing, I saw the mark of a naked foot on the sand, and forthwith pulled up. Macarey saw it, and merely stopped to keep the horses from defacing it.

On the opposite bank there was a halt, and Jim was of the opinion that we should change our course, and let the dusk creep on before we fell again into the trail, fortunately for us, there was a collateral creek, sometimes without water, but its course being marked by a chain of trees and brushwood. We kept along its hollows, and found it no great circuit, it was evident there was a party of Indians on our trail, who had been satisfied that the marks of the other party were ours, and who therefore, only thought of keeping within reach of them.

We made about ten miles in this way, when the creek we were following up gave out, and we were thrown upon the open prairie, this would not suit, we must stay till dark, or find a hollow, we preferred to try the latter expedient, and accordingly turned on our heels, it was not long before we found a hollow, but where it might lead to was another matter. However, it was a good hollow for us, as long as it was a hollow, and something near the right direction, and we held on, it became exciting to have two parties to watch, and we each shortened our leading reins, and skimmed the horizon as we advanced. It was now getting dusk, and a considerable creek ahead was the only well-timbered halting place within reach, and it appeared more than probable both these parties must halt there for the night, it had been evident, I thought, that the Indian party were not on the same side of the trail we had taken, or we must have seen them as we came over large spaces of open ground. The wooded creek was still two miles ahead, and we pulled up, I in doubt, and my companion with the intention of halting where we were, it was a little basin on the slope of the ground, which hung toward the creek, but could not be seen into from it.

Jim made his arrangements like a general, he collected the baggage together in a little hollow, where there had been water, he hoppled the two baggage animals and picketed them, and then he led the other two down to the trail upon which we turned back at least two miles, to where it crosses a little steep-sided stream of rather difficult access, here he led us up its bank for more than a hundred yards, and tied the horses.

"The moon is somewhat clouded, and we must wait here, and try and get hold of the animals they ride, as they are passing the grip, they will have done the thing quietly, and will lead each one of the stolen horses, and missing the rider, you must seize the horse he rides or leads if there are but two, if there are more, we will each drop our man, and the rest will try to run away, but whatever horses escape, must not cross, and will therefore take up with those which are tied just above. If there are but two horse stealers, you must see them coming over the sky line, before they dip into the creek, and they will be easily secured, but noise is to be avoided, as perhaps there may be more than we might see at first."

These instructions, however I may have rendered them in this narrative, were given so clearly, that I could not misunderstand them.

"If we have any luck, this will be better than the painter," added Jim, with a low laugh. "Keep within the bushes on your own side, and keep your ear to the ground."

We had been seated at the crossing upward of two hours by my watch, and it was past eleven, in the course of another two hours, they would probably be coming. I had brought my blanket, but still it was cold, and I began to count the minutes, and listen and look with impatience. My neighboring sentinel might be frozen, in respect to motion, I could observe nothing but a dark mass. Slight doubts began to arise in my mind as to the affair coming off in the way we expected, or coming off at all, that night, and the watch became almost irksome.

Jim might be dead, or sound asleep on his post, I was getting desperate, and had determined to move, when I thought I heard the neigh of a horse.

The spell was broken now, they were rushing on. We were both on our legs, but concealed among the branches. Happily for us, they led one a horse and the other a mule, and the other mule followed. Such was the order in which they came.

Jim was to seize the first, and he was already in the bottom of the creek, and I could see nothing. My intended victim lingered before descending, and heard a stifled exclamation and a scuffle below, and turned up the hill, trying to pull the horse he led after him. This however would not do, and gave me a chance. I sprung at him as he held back, and the Indian let go the rope. A loop was tied round his jaw in a second, and I was on his back. He was a free-going animal, of some swiftness.

The night was dark, and had it not been an open prairie we must have broken our necks, or pulled up. I felt I could go wherever the other went before, and pressed on. I had no arms but my knife—my hat was gone, and my blanket—had the sun shone out suddenly on us, I must have appeared like a maniac escaped.

Still we rushed on—he for his horse and his honor, I to escape the disgrace of a failure. I could see him belaboring his flanks with his heels. The animal he rode seemed to have the speed of mine, but being first, had some shyness of rushing on in the dark, which mine had not.

I soon saw that could he get to any place where there was cover, or the means of making a sharp turn, I was to lose him, and though sitting steadily, I urged the animal I rode to his utmost speed, keeping rather the inside next the stream and its fringe of wood. But I was alarmed at the gradual thinning of the trees and shoaling of the ravine. And it was well I kept the inside, for, at the first break, the Indian tried to strike to the left through an open, and throw me out. I had well nigh cut in upon him on this occasion, and gained at least a horse length.

The race now became interesting. I had forced him to take to the open, where he could not take a sharp turn without my having the advantage of cutting off the angle, so I drove him straight out before me. The night was still dark, and I had no idea in what course we ran. The savage was armed, and I did not think, if I had the speed to do it, that it would be prudent quite to close upon him, but he evidently trusted more to throwing me off, and I was straining my utmost not to be left behind.

Something, at this moment, when I thought he was gaining ground, made his horse stumble, and brought me up almost to feel the blowing of his warm breath.

There was an end to all reflection.

I was now so excited that I cared not for any danger, and my object was but to close on the chase. We were on the crest of one of those long wave-like swells which characterize these lower prairies, and down it we rushed with a headlong speed. My horse—I know not how—made some false step, and after a vain effort turned a complete summersalt, I leaving his back at the first blunder, as I was leaning forward.

I found myself pitched many yards ahead, almost upon the horse before me, who had now also met with an obstacle, which placed the riders more on an equal footing. This was a boggy-sided watercourse, without bushes, or any indication sufficient to have warned us in the dark.

The Indian had partly pulled in, which prevented his having a fall, but his horse struggled and plunged, so as to make it impossible for him to use his rifle, and I was by his side. I had presence of mind enough to get upon his right side, that he might not be able so easily to use his arm, but I found he had shifted it, though the plunges of his horse prevented his being able to steady it for an aim.

My own footing was not secure, but I made a bound at the gun, but again I missed to catch it, and the rider had slipped off on the other side. He had now an advantage over me, which rendered flight and a refuge in the darkness almost my only chance. However, I kept moving back and forward, and occasionally stooping down, and the movements of the horse between us rendered an aim difficult. I was desperate, and at the end of my resources, there appeared nothing for it but a rush, and take the chance of the rifle hanging fire.

Chapter Thirteen
Fighting hand to hand in the dark—a captive—companions and counsel—regrouping

I know not what idea of a Spanish matador came into my head, but it flashed upon me that I might make my hunting-shirt a diversion, or even throw it on the rifle, as I made my rush. While I bounded from side to side, I disengaged the skirts of the shirt from under my belt, and stooping suddenly down, passed it over my head.

My adversary saw that there was some new agent come into play, and crouched down to take aim over the horse, now quietly stuck in the mud. I immediately moved toward his head, and shifting from side to side, obliged him to change the barrel, as I moved from one side of the head to the other.

This took place two or three times, as I drew nearer. But there was a little hole, half filled with water which balked my spring, and I had again to shift, and as I did so, made also my bound. But the barrel had already shifted to the side of my attack—the shirt was thrown at the same moment, the smart of a wound in the side, and the explosion of the rifle came at the same time. But I felt the most furious rage, and instead of dropping with the shot, I dashed aside his weapon, and closed with the Caw, now risen up, and resolved to grapple with him to the death.

I had few equals in personal activity and strength, and notwithstanding my wound, I felt I had yet life enough in me to overcome my adversary. He was as slippery as an eel, but I was not to be refused. I threw him, and put my knee on his chest, and a hand on his throat. I felt him search for his knife, but his belt I had burst in the first of the struggle. I could see his dark eyes looking calmly up at me, there was not a word or a sign of fear, when I took out my knife and raised my arm. I did not feel him wince, nor did his look quail. I could not strike, and I lowered my hand.

There had been a lasso in his girdle, which I felt among our feet, I stuck my knife in my teeth, and pulled the lasso, seizing one hand, I tied a part of the rope tight round the wrist, and passed it round below his back, my knee was on the other arm. When I got it through, I tied another end to the other arm, and passed it round the opposite way—something like a straight waistcoat. I then made fast the feet. I know not how long I had been in the chase, or the struggle, but I felt the blood trickling down my side. The Indian lay still, as may be supposed, but the horse showed some symptoms of a desire to better himself, and I turned toward him to see if I could get him up. I folded up the Indian's blanket, and put it under his foot, and having slewed him a little round by the tail, and given a haul round to his head, he made an effort, and finding the thick folds of the blanket sustain him, and having no weight upon his back, after two or three surges, he gained his feet.

I led him then up to where I expected to find his companion, either bogged or with his neck broken. He was, I found, safely eating close to where we fell. I hoppled both, and returned to look at my fallen foe. It was only right to place a small appichimo[i] on a drier place and move him to it. Putting his blanket round him, I left him to his fate for the night.

I knew, for the last half mile, the direction we had come, and I took it, carrying off my prisoner's rifle.

It must have been some time before sunrise, and there could be no use in wandering about in a wrong direction, though it was as well to keep the horses in exercise, to prevent chill, after the previous burst and subsequent mud-bath of one.

I put them upon their own back trail, but I found they did not keep it, so I must trust to my own luck in hitting off the direction. I went a little way, but as I got on the higher ground, was soon at fault. The wind had been pretty steady I thought, and I took my bearing by it, but progressing very slowly.

It was past two, and the day would break in little more than a couple of hours, so I let the horses' heads loose, leading them by a long cord, so that they could eat when we came to a good bit of grass.

Thus loitering, so as not to get very far off the trail, in case the wind should change, I consumed the tedious time, till a slight break appeared in the east, the herald of the dawn.

I never remember to have felt so glad. I had undoubtedly made a *coup*—I had brought in two horses, and bound an Indian armed, and taken his rifle, but I had to search for my own, in case Jim had not thought of it, and my blanket besides.

I could now see, from a height, the line of the stream I had galloped along in the previous pursuit, and edged my course toward it, and in half an hour was at the crossing, the scene of the last night's watch, but there was no blanket—the rifle, however, was under the bushes, from whose concealment I had leaped at the expected prey.

I could find no marks to indicate the result of Jim's scuffle in the creek, nor could I find the back mule track, though I was rejoiced to trace that of the horse distinctly, taking the onward trail, I immediately mounted, and getting the two arms, set out as blythe as a man might be, who, though he is well satisfied with his performance, had not slept the whole of the night before. I found the distance turned out not to be more than about four miles to the next timber, and of course, I was not long in going there.

The morning was about the usual grey of fine weather, an occasional prairie cock[1] skimmed over the horizon, otherwise all seemed still when I arrived at the spot where the trail enters the timber. I had to watch for the signs, and at last I saw a leaf turned over on my right hand, and then a horse mark, it was not difficult to find the track after they entered the woods, and I soon saw the figure of a man, who was leading a mule out toward the grass, I then perceived the other animals, and took a direction toward them, to add my steed to the common lot. Having hobbled them, I returned to look for the camp, which a slight curl of smoke enabled me to see not far off, behind some bushes.

I came in like a Robinson Crusoe, with my two rifles, the fire was in a little circular open, surrounded by a low screen, over most of which a man standing up could see the plain where the band was feeding. They were all seated round when I entered, and I went straight to my saddle, where I also found my blanket. Having sat down, Jim handed me his pipe, I took a few puffs, he said,

"Well! what luck?"

"I've got the two horses," I said, "and you?"

"I got one—are our own right?"

"Yes."

"And the mule?"

"Yours is all right, but the other slipped off, the Caw was riding the horse, and the mule broke while we were in the struggle, I fell on the slippery bank, and the Indian broke too, the mule, however, must be in the creek, or gone back, as he did not go out the same road as the Indian—who dashed away over the prairie on the back trail—unless he turned into the bushes again, the one which was behind, I suppose, is not far off, for I caught a sight of him on this side the creek, as I brought our own beasts back. You have brought the Indian's gun, have you got his hair?"

"No! he lay at my mercy, and I did not like to kill him, he lies up yonder ready tied, however."

---

1. Prairie cock: The bird variously called prairie chicken, sage grouse, fool hen, etc.

"Do you mean to leave him there?"

"I suppose I had better loose him when we start."

"As you like."

Jim was busy with the coffee, and taking a look over the bushes at the prairie, and I turned to the young European, to whom I held out my hand.

"You did not expect to meet me here, I'll bet."

He took my hand, and looked doubtfully at me, as if he expected some reproach, but I was in good humor with all the world, though I know not why. I did not feel inclined to rush into the arms of one I had known in such different circumstances, and whom I knew not well whether I liked or hated, but I now turned to Smith.

"Can you tell me where Heald is?"

"I thought you would ask me that anyhow, we had a sort of difference about starting before the time, and some other matters, and I let him go alone, and as I fell in with Mr. Bernard, I thought it would do as well as go up with Fontinelle[2]. We did not think to lose our horses so soon, but are you going to give them up?"

"I could not keep them, as they are not mine."

"Why you should know, that the mountain law is, whoever retakes stolen horses with the strong hand, keeps them, and if I understand right what happened, you took them back at desperate odds against you. No, they are well earned your own, but if you will lend me mine, I'll have a cart for mules."

"I wish to give back the horses I took, to their owners, of course," said Jim.

We were now at our breakfast.

Smith was a tall, active-looking, yellow-haired Missourian, with blue eyes, a Grecian nose, and a pleasant and eager expression of countenance. The strange face was that of a dark-muzzled, groom-looking youth, who was apparently the hired man of my former school acquaintance, Bernard the Swiss. I could in no way account for the presence of the latter, and I could not shew any great cordiality, where I really felt a certain distrust.

After breakfast, I accompanied Smith to give a little look for the mules, and to have him put a bandage on my wound, which was only from the ball grazing my side.

While the baggage was being arranged, taking a bye line to where I thought the Indian was, I had got to the height above, where I expected to find the scene of the last night's struggle, when Smith made a sign and stopped, I

---

2. Fontinelle: Lucien Fontenelle (1800-1840), an orphan from New Orleans, entered the trade in 1819 and late became an employee and partner of the reorganized Missouri Fur Company. In 1830 he led an American Fur Company brigade, and in 1833 led that firm's train to rendezvous. Admired as a leader, he also drank to excess. See Dale L. Morgan and Eleanor Towles Harris, eds., *The Rocky Mountain Journals of Willam Marshall Anderson: The West in 1834*, San Marino, 1967, and Alan C. Troutman, *Lucien Fontenelle*, in Hafen, *Mountain Men*, V: 81-99.

followed the direction of his eyes, and perceived the two mules tied together behind a little height, Smith immediately started for them, and I followed, as I felt assured that the untied Indian had just laid his clutches upon them, and that the Indian lying wait, would have the best of it. This was true enough, for just as I got within reach, I saw his head cautiously raised, and the barrel of his gun leveled toward the unconscious American, who was eagerly moving toward the mules. I shouted and made a gesticulation, to shew that if he fired, I would shoot him. He dropped into the hole again in which he had been concealed, and Smith came back with the mules in triumph, we were both now within fifty yards of the Indian, still concealed. I told Smith to keep on one side, while I kept the other, and to cock his rifle if the Indian raised his head to shoot at one, he on the other side should shoot him through the head while he was taking aim, which all Indians do very slowly, our enemy now saw that he had no chance, and fired off his rifle, and rose to come toward us. It was to my side he bent his steps, and I begged of my companion to explain to him, that the other Indian was bound at a little distance off, and that he must give up his gun, this he did with a very bad grace, and I saw no more of him, for the others being waiting for us, it was time to be off.

Chapter Fourteen
Spying buffalo, and wild horses—first hunt for buffalo

We were gradually nearing the open country—this part of the journey is not of great interest, unless as indicative of the disappearance of the bison and the wapati deer, whose heads still bleached occasionally by the side of the trail. After crossing the great Pawnee Road[1], we reached the last camp before striking the Platte, and the next day a dreary morning's work brought us upon the low sandy heights which bound its valley on the southwest, it is one of the most singular of views, which bursts upon the eye from these hills —the long straight course of the broad and shallow stream, the great extent of flat, and the line of poplars which mark the great island, almost inaccessible from the shallows of quicksand, which protect it alike from the wader and the swimmer.

In this island have always haunted the great wapiti, and a few of the common American deer, a larger species of roe. We had already fired at the antelope and were beginning to get into the region of solitary bulls. Nothing was attempted in the way of running and we waited to cross the South Platte to encamp, and have more hunting than enough between the forks.

The crossing of the South Platte is not a very easy matter, but the piloting was undertaken by Smith, who went off while we halted to noon, to find a place. After nearly drowning himself several times, he at last came back with some pieces of driftwood for a raft for the baggage, and the news that there

---

1. Great Pawnee Road: Evidently a trail linking the Platte River with the Smoky Hill Fork. See Frémont's map of 1845 in Jackson and Spence, *Fremont,* map portfolio.

was a good enough ford halfway across, and then swimming, but that was but short, and near the opposite shore.

We got over easily enough, and the next day I was to give up my horse to my baggage and take to that famous mule hitherto untried by me.

Considering that it is really dangerous, the crossing of this river, we got over with wonderful ease, and we encamped on a small island for the night, where we were safe from attack, finding on it a good supply of driftwood, and some bushes for shelter and concealment, we had got mixed up together tolerably well. Smith was captain, but the Delaware's knowledge and coolness were almost constantly referred to in any deliberation. The Swiss and his man Friday kept pretty much together, and when it threatened to rain, put up their shanty covered with a piece of oil cloth. Smith lodged with us in a like habitation, when shelter was required.

There was nothing to be seen on the wide plain above, or on the low buttes on either side, and we determined to go over to Ash Creek[2], on the north fork, and come back on to the divide to hunt, should we see any buffalo as we passed over. This was the result of the evening's council, we caught up at five o'clock, swallowed a cup of coffee and a mouthful of unleavened bread, and took the branch of the stream which separated us from the mainland, the sun was yet low, when we were upon the edge of that strangely level table land, which extends some twelve or fifteen miles at this point over to the head of Ash Creek, near the North Platte, it was disheartening to find that chosen spot deserted, and we wended on our way toward the rising sun.

It was necessary, however, here, to have the animals in hand, in case of their coming in contact with any wild horses, which this vast plain either here or further up was never about that time without. Thus we had journeyed nearly halfway across, when Jim, who was a little ahead, as it was my turn to take charge of the baggage, began to make gestures as if throwing something he stooped to gather into the air above his head.

"Buffalo at last," said Smith, and we soon discovered a long line of black on the plain five or six miles off, our whole thoughts were directed now to getting to the point we wished to strike. At the head of Ash Creek, there is not the slightest landmark as a direction, and it is only to be done by course, and we were able to get down without difficulty to the spot at which we were fortunate enough to light.

At the time of which I speak, the main valley and several branches were covered with luxurious wood, the ash festooned by the grapevine, the wild

---

2. Ash Creek: Probably the creek of that name which is a tributary of the North Platte River, near present Oshkosh, Nebraska. The route of the fictional Warren thus far has been up the Kansas to the Little Blue River, crossing the Great Pawnee Road and moving to the vicinity of the *Big Island* shown on Frémont's map of 1845. Big Island is the present Grand Island, Nebraska. That route was a usual one for fur caravans, and became the Oregon Trail.

cherry tree, and the plum below, whole thickets of gooseberry and currant, and cedar in the rocks above.

There were hiding places for a dozen such parties as ours, and in the paths which led from the river up the branching ravines, might be studied the track of every animal inhabiting these plains.

In that day, it was the especial haunt of the wild horse, and the grisly bear found caverns and impenetrable thicket for a winter's abode, the great bison bull, who occasionally seeks solitude in summer, leaves a passage of fur when he winds through these tangled brakes, the argali[3] is found in the rocks, while the eyrie of the eagle and the hawk. It is the first shelter after leaving the wooded banks of the feeders of the Kanzas, and the surest for the chase.

"We may have a grand hunt tomorrow," said Smith, as we wandered together up one of the ravines that evening. "But we had better move our camp the first thing, a little from here, as it will then look as if we had gone on, they will all be wanting out, and I think we had best cashe our booty, and take the rest of the works with us. I do not feel so sure of this place, if there is a vagabond in all these parts he must pass here."

"Nor do I feel very sure of two of ourselves," said I.

"You mean the Swiss and Friday, they do look something out of the way, there is something in the head of Bernard I cannot make out. Never mind, we will shake him off the first people we meet—had you ever any quarrel?"

"Not exactly."

"Well, he has rather a bad eye, and that's the truth, but he shall not do you any wrong by treachery, I'll take care, I owe you a good turn, mind that."

I saw there was no use in making a quarrel with the Swiss, and the conversation dropped.

We had wandered a good distance, and were got out from the groves of ash and cherry, the latter of which, with the vine, were in flower, and filled the valley with an almost oppressing odor.

As we looked down and back toward the river, we saw the long column of white smoke curl from our nest-like camp in the bushy thicket.

The eagle was far above, with his wide circles in the calm blue sky, a colony of small birds, which belonged to the spot—for there was no other shelter for them in many miles around—were caroling, and it was a most soothing scene, and turning upward to look into the next ravine, a hollow valley without a shrub, we saw what at first startled, and then delighted me more than anything I had yet seen, some half-a-dozen horses, apparently gamboling on the opposite side. That they must be wild, was evident from the length of mane and tail of some two or three, who seemed the masters of the

---

3. Argali: The bighorn sheep, a source for meat and skins or clothing. See Ross, *The West of Alfred Jacob Miller,* plate 30 and notes.

herd, they were upon our trail, coming and returning, rearing up and striking out with their forefeet, one in particular of a dark brown, had the great neck, and a heavy mane falling to the ground.

I gazed over the little divide in a trance of admiration, I thought I had never seen the animal before, how different from the conventional race.

"Aye," said my companion, "that is a noble beast, but we may see a hundred tomorrow, if we have any luck, so we'll let them be tonight, that they may not be scared."

"Do you see these ravens to the left," I said, "the Romans considered it was good to see ravens on the left hand."

"We will set that down for tomorrow then."

It was nearly dark when we got back, and we found a little arbor already made, it looked both comfortable and picturesque, and the pilaffe[4], with a few slices of ham and a bull's tongue, set off what was intended to be the last of our scanty meals. We were promised after this to have more than enough of the choicest parts of the cow, if we would hunt, we were never more to want.

"Do you hear the wolves," said Jim.

I listened for a moment, there was an almost universal howl came down the ravines.

"Ah!" said I, "shall we not be eat up?"

"I don't think they are so badly off as that, it is a good sign, however, that there has been no running among them lately, when the bands are quiet, the wolves do not dare attack, unless it is some sickly or stray beast, and they will follow us tomorrow like dogs, or we shall find them waiting for us on the plain."

"It is not the sweetest music," said the Swiss.

"I've bin whar I liked it better than the sweetest song that ever was sung, however," rejoined Smith.

We were all in bed, when we heard a noise among the horses, and I really had no doubt we should be attacked, but on going among them, I could see that it was not alarm which made them neigh, and I remembered the wild herd we had seen an hour before, I took the precaution of hoppling mine, however, and when I came back, I found those who had experience in mountain craft, had made up their minds to the same effect, there was not much talking, and no singing that night, we were all anxious to be ready for the dawn.

After maneuvering the animals in different directions, we left the lower end of the valley, and uniting them together again in one trail, proceeded toward one of the upper outlets, which lead to the table land, the springs were

---

4. Pilaffe: It's interesting that Stewart indicates that rice is part of mountain provision.

not all dry, and near a tuft of bushes and trees, we found still a little supply of water.

It was not difficult to hide our packs, and we allowed the pack-saddles to remain on the mules, that we might each bring back some trophies of the first day's hunt to the camp we had thus casually chosen. Occasionally, a wolf was to be seen loitering about, and I, for the first time, saw the immense track of the grisly bear, almost fresh on one of the numerous footpaths which every where line these dells.

"We may see him above," said Jim.

I observed the Swiss and his man look almost with a sneer at what they would not believe to be the footmark of any beast, the little it was defaced made some excuse for the doubt, besides the great size.

My first feeling was a desire to see such a beast, but it would be beyond the luck of ordinary men to hope to bring in one of these vast feet as a trophy at first sight.

Mechanically, I examined the cap of my rifle, as I followed in file. Jim was leading—he had good luck, and the best eye, we were gradually mounting, but without seeing before us any apparent outlet. At last, a sharp turn to the left, and at a single step from the sharp-sided creek and contracted ravine, we were on that remarkable plain, where the eye looked in vain for an object to rest upon, or a distant speck upon the horizon. We stood still for a moment, and I felt a pang of disappointment.

"Hist!" articulated Jim, as he directed his head to his horse's neck.

The wind blew steadily, but not strong, right across the plain, the way we had come the previous day. I got off my horse, and changed the saddle on to the back of the mule.

We could plainly hear the grunting sound of the bison, so different from the lowing of other cattle. There could be but a slight swell between us and them, and we went down again under cover of the mouth of the ravine, to make our arrangements.

"I do not think I'll run today," said Smith. "My horse is not blooded, and once in for it, I am sure to have a fight with him, so I shall take my chance of a flying shot. We will leave the pack-saddles and their bearers with Friday. Jim will tell him how to keep us in sight, and to keep along the edge of the coter[5,i]. All the greenhorns run, except yourself. Now, you black-muzzled partner, I'll just tell you one secret, and that is, that ne'er a one of us three has a horse to his name, so mind that nothing happens to theirs, as they will put you afoot, I reckon, the first, if they want a remount. Now, put that in your pipe and smoke

---

5. Coter: Stewart's version of the French *côte* or *coteau*, meaning slope or hill. Often used in the area of the Louisiana Purchase to indicate abrupt hills bordering rivers, sometimes indicating a ridge or divide.

it", and he turned toward Bernard, with a look as much as to signify that he might take to himself part of the admonition."

"Now mind," said he to me, "as you have a beast that *can* do it—and I see you are not to be denied—that most of the cows are in calf, heavy, some have calved, a very few are barren, and the best chance is a young cow, as they are easiest known, and have shed their coats. If you should see a long-horned ox, take him by all means—he is sure to be as fat as a friar."

It was a moment of anxious suspense, and having made these arrangements, Jim said to Friday, "You will keep opposite the cloud of dust, when you do not see me."

We were now again in silence on the plain, and Jim, with Smith, was to creep as near as possible, to try and get a quiet shot, but if nothing good was within reach, they were to make a signal, and we were to rush in.

Though there was a gentle rise of the ground, sufficient to conceal the herd and the prairie beyond, yet was it so smooth and gradual that to approach was a matter of some difficulty, and we stood watching and waiting for a signal.

The sounds came still louder, and more from the left. The Swiss took a few steps in that direction, to secure a better start.

I saw Jim raise himself on his two hands, and peer forward, but dropping again spoke to his companion. After a moment, they turned on their backs, and made a signal.

Bernard dashed off, as if for a race, to the left. I bore away rather to the right.

Smith hollowed, as I passed, "Take your pistol, boy, as you get near, and shoot from behind, to break the back or go through the kidneys."

I was already in sight of the vast moving mass, there were none of them eating, but all collected together, as if disturbed, and when Bernard, who was first visible, made his appearance, and then myself, there was no immediate commotion of alarm, a mighty bull or two shook his shaggy head, or the maternal feelings of a cow might be moved, but the herd as a body did not appear scared at our abrupt appearance, and I was within a hundred yards before they were all seriously in motion. The style of deliberate gallop with which the vast body first put itself in motion, by no means promised much difficulty in running in upon any one I might choose to single out, but I felt completely overpowered at the sudden and monstrous display. I had, however, recovered myself after the first bewilderment.

The wind, as I have said, was across the plain, and as the course of the band was along the head of the ravines, it brought the whole dust upon me as long as I remained on the right flank. I, therefore, closed my legs to the mule, and darted at the herd, who gave way in some confusion at this maneuver, and I could see when they laid themselves down to their work, that the speed of the bison is not to be despised.

On entering the band, I could not force my way right across, as I had intended. As it was, I was in considerable danger—those nearest to me being pushed on by the crowd behind, and I was obliged to steer with great care in bearing up toward the windward side.

The dust was now suffocating, to choose a mark would be impossible, or to distinguish sufficiently to follow up the choice—the thunder of so many thousand feet over the hollow-sounding prairie—the ominous look, and threatening approach of those on whom I pressed, the bewilderment of being carried along in the cloud of monsters and a whirlwind of dust, on an animal, though of whatever merits of speed and endurance, was of a height which added dread of being overwhelmed to the other perils of this extraordinary chase.

I had hoped to cut through a narrow rank, but with those behind and beside me, was forced like a wedge among those before, thus making a broader column as we rushed on. The speed was terrific, and had there been a hole or any obstacle in the ground, we must have fallen headlong upon it.

Happily for myself, I thought I saw a large and black-looking cow, her hump seemed less in proportion, and thicker, and as far as I could see in the blinding sand, she had all the symptoms of being fat, as I had been instructed to look for them, and I laid my mule upon her, determined to have blood anyway.

The moment the animal found herself an object of attack, she increased her pace and made a clear way for herself, and for me to follow. Everything gave way before us.

How had I escaped the ponderous heads that sought to hook me as I passed, and was almost grazed by them?

We were going down a gentle slope, where the cow had the advantage, we plunged into a shallow pool at its foot, and then the ascent came of a rise beyond. I had the rapid recollection of having heard of five picked cows being killed in a course, reloading each time.

I replaced my pistol in the holster, and covered the lock of my rifle, as we rushed through the water a shower of which was dashed high in the air by the plunging multitude. But we survived the bath, and in getting out I again saw, where there was no dust to obscure the sight, that my cow was not far off, and that the mule, or my position in relation to the others which surrounded us, had also kept me near her.

There was now a gentle rise, and good fortune had it, that she was forced up the middle and steepest of the swell, and here I found the truth of two things I had heard—one that a bison relaxes in fastness up hill, and the other, that if a mule chooses to put it out, he has always some reserved speed for an emergency.

Three or four bounds brought me up to the croup of the cow. I rose in my stirrups and delivered my shot. She did not exactly fall with a broken back, as I had intended, but I saw that she was mortally struck in the region of the kidneys, and that she faltered, and I passed forward, in my headlong course, to challenge another.

I had got on the crest of the height, and it served to show me the immense scattering that had taken place, and also to remind me not to let my ardor overcome me so far as to forget that I had but one mule, and how well she had answered, when called upon in the last burst, and I pulled up, to examine the appearance of the field of battle.

There was a great string winding along far ahead, there were scattered compact bands in all directions, and a few singly, but the main body was still between me and the cliffs and I was too windward of them. I dodged the herd for more than half an hour, my mule, I thought again fresh, and I once more edged toward the herd, but on the same side.

It was now less difficult to distinguish individual forms, but I could make out nothing to please my idea of a barren cow, there were some magnificent bulls, who galloped lazily with the rest, but still no cows worth killing, unless there might be one leading, which I could not perceive, and I had to quicken my pace, to examine the first of the band.

They took a slight turn toward me, and I could see the leader, she was short and thick, and black, and therefore fat to all appearance, and had shed her wool. I let her take her circle, and eased my hand, the mule sprung at the first release, and I made the string of the bow which was formed by the course of the herd. As soon, however, as it was perceived by them that I was gaining, their speed again increased, and I bore right toward the leader.

And well worthy she was to lead. Away she went like an antelope, an even, steady pace, which kept my mule at more than three parts speed.

I did not know then that you must break down this sort of pace by a burst, which they cannot support, except downhill, and I only gradually gained, while the chase seemed not in the slightest degree distressed, and not yet pushed.

She had so evidently the heels of the others, that there was no chance of journeying her up, but I must run in upon her in the open field, and perhaps have a fight. I shortened my stirrups, and threw the stock of my rifle over my bridle arm, instead of letting it rest a dead weight across the pummel of my saddle, leaving my right hand at liberty, and I cannot say I blessed Mr. Heald in my heart, at having deprived me of my favorite roan.

But the mule showed no signs of distress yet, and I pressed her on.

The dust was wafted over the heights toward the north fork, and the leading cow and I were fairly to have a match of speed. The lumpy appearance had disappeared, and she stretched out at a pace of which I thought such a form incapable.

I touched the flank of the mule, for the first time, with the whip, but that was not the key. I pricked her flank with the spur—but that was not it, either. I was almost in despair, and dreaded she was beginning to tire.

The lasso, the coil of which was stuck under my belt, came loose, and to gather it up, and at the same time animate the mule, I swung it over my head. The Spanish blood was moved with the memory of her native plains. I found her lighter and stronger in the bound, and I was insinuating myself in between the leader and the panting followers. The cow now saw it was a run for life or death. We were separated from all the rest and but a few yards asunder.

Again I had recourse to the lasso, again it touched the corresponding cord, and a few bounds, and I rose in my seat to deliver my shot. The cow swerved at the moment, and she was but struck in the flank. I put up my pistol, and prepared to try my rifle, but I was a little on the left, so I had to shift my position. The animal was already the more shy from the wound, and I was again losing time, and a turn threw me out.

Of course, I did not like to pull up and take aim, as that could not be counted running, so I forbore, and again I tackled the cow, who, turning sharp to the right, had disappeared in a deep gulley, which here indented itself into the plain.

I did not attempt to pull up, it would have been vain, but I shut my eyes as I dived after my game, she had now taken to that sort of work, which rendered it fair to take ever advantage, if advantage there was to take.

I had already almost fallen over a precipice, the cow was rushing wildly down a watercourse, and I got another chance on the smooth bottom of a little valley. I shouted, and again, the gallant mule made an exertion, and I was a little behind her on her right.

There was every appearance of an almost impassable gorge beyond, and as a last effort, I gave my last shot. It was again badly planted, and while I thought on the humbler method of dodging and waiting, that the tired beast should stop to receive her death-wound from a steady aim, a horse flew rather than galloped past me, and I saw an Indian with long flowing hair, bending a bow at the flank of the cow, as she went over another precipice beyond, the horseman followed, and an unperceived hole laid myself as well as my mule in the dust. The sand had so given way to my weight and impetus, that I must have left in it a cast for an alto relievo[6], but I was not hurt, for I was on my legs again as soon as the mule, and rushed to the spot where my cow and her new enemy had disappeared.

---

6. Alto relievo: Sculptor's term for high relief.

Chapter Fifteen
A beautiful Indian youth—butchering a fat bison cow—taking leave

From thence, I saw commence, after the short but rugged descent at my feet, a small but verdant valley, watered by one of those pure and sparkling streams which are so short-lived in that arid soil, and a hundred yards down its side stood, without saddle or anything but a small apichimoe, a horse of that golden hue in which Guido[1] chose to represent the Horses of the Sun. A blaise like theirs marked the neck and part of the shoulder and head, giving a flesh color to the large distended nostril, the head was short and square, and the eye large and luminous.

I had leisure to remark this magnificent animal, as he stood the prominent object of the picture.

The Indian was on the other side, bending over the spoil, and in the act of extracting the fatal arrow.

I led my mule down the bad step, and dropped the trail rope and loosened the girth, and then proceeded, with some wonder as well as misgiving at the sudden appearance of this second actor in the scene.

The Indian turned round as something signified my approach, he still grasped the short bow, but the arrows were all in the carquois[2], save the one which he held headless in his hand. I lowered my rifle, which however, was unloaded, as I could only re-charge a pistol while in mid-course, and I

---

1. Guido: Probably a reference to Guido Reni (1575-1642). An Italian painter of the Eclectic school, Reni represented golden horses pulling the chariot of the sun in his celebrated *painting Aurora*, or *Triumph of Phoebus*, on a ceiling in the Rospigliosi Palace in Rome.
2. Carquois: French for archery quiver.

expected no hostility, as there had been already ample opportunity of planting an arrow in my back, instead of in the cow, had it been wished to do so.

Slightly formed and under the middle size, the Indian stood in an attitude of complete repose, as if awaiting my approach, the head bare, and the long hair confined by a small strip of beaver fur, very fine beads, of the blue of the turquoise, were strung on a lock, above the separation of the longer tresses which fell on either side, the brow was paler than that of the tribes I had hitherto seen, the hunting shirt was somewhat longer than mine, and left the arms exposed, the hands were beautiful, as well as the feet, which were remarkably small, the leggings were of deer-skin, full and long in the fringe, with a rich stripe of small bead-work down the seam, the legs appeared to be beautifully formed and fuller than usual.

I was so pleased at the survey, that I was in no hurry to break first the silence, and raised my eyes again to the countenance, to read if there was any sign to lead me on.

However, I may be alive to surprise or admiration, or to those mysterious sympathies which are electrically conveyed by the touch as well as by the sight, I have never been conscious of betraying it by outward emotion, but I must confess that now I had to controul an exclamation as well as gesture of surprise, which I felt would be ill-bred. That countenance, on which I now gazed with fascination, was of the most faultless beauty—the finely penciled eyebrows, arched over those almond-shaped eyes, for a moment, opened upon me with darkened fire from between the long lashes, which again reposed on the cheek, through whose tint the late exercise had brought a warmer hue.

I had never seen anything to give me the idea of a perfectly noble head before, and I suppose my admiration also spoke through my eyes, for a smile, somewhat wanton and scornful, stole over the features and curled the lips of the Indian youth, but he did not move.

If it was, however that was the intruder, he was on his native soil, on which I was the trespasser, and I resolved to acknowledge it. However poor my politeness, compared to the grand simplicity of bearing before me, the conscious patience of attitude and manner that so imperiously bid me speak, were not to be resisted. I was so completely enthralled, that I adopted at once the type before me, and without any *white man* salutation, addressed to the patient youth *a hope that I had not interrupted his sport.*

This I did in French. Without feeling certain, it had flashed across my thoughts that it was a young Metis[3] to whom I spoke, and I saw by the awakening smile which answered that I had been understood, but I also saw those eyes turned toward the neglected cause and trophy of the rencontre.

"Are you not going to take any meat?"

---

3. Metis: French Canadian term for persons of mixed European and Indian blood.

"As you killed, I left it for you."

"The first blood takes, and you had given her two shots before."

I was as ignorant of European butchering as might be, and only knew in a general way that there were pullies, and that the animal, after being partly skinned, was hoisted up and sawn in two down the middle of the back, and then quartered, but what to take I knew not, nor how. I suppose my ignorance and embarrassment were quite apparent.

I took out my knife, but the half-breed said, "Perhaps you had better go up to the prairie first, and see if everything is quiet, but take care! Don't show yourself, look first that the herd is still."

It was a great relief, even the short respite of that little distance. Everything seemed quiet above, the animals had gathered together again in some places. I thought I could see a herd of wild horses snorting about the plain, but there was no appearance of any fresh alarm, and the whole space in sight was so covered with living creatures, that no general enemy could have entered among them without causing alarm to some.

Having satisfied myself thus far I returned to report, secretly hoping that the dreaded operation would be begun, or the way of beginning indicated by some graphic cuts.

I found my mule had formed a close attachment to the horse, and they were browsing together like Siamese twins, the Indian was just hanging the tongue of the cow on the pummel of my saddle.

"Now come, for I cannot get up the beast out of the hollow without help."

We then set ourselves to the task of turning over the cow. In no way whatever could I comprehend the operation—an animal to be ripped open with the legs doubled under the body, and back uppermost, I could not understand. However, I was not long left in suspense, the cut was made along the back with the quickness of thought, and one side was being skinned and stripped down, in which I now began to help, but was removed by a sign to effect a similar operation on the opposite flanks. My guide now took off the shoulder, and commenced to remove the mass of flesh which lies in the angle between the ribs and along the backbone, which is called by the Americans, the fleece, and by the French the depoulée.

Being considerably behind in knowledge as well as execution, my operation, which I tried to make a faithful copy of the other, went slowly on. The thick yellow fat which covered the loin, seemed to give great satisfaction to my companion, as he pointed out nearly three fingers' breadth before laying it down on the part of the skin which lay spread out, though still on one side attached to the belly.

"Take care of the sand, keep the fur to the ground."

I obeyed all these directions.

Detaching a small axe, called a casstete[4], from his girdle, he cut the ribs along their root, thus opening a door to get at the pudding-gut—the same as that used in the red deer in Scotland, but in the case of the bison, it is stuffed with the meat inside the loin cut small, and is considered the greatest luxury in mountain cooking.

I was now far behind, laboring with a bad knife and unskilful hand, however, I followed the pattern before me to the letter, so that though the skin was not taken off clean, it was taken off, and though the fleece was notched and unevenly cut, it wanted nothing of the weight or size of its fellow.

The hump ribs were now attacked and severed from their base, and ready to be packed away, the knives were returned to their sheaths, and the Indian went for his horse—my mule followed, I saw the horse was without saddle.

The Indian said, "Can you spare me a fleece and side ribs?"

"Yes! But I must carry them for you also, for you have no saddle."

"Oh no, I'm just across the river. You are in Ash Creek?"

"Yes."

"Our way then lies, for a little distance, together. I came over to get a bit of fresh meat, as we are waiting for Fontinelle, and do not want to disturb the left bank."

"I'll carry the meat over for you."

"No, it is part swimming, and you are a good way off, and have some bad camps for grass about Scott's Bluffs and the Chimney. Don't abuse that rare mule, no ordinary runner would catch that cow. Did you see any others look as fat?"

"There might have been plenty, but the dust was as thick as a wall the first race, and I should not have had a chance to see but for our getting into a pond, but I believe it was a good cow, and something bigger than this."

"She was not down, then?"

"No! But I left her staggering."

"Where was she shot?"

"Down through the loin."

"Well, she is safe enough, if the wolves have not got her."

While this conversation was going on, the Indian had tied together two bundles of small twigs, and laid them one on each side the horse's withers, with a piece of skin beneath them, then the meat, equally divided, was thrown across, tied together by a strap of hide. Leaping up behind this provision, he took the way gently down the slope. I bundled up my meat and followed.

"You are on the opposite side?" I began.

"Yes."

"Are there many in your camp?"

---

4. Casstete: Stewart's version of the French *casse-tête*, a small camp axe or tomahawk.

"No, only two lodges of us, keeping as quiet as possible on account of the Sioux. We are not certain that there is not a camp between us and the Little Missouri. How many are you?"

"Five."

"That is not a great force. You have some among you who know the country?"

"Two."

"Well, we shall meet at Rendezvous, I suppose, you had better take down that other open to the right, it will lead you to the riverside in a mile, and then you have but to follow down its banks till you see the cedars on the Bluffs, and you are at home."

I was anxious to have made some propositions about meeting again, but there was a something about my Indian friend that checked any advance, and I was both attracted by a hidden spell, and repelled by a half-haughty smile.

I followed the direction pointed out, and took leave with an imitation of his smile, at the same time making a silent vow that I would overcome his pride, and make him return the liking I had taken for him.

Chapter Sixteen
A false claim—feasting on boudins and hump ribs

It was well on in the afternoon, when I found, by following the morning's tracks, the place where we had left our baggage, no one had returned.

I hid the mule in a brake at a little distance, and dived into the thicket, where I immediately set to work to form a sort of arbor of boughs for our camp, I then collected some dried wood, and got out the kettles, and lit a very small fire, and having smoothed a dry branch and pointed it for a spit, I stuck it through various pieces of meat and fat, strung like beads upon it, and thrust the pointed end in the ground, but allowing it to hang over the fire sufficiently near not to burn, and loose enough to be easily turned when required.

Thinking of that strange Indian youth, his waywardness and his beauty, I plied my household cares, laid out the meat, swept the floor, and smoothed the couch.

It was not yet late in the afternoon, and the sun was hot without. I had eat what should have been my midday meal from off the spit, and laid myself down to enjoy the green shade, there was not a breath of wind reached the little vale, and there was not a sound—not of the smallest bird, the fire was burning out, and I fell over into a quiet, dreamless sleep.

I was awoke by the sound of voices without, it was the arrival of the others. I went out to take in Jim's saddle, and look to my horse, they had the meat of one cow, but it was fatter and larger than mine.

"Well boys," I said, "what sport?"

"The Swiss killed a fine cow," said Smith.

"Who gave you that meat?" said Jim.

"I killed it."

"How! Only one fleece."

"You see the tongue," said I.

"That's no evidence," returned Bernard.

Smith brought in my tongue.

"And did you not find my cow, then, in the first herd? You saw the direction I took, she fell not far from a pool of water, if she did fall."

"Then you did not see her down?"

"Not quite."

"Where was yours hit?" said Smith to Bernard.

"In the heart, or thereabouts."

"But where was you by her, when you fired?"

"Oh, just alongside."

Smith looked at me.

I pointed just over Jim's kidneys, as he lay on his face beside me. He nodded, and I saw that my first hunting feat was to be half set down to another, but the only two of my comrades I cared about were now convinced of the imposture, and I rather enjoyed this hidden hold I had so easily got over my rival.

"Let us have some boudins[1], boys," said the ever-active Smith. "Whar's the tenderloin, aye, here it is. Get powder and shot, Black-muzzle, come, muster something to chop up this meat on, before the gut gets hard!"

He set them all to work.

If there is nothing in that country so good as these puddings, neither is there anything more easily cooked. Everyone had a pile of meat cut half the size of dice, Jim had his in long thin strings, cut with the grain, in the Indian fashion. The other heaps were put together and crammed into the gut as it was turned inside out, and tied with a whang[i] at regular intervals, so that, when cut into portions, it should not lose the juice. This was set to boil, while the delicious hump rib was set up to roast.

We were, for the first time, to dine on the produce of the plains, and of the best. I might be considered as free of the mountains, as I had made a respectable figure in my first hunt, so that I was in high spirits, and I knew of no reason that the others should be sad.

After the meal, the pipe, and then I was to tell my tales.

I described the faults of my running, as they had been proved by my successes too long spun out, and tiring my mule. This was evidently the opinion of my two critics, who wedged in their hints in good-natured frankness, but when I came to the scene of the death of the last cow, both Smith and Jim started on their elbows, and looked surprised and alarmed. When I

---

1. Boudins: French for blood sausage. Here we have a fine description of one of the classic mountain-man delicacies.

had explained that it was but a half-breed youth, armed with a bow and arrow, and that there were but two lodges, I thought there was no more to be said, but Smith shook his head.

"I do not say that you should have shot the fellow and taken his horse, I would not either, though many would, but mind this, never tell your whereabouts to the first comer, that is a rule." After a moment's further shade upon his brow, it cleared up.

"Don't take amiss what I say, Ned"—for so they called me—"for I don't want that fine scalplock to be carried into a Sioux camp—I've had a warm side toward you ever since you made those coups on the Kanzas. How many should he count, Jim?"

The Delaware said, "Had I done as much, I would not have taken four, I would have counted five coups, a gun, two horses, throw a man down and bind him, he having a loaded rifle, and me unarmed, I would not thank anyone to allow me to count two for that."

"Nor would I," said Smith. "We will keep the heights tomorrow, and we shall be more out of the way, and it is a deep sand, the road by the riverside for two camps."

Chapter Seventeen
To the Black Hills—meeting Old Bill Williams—
talk of Rose

While this was going on, I could not help remarking several times, looks of intelligence pass between Bernard and his follower.

We changed the place of our cavalry, and tied them to their pickets as the dusk came on, it was a question whether or not there ought to be a guard, but it was decided that as the horses were some little way off, and in a nook sheltered from rain, it would be needless, and we lounged by a circuitous route back to our sheltered retreat.

There were no wolves to howl that night, they had got the great herd broken and dispersed, and were sure to fall upon some unfortunate stragglers, or some lame or sick, in so vast a mass.

Everything was still, and had I known where to find them, I would have crossed the river, and had a look at the lodges of my new Indian friend.

In three nights, we were within sight of the chimney[1,i], that strange remnant, a hill having wasted away until it left on the top of a circular mound, an obelisk of clay to record the loss of the rest, the hills of the same composition around, have in parts been cut into architectural forms, and I Jiave been told, seen in the mists occasioned by the evaporation of a wet region around, represent Parthenons and Acropolises, fortifications or cathedrals, according to the point from which they are viewed.

Scott's bluffs[2] form an obstacle to be surmounted, through the cuts and ravines of which, as we threaded our way, there were sometimes visible,

---

1. Chimney: Chimney Rock, an Oregon Trail landmark in western Nebraska.
2. Scott's Bluffs: An Oregon landmark named for Hiram Scott.

embedded in the white clay of which it is composed, almost the only fossil remains to be found in the region of the Platte.

A day further, and we were on the Larrame[3], a sluggish stream in those days, full of catfish and soft-shelled turtle, lofty cottonwoods formed a shady grove, from where now stands the fort to the junction of the river. The great expanse was now changed into broken ground, the commencement of the Black Hills. There was in this grove the remains of a camp, probably of some trading company who had preceded us, in fact, I afterward learned that it was the company of Campbell[4], which that season so completely beat that of his rival Fontinelle, but they appeared to have gone on more than a week from the sign.

We had the luxury of fish here, and almost the best I ever tasted.

It was an Arcadia then, the country we were entering upon, confined on the left by a perpendicular rock, about four hundred yards from the river, the vale extends several miles, full of fine timber, bound together by festoons of all the vines of the region, covered with fragrant flowers bedecking the mournful scaffoldings above, upon which the Sioux had built the nests of the dead, where waved the decaying blanket, escaped from the thongs which had tied it, with other household goods, to furnish out the last array of the departed brave. There were many such relics in this sacred grove. The living Indian left it for the dead, until it became the source whence fuel was procured for the forts afterward built below, and could Antoine Goddard, or Joe Pourrier look up, or Pierre Clement, they would not recognize the harbor of the Wapati and the black-tailed deer, nor the garden of currants and grapes, where they had killed the grisly bear at his feast of fruit.

We did not camp among these sad relics, but sadder still it was to find no relic there.

From an open at the timber of the warm spring, near those bluffs where the cedar and the pine come down to meet the cottonwood and the ash, you first get a distinct view of that finely shaped mountain, since called the Butte

---

3. Larrame: The Laramie River, a tributary of the North Platte River in present Wyoming. Here Sublette & Campbell built Fort William, better known as Fort Laramie, in 1834. Since the fort was not yet built at the fictional time, and Stewart remarks on the race between the Campbell and Fontenelle caravans, this represents Stewart's first Western trip, in 1833.

4. Campbell: In 1833 the fur caravans of Sublette & Campbell and American Fur raced to the rendezvous at Horse Creek on the Green River, each hoping to get most of the business of the trappers. Robert Campbell, leading the outfit in which Captain Stewart traveled, beat the Company train led by Lucien Fontenelle handily. Stewart's *Edward Warren* follows Campbell's route from the North Platte up the Sweetwater, through South Pass, and on to the upper Green River.

du Fort[5], so as to trace the hollows on its pine-clad sides, its valleys, and its kenyons,[ii] its fantastic peaks, and its verdant glades.

I remember well I lay, during the halt at noon, surveying through a telescope the intricate defiles and the monumental formations of rock, which appeared as if exhibited on a map, on its varied side, it is the first and the most beautiful of the mountains eastward of the divide. We were moving next day from the warm spring, to fall upon the river again two camps higher up at Deer Creek, and had in the route before us that succession of streams which flow from the Butte above.

They are all well-wooded, and the distance between each is not more than six or eight miles. This was, at that time, one of the great passes of the bison from the parks, and the western country of the Sioux and the Arapahoes, and unless it has changed within a very short period, it is still one of the richest regions for game in the mountains.

I knew the direction we were to take, and at which creek we were to noon, so I had taken a course of my own, a little to the right of the trail, where the creeks cut through the rocks in deep canons to join the river, here a cascade where Scott[6], who died at the bluffs below Larrame, was wrecked long before, and Freemont, who would not take warning, lost his boat[7] and its freight some fifteen years after.

The scenery is romantic, and such is the steep and rugged nature of the rocks, that the beaver exists, I have been told, to this day in its cavern-like pools, unattackable by Indian and white, who had almost cleared out all the streams around. I had had a glimpse of a cougar, and two or three wapatis were sunning themselves on the upper slope of a cliff, but they were in velvet, and their meat is white and tasteless, so I let them be. I had had several opportunities of approaching on our way from Larrame, and had brought in some pretty good meat, but I had not got a shot at the bighorn, or the grisly bear, therefore it was in their behalf I was now most interested, but I could not find a chance, being obliged to go in and out by the indentions of the chasm, through which the creeks forced their way into the cataracts of the Platte.

I could see the trail every now and then. It was on one of the occasions, as I had come up the steep bank of a stream to a point fit for crossing, I found the

---

5. Butte du Forte: The context indicates a location near the intersection of 43 degrees north and 106 degrees west on Frémont's 1845 map, the area of present Casper, Wyoming.

6. Scott: Hiram Scott (1805?-1828) was one of the original Ashley men of 1822. He gained recognition as a trapper and responsible leader rapidly. In 1828, while transporting furs down the Platte River route, Scott fell ill and was abandoned by his comrades to a lonely death in the vicinity of the bluffs which today bear his name. See Merrill J. Mattes, *Hiram Scott, Fur Trader, Nebraska History*, 26 (July, 1945): 127-62, and Mattes, *Hiram Scott*, in Hafen, *Mountain Men*, I: 355-66.

7. Lost his boat: John C. Frémont tried to navigate the rapids on the Platte in the vicinity of Devil's Gate and Goat Island in an India rubber boat on August 24, 1843 (see Fremont's map of 1843 for date and location). This was the first rubber boat to attempt Whitewater in the West.

animals turned out and the other evidences of a halt, I took off my saddle, and descended into the hollow, I there found three persons added to our number, who were all busy answering and asking questions. They each eyed me askance, as I gazed openly at them—the nearest was tall, young, yellow-haired, blue-eyed, and sunburnt, with a most good-humoured expression, and was called Bill Doty, a Kentuckian, the next was shorter, older, and of a more reserved appearance, the third was tall even as he sat, his long legs crossed under him were covered with shining leather pantaloons, once fringed and of a natural length, the fringes now few, attenuated, and far between, shorn of their growth by the wants of the times, the knife had been busy clipping their proportions, and polishing its greasy sides on what remained, until they were lustrous with the fat of many seasons, the shirt partook in character, treatment and texture, an old black beaver covered the head, and through a hole in the crown, obtruded a mass of bright red hair seasoned with white, the features were small and intelligent, the eye of a rich blue was restless and eager, and both hands and face were covered with freckles, bony and dirty—this was Bill Williams the divine[8], who, having preached and taught all the religion he knew in the States, naturally appeared without in the mountains of the west.

"Are you to be on the Susquedee for rendezvous, Bill?" said Smith, addressing the reverend Rufus.

"If you knew that, you would know more than Bill Williams."

"I know you have promised Bent[9] your beaver, is there enough to divide?"

"Thar's more than ever you seed thrown by any white man."

"Aye, you mean bought and caught together."

"I mean that you can neither buy nor catch."

"Well, spit straight, can't you, don't you see you are covering that stranger's legs with your spray?"

"And can't that stranger speak," said Bill, looking hard at Bernard with his keen eyes.

Bernard nodded.

"You've come to see these parts, I reckon, and learn to set a trap?"

---

8. Bill Williams the divine: William Sherley Williams (1787-1849) was one of the most celebrated mountain men, mentioned in many accounts of the heyday of the trade. Williams had been an itinerant Baptist preacher back in the States, and later acted as a guide for Fremont. This amusing description of his appearance is rare first-hand evidence for the dress of free trappers of this period. His presence here on the way to the Horse Creek rendezvous is consistent with what is known of his travels in 1832-33. See the biography of Williams by Alpheus Favor, *Old Bill Williams*, Norman, Oklahoma, 1962, p. 104.

9. Bent: No doubt a reference to William or Charles Bent, brothers and proprietors of the firm Bent, St. Vrain & Co. In 1832-33, this firm built a large adobe fort on the Arkansas River, formally named Fort William but generally called Bent's Fort, later Bent's Old Fort. It became a major trading post and way station on the Santa Fe Trail, and is now a national historic site near La Junta, Colorado. See David Lavender, *Bent's Fort*, Garden City, 1954.

"To see these parts, yes—to set traps, perhaps," said the Swiss.

"Well, I guess you have seen something on your way, which would open your eyes."

"Yes."

"Is that all?" said old Bill, furious at the calmness of the other, "I have just come from the Taos, and have seen in a month more Fandangoes than you ever saw in all your days, and murders enough to have kept the old country in a revel for a year, newspapers and all."

"Go ahead."

"No, I won't, unless I like." And the old trapper lit his pipe, and shut up.

"You expected to cut off some mule load of alchahol from one of the parties going to rendezvous," said Smith to Reece. "We might just tap a company, and there are some more of you lurking about." Ned there saw a half-breed near the forks. "Waiting on the north side," he said, "for Fontinelle's two lodges."

Bill's eyes turned toward the speaker, and then toward me. "What sort of half-breed, and what sort of horse?"

I described them.

"Rose's horse to a hair, I know where they'll cross, not more than a camp above, I knew old Diego would be lurking about."

Reece colored and turned his head another way—they all seemed moved by the news of this party.

"The old man will fort,[iii] I reckon," said Doty.

"I think we'll catch up," said Smith. "It's but a short way to the next creek, it is heavily timbered, there is hiding for ten such camps as ours, and driftwood to roast the mountains."

They were sorry-looking steeds which rode our new allies, but hardy, the four mules, which followed these three men, were loaded with beaver, and each a small kettle, and we jollily crossed the rich meadow, through which wanders one camping stream in devious course, never two seasons in the same bed, which it changes without anger at the instance of any obstruction of driftwood choaking up its wonted way, spreading out like a lake, until it finds another hollow for its track.

At the period of which I speak, this was almost the finest part of the west for every species of animal the country affords, excepting the moose deer, which is to be found no lower down than the hunting grounds of the Blackfeet and the Assimboines, on the far sources of the Missouri.

The sun was yet high, when we arrived at what appeared a complete enclosure of several acres, surrounded by the small-leafed maple, the cherry, and the plum, feathering to the ground and full of flowers. The grass, rich and tender, grew already rank in this sheltered and irrigated plain. The animals scarcely moved from the spot where they were unsaddled, elbow room gave them plenty, and plenty gave them tranquility.

I strolled out on foot, and as a precaution, stuck in my belt a large-bored but short pistol, the first double-barrelled rifle had not appeared in the mountains until 1837,[iv] and it was a resource to have a pistol for a second chance.

Jim, who saw my preparations, quietly followed, and we threaded the surrounding thicket. Our way was silent, and the shadows were deep, the tender leaves canopied above and curtained around on the path of the bison which we followed, the marks were fresh, but nothing living was to be seen, not a hoof, though we had come several miles.

"Let us go out into the prairie," said Jim. "That timber is too empty."

There were some rocks which projected from the smooth green on the left bank, and one or two branchy cedars There, we sat down, with a view of some extent to the right toward the mountain and across the valley, here wider, and not so deep, the pipe was lit, and Jim, who had evidently sought an opportunity for a talk, opened.

"Do you know if they mean to wait for Diego?"

"You heard all that passed."

"They should go on a camp, for he may have crossed and be before us. The buffalo have been moved out here, but yesterday or this morning, should they fall in with these two lodges, there will be hell. That Rose is just the finest squaw in all the red man's country, and she is as wild as the wind, and as free, she might have had all the beaver in the mountains offered for her, the boys are right foolish the moment they get near her, and I think we may as well be off alone if they halt."

I had never known the Delaware make so long a speech, and could not but laugh at his evident alarm.

"Have you ever seen Rose?"

"No, but I have heard enough of her. They say she has taken a fancy for a young fair-haired Jew, called Phillipson[10], the most beautiful boy I ever saw, and he has a squaw already, and the Spanish blood pretends to be cold,

---

10. Phillipson: There are hints that this may have been an actual person: A Phillipson was evidently a member of the Stewart entourage in 1837, when Stewart took the painter Alfred Jacob Miller along. Miller's notes to plate 11 in *The West of Alfred Jacob Miller*, a sketch of a pretty Flathead woman, describe an unrequited passion that *Mr. P.* developed for the woman. According to DeVoto *(Across the Wide Missouri, p. 447)*, William H. Gray of the mission party also mentions *an L. Phillipson, a name given to a minor villain in Stewart's Edward Warren.* And David L. Brown wrote that in 1837, on the Kansas River in modern Kansas, *We were joined by Captain Stewart, of the British Army, Mr. Miller (artist), and a Mr. Phillipson, both of whom were in the Captain's suite* (Brown, *Three Years in the Rocky Mountains,* Cincinnati, 1845, reprinted by Edward Eberstadt & Sons, New York, 1950). Of course, Stewart may also simply have borrowed the name without meaning the historical Phillipson.

because there is something it cannot have, and so she keeps the young men about her, and jeers them right smart for being such fools as to think of her."

"But I should like to have my chance, too."

" Aye, that's it, I know of none with a better if that be all, but a man might as well have his life in his open hand, as have the sharpest knives and the surest rifles in the mountains to deal with."

"What! Would they stab a man without doing it to win the stake?"

Jim shook his head.

Chapter Eighteen
Hunt for a grizzly bear—several surprises—an observatory—a camp spied—felled by an antelope

The morning after this conversation, we were to move on a day's march, where the signs of the crossing the Platte would be seen if it had taken place, or the passing up on the opposite side. There was a slight cloud upon the mountaintop, and the air had been freshened by a thunderstorm and a heavy rain the night before. The animals were evidently the better of this halt, and we mounted in some glee, from the influences around as well as the expectation of the company we hoped to join, no one was in a hunting humor except myself, and I took my way up the stream on which we had lain, and toward the base of the butte from which it sprung. I was on my favorite mule, there was plenty of meat in camp, but it was never amiss to have more, so I made Friday follow with a led mule, upon whom might be put, in addition to what he might carry, sufficient to ensure us against the idleness of several days to come. He had never been out but once, nor his master, so that it was but due now.

These huntings are not jovial, neither song nor converse enliven them, the senses are in a state of tension, and the mind is occupied in visions of success in the chase.

After following up the stream some considerable way, we passed over to the right on to a succession of broad ridges, hard, and of even surface, the scene of many a hunt, and a country seldom blank. From one of these heights, I showed Black-muzzle a landmark on the opposite side of the Platte, to guide him in case of his missing my trail when we separated. The appearances of deepening ravines to the left as they approached the furrowed base of the mountain, indicated that there might hide secure the bear and the deer, though the passing of a camp should clear the open grounds, and I told my companion to keep on the left slope of the swelling ridges to the right, so as to be unseen from the Platte, and yet never lose sight of the landmark. I then bore away to pry into the mysterious coverts in the opposite direction. The absence of wolves convinced me there were no bison in the immediate neighborhood, so I yielded to the desire I had always felt to kill a grisly bear alone, as such an act is considered a coup by the hunters of this country, as well as the Indians.

Everything was cool and still around, the power of the sun was sufficiently great, but there was a freshness in the earth which it had not dried. I bore still to the left, and the gorges grew deeper, and occasionally a wide valley, as if once the bottom of a lake which had burst its barrier presented itself, and I caught a glimpse of some big horns, which had descended from a precipitous cliff to feed below, but they were off to their fastnesses. Thus I was drawn a considerable distance round the base of the hill, but without seeing a bear, which was the object of my search, and I began to examine all the paths in the frequent passes for a footmark. This quest was equally unsuccessful, and I was about to turn again toward the river, when the footmark of a horse, apparently of that morning, attracted my notice. I got into the first hollow I could find and dismounted, leaving my mule, to look over the next ridge, and then going back for her, I made wary approaches in the direction which had taken the track, there was no foil on the dry grass, and I could not find another path, but I kept gradually advancing, till again a pass presented itself between two rocks and leading upward, there was no track here, and what I had seen had broken off before. I must therefore return and take the heel as it was of this morning, and was evidently outward bound, it was easy to find it again, but not so to keep it. But the nature of the country showed that their were grassy valleys to the eastern side and to my left as I had turned back, and as I had not previously found any trace, I inferred that the animal, whether astray—which was not probable—or mounted, must have come from the eastern side, and had made a cast back on the mountain to show a track in a wrong direction, either to be traced back or forward.

Having come to this conclusion, I set about getting under cover in some deep stream as fast as I could, and felt already interested, the more in the danger of hunting a camp, or plunging among unknown enemies, who themselves might be on the watch for me, but I got safe into the bottom of a dell in which the bed of the torrent was dry, but there were pools occasionally full, and clear, and calm, above, hung rocks of a hundred feet, and bushy banks. There was no sign of life, and I now, somewhat anxious held on my way.

The pines appeared on the banks, and the scene was changing to a more Alpine character, I was brought up by a sudden turn to the left and a waterfall, that is, a rock from which trickled the attenuated thread that now represented the foaming flood, which in the time of storm thundered over its side. I must look over the height, which was the left shoulder to the deserted cavern-like recess, again the mule had to be left while I clambered up the rugged side, a lynx was all of animated nature I found on my way, and I got to the crest stony and bushy. I took a cautious peep through the branches of a distorted pine, a valley was beyond, curving to the north round the greater hill, and running its tribute of smaller streams, much indented and swelling out occasionally, and then suddenly contracting: it was impossible to form more than a guess at what it contained. Groups of trees hung on an open slope, or fringed a watercourse—jutting precipices at other places obstructed the view, but when open to the eye, nothing was to be seen but a scene of solitude and beauty. I took my glass, and laying it on a granite block, again went over what I had just surveyed, there was nothing which could be detected even by an ancient Dolland[1], and I must explore in detail, or crossing over, throw myself openly on the eastern ridge.

I was nearly drawing lots between the two plans, so much had all reasoning become fruitless the dilemma, when something black for the first time struck my eye, as if emerging from behind one of those projections which formed one side of a bay in the extended bed—the telescope at once shewed me a horse, there were two white ones nearby, and I put down as an axiom, what I afterward found borne out by experience, that black is usually seen further than white, or any intermediate tint.

These animals were quiet, but they brought no quiet to me, among all the tales of mountain adventure which had often so appropriately beguiled on our way the hours of travel, and the evenings of repose, I had heard the danger of reconnoitring an unknown camp, held as the most supreme, into that I was now fairly launched, and I must here do myself the justice to say, that however I might feel a dread steal over me at such an undertaking, I never for a moment thought of turning back. That which appeared the boldest seemed also the safest course, to cross over to the opposite side, and taking every advantage of the ground, proceed directly for the intervening promontory, leaving my mule to botanize in the deep and secluded basin, where she already culled that fresh verdure, which the sun visited but when young in the east.

I hid the saddle, burnt some powder on a fallen tree, and picketed the mule in such a way as to enable her to break loose if suddenly alarmed, I had prepared to hopple her, but should she be attacked by a bear or some hungry

---

1. Dolland: A telescope. John Dolland (1706-1761) was an English weaver turned optical scientist who, with his eldest son, Peter, refined and popularized the achromatic telescope, which reduced color distortion. See a contemporary reference in Washington Irving, *The Adventures of Captain Bonneville*, ed. Edgeley W. Todd, Norman, Oklahoma, 1961, p. 36.

wolves, I felt that it would be ever after a reproach to me, to think that I had delivered her to a death of torture, to save my self the walk back to camp, where she was sure to go should she have broken loose.

On foot I found myself, after having submerged among the swells and inequalities of the ground, which the eye would have plained over on horseback, and thus I the more easily effected the crossing of the valley unseen, unless from a point exactly opposite. In the trough of these undulations, I had gained one half the distance to the west of the eastern ridge, when I found a sudden turn brought me to an unseen dell behind a mound, and filled like a nest with a thicket of willow and thorn, with a few tall pines domineering over the minor growths, the wild strawberry was in flower, and the moisture of the late rain levelled the mossy carpet between the bushes.

The head of this thicket, where from the appearance also sprang the water which rendered it almost a marsh, rose up against a ridge which must command a view. There was a well-beaten track beneath the shade. I looked at my gun, and entered a few paces, a turn, and I faced a bison bull, which appeared of gigantic height, occupying the entire passage, he had not got my wind, and possibly his shaggy mane hanging over the forehead, and the darkness of the shade obscured his sight, he had heard the sound of my approach, and stopped as if uncertain. No wild animal will attack, unless in the agony and rage of pain, a foe he cannot distinctly see, and whose strength he cannot measure, the mighty mass stood still, and I shrunk involuntarily at the rencontre, to turn, should he advance, was certain destruction, and I remembered the Jesuit rule, *when in doubt, abstain.*

The monster shook his shaggy head, as if to disdain the precept, but also to clear his vision, firing a shot was at once to proclaim an intruder by a thousand echoes, and to start me on a race against time to recover my mule, and fly —no, I must retreat with a bold front. I had not made many steps backward, when the bull, restored to intelligence, rushed upon me—the dead branches cracking, and the living ones yielding in his way. It was too late to fire where there was no time for an aim, a bull, like a wild boar, is brave in a pass, though he avoids a combat in an open space. Genius and thought, the superiority of man, were gone, but instinct came to my aid, though still fronting my enemy, as I bounded back, I felt there was a space on my left where I might squeeze in behind a bush, which grew out from a mound in a tuft of a hundred stems, which united became the substance, as well as the emblem of strength. The breath of the beast was warm upon me, and even that acid smell which is peculiar to him, I thought myself gone while I fell behind the protecting mass, and how I escaped I cannot yet conceive, as I believed myself already among his feet, but he rushed on, as I gathered myself up from the ignoble position, and followed to see the line he took in his flight, he was galloping in the heavy plunging gait of his tribe, and took a course directly for the Platte, and I now was content to make the circuit of the covert, to get at the point I intended.

The view disclosed nothing but a clear furrowed space between me and that ridge, from behind which the horses had appeared to protrude. Was I to wait until night, or risk the open? To wait, would have forced me into contact to gain information, which in the day my glass could give me at a safe distance, I looked down to the left, there was a deep furrow, and opposite, the wood came down in a point from the mountain, as if growing on a morain, to meet the stream, and pushed it past the centre of the valley, obstructing a clear view up or down. A long look shewed nothing on the bare side, and to guard against all the hidden dangers incident to the life in which I was embarked, was not to be expected from a youth of my age or temper.

Rolling over the bare divide, I got into the hollow on the other side, and dashed down its course, at least to be nearer a concealment in the opposite wood, and to give myself up the shorter time to observation. I now found that by means of this wood, there was a way of gaining a complete view of the side I had left, though a bald ridge running parallel cut me off from getting exactly opposite to where I believed the camp must be situated. It was a toilsome progress up the thicket, and but for the occasional opens, I should scarcely have been able to keep a course so as to ensure not entering too far into its depths. At last I fell into a glade, by which I crossed toward the further edge, but then I found a dip behind the bald ridge I had before remarked, and had to ascend again, but the walking was easier, and I proceeded gallantly for some hundred yards, until I saw a rocky height like a beacon rise out of the wood, I again entered, and almost forced my way through its entangled mosses to the foot of the desired landmark.

Taking a few minutes to cool and collect myself, I now mounted what almost appeared made for an observatory. It was a rock, which might have been detached from the masses above, and having found a resting place had stopped, a certain quantity of debris on the upper side forming almost a viaduct to the great mass, the summit of which otherwise would have been inaccessible, this communication was narrow, like a wall at the top, on which there was a sort of dry turf, the sides composed of rough blocks which had been washed bare more recently, leaving the rock and its access only, of the prior disruption.

I almost bounded up at the view which was opened to me, and for the first time, it must be remembered, that unless in the Alleghanys, I had never been on a mountain, and there in the gorgeous pallet of the autumnal woods, there is nothing of the character of the valleys of the Fort Butte. Behind, I could see crags overhanging as if from the clouds, on the left numerous lines cut in the side by the spirit of the storm, before a rolling expanse, divided by timbered streams, the ridges of the Platte, and the broken country of the Sioux beyond, to the right the long meandering lines of the waters we had passed, the gorges and cataracts of the Platte, and still further beyond, as far as the sight could span its placid and broad expanse, a sheet of silver in the distant view.

But among these divers scenes, which might well have engaged an unoccupied eye, my gaze fell full but on one spot, nor was it quite easy to find where the indenture, that appeared a barrier below, was smoothed down into a level bank from where I stood, but there was a fringe of wood which marked a watercourse, and a plain like a shelf, round which half circled a perpendicular rock partly concealed by the trees, and under them I could with my glass make out several huts called shanteys, and a horse pen. The horses were still scattered, the shanteys were to me Indian-like, and I was unable to distinguish any guard or the people about the camp, but the sun was high, and those who might be out hunting were of course not returned, the horse guard could watch the horses stretched under the shade, and though there was nothing visible to alarm me, the evident concealment and total calm were suspicious, and I might lie there till it became too dark to find the way to our camp, before any one moved.

But I now saw my way, and knew how to proceed, the fringe of wood might conceal my approach, as well as my retreat, in case of need. I looked long and carefully over the ground by which I had to pass, I then cast my eyes over the glorious landscape, and bounded down through the wood, up which I had already toiled.

The ledge of rock, fringed on the top, bordered and partly concealed below by different kinds of trees and shrubs, overhung the bed of a stream almost dry, which, trickling in places over the slimy slope of the granite, and in others forming a clear pool in its bed, took a course in one bend from the bottom to what appeared to be its source.

It would have been easy to have reached this at first, but like after reflections in general, which always disclose a shorter path, and from which there is little to be learnt for the future, they were heeded but little, and I pursued my way up through the cover on the top of the rock.

The horses were quietly grazing along the slope, some half a mile off the line I took to get within ken of the camp.

It was necessary to watch minutely on the left among the bushes of the brook, and at the same time to have an eye to the open prairie on the right. With a pace thus slackened I was proceeding, when my attention was attracted by the approach of an antelope, which, in its curious way, was circling round, and then making advances toward me, until I feared there might be something besides myself to create the attraction. It seemed almost unnatural to see a creature, whose safety depended on its wonderful speed, throwing itself into the way of the hunter and though having the wide bounds of the prairie to scour, offer itself a victim within pistol range. I was seated under the trees, and had been looking over the precipitous rock, and turned round in reciprocal gaze.

There is no animal known in the world, which has the same large lustrous eye as the antelope, except the giraffe, and seen thus near and in wanton curiosity, it had a fascination quite unaccountable.

I had heard stories of these beautiful creatures being allured to within twenty feet, by the exhibition of any contorted attitude, or a hat stuck on a loading-rod, and I commenced my maneuver, boy-like, to see how near I could bring this animal, which seemed so little to dread my presence. I stuck my ramrod in the ground and placed my hat upon it, and changed my attitude, and the creature, after one of its swift circles, came up again almost as near. I thought I would still try how much closer I could bring it, and drew myself under cover of a hillock just at the edge of the rock, but more intent upon the antelope, than careful of the nature of my position, I felt the ground give way, and was precipitated from the height.

Chapter Nineteen
Rescued by one both stranger and friend—
buffalo medicine—schemes and omens

How long I remained insensible I could not tell, but on returning to a state of consciousness, I found myself supported on the knee of a man in a hunter's dress, and whose face expressed some anxiety.

"How came you to roll over the rock?" was his first question. "Are you much hurt?" was the second.

I felt stunned, and put my hand to my head.

"Oh, if it is only the head, I'll do the head-work for you, till you get round."

I explained that I had laid myself on a rotten bit of turf, overhanging and undermined, which had given way. The stunning sensation was almost gone, and I was glad to find there was nothing the matter with my limbs, and I raised myself on my elbow to see into whose hands I had fallen.

The noble head which had been bent over me, was of the true type of the inhabitants of the western settlements—finely chiselled features, good eyes, and magnificent hair hanging in chestnut masses on either side, and kept in place by a band of bright brass.

"You belong to the camp whose horses are out beyond," I said.

"I reckon I do, and you?"

"Oh, I have lost my way, out hunting, and took you for Indians, and it was as well to make sure."

"Well, there is another question I have to ask." He fixed his eyes steadily upon mine, "How came you by that tobacco case, which came out of your pocket in your fall?"

I saw he pointed to the token which had been given me by the old farmer, whom I had found in the wood near the Kanzas with his waggon upset, and I told the story.

"I suppose you will not believe but that I want to raise it, or I would tell you that it is intended for me."

"Are you the son of the old farmer?"

"I am so, but you may keep it till you have proof if you like."

It was impossible to doubt that open brow, and that clear look of careless courage, and I gave the tobacco case—not the less welcome to be full.

"Now we will go to camp, and you shall have a salad dressed with bear's oil."

I laughed at the temptation. "I have been on the look-out for that oil, to make one for myself, and I will find you out as soon as I can, but it cannot be today, as I shall miss the other people I have left on the move, so I must be off, and see if my mule is still where I left her." I prepared to turn away.

"Well, lad, if I can ever do you a good turn, for the old man's sake I'll do it. Will you have a mount to get your mule?"

"No, it is hardly worthwhile. Are there any Indians about?"

"No, I believe the Sioux are not out this way yet."

"If you take a ride over to the Platte, we shall be there for a day or two."

"Are there many of you?"

"Oh yes, several more than we want, and there were many more who would have liked to come along, had they found means, but you will hardly believe there was not a running horse to be found in all Jackson County."

I was on my legs, and the last words were said as I was moving away. It was rather my object to avoid any explanations, I already knew that Joe Heald was there, and had nursed a desire to regain my property, and avenge myself on this traitor, and it would be quite as well that he was not aware that I was on his track, I was bounding along toward my mule with these reflections.

After I was mounted, and had got back to the quarter where I had left Black-muzzle, I was first aware of the sun being two hours after noon, and though I had an idea of the direction which should have taken the camp, there might be some several hours of search before I found it, to waste time in looking after my unamiable companion would be useless, as I felt he had long since set out to return. I struck the trail a few miles from where we had started in the morning, and found the camp on the river in a grove of poplars, five or six miles above where the rapids commence.

There were signs of a recent crossing, and I learned afterward that Campbell's camp had here passed to the opposite side. The bison had been driven off by some hunting parties, or had voluntarily deserted the neighborhood, and the river was too deep to ford, and they were in a hurry, there was no dry wood for a raft, and the hunters were ordered out, and it was determined to remain there till they should return with hides for what is called a bull-boat.[i]

The hunters set out, and the camp, eager to get on, lamenting the bad luck of finding such a country deserted, were preparing to pass the weary time that might intervene till their return, when there appeared among the sage bushes of a neighboring butte, what seemed to be three ravens. Either to kill them, or to see upon what they had been feeding, someone or two men darted off, but were not long of returning at a run, elated by having found, instead of three ravens, three bulls recently dead.

No one knew what medicine[ii] Campbell had made, but there were the bulls killed, it was supposed, by lightning—not a hole in their tough hides. Three mules brought them to camp, while the raven and the bald eagle, from unseen distance, were already circling above. It was in this camp, noted for having been the locality of the above event, that I found our people had made their halt, and held high wassail over a kettle of punch, the foundation of which had been in the contents of a small keg of brandy brought up by Bernard.

My thoughts had been occupied by the discovery of the other camp with my stolen property, and I had come to the resolution of seizing again what was my own, and forming plans for the execution of my project.

I know not why, but I had a distrust of some of my companions, and though I could not suspect Jim Macarey or Smith, they were in the habit of blurting out everything, and I feared to entrust them, there was also a lurking wish to do this without aid. I was alone in the world, and had a name to make in this wild country.

I entered the bower, in which, under the boughs of the young willow, a circle sat or reclined, above which hung the misty vapor of tobacco and the fumes of shrub[1].

Jim's eyes sparkled, and Smith said, "Well done, lad, you have not been caught yet, Friday has been run into camp by four Indians, and we are celebrating the event at his Boss's[iii] expense."

"Don't take it amiss," said old Bill, "that we did not wait for you, as they thought it might be too long."

"Better the latter end of a feast," I answered, "than the beginning of a fray."

"Pass the cup," said Reece.

I turned and sat myself down by a rod stuck as a spit in the ground. I had tasted nothing since morning but the tendrils of the vine, and devoured my dinner under a volley of jokes. The Swiss, when he saw that I had finished, made room for me beside him, and I composed a part of that circle whose spirits had far outstripped mine.

I found that it had been a question of going to join the lodges of Diego on

---

1. Shrub: A beverage said to consist of liquor, fruit juice, fruit rind, and sugar.

the other side of the river and that the fumes of the peach had brought forth sundry declarations of love, as well as hatred.

I had joined the drinking party some time, when Smith, who had been out, came back and sat down, it was easy to see, by his manner, that he had something to say, and it was not long before they hushed up to give him a hearing.

"I have seen a herd of buffalo just crossed the river, and the buttes are black with them just out of the wood. It was little more than twilight, and a late run could alone have moved so large a mass after dark."

"There is something astir," said old Bill, with an expression in which some inquietude was evinced.

"Yes," answered Doty, "but it is on the other side—some of the Free Trappers of Fontinelle, but this later running is strange, for I can hear the band grunting from here."

"There has been something beyond the hunting of a small party," added Smith. "Has anyone a mind to go out and kill by moonlight, I see the light on the patch of snow on the mountain, it is clear enough to kill as they run past at the Gulleys, and if the sign be true, they may be the last we shall see till we can get ahead of the other camps, which appear to be all round us. Ned is tired, but you can come, Jim."

"I don't care if I do," said the latter, and shaking the ashes out of his pipe, he got up.

Reece and old Bill both remonstrated, but the others were already girding on their belts, and looking at their priming, and soon were lost in the dusk, as they went to get their horses.

"Now," said Bill, "we may finish the keg, there will be no going over the river tonight, and Rose must go without our company till another time."

"Do you think, then," said Reece, "that it was Diego's people he saw?"

"Yes, sure, and no other, as you will see tomorrow."

I sipped my cup, which was not unwelcome in the high and keen air of night. I looked out, and saw the patch of snow on the northeast side of the butte cut by a dark mass of rock, of which it gave out the profile. The eyes of the old Trapper followed mine.

"Aye," said he, "if you had to make a night march, as I have had to do, that would be a beacon for you, as long as you keep in the line where that rock cuts less than half the snow, you have good ground to the mountain base and clear, if you keep to the right, and see all the snow, you fall into the deep ravines of currant bushes, without a drop of water and double the distance."

Chapter Twenty
A risk decided on, with trepidation—a stealthy approach—conversation overheard—the deed done—flight

It was strange that the old man should have tapped my thoughts, and I took it as an omen that they were to be followed out. I did not think I was much needed to assist in the night's libation, and moved away, without being observed by those I left, Bernard's large eye excepted, which seemed to follow me wherever I went. I took a piece of meat with me behind the saddle, a horn full of powder I had, and balls, a pair of moccasins, and some tobacco.

Mounting my stout Delaware horse[1], I took my way over the butte nearly at right angles with the course of the Platte. On gaining the height, I saw before me plainly my course, and pricked on, that there might be as much of the night for escape as I could spare from the capture, and having no difficulty in seeing my line, I had leisure to consider the danger of the attempt I was about to make. First, there was the general resistance always to be looked for in a night attack, next, the want of knowledge of the country to enable me to make off with my booty, next, the dangerous nature of the enterprise, on account of the desperate character of the men with whom I had to deal, and that though I was only to take what was my own, the manner of taking gave it the character of a theft. If found in the act, I had no chance of quarter but from Brent, and even he did not know that I was the owner of the property I

---

1. Stout Delaware horse: Note that this animal becomes a Shawnee steed a few pages on. This is not quite the error it might seem: The Shawnees and Delawares were neighbors in the East, had been associated since the French and Indian war, and underwent removal to Kansas together from 1832-45. They were frequently trapping companions of the whites during the heyday of the Rocky Mountain fur trade. Stewart's usage may imply a measure of interchangeability of the names at this time.

sought. With any other who might be on the look-out, it must be a mortal strife.

All this came into my mind, but I also reflected, that to go back to civilized life, and fight my way to every day's bread among the common herd, would be worse than a thousand deaths in heated blood. Here I was to be free, and to enjoy a freedom equal to that of the most wealthy, provided I could hold my own, thus far, I had done so, and this night was to show whether I was to peer with the best of the land, or to leave my bones to whiten where I fell.

My short and strange career came presented to my memory in one review —the strange influence of that evil-boding eye, which I had seen twice—the odd coincidence of the Swiss being at my side, and the doubtful feelings he seemed to have for me, sometimes I could feel his eye fixed upon me with a look of almost affection, and a strange shade, as if of pity in it—at others, there was a scowl of hate—then came the memory of him I had so loved, the noble and spiritual Fernwold—also, mixed with all these, came the softer memories of Isabel, and the fiery love I bore her who had so betrayed me, and the disinterested and soothing affection of Miranda.

While I pursued my way, several times I saw the dark band of bison, like the shadow of a cloud, pass over the open slopes, and I heard occasionally the wolf howling on the trail. I kept on my way.

Once, my horse, in crossing the bottom of one of the winter streams, dashed off, terror-stricken by what I supposed must have been the wind of a grisly bear, to satisfy him, I let him run till we cleared the covert a hundred yards. Again, I was almost run over by about fifty bulls, who came over a steep descent upon me all of a sudden, and I escaped being hooked only by a miracle, as I was obliged to go with them down the precipice.

This, for a time, broke the current of my thoughts, but still I found myself making up my recollections—as if in a last account. But I was now nearing the scene of the intended exploit, and it would be necessary to leave my horse, in order that he might not give the alarm.

There being but one ridge to cross, there loomed at some distance a rock, jutting out from the prairie, with some trees, and I bore up toward it. There was grass, and water, and shelter, and having tied my horse to a picket, I crossed over to get a view of the valley in which I expected to find my long lost roan.

I had intended to come upon the camp from the top, and descend the fringe of wood, to conceal my approach, but it was also necessary to examine the ground on the open side, opposite to where I had been in the morning.

There must lie my course, to escape either a close pursuit, or to gain a sufficient start upon a more tardy action. Having tied my steed, I took my way to the right of the ground where I had seen the horses graze in the morning, it was open, but there were occasional hollows with trees, all, however, giving out near a long transverse ridge, from which they sprung, and which, with a deep chasm on the right hand, broke off the smooth featured swells which I had passed from the rugged and precipitate hills and ravines which form the extreme to the northeastern base of the butte.

Thus, I could see that, keeping this marginal ridge, I should have good ground to gain the Platte, or crossing it, I should have to find my way through difficult and dangerous defiles. There was no time to be lost, and I descended to the left of the grassy slope, from which I could see the low dark shadow of the line of trees bordering the curved line of rock, in the center of the band of which was the camp of these lawless men—the spot where I had chosen to set my life against the possession of a horse.

There was not a breath of wind, the night was clear, and the air was cool. I sat myself down to reflect and to observe.

The eye of one who has watched in the night becomes accustomed to the want of light, and the ear grows fastidious when its powers have been some time intently strained, but I could detect no movement and distinguish no sound. The trees of the upper end of the line were about four hundred yards off, it did not require much exertion to get under their shelter, and there I found no obstacle, and proceeded on my course. My reflections on the undertaking had ceased, and I was now solely occupied by the immediate difficulties of access, and the days of fruit-stealing came back to my mind, which had resumed its reckless elasticity, and I had almost broke out into some wild strain, as I blithely strode to regain possession of that animal, with whom I had first made acquaintance with the forest, and who had carried me many a weary league.

There was a well-beaten track in the shade, and many a bison had threaded through these trees the tortuous path, to drink at the occasional pools left by the shrunken stream.

It was now on the verge of midnight—all was still, not a leaf stirred, and a whisper seemed as if it would be heard over the whole plain. I thought I must be now near the camp, by the distance I had already made in the grove, but there were yet no signs, as, with a stealthy pace, I advanced as if each tree might hide an enemy.

As the time approached, I felt less and less the danger I ran, and more than ever, that Arab love for my steed. There must be much more belonging to me there than the one horse, and I resolved to take a second at a venture, in part payment.

Out of the shade I might see some distance, but could perceive nothing, they must be forted within the cover, proceeding, I at last found there was a thicket, and could distinctly hear the snort of a horse, as also the beating of my own heart.

I was not nineteen, and there are few who can say that even when more accustomed to trying moments, and of greater age, they have not felt that palpitation on an occasion of excitement.

Through a gap in the bushes, I could plainly mark the thick logs which blocked up the way wherever there was an open, as I cautiously crept round, the same care had formed a fence till I had got to where the shanteys were stuck up, and by that was the only open way. The logs were all trees felled at three feet from the ground, and not totally severed, with sufficient art to fall in the line, and were beyond my power to move. I retraced my steps, until again the circuit was completed, it was a perfect fence of impenetrable bushes or immovable trunks.

Several times the animals had started as I crept by, but I had seen no guard, they slept, and their shantey was almost a gate, though there was a large branch which helped to fill the space, and make security doubly sure. This I discovered after having crept into the pen. The horses, having become accustomed to me in a certain degree, did not shew much alarm, as I was similarly dressed with those to whom they were accustomed, there was no move from within the shantey. I took out my knife, and cut off the greatest part of the smaller branches of the bough, which served for a door, and threw them back among the horses' feet, and the way was made clear enough to be stepped over —now to find the roan.

I had almost a pang of anguish, he was nowhere to be seen, and before I completed the search, I heard the neighing of a horse without, those in the pen cocked their ears, and I crept under a bush close to the door. A voice from within the further shantey hailed, though not very loud, and was answered by a horseman, whom I could now distinguish coming up at a quiet pace, he dismounted, and looked into the shantey which was closest.

"Ha, I thought you would be all asleep, come give me a hand, I'm right tired, I've been all day in the cut of rocks of the Platte and its creeks, and have had to carry my beaver and traps on foot."

"Well, and I reckon they were worth the toting," said a voice, which I thought I recognized, in a half yawn."

"Whar's the other horse, is he cashed out[2]?"

"Yes, whar you left him, or nearby, I changed his picket twice, and took him out after dark the last time."

They seemed to be busy with the saddle, and taking in several beaver skins. "Any news?"

"Nothing particular, I saw a greenhorn from one of the camps going up to

---

2. Cashed out: Hidden. *Cashed* is Stewart's version of the French verb *cacher,* to hide. Common usage was *cache,* a subterranean pit dug for storage. See a good description of how to make a cache in Warren Angus Ferris, *Life in the Rocky Mountains,* ed. LeRoy R. Hafen, Denver, 1983, pp. 10-11.

rendezvous, he was out after meat, and got scared at the horns, and crawled in to see what we were."

"Yes, and what sort of a greenhorn?"

"Why a likely enough lad."

"I think I have a guess, tall and strong for one so young, light brown hair, dark eyebrows and eyelashes, and eyes the color of a chestnut, no beard, a biggish mouth, and a sort of smile at the corners, and good teeth. Is that like him?"

"The boy himself, did you meet him too?"

"No, but I divined. Just throw in that blanket, I'll take the horse out to the other, he's not far off from where he was this morning."

"Oh! You will see him before you are fifty yards off."

The last comer, who was Heald himself, was leading the horse he rode out on to the prairie, the other, whose voice, for his face, I had not been able to see, was like that of Brent, whom I had seen in the morning, crept again into his place of rest, and I lay dreading some new alarm, or the discovery of the pruning of the branch at the doorway, but determined to see the adventure out, lying with my ear close to the ground, I could hear distinctly any sound, but all was quiet for some time, and at last, I observed one of the mules cock its long ears, and the attention of some of the rest was also excited. I could see nothing, as my bush was thick and close, but presently heard the snort of a horse, and some muttered words, and the pulling down of the barrier close by, accompanied by sundry oaths.

"He shan't get you this night any how, to throw the dust in our eyes," said Heald, as he patted the neck of the roan, whom I recognised, he passed his hand over his legs, gave him a slap as if in security and triumph, and turned back toward the gate, which he carefully closed after him.

I had to lie still for some time, not to think what I was to do, for the thought ever comes close upon the action in emergency, and things looked bad enough for my success, the more so as I had to lose an hour at least of the night, so valuable for escape.

He did not enter the nearest shantey, and I got on my legs immediately, and took down the bar at the entrance, and dragged away the branch, taking the risk of being heard, in the hope that the noise might still be attributed to Heald. I thought my horse knew me, and he rubbed his head against me, and made a sort of sound, as if of friendly recollection for all the feeds of corn, and the drinks of meal and beer which I had given him in the course of our wandering.

Now to choose a companion to change and relieve in the race, and also to make up my account. I found a strong horse, whose sleek appearance shewed that he had not been over worked, and led him to the side of the other, a rope in the mouth of each, then bounding on the back of the roan, on whose speed

I could trust, and leading the other, I gathered the rest toward the open gate, swinging the lasso over my head, my intention was to have gone out first and left the rest to follow, but a mule, after a snort or two, started off through the open, and the die was cast. I rushed the rest on, and urged my own horse into the throng, two-thirds of them, however, were before me pressing out, the alarm might be given any moment. I let my hand fall with a coil of riding cord on the flank of my horse, who bounded to the unusual stroke, and jammed me among the rest, so as to shove one or two on to the shantey, more followed, I heard a shout either of alarm or pain, down went the frail shelter upon its inmates, but I was clear. The animal I led came along willingly, a ball whizzed past my head, then the report, shouts followed, but the greatest part of the band were already out and careering about the prairie, I dashed on, a mule or two followed, but I distanced them, and held on at a killing pace for the height which I had left, and which was my landmark, but I found a sudden declivity, almost a chasm in my way, I could not venture on it in the uncertain light, and wheeled to the left to get round, but the angle was a great loss of space, as the check had been of time, a horse appeared as I got round the end coming up, and a shout, and then another. There were a few bushes at the shallow end, I dashed through them, but my leading rope caught, and I must lose my second horse, I pulled up to extricate him, and now felt that I must change my course, or have a fight—hesitation was certain destruction. I turned back through the bushes under the brow, along which I had just come, it was absolutely running my own heel on a shelf a little lower down, and under the shade I urged my animals on with a shortened rein, and brushed through the cover.

Just after I had turned, I thought I heard a shout, they had gone on, what was I to do? The moon was lowering, and I knew little of my way, but I thought I had turned back short of the little butte, where I had left my Shawnee steed, and I as quickly turned as I had come, and crossing the wake of my pursuers, I saw the rock just ahead. I was not long of getting my other horse and taking my chance, drove him before me right toward the great butte, over ground so dry as to leave no trail, to take my chance of the intricacies of the mountains, as I had failed to get such a start as to ensure safety by the open course.

Away we went, the horses well together, the ridge was broad and open, and if there was a pursuer near, I could not fail to be seen, but I ventured for more than a mile, there was no change in the nature of the ground, but then we came suddenly on a brink, which showed a bushy precipice running across, and cutting off from the mountain that long mound, which extended with slight deviation all the way from the river Platte. The chasm was deep below, and dark from the nature of the dusky shrubs which covered its sides, there neither appeared end or outlet. Faithful to the system I had pursued hitherto, I took the opposite course to that of one flying from the camp, and bore to the left, which was rather in its direction, until I perceived a path worn down the steep side of the valley, evidently made by the herds of bison, of which there were almost abundant signs. I pulled up, and getting a hold of my loose horse, I took my riding cord, and putting it round his neck, attached several loose branches in a bundle to it, driving my other before, let the Shawnee follow, making a trail as if of lodge poles down the precipitous descent to cover the horses' tracks, or altogether deface them. At the bottom, there was a green sward along the bed of the stream, I untied my bundle, and scattered it about behind some rocks, and took my way at a trot up the stream. Half a mile further on, came a spot where there was a dell, on the right hand tolerably open, here I found no trail to disturb me, but I dreaded on that account that there might be no outlet, which was the case, again I had to retrace my way, but with reluctance, searching on each side for some means of escape. The character of the scene had become more rugged, and I looked behind the occasional masses, to see if there was no other way.

My horses were shod, which if it helped me to cross rugged steeps in my course, also obliged me to avoid places where they would leave their mark.

There appeared at last on the mountain side of the ravine, a sort of hollow slope as if occasioned by an avalanche, I took up this, and with some toil—being on one or two occasions obliged to dismount, where the steepness prevented my being able to lead the two horses—I had to pass on one, and follow with the others, suffice it to say, with infinite difficulty, I got to a high pass, where there was a confusion of hollows, green dells, and clumps of pine, and quaking ash, but the moon was gone down behind the over shadowing height above, I felt myself secure from pursuit, but at the same time ignorant of the run of the water, which, if followed, might lead back into the danger I hoped I had for the present escaped.

Chapter Twenty-One
A cautious return—unplanned bear hunting—
a great leap—furious fighting

In a sheltered hollow, then I once more secured my band by hobbling, and having taken off the piece of meat which hung behind the saddle, transferred it to a branch above my head, and gathering my blanket round me, laid myself down. The breeze whispering through the pines above my head, lulled me to sleep, and the sun was two hours high before it was broken. I started up uneasy, expecting the punishment which awaits the sluggard, but found all quiet, the short neigh of the roan, however, showed that they had expected an earlier attention to their wants, and I immediately went off in search of some water.

There were many thickets of dwarf willow in the green dells, which smiled among frowning rocks, in these there must be springs, I thought, and of course there were, having dug out a place by tearing out the watercress and moss which encumbered it, I went back for the thirsty animals, and having led them to it, I thought of myself, and going up to the shelter of the dry ground lit afire, and set half my meat upon a spit, that I might sally forth with something to sustain my strength, the dry branches blazed and crackled without smoke, and the meat was browned, I cut off the outside and eat while a relay of brown was forming. Eating coat after coat, I got nearly to the spit, and had, with the aid of watercress, made such a meal as ought to content the taste as well as the appetite, looking the while for encouragement at the voracious eagerness of the animals among the rough rushes and tender grass.

I now resolved to look over the height above, and try and discover my way, which I wished to be nearly parallel, but converging to that which my companions would follow, if they left their camp that morning.

A short time brought me to one of those naked ridges which the action of the weather has laid bare in all pre-eminent positions, and from thence I could ascertain that there were a great number of valleys running north west, none northeast, which was the course I wished to follow, but as they seemed to extend or become shallow, so they increased their distance from the great butte, I saw that my way would be clear so far, and that there was a continuous ridge parallel, and not very distant from the Platte.

Saddling, I boldly proceeded to descend into the nearest and deepest of those, whose waters, however, if they reached this branch of the Platte, must do so through the Larrame', or if not, must ultimately fall into what is called the south fork. It was a lovely vale, a mixture of verdant slope and rugged descent, the picturesque pine above, sometimes the pendorosa, and at other places, the flexibilis[1], and in the bottom, the maple with its refreshing and tender green shaded the grassy glades. Without being full, the streams were still supplied from the springs, and in many of the higher ranges, large masses of snow were gradually giving way to the summer sun, and yielding to the parched plains below their refreshing tribute, often, however, swallowed up in the thirsty course, before mingling in the broad channel of the Platte. That which I followed sometimes wound about, luxuriating in its bed till an obstruction came, over which it bounded in a cataract, or leaped as from a spout, still, I was faithful to its side.

The big horn occasionally crossed my path, I was encumbered with the care of my newly acquired steed, and saw them too late. My eye was uneasily bent on the skyline, as I expected at least to see the bison of the night before moving over. It was nine o'clock and there was, as far as my glass could range, no appearance of stir, and I again moved on, as the stream approached the first table land, where it was to leave the character of a mountain rapid, and adding itself to others, lose its integrity, and shape its devious and shifting course to a destination which no map had at that time traced, it had to rush brawling over and between lofty ledges and towering crags, and I had to search for the well-trodden access of the herd, which pays its passing visits to the mountain above. These paths, I had learned, were always to be visited, to see what sign might be on them, even should there be other means of following your course, here there was none, so I drove my horses before me down the winding way. On one spot, I thought I could perceive among the hoof marks the print of some large foot, and regretted not having myself gone first, however, somewhere it might be more distinct, and I kept my eye on the ground to watch, but there was nothing more, and we got to the bottom.

The fork, formed of two or three branches, of which that on which I had come down appeared the chief, was met by others from an opposite range,

---

1. Flexibilis: The limber pine, which grows in the Rockies from Canada to northern New Mexico.

they united in a wide basin, which seemed, however, more like a vast shelf between the mountain I had left, and the chain which ran north from it, apparently bordering on the Platte. They were willow fringed till they united, and then they ran under the shade of a grove of the small-leafed maple, and tufts of plum and cherry bushes, to this grove led the trail I had followed down the steep, but the horses had here disdained to follow it, and galloped on, stopping to browze till I came up, riding along after them, with my eyes cast down, to look for what might be seen on the track.

I came once more upon that footprint, partially only left on the light dust of the path, a few paces further I found it again a complete impression, my heart told me, before I could modulate my thought, it was a bear. I dismounted and examined, it did not appear to be older than the night before, but its size was what filled me with wonder, it seemed about two feet long, and occupied the whole breadth of the narrow track. I turned back my horses to the foot of the rocks, I was mounted on one I did not know, but felt sure he was a good one, from the springs he made when I had to turn the rest, all I cared about was to get a chance at this monster, the horses might be lost if he charged and scared them, I might be discovered in the skurry from the distant heights, but I felt that this time this object of my thirst should not escape without a chance of my tackling. The wind was ahead, and I kept under the lea of the thicket, that my horse might give me warning as I edged along with my left to the covert, the pistols under the fold of the blanket which covered the holsters were ready, and the rifle cover was tucked under the surcingle, the end of the long lasso, the coil of which was gathered under it, was made fast to my belt, in case of a fall that I might recover my horse. All this preparation was made mechanically, like the silent arrangements of the cavalry soldier before a charge.

There was no shelter near, but on the mountain behind, and I felt secure, the grove before me held the monster I had tracked, passing slowly along the front, and watching the ears of my horse, I looked intently for some sign, there was nothing but an occasional neigh of impatience by which the animals so accustomed to go in bands, or if away from camp seldom alone, are in the habit of expressing their anxiety at a separation.

I had gone along two-thirds of the side next me, and had to return to look at the portion I had at first left unexamined, when I had turned to the right, not having exactly marked the spot, I was looking on the ground for the trail, when my horse wheeled round with a snort, which very nearly unseated me. I had been almost close to the bushes, my back was now turned, and it was all I could do to govern my panic-struck steed, who plunged and bounded as if to get rid of his rider, and put the broad plains between him and the danger he had just perceived. When I got him so far mastered as to be able to turn, I heard the crash of the bushes, and the huge monster rushed out, his ears back, and his great stride appearing to come right upon me.

There was no horse to face this charge, unlike the king of beasts, who terrifies by his gaze, assumes imposing attitudes, and lashes his side with his tail when open to view, or who takes a stealthy bound on the unwary, and is ashamed if he fail, this monster of the west at times rushes fairly out upon his foe, and dares him to combat on the plain. Confiding in strength and speed, we had taken fairly to our heels, my frightened horse bounding under me with the desperation of real fear, with a strong effort, I bore him away to the left off from the mountain, which gave me a fair field and a smooth course, though at my horse's tail, I had but seen my enemy for a moment as he rushed out of the bushes, and now I was tempted to look back, to see if I could have room by a double to bring him to such a bearing as to be able to fire, but all I could perceive was his open mouth, and that too close for anything but a straight course and the greater speed. I closed my legs, the horse was at his best, I shook my rifle useless over my head, as if it had been a twig in my rage, my horse had been accustomed to all that, the spur brought the blood, but still I could find no answer, I tried the whip, a single length would clear me, but the handle broke, the ferocious pursuer was dead behind, and my rifle useless in my hand. I flashed across my thoughts, that a pistol might have some effect, should I slue myself sufficiently round to take an aim, and I took my rifle in the crutch of my arm, and bent forward to get at the holster, when I saw gaping before me one of those deep chasms with perpendicular sides, which are so often to be found in that country, it was a frightful looking leap, but it appeared the only chance to throw off the monster, whose stride seemed to gain instead of lose, my horse was at his best, I had the splinter of my whip handle, and I dashed it at his shoulder as if I wished to transfix it, expecting to roll into the yawning fissure. There could be no gathering for a leap, it must come in the stroke of the gallop, or there would be no footing for the stride, all this came rushing through my brain, and my eyes strained over the opposite bank. I even sat loose in my saddle, that I might be thrown clear forward, the strangest part of my sensations was, that there had been no leap and no variation in the straining speed.

I was over, and my enemy was thrown out for the moment, I was now five or six horse lengths ahead, and could see the monster scrambling out somewhat to the right of where I had leaped, it was not so difficult now to moderate my horse's pace, and pistol in hand, I rather verged toward than avoided him. It was now that I could observe the vast size of the animal, and his extraordinary stride, the tongue out and the distended jaws, the hair on end all along the back, he appeared as high as an ordinary horse. Fearful of not getting so good a chance again, and fixing my eye steady on the spot, but without looking at the pistol, I fired, he was struck I knew, by the roar of rage, and stopping to tear at the top of the shoulder indicated where. While I put up my pistol he again charged, and the chase was again converted into a flight.

I soon discovered that my horse had recovered from his first panic, and kept his own with less strain, but a false step, and we were at the mercy of an animal, whose rage was chafed by pain, and probably stimulated by hunger, however slight the wound, like the few extra pounds which equalize the speed of races, the hurt seemed to tell, and I could circle round to cut him off from the mountain. I leaned heavy to the right, and urged my horse to his best, there seemed to be a difficult ravine in my way with indented sides, which I dare not attempt to cross, but I made toward it sufficiently far ahead, to have time turn and offer fight behind a point where it jutted out, and round which my pursuer had to pass.

I had now my rifle in my hand, and gathered myself for a shot, but my horse was unsteady, and I attempted to take a sight along the barrel, I fired and missed, my horse turned, and the whole works[i] vanished from the plains, and plunged down a precipice of thorn and willow. A thick bush, I suppose, separated us in the rush, and the side of it I took was easier, for I got down with a good luck I had never expected, but the precipice over which the bear had fallen, had an easy slope on the opposite bank. When I reached the bottom, a perpendicular cliff faced me, however, I turned down the stream at the best pace the thicket would permit, till I found a way out.

My adversary seemed to have abated in his eagerness, I found him going toward the butte with a slow avering gait, looking occasionally round.

"Ha! Nicholas," I shouted, the cry of the Canadian hunter when he tackles this terror of the wilds, and the brute stopped, and getting up on his hind legs, looked round, my head was only visible as I was emerging from a straggling cover. All animals have a dread of a concealed foe, or one but partially visible, and this was exemplified by his immediate flight.

It was now I had to call upon my steed for a rush, the distance was not above three-quarters of a mile to the rocks, and then my chance of victory was gone, the willing animal seemed to second my desire. I kept on shouting, and the bear turning partially round at the sound, I was nearing fast, and before five hundred yards was getting up within reach, I had, however, but one pistol loaded, and it must be a center shot to finish such a beast. The struggle was again animating, there was little doubt of being able to cut off the retreat to the rugged heights before me, but how to run in so close as to make sure, or how to stop him in an open plain?

We were, however, dashing on, and I could mark signs of fatigue as I got closer, heedless of the danger of the act, I was plunging right upon his quarter, when the quickness with which he turned upon me almost brought us in contact, but as I shot ahead, I was between the grisly monster and his goal. He again gave up the attack and fled, he had turned to the right, and he was on my right hand and slightly ahead, now he must get off or never, I slackened pace to drop right behind with the intention of knocking him over in his tracks, but again he swerved, he had become terrible in his menaces, mouth open, and glaring eyes, but the pace was slackened, though I had done nothing yet to impede his retreat, it was evident we were to have a struggle for the last coup.

Emboldened by former impunity, again I made a charge just as the bear was turning to the left to cross my way, the horse made a dash away, but the bear had the initiative, and was upon us before there was time either to halt or turn out of his way, the horse was struck down by a blow on his haunch, and I fell forward on the opposite side, but I had delivered my last shot in the fall, and it had struck, and happily diverted his attention as I got on my feet to run, but I was not thus to escape, the monster was upon me in a bound, and I felt that my last chance was gone, when he again faltered, and I bounded off for my life, he followed, but took rather the direction of the nearest rocks and cover than my track, and I looked round, reprieved from death, seeing him edging off with an arrow in his side, but my feelings of thankfulness for not having been cut off in my career almost on the threshold of life, and enamoured as I felt of its wild liberty in such field for animal joys, soon gave way to surprise.

Chapter Twenty-Two
A saviour—the final confrontation—an idyllic camp—with Sancho—farewell

An Indian dismounted, was at the side of my wounded horse, who had risen and stood trembling with pain and fear, while a black compact animal, strong enough to be a packhorse, long and low, stood saddled close at hand. The Indian had laid down his rifle, it was my friend of the Platte from Diego's camp, he had again come silently upon me, and this time had probably saved my life.

I hastened back, but the few paces I had to make, enabled me to assume that composure, which the quiet attitude of my red friend reminded me of.

"I fear he is gone," I said, pointing to the direction in which the bear had disappeared.

"He can't go far," said the youth, with a smile.

"Oh, he is not much hurt by the balls, and that arrow does not look quite in the life."

"An arrow works silently its way while he moves, and we shall find him dead by the edge of the trees, but how came you up here, and whose horses are those beyond?"

This was but a natural question in these parts, I told him frankly, I know not why I was drawn into this confidence, but I told him all, he stood listening to me with that strange half-smile, which was habitual to him, and with his eyes cast down. In return, I thought I had a right to know something of him, and I told him I heard of the beauty of his camp, and the rage she made among the men.

"But I suppose you must have improved your own chances," I added. "And I dare say have already secured the prize?"

"You know the habits of my country"—for I hold myself to belong to my mother's land—"we do not make love the whole business of our lives, and the winning of a squaw is hardly a pursuit to occupy a young brave."

"But Diego will hardly give his daughter to anyone here, they say he has untold gold in the banks of Cadiz and Mexico."

"That might make it worthwhile, but would you help me, could I try to carry her off."

This was said with a peculiar and anxious expression, and though that dark eye a little faltered, as it was raised with all its dark fire for a moment, and fixed itself upon mine. There was a strange attraction in that wild being.

"If I believed she was willing, I would do that for you," I said, hesitatingly.

I knew not why I felt pained at the thought of his having any love for Rose, but he did not seem hurt at my answer.

"Shall we have to leave your horse," he asked.

"I think he can follow, but he can remain quiet till we look for his friend, who may as well furnish some grease for the wound."

I had reloaded all my arms, stuck my pistols in my belt, and we set out on the trail, he mounted, and I on foot. There were some drops of blood, but even on the dry grass, the vast spread of that foot was not to be mistaken, and it was not long before we got to where we had lost sight of the wounded animal, and here of course our search was more minute, and upon myself lay the chief charge, as I could dive under branches, which impeded the passage of a horse.

My companion feeling that he had more experience than myself, though not greater age, showed some anxiety that I should not run into the jaws of the wounded beast, as I confess the weakness to have almost had the desire to do.

"Drop the rifle," he said at last, in a humid tone, "and take your pistols, he is just before you."

I had just the time to obey, the branches were low and thick, I heard the dead twigs crash, and the brute was upon me. I must powder burn him, or be devoured, there was no time to hesitate, I did not trust to my eyes in the thicket, but held out the pistol till I should find something come against me, and there was barely time for the short passage of the thought to the deed, the twigs and leaves gave way, and the monstrous head was in contact with my muzzle as I pulled the trigger. I felt no further advance, but the bushes cracked, and I saw the huge carcass in the agony of death. I had fired into his mouth, and he had no power to raise that roar of agony, which I have heard has such an effect as to make good marksmen miss the animal, even when incapable to do further harm.[i]

"We may take some fat for your horse, and you should take the feet, as the claws are as long as your finger," said my companion, as we stood over the great beast extended under the green shade, and still by a convulsive jerk of the muscles, showing how recently they had been in possession of their living power.

"The skin is not good at present, and besides, it would weigh down a horse, he is more than three of my strides long."

In fact, he was more than four, for my new friend I thought, perhaps to compliment me on the size of the mighty prize, made what appeared to me, steps which were scarcely to be dignified by the name of strides.

"We have no need to loiter, bring along what you have got, and let us be gone."

I gave him up the paws and the fat, and he left me to follow, my horse limped toward where his comrades had been left, and my Indian friend went to bring him on, while I took the shorter way by the base of the rocks, where they were cut by the level of the prairie.

Making up some grease mixed with powder, I applied it to the wound of the poor horse, to supple it and keep off the flies, having transferred my saddle to the Shawnee steed, I led the roan, so that the other should have the additional stimulation of company to bring him on, as well as the dread of being left to the mercies of the tribe from which he had already suffered.

"We will keep behind the ridge, I know all the camping places, and we can see what is doing on the river toward evening, when there will be smoke, but I do not think you will care to go right down among them, I know Heald, and you may be sure if you give him a chance, he will revenge himself for the affront you have put upon him, and you will have no fair play, so wait till we see where your own people are, we are out of the way of all war parties till well up on Sweetwater, and there are four long days to that."

The way we took was difficult, as we had to cross a succession of ridges hanging to the west, we saw several elk, and the herds of bison began to come over from the river. Later in the afternoon, I got a good cow by waiting at a crossing, and had again to admire the dexterity of my companion, and his beautiful hands and arms.

With lots of yellow fat to comfort us, and the promise of a choice spot, and secure to camp at, we wended on our joyful way, my comrade telling me of mountain adventures, and sometimes of his young remembrances in Mexico, its fandangos, and dark-eyed daughters, occasionally a Spanish ballad came in when conversation failed. There was something inexpressibly charming in that sweet young voice, in one already so brave and active, as he ambled, caroling on before, throwing back his stealthy looks to see, as he said, if his camp was following in his wake.

There were beaver signs floating on the waters we passed, and every covert held some black-tailed deer or elk, or showed signs of animal life in all their sequestered wildnesses.

There might have been two hours of sun remaining when we pulled up in a deep basin with a waterfall at the top, and a pass-through which the stream must originally have burst, we came up this pass belly deep in water, high rocks rose all round, and in this flat was a grove of maple, a spot more charming could not have been selected.

The fire burnt clear, and the stream run by in its rocky bed, sparkling and pure, retaining still the cold of the snows from which it came. I cannot tell how that evening passed, or how the next, all I can tell is, that I never tired, and that no period of my varied life calls up the memory of such perfect joy. There was one thing remarkable in my new friend, and that was the suddenness with which he would break off our gambols without any apparent cause, on one occasion, I had caught him in my arms, and rolled down a bank with him to the edge of a pool of water, it was at the noon halt, he contrived to stop, notwithstanding my efforts, just as I hoped to have soused him. I could not understand his dread of wetting his clothes, I knew he must have been an excellent swimmer, from his having crossed the river, and I said our clothes would have easily dried in half an hour in the sun, while we might run about in the heat without them, but he took a decorous air, and I perceived these little familiarities, if carried beyond a certain point, brought a shade upon his brow, and I had to sing him into good humor again, he was completely spoiled, and to win that smile which came so stealthily from the dark eye, flashing below the long lashes, I would have joyfully perilled my life.

"But will you never tell me your name," I said one evening, after he had come back from a temporary absence, during which I had in vain searched for him. "I could not call you had there been anything amiss, and besides, it is so stupid not to have a name."

"I never tell my name, but you may give me one, and I will answer to it as faithfully as a dog, will that please you?" he said, as he run his fingers through my entangled locks, and looked down on my face, which lay in his lap. "Call me Sancho, that's not long, and I am your squire."

The herds of bison still poured over the ridges to the right, and there was want neither of food nor water. The country became more rugged, and the chain of heights turned to the left, and we had to cross them, and approach the trail which would quit the Platte at the red buttes.

We had made but short marches, on account of my wounded horse, whose lacerated sore had got a coat of dirt forming a protecting scale over it, and had every appearance of healing, and things went on happily with us, I never dreamed of my own prospects. I was learning fast to shoot correctly with an arrow, and was also lapidary enough to chip off thin slices from the agate and the flint, and dress them into heads to tie on to its shaft, and upon which to trace the usual grooves[ii], the bow was more a matter of difficulty, the best are made of elk horn, and backed by successive coats of sinew, such was that of Sancho, short but strong. There was no time nor means to make this, but I got the loan of that of my companion, though he would not allow me to use his good arrows for practice. It was the fourth day we had been together, when we got abreast of the red buttes[1], and Sancho here told me that he must go in search of his camp, and bring the news. I was thunderstruck at the idea of our separation, we went on so well together and that little reserve of his left always something to be desired, and some further intimacy to be longed for, I knew not very well what, but there was an enchantment over me, one of those mysterious sympathies of romantic affection, as well as the most rational and practical intercourse.

It was early morning, and the horses were not yet brought in, the toilet of each had been made at a separate pool in the stream by which we had slept.

"We are not far from where our way should lie across the Platte," said Sancho, "to take up by the Sweetwater, and as you have seen, on crossing the heights for the last two days, the Mountains of the Winds before you, and as to get to rendezvous you must pass round by their base to the left, you will know by the trails what to avoid, though I expect the camp you should shun is on before."

This long speech was made as if to fill up the time, as my astonishment left me at a loss what to say.

"And are we to separate, without knowing when again we are to meet?"

"How can we tell if we shall ever meet, should you go again horse stealing?"

"Well, but if I should be sage and prudent?"

"We will meet at Rock Independence, tomorrow at noon. But you must not follow the trail till you get over the height beyond the buttes—the direction of the tracks will show you where it lies—and you must keep away to the right by a coal-tar spring[2] and a clump of wood, where is a bear's den which perhaps has no owner, there you may noon, you cannot miss it, it lies fair on the face of a slope of many leagues square, and is seen from the first after getting out of the river bank. The camp trail will be up a hollow to the left, you, keeping round as I told you, will come in about two hours before noon to the clump, there you stop till you see all is clear, and you may then move on toward the

---

1. Red buttes: Located on the North Fork of the Platte in present Natrona County, Wyoming. Warren Ferris called the feature the Red Hills, noting *two high cherry-red points of rock, separated by the river, which turns away to the southward* (Ferris, *Life in the Rocky Mountains*, p. 109). See Frémont's map of 1845 in Jackson and Spence, *Frémont*.

2. Coal-tar spring: Located on the south fork of Popo Agie, between present Riverton and Lander, Wyoming. It appears on Frémont's map of Oregon and Upper California (1848). This spring, according to Washington Irving, was highly regarded by mountain men *as an ointment for the galled backs of their horses and as a balsam for their own pains and aches* (Irving, *Bonneville*, pp. 172-73). When Osborne Russell visited the spring in 1837, he and his comrades set fire to the oil that had collected on the surface, producing *a dense column of thick black smoke* (Osborne Russell, *Journal of a Trapper*, Portland, 1955, pp. 57-58).

trail, which you will find by a small mass of cover toward the setting sun. Next day, you take right up toward the snowy mountains, and you will find a small stream in the sage, which you will follow straight down, you will know it by shoals of little fish the length of your finger, its course will be cut by another right across, you hold on—in the same line with the first—there is no more water-mark, but salt, until you have passed a solitary rock rising out of the prairie on your left, then, on toward the mountains, leaving all the pieces of water—which are brackish—on your right, until you come upon the Sweet Water, which will be on your left, and cuts the base of the rock Independence, which will be on the right, it is a good step. Look well round the face of the rock next the river and you will see a twig stuck in the ground, bent toward the mountain if I am gone on, if not, bent in the direction where I may be, and you must search the passes for further knowledge, but if you find no sign, do not go straight on, but look out someplace to hide for a day, and watch the trail from the heights, for it follows the course of the river for three days."

"I think so much geography never was crammed together in one speech, and clear, too, as the air at noon, though it gives you a cloudy brow. Now, give me Godspeed. You see three ravens going over the Platte—they are on our left—the omen is good, so let us mount and away."

I had discovered that my more reserved companion had a certain contempt for my little ebullitions of feeling which I was learning to repress, and I said no more.

The horses' heads were put to the hills, and we silently wended our way to the pass. The rocks of red sandstone, sprinkled with dwarf cedar were on our immediate left, the Platte, with its poplar groves and islands, stretched away to the right, and before us the broken country covered with sage.

There were two gulleys branching from the pass, I took that to the right, and Sancho, who had silently pointed it out as my course, took the other, winding round sharp to the left.

"Don't get rubbed out," he said, as he waved his hand, and rushed down the steep.

Chapter Twenty-Three
Wolves stalk—salvation by death—
Independence Rock and the Devil's Gate

I was then left to guide myself and my horses, and make the point as best I could, where I was again to meet my Red friend, with whom I formed mighty plans in these regions to pass my sylvan days.

It is useless to describe the change, geologically speaking, which here takes place in the country, and the curious intrusion of that solitary Red-butte, which had been the scene of adventurous hidings and hair-breadth escapes.

The Platte I got over half swimming and half fording. I looked for no trail, and almost sought adventure, so depressed was I by the separation, but I felt to a certain degree also the desire to get to that rock of Independence, where I might again meet my companion and form some project for the time to come.

I had learned that arms, ammunition and horses were the riches of the land, and I looked with some complacency upon my roan and the stout steed, who I thought limped already less, and if that was a criterion of coming cure, had not lost his appetite. We journeyed on.

I had formed some idea of the road, and had seen the clump at which I was to noon, and to which I was to make a circuitous route. Nothing living was to be seen but some bulls, to represent their race and mark out the region as their domain. The argali was in his fastness in the butte, the antelope scoured through the tracks in the sage, and there was an eagle circling above, but all unroused, and following their wonted way.

I had got some little distance from the river, when I observed several wolves, who seemed to eye with some covetousness my wounded horse. I hardly heeded them at first, but after a time it appeared as if they increased in numbers, until they became like a pack of hounds, keeping about sixty yards behind, and getting fresh recruits as they came along. I led the roan, and the other seemed to feel that he was the object of attraction, and limped up close to his companions. It was his uneasiness which first drew my serious attention to the pursuit. I had read of attacks on villages by these beasts, and of the eating up of travelers on the roads in the south of France, and in Russia, and began to fear that the gallant beast who had borne me so well in my attack upon the bear, must, however unwillingly, be made a sacrifice of to save the rest. I knew a shot, or ten shots, would be useless, but I felt that I could not abandon the poor animal, who almost looked for protection from me, without doing my best to save him.

Happily, the sage was in some places pretty thick, and there the pack trailed, and while the horses ran on before—for I had loosened the roan—I lingered, to check as much as possible the head of the advancing column, and at the same time kept up a tolerably sharp trot.

A buffalo track, somewhat in the direction I wished to hold, led us on, and while it lasted I had less trouble, but after having rounded a little butte, it gave out, and I had to herd the horses, and bring them back to the course, from which they were continually diverging.

Things were becoming serious, and the leading wolves were not thirty paces behind, and in a charge, I did not feel secure that they would all confine themselves to the wounded of the party, and that I should not, as being on the slowest animal of the lot, become an object of pursuit in the second degree. However, I must say my feeling of horror at being within reach of the wounded horse and hearing his cries, was the predominant one, and I waved my lasso and urged him on before, at the same time shouting to encourage his speed. For the moment this new sound, so strange to these wild wastes, checked our pursuers, but they came on again, as if ashamed of having given way to the voice of man.

The moment was almost come to urge my horse and follow the roan in a sauve qui peut—it had become almost a scurry, but as the pace increased, I felt the distance was never lessened, then came a gulley, down which the loose horses rushed, and as the side was steep, the voracious pack was obliged again to lessen their front to get across at a path, but it was only a moment's reprieve.

It was now requisite to take my line and ride for it, the ground was broken by occasional grips, and was loose and soft, and in so far unfavorable to the heavier animals. We were at three parts speed, the poor invalid went gallantly, but the pain it gave him was evident, and he began to shew by perspiration the dread of his coming fate.

I had never taken my eyes off the immediate spot we occupied, the wolves and the horses, but now, seeing the hour was come, with that sense of the last pang in danger, which those who have seen it near must have experience, I gazed up to the heavens, and then around, as if in search of some unknown aid in extremest need, or eternal adieu—there was nothing, and without further look where pity would be of no avail, I dashed my heels against my horse's flanks to take an independent line, and run for my life.

I saw with what an easy swinging pace my favorite roan cleared the rough surface while I was straining to save myself—of what use to own him now, with his gallant stride, the turn I took to separate from the victim I had destined to this sad sacrifice had also given some advantage to our pursuers, and I could see the red and hanging jaws gathering upon us, but again came a hollow, broader than the rest, and down it came half-a-dozen bulls, who had caught our wind before seeing us, they were almost in a course to cross our path had they continued, but swerved on our descending the bank, the opposite side was steep, and checked their pace, and I was upon them before they were half up. A shot through the lungs, and one of them faltered, spurting blood from his nose, my pistol broke the leg of the last as he crowned the height. I rushed after him, and he turned to fight, the first I found stopped, and staggering in his death throe, and as I left the latter between me and the herd, they were upon him before his attention had been turned to the new assailants—the warm blood had taken them off and saved us.

It is impossible to describe the process of thought from which I acted, it passed so suddenly. We were in safety, my horses and I, a moment before apparently doomed, for I felt that I could not long have held my own over such a course. Happily, I had kept on in the direction in which I wished to go, and when at a sufficient distance, stopped on a height to reload and breathe, keeping a watch upon the feast below.

There, over the sage, I could see the clustering pack, occasionally a fight and a howl, but all intensely occupied. I was still in view.

The loading completed, I again shaped my course toward the lone tuft where I was to noon. There was a spring which occasioned this oasis, and round the thicket the influence of its moisture gave a certain margin of grass, the interior was void—and there was a den, amid a mass of branches. I usually carried a piece of cold meat for noon, and here, from the openness of the spot, I was glad not to have forgotten the precaution.

There was nothing astir within sight, and I was content to suck my paws and doze, like the absent master of this country, till evening, when I was to get as far as the covert of willows, at no great distance on the regular trail.

All camps of any size, whose journeys are not divided so as to noon, must halt here for the night, as there is no place besides in the neighborhood where there is a sufficient supply of pasture and fuel, so that I found plenty of signs, and the grass scanty. But there was a certain snugness in the shelter of these bushes, I could see nothing else of the kind, though I had looked from the height which commands the onward route, and I resolved to be content.

The lame horse seemed to have forgotten his narrow escape. I took the roan in my hand, and sat among the sage looking out, and when the night fell we all gathered into a little glade more out of the way, and defended on three sides by the spongy swamp which surrounded the springs. I laid down ready for repose—cares I had none. Let the night bring its dangers, it brought also its deep sleep. As I laid down I said, "He is to meet me at noon." As I awoke and recovered recollection, this was my uppermost thought.

The great prairie cock[1] was on my path, the first I had seen, with its ruff round the neck and its long tail, but he hardly tempted me. The fishy stream, I know not why, a mere rivulet, and when dammed up only a wet ditch, should be the only one among these mountains which I saw or heard of so filled with fish, though of so small a size. I remarked it more to confirm me in my route, than as an angler or naturalist.

The isolated rock I found rising out of the plain, and passed the wide wastes of salt[2], a soda admirable for punch or lemonade, as I have since learned, they were on my right, and I bore toward certain broken and bushy hills, which I supposed must bound the Sweet Water on the opposite side.

I could perceive the recent track of a bear, there were antelopes skimming about, and there was the ibis. I did not stay to examine the distant landscape, whether the dark shadows on its green were herds of bison, the great mountains, with their snow, were before me, and the rock of Independence[3] must lie in my path. I still pressed on.

There is something strange in this rock—there is one spring in a hollow of its side, there are two or three dwarf gooseberry bushes grow out of its fissures, and except these, no drop of water and no kind of vegetation. It is like the shell of a tortoise in shape, of red granite, and at one point comes down and dips its bare side in the river. It had its name from the celebration of American Independence held at its base by General Ashley, on a fourth of July, and on its face were written then the names of the famous hunters of the

---

1. Great prairie cock: One of several species of Western grouse.
2. Wastes of salt: Stewart may be referring to the vicinity of Poison Spider Creek, west of present Casper, Wyoming. See Morgan, *The Overland Diary of James Avery Pritchard,* p. 89, note 42.
3. Rock of Independence: A famous landmark of the Oregon Trail on the Sweetwater River, Independence Rock is in present Natrona County, Wyoming. Frémont described it as *an isolated granite rock, about six hundred and fifty yards long, and forty in height...Everywhere within six or eight feet of the ground, where the surface is sufficiently smooth, and in some places sixty or eighty feet above, the rock is inscribed with the names of travelers. Many a name famous in the history of this country, and some well known to science, are to be found mixed among those of the traders and the travelers for pleasure and curiosity, and of missionaries among the savages* (entry of August 1,1843, in Jackson and Spence, *Frémont,* I: 245). Dale Morgan writes: *It seems certain that Independence Rock was so named after William L. Sublette's mountain-bound party of fur traders celebrated the Fourth of July there, the year could only have been 1829* (Morgan, *The Overland Diary of James Avery Pritchard,* note 43). Matt Field, *Prairie and Mountain Sketches,* p. 174, offers an account of the same hidden spring.

day, and others who had since wished to leave this record of their passing by, where the weather has defaced the characters of the first invasion, succeeding cyphers and stranger names have, I believe, taken their place, and the slow teamster, who urged his oxen with the goad, has left a record as lasting as he who scoured the plains with his lance in the dust of the bison.

There could be no doubt as to the spot—but there was no Indian. I rushed up the bare rock—it was useless, there could be no one, as all is level around. I strained my eye on the opposite side, where the trail seemed to lead. I pored over the dry sand for footmarks, and gazed upon the heights for signals, while my horses ate on the well-cropped sward which carpets the level space, out of which rises the clean rock. All this I have remembered since, though unaware I had noted them.

There was no sign—I had but to follow on, the trail was plain, and the landmark of the mountains left no difficulty in the course.

The Porte d'Enfer[4], as the French trappers have called it, is in sight, where the Sweet Water has broken through the granite chain, as if between two walls, in a narrow space, once occupied by a vertical stratum of black band about ten yards broad, similar to those which at various distances, from less than a quarter to half a mile apart, seem to strap down the half-risen rocks to the mother earth.

To avoid this gate, which unlike that of Milton, no one has even entered, the road lies over a hollow in the chain, a little to the left, it is, except where the rock is laid bare, a sandy hollow, worn by the hoofs of the thousand herds of bison which pass by, and also by those who would wend their way from the Debatable Lands of the Shoshonies, the Sioux, and the Crows, toward the head waters of the Colorado and the more southern sources of the Columbia. On either side this pass gnarled trunks of the red cedar start out of the fissures of the rock, throwing out their fantastic limbs, or display their scathed and antler-like branches, where the granite has not afforded them a further sustenance on which to preserve life. Detached masses from the heights on either side have fallen halfway down, hanging over the path. It is a spot where an ambush could be concealed to stop an army, and already, against the brute creation, this strategy of war had been tried, for the skulls of the bison lie thick around, as if it had been more than once a scene of slaughter. Small heaps of stones have also been raised, as if in record, and obliterated marks—once Indian hieroglyphics—faintly show that deeds had been done and chronicled in that wild and lonely pass.

---

4. Porte d'Enfer: Devil's Gate, a narrow passage in the Sweetwater River near Independence Rock. See Dale Morgan's comment on the naming of Devil's Gate in Morgan and Harris, eds., *The Rocky Mountain Journals of William Marshall Anderson*, p. 182.

Chapter Twenty-Four
A stranger—sooth-saying—a cavern—
autobiography & philosophy

I was about halfway down, the horses sinking fetlock deep in the loose sand, when my attention was attracted by a figure, rolled up in a blue blanket, laid at the foot of a huge mass of granite, apparently asleep. There was a rifle leaning against a branch of the tree which shaded him, a short bow was in his hand and hanging over his shoulder on the ground was a well filled carquois, his arm was across his face, so as to conceal his countenance.

The wounded horse, who at the moment headed the cavalcade, stopped and snorted, and I pulled up with a hand on the cover of the rifle, and an inquiet glance at the surrounding scene, which might hold many who did not sleep. It was, however, not a red man who thus lay watching in my way, for it soon appeared that sleep had been but feigned, as after a moment's survey, shaded by his sleeve, he quietly removed his arm, and calmly continued his gaze, though the first impulse led me to look round to see if I was beset, the strange appearance of the individual before me concentrated my thoughts and attention, the scrutiny of the one partook in no degree of the inquiring nature of the other, the stranger appeared to be easily satisfied with his investigation, and did not seem to be surprised at or to shun the intensity of mine, but when he saw a certain degree of embarrassment, which I could not help evincing, and not before, he raised himself up into a sitting posture, and by a motion of his hand made a sign that I should come and occupy a place beside him.

The only precaution I took in obeying this invitation was to slip off my rifle cover as I jumped down on the right side of my horse, which was then between me and him, but I felt almost ashamed of my caution when I observed the quiet smile with which he put away his bow, and again pointed to a place beside him.

He appeared to be a man of more than forty, but there was no white in his long dark hair, which was the only part of his person upon which any care was manifested, it was evenly divided from the forehead to the crown, and was glossy and clean, slightly waving as it reached his shoulders, and confined round the temples by a flattened band of brass, as I might suppose, but which from its color might have been gold, upon which some strange devices were engraved on the front where it was broadest, his forehead was high and full, and his eye piercing and deep set under the prominent brow, the nose was thick and Grecian, the lips habitually much compressed, the lower jaw large and square, with a projecting chin, of his form, as he sat, I could only judge as possessing a certain squareness and strength in the shoulders, and of his limbs, as not remarkable for great development of muscle, but well formed. The usual leather shirt and leggings—which appeared as his blanket fell off in the change of posture—were sufficiently dirty to show a season's wear, as was also the small leather tobacco sac, from which he was now filling a short truncheon-like pipe with a grotesque red stone bowl, with the fumigating weed, mixed with the dried leaves of the dwarf arbutus[1]. As my companion had not spoken, and seemed to be deeply interested in carefully performing his task, I took out my box and struck a light, which came in the moment it was required, and he was for a few seconds absorbed in the mystic right of the country. The pipe, when fairly lit, he handed to me, and I went through the ceremony of inhaling several times before I returned it to the owner, a few minutes, and this ephemeral joy was at an end.

"We will go down to the river, now your horses hardly care to stay longer in the pass," said my new companion.

"I was looking for someone whom I expected here," said I. "Have you met a camp, or seen any fresh sign?"

"There are several trails not old, and some I should deem of this morning, gone up the river bank."

We had not far to go, and turning round to the right, under one of the great towers which flank the portal, where the river, dammed back by the blocks which form the threshold beyond, stagnant and Lethe-like, between its smooth and verdant banks, mirrors the beetling cliffs which frown above. The horses ran eagerly on to this grassy mead, and we again sat ourselves down under the influence of the scene.

---

1. Dwarf arbutus: A small evergreen shrub of western North America bearing white or pink flowers and many-seeded scarlet berries. In *Altowan* (p. 142) Stewart includes a footnote indicating that the dwarf arbutus formed a *principal ingredient of Indian fumigation*.

"I think we are the only two within a long ride, or it would not be wise to loiter here."

"I care not for tonight where I go, so, if you know of a safer spot, I follow."

"Yes, when they have had a bite, we can take them round to my den. I have not seen an old countryman for twenty years."

"And have you been all that time in the mountains?"

"Yes, bating a few visits to New Mexico."

"Have you any meat?"

"A little bit. There is a herd behind the rock, they must be in to water presently, and in fact the leaders are already in sight."

The wind was blowing pretty strong down the valley, I took my rifle in my hand, made a sign to my companion to have an eye to the horses, and following a hollow, got unseen within shot. My ball did not stop the cow, who, with the herd, set off back at the first alarm.

I was somewhat ashamed of this failure, and returned to say I had been unsuccessful. My new acquaintance asked where I had struck, and the distance.

"She must have been eighty yards off, but I held steady to the line between the long hair and the short, as she was standing a little toward me with her head."

"She will be dead then before we get to her, so catch up and let us be off, it is all in the road."

He said this with the confidence of a man who knew, and though doubting, I got the animals together, and led them in an angle off from the river, to fall on the track of the retreating herd. The sand was dry and soft at first, and then we got on to a harder crust, with sage and grease-wood in tufts. A few drops of blood, and then we came to more, and a small height showed us the herd a quarter of a mile off, it was not very large, and had collected in a heap.

"I told you!" said my companion.

They dispersed as we advanced, and there the cow was found dead. After taking out the ribs from one side, as we already had thrown the fleeces and the hump bones over my saddle, we moved off in a direction rather backward, on the left of the pass, along a range of rugged granite.

We had not time for examining the entrails, to see what was their portent.

"Having all this cavalcade, must make us cautious, but had I been alone, I could have read something there it might have booted you to know."

"And you think you can read the future from the gut of a cow?"

"You would not despise what you wish to learn, because conveyed in a homely fashion."

"And why should I wish to learn anything of the future?"

"It is but natural for he that is perplexed, the wish to solve, perhaps."

"But the science of the Roman soothsayer is lost."

"How do you know?"

Here I felt the power of the questioner to be greater than that of he who has to answer, and assumed that part on my side.

"Can you show me that such knowledge still exists?"

"When an opportunity offers I will."

We kept along the base of the rocks, which, as they stretch toward the Platte, we found more broken and better wooded than those on the opposite side of the Sweet Water. Still the black bands, sometimes solid and full up to the level of the granite on either side, intersected these rugged heights, but occasionally there was an appearance as if the space they occupied was not filled up to within several feet of the top, and in these cases the hollow bore a covering of wood and a carpet of grass between the walls of granite.

Up one of these I followed my guide to where there was a small grove of quaking ash, the grass was rich, and a trickling spring came out of a small fissure, and after filling a hollow shelf in the rock, dropped down from its slimy lip on to the shining particles of felspar and quartz crumbled below. There was just beyond, a spot cleared of wood, and where a few weather-whitened trunks and branches told of some former tenantry, part of which still retained their position in the line of a horse pen, and part still showed the square form of what had been a fort.

"There has many a cold blast blown since the Gros Ventres have forted here. It was in the time of the Cotillon[2], as the French boys called him, the father of Bracelet de Fer and the Little Chief. They had made a raise in what was then the Snake country, between the Popoagee and the Bad Pass to the right, and behind the Snowy mountains you saw beyond, they came here pursued by the Snakes, and having taken down the bed of the Sweetwater, had left no trail. The whole nation, however, moved round the end of the mountain, and all the young men were out, and they could see from this spot the dust rising over all the plains, the buffalo were driven far over to Green River, by the Pilot Butte, and here, however concealed, they could not stay, hemmed in by the enraged Shoshonies. They had several young squaws with them, prisoners, as well as horses, and finding they could not carry them further, they killed the squaws and the horses, taking each a supply of meat, and in the night made a dash up toward the Mountains of the Winds[3], but I believe, few

---

2. Cotillon: This Shoshone chief, whose name means *petticoat* in French, was father of Ma-Wo-Ma (The Little Chief) and Bracelette de Fer (Iron Wristbands). Although Bracelette de Fer succeeded his father as chief, the younger brother, Ma-Wo-Ma, was considered the more honorable and important in the affairs of the tribe (according to Morgan, *Rocky Mountain Journals of William Marshall Anderson*, p. 58), and he succeeded to the chieftainship on Bracelette de Fer's death in 1842.

3. Mountains of the Winds: The Wind River Mountains, which stretch north and west from South Pass.

ever got to see their own lodges again. Several skulls were yet lying about when I first saw the spot, where these poor things, taken first from their own homes which they loved, were transferred from the embraces of their captors into objects of sacrifice, and the same hands, which not a sun before had fondled, plunged their knives into their bosoms."

After making fast the horses, obedient to a sign, I again followed a little further up, and turning to the right, over some vast blocks of rock, we descended what had scarcely the size of a chimney, and my feet searching for such supports as in the sides they could find, till I reached a round mass, which obstructed the way, and served as a resting place, from which my guide's voice invited me further to descend, sliding over its side, I found a little light coming from one side, and a dark aperture about two feet broad in front.

My eyes were not yet sufficiently accustomed to the darkness to divine what sort of recess was that into which I now groped my way, but there was no damp or noxious vapour.

As the shadows of the place began to dissipate, I found my host, for such he appeared, was busy shaving off thin slices of a piece of wood, which turned out to be pitch pine, and so impregnated as to be transparent like amber. I again had recourse to my flint and steel, and the shavings took fire with a bright flame, and it soon communicated to a bundle of dry cedar, lying in a little cavity, apparently used for a fireplace. The whole cavern was illuminated by the lively blaze, it was irregular and not large, though extending to some length, and mostly of the same height in the middle, the sides varied as bosses protruded, or where cavities intervened.

In one of these, and on one side of it, I found a bed of dried grass, confined by the stem of a tree in front, composed of twigs evenly laid, over which was spread a robe. There I had been invited to sit, and the master of the abode disappeared in the smoke, and after some little time gave notice, by a shrill whistle, that I was wanted.

Upon arriving at the entrance, I saw suspended above, my saddle, which it was evident I was meant to recover. The meat followed, the fire blazed, and all things tended to the preparation of a feast, which in these cases has the charm of solidity—the meat is substantial and the hunger real. And then the dreamy influence of that fumigaton—the first rite of all known religions, and upon whose mystic influence depended, in many, the effect of worships otherwise barren and cold. I had sufficient tobacco to charge high the bowl, my bed had been made—the counterpart of that on the opposite side, the flame burnt clear, the odour of the cedar in the smoke was pungent, but we Roman-like reclined as we eat, and the smoke hung above us.

"How came you to be able to live unhurt among these wild tribes," I said, as I thought it no bad time to learn something of the history of the singular being with whom I had been thrown in contact.

"I early obtained an influence among them which is the strongest. They believed me to be possessed of supernatural powers."

"And how?"

"Have you ever heard of Mesmer[4]?"

"No."

"Well then, some time I will show you, when an opportunity offers, in the mean time suffice it to say, that I was born of a New England mother and a French Canadian father, near the Falls of Niagara. Circumstances placed me much among the aborigines in the neighborhood, and an Iroquois woman was my nurse. My father was of fickle and wandering habits, and at that time there was still some encouragement for the hunter, which occasioned long absences, and the consequent neglect of the necessary husbandry labours for the support of the family. My mother, with a little assistance from her own relations, and from the small portion she brought at her marriage, contrived to live, in some comfort, with such help as she could in her straitened means command, and having but one child, her chief care was for my education and future prosperity. Thus, without a worldly prospect but what chance should throw in my way, I acquired, through the instruction of a worthy man who had come over from France at the Revolution, much knowledge of things he had no intention to communicate—though forming an enthusiastic object of study to himself—and finding the ready avidity with which I listened so congenial to his own tastes. These episodes soon became a relaxation from the less seducing sciences which he had engaged to teach, we fled to these subjects as a release from Horace and Algebra, and I remember well it was often with a conscious blush my master winked at the curtailing by ten minutes of the hours of serious study, to enter upon these seductive and speculative themes. The most abstruse subtleties in moral philosophy formed but the introduction to the vast field opened to me by this strange man. The reading of the stars is but a matter of calculation by some, but with him was an innate feeling, a genius, a perception individually belonging to him, then came the divining by analogies, and the strange power of affinities. The lore of the ancients, in being handed down through the Middle Ages, was much mutilated, and when it became subsidiary to the love of gold, science was diverted and distracted, having also to contend with the interests of religion, and its just and natural desire to shield the vulgar and the weak from influences which might become hurtful to society, in placing power in the hands of men who need have no systematic scruple as to its exercise. Mind, I speak of the divinations and charms of Egypt and Chaldea. Whether the chain had been totally broken, and afterward retraced and joined, from the little I had read of the history of these

---

4. Mesmer: Friedrich Anton Mesmer (17337-1815), a German physician, developed a treatment through hypnotism called Mesmerism.

times, I cannot pretend to inform you, of this only I may vouch, that Mesmer appeared on the stage in the end of the eighteenth century, and claimed as his system a science which, in every probability, had been better understood in days long past away, though its practice might have been more confined. But I speak to one who cannot follow my wandering thoughts—to one whose curiosity is awakened by the first hints of some strange secret."

"Pray go on."

"There is little to tell of the progress of the different means of divination and of their checks, I believe we have made advances in the knowledge of passing events, we are able to read men's thoughts, and draw from them their most hidden secrets—but in reading the book of fate and penetrating into the future, I fear we are rather gone back than forward upon the knowledge of the ancients. I have within a sun met men wild with anger, and I find you perplexed, it requires no supernatural art to trace the commotion between you, and I knew that I should find you, and take deep part in your fate many hours before I came to the spot where we met."

"But how?"

"I did not dream of you, there was no reflection of the past, I knew you must be here. I then was chased by three whites, I stopped and laid myself down in a hole, and they came up, they hailed, and asked if I was an Indian, as they were sufficiently near to see my dark hair, I answered 'No', they then asked if I would allow one of them to approach unarmed, to see if he recognized me, I answered 'Yes', the man came up and shook his head, I was not he they sought. They then all came round, and I learned that they were in search of a horse stealer of the old country, I knew no such man, nor had I seen a white since spring. Magnus est veritas[5]—they believed me, and besides had no care to disturb a solitary man, when they had the rest of the human race and the elements to contend with, and I went my way, as also they, with the air of men who felt that they had wasted time. I pursued my route, and you know the rest."

I was some time silent after this long apostrophe. The flame, fed by an unerring hand in the time of need, burned occasionally with a brighter flare, but never fell to leave us in darkness, my companion drew from me all I could tell of the state of society and science in England, and communicated what came in contrast, of the noble manners of the red man—his grand simplicity, his self dependence, and his courage, never uselessly displayed.

But there was one point upon which, as a man of observation, and one who loved to read into the recesses of human nature, he most dwelled—the wonderful command these aborigines held over their physical senses, the calm endurance of pain, and economy of courage.

---

5. Magnus est Veritas: The Latin saying *Magna est Veritas, Truth is power*.

"An Indian shrinks from no torture, but he avoids unnecessary peril, and sees no good in the chivalrous sacrifice of an advantage, to give an enemy what we should call fair play."

The night was drawing on without tedium. I went out to look at my steeds, all was quiet, they were standing still and full, and I changed their position, that they might have fresh grass when they might again fall to.

The wind had increased to a stiff breeze, and thin fleecy clouds straggled over the deepening blue of night, there is something in the heavens of the mountain regions so clear and grandly distinct from the petty influences below, when it blows a gale above, and the white clouds are racing through its vault, we are in calmness far beneath, and when a storm below raises the earth in one vast cloud from the plains and tears up the pines of the forest, above the blue serene is calm, and its clouds drift lightly another way, so far and high you may see in that clear atmosphere.

It was some time before I returned to the cavern, its solitary inhabitant sat with his head bowed upon his knees, brought up as if to prop it and its many thoughts, the fitful glare of the cedar blazed up at intervals.

"You are here," he said, "at school, as far as the senses go. Are you good woodsman[i] enough to find your way to rendezvous without losing your cattle?"

"I think so, provided you give me a hint as to water and grass."

"Of that tomorrow. I have taken an interest in you, but we separate here for the present. I will light upon you before you have rounded the end of the mountains. Now, good night, but place the hair rope round your bed back to the rock, or you may have a rattlesnake for your bed-fellow before morning. So good night."

Chapter Twenty-Five
Solitary travel—enemies—terrible suspense

I might have slept in the womb of the earth, so still and calm, and even the temperature and the repose, it had been sealed with the thought, that whatever storm shook the walls of houses, and much more, the frail tenements of the wandering hunter, I lay here unrocked by billow or by blast, and ignorant of their fury. When I awoke in the morning, I was alone, sitting up in my bed, after the eye had become accustomed to the gloom, I could see that there was meat laid out on a piece of skin. I got up the chimney-like entrance, and went to the horses, and they were quiet and full, I made my ablutions at the spring, and came back to my hurried meal. What had happened? There was no treason in that man of dreams.

I took out my gear and saddled, the sun was not an hour high as we picked our way down the rough descent.

Just as I mounted, I saw a twig stuck in the earth, it was fresh and partly peeled, and it bent toward the snowy tops of the Mountains of the Winds.

That then was to be my course or had been his who placed it there. I took up the twig, mounted and pursued my way. The argali had not retreated to the rocks, the herds were far out on the plains, the heat had been such, that the rattlesnake had not waited for the sun being more high.

I could trace no track of man, nor see his sign, till I got to the trail, which without following the windings of the river, touches at its places of halt.

I had to find a resting place as best I might. The noon had passed, and at evening I was beyond the narrow passage of the river, which was then on the trail, but has been avoided since, for a line less difficult for waggons. There is a shorter cut to avoid a bend of the river and this is an affair of some four hours, and was too much to undertake at that time of evening, and the bushes of willow hid me for the night. Next day at noon, I should be at one of the most dangerous spots in the mountains, it is the high road round the base of the great ridge, and leads into the country of the Crows, as well as that of the Cheyennes and the Sioux on one side, and the Arapahoes and the Archarahs —or Rees as they are generally called—and snakes on the other. I was to avoid halting here, and was on that account to stop at noon, at a point lower down the river, and from thence at once take up the base of the mountain to a table land, until I should see some appearance of agreat camp to offer me security in coming down. This was the plan I had been directed to pursue.

The third day from leaving the cavern, where I had passed the night, under the care of my unknown protector, I stopped at a lake[1], from which rises the first fork, after passing westward of the Big Sandy, it is marked with a few scattered trees on its sides, and huge boulders of granite, in most places with a smooth sandy beach, at others abrupt masses of rock, it is an open basin, and comes down in its lower end almost to the plain. A winding and foaming cataract leads to a smaller lake above, whose banks are pine clad, and the mountain range upward from its waters to a great height, and between them intricate and unknown hollows with their sparkling streams.

It was early in the afternoon, and I had time to hide my horses in a grassy nook, and wander to several of these openings, and look in at the doors of the chambers of the mountain group. After satisfying my curiosity amongst the fallen trunks, and the shivers of rock, which obstructed the narrow entrances, I got out on to one of the spurs of the mountain, which like the bare root of a vast tree, ran down with the lake at its side, until it lost itself in the plain beyond, but at its upper end is high and barren. The wood has been shorn off from the bottom of this range by tempest or fire, a few scattered trunks stand desolately, and here and there a pine, that had been spared, still lifted its stubborn head on the eastern bank.

I had climbed to where the forest commences, and the view extends far over the rolling prairies, through which the Susquedee—the river of the prairie cock—winds its way toward the region of gold and silver then known, though neglected.

There was a red light from the evening sun upon the pilot butte, and also upon a small detached hill, by the base of which runs the waters of the lake below, and close to what is the course of the mountain caravan, when it passed toward the great hunting grounds of les trois tetons, the horse plains, and the

---

1. Lake: Local sources say that, both from the logic of the route and the description of the lake itself, this is probably Boulder Lake, the *first fork, after passing westward of the Big Sandy* would then be Boulder Creek.

upper waters of Snake River. A new road[2] has branched off just westward of that spot, along which the Mormons and the hunters of gold have since toiled their unromantic way, and the trail at the foot of the isolated butte, round which flows the clear mountain stream, which was then in the latter days of June, the scene of halt for the Oriental-like caravans which yearly came for the supply of the wandering hunters, in passing on their joyous course, and arriving within the bounds where rushed together their purchasers in every strange variety of guise to hail their coming, and raise the yell of joy, which echoed to the distant rocks, till it was in vain to proceed, encumbered with greetings, which the dust ever rising in the distance, still announced anew, while herds of wapati fled to the mountain fastnesses, and the perturbed herds of bison ran to and fro among the coursers, astonished at the sudden calming of the passion for the chase, which alcohol, the supreme spirit of the day, had superseded.

A man may sit behind that grey stone now, behind which I sat then, and the month shall be the blithe month of June, but the caravan and the shout of welcome are no longer there, there is no dust on the plains to guide the hunter to his prey, or to herald the coming of some new enterprise. But as I sat there, and looked out on the plains and ridges below, a prairie cock of the larger kind, with the long tail of the pheasant flew past me, and lit in the sage of the first ridge beneath. These birds are not easily made take wing, and are often killed by the arrows of the Indians running on the ground, or when first roused to their heavy and unwilling flight. The appearance of this bird, not flying down to water but evidently scared, at first did not excite much attention, but one of those strange second thoughts which the proverb has designated as the best made me turn to look from whence the bird might have come, where I saw the black head of an Indian in the sage, not two hundred yards behind where I sat, happily for me unseen, on account of my recent contemplation and consequent stillness.

The red man was on foot, painted black, the sign that blood and spoil were in his path. I had but a moment regretted not having my spy glass, now in a race for life or death, it might have turned the scale. I gathered my rifle without gaining my feet, they had not seen me, nor yet discovered the horses, nothing but the brow was visible, and it would have been more dangerous to have ducked than to remain exposed, and the contrast was not very great between the heated forehead and the ruddy granite. I was yet undiscovered, and only one redskin had as yet come in sight, he searched about with a bent bow still in his hand, as if he looked for something on the ground, he was not many yards from the edge of the pines, where probably the remaider of the

---

2. New road: The section of the Oregon Trail started by the Mormons in 1847, and followed by the gold-rushers of 1849.

party were, it was a chance how soon they might discover the horses, and steal down toward them while my attention was fixed on the one who had appeared.

It was the first time that I had come in face of a war party, for the accounts I had so often heard of them, left no doubt of the nature of the pursuit of a savage so painted, skulking near the great pass at such a time, however, it was evident they were on foot, and there was the chance still of the struggle of a race. I looked at my moccasins, they were not yet worn out, and I thought for a moment to stuff a fresh sole, cut off my hunting shirt into the inside, but I dared not take off my gaze, the Indian seemed still occupied in his search, looking up occasionally toward the cover of the forest.

It was a time of suspense, which the more prolonged the chances became, the greater were they against me, and I already began to feel the oppression of spirit, incident to one about to be fully overmatched, when I heard a raven's note repeated three times. There was no bird to be seen, and again all was still, but the head of the Indian was in a moment lowered, and he turned his search toward the wood, and I was satisfied, as he fairly showed his back, that he had not seen me.

I had but a few bounds to be out of sight, I wheeled round, and keeping the largest of the blocks as a mask between us while in sight, like a hound from the leash, I darted down the stony side, toward those earthly treasures, which even the missionary of religion himself is taught in these parts to prize, almost beyond the hopes and promises of his faith.

The roan and his now convalescing companion were quiet and full, when I came in sight, and it was almost with agony I remembered they were hoppled, the saddle, ammunition, blanket, and holsters, all my property of the second rank, lay on the ground, and down the declivity behind, raced some half dozen of painted savages, two leading, and the rest a little further behind, they came down in a succession of leaps, to avoid, as I afterward learned, the aim of that rifle, whose unerring ball was so much dreaded in the hands of the Kentucky hunter.

I was a hundred yards nearer the prize, but scarcely dreamed to have time to cut the hopple, and leap on the back of one, before my enemies must be upon me. It was to be a struggle I felt, and though there could be no reason in that never dying hope, inspired to kindle the spirit to such an uneven strife, yet I looked for a position to make a stand, and by instinct it was by a stone, beneath which lay my saddle, and there I dropped as if shot, and pulled out the pistols from their place, preparing for the charge I had to encounter, rather than suffer the ignominy of submission, and afterward a cold and torturing death.

There was an immediate halt of the leaders of the attack, as soon as I had sunk into my place. The next move was to get down close to the horses, not more than ten yards off, there was an abrupt bank, and then a green fringe just upon the border of the lake, and upon this they had been feeding. With the saddle and other gear on my back as a shield, I rushed down to the last point of retreat, and under this last declivity came to bay. There were some low bushes on the brink, through which I could see without being seen.

There were two short guns, such as the traders sell, in the party, and the rest, who had now come up, were armed with bows and arrows, a council appeared to be held, and I had time to breathe.

The measures which I had taken on the moment's spur, now when I had time to think, were really the only ones, and I watched through the sage the dispositions taken for the attack. The two Indians, men of great statue, who had the fusils, divided, and one took toward the higher end of the lake, and one to the lower, so as to be on each flank, the remainder making their approaches by the shelter of such stones and inequalities of ground as might favor them. But in the face of the booty, no one seemed to care much to expose himself to be shot, to ensure the success of the rest, and the advance was almost imperceptible. Being in a sort of bay, those who had got down to the water's edge, must be exposed, after they should reach certain points projecting like capes on either side, however, my eye could not be every where, and it was evident that I must become a victim to such an extended and cautious attack. I began to count the moments of my existence, and for the first time my heart began to beat as if my frame itself, in its matter became aware that there could be no longer any hope, and that its functions were about to end.

I had once looked at the lake, it was too broad to swim unstripped, and then unarmed if I should succeed, the mark also in the water to the aim of the two guns—that was not to be thought of, and I made up my mind to sacrifice three of my foes and meet my destiny. Eagerly looking out for the approach, within pistol shot of some of those nearest, I pushed up upon a bush a part of my blanket, to which I gave occasional motion by means of a stick, to form a false object of attraction, while I kept an eye upon the others by the lake side.

It was an awful moment of suspense—my three shots, and my sand was run, and my scalp was to adorn the belt of the conqueror, and my fair hair, upon whose thick and waving masses all the pains of my toilet were expended, was to be weaved to vary the fringe on the shirt of he who slew me, with the alternate locks of the Blackfoot or the Snake.

The ominous cry of the raven again repeated as before, prepared me for some new maneuver, and I was intently watching to discover what it should be, when the roan was taken with a sudden desire to drink, and slipped down the bank close to where I sat.

The thought came through my brain with electric rapidity—the cord which trailed past me was caught and tied in his mouth, and his hopple cut, a stone helped me to step upon his back, though encumbered with my arms, his head was already turned down the lake, the sand flew from his hoofs along the beech, and I thought I was again free on the plains.

Chapter Twenty-Six
Headlong flight—surprising sights

It had hitherto been sandy and hard, but as I neared the point where was stationed, I believed, the lower Indian with the gun, there were occasional masses of rock, which obstructed the way, and the shore became rough and stony, the roan was shod, so I rushed him along over everything, feeling that nothing short of giving the sentinel an uncertain aim could enable me to clear the cordon with which I was surrounded.

I was almost exulting in my escape, and in my selfishness had not thought of my poor wounded bear-horse. With head down and legs closed, and the arm raised to urge on the horse's speed, and eyes straining for the ambush and the aim I had to encounter as I ran, I thought I saw the black head and the gleam of the gun-barrel in the fringe of sage bushes which skirted the high water-mark, and bore my bridle-hand powerfully to the right, to ride over my opponent, or at least spoil his shot.

The roan answered to the helm, but not in time to save us from the fire, my horse fell, and I happily came off clear of him, almost vaulting over his head, to avenge him, as much as to clear my path, I pitched the muzzle of my rifle right into the breast of the Indian as he was rising to make at me. It must have smashed his ribs and driven them into his chest, as the blow was given with a will and all my might, and met by his forward movement, he fell, and I passed by. There was nothing for it but flight, and I rushed along the edge of the water.

I could see to my right the naked face of the slope and my speed was such, that the second gun, which had been stationed on my other flank, had not time yet to come within range, so I sped for my life. A yell rose in my rear, but

I heeded it not and kept on, bounding from stone to stone where the way was rough, and stretching out the faster where there was a sandy strand, still no pursuit, and after the yell no sound.

I had approached the lower end of the lake, and there was a round mound on the side of the stream just as it broke out, and a pass a little to the right, lower and somewhat smoother, toward this I rushed, almost blown by my exertions, and determined to pause on the top and see what dangers I had still to expect, and the distance of my pursuers.

There was no one in sight, and I dashed onward, more alarmed now than I had hitherto been.

There is something suspicious in the caution of the Indian, and his patience and cunning are most to be dreaded when he is not in view.

Panting, I sped on, taking a line toward the butte I have before mentioned, where from above I had seen the banks of the stream clothed with a thick border of willows. It could not be far, but I felt the forlorn position of a man on foot, let down from his high estate to a humble mediocrity, and all I had gained torn from me by a hand stronger than mine, forgetting for the time the hair's-breadth escape of the hour, and that I still was able to take the field, when I could join the comrades I had left, and find my mule fat and ready for use.

The ground was favorable for concealment, and the Indian is careful of running in upon a well-armed white in a place where he could stand at bay, with a fatal result to the first pursuers. But I was again to be perplexed by. the signs of danger in front, the head of a hind of the Wapati deer, or as they are called, elk, in the mountains, showed itself over a brow, sideling along at a swinging trot for the woods, and presently after a mighty hart, the head full grown, but not clean, seemed in its velvet between me and the sky to be of incredible size, a few shreds hung from the mighty beam, already partially frayed[i], the mouth open, as he lumbered along, and his glossy coat showed him oppressed with thus being roused in his pride of grease to take the steep mountain side, several hinds and calves and younger stags[ii] followed. The parcel was not more than fifteen, but notwithstanding the risk, I could not help stopping to gaze on the mighty-antlered beast as he showed clear upon the sky. Perhaps it was from early impressions of the red deer of England that the Wapati has always had a stronger attraction for me than any other of the animals of the West. There is more excitement in the race after the bison, and there is the rage of conflict in hunting the grisly bear, but I never felt inclined to loiter gazing upon a fat cow, or a bear, when there were Red men on my track.

But whence had they been driven, and by whom? The evening is not the time they seek the heights. They had been started from the plains, and I had to face this new enemy, if such it should prove, rather than linger to give an additional triumph to the captors of my steed. So, without slackening pace, I came upon the last ridge of the undulations, which might be considered the almost inarticulate base of the stupendous range above, and looked upon the placid stream meandering through its willow bed, and suddenly as I came upon the view, as suddenly seemed to have arisen a vast troop of horses and mules, which appeared to cluster thick on one of the meadows of the fork.

It did not require much thought to recognise a white camp, I was safe from the Red man, and in the power of the trader.

Chapter Twenty-Seven
Friends—property recovered—the Snake Indians—accursed and attacked!

Moving on at a less fatiguing pace, I passed the horse guard, and learned that it was Fontinelle's party. There they were, with their bales ranged according to messes of from six to ten, each man having two loads and a top pack. There was one tent belonging to the Bourgeois, as he was called, pitched near the river and round it was all the bustle of a little court.

I walked straight up to this spot, near the door stood a large heavy man, with a ruddy face, bearing more the appearance of a mate of a French merchantman than the scourer of the dusty plains. He looked at me, but did not speak. A number of French Creoles of St. Louis, of whom I recognised the cut, were rushing about with bales, and displaying their usual voluble activity, but the voices within the tent, as also of that portion of the circle which sat at the expanded doors, talked in no mitigated phrase that language in which Wellington informed Mr. Hutchinson *there was no mistake*.

A certain sense of diffidence, not untinged with the humiliation of the late disaster, checked me, and I paused before arriving directly in front of the council, who sat round the great white iron kettle, which Old Provost[1], the

---

1. Old Provost: Etienne Provost (1785-1850) was an illustrious brigade leader. Born in Montreal, he was in St. Louis before 1815, when he left with the Chouteau-DeMun party for the upper Arkansas River. After imprisonment in Mexico, he took Mexican residence, led trapping parties north into the Rockies, became one of the first white men to see the Great Salt Lake, and attended the first rendezvous, in 1825. He was associated for about the last twenty years of his life with the American Fur Company. Bartholomew Berthold called him *the soul of the hunters in the mountains*. In 1837, when Provost was a sub-leader of the caravan in which Captain Stewart and Alfred Jacob Miller traveled to the West, Miller quoted Shakespeare's description of Falstaff to describe

burly Bacchus I had before remarked, placed with affectionate care in the middle of the tent.

A voice from near the door now called out, "Stranger!" with an invitation to sit down. I moved a little forward for the purpose of doing so, when I came in sight of the open-handed and liberal trader, who seeing that I was the greatest stranger in the place, made room for me on his own blanket, and called to enter.

"Aye, do so, lad," came from the mouth of old Bill Williams, from behind a cloud of smoke, now shaved and looking as uncomfortable as possible in a new capot, trowsers, and hat, in which, with the help of his fame as a trapper, he had been immediately rigged on arriving in camp.

I passed on to my seat, stepping among tin cups and tobacco pouches, and giving my hand to all within reach, Fontinelle reached me a pipe, and the session was thus opened in form. There were many questions to ask from the last arrivals, who were to be distinguished by not having had time to change the winter-worn clothing of the country for the gala costumes into which the others had thrust themselves.

Fontinelle was asking Phelps, an old trapper, who with Meek had been on the waters of Louis's Fork[2], the southern sources of the Columbia, if he had heard anything of the new fort on the Maria[3], in the Blackfoot country, or seen any trappers from the Yellow Stone waters.

"No, I don't covet news at that cost, nor beaver neither," said Phelps, "so I kept my own side."

"What do you call your own side?"

"Perhaps you would like to look into my books?"

"I would so," shouted several voices.

"Then wait till I show you," said old Phelps, with a grin.

"Whar are the horses, lad?" broke in old Bill.

I shook my head.

"Well, let's have the history, nothing like historical truth."

Provost: adipose & rotonde—*larding the lean earth as he walks along* (see Ross, *West of Alfred Jacob Miller,* note to plate 197).

2. Louis's Fork: Lewis's Fork, now called the Snake River. Rising above Jackson Hole, Wyoming, this spectacular river was prime trapping ground and played a significant role in the political-economic struggle between the United States and Great Britain for domination of the Oregon country, then the northern half of the United States west of the continental divide. The Oregon Trail followed the course of the Snake River through much of present Idaho. The Snake River produces about one-fifth of the annual flow of the Columbia River.

3. New Fort on the Maria: Probably Fort McKenzie, built in 1832 six miles above the mouth of the Marias River—in present Montana—by the American Fur Company. It is possible, if the news is out of date, that the reference is to Fort Piegan, built at the mouth of the Marias a year earlier, and destroyed by Indians in 1832.

They got from me the story, which I made as short as I could, almost in the hope that someone would offer to help me in the pursuit of the party.

"Some of us may see them on the Big Horn," said Meek, "but for this rendezvous, they might as well be in Tennessee."

This was not encouraging, and the appearance of two great tin dishes, piled with boiled tongues, put an end to my thoughts on the subject.

The mastication of food in a country where there is no dyspepsia, or rather no one who dreads it, glides past as a matter of course, and though the pile of roasted ribs, and the loads of marrow bones which succeeded, varied the action of the feast, and gave time for the terse jokes which passed round, yet the party was rather marked by the intensity of direct physical enjoyment, than the titulating seduction of more refined gastronomy, the well-scraped bones disappeared and the bowl and the pipe supervened.

I learned, in the pauses of eating, that my comrades and my mule were on further, and had encamped near Captain Bonneville's trading house[4], which he had made of logs on the plain at Horse Creek, where were the Snakes and part of the Utes, or Uttowas, amounting to five hundred lodges.

Bill, as well as they, had seen my host of the Porte d'Enfer, and he had given them the history of my adventures since I had left their camp. Joe Heald was furious, and roamed about, swearing vengeance, and was also on near the Indians, waiting my coming. I got all this out of Bill in a rapid undertone.

The palatable shrub—which though delicious, was too strong alone—diluted with water and that ice-cold, made a most refreshing potation, and we were waxing merry, when a certain excitement was apparent without, and Carlo Crevier, a magnificent looking young half-breed, brought us the news that the Little Chief of the Snakes[5], with a war party who had been out against the Crows (Bill whispered, "That is the reading of the raven's croak you heard,") were arrived in camp with some scalps and horses.

One or two men, more eager than those accustomed to the country's ways, had lifted the side of the tent and gone out to hear the news and see the trophies. Meantime, on a signal, Carlo had turned to bring the chief and some of his principal followers, who appeared at the opening of the tent, and

---

4. Captain Bonneville's trading house: Called by some Fort Nonsense, this post was built by the interloper in August 1832. Warren Ferris notes that the fort got its name because it was abandoned a few weeks after completion. It was located on the right—south—bank of Green River five miles above the mouth of Horse Creek. See Ferris, *Life in the Rocky Mountains,* pp. 273-74.

5. Little Chief of the Snakes: Son and brother to Shoshone chiefs (Cotillon and Bracelette de Fer, respectively) and a chief himself, Little Chief, or Ma-Wo-Ma, once assisted in the recovery of some horses of Stewart's. Commenting on Little Chiefs beauty and carriage, Alfred Jacob Miller made a portrait of him in 1837. Ma-Wo-Ma in return painted a representation of one of his battle experiences and gave it to the artist. See Ross, *The West of Alfred Jacob Miller,* notes to plates 25, 35, 199. For Miller's reproduction of Little Chiefs drawing, see *Braves and Buffalo,* The Public Archives of Canada Series, Hugh A. Taylor, general ed., Number 3, p. 65.

silently proceeded by the left side to take their seats in the places which had just been so luckily vacated. A small hole was dug, a piece of burning buffalo dung was brought, and the pipe so lit was handed by Fontinelle, not without some appearance of deference and ceremony, to the Little Chief, now seated on his right hand. Not a word had been spoken to them, and the pipe having gone its rounds, the ashes were placed in another hole somewhat smaller, and both were covered up with the sand which they had originally contained.

Though this chief was a strict observer of medicine, he did not in anyway wish to prolong it, so as to interfere with the sensual pleasure of the bowl, and after quaffing the contents of the cup, he said his heart was glad to see the French chief.

Fontinelle answered that he hoped to be near the Snake camp by the afternoon sun of tomorrow.

While these courteous speeches were being made, I had leisure to remark the red guests.

The chief was a man of about six feet, not thirty years of age, with a countenance whose simple and grand expression was not in anyway weakened by the mildness and gentleness so clearly stamped upon it. He wore one middle lock, cut square, in the centre of his forehead, ornamented by a knot of small turquoise beads, the division of his fine hair along the ridge of the head was filled with Vermillion, with which his face was highly rouged, and certain figures marked on it with great care and accurate drawing in bright yellow ochre, his arms were loaded with bracelets, all but one of shining brass, that one was of iron, it was the distinctive badge adopted by his house, and his elder brother, the principal chief, took his name from it, Bracelet de Fer. But in all matters of importance in war, in the sustaining of authority, and the repression of theft, the voice of the younger brother, the Little Chief, was alone that which insured obedience in the Shoshone camp.

While I remarked this last brave of the once great tribe, who was in a few years fated to die of chagrin at the decadence of his people, and of unavailing wounds in their defense, the attention of all was suddenly drawn to the parade of the captured horses and the scalps, which accompanied by the French boys of the camp, and their wild cheers, were approaching the door of the tent. But what words can describe my astonishment, at beholding my own horses brought up in triumph, mounted by Snakes in full dress, and three or four scalps stretched on hoops, and borne on long willow poles, waving before them in the evening breeze.

I rushed out, not quite understanding the scene before me, or that the horses had been recaptured by friendly Indians, from the robber band who had dispoiled me, the Indians each received a cup of shrub, and then continued their tour round the camp, and I resumed my seat.

Fontinelle, who had learned that the horses had been mine, presented me to the Little Chief, who, looking hard at me, held out his hand, and kept mine locked in it for several seconds, while the scrutiny lasted, he then made a sign that I had struck the Crow in the chest, and that he was found nearly dead.

Fontinelle then proposed that he should trade back the horses, but this proposition did not seem to be received with much favor, I then remarked, that had I not knocked over the Indian, and prevented his mounting, the Snakes would never have touched the roan, however after some difficulty, it was agreed that Fontinelle would advance three muskets, three blankets, a rifle, and a certain quantity of powder, and I was to have my animals restored, with my riding gear, &c. A signal brought a clerk, who soon produced the goods, and the barter was completed.

The young brother of the Chief went out, and in a few minutes, returned, leading the three captives by their trail ropes, and gave the ends of the cords into my hand. I immediately went out and cut my pickets, and planted them in a good green spot near the middle of the round, feeling well assured that had the Snakes, who were great lovers of horses, known the speed and spirit of one of mine, they would not so easily have parted with him.

Meek then came up, and said, "This is a fair purchase by the stranger from the Little Chief, so that settles the affair with Joe Heald, and as I was once a sheriff in Tennessee, or very near being one, which shall be the same thing, I ought to know something, so apply to me for a warrant, should anything go wrong." Meek rode off, looking down on the jaded mules, and making his charger perform demivaults and gambadoes[6] among the admiring French, their loads of merchandise and blazing fires.

Some new yells were now heard in the distance, and off he dashed toward the west, with a shout which echoed from the butte, and this was met by counter yells, and then a discharge of firearms, and the dust of horsemen tearing along at reckless speed, would anywhere else have been a token for urgent news, or headlong flight. It was the coming of John Grey[7] the Iroquois, and some French free hunters.

This Iroquois was a most successful trapper, but a drunken and treach-

---

6. Demivaults and gambadoes: A demivault is a half-turn made by a horse with its forelegs raised. According to the *Oxford English Dictionary*, this sort of gambado is *a bound or spring (of a horse)...a fantastic movement, as in dancing or leaping about*. So Joe was showing off in the style of young bloods.

7. John Grey: Grey, or Ignace Hatchiorauquasha (1795?-1844) was of mixed Iroquois and American ancestry. Apparently, he was involved in the fur trade by 1820. He was considered the leader of about a dozen free trappers who deserted from Peter Skene Ogden's Snake River Brigade in 1825 to join the Ashley men for the sake of better prices. An excellent hunter, Grey is known as the discoverer of Grey's Hole, Grey's Lake, and Grey's River along the present Idaho-Wyoming border. Retired from the fur trade' in 1836, he made one more trip west in 1841, acting as guide and hunter for Father Pierre Jean DeSmet and the Bidwell-Bartleson California party. See Merle Wells's biographical sketch in Hafen, ed., *The Mountain Men and the Fur Trade*, VII: 161-75.

man, who, however, had this vast merit in the eyes of a trading company, that he drank almost all the price of his beaver in brandy, at thirty-two dollars a gallon.

This party were received with uproarious welcome, and while their first noisy greetings were going on, I selected the side of a small bush to spread my recovered apichimoe and saddle, thus to mark out a place of repose. The younger Snakes, who were dandies, and some of the handsomest youths in the village, paraded up and down in their buffalo robes, on which scalp hair in tufts, embroidery in beads, and hieroglyphic painting of fights in which they had been engaged, formed the ornaments, and their leggings, which reached above the knee, and nearly met the hunting shirt, leaving but a portion of the thigh exposed, were each down the outward seam, garnished by broad stripes of small bead-work in blue and white, with a full fringe of buckskin cut in strips, which trailed more than a foot on the ground behind. They had fans of eagle wings in their hands, and under the left arm, with the mouth turned down, the cock resting on the arm, and protected with loose covers, decorated with fringe, reposed short and light muskets, their heads, which they bore high, were painted with the utmost care, and their rich black hair fell in glossy lengths on their shoulders, their walk was peculiarly dignified, and their step firm.

I allowed them to turn twice, in order to have an opportunity of watching their gait, and admiring their appearance, and could not help owning to myself, that in thorough bred, look and bearing, I had never seen their peers. This was the more strongly, because unexpectedly impressed upon me, from having looked upon the miserable specimens of the race which I had seen in New York and in Missouri, as a fair type of their kind. It is not to be inferred from this, that all the Snakes were of this stamp, but there were, I afterward found, a fair proportion.

These young warriors walked up and down in the camp, with an air which strongly contrasted with the vivacious little Frenchmen, and the negligent air of the carelessly clad Americans.

But the sun was already down, and a certain degree of quiet seemed to have taken possession of the camp. The tired and miserable looking pack mules were being slowly congregated to feed till the last moment, before being picketed, and the shout and occasionally a few notes of some wild song, came from the tent of the trader.

I was about to lay myself down to repose, when I got a message from Fontinelle, that he expected me at his tent, I found the circle had been augmented by the newcomers, but I got a place between Shunar[8], the champion of the French, a good-natured stupid-looking man of great apparent

---

8. Shunar: See DeVoto's amusing account of this blend of fact and fantasy in *Across the Wide*

strength, and John Grey, whom I have before mentioned. The potations had to a certain degree done their work, and I found the chief of the revel with evident marks of hilarity, partaken in greater or less degree by various others. It was somewhat difficult to discover what was the subject of discourse, even amongst those closest by where I sat, much more to trace the various themes which were discussing in different languages around, for there were Mexicans in the group. But some feeling, which it is difficult to trace, led me to think that I had been the subject of some of their discourse. In these unexpected scenes, where the passions are suddenly raised, and where the language of dispute is not the most mild, it is not to be expected that young blood should flow with even calmness, and that reason should have its full command over words and acts.

It appeared that Joe Heald's conduct had been taken up in a sort of debate, that Fontinelle, as I afterward learned, had taken my part, but his head was fairly upset, and his interference was unheeded, and it appeared I had been brought in to be baited, and John Gray was the first to begin, and the coarsest in his attack.

Driven to say something in my own defense, I exclaimed, "If I am a horse stealer, I had long odds against me, Heald is a betrayer of trust, who ran away with my property, part of which only I have taken back."

Shunar then said I was a liar, upon which I knocked him over, and a struggle ensued, and while engaged with this powerful adversary, I felt struck in the back by some traitor hand, the confusion became great, and old Batiste called out Villiame[i], Villiame! which was the cry of several French lodges who had William Rodgers, a half-breed with them for their warrior.

I believe nothing saved me, but the crush and the extinguishing of the wax light, a heap of the hired men, and some stray Americans came rushing in, my feet had got turned toward the outside of the tent in the melee, and I felt myself pulled out from under its cover, it was old Williams, who whispered, "The other boys told me to have an eye to you, come along."

I went with him to his fire, and then found that I had been struck with a knife in the back, it was little more than a scratch, the blade having glanced off, but it bled, having been doctored with buffalo marrow and gunpowder, I pulled down my shirt, and laid myself down to sleep, while they held on their revel under the light of another candle, there was no enquiry made for me, and my spell of sleep was sound and long.

Missouri, pp. 226-30. Little is known of Shunar (Chouinard?) except that he was a bully and fought with Kit Carson at the 1835 rendezvous, perhaps to his death.

Chapter Twenty-Eight
The decorated Snake steed—philosophy of hunting, and Indian conservation—an elk hunt leads to a cougar camp

I have often, I remember, been tormented by dreams on other occasions, where I had been subject to the effects of anger just before lying down, but in this case, there had been no anger, the whole affair was sudden, and its effects were almost forgotten, when I began to collect my thoughts on the morrow. No one seemed to recollect that anything had occurred, nor had there, save that mysterious attempt at stabbing me in the back, and the scuffle with Shunar, and both these were not quite unusual events when alcohol was rife in the trader's camp.

The *turn out*, shouted twice by the camp leader in the American companies, was replaced by the *leve, leve*, of old Provost, which created a strange resurrection.

From beneath blankets of every color, appeared unshaven beards of every hue, the miserable mules, with their backs humped up and raw, hung their ears, and shivered in the chill[i], it was a strange contrast to the jollity of the night before.

The Indians had retired with their horses some distance up the stream, and there, after bathing, commenced that interminable painting and decoration, which occupies so much of the time of a Shoshone fop.

It may be supposed, that the small quantity of meat which hung at my saddle-bow, was left behind, after the scuffle with the Crows, so I was not sorry to be offered a bowl of coffee and some meat, by the nearest mess to where I had lain.

We were to halt for the night on the Susquedee, a little below the Snakes and Bonneville, and about four or five miles from Campbell, and Meek proposed that we should ride on, but I thought this would look too like flight, and asked him to put off the proceeding till after the halt at noon. The curious procession of the mules in their lengthened string, began to wind along, the party of Indians had divided on either side, and rode to the heights, where they halted until the camp came up, and then took their course to the next similar position.

Nothing could be more wild than their appearance in all their vivid hues. The horses were painted and decorated with feathers, the bay and black with white clay, and the white with red and yellow. The long robes floated behind, and the fringes hung gracefully from their limbs, the fan of eagle's wing shaded the sun from their eyes, as they looked back on the following | caravan, thus protected on either flank. It was to us, who saw it from below, a succession of the most picturesque and varied attitudes and dress, upon the most appropriate and commanding positions, and whenever the eye rested on a height, it was crowned as if by enchantment, with the wild savage and his steed. More of the whites from the Susquedee, kept emerging from clouds of dust, which came rolling along the prairie, and many Indians joined in the flank escort, it was a triumph equal to that of the return of a successful expedition, but came doubly valuable to cover a signal failure, so we held on.

Fallon[1], in a Mexican dress, the finest looking man in the mountains, came dashing forth, the bison, which blackened the plains, rushed about in consternation, grisly bears were raised in the route, but all unheeded, the two months' journey had satisfied the one party, and the others did not destroy for destruction's sake.

The beautiful antelope fled in strings across our path, and returned with the air of having left something behind, no one heeded them, the prairie dogs barked from the doors in their villages, as we passed over the hollow-sounding ground, under which they had dug their subterraneous homes, the rattlesnake reared his open jaws unheeded, and their prey, the rabbit and the dove, even left to their fate, and all this, where many hundred hunters were prowling, and parties had been passing for more than ten days.

One half-breed dashed off after a wolverine, thinking it a young bear, which he wished to tame, and we arrived at the Pinney Fork[2] to noon, at the

---

1. Fallon: William O. Fallon (?-1848), is often confused with Benjamin or John O'Fallon, but is neither of those Indian agents nor of their family. Warren Ferris says Fallon was at Taos during the winter of 1832-33, which may account for his appearance here in *Mexican dress (Life in the Rocky Mountains,* p. 274). Joe Meek calls him *a big bullying Irishman,* and says that when Fallon threatened to horsewhip Meek's wife Mountain Lamb, she got the drop on him and humiliated him publicly. Fallon is mentioned by Edward M. Kern, of Frémont's third expedition, as *Big Fallon,* an old mountaineer, known more commonly by the sobriquet of *Le Gros*—meaning *Fatty* (Morgan, *The Rocky Mountain Journals of William Marshall Anderson,* p. 299). Fallon was active in the Bear Flag Revolt (1846), and was killed en route to California from Fort Hall in 1848.
2. Pinney Fork: A principal tributary of Green River rising from Frémont Lake (called by Matt

moment of the grove on its banks being filled with strawberries, and its transparent stream sparkling with life, it comes from one of the most beautiful of lakes, filled with the most delicious trout, who, in their ignorance of man and his ways, took in its pellucid waters the most clumsy bait, unscared by the coarse lines, the naked legs, the rash pulls, and awkward misses of unpractised anglers. The banks of these waters were encamped upon but once by white men, and navigated but once, and that was years after the present date. There is not now a live bison, a wapati, or a black-tailed deer in the region, otters are scarce, and beaver gone.

There is a religion in hunting, and like the fire worshippers, or any other culte, it should form its own government and its own laws, nothing gives rise to strife like disputes in hunting grounds, death ensues, and the race of man having fought for their prey, rendering the chase, that of the hunter being hunted. The animals have in their vast range, hitherto had a strong diversion in their favor, besides the sense of their value, and the necessity of regulation in the slaughter of game, which has found its way into the councils of the wiser tribes, there had been no common cause made against the bison and the elk, till the white man came with his reckless destruction, so that in the debatable hunting grounds on the southern and western sides of the Mountains of the Winds, there was sufficient danger to prevent indiscriminate slaughter, it was only the braves, and that under the sanction of the chiefs, who hunted, and in the Crow country the law was most severe, no animal was touched save on certain days, and then so complete the destruction, that no one of a herd lived to warn the others of the danger of that deceitful care with which they were preserved from petty injury, to be consigned, in what is called a surround, to their unsparing wants.

But the year of which I speak, was the last that the bison was found in herds on the upper waters of the Susquedee.

No one who had not seen it, could form an idea of the mass of game which was to be found there in that day, the mountains were such, as the Indians said, the birds could not fly over, so that everything had to pass round between the vast plains of the southwest, and those of the northeast, and the supply seemed inexhaustible. Loads were being brought in by Crevier and Joe de Noyer, there was not a moment that there was not some fresh arrival to welcome, or fresh supply to feast.

After the halt, I could not restrain myself to keep with the camp, but dashed away on the roan toward the gorges of the mountains, where I hoped to fall in with the wapiti, I had not yet shot at one of these grandest of the

---

Field in 1843 Stewart Lake), Piney Fork was a favorite hunting area of Stewart's. See Field, *Prairie and Mountain Sketches*, pp. 34, 135, 139. A sketch of Stewart Lake appears opposite 139. See also Morgan, *The Rocky Mountain Journals of William Marshall Anderson*, pp. 163-64.

antlered tribe, as I considered it wrong to kill anything not in its prime. I had the whole mountain side to myself, and I thought I had discovered a hart of the first class, near a green spring on the side of a butte, which separated the larger and more beautiful lake from which the Pinney rushes in one foaming cataract for a mile, from another smaller one further on. It was rather a difficult spot to ride, but if I stalked on foot I must lead my horse, it was no place for running any risk, a horse stealer of the Snakes, friendly as this village was, might ride off and join the Gauches band[3], who were not very far off, and I felt that while I was to try to creep in unperceived upon my noble quarry, I must exercise all the vigilance I was capable of against a similar design upon myself.

Below, while I paused in a hollow to look out, and also to bring on by a false calculation any sculking savage in pursuit, I could trace the course of the camp, and the wheeling bands of bison and antelope which were careering round, raising clouds of dust which marbled the plain. Occasionally a small puff of smoke marked an arrival, until the head of the line got up to the ridge which forms the left of the valley of the Susquedee, over which the heedless hunter scours, his horse's heels showering back the onyx, the calcedony, the crystal, and perhaps the diamond[ii], which gravel his way.

But, like a dissolving view, the line of Fontinelle's camp had passed from my sight into a small ravine, which conducted it to the brink of the river at its bend, it had previously ran almost south, but here, meeting the debris thrown up between it and the Pinney Fork, it at once takes the course to the west, which brings it to the ocean.

The direction this camp had taken was plain, the region lay like a map beneath, and I withdrew my eyes from the contemplation of the disappearing train, to look out for my own safety and my own pursuits.

Peering out from the hollow where my horse was culling amongst the aromatic herbage what best suited his taste and constitution—for most animals are superior to man in the power of abstaining from what may do them harm—I could not detect anything in my rear, below there appeared to be but the slope and the half-covered boulders of granite and the plain, where the wolf was prowling among the antelope, and a few old bulls were rambling about, undecided as to which course they should take to find a herd of cows. But above, I saw that the great hart which had lured me to the mountain's base, was not, as I had supposed, unattended and alone, there was a hind and a calf in sight, and not far off where he ungallantly reposed to windward—for

---

3. The Gaudies band: A band of Shoshones led by Mauvais Gauche, also known as Bad Gocha, Bad Gotia, and Bad Left-Handed One. Warren Ferris says that Gauche tricked a brigade led by Etienne Provost into laying down their weapons to smoke the pipe, and then treacherously attacked them, killing ten or eleven while only three or four escaped *(Life in the Rocky Mountains,* p. 385). In a footnote in *Altowan* (p. 178) Stewart says Gauche was a *Chochocoe* or Digger chief and his band inhabited the valleys of the Wind River Mountains.

he had lain down since I first discovered him—and they completely cut me off from approaching from above.

I was about to try to get round from below, when I thought I could see another head over a rock clear upon the sky line, but before I had time to use my glass, the head of the hart was to be seen on the horizon, and he moved downward.

Having watched for a half an hour his careful descent, and the looks he turned toward the attentive hind, I traced him on to a small height several hundred yards below the fountain where I had first seen him. Here he was on a sort of ridge where the winds met, and down which I saw it would be easy to get at him, provided the hind was out of sight. She I perceived also to be in motion, but moving upward. I took my spy glass and brought it to bear, it seemed to be the flies which tormented her, she stamped and flapped her ears, and the calf kept running about, evidently uneasy, but as I watched to observe whether there might not be more come in sight, as she moved, I again detected the head I thought I had before seen, it was immovable, but it was a head, (though no head of game, the cheeks were thick and the ears were short—it was no bear—it was not the size—and no bear would lie out there while the sun was high), evidently watching the unsuspicious calf, which was edging toward the shelf below.

The calf was very young, and hardly very much occupied with browsing, though it picked with appetite such things as seemed to please it, and then moved about, in a half-playful, half-fretful manner, to rub its head against its dam, who was still uneasily gazing about.

They were some distance from the shelf on which lay the animal I had detected, and were now moving backward, and downwind, they took a few bounds and were out of sight, but I could now see the form of the animal which had watched them from above—it was a cougar, and it crept along the rock to spring upon its prey when they should come within reach.

I believed the hart now to be in a place of safety to be got at, but I could not reconcile myself to sacrificing the hind and its young to the gratification of killing him, noble game as he was, so I took the chance, should I miss getting a shot at the panther, and having scared him off the field, to return to my first pursuit.

But I must now take a course below, as the movement must be in that direction, not to give her, already to leeward, my wind. She naturally looked that way, but I got almost past her, when there came one of those strata of rock which often occur in these mountains, where the vein is vertical and the formation different from the rest, they are even on the surface, and there is seldom soil or boulders upon this extent.

This formation running on a sort of ridge, formed the salient angle of the butte, and here I could not pass undiscovered, and had to sink down. The hind was almost within shot just above, she had paused some time before coming upon this abrupt angle, and I was looking out for the cougar on her steps. Something, however, had warned her of the presence of an enemy below, and her eyes were fixed in my direction, with an occasional half-turn toward her calf, when I saw the hind bound up in the air, and the calf, with a faint scream, borne under her feet, so as almost to upset her, in the fangs of the panther, the poor mother, her coat raised, with her large eye and the opening below it distended, from which I thought I could see large drops of agony distilled, came past me almost without fear in her uncertain trot, halting to gaze, and turning away in desponding grief, and I made a vow that I would do my best to avenge her.

The panther did not seem disposed to gorge himself immediately, but life being extinct in its tender prey, licked the blood which bubbled from its nose and mouth, and took it up to drag it to some more suitable place, exposing the full side. This was not quite sure enough for my vengeful humour, and I did not fire, but I thought the brute would not go far, and slunk back to get at my horse, and not leave him exposed on the hillside. It was not far, and I threaded my way among the rocks with some trouble, until I came back to the place where the blood marked the cougar's path, the ground, happily, did not on that side the angle of the hill appear so difficult or rocky, and I urged my horse on among the boulders for some time, apparently without giving our wind, but I saw a line, in which there appeared a grassy slope, toward which I bore, and in doing so, I suppose fouled the breeze, for I saw the panther, who had left his prey, bending along before me toward the woody fringe which bordered the lake.

I sped along after, with an ardour which few passions give save the love of vengeance, my horse was famous for his strength in galloping down hill, short in the forelegs and firm, with a deep chest and shoulders. I laid my weight well back in the saddle, and left him free to choose his path, and once or twice shut my eyes when it appeared we were going headlong down. Sometimes his hoofs rung where he had topped a boulder, I was yet fifty yards behind.

There might be caverns on the lake shore, or crevices in the piles of rock or thickets, where he would be lost, and I bitterly grieved before I was half down that I had not taken the more than fair chance previously offered, but I still pressed on. The long bounds, which in the more rugged and uneven ground above had so much favored his flight, were now changed to a rush for the trees, the whole hair on the back and tail was bristled. I was gaining fast, and already almost upon him, and uncovered my rifle, which was already pointed, but a sudden spring of my horse almost unseated me as I fired, perhaps saving my intended victim, but at the same time baulking his vengeful spring. This, for a moment, threw me out, and I had some trouble to turn again. I had, however missed the chance of a running shot, and when I got again on the track the trees were within fifty yards, the ground had become encumbered with masses of stone, and I was obliged to pull up as I lost sight of my quarry in a small thicket of sage, which fringed the elevated terrace which hung over the shore.

It was now necessary to look well among the crevices of the piles of rock, as there was an almost open space a little above. I felt confident the panther was concealed within shot, and therefore rode almost all along the edge of the clump of trees, the line of which for a short space gave out on the lake's edge. There was a buffalo path of smooth and beaten sand along the terrace, but no sign. I felt assured that the animal lay concealed under its edge, or among the roots of the rugged pines, which torn by tempests, extended such limbs as remained unscathed above my head.

What would I have given for five minutes of Solomon, an old hound of one of the Cheshire packs, which we used occasionally to follow from school, when we could get a mount. But a dog in these wilds for a hunter is forbidden, in no case is it safe but for a strong party, and however useful in some cases, would be fatal to all concealment, which so often saves him, where a dog would otherwise be most required.

It is true the grisly bear could be hunted in comparative safety with dogs to bait him[iii], but how seldom is he found when he can be thus attacked, and in some cases has he been known to carry off a man from his campfire, as if not the weight of a mouse, and if in such a humor, I doubt if dogs would stop him before the mischief was done.

However, I felt that I must do the part of a sleuth-hound through this small cover, or go without my promised vengeance, and having come to the end outside, I had now to enter beneath the trees and below the brink in trying back, had I known as much, I ought to have dismounted in such rugged ground, but there is a natural tendency to keep to your horse, which on more occasions than one I have found to my disadvantage. However, in this case, I held my rifle ready, and moved deliberately forward. There appeared no hiding for an animal of the panther's size.

I was almost at the end of the search, when the ear of the roan betrayed by a certain back and forward motion, that there was something. I pulled up a moment, not quite at ease that I might not be mounted. Some slight sound made me look up, and on the crooked limb of an old contorted pine I saw my enemy crouched for a spring. The tree was on my right hand, and I had not time to turn my rifle, if I could have used it correctly with my left. There was not a second for thought, but a branch had laid back the blanket from my pistols, and getting one out, I covered the breast of the cougar, just as he sprang—the animal fell short, and writhed out his last at my horse's feet.

I took a long breath, and dismounted, tying my horse to the point of a pliant branch[iv], and took the skin from my prey and laid it across my crupper, tying it to the cantle with a thong cut off the end of my shirt, already somewhat curtailed, to aid the sun in the work of tanning, visibly begun on my skin.

I could not help thinking of the poor hind, and turned my eyes often toward the scene of her loss. I had taken the shortest cut to cross over the shoulder of the hill, and I readily found the bereft mother warily approaching the spot. There was something painful in her distress, and in being unable to show her that I had no desire to participate in inflicting the pang, she fled, however, in distrust and grief, and I went on my way[4].

---

4. Went on my way: For a visual interpretation of this panther-hunting story, featuring not Stewart but a generalized *mountaineer* as the hunter, see Ross, *The West of Alfred Jacob Miller*, plate 27. Miller also did a painting of this tale in 1840-41 (said still to hang in Murthly Castle) that showed Stewart as the hunter. And he did yet another painting showing an Indian as the hunter. See Ron Tyler, ed., *Alfred Jacob Miller: Artist on the Oregon Trail,* Fort Worth, 1982, plate, 51.

Chapter Twenty-Nine
Rendezvous—Kit helps out

Whether we had been late at the noontide halt, or that I had passed a longer time than I expected in lounging about, I knew not, but the sun was getting low, and though the peaks aloft on the mountain ridge were fiery red with his evening beam, the lower plain was coming under the influence of a gradual shade.

There had been a slight breeze during the day, which had sunk as the evening fell, and now all was so still, I could hear the occasional howl of the wolf and the short low of the bull, as the herds were spreading abroad for pasture, and again, the murmur of the distant cataract, as musingly I tracked my course toward the scene of rendezvous[1].

The camp of Dripps[2], to which Fontinelle came with supplies, was placed

---

1. The scene of rendezvous: Stewart here describes the rendezvous of 1833, on the Green River at Horse Creek. Many of the particulars of his description can be verified. For other first-hand accounts, see Washington Irving, *The Adventures of Captain Bonneville,* pp. 154-58, Warren Ferris, *Life in the Rocky Mountains,* pp. 273-80, Victor, *The River of the West,* pp. 142-43, Charles Larpenteur, *Forty Years a Fur Trader on the Upper Missouri: The Personal Narrative of Charles Laprenteur, 1833-1872,* (Ed. by Elliott Coues) New York: F. P. Harper, 1898. This is the rendezvous which Nathaniel Wyeth, the New England entrepreneur, said was made up of a small village of Snake Indians and about three hundred white men—"agreat majority of scoundrels" (quoted in Hafen, *Mountain Men and the Fur Trade,* I: 130).
2. Dripps: Andrew Drips (1779-1869), born in Ireland, was a longtime leader in the Western fur trade. First employed by Missouri Fur Company in 1820, he became a partner in 1822. After Missouri Fur became part of the American Fur Company, he led that firm's invasion of the mountain beaver country in 1830. Following the Battle of Pierre's Hole (in which he fought), he and William Vanderburgh led their trappers on a pursuit of the men of Rocky Mountain Fur led by Bridger and Fitzpatrick, resulting in Vanderburgh's death. From 1842-46 Drips was an Indian

in a bend of the Susquedee on the left bank, and a few hundred yards before it turns from the bases of its parent hills, that of Campbell had moved from the mouth of Horse Creek back to a spot also on the left bank, and about four miles from Dripps, and Bonneville, with the Indians remained on the edge of the river above Horse Creek, with its vast plain stretching to the west.

As I have said before, the evening was still and calm, few stragglers are abroad at a moment of festivity, and I met nothing till the night had closed in, when as the trail had narrowed as it approached the river bank, and I followed it threading my way among the bushes, there was light enough to distinguish a gaunt white wolf of unusual size, in my way, who did not seem inclined to yield the path. My horse snorted and jumped aside.

There was something terrible in the look of that wolf—the haggard eye and the hanging jaw—the indifference with which it approached in a narrow path alone—not to attack, but not to yield, the lurid glare of the eyes was never turned toward me, but it passed slouching on.

I knew not why, but a shudder came over me, and though I should have punished my horse in any other case for having transgressed against the rules of forestry in giving way to a single wolf. I felt as if I also had quailed before this ghost-like beast, who looked not right or left, but carried those terrible eyes, as if intent on some errand beyond[3].

I regained the path, but never looked back, I felt that the ominous animal was bent on some other dole, and it was not me or mine he sought in this night's prowl.

The guard is not very strict at such times, but as I rounded the next bend of the river, I found myself on the outer bounds of the camp, and was challenged by old Sipiot, who kept that barrier against all comers, I cannot exactly say he was sober, but he saw I was not an Indian. I heard afterward that he thought I was too drunk for fanfaronade[4], and let me pass.

It was somewhat difficult to thread my way among the cords and pickets of the thickly tied animals, and now that I had passed the close brushwood which had hitherto shut out the camp from my view, its whole glare of fires and tents and lodges blazed before me.

The saints of the House of Commons would have been stupified at the scene, for it was a Sunday night. I paused involuntarily, and old Sipiot recom-

---

agent, then once more a trader into advanced age. Harvey Carter argues that Drips should be *well toward the top of the list [of mountain men] because of his long and successful career, his mastery of all branches of the business and his ability as a leader of men* (Carter, *Andrew Drips* in Hafen, *Mountain Men and the Fur Trade*, VIII: 143-56).

3. Errand beyond: Stewart's account of the mad wolf and the ill-fated George Holmes is particularly valuable because, though several first-hand accounts mention the wolf scare, only Stewart and Larpenteur give the identity of the trapper killed. Holmes is said to have died while with a brigade led by Moses *Black* Harris into Crow country in the fall of 1833.

4. Fanfaronade: According to the *Oxford English Dictionary*, fanfare.

my unsaddling on the brink of the water as he said it was difficult to find a clear space, he seemed surprised at the equilibrium of my movements, and I hoppled and tied the roan on the spot, and then proceeded toward the interior throng.

No one seemed to be sober, the glare of the fires lit the different scenes of gambling and debauch, unless where a monster blaze had been raised to show a fight, the air was an atmosphere of oaths. I felt stunned and bewildered, so different the scene from anything I had ever witnessed, as well in contrast to the solitary nature of my wanderings on the several previous days, as in itself unmatched in any part of the world.

As proceeding, with no very certain purpose, through this throng, I met old Baptiste staggering along with a cup of some spirituous mixture, which trickled from his unsteady grasp.

"Bois done!" he stammered, giving the vessel into my hand.

It was a mint julep, strong as poison, but containing at least a handful of moist sugar. It was not an unsavoury syrup, and I swallowed a mouthful, while Baptiste explained that there was an American who threatened to jump upon one of the French boys of his mess, and he was in search of help, and he tottered off, hollowing the war-cry of his lodge for his champion, "Villiame! Villiame!"

Meantime, the scene of confusion went on, and I threaded through almost unnoticed, until a man rushed out from a shanty[i], naked to the waist, and aimed a blow at me, which I eluded, but was about to return, when someone on a bare-backed horse, pushed in between us.

"Easy, easy, Shunar, that stranger belongs to me for this night, you shall have your will of him tomorrow."

There was a pistol in the hand of him who thus claimed me, and Shunar hesitated.

"Jump up behind," said my mounted friend, in a low voice.

But whether this was taken for an evidence of fear by the bully of the camp, or that he now felt himself backed up by the gathering of a crowd, it was difficult to say, but he made a rush as the horse moved, and I barely missed getting into a regular fight.

It was evident, however, that no one there wished to seize the horse or come in contact personally with the rider, who, replacing the pistol in his belt, sounded the shrill yell of the country, and made his charger curvet through the mass which had surrounded us, who swore they would make us into small pieces when we should meet again.

The light of a fire now showed me the face of my new friend[5], who I could

---

5. My new friend: This is Christopher Carson, better known as Kit (1809-1868), and the description of the appearance of this celebrated mountain man and guide is interesting. Carson, though,

perceive as he sat before me was of much shorter and slighter stature than myself, his head, without other covering than waving locks of light brown hair, was occasionally turned to me as he carolled some stanzas to the air of Bruce's march, then much the fashion among the American boys, and showed a pleasant and open countenance, with blue eyes.

After a sort of parade round the camp, during which our horse's feet often got entangled in the cords of the others, and created considerable confusion as well as occasioned some abuse, we arrived at a lodge somewhat apart and near the grove of poplars which shaded the river, dismounting, we listened for a moment as we peeped through the crevices of the door.

There was a game of cards going on upon a clean apichimoe, by the light of a fire of pitch pine cut in small pieces, which continually fed, kept up a bright blaze, and there were several persons round a tin kettle of shrub.

"Bill, you are a confounded bore with your spitting," said an English traveler, who had come over from one of the other camps.

"I'll tell you what, Captain[6], the human race, that is the white people in Americay, are divided into two sexes."

"You don't say so!" said a voice.

"Shut up," shouted Bill, "they are divided into two sexes, one spits and the other doesn't, and has no call to spit. Now, those who spit will not be stopped by any Englisher, and will go on to the end of the chapter."

"Well done, Bill, is that out of your last stump-sermon?"

"And if it waar, more the pity."

"How so?"

"Because, had that not been a last sermon, there would have been less lost sheep down yonder, and fewer lost hosses up here, by a long sight."

"That's a fact," said Fitspatrick[7] gravely, who was playing at ucre[8],[ii].

Bill seemed uncertain of the import of this last assent, when we entered.

"Holla Kit," shouted three or four voices, and the cup replenished, and a fresh bunch of mint thrown into it, was immediately handed to us.

---

was not at the rendezvous of 1833. Stewart seems to have met him at the rendezvous of 1837 and 1838. DeWitt C. Peters has Carson recall Stewart thus: *For the goodness of his heart and numerous rare qualities of mind, he will always be remembered by those of the mountaineers who had the honor of his acquaintance* (Peters, *Life and Adventures of Kit Carson*, p. 23).

6. Captain: The use of the title Captain and the reference to *an English traveler* suggest that the complainer about spitting is Captain Stewart himself, and that this dialogue with Old Bill Williams is based on something actual.

7. Fitspatrick: Probably Thomas Fitzpatrick, (1799-1854), a leader among the mountain men from the early days of the mountain trade, later a partner in the Rocky Mountain Fur Company, still later a guide—for Frémont and DeSmet, among others—and an Indian agent. At this time Fitzpatrick was struggling, futilely, to pull the Rocky Mountain Fur Company out of debt, much of it to Sublette & Campbell.

8. Ucre: Euchre, a game with thirty-two cards which was the most popular card game in the United States before the introduction of auction bridge.

"Go it boys, I've got to finish this stranger tonight, or Shunar is to have the choking of him tomorrow."

"Come out of that a little faster than lightning, or I'll be upon you quicker," shouted Bill, as he struggled to get at Cotton[9], a curly-headed greenhorn of the last season, who was groping behind a saddle for the old trapper's medicine box.[iii]

"I wish you had stayed in your pod down South, no reasonable beaver would come to medicine, fingered by such a varmint."

"How's Rose, Bill?" said Kit.

"If she's not all right, it's not for want of people to look after her, there's a Swiss boy clings close, and Reece and Doty, and a lot like a string of beads."

"You mean a rosary," said the Englishman.

"And what if I do," said the crusty old trapper.

Mean time I had got some dried meat for supper, and the dried fruit of a sort of service tree, and a handful of biscuit root[10] to eat with the sun-cooked fat. I had never made so curious a meal, or one I enjoyed with more relish.

We were all bound next morning for the Snake Village and Bonneville's store, where the Generous Walker[iv] was lavishly kind to all comers, and near which I expected to find my comrades established, where it was almost time to get to rest.

Kit's horse was at the door, and having crept out of the circle, we again, as is customary in these camps for persons of condition, rode home on a prancing steed, Sipiot was still on the watch, and had well nigh shot at an Indian, who was skulking about.

Kit and I lay down together to be lulled by a slight murmur of the stream at a casual obstruction of rocks close to our simple bed. All the desire for reflection, which, however unhabitual to my age, ought to have been forced upon me by the forlorn situation in which I was placed, was put off when it crossed my mind by day, to that period when sweet sleep comes to lull, rather than foster thought, and however I had arranged to meditate in the deep stillness of the night, scarcely had the muscles of the limbs been relaxed, and the head searched out on its hard pillow the easiest spot to rest, when a gentle oblivion stole over the senses and care was suspended until it could thrust itself among the pursuits and occupations of the coming morn.

---

9. Cotton: Probably Cotton Mansfield, a little-known trapper who was a companion of Joe Meek and Kit Carson. In 1837 Carson seems to have saved Mansfield's life in a conflict with the Blackfeet (Peters, *Life and Adventures of Kit Carson*, pp. 20-21, and an illustration opposite p. 120).

10. Biscuit root: Edgeley W. Todd, in *Captain Bonneville,* says the biscuit root is *Lomatium cous.* The better known camas seems not to be indicated here. In *Altowan* (p. 141) Stewart notes *the kammas, which is of a sweet and glutinous nature...[and] the biscuit root, tasting exactly like a New York cracker newly baked.* Presumably *the dried fruit of a sort of service tree* in the previous phrase means service berries.

Chapter Thirty
The hand game—a mad wolf—face to face with Heald

It was high noon, the heights around the great plain were crowned by videttes, the vast herd of horses which were scattered over it were in the repose that a hot sun brings upon all the animals of the plains, a few Indians were scattered listlessly about, and a squaw, who sought a pack animal for bringing in wood for firing, or who required lodge poles from the younger growths of the forest, might be seen carrying out her saddle to search for her horse. A few children also might be found with their bows and arrows, practising at the turtles, the serpents, and the lizards, which they found in the way. But the aspect of the plain was that of tranquillity and peace.

The river here runs at the base of the mountains, and along its banks groves and thickets appear occasionally, where a former course has been abandoned, and its bed filled up. Among these groves and thickets, and along these banks the lodges of the Snakes and Utes were placed, without any attempt at regularity.

The trading house and camp of Bonneville was at the upper end of those which were scattered nearest to the river bank, and where the timber gave out. We rode through the plain, until we came toward the store, which was surrounded by Indians and whites, and amongst the rest, I perceived my friend Jim, who with Black-muzzle and Smith, were looking on at the purchases of some Indian squaws, the bucks, as the young Indian fops are called, were parading up and down the camp in all their bravery, the painted robes and shields, the household gods of each lodge, were hung out in their gaudy colors.

No wonder if the charms of Jacob had effect in other climes, and that the horses here were scattered about in every color and pattern, spotted, pyed, mixed, dun, yellow, red, blue, and violet, if they were at every moment surrounded by objects of the brightest and most varied hues.

"Hollo Doctor[1]," said Kit, addressing a good-looking man. "when did you come from the Crows?"

"About as long as you have been from the Wintey, I guess."

"And what luck?"

"Fairish, but lost a good number of traps, and well nigh my hair."

"What, they didn't much encourage you?"

"No, I can't say as they petted me unreasonably."

"And lots of braves?"

"Yes, baddish ground to ride, but fairish signs."

"And whar abouts?"

"Why near by where Fitz once saw a bull as big as the trading house."

"Of course."

"Are they giving things away here?"

"Right smart."

And the doctor proceeded toward a group of gamblers, who were seated in a circle, and chaunting the air which accompanies their game[2]. A small piece of carved bone, often taken from the body of the fox, was held by the gambler, who joining his closed fists together, one above the other, could thus pass it into either, he then separated them and threw his arms wide apart, singing and jerking his body up and down, and again bringing his hands together, and changing or pretending to change the bone, the gamblers choosing only when the hands were held wide apart, if the guess is right, the guesser pulls away his pile with that of the bone holder, previously arranged beside it, and if inclined a new bet is made, when the juggler or the bank, as he might be called, has nothing more to bet, he gives up the bone, or if the successful guesser chooses, he may, as is generally the case, take his place[i]. The scene is particularly animating from the exciting song and action, being joined to the deep and desolating passion of play. We looked on a minute, and Kit threw down a handsome dagger-knife, a considerable bunch of beads was placed against it, the youth who played had lost the dignity and calm usual to his race, his dark eyes flashed, and his body naked, but for a slight girdle round his waist, was jerked up and down from the hips with frantic eagerness, and his wild song rose high as he eyed the tempting stake. Kit having clapped his hands, and threw out the left, signified that the bone was to be found in that opposite, the

---

1. Doctor: Perhaps Robert *Doc* Newell, friend and frequent companion of Joe Meek.
2. Game: Here is a fine description of the bone game, a game of chance popular with Indians and trappers alike. Compare with George Frederick Ruxton, *Life in the Far West*, ed. LeRoy R. Hafen, Norman, Oklahoma, 1951, p. 101, Irving, *Captain Bonneville*, pp. 331-32, and *The Journal of Rudolph Friederich Kurtz*, ed. J. N. B. Hewitt, Washington, D.C., 1937, 200-01.

Indian opened the other where there was nothing, Kit had won, and drew back his knife and beads, making a sign that he did not wish to play, and the game went on. A young squaw of the Utaw tribe, who had lost everything of her dress to a scanty shirt, stood looking wistfully on, her small hands clasped, and her beautifully formed limbs crossed one over the other, she never took her eyes off the ring, in which her whole desires seemed to be concentrated. My companion threw the beads he had won at her beautiful feet, and with an almost imperceptible look of thanks for the gift, she flung them down again to be risked in the chance of the game.

"Where's the Doctor," said Kit, as after in vain attempting to catch her eye, he turned away.

"I don't know," I answered, "but is he a medical man?"

"He knows beaver medicine from horse dung," said Kit, laughing. "But why is he called Doctor then?"

"I believe he poisoned someone in the States by mistake, which is reason enough to call any man Doctor. The fools there talked of culpable homicide, or some other grand name, and the Doctor cut them, and brought his diploma up here."

The chief of the Snakes, Bracelet de Fer, sat near the distributor of alcohol and goods, behind a sort of bar or counter, he was a good-natured cunning-looking Indian, who did not much meddle with the more important affairs of the tribe, and contented himself with interfering in the intrigues of the women[ii], and the profits of trade.

From a dark corner of this emporium, a figure came toward me, whose warm greeting was not to be mistaken, though the darkness obscured his features, it was Jim Mackarey, bedecked in a blue capot, scarlet vest, and a white hat, my favorite mule was fat, and he had brought on all my pack safe.

The Swiss had gone to Diego's hiding place on the other side of the mountains, where he had followed their trail, in fact, Jim had seen nothing of them since leaving the Sweet Water, had himself got round the base of the mountain, and was now with the Bonneville camp. He had heard of Joe Heald's threats, and kept himself quite dark, stating the animals and goods with him to be his own, we accompanied him to his shanty, where we found a parcel of Indians hanging about, who disappeared at our approach.

"It is well you have come," said Jim, as I had hard work alone not to be plundered, they tried to pull everything about, under pretence of curiosity, and then abstract what they can.

Heald, it appeared, was out after meat. I rode to a spot a little up the river, where there was better grass, and where, with some other horses belonging to the Snakes, Jim's two and mine were grazing under an Indian guard.

On our return to camp, we found some of Campbell's party, who had returned with Phillipson, they brought news that a mad wolf had come into camp the night before, when most of its inmates were asleep, and bit several persons, and also a bull which was being taken up with some cows for the use of some trading fort on the Yellow Stone. The confusion and panic which this nocturnal attack had occasioned was described to have been very great, and as most of the persons who had been bit were lying down, the wounds were all in the head, and in one case, a man's ear, and part of his cheek had been torn off.

Bracelet de Fer had returned before, not without some feeling of contempt for the whites, who had been so completely dismayed by a single wolf[iii]. It was a white wolf, and the hour and direction of its course left no doubt that I had myself met this beast on its errand of death, and a shudder came over me, as I remembered the hanging jaw and the haggard eye.

While musing at the news of this disaster, which was to keep for some time in suspense the lives of so many, and which cast a gloom over all the whites, the doorway behind me was darkened by some new comers, and I turned to be confronted, face to face, with Joe Heald. We mutually gazed upon each other like wild beasts, and I felt for a moment the life blood rush back to my heart, but my eye did not fail me, and his, after a struggle, faltered, still expecting that his object was to rush upon me and make use of his great strength, I kept on my steady gaze, ready for the attack, while things were in this position, a form of great bulk inserted itself for a moment between us, but Heald shifted his position, so as to be again open, when Walker, for it was he, said, "What's the matter, Joe? You look savage."

"And not without cause, a man comes a horse stealing in the night, instead of saying what he has to say honestly in the face of day."

"I only took my own, and much less than my own, if accounts were squared."

"And who refused to square accounts? every one knows me—man and boy in Illinois, and I've credit here on the books, if I wanted it."

This was an indirect challenge as to character.

I felt that I had never done anything dishonest in my life, and had never thought of such a thing, yet I could refer to no one, and had I been arraigned in my own country, and had my cause depended upon producing testimony as to who I was and what I was, I should have felt it difficult to say, and impossible to prove. For a few seconds then, Heald's triumph was unopposed, and his disagreeable eye expressed a sinister satisfaction. I at last—for Heald's triumph, however short, I held to be all too long—broke out.

"I have come here openly, and paid my way, all your references to your state are useless to me, as mine would be to you, and as to credit here, I owe nothing, I have my hands and my head, and I can get as much credit as anyone else I suppose, who is new in the mountains."

"Well, you do acknowledge to be a greenhorn."

"I think no one but a greenhorn would have intrusted his property in your hands."

I had got the laugh on my side, and I could see that Walker had no wish that a friendless stranger should be bullied under his roof, and Heald perceived so also, and it is never wise to quarrel with a trader, until a considerable debtor in his books.

With what money I had over, and my animals and goods, I felt I was not in an unfavorable position for a start as a free trapper, and my object was to find out the best party with whom to associate myself, and penetrate into the more unknown haunts of the beaver and the otter, with those who best know the country.

Heald was one of those who had the most general knowledge of the best hunting grounds, without being himself a first rate or lucky trapper and though no one had any clear case of evading payment against him, he was a debtor to a small amount in every company's books in the mountains.

I was considering what was to be my line of conduct, and to what this dispute, though at present suppressed, might lead, while the crowd was thickening, and alcohol and beads were being diffused with a ready hand, when I felt my arm touched gently by someone behind, and I found my friend of Hell's Gate standing close to me. His deep and expressive eye invited me not to any demonstrative recognition, but I kept my eye upon him, and remembering that it is somewhere said, "knowledge is power." His presence seemed a protection.

Chapter Thirty-One
Snake Village described-arrival of Diego's band-spectacle and pageantry

It was evening, and Indians and whites were flocking back from the excursions of the day, whether those of hunting or pleasure, a war party had returned from the side of the Blackfeet country with scalps, the drum was beating, and the squaws and some of the braves had already begun the dance to its slow and measured music. The Snake camp was full, and the games of the young, as well as the grown-up, the shooting with the bow and arrow, as well as throwing an arrow like a javelin, diversified the scene, the bucks paraded in full paint, and the gamblers dotted with their groups the varied scene.

The sun was getting low, and the Arab-looking guard was already scouring round the outskirts of the pasture ground, and collecting such of the herd as had strayed, with the circling lasso and the wild yell, altogether, it was worth the journey, to wander unnoticed through the village of that noble nomads race, spread out on this plain, under the base of the great range which forms the backbone of half the world. I had gradually left the whites, and absorbed in what was passing around, hardly felt myself alone, wandering through the streets of lodges with their trophies and medicine hung out, the Lares[1] alike for protection and display, among hieroglyphic paintings, captured arms and scalps. While I roamed through this scene of a life, equally new and interesting, and the dogs barked at the stranger, a cloud of dust was rising in a continuous line at the lower border of the plain, and already there the eager eye of the Snake was strained, and those who had horses up, which it is the custom

---

1. Lares: In Roman mythology, household or tutelary gods or spirits.

of the rich to have ever ready at their door, were mounting and galloping forth to meet what seemed to be a gay cavalcade, who were prancing over the sandy prairie.

As I stood, a white horseman came past at a gallop, on his bare-backed steed, but pulled up as he saw me, it was Brent. "Jump up, and let us meet them."

My mood of contemplation was at an end, and full of the animal life of youth, I bounded up behind upon his impatient courser, and we sped on to meet the new comers, circling round, and performing such feats as were within the compass of the manage education of our steed, subdued to a certain degree with the double weight of his riders.

The party we found approaching was gay and gallant in trim, the horses were of every color, and the squaws who were with them, shone out in the most costly jewels of the land, and their housings and horse gear glared in flaming red, or dazzled with embroidered white, upon various colored and painted palfreys, while their admirers curvetted their running horses around to attract attention, and the husbands or fathers alone maintained the sedate demeanour which they wished to be an example to the joyous spirit of youth, so hardly to be restrained.

There was but one husband in all that group who rode not sedate and solemn, and there was but one squaw whose eye did not encourage some favored glance or covet some bounding steed. That husband was young Philipson, bright and fair, with his neck white as snow, exposed to the burning sun untanned, begirt with a sash of silk and decked in the holiday garb of agumbo ball, and his wife followed him, unheeding the costly finery with which she was decked, and never leaving with her eye, for a moment, the form she loved. And that other, whose eye searched not for conquest, nor sought to retain, who rode simply on her folded saddle-cloths, a platted rein guided her horse, a bow and quiver hung from her side, and whose seat was as firm, and hand as light and true as of the strongest man, and by whose side rode a noble-looking Spaniard, in his loose trowsers and sombrero, who was in animated conversation with Bernard. These were the personages I singled out as we circled yelling round, and it was from among a crowd, whose orbit was continually in motion, that I could see without being seen.

The first glance at that young squaw had made all my blood rush back to my heart. Was she the sister of my Indian of the Platte? And I urged Brent to circle nearer the group, but the crowd was thickening, and it was in vain I desired to approach, and they passed for the time onward on their way, a slue and a thicket now separated us still further from them, and Brent said, "Let us get back, and I'll mount a fresh horse and you another, to show ourselves anew when the band[i] comes in." So we stretched out on our return toward Bonneville's camp.

"We had best make our way good while we can," said my fellow-horseman, as the stout steed bounded under the rope's end that fell upon his flank. "I see the dust rising thicker, and we shall have the works upon us before long."

And, in effect, the setting sun shone in flames of red through the thickening atmosphere, in which the dust hung like a rising mist, the breeze had fallen, and occasionally the distant yell of a horse guard was heard, yet afar, as they collected the scattered groups, and further beyond might be seen a naked youth, discharging his gun behind the crowding throng, and waving the short robe he had taken from under him above his head.

I stood upon a little mound of gravel by the riverside, and looked out upon a scene, the like of which is only to be beheld in that wild land of the hunter, the squaws had been already busy in taking in the meat, which hung in festoons on bars to dry, and which had been brought in from the morning's hunt, alike to rescue it from the dust and the chance of being overthrown by the gathering rush, which was now drawing together into one mass, and behind which rose and spread as it came on, the curtain-like mist of fire, extended in all its gorgeous panoply of red, to veil the sinking sun.

Urged on from behind by the wild whoops, the dense charge came thundering on—the eye became bewildered, and the ear was stunned—the plain trembled, and it appeared as if the charge of five thousand horses must trample down everything living in the camp, as well as its abodes—the dogs howled, and rushed into the lodges for shelter, and as I looked out from my height to see everything overthrown and trampled under foot, as the headlong column tore onward in mad career, the dust changed in its color to a sober grey, had intervened to hide the general rout, and gradually thinning while I gazed, left but a gauzy medium, in which I could see the squaws and the boys tying up their horses, panting and snorting from the race, and apparently each stable congregated at its owner's door. The whole thing appeared more like the shifting scene of a theatre than a real event.

But it was time to look for my own in the throng, the lodges, which had appeared uselessly far apart before, seemed now to leave but sufficient room for the tying up of the animals between them, whose cords encumbered the ground. I could see no one I knew, and at last returned toward Bonneville's tents, where I found Jim had secured not only those he had had with him, but by means of the Indian horse I had taken with me, recognized the roan and the other as they followed him, I started to ride in search of the party which had just before arrived, and which could not be but Diego's. Brent had mounted his best runner, and was curvetting near, as if waiting for me.

"I want to show you the humours of the place," he said, "so come along." And we rode through the crowded streets.

It is a moment, in one of these villages, when every one is astir, those whose stud did not afford a horse to starve in his turn, tied ready at the door, could now parade about in all their bravery—a creek near supplies white and yellow clay, and the period is rich in vermillion, so the horses prance about smeared with the most brilliant hues, and toss their proud heads, as if glad in the sound of the human voice, while from the tail flies the falcon feather, the sign of speed, as from the only part visible when it is put forth, the distinction of the courser from the beast of burthen. The chiefs and the braves were riding forth, and often a friend jumped up behind, the more secretly to hold a confabulation, or the more lovingly to enjoy the society of a brother or a companion.

I had rode round that part of the camp which was next the river, and having discovered where Diego's lodge had been placed, I left Brent, in order to get rid of my horse and be more independent, and was returning toward the quarter, when something told me there was a strange riddle to solve regarding my young Indian friend. It was by the banks of the river I had to go, which is here broken into different courses, and rushes rapidly beneath the bushes on their banks. I had, in following their windings, often nearly to retrace my steps, and sometimes to intercept the secret conferences of lovers, or at my approach to cause a disappointment in some beating heart, my blanket, which I had thrown round me, was a sufficient disguise, and my head was bare. I bore it high, in a sense of newly acquired freedom, so that I should not be easily recognized in my mission of curiosity, and Indian-like, I stalked along.

It was on a grassy bank, close cropped and lined by a row of tall poplars, that I found myself, somewhat distant from the lodges of Bonneville and out of the way of those of the Snakes, it was nearly an island, and I had, in following the stream into its curve, almost lost my way, and while hesitating whether to pass over the narrow branch which lay before me, I saw a figure, apparently of a squaw, almost directly opposite, who appeared to be carrying a load of wood, and making evidently for camp. This seemed to show in which direction it was, and I turned to proceed in a parallel course, when I was met, where the stream took its reverse bend, full in the face by a figure closely muffled in a robe, we both stopped for a moment, so sudden the meeting in the narrow buffalo path through the thicket. There was no light to shine on a known face, and no voice to tell on a friendly ear, and yet one of those mystic instincts which communicate between certain persons, told me plainly through every fibre in my frame, that the Indian I sought was before me, and I held out my arms to embrace my wild friend with the ardour of real joy. We had never been, while together, in any state of emotion, there had never occurred anything to call forth any unusual demonstration of regard, but this meeting, so sudden and unlooked for, had destroyed all forms and reserve, and I strained my friend to my heart with unalloyed delight, neither of us spoke—my heart was full. A moment, and I felt the arms that in the first surprise had encircled my neck, withdrawn. The robe fell, and my fingers rested upon the beaded zone of a woman, as the gentle pressure of that soft hand tried to remove my embrace.

Chapter Thirty-Two
Rose revealed-introduction to Diego—a song for Rose

"This is foolishness," said my recovered companion.

"Are you then Rose, that I have taken for a boy?" said I, the truth flashing at last upon my bewildered senses.

"Would you have had me make myself your companion, had you known I was a woman?"

"And why not?"

"We must have quarreled, or you would have despised me."

I was silent.

"And would you have been happier had you known me?"

"No," I answered, after a moment's pause. "I would not have changed a thought I had, or a feeling I bore toward you then, for a province."

"There you remind me of the gulf which separates us, in that word *province*."

"And what gulf shall separate us now?" I said, impetuously.

I was about to take her again in my arms, as if to enforce my words, but she caught my hand, and said, "Listen. Do you know why I sought you tonight?"

I was silent, for I trembled that it should not be as I desired.

"To ask a boon of you."

I laughed clear and loud as I corrected her. "To give a command!"

"Be it so, for I know you will obey. We must appear never to have met before. There may have been some of the young people about camp who had taken my horse the first day, and no one knows of our journey together to the Red Buttes."

"But the medicine man," I interposed.

"Ah, but he is no gossip. Now, you are coming to see my father?"

"Yes, I was on my way."

"Well, in half an hour."

I wished to have taken her in my arms, but she slipped from my grasp with a quickness and strength which reminded me of some of our little struggles before.

"I will play with you like a sister," she said, "as we were wont in those—" she hesitated for a word.

"Oh, call them happy days," I said, imploringly.

"Well, and they were happy days," and the first tone of sorrow tinged that melodious voice.

"Is it a bargain?"

"Yes"—and she gave me her hand, and parting my hair, pressed her lips on my forehead—"and now for the present, *Brother*, good night."

I did not dare follow, as she bounded like a fawn through the deep shade.

I could be in no humor for companionship after such an interview, so I paced up and down the busy stream, and watched its black eddies and silver foam, as they shot swiftly by. Every thought was restored to harmony. The happy influence of joy diffused a balm over my misfortunes and my wrongs, and the half-hour that I lingered by the spot we had met and on the path she had trod, was one of those periods which—almost too presumptuous for hope, and too intense for imagination—I thought memory only could enjoy.

I stood by the entrance of Diego's lodge above the usual low door, the lacing had been loosened, and the sides thrown back on the adjoining poles, giving air and exposing the arrangements within, round the base of the inside hung a border of scarlet cloth, filling up the angle between the ground and the slope of the roof, and against this were ranged piles of blankets and robes, forming a sort of circular ottoman, in the middle, but near the door, blazed a fire of pine, and round the circle was passing the cup, whose costly contents made the entertainment one of extravagant hospitality. The dark Diego sat calmly in the centre of the crescent, and near the door, with a couple of squaws, was his daughter, the acknowledged flower of the western plains.

Crowds were riding up, and several horses stood by the lodge, whose cords were in the hands of the owners seated within, and many, seeing there was no room, were content to prance about, not to be unseen, if still unnoticed, by the fair ones within.

Crosseagle sang the Kosciusko song, which he finished as I came up, and then the voices of all were mixed up in a common din. Many had just met after a long separation, and news was exchanging from the Dardanelles[i] to the Sandwich Islands, from the church-going citizen of New England to the unbridled wanderer of Texas.

Meek charged up in cuirass[ii] and helmet. "A horse, a horse, a kingdom for a horse.[1]" And rushed past, looking for another Richmond.

"For what king, Besonia, speak or die," shouted Bill Williams, as he slapped me on the shoulder to arouse me from my trance. I turned to the old trapper, who led me, not quite unwilling, to present me to the master of the lodge.

It was, however, no easy task to penetrate the crowd, who, if not anxious to make acquaintance with the host, eyed with eager covetousness the handsome squaws, and the inviting goblet.

"By the mark, seven," said a sailor near the great kettle, as he sounded it as far as his long knife could reach, and dug his elbow into the side of his neighbor, a mild-looking, handsome youth, with yellow hair hanging over his shoulders, who seemed to take the joke.

"That is Mark Head,"[iii] said Bill in a whisper. "The best and most reckless trapper of these parts except one, but we must creep round behind, for they are packed like a nest of kettles, almost into one another."

We accordingly got round outside, and having lifted up the edge of the lodge, crept in from beneath the hangings. The host, who seemed to like Bill, received me very graciously, and after a moment's scrutiny, in the courteous phrase of Mexican greeting, told me his lodge and everything in it were mine.

There must have been something imposing in his manner, for I felt it, I remember well, as being the grandest reception I had ever met with, though under the disadvantage of the squalid position and boisterous mirth of all around.

Not having risen, there was a great part of the circle concealed by those who sat thick beside and before me. I quaffed of the cup of welcome, almost stunned by the noise of the carousal around, and hardly detaching from the converse of various languages the separate sense of any. My companion, instead of aiding me, helped the confusion like a polyglot, as I found Spanish, English, French, Snake, and Crow, mixed up in his voluble discourse, but the sound that interested me was the voice of Bernard, which came all at once clear and high above the din, in one of the wild songs of his mountain land, and was listened to with an attention which the fine execution and more beautiful air of the German who had preceded him failed to command. I leaned forward to try and catch the eye of my comrade, for a strange attraction seemed ever to draw me toward one who scarcely received my advances toward the renewal of former intimacy with graciousness, but I failed to get a sight of that part of the lodge, though I knew from the quarter whence came the sound that it must be near where the squaws were seated.

---

1. Kingdom for a horse: Meek is slightly misquoting Shakespeare (*Richard111*, V.iv.7), so is Bill Willams, in his shout (*Henry IV*, IV,iii.ll7).

I do not know what took old Bill, but he whispered to Diego something about a guitar[2] and a Spanish song, and a signal produced from among the squaws of the guitar with one or two broken strings, in the hands of Rose, who, beckoned by her father as if proud of the child he adored, bounded sylphlike over some of her companions, and getting through what had hitherto appeared an impassable throng, presented herself before him.

"A guest, my child," he said, pointing me out, and I felt the blood run back to my heart, as I looked up and saw that proud dark eye almost closed beneath its long lashes, which graciously bent upon me for a moment, was already calmly withdrawn.

Old Diego was busy with the guitar, and thinking he might let me do this mending for him, I took it from his hands. Whether he had intended to have touched it himself or no, did not appear, but after I had tied the broken strings and put it in tune, I would have returned it to him, but he said, "he must hope that I would let him hear me accompany myself. Do you know any Spanish song, for my voice is gone, and I should like Rose to hear the music of her father's land."

There was an old Spanish air which had been set to English words, but I had, from a strange liking for it, learned the Spanish as well, which though not so expressive, sounded better with the instrument for which they were made, the sound of the guitar in the few chords I struck, had created a silence and expectation, so I felt bound to comply and be done with it, as well as a secret desire to please her, who in my young delight, was the idol of my heart, and I began the air of *Meet me by moonlight alone*. I felt every word I uttered, and addressed the whole though looking up at the starry Heavens peeping through the opened roof, to that star I loved, to that flower, which among all others, I proclaimed their queen.

Old Diego embraced me, and there was almost a murmur of applause among those who hardly cared for any song in an unknown tongue, however, I felt it had been a success, and as if to indemnify themselves for these moments given up to song, out rushed again the pent-up words for a time suspended, and the Babel of before was commenced again.

---

2. Guitar: This is a very rare, perhaps unique reference to the presence of a guitar at rendezvous. See *Guitars for the Mountains, Museum of the Fur Trade Quarterly*, Vol. 19, number 4 (winter, 1983), pp. 4-15.

Chapter Thirty-Three
A promise of murder—a surround

The sinister look of Heald I saw for a moment, as he sat himself down near the door, and then I gave myself up to a complete absence of mind, and wandered back in not unpleasing memories of my intercourse with Fernwold, with unavailing regrets that his hard fate had not permitted him to come to this healthful clime. While thus following back the chain of events, which linked together in my short history my sorrows and my joys, and dwelling on the former with that strange feeling, which makes them a dear and constant theme, I saw a movement in the squaw's corner of the lodge, and as I still reclined on my elbow, with my head lower than those who sat up, the figure of Rose appeared through a momentary opening of the crowd, her eyes were fixed upon me, and they seemed to express, accompanied by a slight motion of the head, that she wished me to leave. There was no difficulty in withdrawing under the hanging behind, and it was not without the hope, that further off, on the way I had come, I might again renew a scene which there are few who would not have desired to repeat, but it seemed there was no such happiness in store for me, and I was with lingering tread winding my way toward Jim Macarey's abode, when someone's steps behind sounded in displacing the pebbles of a gravelly bedded shore now dry, and I turned to confront whoever it was.

"No one but a friend," said a cheerful voice.

"Ah, Harry, is that you?" I wrung the hand of my fellow traveler.

"I wanted to tell you," said he, "there is to be a great surround down near the river beyond Horse Creek, the Snakes have kept it quiet, but they find that the whites are always out, and have run off all the game, there is a band of cows, however, seen late this evening, and they want to make a clean sweep, it will be something to see, but they will be early astir."

I said, "Yes, and I'll be with you at the turn-out, and we can go together. Good night." He was in a moment lost among the bushes.

I pursued my course, keeping still out of the way of the throng, for I heard in the still night, when the hoarse voice of the stream was more remote, the beating of the drum for the scalp dance, and the song of the gambler, and the bay of the faithful watch. Suddenly, however, I came on the sound of voices quite close, and before I had time to turn away from taking the part of a listener, the words I heard arrested my whole attention.

"I've sworn to be his death, and when we get to the lodge, I'll take my oath again on the Bible."

"Mind what you say, someone will hear you," said a voice I did not recognize.

"I care nothing who hears, if half the camp come, I will take the oath before them."

I thought I knew the voice, but to make sure, and also to learn who was to be thus publicly doomed, I quickened my pace, and at the end of the brake, which had before separated us, joined the persons I had heard. The companion of the last speaker eyed me askance, as if thinking I had been an eavesdropper.

The other, who I found was Reece, said, "Where are you bound for, Ned?"

I answered, "Toward Jim Macarey's."

"Well, that lies near our quarters, so come along."

I saw he was flushed with the revel of the day, and we entered after a short time the lodge where Reece had taken up his abode, with some free men of inferior note as hunters, among whom I recognized Phelps and Joseph Gale[1], and the colossal Ruben Heron[2]. It was not long after our entrance that Reece reverted to the subject of his intended victim.

"You know the poking scoundrel who stands between me and Rose."

I answered by shaking my head.

---

1. Joseph Gale: Born in Washington, D.C., and orphaned, Gale (1807-1881) became a trapper in the Southwest about 1830. He trapped with Ewing Young out of Taos, was a member of Joe Walker's California expedition of 1834-35, and moved to Oregon in 1838. He settled there on the Tualatin Plains, also called Rocky Mountain Retreat, where he was joined by Joe Meek, Doc Newell, and others. See Kenneth L. Holmes, *Joseph Gale*, Hafen, D., *The Mountain Men and the Fur Trade*, VII: 107-19.

2. Ruben Heron: Valentine Johnson *Rube* Herring (1812-1883), born in Illinois, became a trapper in 1831 with John Gantt, and went on his own hook in 1835. He and his Hispanic wife, Maria (?) Nicolasa lived in the Hardscrabble-Pueblo area from 1845-49, and then moved to California. A sometime Mormon convert, Herring provided George F. Ruxton, Rufus Sage, and Isaac Rose with colorful material for copy. See Janet LeCompte, *Valentine Johnson (Rube) Herring*, Hafen, *The Mountain Men and the Fur Trade*, IX: 203-09.

"Aye, you were gone when that damned Swiss came in between us, but I'll throw him cold the very first chance. Rube, there, has got the book."

A discussion arose, but to humor the excitement under which Reece evidently laboured, Rube produced a dirty-looking Bible from the foot of an old stocking, and Reece, to my great horror, took his oath to shoot or otherwise destroy the Swiss the very first chance.

I got up and left them with a shudder but not before I had been authorised to inform Bernard that his days were numbered.

At early dawn the next day, I was mounted on the mule, and leading the roan, to join in that great hunt, of which I had so often heard, the Indian surround[3].

Whether the potations of the night before had kept most of the whites in bed, or whether they had not been informed of the event, I knew not, but there were few of them on their way to cover, that early morn, and the few that appeared, shone not as wont in ruddy health, as they almost unwillingly came leading their running horses quietly along, unlike the meet of foxhounds in old England, where the circumstances of the cover side, and the triumph of the find make the most striking picture, and the spirit of the chase is conjured forth by means which here would be wanting in their effect. Le Blanc was on his packhorse, and as the one he led looked forward over the low intervening ridge and pricked his ears, and snuffed the morning air, the old Canadian cried out "Il dit vrai[4], il dit vrai." He leaned over, caressed the impatient steed, and this was the first note of animation of the meet. We had been somewhat later than our Indian friends, and as we came along, were mixed up with the old men and the squaws with their pack horses to bring in the meat which the slaughter of the day was to produce. But on crowning the height, a long line of red hunters were to be seen to the right, down parallel to the river and another to the other hand progressing at a right angle, the wind being right a head between the two, these forked lines were headed by the swiftest runners, who as soon as they should be getting to a point sufficiently beyond the herd, were suddenly to converge, and those in the rear coming up, were to form a complete band round the herd, which getting the wind, would be set in motion, and the onslaught would then commence. This species of hunt is intended alike to secure a large supply of meat, and to protect the bison from

---

3. Indian surround: This description of one of the standard Indian methods of making meat conveys the excitement of the surround and is filled with good detail. The story about the white bull may have originated during Stewart's final trip to the West in 1843. William Clark Kennerly, along on that jaunt, said that he and a companion saw such a beast and attempted to kill it, but failed. *These white buffalo were as scarce as white elephants, and we had only encountered one man in all of our travels who had ever seen one* (Kennerly, *Persimmon Hill: A Narrative of Old St. Louis and the Far West*, Norman, Oklahoma, 1948, pp. 157-58).

4. Il dit vrai: French literally meaning, *He speaks truly*, idiomatically, something like *He's telling us*.

that harassing and continual depredation which the system of individual hunting practiced by the whites inflicts upon them, and which has since driven the game off from the Snake country.

The herd was yet unroused when I got to the height, from which could be viewed the black mass, apparently about fifteen hundred, quietly feeding, and I dismounted from my mule, forgetting that I had no one with whom to leave her, when Smith, with kind consideration, took charge of her, making her over to an old Snake, who had come out behind another, but was now afoot, while this was going on, a total change had come over the spirit of the dream, the black herd was enveloped in a white cloud, the flanking lines had contracted, and the dusty mass was instead of going up wind, diverging from the taint of unseen danger and came wheeling suddenly backward, and having found itself hemmed in on one side, was madly charging toward the other through the dust, and before it had time to rise above the level of a horse's back, were seen the forms of the Indian hunters as if borne on its surface, their long hair floating, and the arm continually raised to deliver the arrow or point the lance, outside were individual conflicts, where a single rider was dashing up to a bull broken out from the band. Horses were already upset and gored, by a toss of the head of an enraged victim, and one or two cows in the prime of grease, had been got out of the throng, each keenly followed by a pursuer.

It is impossible to describe the total change of scene during the few minutes I had been occupied behind the butte. The mule was forgotten, and all else, as I rushed into the field, gravel, and dust flew everywhere, and races and combats filled what had now become a vast confusion, those worse mounted playing the part of Tauridors[5], held their wounded quarries at bay, and as ammunition or arrows were exhausted, sometimes on foot attacked the dangerous and maddened bull with the knife. My first shot told on a cow, but I hurried on, leaving her to those who might pick her up, a ball was in my mouth, and when the powder, which I measured in my hand, was in the barrel, so much of it stuck to the wet ball, as to prevent it rolling out when lowered for the next discharge[i]. Again I fired, but I got impatient of this kind of sport, the effects of which were not to be seen, I longed for a bow and arrows, that I might see the shaft stick, and the barb, drawn in by every heave of the lungs or movement of the body, eat silently its way to some seat of life. And again a monster cow was before me, and I broke her down in her tracks by a shot in the back, and felt myself flung over my horse's head into the middle of the throng. Happily, my riding cord was under my belt, and I gathered it as my horse struggled to his feet, the cow was still in the use of her head and forelegs, and it was well I had been pitched so far, as with bloodshot eye she tossed about her head in impotent rage. But the pause protected my

---

5. Tauridors: Toreadors.

prey, no one of the followers touch any animal you remain beside, or by which you leave a mark, several looked wistfully as I was preparing to remount, but at last I discovered my mule, with the old Indian, in search of some worthy spoil. But all that I remarked was a stout lance in his hand, and upon that I pounced, giving him my gun in exchange, he equally eager about the meat, which seemed that of a barren cow of the first class.

I was again in my saddle, it was now about to be a joust, and knight-like, I surveyed about me the increasing dust and tumult, though most of the animals had wheeled round to another side of the ring, it became now for me a series of separate conflicts, and my horse was getting somewhat dead in the mouth when I felt the rein, and I slackened his speed for a moment, to breathe him, as well as to pick out something better than indiscriminate slaughter.

There was a white bull known to be in the country, and in an open of the herd, I saw for a moment what I at first took for a horse, rushing across to try and break into the mass in which he was, while my attention had been thus attracted, the roan, as I thought, kicked suddenly up behind, and then faltered a few steps and fell. I had but time to see the mighty black and shaggy head, as intent on further destruction, it plunged toward me, my lance caught him on the neck behind the horns, and we all rolled together on the plain. I dared not look at my gallant steed, his groan of agony was sufficient to tell his fate, but I plucked the weapon which had been stuck with some force in the bull's vertibrae, and ensconced behind the huge mass, which had fallen with the legs doubled under it, and resting on its chest, the shoulder, as high as my chin, waited for some chance of extricating myself. At last, through an interval of dust, I discovered my mule and the Indian butchering, and the first moment I thought there was a chance of not being trodden under foot, I was by his side, and the next the mule was bearing me again into the panting throng, which with mouths open and tongues hanging out, were still being followed by their exterminating pursuers.

Chapter Thirty-Four
An admonition-Bernard warned-unhorsed

Still in search of this white bull, whose vision I had seen, if not himself, I was galloping on the flank of the diminished band, when I was overtaken by a horseman, of whom I took at first no notice, but finding something like pertinacity in the manner in which he hung at my quarter I looked round, and found it was my medicine friend, his dark and serious eye unlit by any ardor of the chase, was fixed steadily on me, and I involuntarily checked my pace.

"Have you seen Bernard," he said, and there was something strangely earnest in his words.

"No!" I answered, not caring to stay my sport, but remembering the oath of Reece. I added, "Why do you ask?"

He must have noted some interest in my manner, but said nothing, I then hurriedly narrated how Reece had sworn to destroy him, and my intention to warn the intended victim of his danger.

At this moment, again I thought I saw the white phantom ahead, and I shot forward, a wounded cow struggling on the ground made my companion's horse swerve, but he held up his hand and called to me,

"Inform him of nothing, leave him to his fate, your own—"

I could not hear the remainder of his words, but I felt that every duty enjoined me to act contrary to the warning of this strange man, and I was the more eager to warn a stranger, who seemed to have already made too many enemies, and for that reason, instead of undivided attention to the hunt and all its furious interest, I was allowing my eye to wander among the runners and among the groups around, who watched for such animals, as driven to desperation, fled like projectiles from their circling orbit.

The spirit of the chase had to a certain degree subsided, the ground was encumbered with the killed, while the wounded held out to the young followers of the hunt, opportunities seldom neglected of practicing the art of Tauridor, and inflicting a slow death of torment upon animals already incapable of making their escape. The young savage, as he is called, having a total disregard to the pain he inflicts, it must be admitted also, despises that inflicted upon himself. The young white, as he is taught, contrary to his natural bent, to spare from pain the fly or the helpless bird, is also carefully learned to feel acutely such hurts as scarcely would be noticed in a less finely tempered nervous system.

There was a broken watercourse through part of the ground, upon which this strange and exciting scene had taken place, its sides were steep, and in some places it had broken through the indurated clay, leaving a perpendicular bank or precipice, under which the eating course of the torrent ran when swelled from the melting snow, leaving a bed continually filling up from the crumbling banks above, for a flood again to undermine, but in which there was now but little water—here stood a mighty bull at bay, the shaggy hair of his deep chest almost touched the ground, he was not of the long-headed breed of bison, but of the larger wide-horned and broad-fronted race, the inhabitants of the higher plains, with longer manes and greater speed and strength than the other. Around him, on the open side, was a half circle of youths, but in front of them was a white man, to whom they seemed to have left the task which he had undertaken, of finishing him with his knife.

"You will never get in upon him from before," I hollowed, as I saw the mad attempt, and leaving my mule, rushed to save the Swiss—for I saw it was he—from certain destruction. But instead of having the effect of a warning, my words only seemed to be a stimulant, and he was in the act of trying to get round, after having thrown his capot as a lure, when the enraged animal made a rush forward, and only missed by a few inches falling upon his opponent. It was now my time, and I dashed in behind, and with one sweep cut one hamstring and so weakened the other, that the monstrous beast fell.

Bernard's countenance at once showed his anger at my interference, he did not speak, but turned away, and getting on his horse was hastening off.

Leaving the prostrate buffalo to his fate, I mounted my mule in pursuit, as I saw his horse, urged to his speed, dash into the diminished herd, the loading delayed him until I had time to come up. On seeing me, he again, trusting to his horse's swiftness, made off to avoid me, but the mule was to be left behind by few horses of these parts, and I was not long—cutting across a double—in overtaking him, still he seemed uninclined to attend to me, though I shouted to him that I had something to say, however, I was at last alongside.

"Don't let us lose the whole day, listen to me a moment," I said, as I laid my hand on his arm, in one rushing speed.

"Well, out with it, then, or let me alone. I don't want your help," he said, without looking round.

"I don't want to help you, but to warn you. Reece has sworn to shoot you the first opportunity."

"What, you believe that also?" he said, turning round. "And why not let him? I should be out of your way."

"I did not know you were in my way," I said.

"We will see," he answered.

"Not if he gets a chance at you, for he has sworn it as publicly as if he meant to do you a favor, and on the Bible, if he respects that, so keep the open plains and the broad day, or you will be but a small potato before long."

I left him to take his own course, but I saw that my words were not unheeded, and was so far relieved from my apprehensions respecting this ungracious youth, toward whom I could never bring myself to feel the indifference his churlish and almost hostile manner would have inspired on the part of another.

We had not got out of the ring formed round the devoted herd, scattered and exhausted, there was still a considerable number in useless flight or desperate resistance, but by degrees those who had hitherto hemmed them in had mingled in the fray, and there were beginning to be escapes from the surround.

Again I thought I saw the phantom-bull, but it was only one whitened by having rolled in a slough of white clay, but he was a grand animal, and had hitherto kept where the masters of the band always shelter themselves, in the center of his harem. Seeing an open toward the south, the point farthest from camp, he was galloping away with that high gait which, until hard pressed, is the action usual to the animal.

He was on a wind which blew a gentle breeze from the mountains, and no Indian had as yet started to pursuit, my mule was comparatively fresh, and I slackened the rein, his course was toward the trail, and we were below where the Piney Fork enters the Susquedee[1], the ground was a rolling prairie, covered with dwarf sage, and a low ridge running parallel to the mountains repelled and collected two or three of the torrents coming from them, which we had crossed on the trail to rendezvous, and turned them almost at right angles into the river, this accumulation of waters at last receives the Piney, and is for some distance clothed with wood.

---

1. Where the Piney Fork enters the Susquedee: Stewart seems here to mean the area near present Daniel, Wyoming. As evidence see Field, *Prairie and Mountain Sketches*, p. 139, where Field notes: *We were encamped upon the edge of a magnificent mountain lake [Frémont Lake—ed.] at the head of Piney Fork, one of the streamlets marked as* New Forks, *in the map of Lieut. Freemont [sic]*. Field refers to the Frémont map of 1842, reproduced in Jackson and Spence, eds., *Frémont*, map portfolio, map 2.

The last I saw of this bull was going over the ridge which forms the left bank of the waters I have mentioned, I plunged down a less steep part of its side, but instead of the bull came upon a bear, whose almost white sides made it, for a moment, doubtful to me what he was,[i] not so the mule. We were going down a steep descent at a gallop, and as soon as she perceived our common foe, who was making down in a direction that would cross us a little below, her back was humped up, and as I swayed a little to one side, to avoid a strong branch in the way, a succession of bounds and kicks-up, which would have thrown a horse a somersault, sufficed to throw me, taken off my balance, over her head.

I did not lose my consciousness with the fall, though pitched a considerable distance, but without being able to recover myself or check the impetus with which I was propelled, was plunged over a cliff concealed by bushes into the water below.

Why the bear preferred the mule to me, I did not wait to inquire, my rifle would have sunk me, had I not found bottom in a single plunge, for I clung to it in the way men with less need are said to cling to straws. A moment, however, I looked back, the stream ran a deep blue under the rocks, and of a considerable breadth before it shoaled, and I owed my escape from drowning to the struggles I had made, before coming over, to recover my feet, and a bound had carried me well into the current below.

The mule had escaped in some way, and I saw her speeding across toward the mountains, in a way which left no chance for me, on foot, to overtake her.

Chapter Thirty-Five
Concealment—a rattlesnake—a corpse

Thus had I gone out that morning in possession of the best horse, as I believed, in the mountains, and undoubtedly of the best mule, and was now, having lost my roan, with my mule run off, and with a wet rifle, in the midst of every kind of danger. There was no use, however, in reflections, the object was first to dry my arm, and then to try and find someone to go after the mule. The drying of the rifle was not so easy a matter, it was necessary first to draw the ball in case of accident, then to prick the nipple and fill it with dry powder. My horn was sufficiently water-proof for the short immersion, the few grains introduced into the touch-hole were exploded by a flint and steel, which operation was repeated until it communicated with the charge, which at last went off, a little tow, changed when wet, in time dried the barrel and breech.

During all this time it was with an anxious eye I covered all the ground within sight, and listened, with an ear distended to a sensitiveness at which no professor or even critic of music ever arrived. But I was armed, and though on foot, I felt not unconfident of the power to protect my life, and there was but little more apparently left.

As far as I could guess, it was some twelve or fifteen miles to the Snake camp, but it was still some two hours to noon, and if there was any haste, it was to send after the faithless mule, who had cast me off to escape danger to herself.

Meanwhile, sundry animals seemed to be forced in the same direction I had taken, and presently, a few Indian scouts appeared, and then a troop of warriors, some naked and smeared with black, others in full gala costume, painted and plumed and armed to the teeth. The first scouts I did not recognize, I had hid myself, to try and knock over some of the flying herd—wedged between two blocks of stone, with some sage in front.

I lay perfectly concealed, unless to someone on foot looking closely under every bush. The party, for it was evidently a party of some force, moved at a rapid pace, and happily did not ride over the ground where I lay.

I could not tell that they were Snakes, not having recognized any individual, but I saw there was something more serious than a mere parade or a surround. The course was such also as to show no decided line, as it was in a direction to gain the trail at the foot of the mountains, and indicated neither a tendency toward the rendezvous nor a flight from it.

These parties, like the light troops of an army, assume a certain license, and to use a homely expression, everything is fish which comes into their nets. Of this, I was well aware, and rejoiced to see them pass, but the heights were all crowned with videttes, and I felt assured that the main body was concealed in some hollow not far off. It was my doom, therefore, for the present to remain, and I should have passed the time uncomfortably enough had it been cold, but the sun shone upon me, the soil was as dry as tinder, and I fell into a profound sleep.

Just as I began to doze, I felt something move through the fibers of the sage-bush which served me for a pillow, but feeling secure, and also being certain that it would be rash to move, I yielded to the peaceful drowsiness which this comparative security inspired, and let myself fall over in that mood of not knowing whether I might ever awake again, with as much calm as a man could throw down a stake at play, which it was indifferent to him, from its smallness, whether he should win or lose.

It was at first a dead dreamless sleep—a complete loss of life, as far as the spirit is alive—though a feeding and strengthening balm to the animal man, but that need being satisfied, a certain consciousness became the prelude of returning life, and I again felt the sensation of something moving through the bush which bolstered my head, it appeared but a moment since I remembered the first perception of the same kind, and I felt somewhat provoked at its early repetition.

The sun, however, which had shone warm upon me before a little from the direction of the feet, had now passed round, and was almost got behind my head, this brought me round to a certain consciousness, I sat up leaning on my elbow, the sun was low, no living thing appeared to move, I was alone as far as I could perceive, but in rousing myself, I had displaced my pillow, and the clear rattle of a snake sounded close as he coiled beneath.

Not having anything but a cotton shirt on my breast or arms, it was not likely I should feel secure from a bite, I shuddered in that pause, which in such near contiguity was anything but fascination, but is the best means of dispelling the fears of the reptile of being himself trampled upon or crushed, saved me, I believe, in this case, for after eyeing me for a few seconds, he crawled away under a stone, which appeared to be his usual abode, and in gratitude I did not attempt, as I might, to destroy him.[i]

I had learned a sort of code to prevent waste of life in hunting, and in regard to noxious animals, I felt that the snake would have no desire naturally to attack man, whom he could not devour, and that, if not in dread of his own destruction, he could never wantonly be the aggressor, unless prophetically knowing that the presence of the master of the animal creation boded the ruin of his race. Suffice it to say, that I have since lain watching a herd of bison, of whom only some lean ones were within reach, and not daring to disturb them, could not move from a prostrate position, and a rattlesnake was coiled within striking distance of my head. We lay looking at each other, and I remained in possession of the field, at another time, I have been stopped in a buffalo path, until time was given the reptile to get away[ii].

But I am diverging from the thread of my narrative.

The camp was at some considerable distance, and I had still light enough to get to the Susquedee, having only to cross one feeder on my way, which could not be far distant.

There was occasionally a well-beaten path along the stream, and I arrived at and crossed the Piney fork. Here I came upon a wolf-feast going on under the commencing twilight, little seemed to remain of the carcase but the head, and they slunk away with their coward gait and disappeared, my feet were getting sore from the wearing of my moccasins, and opportunely I remembered having been shown by Rose in those happy days when she played so well the part of a boy in courage as well as woodcraft, what comfort it was to stuff the moccasin with hair from the scalp of a bull.

To this resource the wolves had done no injury, and there was abundance of hair for all my wants, and I was not long of making use of it.

The way was clear, and I steered my course to strike the river just below Campbell's camp, and crossing it, proceed by the shortest cut to the Indian village. All this I accomplished, and it was well on in the night, but the sounds of the drum and the chant of the scalp dance had ceased, and as I neared the outskirts of the lodges I hesitated, not knowing how far it might be safe to intrude at such an hour. At intervals the howl of the medicineman over the sick rose in the night air in mournful wildness, but there was no other sound.

It was not difficult to keep round to the right, and pass between the river and the main body of the lodges, and I took that line. Diego's lodge lay in my way, but it was silent, and scarcely a gleam of light shone through the joinings of the door, however I might have desired to enter, I felt that it would be an indiscretion, and I lingeringly passed on, but there was nothing to prevent my going by that spot where I had been made acquainted with the sex of my

Indian companion, and first could read the signs of that strange attraction the supposed youth had for me.

The Susquadee had its eddy yet by the spot which still boiled silently under the branches on its brink, and the light, cold foam still whirled in mockery at the unceasing eagerness of the contiguous stream, itself ready to be dissipated or carried off into that rushing course, which was but to be stopped by the distant ocean.

I know not why I lingered on that spot, the memory of it to one who had the hope of a renewal of the scene it witnessed need hardly, under the circumstances I now found myself in, have caused me to dwell upon it, but I looked at all I saw around, the trees, the mountains, and the stream, as if to call them to witness my former bliss, and to feed my memory until such a scene might come again.

Fatigue and hunger, however, are not co-partners with romance, and I already had taken the first step toward my destination, when some dark object seemed to encumber the path, and I stooped to ascertain what it was. I had heard much of death, but never had seen it, and a body, cold and stiff, lay before me, the pale visage looking up to the stars, and the hands stretched out on either side, which had been grasping the grass and the underwood in the last agony, I felt the clay-cold countenance, and then for the beating of the heart, but it was still, but a sticky and clotted moisture left the dark stain of blood on the hand I drew back, which with a shudder I wiped on the leaves of the thick bushes near. I stooped down, the eyes stared wildly open, the mouth was but slightly contorted, the stature was that of middle height, the hair was long and brown. In that light there was nothing for a stranger to recognise, but a small embroidered pipe-case[1] was suspended round the neck, I took out the pipe, and thought I remembered a small red stone carved in a peculiar way, I had somewhere seen it before, there was also a red silk handkerchief tied round the head and over the brow. A vague feeling came over me that I ought to know these tokens, but the memory of them was not to be awakened on the first call.

I began to reflect that I could not bring the dead to life, and that my being there was not in itself more likely to convict the guilty—if foul play there had been—than to inculpate the innocent, so I moved on, not quite at ease at having such a crime as a supposed murder in my keeping.

---

1. Embroidered pipe case: The pipe and tobacco case Alfred Jacob Miller calls the *gage d' amour* (See Ross, *The West of Alfred Jacob Miller,* note to plate 1, plate 29). The red stone pipe Stewart mentions is probably of Catlinite. Many observers noted the use of clay pipes by mountain men. See Field, *Prairie and Mountain Sketches,* in which a photographic plate opposite p. 171 shows George W. Christy wearing such a case around his neck.

Chapter Thirty-Six
The mule recovered-the murder discovered—council with medicine man

Justas I neared Macarey's shanty, I had to pass the lodge, where the previous night I had heard the threat against the Swiss, and the first feeling I had was to examine my memory. Could the dead body be his? But he was taller and darker, and had but a slight beard—that of the dead man was partially shaved, but what remained was strong and characteristic.

I paused and looked in, nearly the same persons were there as before, but one was absent.

Had Reece gone out on his declared mission? It was thus I began to reflect on what might have been remarkable about the dead body, and it was not without a start that I remembered the handkerchief, and the appearance of him who had sat there, high-colored and swarthy, not twenty-four hours before, impiously swearing upon the holy Book that he would destroy his fellow-man. It was he I had seen cut off in his prime, the pallor of death more ghastly pale by the light of a waning moon.

I felt convinced now, and passed on. Macarey had not come in. I struck a light, and finding some cold boiled meat, made a hasty though not a hearty meal, and threw myself on my bed.

Some meat, probably brought in from the surround, was hung over a tripod, it was a magnificent depouillie[1], lined with three fingers of fat at least, so I saw they had had the news of the hunt and of my loss, but as well as having lost my horse, I had for the present also been deprived of my saddle.

---

1. Depouillie: A *depouille*, according to John Francis McDermott, *A Glossary of Mississippi Valley French, 1673-1850*, is *Buffalo tallow, the layer of fat under the skin along the backbone*.

The hunt had been performed, as far as my ill-fated roan was concerned, barebacked according to Indian fashion, and I had to lay a couple of logs, and cover them with a piece of folded skin, to form a pillow, and I cannot say I felt sufficiently impressed with the sight I had just seen to keep me long from sinking into complete oblivion[i].

Next morning the boys were all early abroad, and someone had caught my mule with Campbell's band, and both she and the saddle, &c. were forthcoming. This was so far good news, but we also heard that four more persons had been bit by the white wolf, and that all the camps proposed to move very soon.

Meanwhile strange scenes had taken place, as I afterward learned, in Diego's lodge, and as I went out to get my saddle, and take the truant mule to the band, I met old Bracelet de Fer close to his lodge, as if busied by some important news, he had in his hand the rifle of a white man, and the horn and bullet pouch. He stopped me, and pointing to what he carried, made a sign of the owner being dead, by closing his hand and turning down the knuckles, and pronouncing the word *Tabibo*[2], making me also understand that he was on his way to Bonneville's store to report.

It seemed the body I had seen had been found by some Indian, who, fearing to appropriate the arms to his own use, had related the circumstance, and had delivered the rifle to his chief.

I kept my own council, I had no friend near of whom I could ask advice, and I did not feel possessed of that avenging spirit, which characterises the public of England, where the vindication of the law has become a passion. There is no more generous or forgiving character in the world than that of an Englishman, individually wronged, and no more savage bloodhound in bringing to trial or punishment, those accused of wronging or injuring others.

It was near midday, it had been a party of Arapahoes[3] who had come near the rendezvous from their village, which had come to the neighborhood of Snake River, a couple of days' march further down. There had been some horse stealing on the part of the Mauvais Gauches band of Snakes, and they had followed them, and would have made reprisals, but for finding so many whites about, who would not quietly submit to any injury in the mêlée, and they had retreated without making any attempt, but a war party of the Snakes having no such reasons for restraint, had that morning gone out under the

---

2. Tabibo: Apparently Stewart's transcription of the Shoshone word for *white man*.
3. A party of Arapahoes: Perhaps a band of Atsina, also known as the Gros Ventres of the Prairie, who lived and allied themselves with the Blackfeet and were also affiliated with the Arapahoes proper, who lived in modern Colorado. When the Gros Ventres periodically visited the Arapahoes, they preferred the route down the Green River valley (Chittenden, *History of the American Fur Trade*, II: 852). And Chittenden says that no Indians called Arapahoes *are ever spoken of as dwelling in the northern mountains. When the Arapahoes are mentioned the tribe in the valley of the South Platte is always meant* (II: 878).

Little Chief, to make such a demonstration as might induce the other village to retire from their hunting grounds, and leave them to be pillaged only by the whites. But as I was from different sources collecting this intelligence, I recognised my medicine man, who stood looking fixedly in my direction. I was too glad to profit by his knowledge, not to seize the opportunity he offered.

"You told the Swiss, notwithstanding," he said, as soon as I was within reach.

"We were old friends," I answered, "and I could not do otherwise."

"It has made no difference, but you would have been freed from him sooner."

"And why?"

"I will tell you at a more fitting time, that fool Reece has caught the fate he deserved."

"But by whose hand?"

"I suppose by his whom he swore to sacrifice, Joe Heald, however, has doubts."

"Ha, does he mix himself in it?"

"Yes! but Diego has gone off for the Crow country at dawn, and you will see the avenger follow, so keep quiet till you hear further." And he passed on.

Chapter Thirty-Seven
On trial for murder-a verdict of guilty?—
sentenced to be hanged

I felt that I might be compromised, had anyone seen me pass by the spot where the body lay, it was an uneasy thought, and I turned toward the shade of the trees, where the river ran, to reflect upon what I had best do, whether openly to declare what I had seen, or abide the result of things as they were.

Most of the Americans had gone down to the other camp, and I had climbed one of the bluffs across the river from which there was a view of the bustle below, it was a scene to dissipate anything like care, and I gazed tranquilly down on all that array of busy life. While thus occupied, I was accosted by a squaw, who made me understand by signs, that she had seen me the night before near where the white man had lain, this news at once broke up my reverie, it was as I had feared, and I came down determined to court inquiry, and know the worst at once. I came down to find every one gone, the body lay, I was told, in Heald's lodge, and was to be buried as soon as some inquiry could be made as to the cause of his death. Old Bill Burroughs[1] remained by it, and a blanket was laid over, and a piece of white cotton beneath, intended to be used as a winding sheet. I came into the lodge, Bill seemed astonished, and asked me what I wanted, I answered to see poor Reece's remains, and I lifted the blanket, and took the lifeless hand, the ball I found had taken effect under the armpit on the left side, and had passed clear through the body, the face

---

1. Old Bill Burroughs: This trapper, whose last name is also spelled Burrows, is little known, but he was sketched by Alfred Jacob Miller in 1837—see DeVoto, *Across the Wide Missouri*, plate LXXVIII.

was little changed, though a certain blackness was beginning to gain upon it about the eyes, which had acquired a sunken and withered stare, it was altogether not an agreeable sight, especially to one who never saw a human being dead before, save in the cloud of night. I dropped the hand. Burroughs, who had a certain portion of mint julep before him, gazed at my proceedings with some wonder, and I walked away in quest of someone to consult.

It was evident the squaw, who was young and handsome, and the wife of John De Villie[2], had not been out alone, and it must have been to her companion I owed the testimony which implicated me, still there was no one in Bonneville's camp, and I was left in that disagreeable solitude, which not even conscious innocence can bear with equanimity, at last I resolved to place myself under the protection of Captain Walker, and proceeded to the store for that purpose. I explained to the worthy Captain what I had seen the night before, and why I had determined not to mix myself in it, he heard me patiently, and said, he did not think there was any proof as yet, but that as far as he could he would see fair play, and invited me to stay where I was in the mean time.

It was not long before several of Reece's friends came back from the other camp, and some looking in, left again in ominous silence, more arrived, and I could see groups talking together, at last half-a-dozen made their appearance in the store and passed round behind the counter, and then as many more, it wore all the appearance of a trial, there were twelve men, and then in came Joe Heald and Doty with Phelps, who being the senior trapper present, took upon himself the office of judge. Doty had been the comrade of the deceased, and acting as prosecutor, at once accused me of his murder, stating that jealousy was the probable cause of the act, he himself having heard me threaten him, and seen me coming out of the thicket where the body had been found in the morning, and by a path bordered so thickly by wild rose bushes, that there was every reason to believe that I could not but have known that the body was there, that he had seen me look suspiciously round, and go stealthily away, crouching beneath the bank, when the way was open. He had passed the night in a sort of shanty made close by, and no shot had been fired after, or he must have heard it, and the murder must have taken place there, as it was as he described it, *a centre shot, from which there was no walking away.*

This was the case for the prosecution, and I was called upon by Phelps for my defence.

I stated that I was innocent, that all that Doty had said was quite true, accounted for my being so late by the loss of my mule, and declared that I had

---

2. John De Villie: John De Villie (?-?) is little known but may have been the John DeVillier employed by William H. Ashley in 1827. See Dale L. Morgan, ed., *The West of William H. Ashley*, Denver, 1964, p. 172. Stewart later (p. 216) seems to spell this name DeVilder.

no enmity to the murdered man. I had no more to say, stating that I neither begged mercy nor fair play, I did not choose to suppose guilt in the first place, and hoped that there was no reason for doubt in the second.

Phelps asked the jury for their verdict, it was some time, and during a breathless silence, before the foreman asked to retire, they went out into the open space in front of the door, and sat themselves down in a circle, even the Snake children, respecting the talk of the white men, held suspiciously aloof. Within, Phelps smoked with an air of indifference, if not of impartiality, and Walker once interrupted my thoughts, which were far away, by asking me if I could recollect nothing more to exculpate me. I could but shake my head, a period was about to be put to my adventurous fate. I had not even the satisfaction of complaint in point of justice, I had threatened Reece, and bade him take care of himself, when he had sworn to destroy the Swiss, and I had been seen stealing out of the patch of covert in which the body had been found, and I had to no one mentioned that I had seen it, all the facts to constitute circumstantial evidence were against me, and I felt that my doom was sealed.

The jury returned, and of all the persons comprising it, not one seemed unmoved.

Phelps took the pipe from his mouth, and the hat from off his head, and asked in a voice not unmixed with anxiety, "how say you?"

The foreman in a low tone, and looking down, gave the verdict, which I did not hear, but I read it in Walker's eye, there was again a pause, they seemed now for the first time to feel that all the proceeding had not been a terrible mockery, and every eye was turned upon Phelps, who almost appeared inclined to throw up his office.

Walker said something to him in a low voice, and it was not with an unkindly look that he now again addressed me,

"Prisoner, have you anything to say why sentence of death should not be passed upon you."

There came a flash of hope into my mind, and I felt that I could not abandon my young life without a struggle.

"What motive could I have had, having seen Diego's daughter but on the previous night?" The question seemed to have some effect.

Phelps turned to Doty, who seemed to have nothing to reply, and Walker's eye shone for a moment in benevolent hope, when the sinister look, and gaunt form of Joe Heald appeared as if suddenly risen from the earth.

"He has rested his defense upon the impossibility of there being a motive of jealousy, I am compelled to say, that the evening before, in the very thicket where the body of the murdered man was found, I saw him have a conference of some length with the object of poor Reece's affections, and I saw them embrace on taking leave, and heard them allude to intercourse they had had together before."

The judge turned round to me, but as I saw him do so, I hid my face in my hands, I felt that this last appeal had in fact, taken away from me any chance of escape, and had sealed my fate. The taste of Phelps, it must be supposed, did not run in dress, though a judge more powerful than one constituted by law, being chosen, as well as upheld, by those who were to carry through his decisions. There was nothing imposing in his manner or appearance, yet when I looked up, feeling that I owed it to innocence, and to the character I had hitherto held for courage, to bear a good front in this last proof, I could not help feeling an awe indiscribable at the silent solemnity of the scene, which was to herald my doom. A short consultation was held apart with Doty, it mattered not to me what it was, and I awaited the words, which however homely, were to consign me to an ignominious death, the pause was not long.

The Judge, with an effort, began: "Edward Warren, you have been found guilty of murder by a jury, without any mitigating circumstances, and your own admissions and defence seem only to have added to the testimony against you. I feel that I am called upon to sentence you to the penalty of death, and the sentence of the court is, that you be hanged at the hour of seven this night."

Chapter Thirty-Eight
A terrible wait-the gallows tree—a confession

I feel that I can say, with truth, no muscle of my face altered, and I looked the sentencer calmly in the face, until his eye fell beneath mine. Two of the jury constituted themselves my guards, my knife, the only weapon I had about me, was taken away, and I remained in front of Walker's counter.

There were few men who possessed the bodily strength I had in a personal encounter, and not many who could hold their own with me in a trial of speed, either of these means successful, and it would be well, but a couple of sure rifles were odds against me in either case, and the unsuccessful effort would take away from the heroism of my sacrifice, and from the dignity of my courage.

I offered my hands to be tied, but Joe Gale, one of my guards, pointed to his rifle with a meaningful look, and I sat still. It was not far in the afternoon as yet, and I had to wait the hour appointed.

The delay, I learned, was owing to the difficulty in finding an executioner, and while I waited a certain drowsiness came over me, and I fell into a horrible sleep, in which I seemed to live ages, and the commonest incidents of life became tortures.

I must have remained some hours in that state, though it seemed to me, with a strange contradiction, but a few minutes. A hand roused me from my position, inclined between two bales of goods, and I looked upon the sinking sun, which I confusedly remembered was to be my last.

I know not how I was prepared in other respects, but I was blameless in regard to that for which I was about to suffer. I roused myself, however, with as good a grace as I could, and prepared to precede my guards to the place of execution, which was near to the spot where the body had been found, a solitary poplar, which having been left untouched among the surrounding havoc, marked itself out as the tree of doom.

I remember that my step was firm, and I almost looked with curiosity at the rude contrivance they had made for a ladder, upon which I was to mount, and in that hour, when there was but little time to bring together my thoughts, I recollect well the uppermost was that of Isabel, who had betrayed me. The remembrance of Rose came after, more as an accessory to my present fate than a distinct feeling of regret, I remembered the beautiful tresses of my tempter of Wimbledon, and the first joys of dreaming I was beloved—and I was at the foot of the gallows tree.

A crowd of Indians had gathered to see in what way the strange preparations were to be used, which they had observed going on. I was about to kneel to say a short prayer, I fear more to ask for fortitude to bear this trial becomingly, than to seek forgiveness and to acknowledge my sins, when a stir showed itself among the lookers-on, and a cloud of dust rose in the distant plain.

Doty and Walker both seemed inclined to delay the execution for a few minutes, but it hardly appeared they could have carried their point, but for the state of the last officer of the law, a man called Dempsey[1], who had been filled half-drunk to induce him to undertake the office. Meantime, as I was hurried to the foot of the fatal steps by some, there were certain essential preparations wanting, by which Walker was enabled to delay my ascent, even after I had got a few steps up the rude ladder, where I was almost glad to rest, in order to see if, when at the extremest need, any incident might arise to mitigate, as none could render more cruel, my fate, when Brent sprung forth like an apparition before us, his horse black with perspiration, and his sides yet bloody from the spur. He seemed to think that the rope was already round my neck, and that, according to the fashionable phrase, I was about to be turned off.

"I'll put a ball through your brain if you stir a hand," he cried, aiming at the fumbling functionary. "I have got proof coming that he is not the man, there is one horse dead in bringing it, and that is more life than the affair is worth."

And to back his words, another cloud of dust, rose and several horsemen, were rushing headlong on, in front of whom, and with an appearance of eagerness which could not be feigned, came the Swiss. He had borrowed an Indian horse when his own had fallen dead on the way, and all the Indians

---

1. Dempsey: A trapper named Dempsey worked out of Fort Hall in 1835 under Joseph Gale, but may or may not have been the same man. See Janet LeCompte, *John J. Burroughs*, in Hafen, *The Mountain Men and the Fur Trade*, III: 62.

who were about, and had the means, accompanied him, to see on what momentous errand he was bound.

He threw himself off his horse, and declared he was the slayer of the deceased in self-defense, stating that there was proof that Reece had threatened his life several times, and that if this could not be considered as sufficient excuse for the act, he was the person upon whom the doom must fall, and that I was innocent[i].

I cannot say I felt the instant relief this declaration was calculated to inspire, it, on the contrary, rather stunned me, and I mistrusted the motives of Bernard.

Those of the council who tried me, who had hung back from witnessing the execution, now came forward to support the acquittal, and I must say that, with the exception of Heald, no one appeared sorry at the new light which had been thrown on the affair.

I advanced to thank the Swiss, and offered him my hand, that I received was deadly cold, and I turned to receive more welcome and more cordial congratulations on my escape.

I never knew until long after how this opportune appearance in my favor came about, but I was again a free man, and this mountain-life, with all the buoyancy of youth, was again to me full of its former charms.

Chapter Thirty-Nine
A solitary journey—an encounter-in hiding

There are few small birds in these parts, the drop of water, which through a microscope illustrates our social state, shows us one animal continually preying upon another, those ferocious beasts who are the enemy of man, are destroyed by him, and he may extend his protection, and proclaim, as in civilized countries, his monopoly of the eatable part of the brute creation, whether beast or bird. Where the first wants are only to be supplied, the larger animals of prey are alone the rivals of the human race, in a land where vegetable productions and fruits are rare, and little esteemed, and the constant hostility of man has thinned the bears, and the panthers, and the wolves—but of the birds, the eagle and his subordinates are unmolested, save to furnish the feathers necessary for a fop or the fledging of an arrow. The martin, the weasel, the snake, the owl, live upon the winged tribe, who besides, were they not migratory, could not exist in winter, so that the forest which clothes the bases of the Mountains of the Winds is not what a similar portion of wood would be in England, in regard to the birds and beasts which it might be capable to contain, their dark solitudes are almost devoid of life.

It was the third day after the events just described, when I had so near become a victim to circumstantial evidence, and little before the sun was at its height. I had quitted the breaking up of the camps before their final move, and acting on the information I had gathered of the different countries about to be hunted in the opposite interests of the traders, had chosen that which was perhaps the most productive, and which was certainly the most dangerous.

The Crow Indians, whose lands begin immediately on the eastern side of the ridge under which the rendezvous had been held, have, since the visits of the white man to their country, begun a systematic protection of their beaver and of the game which affords them subsistence, and they recognise no right of devastating their hunting grounds by the whites more than by any hostile tribe, and from the care they took of it, the beautiful region in which they roamed was stocked with every animal the mountains produced, and in a quiet state, unharrassed by the constant and wasteful destruction which went on in the countries to the south and the west.

It was toward this land of the bravest and the most enlightened of the Indians, that I was bending my steps, but I had not got far, I was alone. My mule I rode, and the packhorse I was obliged to lead, to save his load from being brought in contact with the trees and rocks which encumbered the way. The mighty pines made a continuous shade even when less crowded and of greater girth.

I had passed by the back of the lake at which I had lost my horses before, and was now slowly ascending toward a pass seldom or ever used unless by the diggers, who haunt the most inaccessible precincts of the cliffs, hiding themselves in caverns and clefts from the search of all the human race, and the more especially when there are camps on the plains beneath, do the debased and miserable Chochocos[1] shun the danger of being found out, and the light of day.

It was what is called a family journey, all its cares coming to be performed by one person, but I would have been glad that it had been in the open, where, though more dangerous, I should not have been tempted to muse in the solemn mysteries of that dark wood, and be recalled from that sweet absence of care by the commonest drudgery of travel.

The packs were getting foul of the trees, in spite of my intended caution, and while they were adjusting, my spare horses were getting out of sight. The pass, which like the hollow between the bumps of a camel's back, had been easily discernible from below, and must, I knew, be nearly right above, and though being obliged to tack in the steep ascent, I might have missed the direct line to the hollow, it could not be far to either hand.

After fighting through these natural difficulties for nearly a couple of hours, as well as those occasioned by the animals, I heard a short whistle right above, as no Indian whistles, I knew that, friend or foe, it was a white. I gave a shout, which I hoped Would not reach farther than the signal I had heard, but I had got cautious, and collected all my worldly goods below a rock, on each

---

1. Chochocos: Shoshokos were poor Shoshones also called walkers, or diggers, *from their subsisting*, according to Irving in *Captain Bonneville* (p. 224), *in large measure, on the roots of the earth, though they likewise take fish in great quantities, and hunt, in a small way. They are, in general, very poor, destitute of most of the comforts of life, and extremely indolent: but a mild, inoffensive race. They differ, in many respects, from the other branch of the Snake tribe, the Shoshonies, who possess horses, are more roving and adventurous, and hunt the buffalo.*

side of which was a slope, and sat myself down with a cocked rifle, watching the long ears of the mule, which would be sure to point out the least movement within ken.

This inactivity did not remain long, the mule, faithful to her fine senses, looked up. I still lay ready, nothing could drop over the rock, and live. In a few minutes the ears of all my beasts were pointed to the east, and I could myself detect by the noise of the crackling of some dry stick, that someone was descending in that quarter.

"You are nearer the summit than you think," said a voice I easily recognized, even before I saw the speaker.

"I have had toil enough for any summit," I answered.

There was no good in stopping where we were, so I began to prepare for a further progress. The medicine man, for it was he, gathered up the rope of the packhorse, and I led the mule, the others, as we got into a sort of path, followed in a string.

But our course, I was surprised to find, was not now upward but along the face of the steep, following occasionally what appeared to have been paths long disused, at last we came upon a torrent, which rushed foaming down its stair-like way, and here, on the shallow margin of an eddying basin, our conductor made a halt. This piece of water was of some twenty yards long, and by entering close to the upper end, a horse, notwithstanding the current, might swim across and have room to land safely above the cataract below.

"Follow me exactly, but first tie the other two to a tree." I heard, notwithstanding the torrent's roar, and he entered the edge of the stream on foot, leading the horse after him, and I looked with some apprehension to my baggage, and the idea of swimming, encumbered thus, seemed madness of the wildest kind, but instead of attempting this, the animal, trembling and reluctant, was led with shortened rein along the edge, and emerging at the confluence of a small feeder coming in from the same side over a bare rock, he proceeded up it until he found a bush growing from the rock, to which the horse was tied. When I got up, I followed the example, we then led the other along in a similar way.

The almost dry course up which we now took our slippery way, was sunk deep in the mountainside, the banks were almost of inaccessible steepness, and we had at last to take off the pack, and leave it to be carried up after on our backs. However, the whole course, though steep and difficult, was not more than three hundred yards before it emerged upon a green flat of the richest verdure, dotted with birch and quaking ash, and surrounded by scaibre pines, which, head over head, rose up until the blue sky defined their outline, no rock overlooked them on any side, so that to peer upon this spot of verdure in the surrounding gloom, it must be from beneath the shade and close to its border.

But our precautions were not ended, and again the loose horses were made fast, while we waded onward through the now almost stagnant watercourse, at last, near the middle of the plain, we got out, and with a good trail rope I let loose the glad mule in the rich and tender herbage. The getting of the baggage up, and the other horses, was a matter of course, and it was not long before a fire was lit at the opposite end of the open, and the first meal of the day was in progress.

"When are we to get across?" I said to my companion, as we watched the crackling blaze over which the roasting sticks affectionately leaned.

"Did not I tell you, last night, that it would be two days before we saw the Popoagee and the country of the Crows[2], and you do not suppose we are here taking an excursion of pleasure?"

"And why not, as we are not trapping, and there seems nothing to hunt?"

"And you really suppose that it was merely a little practice in the art of escape, that took us into that snow-water, and up the small ravine."

I looked at him in some surprise. "Do you suppose we are pursued?"

"And why not, are we not worth the capture, should it be Indians? Or are there no well-wishers who might like to look after us among the whites?"

"And you really think. that there is some risk?"

"It is rare that there is not about here. But I do not think on the matter—I *know* we are pursued, and though all has been done that can be done to throw them off the trail, it is not a sure matter that they are not now looking at us. And where is your horse?"

"Oh, my horse, if we have luck, we will see tomorrow."

"I'll tell you what—we will picket the beasts, they may get too near the trees. Bring them this way, and we will go down and eat in the middle also, and put out the fire."

With the roasting sticks in our hands, we sallied forth, and deposited them by a thicket of dwarf birch and willow by the stream side, and nearly in the centre of the little open. The horses eat eagerly—and so did we—and the picketing them did not appear a hardship, so close and rich was the sward.

But I could not but remark an unusual earnestness, as well as anxiety, in the appearance of my companion, whose eye was never still, and I remarked, that I saw he was uneasy, and that we had better *put out*.

He then said, "Aye, that is just the matter, if they be upon us close, to move onward would do nothing more than put off the evil hour. But I know a place

---

2. Popoagee and the country of the Crows: Warren seems to be heading northeast over the Wind River range, possibly over Washakie Pass in present Sublette and Frémont counties, Wyoming. Absaroka, the Crow homeland, embraced the Wind River Valley country as far west as the valleys of the Wind and Popo Agie rivers.

where, with a watch, all is safe enough, even should they track us there, but I would not, for ten horses, it were found out."

"Well, for that matter I have not ten horses to give, but if we move quickly, the odds are in our favor that they have not yet made out the trail."

"Let us be off," was all the answer given, and the packs were up and the saddle and all ready in a twinkling, and again we strung our way down the brook into the ravine, and not quite halfway down there was a small place, very steep and rough, up which I succeeded in taking the mule, after an ineffectual struggle with the packhorse. A mule has always the advantage in these passes, besides that horses always follow them, and we got up again almost on to the edge of the little prairie so abruptly quitted.

Keeping on the border of this, we approached to a side where the pines grew strong and high, and where there seemed to be some moisture, but passed on, and a flat space of wettish ground, this we also skirted. At last we came to a stream, and into this took our course, winding along until we heard the sound of a cascade not far off. Near this we quitted the watercourse, and getting across a piece of soft turf, where we left a plain trail, found a bare spot of rock covered with moss. There was a border still to pass, and we got over it and into the bed of what appeared to be the brook of the little prairie where we had dined, if such hurried meal could so be called.

We were no sooner there than our conductor, casting about him a glance that might seem to pierce through the skirt of forest which intervened between us and the glade, and allowing time for collecting the animals—this curious man, whose knowledge he so well knew how to put to the best advantage, told me to remain quiet, but to follow him when he moved, the din of the waterfall being so great as to drown all other sounds.

There was a considerable space of shingle and driftwood, brought down by the torrent at times of flood, and on this I stood, while our guide, taking the mule by the rope, led her behind the spoutlike fall along an almost cavern-cleft of the rock, into which the stream poured at right angles, nearly meeting the opposite side. It was a dark and slippery way, and wet, the rock also was slippery. But all this I discovered when it became my turn to pass in, leading the packhorse, and followed by the others, who finding it a case, crowded after me as fast as they could. But we were through this pass and in a small narrow valley, steeply rising and fenced in by overhanging rocks, continuing the character of a crack in the mountain side which it had borne at the more narrow entrance, sufficient moisture rendered the bottom of this contracted spot—for it did not seem three hundred yards long, and not fifty broad—green and pleasant, the herbage was in its prime.

Chapter Forty
A visitation—mystic vision?—conflagration

"You may let the rest loose, you see the mule is already eating, no need of a guard here if we sit ourselves down near this entrance." And there we were.

Although the light was bright of the evening sun where it shone, the shadow of the cleft was to us like night, a slight ruddy tinge, half yellow, touched the pine tops far above, and told us, needlessly, of the coming night. It was now we kindled a fire, and its bright and fearless beams lit up the rocky walls, which rose red from the green sward where we lay.

The precious weed was not wanting, and we were soon enveloped in its fumes. The time had hung on drowsily, for though I might have heard much I wished to learn, there was also a disinclination to enter on the subject nearest my heart. My companion sat absorbed in his pipe, and a small kettle simmered on the blaze, his eyes were turned toward the entrance, and mine nearly in an opposite direction, the animals eat greedily, and the light in the upper air had given way to a cloudy haze.

We had been thus seated an hour, and each had taken from the common store his want for the evening repast, and I had lain myself down to enjoy that rest which it might be as well, under uncertain circumstances, beforehand to secure, when a form, not of very lofty stature, but enveloped in a short robe, came between me and my companion, and stood as if it had grown out of the earth then and there. I did not move, though it required my utmost self-command to restrain an expression or gesture of surprise, but it could be no unexpected visitor, from the sign made by the other that the strange figure should sit down, which he did.

By the light of the fire I saw that it was a youth, apparently about eighteen, but under-sized, he was paler than the Indians I had hitherto seen, and I judged of his age from the finished form of his limbs, rather than from any appearance of maturity in anything else, the hair was very long, and tied by a simple cord, and no lock as is usual with the Snakes, was cut and brought down in the middle over the forehead, the eyes were near the nose, long, almond-shaped, and not without a certain look of cunning, but the mouth was really pleasant in its expression, and gave an assurance if there was a want of determination, there was at least a blithe guileless spirit within.

My companion looked hard at the new comer, and as he did not look behind during his survey, I concluded he was alone, at last he was interrogated, as the pipe was handed to him, by that expressive *Ha-gane* of the Shochone tongue.

"They have set fire to the forest," said the Indian youth, quietly.

"And your people?" said the other, almost starting from a mixture of anger and surprise he even was unable to suppress.

"Oh, it is only about here, but it will burn clear through the pass. Look!"

And, as they both gazed up at the gloomy heaven, I also saw clouds of a darker hue beginning to flit across, and with a swiftness which denoted a storm, the wind had risen, and blew a gale, I distinctly heard its roar. The animals which were near enough to be observed, looked up and pricked their ears.

I looked for an explanation, and the conversation contained in the previous words was rendered to me.

The Chochoco—whose name was Hy-Hy—was the son of a Nezperce' squaw, taken by some wandering diggers, and received his name (which signifies white in that language[1]) from the fairness of his skin, and having become known to the medicine man in some of his visits to the rugged recesses haunted by these miserable bands, had been glad to act as a sort of familiar spirit to this master, both from affection for himself and a dread of the mysterious powers with which there appeared ample evidence that he was invested. His great passion and aim in life was to get a sufficient supply of horses for his tribe to enable them to join the Indians of the plains, emancipating themselves from the necessity of labor for subsistence, and enabling them to obtain from the spoils of the chase the skins, which, as a medium of barter, form the riches of those who have acquired foreign wants.

Inhabitants of caverns and inaccessible dells, and living upon grass-seeds, and such dried meat and fruits as they can procure for winter supply, they

---

1. Which signifies white in that language: The Reverend Samuel Parker, in an appendix to his *Journal of an Exploring Tour,* included a brief vocabulary of the Nez Perce Indians, including the word *hihi,* meaning *white* (p. 398).

prowl about in summer, with the arrow, the stone-axe, and the spear, and are treated as vermin by the surrounding nations, and in some instances have been shot down in cold blood by the whites.

It was easy to occasionally perceive a certain light in the eye of this young savage, which lit up as if from some hidden fire, and gave to a countenance usually calm the air of a wild enthusiasm. But now he looked up at the hue of copper which was already stealing over our canopy, and listened to the distant wind as if a convulsion of one of the terrible elements, borne on the wings of another, was a matter—did it even involve personal safety—which had no power to ruffle his aspect, or disturb the serenity of his brow.

"Do you see that tree?" said David, for so I had learned, at rendezvous, my mysterious friend was called, though to none had he been so communicative about his own history as he had been to myself.

"Why should I not?" I answered.

"It is sufficiently lofty to let you see over the gap by which we entered, and you will observe if the forest burns on the other side of the pass."

Be it remembered that we were on the eastern side, and just at the commencement of the hollow to which I have given the name of pass, from its shape, rather than its practicability, and its small distance gave a certain height to add to that of the lofty pine, which stood alone and flourishing in its might. As I moved, I saw, for a moment, a flash gleam from the eye of the dark youth.

"You will see something in the branches, give it a wide berth, it is his mother's remains."

From the high bough, which scarcely waved to the tempest blowing without, I could see nothing but the reddening glare, as it seemed to sweep as if from the side of the mountain where I had first been joined by the medicine man into and across the hollow. On descending, I approached our fire, whose light was easily kept up from the dead branches which had fallen over the rocks, and there I beheld Hy-Hy leaning against my pack-saddle with a countenance of supernatural calm, the eyes slightly closed, and altogether the expression of peaceful death.

David held up his hand as I came near, and pointed to a place beside him where I should sit, I mechanically obeyed.

"You are in the lodge, and who do you see there?" he continued, as if following up some previous inquiry.

"I see Rose, and a squaw of some dark nation I do not know."

"What are they about?"

"Rose embroiders a mocasin, and the other looks at a kettle of meat, and puts a stick occasionally in the fire."

"Look, and tell me what happens."

For some time there was no movement, but presently a sort of expression came over the countenance, and the medicine man took the hand of the youth.

"A man comes in."

"Who-her father?"

"No, a dark-haired young white, whom I never saw before. They talk, he sits down at her feet."

"Repeat what they say."

"He says, 'You promised.'"

"She says, 'Yes, but I did not say when.'"

"'But I saved his life, and am here to ask you to keep your word.'"

"'And I will. But you have set that rascal Heald upon him, and he cannot escape, so that your object will be come at still, as soon as I consent. He shall go home safe.'"

"'And what will my father say?'"

"'He must look out another wife for his son.'"

"'You say he has bribed high?'"

"'Yes, but there is no danger from that, Joe will do all he can to thwart, or rob, or keep him here, but he won't be paid for taking his life, therefore all is safe as to that.'"

"'But why not let him be, and inherit his own?'"

"'Ah, with that I have nothing to do, I am, as you know, content. Let your father then—'"

"Here, the conversation ceased."

"What more?" asked my companion.

"They have gone out."

"Are there any more?—but follow them."

"They are outside the door. He says, 'at the Yellow Stone.'"

"And she answers, 'he must start safe from them, I will get my father to give up his hunt.'"

"'But you love this stranger.'"

"'There are things which you cannot know, but this may satisfy you, that I shall never see him, if I can help it, again.'"

"'And will never—'"

"They are interrupted by Diego."

"'But you feel tired?'"

"'I wish to sleep.'"

"'Well.'"

"And the youth's head sank back, and his eyes closed."

I looked with speechless surprise at my companion.

"And do you believe in all this?" I asked, after he had explained this conversation. "That he really has seen what is doing in a distant spot, and has conveyed his spirit there, and told you what has occurred?"

"You will see, when we get to the other side," he said with a smile. "But see how the flakes of fire are borne through the sky, it is well we have got this quiet spot."

In fact, as he spoke, the growing roar and lurid light were gaining, and it was a scene whose influence was calculated to destroy entirely all thought. I have been in danger of my life more than once, and death appeared inevitably near. Still the mind flashed far to other scenes, thoughts alike of the future and the past, but on two occasions, where the voice of the elements spoke, all thought was hushed and absorbed, one was when drifting under the spray of the fall of Niagara with a drunken boatman in the night, and the other was when chased and surrounded by the conflagration of the forest[i].

The boy slept, and we, his companions, watched until the glare was so near and great, that to us, the universe might be in a blaze. The few trees which stood visible on the ridge above, were tempest tossed, and waved their arms against the coming light in wild despair.

The waterfall had long ceased to be heard, and the warm air came up the gorge, in place of its refreshing sound, the horses had ceased to feed, and had clustered round, submitting as in desperate emergency to that power, which has but to be known, to be obeyed. The air heated and rarified was disagreeable to breathe, and I laid myself down on the cool earth, and closed my eyes to that dreadful scene. I would have given a world to have had the fire around me on a plain, careering over the wide expanse, though followed at rushing speed by the scorching wind and devouring flame.

There is action to the last, and in the terrible race, the relentless element may be foiled, and the victim snatched from his grasp by a damp spot or a leafy grove, though the bloodshot eye, whose ache is all unheeded, in vain would penetrate the murky smoke, which precedes and accompanies him to his doom.

Occasionally looking up, with some such troubled dream, I passed what must have been a long period, for when the friendly hand of David roused me to look again, the wind still roared, but in comparative darkness, and the ravages of the fire were stayed, the horses shook themselves, and put down their heads again to taste that sweet herbage, but it had been sprinkled as if by a shower of snow, with portions of brands and ashes borne by the gale. How small appeared our little fire now replenished, and how insignificant we seemed, awoke from this terrific scene, but the wind was still rushing in wild tumult, and every now and then the fall of a stately tree might be heard between the blasts, but a certain exhaustion was stealing over me, and I slept.

Chapter Forty-One
Through a wasteland lone wayfaring-an incubus

Morning might have sometime dawned, and we know nothing of it, in that sunken spot. The black forms of the pines which crowned the ridges around still looked down dark and gloomy upon us, for the rocks immediately to windward were bare, and the devouring flames had there died for want of food, a bare face had also stayed their course all along to the other side of the pass. This was discovered from the lone tree, which the evening before had been my look-out place.

Hi-Hi, disenchanted, was busy aiding in the preparations for departure, and soon we had passed under the fall, restored to its voice and its local importance, but the scene without had changed, the little prairie, where we had rested. The afternoon before, was a discolored grey, but all was black around, the wind was still high and mournful, part of the wood to the leeward of the grassy open had remained untouched, but beyond, to our right, toward the other side of the divide, the desolation of black stumps, and still smoking trees, which had longer resisted the flames, presented a scene, which with the cloudy mist hovering above, was of black and hopeless desolation. Many trees, when we got into the region of ashes, had fallen and barred the way, and others tottering, fell before us, some on which the gale acted, waved to and fro unwilling to give way, neither bird nor insect, nor living thing was to be seen.

Hi-Hi picked up a roasted porcupine and threw it into a kettle, and we passed on, the horses crouching as if in dread of this forest of blackened masts, which gave no warning, but fell. Thus we went without a word. It would have taken a bold man to follow on our trail, the hours seemed lengthened.

Hi-Hi led with agile step to avoid what was in the way, as to avoiding what was doomed to fall, that was beyond his ken, but the day, or rather the end to the smouldering smoke at last appeared to brush before us, and in a short time we stood on the brink of a rocky precipice, which there suddenly began the fall of the waters to the Missouri, but there was then no view, and relieved from the dangers of the still falling forest, we thankfully kept along the ridge. A crashing sound heard through the whistling blast every now and then reminded us of the dangers past.

The Indian boy sat down on a rock, and wiped the perspiration from his brow, the horses let down their heads, and shook themselves with a shudder, and my companion gazed upon me with a look of calm relief, as if an acknowledgment of having passed through imminent danger.

"We have now to contend with our own kind," was all he uttered, and resumed our way.

There are many spots, where some landslip or fire had laid low the older wood, and upon which a younger growth sprung up thick as a wheat-field, tall and slim, it was from such nurseries of the pine, that the Indians supplied themselves with those long, light, and straight lodge poles, upon which are stretched the roof which shelters them from the heat, as well as the cold on the plains below.

It was on the eastern side, there was a road, or rather track, by which were dragged these stems, which might in all but size be justly called the roof-trees of those nations, and downward by this path, only trod by the squaw, who is the architect of these tribes, and forms with wonderful taste and skill the shape of the tall tent to resemble the base of the lighthouse, in the commencement of its graceful curve.

Down this path we also led our way, as it slanted to meet a valley, through which rushed a tributary of the Popoagee, not at right angles with the great mountain line, but slanting toward the south collaterally, and collecting in its course the streams and rills, as they came from the highest points of the range, as well as off the spur, running out bastion-like from the structure above. When we had reached a spot where there still remained the trace of a retrograde path, as well as one which tended toward the lip of what appeared the basin of the upper part of the valley, and which contained a lake, not of great size, but of picturesque beauty, which we had seen from a point above—a halt was called.

"You will have to pass over as best you may, leading your horse, and followed by the other, except the pack animal, and he cannot get through the trees, or past the rocks with his projecting burthen, and you must trust him with me. When you have to ride take the mule, it is hardish ground to get over, but it can be done, when you get to the opposite ridge beyond the end of the lake, you are in a spot where there is a curtain of wood on the upper side, and precipices over which you have to pass, you are safe in the margin of this cover, and there is no want of grass, without coming far down the plain. There is another impracticable canon on the left, which converges toward this at the base of the mountain, and the Crows have been known to get a great herd of buffalo between, and lighting fires, and forming their camp below at the narrow neck, live there in ease, until the whole herd was destroyed. It is quite a country, and I have heard a report, that the village of Long Hair[i] is somewhere about, but I shall probably know more by tomorrow at noon. Hi-Hi and myself will be with you, God willing, at a spot before the junction of the Popoagee, and the other stream which you see below. You cross the waters on your right hand, and keep up the valley, there are some small streams, but you have only to look out for the fork that takes up again to the southwest. You understand that you are to suppose yourself on the other side of the ridge now opposite us, the wood does not extend far down, there hangs below a vast grassy slope, enclosed on either side by the cut rocks of the two river courses, joining in the valley below, and which are impassable, the only entrance being at the bottom, where the rocks have run out. It is a triangular space, with its most extended side formed by the line of the pines, within the edge of which you should keep. Within these bounds meat has been supplied for many hundred Crows, when the herds were here penned up in early winter, and the village encamped across the only access from below. Do not let your horses range far from the pines, and they will never be seen, unless by accident, against which no man can provide, collect them in the morning, and come down, or rather move down before dawn, but be wary of fire. I am spinning this out as if you were a child, but it is no very easy spot to deal with, and when you get below, you are on ground where no man is safe, were he the best that ever strode the prairies."

"I think I understand, and God willing, I'll be with you by noon."

I was going, when he called after me, "If you see any whites, ask for *the grave of Bray*."

I was again cast loose, and it was not in such a country that I parted with my baggage without a pang, however it is the character of journeying in America, to trust in a great degree to what may be considered the best chance rather than hesitate, however poor the prospect that best may afford, and I followed on the upper trail, leaving my companions descending that which turned down, and backward to the meeting of the waters in the vale below.

There was a lake, I had been told, above me on the left, but I soon found that it was no matter of choice to steer my course, there was a perpendicular crag which showed its ruddy face on the opposite side, continuing the whole distance I could see, I therefore zig-zagged upward to reconnoitre, at the top I found a densely wooded mound, which dammed up the water and formed the lake, which it was sometime before I could see but by glimpses, at last I got to an open, it was a singularly wild and beautiful piece of water of that bluish green, which is found so often to tint the streams which flow from mountains where great portions of rock are continually crumbling, and of a whitish substance, the friction of particles as well as the decomposition give an aquamarine color to the first resting place of these torrents, which by degrees is lost, as it has time to deposit.

The pines about were black as night, and the almost milky blue of the lake was a strange, and not disagreeable contrast. The length of the expanse was not great, and while the animals were picking up the scant herbage around, I took out my spyglass to survey the opposite end, where a low mass of wood ran into the ridge which cut perpendicularly down on the opposite side, not only on the left of the outlet as I had seen before, but forming a wall along the whole opposite side, running out as it got to the further end. I thus found myself obliged to follow the margin which was on the left, or on the side next the mountain ridge, to get over from above the opposite end, to the great prairie face to which I had been told to go, and turning, I got along through the trees, once I saw an otter dive as I passed, and a herd of argali rushed up an inaccessible promontory, amazed at being disturbed, and I was nearing the other end, when a small coil of smoke curled up from a point beyond, shewing white against the dark mass of firs. I rushed at my loose horse, and caught up his trail rope, and put myself in a state of preparation as fast as I could, that is, I made up my mind for the worst, tied the animals within the shade, and took out my glass, which had saved me so many a weary mile of investigation already. The smoke had vanished, but I had marked the spot where it had appeared, there was nothing to be seen, again I looked my best, was it a tree laid down by the wind, but it was longer than one tree, I looked again, there was a sort of barricade across an isthmus, it was so much to learn that, and by dint of following up the hint, I could see other indications of the interference of man in this one of the most remote and desolate strongholds of nature.

I looked about for a grassy open for the horses, a little watercourse which joined the lake furnished me with a place to picket them, and devote myself to watch.

I had never been able to understand how the unseen power of an enemy, whom it was evident I had, should be able to affect me at such a distance from England, or how it could be worth any one's while to follow a youth now utterly destitute in this relentless way, to such distant parts, but that terrible head I had seen twice, it was not the countenance or the expression of a mortal, it was something darker and worse than ordinary hate or evil purpose, but there was a hungry vengeance in it, the remembrance of which came over me at times in a strange way, and formed a sort of mood, which I recognised and tried to shake off, but in vain, it must have its time, and sit like an incubus upon my spirit.

Chapter Forty-Two
An engaging surprise—flight—struggle for life-surgery

Under this gloomy influence, I had lain for a while, looking now and then mechanically through the glass, but not observing, when something on the promontory caught my attention, and awoke me to a consciousness of my own position. Concealed, however, by a broken branch, it was not probable I had been perceived, and I continued my scrutiny. It was an Indian I saw, but not in war-paint, and it was difficult to make out what the strange movements were, at last I saw a horse between the trees, it was the favorite steed of Rose, the sun shone upon him a moment, and there could be no mistake, and now I could recognize his mistress, the distance could not be more than a mile. Without casting a glance toward my animals, I sped along through the trees, and happily the way was not difficult, nor was it long before I stood panting by the side of her to whom I owed my life. I could see the red blood glow, and mount to the roots of her hair, but she was the first to speak.

"Have you met no one, or have you heard of our loss?"

"I have seen no one, and know nothing."

"The Crows attacked our lodge when I was out, and left my father badly wounded, and one of the squaws killed, my poor father stuck up a hat, and as he was behind some cover, they made off with the horses, and did not risk entering the shelter we had made, I returned from being out hunting, and found what had happened. I got my father away on a raft of dry sticks, and he is in a cave in that face, a hiding place of the medicine man. Now I must hide our only horse, he is here in the fork, where he has left no trail, and the camp was a little bit higher up. Where are yours?"

I pointed out.

"Well, take mine to them, along the lake side a certain distance, to make no trail, and be back as quick as thought. I'll wait for you after I have been to get some things."

All my energies were roused, and I did not require a second order. I mounted, and followed the creek to where it entered, and then the shore for some distance, until it became too deep, and then got away at once, and happily where there was little chance of leaving a track. The horses, after the usual greeting, became quiet, and I took again the way back to the upper end. I found Rose busy working at a forked log she was trying to move, and she made a signal for me to hasten my speed, it was evident there was something new, and in fact, I heard a shot at some little distance.

"They are come back, I could only bring away a little bag of kammas."[i]

Another shot! There was no time for thought, the log was large, though light for its size from partial decay, and had been evidently cast up by a strong wind, when the water had been higher also. We were getting it afloat when the cry of the raven, the watchword of the Apsaroche[ii], and the answering wolf howl, came distinctly near.

"They are upon us," said Rose, and a pallor of anxious dread came over her face, as she raised her eyes toward her father's refuge, with the eager look of one who had still something to live for.

"Launch, Ned, launch." She strained to pull on the timber, which was to doom or save us.

I gave my rifle into her hand, and applying all my strength, the tree was impelled before us.

"Get it into deep water before we get on," I said, as I tied my powder horn round my head upon the brim of my hat, and we waded the while, she pushing on the trunk, and holding up my gun.

"But it will require something across," she said, in an accent almost of despair.

The thought had well occurred ere it was too late, and with all the speed I could muster, I rushed back through the water for a couple of spars, of which I had observed several among the driftwood. But the cautious signals, imitating the voices of animals of the wilds gave way to the shout, as several Indians were rushing down through the trees, I had my pieces of wood, but getting through the water was by no means so easy a matter as that of bounding over the springy turf in pursuit, but I rushed on till I got to what was to be our raft, happily I never stirred without my lasso, in an instant I was making fast the spars across the broken ends of the fork upon which Rose with my rifle already was placed, but a dozen naked savages were splashing through the water, while our course was retarded by the object in tow, and the operation of tying on the cross bars, several arrows were fired, and one grazed my cheek, but we held on though the pursuit gained upon us, and I saw, when too late, that my desire to save my arm had put us in a position, where there was not left a hope.

A few yards, and we must come to turn for a last struggle.

Rose clung fast to the raft—I urged it on while I still had footing, and gave it an impetus, but they were upon me—one had seized me behind. I still felt bottom, but the water was much above my middle, and I suppose in the exertion of catching at me, he had overshot his balance, for I still felt the ground firm under me, he floundered, a back-handed blow with my fist on the side of the head, and he let go just as my footing failed.

I had to get up as best I could, however our tree had gathered way, and Rose was lying flat upon it, paddling with both hands, and the little wind there was, was in our favor.

By the time I was in a state to take a part in the struggle, we were already in deep water some time, and the Indian I had the tussle with had been in the way of the others, or some new idea had taken them, for they ceased firing their arrows—though we were not fifty yards off—and returned toward the shore.

The wind blew us toward the cut rocks, and I sat up, riding on my seahorse, a few minutes, and we came against them, there were some sunken reefs, but on the whole, it was a sheer perpendicular, except at a very few places, and then there was hardly a footing. Guiding ourselves along by our hands on the rock, we at last came near the cave, but I had, for a moment, forgotten the Crows, in my joy at having achieved our escape, and looked round just in time to see them rushing round to the other end of the lake, thinking we made for it to escape, but seeing us stop and clamber up the rugged footing which led to the cave, they stopped also, and there seemed a council held, but it was time for us also to hold one.

Here we were, a faint voice we heard calling to us, "Rose beloved! come here. Are you safe?"

"Yes, father. How is your hurt?"

"Why, baddish, you must try and get out the ball. But who is with you?"

"Don't you remember him at rendezvous? Had it not been for him, you had never seen your child again."

The old man looked round, for I had now appeared in the entrance. His feeling, so long strung in anxiety—for he could not see the operation of coasting along the crags—now gave way, and he dropped his head on the bosom of his daughter, and large tears chased each other down his cheeks, as he silently held out his disengaged hand and wrung mine.

Diego's wound was not a dangerous one, though it had disabled the right arm and made a lodgment in the muscle under the shoulder-blade. An examination showed some little inflammation, and there was much pain on the slightest movement, the ball was three inches deep at least, from the probe he had with great resolution made to search for it. But how to find a forceps, or what to substitute?

My talent for mechanical invention was not of the highest order, that of Diego, possibly, had no right to be classed much above it, but he had profited by the inventive genius of the Americans he had been among, and already planned the means of performing the operation. Two splints were reduced very thin from a split splinter of our raft, rounded outside, and a sort of notch cut close to the end of each, and hollowed like a spoon. After rubbing the outsides of these two spoons, if such they might be called, to smooth them, one was introduced until it got on a par with the ball, which was lodged against its small cavity, then the other was run exactly in face of it, until—which was the greatest difficulty—the second spoon lodged itself so as to have the ball between the two, it was then that some of Rose's rings became of use, one being easily passed over both hafts some way into the wound, and then a wedge was introduced between, so as to form a lever against the compression of the ring, and to give a firm seat to the bullet between the two. The pain of this operation was excessive, but otherwise a great gash must have been made to get out the ball, and we were not sure of the safety of such an opening, this was discussed, and as I was to have been the operator, I was too glad to dig with the spoons rather than run the chance of a dangerous incision.

The wounded man set his teeth, and bore the operation with a fortitude I did not think possible, his dark eye flashed, but he neither winced nor groaned, and I could have wished to stop the process, to note the bearing of his heroic child, but the ball came out, and the wound bled profusely. We bound it up with a part of a shirt, and Diego insisted upon its being beat sharply several times with a loading-rod to create an inflammation.

Chapter Forty-Three
A plan-a daring try by darkness—stealing away

Kammmas is not the best food for an invalid, but it was all we had, and we sat back into the shade of the cavern, which was not very much larger than a small chamber, so as to give no clue to our movements or intentions, and in fact, though I had no wish to broach the subject, our danger was far greater than I had any wish to own.

Diego fell into a doze as soon as he was relieved by the extraction of the bullet, and I looked at Rose, and by a sign showed I wished to confer with her. There was a simplicity in her movement, though she did not look up, as she made room for me on the edge of her blanket.

"We have no more meat," I whispered.

"No, but we must let my father have his rest, as he has to be moved too. Is your rifle dry?"

"I think it is."

"But you must make sure."

I looked, and found all right, but put on another cap and stuffed a bit of blanket into the barrel.

We chewed some pieces of kammas, which resembled jujube[1].

"My father will have an idea," said Rose, "all we have to do is to keep quiet."

"The breeze makes but a ripple on the water and they can see our raft."

But my glass was at my saddle-bow, and they were not going to show

---

1. Jujube: Jujube is the edible, plum-like fruit of many of certain Old World trees of the genus *Zizyphus*.

themselves to the naked eye—those who watched us—and our calmness made them think we had some other means of escape, but the great risk was, that they should find out the horses, and that was a hit or miss sort of affair, which would turn upon the slightest accident. It was a matter of doubt whether or not we should make a demonstration in daylight.

There was a singular firmness and decision in this wild girl, and I felt a delicious pleasure in making her show off in all her courage and independence. The time flew, and at last old Diego awoke, there was not more than an hour of sun, he rubbed his eyes, and seemed as if awoke from a total insensibility, but on recovering, addressed himself to the subject of our situation with his usual promptness.

"If we could make a feint, or run our chance across to the horses."

"The lake is like a mirror, which tells for and against us, had there been a slight ripple, a dark object is easier seen," he muttered. "But I think I have it."

The sun had sunk low, and the deep shadow of the great chain loomed over the death-like water, not a sound—no bird—not even the owl was to be heard.

Though there is scarcely a twilight in that latitude, there was still light enough to see with some distinctness across to the opposite shore.

"Now, let us be off, my daughter, we must have a cruize."

I could not devise what plan was to be followed, but I started up to bear a hand.

"First get up one of the cross spars," said Diego, "and see if we can split it."

It turned out to be a clean and dry piece of wood, and the admirable lessons of American woodcraft which the Spaniard had learned came into play, a wedge was soon made, and then another and a casstête made the first insertion, a piece of rock drove in the first wedge, and then there was a second and the rent began, and the spar gave off from its thickness a smaller piece, nearly as long as the original, this we lashed across at the opposite end from the two first, and then we all got upon the raft, enlarged and made more buoyant by additions from the one which brought Diego—Rose having swum back, my rifle and Diego's tied up in a blanket, like a baby, were laid safe and strapped down, all was quiet, and we started, moving along by paddling with our hands, lying on our faces—Rose before and I behind, her father could not be of any use in this, and when I had a chance to see his face, I could perceive the workings of suppressed pain. We went on, touching the wall of rock on one side, toward the upper end where we had embarked.

I have glided silently since in the black gondola, threading its noiseless way through the intricate waterpaths of Venice, where the shadow was darker, and mystery and hope—perhaps some danger—gave an interest to the midnight way, with the risk of vengeance or the uncertain issue of an adventure, yet here was the intense and wild hope waited upon by despair, with the influence of a silence it were death to break, and the knowledge of how little it needed to awake the wild yell around, or have the noiseless arrow come upon us from the unseen hand.

The rock was lowering, and we were approaching the end without a sound, and my heart, I do not hesitate to say, beat almost audibily, though hardly for myself, as I saw the light line which the sandy strand marked below the gloomy pines, but a motion of Diego's hand directed the course close into the corner where the rock rises out of the shore, as it had hitherto done out of the water.

The shadows of the lowering crag, and the deepening night, and the silent fin-like paddling of the hands, which also pulled us along, catching by the unequal surface of the overhanging wall, caused our arrival to be unperceived, and I really believed we were about to land, when a motion of Diego's hand stopped our course, and intimated that we were to back. There were several large masses of stone about this part of the lake, and there was a danger of grounding, we touched, but passed, and just after doing so, got into our old track close to the perpendicular rock, and as we did so, the old Spaniard yelled forth one of those shouts which are generally marks of defiance or triumph. The echoes gave it out with a repetition and a loudness that startled me, and made Rose look round, but when the echo died off, all was again silence, certain croaks as if of the raven, and a suppressed howl as if in answer to the challenge, was all we could perceive.

Again we paddled up within the sunken rocks to very near the shore, and again out came the yell, confused in echoes. This maneuver was a third time repeated, and then we bore away under the beetling cliffs with a will. The darkness was such as to let me use the spare spar split off the other in shoving along, and we got to the outlet end of the lake, when another shout, followed by the raven's note, was given out, and then we were directed to resume our silent labours, and for the first time Diego showed an eagerness and desire to stimulate our speed. We appeared to shoot along wonderfully while close to the rock, where we could note our progress, but after keeping some time along it, we stopped near the cave.

"Now for a straight shoot across. Do you remember where the horses are?"

"I think a little higher up that opposite the cave."

"Yes, on a watercourse."

"Ah, that runs in on a low open strand. Well, we must risk it, keep the star near that point till you can get a tree. Now I regret that accursed ball, but you must work, boy, for your life. Are you tired Rose?"

All the answer we gave was to put our vessel in the line for the opposite shore.

There was nothing to note our progress, and there was a slight breeze against us, I never thought a pull so long, and strained till I felt the blood rushing to every vein of my head, I shall long remember the agony of that terrible hour, every stroke was to relieve one I loved well of some mite of labour, and do a little toward that small hope which still remained to struggle for. Out of the shadow of the louring mass, under which we had hitherto been, and with the slight curl on the water a dark object would be tolerably distinct at a considerable distance, and should any watch be kept, we were discovered and lost, of all this I became sensible, though there was nothing better, or nearly so good to be tried, though I racked my brain as I strained my arms in the hope of finding something else to be done, ere we were committed on that dismal shore. The stern old man had sat without a sign of life, and I could perceive his unquenched eye glaring upon the low line which skirted the forest, we could not be a hundred yards off, it was now danger was to be detected before it should be too late, and I instinctively slackened in my efforts, and my hand fell more noiselessly in the water, which was yet black and deep, no sign was heard, and we came to land.

"Now for the spare spar," said Diego, in a whisper. "Get off some of your rope for a stay to the point of the cross beam."

"I have got off some of the other rope, and fastened it with a thong cut off my cotillion," said Rose, who already understood what her father meant, who was habitually sparing of words, and to my astonishment, who wished to crawl away like a serpent, I found myself aiding to put up a mast, and hoist a blanket on a yard, which they had found on the spot, there was no word spoken, and the mast was stepped on a branch cut short below the angle of the fork, it was all simple enough. I remembered floating small craft at school, and trimmed the sail to answer the wind. Diego pointed to the outlet where we had last touched, and with the sincerest wishes for its safe arrival, I waded as far as I could to start the lightened raft on her voyage, the sail hardly filled, but she drifted away, and was a hundred yards off before we lost sight of her in the trees. Diego leant upon us, and I carried both guns.

"It matters little for a trail, we must be far from these waters before a trail can be seen, or..." The old Spaniard checked himself, and I believe muttered a prayer.

I had never learnt a prayer, and English-like, did not care to show any outward sign of thankfulness for an almost unexpected deliverance, though in my heart I hope I felt as grateful as they.

There was much encumbrance of fallen wood upon the ground, but we struck the little stream which ran along the crest of the debris of its own formation, presently the trees thickened, and the gloom of the forest prevented our seeing our way, and it was by the sound of the brook we were guided, the line of watch, if it ever had been on this side, was passed, and we felt in some degree safe, provided our horses had not been discovered. Our anxiety could not be quite suppressed, in advancing toward where they were left. Nor could I be quite sure of the distance, but we toiled on, a low neigh at last led us hurriedly forward. Rose left her father with a bound, and his whole weight came upon me, it was with a pang I saw this act, as she muttered something about her favorite, and I felt for her father as he tottered with the pain of his wound.

"Yes," he said, "I have always told her that horse will some day be her death, he cannot keep quiet when she leaves him, and there again, he'll wake the whole country with his noise, but she will quiet him now."

And we got to the edge of the open, where we could distinguish only one or two dark masses at first, but afterward the old man could make out his daughter soothing her steed. I helped him as he let himself slowly down on the grass, and ran to my saddle, from which I got a piece of dried meat for him, but he shook his head.

"There is fever upon me, boy, perhaps the cold may check it, but bear a hand."

It was but a moment, and the saddle was on the mule, and I had got her to the side of a large stone, but the wounded man pointed to the stream, which run deep under one of its banks, we got the mule into it with some trouble, and Diego bestrode her without exertion.

Rose was at his side in a moment, and they seemed by instinct to take their course giving the lake a wide berth, it could be but little after ten o'clock, at least so said the Pointers, as those two stars of the Plough are called, which line with that of the north, it is by their positions in their almost diurnal revolutions round it, that the mountaineer reads the watches of the night.

Rose led, and I followed last on my horse, having no saddle, the night wore on, every now and then we had to look for an open to maintain our course. When, however, we had got over the flat space at the head of the lake, and had to ascend the ridge, which is a continuation of its rocky boundary on the east the direction was easy, and we had only to look out for the openest part of the pines, and the best footing. On getting over the ridge, there is still a considerable space of timber as a fringe to the upper part of the slope, and it was there I was to have gone, had I not been taken off from my course by the events previously related.

As far as I could judge, it was past midnight, the moon far in its wane, had not yet risen, the plain which hung down before us was still as a calm sea, not a sound escaped the wood, but that continued murmuring air, which breathes through every region of the pine, there was not a cloud on the sky, the night was cool, for we were far above the ordinary level of the land. There was little to choose in point of course, we had to slope our way toward that isthmus between impassable ravines, which is the sole outlet below. On getting to this neck, we had the whole country of the Crows before us, rivers pouring in from either side to feed the Big Horn, which runs across two broad vallies by forced passes, had there been light, we must have seen from above that noblest country of the hunter stretched out before us, but as we were, there was nothing but a dark mass, the groves of the Popoagee being in shade, as well as the heights beyond. There was nothing yet certain, we had to pass the right-hand stream, so as to follow afterward down the right bank of both after they joined, and here a short confabulation took place between the father and daughter, in their native tongue.

"You said you were going to join Fitz's camp at Bray[i]'s grave?" said Diego.

"That was my plan."

"Well, here we must part, for I am nigh done, and her"—pointing to his daughter—"and I must cashe on the other side, leave your trail broad here and there, we will cross the other stream, and hide where we can. You may bring some of the boys this way, it will make a diversion, let me have the little kettle you have behind the saddle, a sick man requires slops."

"I have never taken it off," I answered.

I saw there was but little time to lose, in getting them off toward a place of safety, the old Spaniard, as I took leave, said, with one of those looks which the wan hue of suffering could not subdue, or rob of its Castillian grandeur. "I have accepted your mule and your saddle."

Rose bent down her looks for a moment, and then pointed to the woods of the opposite hills.

I gave her my spyglass, and said, "we will light afire down here, you can answer it."

Chapter Forty-Four
Recoveries-the supernatural?—conversation with Old Bill Williams, Doc Newell, and others —fandango

These were the gay moments of the year, the first move of a camp into new ground, the fountain of forbidden waters[i] still alive, and the new recruits, redolent with horses and gaudy trappings, make a scene of more character and variety than is to be found in the ordinary movements of a trading party, the daring wanderings of the greenhorn often shew bright against the vauntings of experience, and the romance of the hunter's life, as exemplified in the ordinary occurrences of the day. At first the lip curls in unbelieving scorn at sober warnings, when a man is told that he has been hunted while he followed the chase, and that had he for a moment stopped to give a fair aim in such a pass, a ball had been driven through his brain, yet does it require a nerve of steel not to remember it next day, or what is better a disregard of life, such as he may have who has nothing to live for. But I crossed, while my companion went down the shallower part of the channel to ford the Popoagee. The swift blue waters divided us, and I turned my course to cut off the angle formed by the stream I had left, and its feeder, on which was to be the sought-for camp. There was a beginning of the grey, which precedes the dawn. I took a beeline in the direction which had been pointed out, everything was still, occasionally a wolf stole across my path, and I heard the grunt-like lowing of the bison, and once the rush of a herd which had got my wind. I had no horse to take care of, feeling assured that the Crow party would not come out of their way to follow us, encumbered with the valuable booty they had secured from Diego's lodge. I came to a little hollow, without trees or water, but basin-shaped and grassy, in this I tied my horse, and overcome with excitement and fatigue, gave myself up to sleep.

I need hardly describe a repetition of former scenes, that awakened by a thundering noise, two hundred horses passed almost over me, that gay and gallant hunters, and women bright in gaudy hues and needful baggage, and all the caparison of a roving band, bent on the joys as well as the fruits of the chase, were on the wing, that I was greeted with welcomes before I well understood that all this pageant-like array was other than a dream. My horse had broken loose and I stood in the midst of all an object of curiosity and mirth, how I had a saddle lent me, and how I told of Diego's robbery, without mentioning the mode of his escape, how I learned that a party, headed by the medicine man was out since dawn after the Crows, and that the whole camp was to stop a little lower down than I had crossed on my way hither.

It was in that day a beautiful and rich country, full of game and fruit, and be the success of the beaver hunter's what it might, all were now glad in the hope of passing the autumn in a region of almost unequalled resources, and profiting by those strict laws in regard to game, which secured to the Crows a constant supply for food, and also for the sale of robes. To run riot then among these herds of bison and wapati, which covered the prairies and filled the forests, was a prospect which had its charms for the idle and indolent, as well as the active and persevering.

We signaled Rose from her mountain nest, and Diego, tended with every comfort and care, recovered fast, the party who had robbed him, were overtaken before they left their camp, where they had first lodged the horses on their capture, meaning to start for the village the following night, a great part of the goods had been retaken, and but for the wound, there was little to cause any annoyance to one accustomed to a life of peril and change.

The party which was afterward to lose small detachments, and also the returns of peltries going down the Yellow Stone with Campbell[1], now numbered more than a hundred loose horses, besides the beasts of burthen, and therefore, a large space was required, and constant change.

The principal Crow village under Long Hair, was expected to be met with on some of the waters of the Popoagee, and we were to take short camps, until we met in with some indication of its vicinity. During several days there was almost an air of sulky defiance in the manner of Bernard, and once or twice this was so apparent, as to be remarked by those present, he had been forced to come forward and tell the truth about Reece's death, and it was now pretty well known that he himself would have left me to my fate. Heald had believed me to be the person, and it had suited him to carry out a certain system of law

---

1. Down the Yellow Stone with Campbell: Campbell *left rendezvous on July 24 and reaching the Bighorn on August 12, 1833, he constructed bull boats for a voyage down the river and the Yellowstone* (Hafen, *The Mountain Men and the Fur Trade*, VIII: 55). Like Fitzpatrick and Stewart, Campbell encountered a large party of Crows, but managed to get away unscathed.

in my case, probably for the same reasons which induced him to act so unfairly by me in other matters, but he was very angry at having nearly been allowed to commit a judicial murder which would have clung to the American camp as a disgrace, from the dastardly backwardness if not ill-will of the Swiss, who having been reproached with this, shewed that dislike which is never so strong as toward one who has been the object of injustice or injury.

Diego's manner was perhaps also a cause of uneasy jealousy, as he invariably shewed a marked preference for me to anyone else present, when I went to his lodge.

It was on the fourth day after I had joined the camp, we were upon one of the feeders of the main branch, which came in from the left bank, it was a rich grassy plain, between hills covered halfway down the side with pine, and the creeks and streamlets fringed with maple and birch, a lovely vale where our band of horses had displaced herds of bison and of deer. For a couple of days my friend David had disappeared, not as I learned quite an unusual occurrence for him, and I looked for his return with some anxiety.

Animal magnetism was a science to the general run of men, of whom I formed one, perfectly unknown, and I could scarcely believe what I had seen of its effects, besides, I had learned that the medicine man had known of the lake affair by its means, and had in consequence started to come to our assistance. This appeared to me bordering upon the supernatural, and added a feeling almost of awe, to that affection which it was natural I should feel for one who evidently liked me, and had been the means of putting it in Rose's power to save my life.

We were to move next day, and were to visit the Crow village before there was to be any separation amongst us. I sometimes eat with one mess, sometimes with another, but generally tied my horses near, and shared the shanty with Brant. I was free to go where I liked, and had passed muster as a hunter, and the exploit of recovering the horses on the Kanzas, had enabled me to count coups with many of those who had been long in the country. So that I was not considered as an intruder, or an encumbrance, which one more helpless might become.

The evening was fine, not a breath of air stirred, and the lodges and tents were abandoned for the open air, large fires of resinous pine illuminated the circle of the camp, lighting it up as if under a summer sun, some conversed, and a few slept, others kept alive the flames.

"I would not give a straw for your beaver caught among these poor Nezpercees, it is dear," said Dr. Newell, "where men's eyes look large, and their cheek bones are high."

There were some of Wyeth's people[2], who looked right ghastly for a month

---

2. Wyeth's people: Nathaniel J. Wyeth led an expedition to the Pacific Northwest in 1832-33.

after they got back, and smelt of fish. They had ground their teeth down to stumps, with eating sand on the Columbia.[ii]

"Yes, but men may have to do worse to fill their pockets," said another.

"Well, boys, I have seen something of hunting beaver, where there is no cow meat, and though it is to be done, it is no great fun, I say," said old Bill Williams.

"But you do not call the Big Hole and the Little Horse plains, and the divide, a country without buffalo."

"Not without buffalo," rejoined the other, "for I have heard say, when a party of the North West were on the lip of the Big Hole, where they expected meat, for they had been living on biscuit and moss from the trees, some in front sung out that there was not a buffalo in it, but 'the captain,'[iii] who was with them, took out his glass, and saw it swarming. So there are manythings that you can't see, no more than they."

"Well," rejoined Newell, "the country may not be without buffalo, but you wear out a horse upon an old cayack."[iv]

"There is Crosseagle, who is thinking of the Rhine all the time, or singing about it, though he never saw it, as it does not run through Brandenberg," said old Bill.

"Well, and you never saw the Delaware," said the German.

"No, but no man ever heard me sing a psalm upon it, you think there is nothing like your river and your split bird."

"Yes, our eagle has two heads, that is true, and yours has but one, and that is bald," said the Teutonic champion, reddening with wrath.

"Bill is too strong for any of us at present, with a hundred beaver skins at his back."

"Is John De Vilder making soap, Bill?" said Doty.

"How should I know."

"I didn't say you did."

"No, he is washing for Dr. Harrison[3], and all the squaws are learning."

"He promised to make me some dumplings," said a greenhorn, "and I bought sugar and flour, and some brandy."

"You had best look after them then," said Newell, "unless you would like me to do it."

---

3. Dr. Harrison: Dr. Benjamin Harrison, son of William Henry Harrison, ninth President of the United States. An early dude to travel the West for the sake of health, Harrison was a member of the Sublette & Campbell caravan which also took along Captain Stewart. According to Larpenteur (*Forty Years a Fur Trader*, pp. 16-17), Harrison went *with a view to break him from drinking whiskey*. Davenport and Porter indicate that it was Stewart who persuaded General Harrison that a mountain excursion might cure his son's alcoholism. Sublette & Campbell charged a thousand dollars (*Scotsman in Buckskin*, pp. 27-28). Dr. Harrison is said to have treated George Holmes, the trapper who was bitten by the mad wolf at rendezvous and later died.

"No, they are well enough off at present, thank you." He went toward John's mess.

"Come Crosseagle, sing us a hymn," shouted Harry Smith, and imitating a Tyrolian air, broke out to be joined by most of the rest, and now song and chorus succeeded, and the wild yudle rung through the neighburing pines, while occasionally a better voice came in a solo in milder tone and more delicate harmony, and even Bernard forgot his unsocial mood, and joined, each contributing when his turn came. Had they had Stein wine to match the music, Paradise would not have been envied to any one else. Fallon at last started up, and approaching Rose with castanets, and the gesture of the Fandango, she accepted the challenge, and that graceful of all movements, drew round them all the singing tribe, who took up the air, and never was there a grander music than these manly notes. Fallon's noble figure, and his partner's beauty and grace, called forth shouts of approbation, I saw Bernard's lurid scowl, which appeared as ready for another as for me, while I leant against a tree, absorbed in the pleasure of the moment.

Chapter Forty-Five
Visions—a storm—horses stolen

I caught but one glance of Rose's eye, it was one not of triumph but of a melancholy reproach, for I had been gazing raptly at her, with perhaps a little too much of inward feeling in the outward gaze, when a gentle touch claimed my attention, it was the Chochoco, his light short robe gathered round his slender frame, calmly he stood at my side, but an eye of flame lit up the pallid face that was raised toward mine. Without a moment's hesitation I turned from the scene, and the Indian youth shot on through the line of fires, and we were alone on the slope of the mountain's base behind the camp.

Contrary to the habit among the whites, the Indian speaks best seated, and that cross-legged on the ground, and I felt that my companion had something to say of unusual import thus to overcome his reserve, so, setting the example, we were soon squatted on the turf. He told me that his spirit was troubled, and that he had seen his father, so he called the medicine man, in a dream, and blood was trickling from his breast, but he could see no more. I eagerly enquired if he could form no idea of where he was, he shook his head. But I saw there was something yet unsaid or untold.

At last I got him to say that he knew he told manythings when he was put to sleep by the medicine man, and that if I could do it he might be able to tell something of him. Finding that he had a lock of his hair twisted into a strange knot, which he always wore on his breast, suspended round the neck by a collar of beads, I began to make passes as the process had been described and shewn to me by him in whose behalf it was now to be exercised, and Hi-Hi soon sunk under its influence.

In the command I then obtained over his mind, I had not to feign a strong volition, it was already there.

"Do you know where your father is?" I asked.

"I cannot see more than a dark hole in the rock, and he is sitting making the writing of the white men."

"Is he wounded?"

"No, I see nothing. A fire burns at the entrance, and shines on a black stream."

"What does he write on?"

"Thin white pieces laid flat on each other and cut straight and even at the sides. There is more light, the moon shines on the rock and on water below. I cannot tell where it is."

"What does he think about?"

"He is tired counting, and he thinks about Edward."

"What does he think?"

"He wishes to find out who he is, that he is kept away from his country by enemies."

"Does your father love this Edward?"

"Yes, much."

There were several more answers, but nothing more explicit, and I disenchanted the poor boy. When he came to himself, immediately told him what he had described, and that David was now well. He made me repeat the description of the cave, the rock, and the deep black stream in front, and dropped his head on his breast in helpless despondency.

My friend then was well, but I felt still the desire to find him out, perhaps at the moment when his midnight lamp was trimmed. A watch was set round the retreat, the strange pertinacity with which the boy, for so his small stature caused him to be called, clung to his belief in the fulfilment of his dream, though deferred had its effect upon me almost as strong as the belief I had in the extraordinary knowledge thus acquired.

The Chochoco came back with me to my lodging under a bush of buffalo berries, over whose boughs had been thrown a piece of lodge skin. He spoke not a word, nor was there any outward sign of grief. The sounds of revelry had ceased, the winds breathed through the pines above their low moan, and the thin upper clouds were driving over the clear sky. The restless river murmured along its course.

How long I had slept I cannot tell, but I believe it was a flash of lightning first awoke me, for a second it lit up the small space into which I had nestled myself and my gear, as if it had been on fire, and a crash came after, such as I had never before heard, it shook the earth on which I lay crouched. Somewhere near it must have struck, or there hardly could have been such a shock, and this had scarcely ended, when a flood of light came again, such as by which I thought could be counted every leaf above my head, so impressive and intense was the glare, and then poured down a torrent of such rain as deluged the earth around in a moment.

One part of my bed was already under water, before I had time to roll it to the highest side. The storm had reached its worst, and the succeeding flashes came longer after the thunder. The fires were out, and I had covered myself up again to make the best defence I could against the chill. Hi-Hi had nestled himself close to me in a sort of ball, his head against his knees.

It might have been an hour after the worst of the storm, and a broken sort of sleep had taken possession of me, when I was awoke by my companion, who whispered gently, "There's something coming."

But fancying his nerves, always in such high tension, had been over excited, I turned over to dispose myself to sleep, when the short sharp bark of the medicine wolf sounded as if close to camp. This evil omen, however, had not over my mind the same boding power which made it so dreaded by the men of the country. I felt the young Indian shudder, and I knew his affectionate heart was wrung by the belief that some evil was hanging over his friend and protector, but sleep, which comes so welcomely upon him whose habits must be those of activity, and whose food is the most simple and the most wholesome, stole over me.

The discharge of a couple of shots in close succession, and a yell, aroused me at once from sleep and bed, I had never heard the yell of the savage as a foe. The night was dark, and the wind howled in a chilly blast, with a drizzling rain. The horses were already in motion, rushing and snorting, ropes had been broken, and the unearthly cries of the savage, mingled with the blast, and rising wild and high over the general din.

The guards had sought shelter, so that the surprise had been complete. The herd was swept away as if by a whirlwind. I plainly heard the thundering course, and in the murky starless night could only meet half-naked figures rushing about in consternation. My companion had disappeared on the first alarm. Brent brushed past me almost naked.

"Did you observe which way they went?" he said.

"No, the sound seemed to come as if from above the camp," I answered.

"If there were none broken before the first din, they have made a clean sweep," added Harry Smith, who now joined us.

"Who was on guard?"

"I don't know. The Swiss for one I believe," I answered, as I tripped over a rope and fell.

On returning to my recollections, for I found I had been rendered for a time senseless, I was lying among some dwarf bushes. Approaching voices, and the sound of my own name uttered at no great distance, arrested my attention, as I began to collect my thoughts.

"But what would you have me do, you do not suppose I am to stick a knife in his back without a quarrel!" said a voice I recognized to be Heald's.

"You have tried to do nearly as bad for him already."

"More time to stop, his medicine is stronger than ours."

"Yes, but if we leave the work undone."

"I know not what work you mean," broke in the other roughly. "I have let him in for every chance, and there was the hunting party, but this cursed raise of the Crows has baulked that, though he is gone with the others in pursuit. It's but a wild night, and I scarcely think they can overhaul them."

"You know they were Crows?"

"Yes, there was a moccasin left, and old Margot thought she knew one, or heard some Crow words, but if so, we will have to go on foot to the village, it is near the hot springs I guess. The medicine man is well away any how, but you had best to bed, the night's work is done, and you have made but a botch of your guard, so you may reckon how you are to foot it when you are awake."

The weather was chill and damp, cold gusts came fitfully, and I lost the remainder of the conversation as they turned out of sight. I had now got up from my concealment, and wiped the blood from my face, and turned into a hollow to get back to the camp by another direction. There were but few dogs with us, and they belonged to some squaws of the northern nations, but they had been thoroughly alarmed, and were now keeping up a continued bay. All besides seemed still, the fires had been drowned out, and a general black blank had traced to the scene of suspended life, which is presented by a camp in repose.

Part Three

Chapter Forty-Six
A Hunt with Bill Williams—danger

The later portion of Autumn, Winter and Spring, have passed away, it boots not to tell of the snowings up, and the want of meat occasionally, and the long evenings, and their histories and Canadian songs. Summer had come again. We had recovered our horses from the Crows, on condition of leaving their hunting grounds.

I had long left the main body to make a hunt with a party, of whom old Williams was the head, toward the Utewa country, and from there across Snake river to the Titons, and the horse plains.

Rose had gone to live with Bernard in a separate lodge before I left, and the interest I took in trapping and hunting occupied my mind, leaving but little room for sentiment and imagination. Better success than need have been expected crowned my fall campaign, and I was an expert beaver hunter by the spring. Bill had not the reputation of being rash, and we avoided a great deal of danger by a great deal of caution. We had been a part of the winter with the Snakes at the little lake, and passed on from thence by the Blackfoot river, to cross Lewis's Fork toward the Titons[1].

---

1. To cross Lewis's Fork toward the Titons: From winter quarters at Bear Lake (*the little lake*), according to Stewart's summary here, the party moved north onto the Blackfoot River and down it to the Snake (Lewis's Fork), then east across *one of the passes which lead to Jackson's Hole*, perhaps Teton Pass, in order to meet with other trappers and proceed south to rendezvous on Green River. The reference to a *pass at the end of the mountains of the winds* is confused or confusing: South Pass, far to the southeast, can scarcely be intended. The indicated crossing of Snake River would be necessary to get to Union Pass, at the northwestern end of the Wind River Mountains, but that would involve backtracking.

The whole of that country was then filled with game. The Missouri Indians sometimes came across, occasionally the Flatheads and the Snakes, but it might justly be called *war ground*, and therefore was not a quiet or a safe region.

It may be necessary to explain that Bernard had accounted for his appearance in the West, by a desire to be emancipated from a school drudgery he detested, and that a national love of his own deep valleys, their torrents and their rills, had pressed him onward to seek for kindred scenes in this range of the northern Andes. We were all to meet who might be on this side, at some given spot not far from Jackson's Hole, about the end of June, and proceed together to rendezvous, which it was conjectured would be somewhere near Green River.

After recrossing Lewis's Fork to take the pass at the end of the mountains of the winds, it became a matter of the most intense interest to look for traces, as well of those who hunted them, as of the animals themselves, to read the hieroglyphics of the great war-path, and look for the most recent sign.

We had left the horse plain, and not without risk as well as trouble crossed the swollen waters of Lewis's Fork, the most southern branch of the Columbia. It was early, the camp was struck, and the summer morn hardly lit by the coming sun, and we were under way for one of those passes which lead to Jackson's Hole, it had been an object to get over an open shoulder of the mountain, before there should be light to let us be seen from any great distance.

Jim Macarey was in front, having preceded us some distance, and we wended on our way in that silence, which is often found to characterise travelers in the earlier hours of the morning, and under the influence of a certain degree of cold. It was a fresh and balmy air, a heavy shower during the night had left its traces, some of them still hung in the sparkling drops, which gemmed the sage through which we passed.

Smith and Brent were out, they had gone on further than the rest of the party the night before, to set their traps in some gulley in the mountain side, within the range of the woods, where they expected beaver. I was muffled to the mouth in my blanket, the thoughts of the party seemed to be absorbed each in its own direction, and like diverging rays, were probably directed toward various parts of the earth. We followed in Indian file, and I found myself up against my front man, by the sudden check of the head of the column.

"Had there been a distillery of half the sage of the Susquedee, we could not have had it stronger, it is the incense of this very morning, and the dust could not have been but just laid. I actually hear them, they must be settling over the ridge."

This speech came from old Bill, who had stopped like a pointer, dead on the scent, but his eye was directed, not toward where the bent and torn sage pointed the course of the herd, but to the direction from which they had come. I had crowded up to the front, to inhale the fresh aromatic odour, and hear the opinion of the wary upon what might have been but an accidental move.

"Smith and Brent are out on our right, and they come from the left of our trail, and they are roused," said Chariot Cuvier. "Keep the hollow, boys, and get hold of the loose horses, the loaded ones won't stray far."

The lassos were already circling over the band, running on and snatching a moment's bite at the small tufts of grass, freshened by the previous rain, and we were soon ranged as if we had been going, each with our string, to a horse fair in England.

Jim had stopped on the nearest rise beyond the bison trail, to see if any change might have taken place in our advance, but seeing that we followed on, he disappeared over the height. Looking back, I could see a slight blush light tinge the tops of the Utewa mountains, and yellow their snows with a hue of gold, but we were as yet in the shadow of the pile to the east, and not far from where it began more abruptly to rise, and show the hollows which furrowed the base, and divided what have been called, I know not how appropriately, its spurs, and every eye was strained to see if there might not be something astir before, but we were nearing one of those glens, three of which headed close upon the pass, it was the middle one, and both rough and long, partly a bison path, and partly a trail.

"We are in for it, either for the plains or the mountains, and I think we are safest here, the Blackfeet would pass for the Arapahoes by Ham's Fork, and the Bad Gaushey is on the Bear River."

"We are altogether best on the other side," muttered our leader, half in soliloquy, as I came up by his side. But I could see something like irresolution in the half glance he turned toward one who could so little counsel him, we had held on for two hours, and the pines began to thicken, and Jim, uncertain that he might not go too far, halted till we overtook him.

"Look out for a brake, where there may be some grass and water, for we had best let those that started that band, go over before us." And with whip and herd, Jim again took his place in front, and was lost to our sight the first turn.

It was evident things were in a serious position, and every startled bird, or echo of our own steps, might be mistaken for a warning of danger, these journeys are seldom conversational, but silence on this occasion wore a more portentous gloom, the hoods of the capots were thrown back, and the gun covers tucked under the belts, the animals instinctively let themselves be led close, and those loaded, which were loose, squeezed in amongst them, as when alarmed by the scent of the grisly bear. The eager eye and the bent brow took place of the usual reckless bearing of the band.

"I wish the two who are out were back," I observed. "We are enough for small odds, and they would not save us from greater."

"Whose horse is making that damned row?" Bill pulled up short, and beckoned to a horseman who had separated from the band and taken a line on the opposite side, thinking probably to be of use as a flanker.

"You want to bring the works upon us, with your noise?" said Phelps, for it was he, was beginning.

"I thought—"

"Yes, I know you thought it is an advantage men say they have over brute beasts, but your thoughts, though they might put us to sleep, cannot keep your horse quiet."

It was no time for disputing.

"I wish we had the sun at our backs, and low, I should like to see a little clearer under the trees," said Phelps.

"That is, you wish it were night, and all were well," said I, not so fully awake to the general anxiety as I might be.

"Keep back, you are not to be trusted in front, but keep your eyes skinned all the same," said Bill, and we resumed our sombre march.

About a mile was made in evident expectation of an attack, the occasional movement of a martin, or a porcupine, being noticed almost with alarm.

Just as we made a turn, which exposed a longer vista, less encumbered with trees than before, I perceived an Indian standing calmly on a mound in our course, as if waiting our approach, and with a sort of low half-whistle, arrested the attention of the old trapper, who was on his feet, and his rifle ready behind his horse in a moment.

"They must be in some force, to show so plain," whispered Chariot, as he also jumped down. "Its but an elk, however now that I am low enough to see his head gear," he added, "but let old Bill alone, see what he will make of it."

"He is not looking back, and has been coming down wind," said our leader, after drawing a long breath, and he remounted.

"Well, lad, that's a good eye-shot, there is nothing just to fear on that side, there he's off Chariot, go and find if he has not come from our left, you'll easily get his foil on the grass, or the turning up of the dead pine leaves."

The whip came down with confidence on the shaggy flank of his Indian steed, as the half-breed launched off at a swinging gallop. There was an evident relief in the expression of every eye.

"Why should he look behind, if he has the wind in his back," said a voice, in something of a French accent. "Make beaver medicine, Bill, but you cannot read the signs of woodcraft."

And a figure rose out of a little crevice, caused by the water in time of rain, it was but a crack in the earth, and tufts of grass grew on its lips like mustachios, and though he rose without hurry, there was a suddenness in the apparition, which startled our camp leader's horse, and belied the circumspection in which we had believed ourselves advancing.

Chapter Forty-Seven
Antoine Clement—a message—travel

The figure which stood before us, was that of a youth under twenty, a half-breed, with light-brown hair worn long, and the almond-shaped hazel eye of his mother's race—the fine formed limbs and small hands, with a slightly olive tinge of skin. His dress was almost Indian, consisting of a leather shirt and leggings, coming a little above the knee, almost to meet it, and tied up to the waist belt by a small strip of leather, on the outside of each thigh. The skirt of the shirt, though full, did not reach far down, thus forming a short Scotch kilt and coat all in one, which may probably be the original shape of that species of attire.

"Well, I reckon you're afoot this morning, being so sharp set, Mr. Clement?"

"No, sir, not by a long way." Antonie vaulted on to the back of a loose horse.

"Now, boys, don't be afeard of being surprised, old Bill is himself that sharp, a Blackfoot would sneeze at the sight of him a hundred yards off."

Our leader did not seem much put out by this attack, notwithstanding the laugh it raised, and a general sort of string of questions and answers went on between the newcomer and the others in an undertone.

The old trapper looked round at Antonie, whenever he saw an opening, but still held on his way, at last, one of those looks was answered by a nod, and we turned off sharp to the right, over a bare shelf of granite along a grove, in which trickled a thread of water, and winding through a few boulders, we at once found ourselves in a small marshy meadow, interspersed with bushes of birch and quaking ash, it seemed long and narrow.

Four good men for guard, each with a horse in his hand, the rest set to work at a pen. We found old Le Blanc fast asleep, and Antonie Goddard on guard, but Jim Macarey had passed on unobserved, and the sun was low, when he got into camp, he had been on as far as the pass, and had there found a piece of bark, newly peeled off, on the white side of which something was written, and as it was so freshly done, he had brought it to have it read. I was out on guard when it arrived, and when I came in, saw that something had happened, by the group which was eagerly scanning the document.

Bill said it was neither Latin nor English, and it did not appear to be considered much better than a hoax.

"Perhaps," said someone as I came up, "it may be a joke of Black Harris, to humbug some Snakes into the belief that he could write, and I see a B at the bottom."

"Well, B stands for bottom," observed Black-muzzle critically, who had become a camp keeper, since Bernard had joined Diego.

"And for Black-Muzzle also," said Bill, "so you may shut up."

I had squeezed in to get a peep, and perceived at a glance, that the language was French, though the charcoal was somewhat rubbed, and the words run into one another too close.

"I bet a beaver, Ned reads it right away," said Antoine Clement, over whose shoulders I was leaning.

"Well, and whose hindering him," said our reverend leader, and he handed me the scroll—for it was curled up by the heat—over his shoulder.

It was merely to say, that Diego and John Gray were on the west side of the lake, below the pass, and I conjectured by the initial, it had been written by Bernard.

"I heard that Rose had had a boy," observed Goddard.

I do not know why, but I felt a sort of shudder at the announcement, I did not like Goddard, and—though it was to be expected—-did not like the news.

"There are to be lots of strangers at rendezvous," Goddard continued, "and money is as good to the Bosses[i] as beaver, so I rather mean to make myself scarce, and I dare say so does also Diego."

The wind blew a gale the next day, as we were on the way to get to the other side of the pass, and to the lake along the northeast shore of which ran the trail, the only practicable passage for horses from the headwaters of the Colorado to those of the Columbia[1]. We were keeping compact and close, and

---

1. The only practicable passage from the headwaters of the Colorado to those of the Columbia: The geography of this section is confused *From the headwaters of the Colorado* must mean upper Green River, and *those of the Columbia* must mean Snake River. But the party, in fact, goes down Wind River, which indicates passage to the headwaters of the Missouri, not the Colorado, it is consistent with the reference *northern feeders of the Big Horn*, below. In that case, the *practicable passage* is Togwotee Pass.

had got over the ridge which forms the divide, with its marks and hieroglyphics traced in black paint—made of pounded charcoal and grease—upon the great walls of granite, which occasionally lined the road, here and there a heap of stones marked a spot on which a bloody death had occurred.

The two Antoines, as they passed, had read the histories which were recent, that is which they had not seen before, and the Blackfoot, the Crow, and the Snake, had each been there. These races were as different from the wretched specimens of the red race, which are to be found in the Eastern States of the Union, or in Canada, as the limits of human character will admit, they have a taste for quaint, but expressive painting[ii], and can make themselves perfectly understood by signs, their languages being all totally different, and having only one common characteristic in sound, if a want can be considered such, which is the want of the letter *r*. In signs, they are both elegant and expressive, and it is really beautiful to follow an Indian, who expressed himself well in signs, not only from the correctness and precision with which they are made, but by the classic elegance of the attitude in which his thoughts are represented. It is impossible to mistake the meaning of an intelligent Crow or Blackfoot with ordinary perceptions and imagination.

It was not far in the day, when having avoided the opens as much as possible which lay in our course, the lake appeared beneath all agitated, but partly white with drift and foam, and the curve of the valley had conducted the wind, so as to throw it on to the water from the upper end, and it swept down the entire length with unopposed fury. It is probable we should not have moved camp, had the morning been less serene, but being afoot, it was as well to get on to some spot, where we could decide on the next movement, which, in whatever direction, must take us out of the limits of the pines, and throw us on to those plains in which the great tribes camp, and which small parties avoid, until they know that the coast is clear.

For a considerable time, the half-breeds were riding ahead, occasionally in conversation with our partizan, and from an occasional turn of the head, and pointing with the chin—an Indian never points with the hand—it was evident that the subject of debate was where we might best be sheltered and lie by, for both a lull and a look-out.

"I don't know whether the day is in our favor, or against us?" I asked Antoine Clement.

"In our favor," he answered, "out looks are not so sharp, and there is more chance of the moving of a lock of hair or a feather, in such a wind."

There was something to be liked about this half-breed, and I had kept by his side all morning, there was not much to be got by direct questioning, but occasionally he put forth some symptoms of the most extraordinary sagacity, as well in respect to hunting as to the ways of the man and the brute with whom he was in the habit of coming in contact.

"We shall see nothing here that is not roused."

We had almost reached the lake, the boisterous storm obliged us to be close together to hear each other's voices without shouting, but Antoine leaned closer toward me as he said low and quickly, "We have no business down that way. There is a camp somewhere on this side the Blackfoot, I know by signs of stragglers for the last two days."

"Why did not you speak to Bill before?" I inquired.

"I have not picked up marks enough for the old one."

"Well, but the sooner we turn, the less we shall have of this cursed wind to face in getting back."

"That's it," said Antoine, by a sign and a smile, and I quickened my pace to communicate what I had learned to the local and moral head of the party, who, when he heard who was the suggester of a return, and the observation which led to it, halted at once, and as the others near the front closed up, he told them that there were appearances which indicated a camp of Indians not far off, probably Blackfeet.

The announcement, as might be supposed, produced considerable murmurs among those whose eagerness to arrive at rendezvous and lose nothing of its pleasures, made ready to rush on at whatever hazard. God-dard, and old Le Blanc, and Phelps, even, of the number, and Chariot Cuvier, they made a struggle to get the rest to despise the prudence of a backward movement.

"We are good for a war party, but ten men are not a bite for a camp, and I, for one," said Bill, "do not want to fight for my horses and beaver, that I may lose my hair into the bargain, whether you approve of its color or not, and should we have a battle, it is my opinion that there might be more of the same hue."

"That might happen just as well on the other side as this," said someone. "I have a better opinion of the Crows, however."

"Oh, as to opinion, we may have our'n also," said Phelps.

"I conclude you have, or there would hardly be a talk."

"Well," said Goddard as he made a movement onward, "we are as well shot of an old fool."

"As there seems to be only a difference of age then between us, let us sink that, and part friends," said Bill, as he made a half-courteous salute in passing back, leading his mules, more precious from their burthens.

"We are safe for a while, taking the back trail."

Nothing appeared to move among the trees but their own tossed and breaking boughs, and it was not probable anything would be afoot on the plains, should the tempest rage without as it did between the hills.

The lake was a sheet of scud, all but its few sheltered bays. We were recalled to a sense of our position, however, by the gale, which nearly blew some of the nearest over the open brink, on which we had turned to look upon the waving woods and raging water below, dark masses of careering clouds, by their intervals of passing, varying the scene with glare and gloom. The animals were gathered close, and in fact, did not seem inclined to stray.

"Let's get out of this, boys," said Antoine, "if the wind breaks down but a tree, there will be a clean sweep—the first one does it, and there is also a good thing in our favor, old Le Blanc is sure to make the biggest smoke in the west, when they halt, if he does not set fire to the works with his pipe before."

The pace was slackening, and a course taken to the right, leaving the trail we had quitted on the other hand, and descending as we turned into another valley.

"I believe we shall have a portage to get over the divide," said Bill.

"No, sir," answered Antoine, "I know a shelf above." And he got to the front and passed off the almost blind trail up a piece of bare rock.

I was about to cut off an angle to join him, when I could distinguish the word *Gare*[2], and a sign to follow file. He dismounted as soon as I was by his side, and showing me, by a sign of his head, a sort of level which was really a shelf with a precipice above and below, gave me his leading cord into my hand, and with a sort of chuckle disappeared over the ledge beneath at a single bound. The old partizan passed me without a word, and I felt that I was intended to take care of the horse.

In this way, after proceeding three-quarters of an hour, for the most part ascending, we came upon a large mass of boulders and broken rock, fallen from the upper cliff, and the way was stopped, and there was nothing for it but to return.

While I was thinking that we might have been a little better instructed, and had got but a few yards back, Bill turned up another bare rock, shining with wet moss, which pointed itself out as leading to a stage above, and soon after, we were upon the brow of the hill, some distance above the lowest pass.

From this bald spot, over which the tempest swept without a blade to scathe, we could see the ridges of the vallies down which flow the northern feeders of the Big Horn. I know not why, but a sense of sadness came over me as I looked in vain to behold again any part of the great plains we had so recently quitted, their wide though bleak extent had had its charms as well as its perils.

---

2. Gare: From the French verb *Garer*, to take cover. In this context, *Look out!*

Chapter Forty-Eight
A nocturnal encounter—song—ambition—Blackfeet

The season was but growing on to its prime—the region before us was thick with game—yet well I knew where these waters flowed, and how soon they arrived among the ordinary herds of the human race, with their vulgar toil after wealth. I was leaving the vagueness of the West for a country through which—whatever its own charms—every step I took led nearer the spinning jenny and the exchange, but these thoughts were broken in upon by the sudden appearance of Antoine, who again stood before our leader, as if sprung out of the earth.

"A small party are through before us—last night, I think. I can't tell till I see the sign again," he added, to a look of inquiry, and by a sign, further explained that they were whites. He was now on his horse, and leading down the slope among the trees.

It was high noon, and we were well over the divide. The gale, in reality from the northwest, still blew with its former fury, but the valley we were leaving, running nearly east and west when we got out of it and turned to the right, the storm was from behind, and its power considerably broken by the abutting heights, which ran out toward the Popoagee above, but a little out from the mountains we could occasionally through an open observe the effects of the wind—columns of dust and the sage bending over and wavering to the blasts.

As the trail was found to be of the early morning, it was decided not to get too close, and we edged downward to where the waters were less precipitous in their descent, and there was more chance of grass. Finding a small flat of tolerable extent and verdure, through which, often lost under its hollow overhanging banks, ran a small stream, the camp was formed, and a horse pen.

The heat of the day had long passed, and was fast succeeding to it the coolness which evening brings in that elevated region. The wind had died away, and the leaf of the aspen hardly fluttered, out of our own camp there appeared no living thing, and was to be heard no sound.

Antoine, impatient of inactivity, had gone out to look among the crags above for a reported lake and a colony of beaver, and having no one with whom I particularly felt inclined to converse, I sauntered about, a vein of fat blue clay had enabled me to do a little washing, and my gaudy cottons having confronted the glorious sun until it sunk from the contest, were ready to be reconsigned to the possible sack.

Some dry sticks had been got, and a small smokeless fire was beginning to crackle, at last came the night, and I was sitting by this attenuated flame, which I allowed to flicker and faint, and then but feebly revive. Every now and then I cast my eyes upon such of my charge as whose heads were visible over the fence, at the door of which I sat.

The early part of the night is that in which the horse takes his rest, and many of them never lie down. The shanties of the party were formed round this enclosure. The darkness was to be divided into two watches, the first extending to nearly one in the morning. Though I had a small Briguet[1] which, according to a compass with which it was occasionally consulted, kept pretty good time, I looked up upon the sky, leaning back into a stunted bush of dwarf willow, and watched the position of the pointers in their course round the North star, they were in the direction of two on a clock dial, and that year this position indicated nearly about eleven. There was occasionally a meteor, and I was thinking of the phenomenon of the falling stars[2], which in the preceding November, had made us believe that heaven and earth were coming together, when the low notes of a subdued voice struck me as if borne by the regular breathing of the pines, in strange Aeolian wildness, but human tones. The ready rifle was in my hand, the night was clear, and the moon was high.

I turned softly, and my head was now where the back of my neck had rested, and I could see a gun-shot length to take accurate aim, concealed by the boughs over my shoulders, I could observe the horses in quietness, one, with ears pricked, looked—but calmly—toward the direction of the sound. The air, for it seemed a song, neither fainted in greater distance nor loudened by coming near. It could be no one bent on mischief or concealment.

---

1. A small Briguet: A chronometer, an accurate navigator's timepiece.
2. Falling stars: Here Stewart places an event that actually took place in 1832.

I listened on, there was, I felt, monotony if not obstinacy in its continued sameness, and I hailed, "Qui va la?[3]"

The singing ceased, and I could hear the clear low voice give the name, "Hi-Hi."

It was a voice I knew so well—there could be no deception, and contrary perhaps to rule in such cases, I bade him come to the fire, in such words of Snake as I thought would convey my wish, but without rising from my position, or changing the preparations for defence I had previously made.

The moonlight showed but the one figure, and the height and air were equally to be recognized, the robe worn short, like the Blackfoot, not to encumber the wearer on foot, and gathered high toward the temples to shelter the face from the moonbeam. At an unhurried, though not a reluctant-looking pace, he was approaching, while I still kept my eye in the distance behind, not from distrust, but for fear he might have been followed.

The young Chochoco was now quietly seated by my side, and after having replenished and lit his pipe, I was free to ask him the news. We had not met for many months, and I was really glad to see him, and I could easily read in the serene brow and smiling though sad eye, that he also was pleased at the meeting.

He gave me his hand, and looked long in my face, on which the pale light fell.

"My brother has had plenty of cow meat in the last snows."

I nodded assent.

"And has got no squaw to make his moccasins." I looked toward my feet, on which the beauty of the embroidery was less conspicuous than the care of the mender.

"Why were you singing just now, Hi-Hi?"

"To prevent your shooting. I saw Antoine, who told me you would be on guard, and I thought you would know the song."

"But I did not, what was it?"

"Oh, it is Cre'e."

There was something wild and mournful in it, as he laid himself down and looked up to the midnight sky, and sang what, when translated, I found to have been almost a prayer, beating time upon his expanded chest.

The words I have endeavoured to render into a sort of rhythm, but the translation is almost literal, as I have no claim to poetic license.

> *My arrow a sharp point hath,*
> *And the brave on his war-path,*
> *From the bent bow, with silent wing,*

---

3. Qui va la?: French for *Who goes there?*

> *The shaft speed is quivering.*
> *Let it be in a big brave heart,*
> *That throbs as the life's streams flow,*
> *Oh, let not the home of my first aimed dart*
> *Be warmed by blood of chillier glow.*
> *Let the dark hair be young, glossy, and long,*
> *Let it be of a head high o'er the throng,*
> *Let its jetty waves have been comb'd by fair fingers,*
> *Let me Watch his wild sorrow while yet life lingers.*
> *And then let the trophies and scalp of the slain*
> *Be sung in the camp of the far distant plain.*
> *Oh, moon, come down from the middle of the night,*
> *And show me their war-path with thy cold white light.*
> *The smoke shall rise, and the pipe shall be given,*
> *And its odor shall breathe in the calm of heaven.*[i]

"Then you want to count a coup, Hi-Hi?"

"To be heard when I speak among my people."

"And you have no fear?"

He turned his eyes toward me as he lay, as if to understand what I meant.

"I have told my brother that I want to count a coup," he repeated, after a pause.

Whether Jim, who was to succeed me in my guard, had heard our voices, or had accidentally awakened, I did not enquire, he was always ready to save me any fatigue, or share in any danger, and though no longer hired by me, lent me a hand as I did to him, at loading or tying up, he showed no surprise at seeing the digger. We made the circuit of the pen, all seemed right, and I took the wanderer with me, and turned in. The horses had to be kept in hand for their short interval between the pen and the saddle, as the scarceness of grass under the trees might induce them to wander.

Jim was to give an eye to mine, as he was up, while I was to arrange the packs, I looked for Hi-Hi, but he was not to be seen, he had slept on Jim's appichimoes, but they merely retained the warmth of recent occupation, he was gone. Such departures were not inconsistent with his habits, but I was vexed not to have had the opportunity of questioning him further on several points, on which he might be able to give information.

A good lump of meat had been cut off a fleece which had hung above our heads on the shanty's bow, so we were not to expect to see him immediately again, he had, I however began to recollect, been unusually excited, and I feared was bent upon fulfilling some of those dreams which occupied his imagination, and constituted his ambition. But he was gone, and my attention was brought back to the evident risks of our own position.

The day was beautiful and calm, the forest still solemn, though not to be called gloomy, as the early sun beat upon the eastern face of the mountains, and its beams came occasionally into the glades through an open, and lit up the neighboring stems. Keeping as near the outside as prudence permitted, we had already made considerable way, when I perceived what I considered to be a medicine wolf stealing along, not far from our course, and motioned to Jim Macarey to observe it, who, after looking for some time, suddenly asked for my glass.

"It is no wolf, it is a dog, there is a burnt spot on his hip, I saw it when he turned, there must be some camp near."

We were a little behind the rest, I looked about as if already to see the signs of danger further confirmed, there was no use in spreading an alarm, every one of the party knew we were in a spot where it was impossible to calculate who were to be found before, or might be following after.

Jim looked about for a moment, and then pressed on past our leader, pointing still forward, and getting almost out of sight. In the absence of Antoine, he was evidently the one of the party best fitted for a scout, the part he thus appeared to appropriate to himself. A certain degree of seriousness had crept over us all, it was evident some sort of difficulty was expected, and all eyes were strained.

The Indian dog had disappeared, not forward or behind, as if following a camp, but upward toward the mountains. The open valley was distant below, and our object was to pursue a course screened from its view, the passing of some ravines was difficult, and there were impediments in the way which caused occasional delay in the thick forest, so that the distance we had made the first four hours, was not very great from point to point, following each other in moody silence. In threading a path among the trees, there was all at once a sudden check ahead, leaving go my baggage mule which I had been leading, I pushed forward.

Macarey was seated on a stone, and under the brink upon which we had halted, rushed a torrent over a rugged bed, between impassable steeps.

"You ask if I know the creek, Jim," said Bill, with some seriousness as I came up. "There are few creeks or forks I do not know in these parts, but it is a different thing knowing a stream smiling and sparkling in its pebble bed in a sunny plain, and tearing along the clift of a mountain canon, there never has been seen a peeled stick float down its waters, and therefore, I have left it free to come from the snows and go to the devil, according to its own fashion."

Jim smiled at this denunciation, but I could see who knew how to read, under his quiet and unperturbed manner, that there was not much gladness beneath.

"I scarcely think there is a crossing above."

"And I know there is not," said Antonie Goddard from behind, who had suddenly appeared, his horse jaded and foot sore, and his whole appearance betokening a hurried ride. "I thought you had known of a place to pass, or I should not have followed your trail up here, we must try and get in time to cross below, before we are seen."

I here interposed, and asked some explanation in French, of the sudden return of this half-breed.

"That can be given as we go down, there is no council to hold, ride on Goddard before," said someone representing a slight sensation of panic which had now evidently taken place of our former uncertainty.

The brink of the canon was less encumbered with wood than the ground over which we had come. I kept in front, and got out of our guide, who hardly seemed to like to acknowledge his having been obliged to retreat after the previous day's vaunting, that they had been surprised soon after they left us by a party of Blackfeet. He had escaped unseen by them, and the others had forted, and had a fight, in which two Indians had been killed, and he believed some wounded, that while they were deliberating, he had fired from a concealed position in their rear, and knocked over another, the smoke had been blown away, and they thought there was an attack from another party behind, and put out for the pass. The affair had occurred about noon, when there had been a halt.

"My horse," he added, "was concealed some way from the spot, and by the time I thought it safe to get out of cashe, and was mounted, the works were gone in a rush. I got two scalps, if any wounded remained, they had crept into covert, and I decided on taking your trail, which I had seen fork off the other on turning back after a cougar, which was the cause of my being separated from the rest before they halted to noon."

Before he had finished speaking, we had got upon a higher and barren spot, and in a few steps more, had a view of the prairie below. The hawk-eye of the native widened to an eager stare, and he reined in, almost throwing his horse back upon mine, the open, parallel to our course this morning and the day before, was dotted with horsemen, the advanced guard of a camp.

"They must be coming strong," I observed. "But who are they?"

"Oh, for that matter, they are bound to be Blackfeet, and will camp at the forks."

"We are in a fix now," said Jim, as he came up and saw us peeping over the bald height, behind which a group was clustering.

"But where is the other trail, I think it must be Diego's," resumed Goddard, and a discussion ensued, in which I took no part, my thoughts were occupied with the danger Rose was running also with ourselves.

At last Bill said, "Ssomeone had better go down to the end of the canon, if they have shot on, perhaps they may get clear, but if not, their best course is to come up higher out of the way, and take a chance of being able to pass with ourselves in the night." And this seemed to have the weight of an order in council, after a moment's hesitation, I offered myself to search for Diego, and no one said me nay. Jim, always devoted to me, took the reins of my animals, and I already knew that I should go on foot.

"If you don't find them near the water before you get to where the trees give out, get back with your hair on your head, keep the edge of the wood, and be quickish of foot and eye, as I think there are no stragglers forward yet, and you may be in plenty of time."

Chapter Forty-Nine
A mission—a bear hunt ending in surprise— brotherhood

I was already plunging through some brushwood, and was not long in bounding down the descent a considerable distance, taking occasional glimpses to the torrent's brink, and it became evident that I ought soon to see the looked-for trail, if they were still in the pines. Entirely occupied in the search, happily the same watchfulness served for this object and my own safety, else I might have sacrificed the one in looking solely after the other.

The space for search was short, and time progressing, and with it dependent events, the camp must be approaching to the confluence of the streams, and the scouts already nearly abreast of the mouth of the canôn.

I was accounted, among the runners, with whom I occasionally tried my speed, faster than the common herd, and I was already down far on the hillside, was I not in a natural eagerness to attain an object, overrunning the scent? I might be leaving enemies behind ready to cut off a retreat.

A small bird, startled from the side of our back trail, flew across toward the canôn, and first brought upon me this reflection, and the ensuing pause served to bring on that instinctive sense of danger which, however, was not in this case, as it often is, a means of paralyzing the energies and the senses.

It is always safer to be still than to move, to escape observation, but it is also offering a surer aim. The porcupine had, with the elk, in grazing, lacerated the bark of the trees, so as to leave them in some places bare, and I thought I could perceive on the white of the wood of one something like a blaze[i] newly made, and this suggested the idea of dodging from tree to tree.

I felt convinced there was something astir near and was not long in perceiving a horse moving upward. My glass was out, and I plainly saw several figures mounted, and a few loose horses going up toward the direction from which I had come. A fortunate open showed me more clearly, and I could make them out to be a small party of Whites, among whom I could easily distinguish Diego.

It took me but a few minutes to get near enough to see that they were hurrying away from some danger. The animals were close packed, and the pace was quickened whenever there was an opener spot that would permit it.

I was concealed, and it occurred to me that I could be of more use watching in their rear than delaying them with a conference, when they were evidently in the right direction to fall in with our trail. I sunk, therefore, into a hollow, caused by the root of a tree blown over, and kept the best look-out the trunks of the forest would permit.

It had not been half an hour since I first saw the party, and were there anything following on their trail, it must be near however, as the torrent's bed guarded the southern side, it was probable the other was that from which any danger must approach, and I accordingly moved cautiously in that direction, at the same time inclining upward.

In one of the pauses which it was necessary to make to observe if anything was moving near, I saw a black mass suddenly fill up a narrow space, which by chance gave me a vista of considerable length. I had by this time crossed the trail, the object which I took for a horse had also stopped, and I had almost felt satisfied that it must be a straggler of the party I had seen, when a change of attitude made it evident, in the brief interval which I had him in view, that it was a bear—he was already out of sight.

I had almost a passion for this exciting chase, and feeling convinced that I had not been seen or winded, laid myself out for a run to cut in upon the course of the huge beast, which did not appear hurried. I caught another glimpse, however, as he entered a small thicket of willow, which probably contained a spring, and was quite a spot of refreshing coolness and concealment for the middle of the day, or might be the regular harbour. Once deposited and asleep, it is not difficult to get at such an animal, but it requires time for him to settle, and this I was already disposed, at the foot of a tree, to give him.

I had one good pistol in my belt, the cap of which I renewed, the Manton was all right, the cover off, and tucked under my belt. I had just finished this preparation, and looked up to watch the covert, when I thought I saw something not very far from where the bear had passed. Again all was still—but an object had moved—and I nestled myself between two great branches of the root which ran out boldly above ground to spread forth thin tendrils for further and deeper nourishment. A withered branch lay by my side, which it was not necessary to move to form a complete concealment, through which it was also possible to keep a perfect watch, but the two spots where I believed were contained both the objects which it became necessary to observe, were sufficiently apart from each other to prevent the eye being steadily fixed upon one without losing sight of the other.

There were certain hollows in various directions about, and I was balancing in my mind how I had better proceed, or whether it would not be best to remain perfectly still, but I am ashamed to confess that all my tendencies were strongly toward the thicket, and that the glances I cast toward the other direction were furtive.

More than half an hour had passed in this position, which was not sixty yards from the thicket, and I was looking eagerly at it, when I was startled by the sound of a shot, and seeing the smoke issue from what must have been a small hollow halfway between me and the bushes, a roar, and rushing motion among the branches, showed me that I had been forestalled by another hunter, and in a few seconds I was by the side of my more successful rival. Having my arms loaded, I had not hesitated to advance.

Though to all appearance the shot had told true, as I reached the spot the hunter had raised himself to a sitting attitude, to reload.

The trappers of the mountains so often wear the Indian dress, that I had no difficulty in believing this to be one of them, and asked him if he had had a good sight, and thought he had killed.

An Indian looked round to see who spoke, but I was the more startled of the two, and stood a moment taken aback. I had plunged upon a danger which I had come to warn others of, and aid them to avoid, and the thought flashed through my mind to sacrifice the intruder on my path, as my eye rested upon his, which never for an instant quailed, in what must have been believed his extremest peril, but a better spirit came over me. I could not quench that noble and fearless spirit, which spoke so calmly through those large dark eyes, nor did I attempt to look him down, but frankly offered him my hand.

He had seen well that I had had time to put a ball through his brain had I wished, and he accepted the offered pledge with a most becoming confidence.

I motioned to him, after he let go—for he held my hand firmly clasped for several seconds—to finish his loading, and while he did so, after having arisen, I had time to examine my new acquaintance. He was lightly clothed in a leather shirt and leggings, and had no robe, and what had probably so much induced me to believe in his being a white, I found he had tied his carqois round his head with the face of a cougar in front, as a means of disguise, the human visage being what alarms everything in the brute creation, after it is known as the portent of destruction among them.

In getting up he took this turban of fur from his head, and let the long hair which it had confined fall free upon his neck. His height appeared to be, by several inches, above six feet, though the symmetrical proportion of his figure did not permit him to seem so, his limbs—what of them were naked—were round, though slight, his head was nobly carried, and the neck long and muscular, the countenance was decidedly Indian, and the tint the red brown sometimes seen in the works of Georgone, the eyes, somewhat depressed toward the nose, were long and almond-shaped, the nose, thick and well formed, without being high, and the nostrils somewhat distended, the mouth large, and the lips rather full and projecting in the middle, but thinning inward into a curve as they extended toward the cheeks, the eyelashes had been plucked out, as is the fashion with the three great tribes, the Blackfeet, the Crows, and the Snakes, but the lids were thick, and gave a deep and strong shadow, and the lower one was well supported up upon the ball by the oval cheek, beard there was none, nor eyebrows, but their lines were well defined, and the brent brow[ii], though not lofty, was full of power. There was a peculiar thickness in the hands, without breadth, and of the fingers, without preventing their coming to a taper point, the nails, long and oval, both of them and of the toes, for the moccasins had been tied to the girdle which supported the legging thongs and the braye[1], the feet were beautiful and the toes healthily articulated and distinct.

It is not to be supposed that I had time to note this description down at the moment, but as the impression of the whole was strong to intensity, the traits were not difficult to remember, and I may as well here, as they were first remarked, record the description of a form which I had but too well the opportunity of examining at an after time.

The Indian finished his loading without hurry, and we proceeded toward the thicket, where all appeared to be still, the bushes were, however, so low and thick, that though you could not see over, it was impossible, standing up, to see under either, and my new friend was preparing to enter on all fours, when I pointed out the inconvenience of a gun in such a position. The Indian looked at me perplexed at first, but smiled with some interest as he examined the pistol I offered for his use in exchange, and as I explained the necessity of his taking care of the cap not being knocked off by the branches.

I listened attentively after he disappeared, for by the ear I first expected to learn whether we should still have a fight for the monster's life, but there was nothing—five minutes more elapsed—and still no stir, until a quarter of an hour must have passed—the hunter could not have been swallowed within ten paces without a sound. The scene, the spot, bore the stamp of irrevocable silence. By an ill-timed interference in the struggle, I might equally baulk another and endanger myself.

I had laid the Indian's gun up against a tree by where I stood. It was more than half an hour since I watched—I could neither see nor hear bear, nor

---

1. Braye: Breechcloth. *Braye* (also *braie* or *braguet*) is derived from an older French word, *braguette,* meaning cod-piece (see McDermott, *Glossary of Mississippi Valley French,* p. 34).

hunter, nor sign. A voice said something in an Indian tongue close by, and I turned to confront the Blackfoot, as he offered the pistol back into my hand, and had taken up his own gun.

I looked a question, almost doubting whether he had ever left my side.

He pointed with his chin to the thicket, and made a sign that the bear was dead.

There was no consciousness of satisfaction in his look at having had me in his power, and feeling that we might be considered quits, after understanding that he was going to take the pattes, as they are called, I was about to frame some excuse for quitting my companion, when he at once pointed out my course upward, and his down toward the probably already formed camp. He then placed the two first fingers of his hand, which he had previously pressed upon his heart, into his mouth, and taking them out again, pointed one held like a limb of the letter V toward his own head, and the other toward mine. I knew that this was the sign that we were brothers, we embraced, exchanged knives, and parted.

Chapter Fifty
Rose & the child—warned—stealth, and a baby's cry

It would have been completely unworthy to look behind, and I was eager to meet Diego and Rose, if possible, before they joined our party, and perhaps, as they were not pursuing the most open course I might succeed, but climbing up a steep was to be found more slow and difficult than running down.

I found a pen and kind of fort had already been formed, and the former was being enlarged by Brent and Harry Smith, who had also joined, all driven in by the appearance of the common enemy in the plain.

Rose was seated with her back toward me as I came up, with her infant on her lap, she was fondling the little thing—that brave and beautiful young mother—tied up on its embroidered board, its bright black eyes were shining like beads, not even its little hands being free—there it was, as it had been hung to its mother's saddle like a single holster.

I came behind her, and she must have heard the footfall, and known it was mine, for I could discern the red blood rush to her cheek as I leaned over her, and took into my arms the baby she had been caressing, and kissed its little brow. Those eyes—almost the only part of the body which appeared to be in use, were fixed upon mine for a moment in an earnest stare, and then were turned upon their mother.

As I was returning the infant to the opened arms and renewed embrace, I saw the eye of Bertrand[1], who came suddenly upon us, follow it with a scowl, our meeting, on his part however, was marked by some assumption of cordial-

---

1. Bertrand: Evidently a printer's error for *Bernard*.

But I hurried toward the very small fire, which Bill sat over, as if to consume its smoke, and made him acquainted with the Indian adventure.

"There is no matter," he said, after hearing my account of the Blackfoot. "The trail of Diego must be seen this evening or tomorrow, and we must be off out of these parts this very night, and show them straight shirt tails before the sun is high, far down the waters of the Apsaroke country tomorrow."

There was some tolerable picking, about, so that the band might be kept pretty well together. All the young men were out on guard except Bernard and myself.

"You had best say as little as you like about the Blackfoot brother you have made," added the old fellow, after a moment's pause.

The sun had sunk behind the high screen above us, and the horses full, though never satisfied, were collecting round, cropping the spare tufts of grass among the trees, they had been watered, and their different owners were hovering round them, as if they felt an approaching danger, or were taking a long and solicitous parting look.

I had got hold of my favorite mule, and was listlessly leading her who led the rest, for she was the bell-mule in influence, though she did not bear about her that musical emblem. My thoughts were full of the new character of mother in which I had just seen my Indian boy-companion of the Platte.

I had always a strong feeling of love for children, even at the earliest and most unintelligent stage of infancy, it was almost a weakness with me. Rose seemed to be amused at her own awkwardness, as also was her help—for she still retained the stout Navahoe girl she had at rendezvous.

I was thinking of all this, when I came up to the pen where I found the object of my thoughts, after having tied up her Aurora horse, playing like a child round the little mummy-looking thing she had stuck up against the enclosure. It seemed that some new and joyful cord had been struck in her heart, and it was also so in mine.

I had never seen the child of any one for whom I bore a strong affection before. It was strange also to see her laughing and playing round the grave little baby with such childish glee, it seemed a new phase in his existence, for I had learned from her father that, still following her former habits—out hunting all day—like an animal of prey, she came in at evening to suckle her child, and it slept the interval, between morning and the hour of her return and the night, as if they were regular periods of torpor, this, however, appeared to be a holiday, and she was enjoying the fun of being a mother, and the quiet astonishment with which her boy regarded her unwonted gambols, and the clear ringing of her laugh, which came, I almost thought, to remind me of former days.

It had been, we found, the intention of the Spaniard to have taken the back trail, but after a full council, it was thought better to run the risk of getting away round the foot of the canon in the night, and shake off the Blackfeet, who would hardly penetrate far into the country of the Crows, and the camp accordingly was to be moved about eleven.

The fires had been dimmed down to a few cinders, all but the guard had lain down for a short sleep. I found on awaking, that Hi-Hi had arrived, and on learning the plan of passing the Indian village, suggested the possibility of taking a short cut by a shelving path down to the torrent's bed, and then following it up a short distance, there was a small feeder, which came in by a crack on the opposite side, too narrow for a horse even with a rider, and consequently impossible for a loaded mule, in fact, it was a path of the Chochocoes, and as a great angle was to be cut off by this way, it was proposed that the Spaniard and his daughter should go by it, accompanied by Hi-Hi, and the rest were to wait, if they arrived first, at a bend of the Popoagee.

I was busy saddling, when Smith came up beside me, and in a low tone, bade me come a little apart when I had done, as he had something to say, accordingly, in a short time, we found ourselves together a few paces from the pen, seated in deep converse.

After explaining that he had long suspected and disliked the Swiss, he added that something in his looks and manner made him feel confident there was some black scheme in his head, and he thought it right to warn me.

"And I believe him," he added. "To be a coward also, as he has just declared that he must accompany his wife, and old Diego must, in consequence, look after the baggage, but he is out for once, as I believe there will be more danger of being caught on the short cut, if there has been any one on the trail, than on the way below, for the line we have taken leads within a couple of hundred paces of Hi-Hi's road, and there must be plenty of Blackfeet who know of it."

I at once determined to be of this party, and with that quickness of arrangement which is taught by a hunter's life, settled in my own mind to leave the favorite mule, which, if anyone led, was sure to be followed by the rest. Taking the stout Indian horse by the cord, saddled, I wrapped a short robe round me, placed my much-battered hat on the top of my baggage, and proceeded toward the spot where I expected to meet the young Chochoco, on his return after depositing the other horses.

It was not difficult to persuade him to take the trouble of crossing mine, and placing him safe in a thicket with the rest, a little above the out-coming from the little stream, and as all the trails tend downward from the crossing, he there considered them safe.

I was now ready to accompany Rose and Bernard on their midnight path, the rest of the party were getting silently into their saddles, in the way men start on a mysterious or dangerous enterprise.

Diego's baggage was borne upon two mules, packed as none but Spaniards can pack, he had left his lodge behind, and the summer campaign was therefore accompanied with less embarrassment, and I saw that he felt confident he could play his part well in the scurry.

They were beginning to file away, and as Harry passed, he again leaned from his horse and whispered, "It was Rose herself told me—and the girl is quick as an arrow—that she had seen something in Bernard's eye, and she is not of the kind to be easy scared, so look out. She will take no notice, as she knows I have warned you. Good luck, and steady hand!" And the true-hearted Missourian was gone.

There were a few drifting clouds, but the night was clear. Rose was seated, suckling her baby, Bernard had gone a few steps to see his father-in-law fairly launched. I stood waiting Hi-Hi's return, as the signal of a move, he and Bernard came up at the same moment, and I thought the latter seemed surprised at my presence. I simply observed, "I shall be no embarrassment to you." And we were already on our way, the light gun of the mother in her hand, the infant slung on her back. Bernard followed Hi-Hi, then Rose, and I brought up the rear.

The entrance to the shelf along which we had to pass was among broken rocks, leaving no trail, and led to the water, turning upstream, so as to meet almost on a level the cataract rushing toward us, and which was roaring beneath. Where this stratum came upon a level with the torrent, it formed a sort of bar, which was easily crossed, though a false step would have been fatal. But, in the presence of greater dangers, this seemed to be unheeded.

We then skirted the pool on the other side from that on which we entered, and followed up under beetling cliffs for nearly a hundred yards, when the crack-like entrance of the little stream presented itself.

There is never need of any injunction in such circumstances to proceed in perfect silence, and even observe to tread so as not to move the stones which might be unsteady to the step.

We had not proceeded far up the sometimes shingly, sometimes bare bed, when something occurred to cause a check, Bernard could not understand what, and the Chochoco made a sign for Rose to take his place.

It may be necessary to explain that this fissure, now nearly dry, came in at right angles to the stream we had crossed, the course from where it gave out, and came upon the general slope of the hill, was in a downward direction, but the horses were a little above the exit, and off the line of our route, as also the Chochoco path. There was a bright moonlight, but the deep cleft was all in shade.

The young Indian held in his hand something which he had picked up, and was showing to Rose, a few words passed in a whisper, and then she turned back to let me know that a moccasin had been found, which had not been there when the horses had been along, or on Hi-Hi's return, and that it was probable there was a guard set upon the outgoing.

This was startling news, and I own I felt at a loss what to do. Happily, there were two persons of the party who had their entire senses at command, and it appeared, were not without resource. It was still some distance to the mouth, as I understood.

Rose turned back once more to communicate the plan it appeared they had been forming.

"He thinks they have come since the horses passed, that is, he is sure, for he is quite confident, we must, therefore, try and pass to get to them. If that cannot be, we must run the gauntlet. But we will have a look." She gave her infant to Bernard, and followed the noiseless tread of the young Indian.

It was the best part of an hour before they returned.

"They are under the shadow of a rock, and the moon shines bright upon the small clearing, but there is a green slope over the brink of the rock, and if we can pass quietly above it, we get behind them up to the horses, but so near that the ruffling of a leaf would discover us to such hungry ears. It being quite open, they will keep close to their ambush under the shade, and the step is but short, so here goes, for our time is measured out to us."

The guide of the party seemed already impatient, his bow was in his hand, and the light short musket slung on his back.

Rose had made the same preparation, and I saw that resistance even was to be silent in its destruction, our steps fell like down upon the rock, there was a partial open, and the moonbeam for a moment fell white on the pallid features of Bernard, there was something made me shudder in the repulsive dread and anxiety which they exhibited, but he had a wife he must love, and their young child, and I felt some allowance might be made, but that dastardly look scarce seemed to be caused by care for others, and I shall never forget it to my dying day. The infant had been slung on his back, and as we neared the opening, there was again a check, and the two first of the party went on again to reconnoitre.

Bernard leaned against the side of the chasm, as if he had quite forgotten his hitherto silent little burthen, a small cry was the first thing made me remember the young creature's presence, and I sprung forward to try and lull it to quiet, he was lustily sucking my finger, when we were again in motion, and but a few paces were to place us on the slope, where the greatest peril was to be passed.

The mother here turned and held out her arms for the boy, but he was in a stronger grip, I could see her face anxious for the first time, but it was no moment for debate, I had been playing with the little creature now awake, and Bernard apparently thinking I would cause it to crow, or make some noise, took it in his arms, we were arrived among some low bushes, and had to climb up to the right to get upon the slope, which hung above the party, and it was only by keeping in a bent position, that we could escape being seen, no horse could turn in the latter part of the pass, and the slightest sound would be heard carried along the narrow passage.

Just as we got among the bushes, an Indian stealthily skirted them and listened, and then sat down near where we had just trod, and in sight of the rest, our own situation was becoming complicated and critical, but there was no time to falter, the silent step had been exchanged during a short time for one in which one hand took a share in the weight, and then we reached a higher and opener growth, whence we were to emerge to that last open ordeal, beneath which our enemies lay concealed.

There was no hesitation, the quiet step was continued, and my blood almost run cold, when I heard a sort of suppressed cry from the infant. Bernard fondled it, and wrapped it up in his blanket, and I almost liked to see the only demonstration of his love I had yet observed. There was another little sob, but he pressed it to his bosom, and we flitted past the open, all was yet hid beneath the shade below, ten steps and we were in the trees again, and the Chochoco had already quickened his pace, and we followed, threading the timber for two hundred yards, when in an open, we found all the animals tied, not a word was spoken, the mother took the baby from its father, it was asleep apparently, its head shaded from the moonbeams, which cause blindness. While the wood was yet thick, Hi-Hi led us downward toward the path we were to strike, it was then easy to follow, and he could himself evade all pursuit, when once again among the rocks.

Chapter Fifty-One
Ambuscade—death—sacred ceremony

It was nearly noon the following day. In the Blackfoot camp there was a stir, betokening some event of interest, the idlers were assembled in groups and the soldiers and chiefs of lesser name were about armed, a council sat in a great lodge, the principal chief, a man of some age, was there surrounded by the men of wisdom and influence in the village, besides those whose personal courage gave them a name of note, and who representing the genius of enterprise, led the young and the ready. Amongst the more aged and sedate, in a place of honor, sat an agent of the American Fur Company, and beside him, another white of a dignified appearance, features strongly marked and stern, the rest, except one, were men of the usual stamp, of imperturbable composure, and of mature years. That one sat with his eye fixed on the door, and occasional looks of intelligence passed between him and the youths who were continually looking in while the sacred pipe was being handed round, he has already been described, it was the Indian of the day before. But it is anticipating events, to describe what was about to be our reception, before narrating how we came to be presented before this high council.

We had reached safely the point where we expected to meet our camp, and before early dawn appeared, were in haste to proceed on our route. No sign was to be found by the acuter senses of our horses, and we were already on the bank of the stream, which ran at this season of the year full and clear, and would not have been crossed unwarily or unnecessarily by the main branch of our party. The line we had to take was clear, and it was well for us to follow it quickly, there was but a moment's pause. Hi-Hi had left us at the giving out of the wood, and Rose turned bridle down stream, were the others detained, our delay would rather cause mischief than good, so we urged our horses into a pace, which might not put them to their mettle, though it was sufficiently fast to get over the ground be times, and not run the risk of being seen by morning stragglers of the village. Rose assumed the lead, naturally enough I kept in rear, but could never get a sight of the face of Bernard, there seemed to be a complete change in his behaviour, shrinking from me, yet not riding near Rose, I was in doubt, whether or not there had been truth in the prediction that he was after some evil, and my watch upon him was the more incessant, when of a sudden, a lasso swung in the air over Rose's head, she was pinioned by the arms, and we were brought up against her horse by the impetus with which we were going. Several dark forms appeared, as if risen from the earth, I was off my horse before I knew what I was about, Bernard was more fortunate. I saw him break through between two who were attempting to seize his horse, riding over the one, and punching the other in the head with the muzzle of his rifle. I was, however myself on the ground and disarmed. Rose was close to me in a similar position, and the attention of our captors was turned to the desperate and determined act, which had set the one of our party free. Rose's horse and mine were immediately mounted, but not before the mother had received the bundle-like figure of her babe, cut loose and thrown at her by the new rider of her steed eager to recover our companion, and avenge the daring act by which he had escaped.

I had still time to fire off my rifle, which I did in the air, hearing that percussion locks were useless to these savages, when I was startled by the despair I saw in the face of my companion, the blood had left her cheeks, her eye looked large and round, and wild in horror and surprise, I gazed still at her, and forgot the dangers of our position. It was still on that visage of hopeless terror and grief, so changed from all the expressions I had ever seen borne by it before, that my eye was bound as by a spell. She held in her arms her young babe, and I approached to see that she was not losing her reason. My voice seemed to recall her to a certain degree, and she pressed to her bosom that poor little creature, which had called up the feelings of woman, and the weakness of mother, in her till now heroic nature.

I saw the Indians who surrounded her draw back, her eye searched from one to the other, and then fall again on the object of her solicitude, but I observed she did not offer it suck, or do more than smooth gently back the covering which still partly shadowed its head. One by one our captors had retired, leaving us alone together, the stream on one side, and a circle of ominous arms on the other.

Abstaining from all exultation, and refraining from any demonstration of anger at the escape of the Swiss, they had left us to council each other, and compose ourselves after this sudden attack, with a decency so simply shewn among the warriors of the great nations. I had come up to my companion in captivity, and she raised her eyes in a strange sort of wild uncertainty upon my face, and then, as if in mute appeal, let them fall again on the burthen she bore in her arms.

Could the child be asleep in such a moment, I looked for its little crowing voice to mock our cares, with an incipient dread that something had happened, its mother removed the piece of silk which had covered the face, with the same glance of almost despairing inquiry I had remarked before. The infant's features were swollen and black, and a small mark of blood had clotted at the nostrils, the eyes open staring and glassy. I rushed and seized the child's body, as I feared the mother was about to sink, it was dead and cold. She allowed me to take it, and as if feeling that it was necessary to compose herself, sat down. I kissed the poor little distorted mouth, which had sucked my finger so greedily but a few hours before.

"Can you guess how this has come about," asked Rose, in a voice so low and clear and calm, that I almost started.

I shook my head.

"It must be buried," she added, after a short pause and with an effort.

It was most painful to see the struggle to seem calm before so many eyes, she looked wildly round, and then felt for the knife which hung at her girdle. I cannot tell how I felt, it was impossible to arrange my thoughts, or to describe them. Rose moved off from the river, and through our guard, and began digging out a crack between two rocks, which were bared toward the water's edge. My alarm was dispelled as to the knife, but I felt myself playing but a poor part, and laying down my lifeless burthen, I hastened to help in this last sad office.

The little thing had been swathed in a piece of scarlet, of course not very bright nor very large, and there was a fillet of clean white over the chest as a pinafore, from this, with that composure which an education to command the nerves can alone give, the mother tore off two strips, and folding up what remained, put it in her bosom, the strips she stitched crossways with her awl upon the small scarlet bale—which had been to her a world of hopes and promise—the white emblem of Christianity. But for the example before me, I must have given way to a burst of grief, the short muttered prayer in Latin, and the angelus pronounced by the mother in a voice of entreaty which thrilled to my heart, was all the rite performed at the infant grave, the bended knee, and upturned eye, hopeful and imploring.

I would have given up church and creed to have been able to join. I knew no prayer for the dead, and had no faith in that beautiful trust in the intercession of the spirit of the blessed mother of God, and I felt as far from partaking of that sacred prayer as the savage, who refrained from, and respected what seemed solemn and mysterious, but the body was laid in its narrow cell, a stone was inserted that fitted at the head, one at the feet, and a slab of some weight was moved to serve as a cover to this simple grave. Rose turned to me after our work was finished.

"We will never speak of this event again, it was nameless, my poor babe, but I ever called it Edward, when I talked to it to lull it to sleep, or prayed for it." And then, as if to cut short the scene, she pointed to the spot we had left, and approached the warriors, who had calmly and cautiously awaited our finishing what they even think a sacred duty.[i]

Chapter Fifty-Two
Prisoners in a Blackfoot village—council—eyes of omen—a friend in need

Bernard must have got to cover, for we could see the two horses returning from the chase, over a height at some distance, and for the first time, looks of displeasure were apparent in our captors, the suspense was not long. Rose, who seemed to be recognised by some of the party, was put upon her horse again, the partizan walked by my side, and we rather hastily took the direction toward the village. It was evident that nothing worse than a ransom was intended, and Rose contrived to learn, as she believed, that there had been some whites about, whom Bernard must have joined, and it was not possible for the two sent in pursuit to make anything of them. It was not far to the village, and it was to be expected that some account might there be had of the rest of our camp, or some negotiation entered into for our release. Various were the wild looking riders who came out to meet us as we got near, and careered wildly round, on arriving within a shorter distance, it was evident something unusual had occurred. A few soldiers were soon with us, and a short conversation with the leader, set them to act as the guardians of order.

It was in a bend of the stream, forming a peninsula, that the village was placed, and there was a closer row of lodges across the mouth, the greater villages of the Blackfeet and the Crow disdain the precaution of a barricade, which is adopted by the Flathead and Nezpercee tribes, on the frontier of their lands.

There was nothing very remarkable in the appearance of the savages who came about, tall and darker than the Crows in their complexion, the young men were not so elaborately decorated as those of the camp of Bracelet de Fer, nor generally so good-looking. One horse at least was attached to every lodge as we advanced, and the tripods were charged with the charms which go under the name of *medicine*. The sun was shining bright and hot, the cow tails and pennons hung from the radiating lodge poles unmoved by a breath of air, a drum, accompanied by slow and monotonous music, was to be heard when not overpowered by nearer sounds, and once or twice we distinguished the howl of the medicine man in an agony of supplication for someone near his doom,[i] the other, more regular and continued, I knew to be the scalp dance.

In the village of the Blood Indians, such sounds to the ear of a prisoner are not without portentous significance.

It was near the middle of the camp their great council lodge had been placed, rising in the curve of the base of a lighthouse over the tall poles, it was stretched to the utmost tension, and unlike most of the others turned up at the bottom to admit the air, was pinned down close, and around were grouped the horses of the warriors within. It was toward this we were moving, and either chance or design had left the line open by which it was to be approached.

I before began to describe the assemblage, at whose door that short delay occurred, which precedes the heralding of strangers into the presence of princes or of councils, during this time some indications of curiosity were manifested, and a young woman came toward us from an adjourning lodge of inferior size, at the door of which sat two others, she was somewhat dark of skin, the mouth grave though sweet, the eye lustrous, and almost joyous, her dress was of the skin of the bighorn, though scanty, elaborately beaded and fringed at the edges and the seams. I looked attentively, anxious to observe everything that might affect my companion, toward whom she evidently came. There was a slight change in the countenance of the youthful squaw as she drew near, a shadow spreading gradually over it, and a slight hesitation in her step, but she took the riding cord from the Indian who held Rose's horse, and not with unkindness, though somewhat with a reluctant step, led it and its rider to the neighboring abode, at the same time one of my companions made a sign, by which I understood I was to enter the other. Room was made near the door, and the chief bade me be seated by one of those gestures, the graceful use of which is one of the first accomplishments of the high-bred Blackfoot and Crow.

Though I cannot say I felt at ease, seated amongst men who are educated to value lightly life, and who have a command of nerve, which enables them to despise pain, yet there was nothing of a hostile feeling apparent in those around.

In similar situations, I had learned that it is equally necessary to avoid a demeanour of pretension, as of diffidence, and as I saw a French trader in the circle to which I had been admitted, who I supposed must[ii] be able to interpret them, I begged him to offer my thanks for having been allowed to see the camp of such warriors, knowing also that I was safe while I remained in it.

"We are glad to see the young white chief"—for so they chose to designate me—"but why did he run off in the night, if his heart led him to our village."

I explained in reply to the grave but courteous answer of the chief, that I was but young in the country, that I did not know whether they were Crows or Blackfeet.

"And why did the white chief's brother kill one of our people?"

"He wanted to get away, but he is no brother of mine, had I wanted to get off, I would have done the same."

I cannot tell why I felt that I ought to disown Bernard, an instinctive repugnance rose up in me for the first time, not to be repressed, as my feeling had hitherto leaned toward him, notwithstanding the general conviction I felt that he was my enemy.

"The young chief is a brave among his people, that he talks of killing a Blackfoot, and escaping as if he had but to have it in his heart, and that our warriors would be nothing."

"I have counted coups upon other nations, who are thieves, and have crossed my path." And as simply as I could, I told my first adventure with the Kanzas, which I believed by the signs my interpreter used in aid of speech, were faithfully rendered. But by some of those feelings of insecurity and depression, by which is imparted by some magnetic influence of the presence of an ill-wisher, I found that there was something going wrong, and summoned my best courage to look the danger in the face, what would I not have given to have been a Nevil or Plantagenet, to have had the memories of the past to screw me up in the slow-timed courage that was here required. I had but the affection I felt for my captive companion, and the natural clinging to a life, whose threshold steps had not been without their nascent joys. I looked up with some resolve to meet the eyes which I believed were reading the resolution of my spirit, and scanning the veracity of my words through my outward bearing.

The countenance of the chief was turned toward the French trader and his to that of a person near him, there was something in this I could not account for, why should I feel disturbed?

There was some movement, and a laying together of heads, a sort of exclamation from the chief, however broke this up, it was something more of incredulity than anything else, and not free from contempt. The heads which had grouped, and the bodies which had bent forward, resumed their proper positions, and opened out the head, those eyes fixed upon me as on a prey, which I had seen omen-like at Fernwold's, and at St. Louis.

For a moment I was daunted, I had allowed this horrid mask to reign in my mind as the omen of evil, as they say of the snake, I was fascinated with this gaze. I did not shun or rebut it, but drank in the rays of those eyes with famishing greed, could I dive through them into what they meant, and the cause of their power?

The acute observers whose attention had been fixed upon me, could not have failed to perceive that I was disturbed, and as something intervened to hide that ill-omened visage, I looked round to note what might be the effect my changed demeanour had produced. The dark forms around were still, but their eyes were fixed upon mine, and I at once rallied to meet them, and turned an answering look from one to another, with a recovered calm.

About opposite, but a little further from the door, at this moment was raised up a form which had hitherto reclined rather than sat, and that behind another.

No one who has not felt the sudden finding of a friend in need, can tell how gladly the hopes and confidence rebound, though sufficiently restrained by the scene and the habits of the personages around, I knew there must be a certain glow on my cheek, and beam of the eye, as it rested upon the handsome face of my recently acquired brother, the force of whose fraternal ties I might have so soon to test.

But there was no answering glance—no coldness—but not a particle of expression in the sedate though not unkind regard which met my sudden joy, and then as calmly was turned toward the chief. I took this slight check as a lesson of restraint. No one seemed to have observed anything unusual.

Chapter Fifty-Three
News—Diego—more news—Goddard—pipe ceremony

The gallop of a horse was at this moment heard without, and soon after, an Indian, squeezing through the crowd at the door, hot and dusty, sat down. He was evidently a messenger. There was no medicine pipe going round, but a few of those present smoked their own calumet, and the newcomer had chosen his place at the side of one so occupied, and having first profited in that position, by partaking of this luxury, which unchains the tongue if it does not open the heart, he submitted himself, by turning toward the principal chief, to the questions he might be disposed to ask.

I learned that there had been a fight, that some two or three Indians had been killed, and one white man wounded and a prisoner, along with some others.

Upon reflection, after hearing the best interpretation I could get of this report, it appeared to me certain that Diego had been wounded, and possibly severely, from the fact of his not being brought to camp.

There was some stir, as if a sudden resolution had been taken, and I had but time to proffer a request that I might go to see, and if necessary, to aid, the wounded man.

The character of a leech is always sacred with savage nations, and as the object of my request was partly understood to partake of the character of medicine, it did not meet with that refusal which otherwise might have been expected.

A few words were said to the French trader, which I afterward found were to ask him if he would guarantee my return. The answer I could see at once was unsatisfactory, and I spoke aloud I would give my word to return, if alive, by the six o'clock sun.

This, I suppose, was made known, though I had been able to make my promise sufficiently clear by signs, still, there was a pause, there was some distrust occasioned by the conduct of the trader and he who sat next to him, when one of the young braves who sat next the door said something, pointing to himself and me.

He was a slight-looking youngster, and it was almost with a smile the older warriors present received his appeal. What was its object?

My acquaintance of the day before, making a motion to be heard, said something in brief but energetic terms, he understood that the half-breed who had killed his father treacherously at a conference was taken, and he would be answerable for both the young brave and myself.

It was not long before we were galloping in a direction toward the foot of the mountain and the forest which covered its base. No distrust was shown by those under whose guidance or escort I was, they sped on in front, and I rode a horse which equaled, I thought, theirs in speed.

It was the father of Rose who lay under the shade of some branches of willow. The wound had disabled his right arm, cutting a vein, and the consequent loss of blood had caused much weakness.

I cared hardly to note those around, the languid look of the Spaniard barely gleamed a recognition, and I hastened to tell him that his daughter was in safety, and that he must remain perfectly still. The squaw help was seated near, awaiting her fate, and I at once put her in requisition to make some soup, as the best restorative. She seemed to take this as a sign that she was to live, as also to be useful.

It was now that I had leisure to look around and observe the strength of the party, who were in shanties, and principally consisted of men. It was apparent that most of them were from the village, and that the party thus separated was in itself an off-shoot but temporarily detached. The men were in groups, there were no fops about, nor were there any games going on, several young warriors, still painted black, had evidently but recently returned from an expedition, where there might, from the doubtful feeling displayed, have been disaster rather than success. The horses were within range, two large lodges alone were up, but there were shanties sufficient for a considerable body.

I had not much time for observation, however, it might be necessary to look about me.

Diego was perfectly known to the French trader, and I felt secure as to his fate, it was a different thing, however, to deal for the ransom of his daughter.

The help had the soup already in progress, and by degrees, I was imparting all our misadventures and the cowardly flight of Bernard, only concealing the death of the child. There seemed, however, to be a link wanting in the story.

Diego, though I would not let him speak much, evidently stumbled at the cause of his son-in-law's flight, he was no coward, and he could in no way account for this desertion. However, a certain degree of lassitude was creeping upon him, and before long, I was glad to see him drop over into a not uneasy slumber. I left the female attendant to watch his repose, shaded by a piece of old lodge-skin from the glare of the midsummer sun, and prepared to lie down myself, when a sudden arrival roused me and my young protector, who lay near, he sat up, and made a signal that I should come to his side. The other Indian who had come with us came up, and we formed a group somewhat separate from the rest, patiently awaiting the information to be expected from an arrival which had apparently spread about some disturbance amongst the party.

It was not long before a man, somewhat older than the rest—who were for the most part youths—came toward us, and in a communication which showed more urgency of manner than usual, told the news, which I soon learned was, that they had had a skirmish the evening before, and two Indians had been killed, but that meeting some reinforcement, the whites had been obliged to get away in the dusk as well as they could. This morning they had overtaken a half-breed and a Snake, and had brought the scalp of the half-breed into camp, and the Snake was taken to the village a prisoner.

I forgot my own situation in my anxiety for the two Antoines and Charlo, one of whom it was evident had met his fate.

The questions about the appearance of the half-breed I put to my brother, induced him to call up one of those who had been of the party which brought the news. It was not Antoine Clement I found, as his hair was between a brown and auburn, and cut square by the nape of the neck, while that of the scalp was black, the two others wore them alike, long and thick, and the color confined the doubt to between them.

There was evidently an unusual excitement in the party, and some little dread of retaliation, as I was told they would probably move immediately, to join the village. My only anxiety was for Diego, but this was quickly dispelled by the assurance that he would be safe, no Indian would meddle with him, there could be none so near, and of course, there could be no danger from whites. There was a good supply of meat left, and another piece of old lodge skin, with a promise that they should be looked after, and we were gone.

There was this difference in our mode of return from that that of my coming, that my friends now rode watchfully one on each side, but it was not, as far as I could see, by the same route we were returning as that which we had previously taken as the most direct, a considerable bend toward the mountain was evident, and the party was led by the more elderly Indian who had before come to give us the news.

Thus much I had remarked, and was riding listlessly along, when the halt of the leading horsemen showed there was something interesting them, round which the others, as they came up, assembled. We paused—my two companions and myself—until the curious had been partially satisfied and had passed on, and in our turn came up to the spot where the others had halted. There, on the brink of a pool in one of the mountain creeks, lay the naked and mutilated body of a man, whose skin, what remained of it, was not fair enough to be that of a white, bits had been cut off the body in various parts, the heart had been taken out, the scalp of course was gone, the eyes were getting dead and glassy, and the face, upturned, was evidently left to show who he had been, rather than from tenderness to destroy it.

I knew the features well—that eye had once been keen as that of the eagle, and swift had been those limbs, now stretched out stiff and bloody-it was Antoine Goddard.

There had been a long account against him, and a sanguinary reckoning. It was no agreeable omen, and the taste of blood and revenge might be too sweet to be withstood.

The distance was not long, and the sun was not low when we got back. The usual parade of the fops, or as the Americans called them, the bucks, toward the evening, was beginning, the soldiers were about, armed, in the council lodge, it was to be supposed the chiefs were still assembled, as the entrance was thronged.

I saw Rose sitting at an open door as I passed, and made as cheerful a greeting to her as I could, I did not wish to challenge the authority by which I was guarded, as I could easily surmise I might fall into worse hands.

Some of the party entered to report as I suppose, and I remained observing what could be noted from the calm demeanor of those around.

My Indian brother's re-appearance, whom I had lost sight of on entering among the first lodges, was like the recovery of a real relative, so strong was the feeling that he was my friend. His eye was calm, and the lids slightly closed, and no sign either of favor or displeasure could be gathered from any feature, the lips, usually compressed in high resolve, were slightly apart—they had but a moment before smiled upon some of the fops who loitered in his way. Intuitively, I followed him, and observed that he was armed, in addition to what he carried before, with a shining tomahawk, his hunting shirt was gone, on his arms were still the burnished bracelets, which its sleeves had partially concealed, and the imprint of a hand, done in black, appeared clearly designed over the left breast.

A little way from where I had waited for him, the lodges were ranged in something like regularity along the back of the stream, by one of these, partly thrown open in front, we paused, and the way was led by my conductor, after asking permission, we received a sign to be seated at his side from the only person it contained on a new red blanket spread over several skins.

There now appeared about a dozen of young warriors, as if dropped from the skies or risen from the earth, they took their places in the usual circle, a light was brought, for the lodge did not appear to have been used, and had no fire, a medicine pipe was passed up the left side of the circle to the most mature-looking of the party, the forms of offering to the sun and to the earth were gone through, and then the smoke was in like manner puffed upward, and then toward the ground, to the right and to the left, and the ceremony was concluded by my new friend holding the stem to my mouth while I inhaled three times, he, after doing the same, passed it round.

It was the first time I had been admitted to smoke at a council, if a meeting where no word was uttered could be so called. The same ceremony was followed three times successively, as the pipe-bowl, which was cut out of bloodstone, did not hold more than enough to make the circuit once.

I knew sufficiently the customs among these nations to be aware that this rite was one by which hospitality and protection was guaranteed to the stranger, if not by the whole camp, by all who had participated in it. But there was not much time for reflection or calculation on the stability of my present position, the sound of the tread of many feet, and the rush of children past the open in front, could not fail to attract notice amongst a people rarely, by any occurrence, to be moved to a demonstration of excitement.

But hardly had this sound of coming steps been heard, when the medicine man David came in, as if he had some express design, and going straight up to the youth whom I have called my brother, spoke, assisted by signs, without sitting down. I could not quite understand what was said, but to the first part, a negative answer was evidently given, to the second, an assent, and then a few words to the young men around, and we all rose, and David passed forward to my side. I felt he was moved by the almost eager pressure he gave my hand.

"Come along," he said, "and witness the last of poor Hi-Hi. He has been taken, he had killed two Blackfeet, and had their scalps beneath his shirt, he killed another of the party who surprised him, and was knocked down from behind and brought in, disarmed, to be tortured. They saw the scalps hanging to his braye-belt as he fell, and knew that it must have been him who killed two men of note in the village the day before yesterday. I have tried in vain to have his life saved, against my own conviction, but his doom is fixed."

Chapter Fifty-Four
Blackfoot scalp dance—Hi-Hi confronted—
wonderful visions

I felt this news almost turn me sick—the poor boy, gentle, brave, and almost innocent-looking, who had seemed so devoted to the whites, thus to be sacrificed, I felt the blood rush back from my heart, and it must have tinged my face to the roots of the hair, with grief and rage, and also in shame, that I should be invited to witness so ungrateful and cruel a sight.

My companion, for he was by my side as we left the lodge—seemed to read my thoughts in my flushed brow.

"I can spare you the pain of thinking of his torments. Have you forgot that I can put him to sleep, and that, though he dies, he feels no pain?"

This remark was made in a calm tone of voice, but there was an expression almost of contemptuous indifference in the steady regard with which it was accompanied, and I own it was more a feeling of shame, than any desire to sustain and support poor Hi-Hi, that induced me to follow this singular man.

The sun was already a quarter of the circle past the meridian, and the evening parade, or rather promenade of dress, was almost begun, a few young men had been making the circuit of the camp, throwing the javelin—a larger and heavier arrow—at a mark, and I observed that they followed our steps as soon as we moved.

David spoke a few words to Rose, who was apparently waiting for the appearance of her father, she turned somewhat reproachfully toward me.

"You did not tell me, Ned, of his wound."

"No, I wished to save you that pain."

"Ah, you thought me of the weak stamp of your enervated whites, who spin all their own miseries from their nerves. However, he will soon be here?"

"Yes."

I observed her, after exchanging signs with one or two squaws, one the wife of the chief, prepare, by taking up her Navahoe blanket,[i] to follow to this scene of cruelty the eager throng.

Toward the outside of the village to which we were moving, there was a small mound with an abrupt bank, once probably washed by the stream which now flowed at a slight distance, round which, and along whose ridge, a dense crowd had gathered, and to the music of the old men the dancing of the squaws before the scalp of Goddard was distinctly to be seen as we came up, and above the heads of the actors in this scene was waving up and down the dark hair and bloody skin, the inside of which, as it turned distended on a hoop, glared red when fronting the sun.

There, upon the bank, sat the great chief and those immediately connected with him, also the same trader whom I had seen in the lodge in the morning. David, while I had lingered, preceded me, and was already seated, and somewhat to my disgust, by that ominous individual, who seemed to haunt me. They were already in deep converse.

The sun shone out, and the busy camp dispelled, to a certain degree, the dark feelings of misgiving or presage hitherto brought up by his appearance, and I found a man about forty, in a dress which might have suited a mountaineer of the Tyrol—the conical hat, the green coat, the Indian leggings, and moccasins, only substituted to suit the fashion of the country. He never raised his eye, but the features were regular, and but for a certain expression which they wore of a character it was impossible to define, otherwise than I have attempted by describing their effect upon myself, might be considered handsome, now that I had a fair opportunity of examining them.

Some of the war party, who had sustained a loss almost amounting to a defeat, had come in begrimed in the sombre hue which is adopted in desperate enterprises. They had been the captors of Hi-Hi, the steam-baths, from which they had emerged, restored them to their natural color, embellished by the rouge and adorned by painted robes picturing exploits which there was not time to mark by distinctive emblem on the skin. They came up in time to claim their place in the triumph of taking a prisoner, if not achieving a victory.

Hi-Hi had been taken by surprise—though not without resistance, and the reason of his being now the object of public vengeance was that beneath his girdle had been found the scalps before mentioned.

On the other side of the medicine man was the trader from the whites, and I remarked that the great chief joined in their conversation, while one of those whom I had remarked in the lodge where I had smoked, took me by the hand and led me to a seat on the opposite side from the whites. Here and there among the crowd I met a friendly glance from someone I thought I had before seen, and the men seated next me each gave their hands, after pressing them to their hearts.

But that eye of evil omen was still there, in some degree blighting this reassuring reception. But a wave of the hand of the chief, as if granting some boon to my friend David, interrupted any reflections I might have made upon my own situation, as a movement among the crowd at the same time drew the general attention to the side from which the victim was to appear. I own I felt my heart beat, as some women were with difficulty restrained from breaking through the compact guard which had formed itself around his smaller form, and as yet concealed it from view, but a word or two from the chief, and the space around was cleared into a large circle, leaving Hi-Hi alone in its center.

"Let us know from whom you stole the scalps which were found upon you," said the great chief.

"Why do you not give me the scalp of the warrior I struck down before the eyes of your braves?" answered the prisoner, with a calm assurance of tone, which first emboldened me to look upon him.

I had felt loath to see the gentle boy in the ruthless hands of these strong and fierce men, scarcely restraining that eagerness for vengeance which is the natural feeling of the savage, if not of the civilized man.

It was barely possible to recognize in the form before us the slight young Chochoco, away from the tall warriors around, and not being brought into immediate contrast with their height, his stature seemed to be increased, his form had assumed a nobleness of port I had thought it incapable of wearing—the head borne high and the eye dilated—he appeared possessed by some mightier spirit sustaining and exalting him above his former self. There was evident satisfaction in the look by which he recognized his friend David, as well as myself, though he never allowed it to relax from the lofty tone it now bore, to meet that ordeal which every Indian looks to as to stamp him worthy of the name of man.

"A great brave," resumed the chief, "may be killed by a creeping snake."

"It was the Snake who stood, and the Blackfoot crept on his belly. Is it so long since two Blackfeet braves were killed by the knife of the little Snake chief, when he had lost his horse and he had no gun? The chief sees things which are passed with but one eye, but I will show him, if he will untie my hands."

"Why should I let your hands be free? Where is your gun?" said the chief, with grave contempt.

"I have left two guns, which belonged to two great warriors, among the branches of a young pine, I took them alone—five Blackfeet took mine. Would the braves of the Blackfeet like to see them, that they might know from whom they were taken?"

"They would be hard to find, and the Chochoco might have to live too long in searching for them. The Blackfeet have many braves."

"Yes, they may have many, I can count three," said the youth, holding up three fingers.

At this moment the medicine man, seeing that it would be difficult to contain the fury which these taunts were inflaming, passed into the space yet open, in the centre of which the prisoner stood.

The great chief said a few words, and the front rank of the circle seated themselves.

"You will tell my people," said Hi-Hi, "what I have done, and how I die?"

"Yes, my poor boy," said his friend, but as he looked at the youth, and saw the proud, reproachful look at the word *boy*, he corrected himself, and added, "My son is a warrior, though so few snows have passed since his birth. I will tell his people."

A beam of satisfaction shone on the countenance of the prisoner—a face though so young—lit by the beams of its last sun coming aslant over those mountains in which he had lived, and those deep vallies he loved, and their fastnesses, which, if his feet were free, would defy re-capture, or even pursuit.

I could see the thoughts flashing through his mind, and how suddenly, though calmly checked, and his friend beside him saw also that if his sufferings were to be assuaged, the sooner he was to pass into a state of present oblivion, the better.

The exercise of the power of producing mesmeric sleep had, by frequent use, become so easy as scarcely to require more than the look of the eye and the volition.

The Chochoco became rigid as he spoke.

"Whose knife is this?" asked David, showing a knife.

The boy held out his hand. "It is the knife of Bernard," said he.

"I do not think it is. But who gave it to me?"

"You took it from a white man, who had it from Bernard."

"Who is he?"

"He is the father of Ned."

Again, his interrogator looked doubtful.

"No," he continued, "Ned's father was his brother. He wants Ned dead, and then he will be a great chief, far away."

"What is he doing here?"

"Come to get the young white chief out of his way."

"When did he see Bernard?"

"He saw him yesterday, but he is gone to look for the whites."

These questions were put rapidly, and though I could but imperfectly understand them, I could learn from their import that they regarded myself, but it was evident that it was time something should be done, to shew that power to the Blackfeet of which a boast had been made.

"Would the chief wish to ask any question?"

After a pause, during which a tobacco pouch was handed to Hi-Hi, he was asked by the medicine man, "To whom it belonged?"

"It belonged to the son of the chief," was the answer.

A slight movement showed that the reply was considered wonderful, and the chief himself asked, "Where is my son?"

"I see him lying near a swift stream, his head bloody, and his hair is gone."

Not a muscle of the father's face betrayed whether he believed this or not, but as he spoke, I saw his fingers tighten their hold of the pipe stem he held.

"How do you know it is my son?"

"I took this from his wrist." He shewed a brass bracelet on his arm, on which appeared an attempt to carve the head of a snake.

The Blackfoot looked for a moment, and shook his head," he had nothing of a snake about him," he said, with some disgust, imitating the crawling of the reptile with his hand.

David seemed inclined to let the matter rest, but a boy said something to the chief, who made a sign that he wished to see the bracelet.

It was easily taken off, and as this was being done, he asked, "Who gave it to my son?"

"Three days ago the chief put it on to the hand of his son, and he made three marks on the inside, and told his son to put it on the arm next his heart."

By this time, the rude and recent attempt at forming a snake's head had been examined by the soldier, who received the bracelet, to be handed to the father. No sign showed that this was an evidence of the son's death, the old man gazed immoveable on the ornament, and though he did not recognize it distinctly, he did not give it back, but held it as if in amaze.

To the throng all this, which had it been understood might have filled the camp with wonder as well as dread, was lost, they saw no more in it than the giving of a trophy taken from the dead. The old man was however moved with a strange grief and wonder, as he gazed at the medicine man, and then at the relic before him, and David seized the moment to try and make some impression in favor of the prisoner. It was—he suggested—a chance for the Blackfeet to preserve among them a person who could see what was going on in an enemy's camp.

The medicine man continued what appeared an expostulation some minutes, and again he received a tobacco sack, whose ornaments had been cut off, to desire to know to whom it belonged, there was nothing distinguishing in it, but to shew how jealously they watched anything which might give a clue or aid in collusion, it was recalled before reaching the hand, or being observed by Hi-Hi, and a knife was substituted in its place, which bore no mark. The prisoner looked at it, put it to his forehead, and his mouth and nose.

"It is the knife of the son of Bracelet de Fer, a young Snake brave."

"And where is he?"

"I see him with many more, part Snakes, and part Crows." The eye of the Chochoco was strained, and his head stretched down the stream.

"But how far, for the country is many moons wide!" say the pale faces.

"Can the Chochoco hear them speak?"

Chapter Fifty-Five
Tumult—fighting—understanding—Rose gone wild

"No! But the chief may hear them before the sun touches the tall trees, if they come on", and a flash of joy shone over the visage of the dreamer.

There was a moment's pause.

Just above this outskirt of the camp, like all the heights around, videttes were posted, and one of these made his horse curvette round in a sort of figure of eight, while the more distant guards, from whom the alarm had been conveyed, were fast gathering their scattered bands. There was a rider came down at headlong speed, and from mouth to mouth was borne the words *they come! they come!* dust had been seen far down the valley.

"It may be but antelope, who scour the plain, or buffalo," said David.

But the breathless messenger said, "No, he had seen the line far back, coming up the valley, no buffalo care to run in a straight line when they are pressed, and there are not antelope in these parts to make such a cloud."

For a moment, I thought the fate of the prisoner would be changed, and that he might escape in the tumult this unexpected news might bring about, but the thought was dissipated, as by a flash of lightning the ring around was broken, and we were all jostled. I saw the tomahawk flash before his face so near, that it seemed to touch. I saw his figure shaken by the slash of a knife down his ribs, but the eye and the countenance were unmoved, and were of a smiling calm, and I felt that the spell had been true.

The confusion and rage of the Blackfeet was beyond controul, and I was borne off in one of these flows, which heaved the crowd from the centre. I had seen the last of my poor friend the Chochoco, and want of time probably prevented longer continued attempts at torture, I saw his scalp between me and the lowering sun.

Horsemen were now mixing in the throng, as those who had a war horse up mounted, and as others had met the gathering cavalcade: the dust and confusion were increasing. I was separated from the chief, the French trader and David, the sore feeling in my heart was in some degree deadened by the stunning confusion around, but I remarked ever near me some Indian face watching, with not unfriendly earnestness. I was beginning, however, to feel that I was alone, that the blood of the savage was roused in all around, a rush of those who had been round poor Hi-Hi came shouting toward me, and I felt myself borne to the ground, it was as I thought to anoint me for sacrifice, that I felt my face rubbed over with what I could see was black grease, hair and all, a robe was thrown round me, and I was once more on my legs, surrounded by several similarly painted for war. I had seen enough to recognize this friendly disguise, and closed the robe over my arms, once or twice I thought myself the object of scrutiny, but my unknown friends swarmed round, and I was again almost carried off my legs. Meantime the horses had been coming in, and were being put into requisition, and the cluster of protectors round me were edging toward the centre of the camp, but the women were howling like demons, and had I been recognized, I must have been torn into shreds.

The more active men were getting hold of their horses for the sally, which was evidently intended, but the chief was already haranguing, and recommended getting in the horses, and ranging a guard behind a low ridge, forming the further side of a dried up watercourse, which running out from the wood came to a head on the river at the bend of the stream, which formed the lower side of the mouth of the peninsula, containing the camp. There had not been a horse out on the eastern side of the valley, to keep fresh grass one portion had hitherto been left pure, and almost untrodden, the attack was to be made on this side, and the object was to get the horses together behind this mound, there the river and its deep cut sides formed the flank, and an attack would be attended with the loss which must result from a steady aim from behind some cover, and if repulsed, there was ready an unrelenting pursuit by men, who were only now restrained by the confidence they had in their chief, and his explicit command.

Already was the river bank lining with armed braves, who could act by signal from that height which we had just left, and as we pressed on, an Indian gun was thrust into my hand, it appeared as if we were to take our station behind the mound I have already described as we bent our course toward it, but suddenly diverging the whole party dropped over the steep bank, and were seated quietly by the river's brink. It was at a salient point, and amongst large lumps of the bank above, undermined by recent flood, each seeking sufficient cover from these, but as near each other as possible, a good view could be obtained of the bend, up which the attack was pouring upon the camp.

I ought to have stated that all the horses not mounted, or reserved to be mounted in the hollow of the watercourse, had been taken through the lodges toward the upper part of the camp, and it seemed the intention of the assailants to follow them, as they had been plainly seen by those in front, who, however, were ignorant that the great body of the warriors were in ambush on what to them appeared a deserted plain. Happily, however, there were a few, whose eagerness, or the superior speed of whose horses had placed them in front, and they came yelling on, expecting probably that the few which might be reserved, would have the impediments of the camp to detain them, and probably that the camp would be abandoned, so much the maneuver of the Blackfeet appeared like a rout. But a shot or two broke the spell, and in the precipitancy saved a greater slaughter, perhaps, a dubious conflict, the line began to pour in its desultory fire, and several horses were stopped, or fell, it was evident, from our position, that there would be no attack from the opposite bank.

The sun was getting low, and though checked, the hostile party were still pouring on, it was time to shift to reinforce the fire of the front, and we were moving to the hollow, when a general discharge and yell, shewed that some change had taken place, the party which we had been to visit in the morning were seen charging on the flank next the forest, and with the now general fire of the rest, seemed to have caused a retreat to be commenced in the same headlong speed which had characterised the advance.

I have mentioned that a great many warriors had their hunters ready in the concealment of the hollow, and had only been restrained from a sally at first by superior command, it was now evident that pursuit to a certain extent might be safe, both producing plunder and affording revenge, and there was an immediate rush among those who had horses.

During the whole day I had looked for the face of my new brother, to read warning and comfort, as well as hope, he had never spoken, but those whom I could see were his adherents, kept a constant guard, while I now searched for that support which his appearance gave me, still were round, close packed, the friendly throng, and I was touched by the side of a horse coming up as if to pass me, there was another behind, a few words pronounced low, arrested my attention, and I saw the eye I had looked for bent upon me, and then turn upon the horse, a cord was placed at the same moment in my hand, the young Indian was in a second mounted and away, the yells were loud, and still some shots were fired at several whites, who appeared unwilling to retreat.

I was cleaving my way through the line which was mounting from the hollow, disdaining further concealment, and it was time. The shout I heard was from a party evidently rushing through the crowd toward myself, but those who had hitherto protected me stood their ground. My horse, full of spirit, answered to the closing of the legs and slackened rein, and I was at the heels of my young guardian. He made me a sign that the horse was mine, and I was free.

This, in the evening wane, was the last I saw of horse or rider as he plunged on, but I beheld in place, a figure it was not easy to forget, darting into the pursuit and I bore toward it.

There could be no mistake, the Indian youth of the Platte was there, urging on his horse among some blanket capots, which marked their owners for whites.

I know not why the Blackfeet had preferred to follow the Snakes, and several had been killed, whom we had passed, and the cluster of Americans ran rather from the desire to get out of a night melee with the yelling reserve we heard behind, than from any immediate pressure. But the horse I rode, though gathering quick, strong, and active, was not equal in stride to that I wished to overtake.

The evening had become grey, and the dust hung on the plain. There was some sort of hail, and I could perceive something pass between her I watched and those before, they had taken a turn to avoid an almost dry but deep-sided slue. I had not speed for such a choice, and I cleared it to make a shorter cut. It turned out a greater saving than I had anticipated, and I came in upon the skirt of some Indians in advance of the whites.

I could see that my best safety would be to bear up toward the trees till dark, and accordingly veered my course to the right. But barely had this change been made, when there came upon me a horseman, evidently a white, urging desperately on an over-strained steed, the head bent down, and the arm raised to apply the whip. No sooner had he seen my Indian-like guise, than he turned rein almost backward, a handkerchief was tied round his brow, down almost to the eyes, the face was pale and haggard with fear, but I thought I could not mistake—the stamp of guilt was there, and for the first time I understood the silence of the bereaved mother, and the dead of the night before.

I could not be known, so much was I disguised, but I slackened my pace to let pass by, one already a prey to tortures too plainly stamped, and he sped on.

But another horse and another rider were coming, and the flying man was now pursued in earnest. I saw the wild glare of the eye, as with a wave of the hand I was imperiously repelled, but my horse had not the speed of the one I sought to join, nor was there in the rider that terrible will, which can communicate its power to the animal in such moments of supreme resolve. I felt I could not come between the mother and that dread vengeance—if such there was—had I the power. Mechanically my course was steered in their wake, and through the dim shadows I could see again a double, and again I was able to cut across, near enough to discern the race of retribution.

When I had first discerned Rose careering through the flying throng, I heard her voice, wild and high, calling upon someone to stop, but there was no sound now, and the deepening dusk shut out the two figures in its gloom.

There were now others coming forward, and the voice of Cuvier was to be distinguished, he was shouting that there were Indians about. It was necessary, therefore, to explain who I was. I hollowed to the half-breed in French, and pulled up.

We were considerably off the line taken in the retreat by the main body, occasional shots had been heard, but the darkness seemed to have put its seal on the pursuit.

"Have you seen Rose?" said Harry Smith, unheeding my strange appearance, and not questioning its cause. "She is raised right wild, and is tearing after Bernard, something has driven her distracted."

"How?" asked Cuvier.

"Why, mad—raving mad—her father would not know her again. I had seized her as she was striking with her tomahawk at him, but she threw off my hold as if I had been a feather, and you know I am not to be just called soft griped."

"She has lost her child," I answered.

"Ah! There it is. But who would have thought of it making such a tigress of her."

"There is, perhaps, fever, I have known such things come upon women giving suck," suggested Brant. "Let us spread, boys, and see and get a hold of her, to stop further mischief. If it is fever, she must be got to camp."

There were some half dozen dashed off in search, I cannot say I was the most eager, as I dreaded it would be but to find some bloody scene, from the thought of which I recoiled.

Chapter Fifty-Six
Regrouping—a search and some signs

The party which had made this attack consisted of a considerable number of trappers, out from the camp of Dripps, and some fifty lodges of Snakes. They would not have attacked the village had they known its strength, and the darkness which covered the latter part of their retreat, served to hide the smallness of their force. They had been induced to believe, by Bernard and the others who had escaped from the skirmishes of the morning and evening before, that there was but a strong war party out, and that the village was far behind.

I got this information in detached pieces, as we galloped on in a direction down the valley, which was that in which had last been seen the Swiss, straining to escape. But the plain was here and there cut by the winding of the stream, as also by its deserted beds, and the fall of De Noyer gave warning that the pace should be slackened.

There was nothing heard of the search, as most of them dispersed on that errand were coming together, from the narrowing of the valley on its western side. An ominous silence prevailed as we proceeded down the stream, which again swept away from the dark wood, and the plain was again expanded. Cuvier, who knew well that river and that plain, took the lead, inclining toward the middle of the valley, and the rest followed warily after.

An hour's ride brought us again to where the stream neared the pines, which also came lower on the other bank, and presently came the roar of water rushing over some obstruction. The path—for here there was a well-beaten road—descended steeply among rocks, and opened to our view the fires of the camp on the plain below. Chariot had been singing some snatches of a Canadian song, a young savage sprung from behind a stone, to whom he said something in Snake, and he darted on toward camp.

I found Macairey, my animals, and baggage, and a roast of ribs at the fire, which employed me like a wolf for the first period of the night, but giving during the time an account of the adventures of the day, though in disjointed parts, as it would be desirable to do something to find out what had become of Rose as soon as there should be light.

"A good number of Indians have been knocked off their horses, if not killed, and there will be a search made by break of day," observed Smith, who had previously arrived.

The fire was allowed to wane, and we laid down to rest, leaving the camp unusually quiet. An evidently painful vigilance was apparent in the Indians, who prowling about, every now and then looked in to light a pipe or to warm themselves at the still glowing embers.

Through the gray of dawn I could perceive that the camp was much larger than I had supposed, and well posted. Jim was with me as I made my way up the path of the night before, tracks of several horses were fresh before us, and I learned that a considerable number of Snakes and some Crows had gone up the opposite side as a look-out a couple of hours before, having crossed by a ford lower down.

Most of the whites had remained in camp, uninterested in taking scalps or the finding stray horses. Chill is the vapor which accompanies the frequent frosts of these altitudes.

Our silent ride had been uninterrupted by word or incident for a considerable distance, when we discovered sundry horsemen grouped on their return, a short examination enabling us to recognize among them De Noyer, who had gone out early to search for his running horse, which he had lost in the mad struggle of the night before, and we drew up to hear their news. There were three horses led, and two scalps were dangling from the ends of muskets, therefore it was probable this cast might have taken in the ground where the event had taken place of which we sought the trace—that terrible race—and this was found to be the case, they had swept most of the plain on this side of the river.

I could not urge Jim to continue what appeared a useless waste of time, but I took a line along the edge of the stream to return, here perhaps something might mark a crossing, especially if made at desperate speed, every moment, however, I was obliged to look up from the quest, to watch that some movement was not being made from the other camp similar to our own, and from which it would be necessary to escape. The water was deep, and there was nothing of a slope on its bank, generally, it was perpendicular.

I had gone along the brink for some little time, when I saw some distance ahead a wolf stealing away from a small thicket of sage in a deserted slue. It is always good to examine what an animal of prey may be about, when found alone, he was one of the large dark grey wolves, which are more seldom met with than the smaller and lighter colored species. On reaching the spot from which he first appeared to move, I could discern nothing, the ground was gravelly, and therefore there could be no trail, but just as I left I thought I observed a stone freshly displaced, and a portion of a bush broken. There was nothing not easily accounted for in this, where so many horsemen had been recently about, but it was the first mark of anything like speed I had observed, the turf dry and thick, however, was close by, and there was no further trace.

I saw the others pressing more rapidly on their return, and did not dismount nor stop, but proceeded in a line for the nearest bend. Though it might have been a satisfaction to have made this examination more complete, I began to reflect that I had better be pricking on, and had already quickened my pace, when, on the very edge of the bank and where the stream ran deep and rapid under it, I saw a fresh fall of earth had taken place, and the plain marks of hoofs close to where it had given way. I pulled up, the soil had been ripped by horse-hoofs, as if in a struggle to stop, and just beyond, where the clay was yet fresh and new, there was the imprint of something having slid down the bank, and I thought an appearance of hair. However, the others were almost out of sight, and I could observe nothing more.

A considerable number of horses were going down the opposite side of the plain, and altogether the indications were not those of security, so I loosened rein and let my horse, already impatient of being left alone, put out his speed to get again into company.

There was a camp of Crows in a neighboring valley, on another tributary of the Yellow Stone, and probably the Blackfeet believed ours to be stronger than it really was, but it was considered best not to press forward at present round the mountains until they had time to retreat. It was accordingly determined only to move a short distance backward, and I found on my arrival this retreat was about commencing.

It was after a hurried breakfast—a meal which, in cases of difficulty it is as well to secure, that Smith came to the fire, for the lodge was down. I saw before he spoke he had some news.

"I believe Rose has made a husband less in the diggings."

"How?" I asked, starting up in fear that some dreadful event had occurred.

"The horse of the Swiss was found by the party we saw opposite, both stirrups were on one side, and he had been in the water over the saddle, his hip cut and scratched, and the lasso still in a coil entangled round his legs."

"And Rose?"

"Nothing of her or her horse."

"Well, but that is no proof even of the death of Bernard, much less of its manner."

"Aye, but there is a part of the blanket over the holsters, which must have been above water—it is black with blood."

My worst fears thus were realized, but I had said nothing of the signs on the river bank, and thought it best to assume an incredulous tone.

"There were Indians enough about," I remarked.

Smith smiled meaningly and shook his head.

Chapter Fifty-Seven
Interview with Rose—a fearful struggle—the confessional—an agony of suspense—appetite

It was again on the southwestern side of the Mountain of the Winds, we met to rendezvous[1]. Almost all the companies and their dependant bands were arrived.

In a lodge, a little apart from the scene of business and pleasure, and close to that tree upon which I had so nearly finished my career, reclined two persons, one of whom I had last seen suffering from that wound of which he was still weak, though convalescent. The other, when we last met, was in the fury of fever, caused by a revulsion of the nutriment of a mother driven back upon the system, and in a delirium directed by the bereavement which caused it, she was seeking the life of him she believed a murderer, with that uplifted hand of vengeance, which I had reason to believe had so truly fallen. A slight tinge of color, scarcely showed she was sensible of my presence. Her father, as usual, held out his hand, and my appearance there was evidently to him welcome and relieving.

He sat up. "Rose is but weak, therefore be tender of her," he said. "And as the heat of noon is past, I may be the better of a ride."

---

1. Rendezvous: The rendezvous of 1834 started above the mouth of the Big Sandy River (which drains the west side of South Pass), and continued in the third week of July along Ham's Fork, another tributary of Green River, near present Granger, Wyoming.

   The rendezvous of 1834 saw the culmination of major realignments in the mountain trade: Nathaniel Wyeth, beaten to rendezvous with trade goods by Bill Sublette, at last was obliged to concede failure. The Rocky Mountain Fur Company, bankrupt, was absorbed by The Company. But that venerable monopoly was no longer the American Fur Company but Pratte, Chouteau & Co., John Jacob Astor's successors in the West.

I helped him up, and he walked out to where his horse was tied, giving him a leg, he was soon mounted.

"Be tender of her, and you may be able to do her much good," he said again, as he went.

I returned, and sat down by Rose, she was dressed in a cotillion, as it is called, of dark blue cloth, which gave almost a livid hue to the skin, the eyes looked large and lustrous, else there was but little change, she motioned to me to sit down, and for the first time spoke, her voice was low but clear.

"Do not speak loud, Ned, I am sadly unsettled, and it is but at times, I believe, I know what I am about."

"Well, but you are better," I hazarded.

"Probably," she said, with a faint smile, "or I should not have known you, it is not long, they tell me, that I knew my favorite horse from a pack animal they put me upon."

Here I perceived she was getting exhausted, and gave her a cup of warm jelly, which was near.

"Oh! that is what they plague me with, and tell me it is to make me well, but it will moisten my throat, don't you feel it cold?" she added. "You have no idea how dreary the chill last night was, after we parted."

"It was bad enough," I answered, and she sunk back.

I pulled a piece of robe over her feet, the attentive help saw the action, and heaped wood on the fire, there was a slight hectic on the face of the sleeper, as if from recovered warmth, and she dosed in perfect calmness, by signs, and a few words of Spanish, I was made to understand, that restlessness was the chief ailment now, and that it was rare she enjoyed tranquil repose, or could be brought to take nourishment, she was evidently delighted with the cup of jelly being swallowed, and the slumber following. I moved gently out, making a sign that I would not be far, when the object of our care woke up.

Notwithstanding that the eye is the most important and expressive feature of the human countenance, there is no position in which the face looks so beautiful as when each muscle returns to its proper position, and a languid harmony pervades the whole as in sleep, which is immediately dispelled on being awoke. I lingered to gaze on that pale but rounded cheek, I looked at those full lips, little parted, but looking ready to form a smile, and that beautiful hand so little like a deed of blood, that I shuddered as I turned away.

Diego had taken a ride round by some of the more distant lodges, there were but few Indians, and he had chosen a place near the outside, to be away from the noise of a closer neighborhood.

I sat down within sight of the Navahoe handmaid, and taking out my glass, surveyed the opposite heights, the usual Indian guard were about, but at one point, I saw a strange horseman, round whom several of the scouts were clustering. Little interested in such an arrival, I amused myself by observing the squaws crossing back from the beds of white and yellow clay, which are to be found on Horse Creek[2], they were to have known by the profuse coloring with which they had smeared the horses which they had loaded. Some time after this, through an opening between some more distant lodges, I perceived the same stranger surrounded by several Snakes, coming slowly onward, bringing the glass to bear upon the group, during a momentary opening, I at once saw it was the medicine man. Eager as I was to meet one who had been to me in this country invariably a friend and support, I could not quit the neighborhood of Diego's lodge, and leave the state or Rose unsolved by one short interview, only taking the character of an episode in the general state of her wandering intellects.

It was some time since I had lost sight of my friend, and I still remained at a point of the brink of the stream, where it had taken a reverse turn, and I could sit facing the water, and watching the collecting and carrying off of the white foam under the opposite bank, and still have before me the lodge, and a view of the camp beyond.

At last, the Spaniard made his appearance, riding alongside was David, he had changed the travel-stained steed on which I had seen him arrive for one I knew at once to be lent him by a brother of the Little Chief, a horse not become white with age, but one of those which are born so with white skin, shewing at the nostrils and the lips he had been profusely painted, the hair of the mane and tail were amber, and various marks in pale blue had also been made with artistic care on his glossy coat, the simple Indian cord of black horse hair tied round the lower jaw, and its coil hanging over the shoulder, and the dark blue capot and leggings which the Indians call black, contrasted well with the rest. Beside him, the long face and high features of the Spanish Don, calm and subdued by suffering and weakness, his horse in the gaudy trappings of the Mexican cavalier, curvetted under a restraining hand, by him in a free walk nose forward and eager eye came his brother of the western plains, his movements almost unheeded by his rider, earnest in look, though calmly bearing his part in a conversation of apparent interest.

They had both dismounted when I reached the door, and the father explained how glad he was to be able to derive assistance from the medicine man in such a crisis, while the other had entered the low door where the patient lay. I told him of the sleep which had soon ended our interview, after his departure.

"It is what we have been praying for," he answered. "She has had a fearful struggle during these last ten days, and had there not come now or soon some repose, I should have had but a sad hope of preserving life with a clouded

---

2. Horse Creek: Here Stewart evidently confuses this rendezvous of 1834, on Ham's Fork, with the rendezvous of 1833 on Horse Creek, some ninety miles north.

reason. God is merciful," he added, reverently, "and I trust in the intercessions of the blessed Virgin." He was evidently affected by what he deemed a crisis.

The visitor to the tent now reappeared, and it seemed there was nothing immediately alarming in the case he had just been examining, and this continuing sleep was its most encouraging symptom.

"Have you sung her into a dose?" asked he, for the first time speaking, in a tone meant to re-assure Diego.

"No, we had but few moments together before she fell off, as if exhausted."

"Well," he said, after a pause, during which he looked steadfastly in my face, "come this way a little, let us sit by that cool waterside, and before I taste food, solve in some way various matters in which you are concerned."

We had seated ourselves on the bank of that stream again.

"Now," he began, "you need not answer me unless you feel free to do so, but there is some terrible secret between you and Rose."

I was perhaps somewhat prepared for this, but with a wariness I had almost learned to adopt latterly to all, I answered, "I left the Blackfoot camp before her, and have heard only in a general way, that she has been in a high fever ever since that day."

"I have told you that you need not confide in me any secret affecting another, but further I may add, should you do so, it is as safe as in the confessional. I could not but be of less use to her, ignorant as I am, or forming wrong suppositions." I had had time to reflect, that surmises and rumours were already afloat, and that it might be better to confide in what I considered the tried discretion of my questioner, and such a well-known friendship for the family of the sufferer, and answered, "I will relate all I know, in the full faith of its being the best thing I could do for her it most concerns."

I then gave a circumstantial account of our departure the night of the child's death, Smith's warning, and the strange looks and conduct of the father, his desperate escape from the Blackfoot party, and the discovery of the death, with Rose's suppressed affliction, and those words which first made the conviction of the murder flash upon my mind, the terrible look of wild vengeance on the evening, and the deadly race of the night, next morning the discovery of the riderless horse, the bloody blanket. "She has been in delirium ever since."

"There can be but little question that she rushed out in that state," rejoined my companion. "That I learned myself, and that well on in the night she came back, and after applying cloths to her father's wound, which she seemed to believe was opened afresh, she sunk into an uneasy slumber, and always on awaking, asked for her child, relapsing into wildness again on his not being brought. I also learned that one of her great anxieties has been to learn what you would think of her."

Here we were interrupted by a call from Diego, though now long after that hour, to the midday meal, and after washing in the clear water at our feet, we repaired to the lodge. There is ever in these climes, attending on the opportunity of a repast the ready appetite.

Diego convalescent, and much reassured by the happy sleep of his daughter, set an example of cheerfulness, and I was not much behind the traveler in feeding from the bones laid before us on their delicious flesh, at last, the pipe was brought. Several persons had stopped at the door to enquire how went on the invalid within, but no one dismounted.

It was getting toward evening, and at last some small symptoms of restlessness began to shew themselves in the breathing of the sleeper, before whose couch a piece of painted lodge cloth had been hung to mark off what might be considered as a dormitory, the help was sitting on watch at the foot of the bed, and we remarked her anxiety, but I had never seen the medicine man shew so much uneasiness.

Diego would have said something, but was restrained by a gesture, and I held my breath, in a few minutes a sudden movement of the squaw made us believe that the slumber was at an end, but she let her hands, which she had reached forward, fall again on her lap.

"If she wakes sensible and refreshed, all may be well, if again incoherent, her reason will be shaken all her life," whispered my next neighbor to me. "In which case go away."

It is impossible to describe the agony of this suspense, again there was a motion of the watch, as if some change had come over the sleeper, but not a breath was to be heard, and the eyes of the poor Navahoe grew intense, I could hear my heart beat, the look of the watcher at last turned, and fixing on me, beckoned me to come to her side. A sign to be quiet, but obey from my friend beside me, and I moved over on my hands and knees, I saw past the end of the curtain that the patient's eyes were open, but they again closed, and a hand wasted with sickness was raised from under the blanket which covered her, and she rubbed them, then came a yawn, and she looked about as if in search of someone, at last she seemed to recognize me, I had wished to draw back, but had not the power, a faint smile shone from the eye, it was a beam of reason. I took a long breath.

"Were you not here a moment since," said a weak voice. "Or was it I saw you in a dream."

I was about to answer, when the cup of warm jelly, as before administered, was put into my hand.

"Yes, it was myself gave you a drink a short time since."

"Ah, now I remember, is my father here?"

"Yes, he is not far off, but we will have more time to talk tomorrow."

"Would you not like something to eat, perhaps?"

"Yes, but I cannot say till you bring it, do you remember, for it seems so long ago, I taught you to cook, and scrape off bits of meat from the bone, when we had nearly satisfied our hunger, and wanted to prolong a meal to that more social stage, when the appetite has to be coaxed."

"Yes," I answered, and at the word, as there had stood by the ever burning fire of the lodge, was handed to me a hump rib, it was almost hissing from the heat of the embers.

"Strip me off a little mouthful, as I wish to eat but to please you."

I did as I was told, and hung the little mouthful, pierced by the point of the knife, over her lips, and she took it, I thought, with some relish, and after a minute observed,

"You forget salt."

It may be easily supposed I was not long in finding some, and applying it to another mouthful, which seemed to be taken more eagerly.

"Ah, that is really good, and I will eat one more bit to please myself."

Then followed the strengthening jelly.

"I must have made a supper," said the invalid, as she covered herself up, and nestled her head on the scarlet blanket spread over a saddle which pillowed it. Her eyes were turned toward me, and I saw their lids gradually drooping, till at last, after a succession of efforts to keep awake, she struggled no longer, and with a smile yielded them up to sleep.

Chapter Fifty-Eight
Palaver—thoughts of England—letters & plans
—an exchange with Rose—Diego's affection

The sun was low, and we went out to see the coming in of our various steeds, each finding out his way to his own home from the general rush. Small white mists of dust were rising near the bases of the more distant buttes, but the real gathering had not yet commenced.

"Rose is safe as to her health, and her mind perhaps may take a melancholy turn, but not a disordered one," observed my companion, seeing me absorbed in thought.

"Well, I think so too, and it is a relief," I answered.

"But you must see her again, and get her to unburthen herself, to secure her in the feeling that she is held innocent by those for whose opinion she cares, and then we must think of yourself. Heald is gone express to the Blackfeet village—I saw him."

"Well?" I asked. "That should rather be a riddance than not."

"I will think the matter over, and we will meet after tying up."

Jim and Brent, who were still together, had pitched their lodge something lower down, and thither I invited the medicine man to go and take up his quarters.

"I do not mind if I do, but I will first take back my gala charger." He rode off to find out the abode of the friendly Snake.

It was not far in the night when I found myself with a knot of Americans, in a lodge of mixed and unmixed happiness, amid whose din my mysterious friend was telling me how he regretted Hi-Hi, and how satisfied he was to have saved him from feeling bodily pain.

"I told the Snakes," he added, "that the Blackfoot tortures had never changed a muscle in his frame, and that I had never seen so great a death. I do not know where the poor lad's spirit now dwells, but if it is given to such to look again upon the earth, his will be rejoiced to find that his bearing at the supreme trial gained him a name which will be quoted among his people."

"Here is the interesting widow Black-muzzle, who is in a maze," said Brent, giving the strangely-changed figure at his side a poke in the ribs.

"I think the further he gets from the stable and little sanded parlour of his thoughts, the more he likes them," said old Bill.

"Tiss distance lands inchintment to the view," said Irish Dick with a wink.

"Like a good number more of us. He has become a great hunter of late."

"How so?" said a greenhorn.

"Why, I saw him knock over a prairie dog and catch him before he got into his house, he had but his hind legs broken, it was a tight race, but the Muzzle won by a neck, and I saw him in wrath dash its brains out against a stone."

"Aye," answered the object of their remarks, "it was a necessary act, as he was only wounded, and I could not bring him home, with both legs broken, without giving him still more pain."

"Yes," said Bill, "with your cant, and had anyone done the same by an elephant, and been big enough to have knocked his brains out against such a stone as the Rock of Gibraltar, your governor would have voted for an Act of Parliament against him. You are all humbugs, mind, I tell you." The speaker, like a heathen god, was hid in a cloud.

"He is too fat to ride a race," said Milton Sublette, pointing to Blackmuzzle. "I must wait for Heald, who takes care of the other horse. I hear the little Dutchman will bet heavy. Kit rides wild sometimes, but if we could get Biggs to ride to order he is the best of the lot, but he loses his head."

"At all events, my horse does not start," said Meek, "till Heald comes, so I'll drink part of the winnings in the meantime."

"Someone has run off with John De Villée's squaw," said curly-headed Cotton.

"Shut up, you varment," said old Bill, who was always at him.

"Yes," said Mike, "It was Antoine, I was there when they started from behind the bushes at the back of John's lodge, they had only one packhorse for both. I don't think they wanted to go very far."

"And what did John do?" asked Black-muzzle, with interest, as he said it put him in mind of a consistory court, and a divorce, and what not.

"Why, John had his best runner tied at the door, and while Antoine dodged down the river among the thickets, to beyond the mouth of Horse Creek, his pursuer, armed to the teeth, rode up the face of the butte behind camp—the only way they could not possibly have gone. The Captain said, when he got down, that it put him in mind of a Frenchman near Paris, who, when he was told his dear helpmate had thrown herself into the Seine, and was carried away by the stream, rushed to the bank and run wildly up the river side, tearing his hair, in search. John did not quite make out the allusion till the other was out of reach."

"Well," persisted the questioner, "but when he did make it out?"

"Oh, as usual, he took his gun to pieces to clean it, and I left him looking death to everyone who passed and scrubbing the life out of the old barrel of his fusee."

"Well," said someone, "he won't be here tonight."

"No, he has sworn that the man who robbed him of his spouse, and he who laughed at him, could both only die but by his hand, so that it would look blood-thirsty on his part to come in the way to meet them. He keeps watch at his lodge door, and sends for a cup of grog every now and then to keep up his resolution to stay at home."

While this and similar conversations were going on, my friend was making me aware that my enemy, whose real motive he did not know, had been at the bottom of the plot to bring me here, and that Bernard had been an instrument, that he was convinced there was something of greater importance than an ordinary inheritance at stake, and that it would be necessary for me to go back to the old country and watch, that the only clue was this stranger, and he might be difficult to trace, but that, at all events, I ought to go to be able to inquire about my father's property.

I paused before I answered. "But there is no means at my disposal, you forget that law in England is the moral torture, which has replaced the Inquisition as a physical one, and that every hair's breadth I may advance is to be paved with gold."

"All that is thought for, and decision must be the order of the day, and if you go, it must be before the others are off. There is a short cut to the mouth of the Yellow Stone, and a canoe must carry you on. You may yet see Rose tonight, if she wakes in time, if not, tomorrow. The signs are altered, and still changing for the worse, nothing but the Almighty hand can stop these Yankees, and there is no longer freedom where a Puritan places his foot, he himself is not free, and no one else within his reach, and all wild animals disappear where they come. You need not regret, therefore, your going, and should things be of worse aspect there than I think, it is not difficult to find your way back."

"Yes," interrupted Black-muzzle, who had crept round behind, "but who is to pay the piper?"

"You hear that reptile," I answered, turning away from him.

"Yes, reptile, I am as well educated as yourself, and am not ashamed of my mother," said the besotted campkeeper, just as Cotton sat down upon him.

"I thought you were a bale, what are you about sprawling there behind backs?"

"Well done, varmint!" said old Bill. "Give Cotton a cup of something soft and sweet to suit his natur."

"Let us be off," said my companion, and we slid out below, amid the din.

"Tomorrow, long before noon, we ought to be ready with our plan. Soon after dawn I will see the Spaniard, there is but that quarter which could cause any hesitation."

After poking about in the embers of the lodge fire, and applying some shavings of the infallible pitch pine, we were enabled to arrange for the night's rest.

I did not concern myself at what time the others came in, but at the turn-out, it was my turn to let loose the horses of the lodge, I went out with but my blanket, the calm though chilly air was clear, and I was amongst the first to answer to old Provost's *Leve, Leve*. The animals were moving off with alacrity, which were already loose, and those tied were exhibiting the usual marks of impatience.

There is no glutton like a horse, eating is his sole natural employment. I loitered for a few minutes, enjoying the shivering of the various figures, called out like myself, and some without even the protection of a blanket. The delight of creeping again into a warm nest, and burying up under the silky robe, I need not attempt to describe to any who have had no similar experiences, but to those who have been in the practice of this nomadic life, sleep is one of the short-lived pleasures not to be despised, and though one of the most innocent enjoyments, we cannot help remembering to have heard it classed with the vice of the sluggard.

However that may be, on looking out again from my lair, I perceived the medicine man was gone. Jim was busy with some coffee simmering by the fire, and I got up at the grateful smell.

I was met by a Mexican who had taken charge of Diego's horses, he told me they were expecting me at the lodge, and passed on. Rose was almost sitting up, that is, she was leaning against a bale of various goods which had replaced the saddle, which appropriately was mounted upon the top, she was much better it was evident from everything about her.

"We all would like to keep you for the fall hunt," said Diego, "but your friend and ours thinks you have a right to know something of your own history, and what duties you might have to perform in your own land, were you allowed to fill your proper place. I have written some letters for you, and will add another, they will furnish you with the means of letting us know your true history, if they do not lead to your finding out anything to your pecuniary advantage. I want no thanks, and you shall give a receipt in my favor to whatever agents of mine give you any supplies. You see it is but a loan, and that we have settled the matter before your arrival. I have another letter to give you, and I will go to Dripp's lodge to write it, meantime, I do not know whether I leave you in charge of Rose, or her in yours, but I hope you will amuse each other, if you do not put her again to sleep."

This was a long speech from the Spaniard, usually so sparing of words, and partly uttered after he had got up to go out. The imperturbable David prepared to follow, and I was at last left sitting at the foot of the invalid's bed, overwhelmed at the disposal they had made of my movements, and the generous —for I knew they would be sufficient—means placed at my disposal, and almost ashamed at the reluctance with which I was about to start upon this, to anyone else, most interesting research.

"You do not look so wild to be off in hopes of an inheritance, as an avaricious man might be," she said, with a smile.

"Because I am not avaricious," I answered.

"Well, you may always come back, my father told me so. But they have not told you yet how useful you may be to us in the old world, so that your generous nature will have to overlook the performance of a task, which however light you make it, is a grave matter for a Spanish grandee. But there has been a short history written out, by which you will learn our position— *Instructions*, it is headed. Now I must leave off, for I have really talked myself out."

I reached a cup, to which as she spoke she pointed, it was tea, cold as ice, for she made me taste it.

I was anxious to ask some question regarding the fatal night, which was ever recurring to my thoughts, and relapsed into silence, from not knowing how I was to begin. This she interpreted rightly, for after a short pause, during which she looked down and seemed to struggle with some unpleasant feeling, she said hurriedly, "I remember but one incident of that night—fit night for such a morning—a gun-barrel was at my breast, and fire flashed in the pan—I saw it. It was then I closed and drove him over the bank, and as we went down I struck the blow. It was not quite deep at the edge, I saw him lie down over his horse's neck, but the current swept us far apart, my horse drifting further down I occasionally remember a sensation of perishing cold, and at intervals unimportant circumstances, but I hardly could tell you how I got from thence, or how I got here. Now, are you satisfied?" And the dark eye for a moment flashed.

"I was always satisfied, but I own you have relieved me by enabling me to state such facts."

"What do people question?"

I saw the red blood rush to her cheeks, and broke in, "Nay, no one has that right, but if such were assumed, you know what a confidence it gives to be well armed, and that is what I feel."

"Thank you, thank you truly, dear Ned, for your thoughtfulness about me, my father also feels you are our friend, it has been a sad short year we have known each other, God grant that the next may be better, at least for you."

"And do you think I should hold any year as good for me, where it was unhappy for you, dear Rose?"

"We will not bandy good wishes further, but believe me, I tell you true, I shall be content with the welfare of my father and Edward."

I almost thought I saw a tear dim the downcast eye. I was afraid to hurt her by further prolonging the scene, and turning toward the door, held out my hand, she saw that I wished to take leave, my heart was full to bursting, I could not speak, she pulled me gently toward her, and parting the hair grown long over the brow, kissed my forehead. I felt that she had more command over her feelings than I had over mine, though she sunk back from the exertion this scene had occasioned, and covered her head, there was a look of almost displeased wonder on the face of the Navahoe, and I left the lodge.

Again seated by the Susquedee, I found the medicine man.

"I have told Jim Macarey of your going, and he says he will go with you, there is also Alik Wade[1], a half-breed, who wishes to go as far as the Yellow Stone Fort. I will come after you with your letters, and we will pass Dripp's lodge to take leave of Diego, as well as him, he is one of the best men to be met with, and his good word, which is never lightly given, will go far and carry weight. The horses and the men will be at the lower end of camp, and if you will put up as light a pack as you can, I will send it and your pack-saddle down by a squaw, it need not appear that you are gone for more than a ride, unless the trading booth, and not the family lodge, should be the scene of your adieus. I will follow the sooner if you can lend me a horse."

"Yes, there is the Indian one to spare, I hope they have some meat."

"O, never fear, Jim will manage that."

My packing was not difficult, but there was a depoullee, which however would go under my riding blanket till it could be transferred to the pack-saddle, and there form the first acquaintance with the kettles and other stores.

We found the good trader in the heart of his family. "He was sorry," he said, "to lose me, but felt sure, that like others, I would come back, as no one ever forgot the mountains, he complimented me also, and said he would give me a letter to the fort at the Yellow Stone, and one to Cherteau at St. Louis. I then took my leave of the Spaniard, who came in, he merely said, Rose, if she

---

1. Alik Wade: Apparently Alexander Wade, a companion of Joseph Gale. Wade trapped out of Fort Hall in 1835 but traded only nine beaver at the fort. Early in 1836, he formed a partnership with Calvin T. Briggs, Moses T. Collins, and Charlie Schriver. See Janet LeCompte, *John J. Burroughs*, Hafen, *The Mountain men and the Fur Trade*, III: 62, and LeCompte's *Calvin T. Briggs* in the same work, II: 62, see also Nicholas P. Hardeman, *Charles A. Warfield*, in the same work, VII: 354.

was able, or the medicine man, was to tell you that you may be able to do us much good in London, by attending to some matters for us there."

"That is my chief motive in going," said I.

"But I hope better things of your journey, than only one half of your errand," he said, "and that of the least moment."

"It will be to me the most important," I said, and this I really meant. But from the style of high flown compliment, which prevails among Spaniards, it was taken as a matter of course.

"Your letters will follow, and so adieu for the present." And the father of Rose threw his arms about my neck.

"I am parting," he said, "with one who could do us much good here, as also where he goes, and he carries our best affections with him."

I was really touched at the regret of the old Spaniard, as I did not in the least doubt his partiality.

It was not far to the lodge where the horses were to be ready, I found, however, only my bear-horse, as I had called him from the first day's hunt I had had with him. He was already saddled, and the medicine man who was within, told me to mount, and I should find the rest a little further down.

Chapter Fifty-Nine
Parting words of the medicine man—toward the Yellow Stone—a tense wait—sneaking by

It was the evening of the night after that we were rounding the southeastern shoulder of the Mountains of the Winds, having left behind the feeders of the Smaller Sandy. There was but little space before we should be on the sources of the Eau-douce, and have passed from the Pacific waters to those of the Atlantic. I had already believed that I had quitted the great west the month before, and had been drawing in toward civilization, but now I knew what ere betided, I was fairly started, again to mix in the race for gold, the ambition of notoriety, or the passion for interference in the concerns of our neighbors, which form the great motive powers of the enlightened world.

There were occasional furrows, and then a space bare of trees, and sometimes of soil, it was on one of these where the horses trod tenderly, that the medicine man laid his hand upon my arm, and said, "Before we pass away from that western sun, which you now see resting near the sources of the Columbia, take what may be your last look, it tints with red gold the tops of the Utaws above the lake, and this side the vast desert which swallows up great rivers, and gives life or sustenance to nothing, it is a region not intended for man or beast, and if it is a curse to be without these and vegetable life besides, it is a region accursed. But between it and where we stand, lies what has been a rich country for the hunter, it was so but last year. It gets darker below, and the pilot butte[1] is but a little reddened, and perhaps you may never

---

1. The pilot butte: Traveling east through South Pass, Stewart sees this landmark, *a high, square, table-like mound* (Ferris, *Life in the Rocky Mountains,* p. III), south of the Sweetwater River (Stewart's *Eau-douce)* between the Big and Little Sandy rivers.

look upon these scenes again, we are on the divide, now let us pass on, for they are pushing toward the next quaking ash and willow, which is to hide us, it is to be hoped, for the night. You have learned that I loved Rose's mother, but she preferred Diego, and that the daughter has loved you, and that the mad jealousy of that unlucky Swiss, has caused much misery and his own death, let this, which is no fault of yours, stimulate you however to repair the mischief done by exerting yourself where I have already told you how much you can serve them, and perhaps, when there are better times, you may come back and see the haunts of some happy days, and many friends, who would be gladdened at your return. I had intended to take leave of you tomorrow, but let us part now, leave me with the setting sun, before we cross the divide, and remember me whenever again you see the red rays sinking behind a mountain chain. I have grown out of forms, but if I am anything particular, I am a Catholic, and I pray you may be watched over and interceded for by your own patron saint, and so farewell."

This was short and abrupt, but I was glad it was over. I was now without friendly ties, unless the good feeling and trustiness of Jim might be called so. The mules were out in the thick short grass, and the fire against the face of a rock in a hollow, already flickered into a blaze, the west was shut out by that cold, dark, bare ridge, and the glow of parting day was gone, my friend was gone, and I was calmly seated contemplating my projected voyage, and all the chances which might affect its issue. The letters I had secured in a piece of parafleche, but as a precaution, duplicates were to be sent down by the caravan returning with beaver.

The animals were all still, the night was calm, and the keen air rendered the fire a necessary as well as luxury, there was no challenge from the wolf, all animal nature around seemed at rest, the ever-trembling leaf of the aspen alone gave symptoms of motion. We lay with our heads to some bushes and feet to the fire, and there was no use in stretching our piece of lodge skin, the embers shone red and warm, the pipe was done, and words had been but few, the stars were bright in the deep blue sky, whilst yet the upturned eye was open to behold.

There was little time in such a journey to hunt, but for a subsistence, nor could the most enthusiastic admirer of nature have been so blind to the danger of yielding to that taste, as to mark the grand and beautiful scenes through which he was passing, with more than a general glance, the shady forest, the bushy crag, was rather to be dreaded for what it might conceal, than admired in the beauty it displayed. At times, the streams deep and leaden-like at the bottom of a chasm, invited us to end the perils and delays, the cares and fatigues of a journey by land, on that silent element, which left no trail on its course, but the roar of the canon further on, shewed how deceitful would have been the calm. Every animal of the land, except the moose, ranged around our course, less wild because less harassed than elsewhere. At last, we emerged, here the Big Horn issues from the channel it has made through the last range which obstructs its course, and becomes the Yellow Stone of the plains.

I may as well here state, that the character of the land is forever changed, and that our way was by open prairies and gentle swells, by the side of a river almost navigable, a letter I had to the hospitable Makenzie[2] at the fort, procured me what little was needed to buy a skiff. Jim found someone of his own people to take the other oar. Alic was engaged to return to the Crow country, I never could learn for whom he was mistaken, but a party of Crows sent out to cut off some obnoxious persons, killed him and another on the track we had followed, and by which he was returning, a very few days after he got to the Big Horn. The express to St. Louis, which passed us, brought this news, the Indians who had done the deed, arriving at the fort before it left, to claim, as they said, their reward.

This account was somewhat confused, as it was given by one of the party, Joe Pourrier[3], out hunting some distance from the trail, which taking a straighter line than the river, is sometimes for a distance of two days' journey considerably removed from its course.

We were under a broken bank mending a small leak, occasioned by the partial staving in of a plank against a snag. Jim perceived Pourrier peeping over the bank, he had not hailed us, and as soon as he gave his news, put out to rejoin his camp.

"I wonder what he wanted?" said Jim.

"Why," I answered, "did he not tell you he was hunting."

---

2. Makenzie: Kenneth McKenzie (1797-1861), called King of the Missouri, presided over the Upper Missouri Outfit of the American Fur Company from 1827 to 1834. Born in Scotland, McKenzie emigrated to North America in 1816 and worked for the Northwest Company before moving to St. Louis in 1822. Between 1822 and 1827 this energetic, skillful, and frequently unscrupulous trader consolidated his personal grip on the upper Missouri. He had Fort Union built on the north bank of the Missouri, just above the mouth of the Yellowstone, in 1828. From there he directed a campaign to monopolize both the river and the mountain trades. In 1834, due to organizational changes in American Fur and his involvement in the distillery scandal, he retired as a major force in the trade.

His acquaintance with Captain Stewart, later Sir William Stewart, was evidently cordial. They must have met in St. Louis in the spring of 1833 see DeVoto, *Across the Wide Missouri*. Stewart felt free to write McKenzie half a year later to protest the theft of Fitzpatrick's horses and furs. Letters from McKenzie to Stewart now held by the Scottish Record Office (photocopies are at the University of Wyoming Library) show that in 1838 McKenzie offered to act as agent for purchase of real estate in the West on Stewart's behalf, and in 1844 he wrote Stewart asking the loan of twenty-five or thirty thousand dollars at a low rate of interest in order to improve some newly acquired property. That suggests a closer acquaintance than previously realized.

3. Joe Pourrier: Stewart has likely based this character on a real person, Joseph Poirier, from St. Charles, Missouri, who accompanied Stewart as a hunter on the baronet's last Western excursion in 1843. See also frequent references to *Joe Pourier* in Matt Field, *Prairie and Mountain Sketches*.

"Yes, yes, but that does not shew me that he was not looking after us. I don't like that, Joe."

"Well, he is a good-looking fellow for all that," I answered.

"Perhaps he is," rejoined Jim, with a musing manner, as the skiff was shoved off.

We were again on the bosom of the turbid Missouri, its stream ran swift and swollen from the mountain snows, there appeared no obstructions in its course within our view, and the deep water in which we wished to keep, inclined to the opposite shore, but at the extreme end of the stretch in sight, there was a white object like a tent, and some horses.

The sculls were in the hands of the Indian who had joined us at the fort, his name was John, and I believe he had no desire to be recognized by any of the fort people.

East side the mountains, Jim took the steering paddle, and told me to take a hand, I saw there was some hurry, and the thowl pin creaked under the strain, as I put on my best power, my slighter looking fellow rower was not to be complained of, either from obedience to Jim's evident desire, or from some feeling of his own, he who had the bow oar was pulling his best, and from the changed position of her head now turned upstream, she soon traversed and regained the right bank, which was that upon which we had seen the appearance of an encampment ahead, and before I was aware, we were run in under some low willows in shoal water. I was going to jump ashore on the sand, but Jim interposed.

"We must leave no trail."

His leggings were off in a moment, and he shoved us before him from the stern, until we had got some way into the thicket, which closed in the rear as soon as the twigs displaced in our passage were again free.

The distance from the open stream was not great, but we were as entirely concealed as if we lay in the middle of a field of wheat. Our propeller seated himself on the gunwale for a moment to rest, and perhaps to reflect.

"You must stay quiet. I will creep on, and see if this does not come to a slue. It is not a place for a horse to pass, we would be, they expect, on the opposite side, and if they want either you or John, they will be on the look-out there, if you hear a duck, it is me, if all is well, answer."

He now left his capot and hunting shirt, and waded warily forward in a direction away from the mainstream, hardly causing a wave in the tops of the boughs he so gently bent, he was gone about an hour. I longed for a pipe or a dose, but no sense was to be allowed to slumber, and nothing was to be done to attract those of others, either by sound or smell.

The sun was perhaps an hour and a half high, and the evening serenely calm. It was no very agreeable mode of passing the time, to sit silently and watchfully in the shade, not covered to suit such inaction, and not wishing to unroll the blankets, in case of getting wet in a scurry, when thrown loosely off.

I had here to acknowledge the superior patience of my companion, though half civilized, but I thought at the same time that he felt himself to be a chief object of pursuit, as he carried drafts from other companies to whom he had sold beaver, on firms at St. Louis, leaving that which had supplied him with goods, unpaid.

I would have been glad to have been a Yankee with a jack knife and a piece of wood, with liberty to whittle, but I felt I must eat the chips to avoid discovery, or keep them inboard, where also was to be sought the material to be victimized, so I sat still, reflecting that my butcher knife, unlike the axe of the Russian, would not probably in my hands be an instrument sufficiently delicate to produce any worthy piece of carving, a sandpiper was running about uneasily on a dry spot by a small open, but there was nothing else which exhibited even life, and the sun was sensibly lowered, the Delaware was in the bow, and I reclined in the stern. At last, I thought I felt some wave come against the bark, and turning my head, found Jim looking grave and calm, and almost doubtful of entering.

"There are both Indians and whites about," he said. "I have seen one a little below on the opposite side." He made signs, by which I know there was someone to communicate with not very far below on this, but they move slowly, as he I saw, searched as if expecting to find us under the bushes, wherever they appeared on the bank.

"We have half an hour of sun," he added thoughtfully, and then paused.

"Are we in the entrance of a slue," I hazarded.

"Yes, and we must take our chance. I knew they wanted to overhaul us," added Jim, "as soon as I saw Pourrier, but we must run the slue at whatever risk, or you two will have to give them a talk, for myself, they don't want me, but I will get you through if I can, so here goes." And I felt the boat shoved gently through the twigs.

"It will be dark before we reach the camp, and if we should pass near, they are not on the outlook on this water."

"But if it gives out or shoals?"

"We must make a raise of horses, or come back and try down the mainstream, where it runs booming, I tell you."

"But we are not launched in the slue," I said, as we grounded.

"Then I must trouble you to wet your feet," he again whispered.

We were soon all three in the water, and when it deepened, a new care was necessary, to serve the thowl pins and the part of the oar in contact, with pieces of skin cut off the end of a robe, to deaden all sound.

The sun was but touching with a last ray the top of a bluff, as we gave way, the slue became soon open at parts, and concealment was for the short period of twilight at an end. While they were examining the river, we were to run the narrow channel, even if it should lead nearer than we expected to the camp, there was but little current, though still sufficient to give hopes of a good outlet, which after the camp should be passed, was our last hope.

We were a mile on our silent way, and had somewhat slackened speed to let the deepening dusk determine into night, when there came between us, and what little there remained of clearer sky in the west, the figure of a horseman, who was making toward camp, or where we supposed it to be. He was going such a pace as a man would take who had something to urge him beyond the ordinary rate, so near as he ought to be, and cutting so directly to cross toward it. The shadow of a bank was all we had to trust to, the rider and his horse disappeared not sixty yards ahead, and we lay in suspense, fearing that he might have missed the crossing, and would have to make a search, and so far he had, as the sound of splashing up the side was distinct, and then that of a horse's feet upon some stones, and then again, though disagreeably near, the same shadow passed on over the plain above, the slue formed then an island, and that was the ford. It was needless to wait for others, this danger was gone, and we had but the delay of half lifting the skiff over the shoal, but that was happily effected without noise, and there were but a few hundred yards before we were in sight of the fires, it was then that the long and quick stroke was to steal us past unperceived, or secure us from pursuit, and my early practice on the Mersey came in good stead.

A dog barked, and a squaw, or some figure enveloped in a robe, looked over the brink, but we heard no sound of alarm, the dip of the oars was as noiseless as if in oil, and their ripple had hitherto been concealed by a friendly shade, but now a sudden turn took us into a broader space of water and less deep at the sides, when it was only safe to deep the middle, perhaps this led without impediment to the stream rushing in its strength, its longer course made the current of the slue, except over the ford where it was rapid, less swift, so we hoped, as we strained to get again into hiding through this stagnant expanse.

Jim was now at an oar, his companion seemed to be considered between them the best guide, and had assured us there could be but little risk of again shoaling before entering the main river, encouraged by this, we were giving way, and the skiff plunged on impelled through the water, on which by her form, she was not calculated to move without urgent force, when I heard the low toned voice of my fellow oarsman.

"Can you make out what these people are doing on the bank?"

There was a moment, when against a lighter spot in the western sky, there seemed to be three or four figures, who might have newly come, or could have been there before, but they were now where that bit of clear sky behind, showed them for a moment, perfectly still.

"They are quiet at present," I answered, as they were lost to our view.

It was not here as it is lower on the river, that the course is obstructed by snags, and endangered by drifts, among which daylight, as well as local knowledge, are required, but before any marked symptoms indicated the change, we found the head of the skiff suddenly in a boiling torrent, and we were carried down it at a pace, which though not over satisfying our wish to get on, called for every vigilance in the steersman.

We breathed again. The river was sufficiently broad, and it was easy to keep in its strongest current, running as it does from bluff to bluff. It might be at the speed of six miles an hour, to which with the most moderate rate of exertion on our part, we must at least have added two more, the principal strain being upon the attention of the steersman, and to do him justice, he appeared to exercise his faculties, if our passing smoothly on was to be a test, thus we went till nearly midnight, and then on the left bank we paused to get out some provisions. We had not eat for nearly nine hours, and the cold repast was most welcome.

Jim and his companion consulted a few minutes, then he said, "I will take the sculls, and you two can lay down and rest in the bottom astern, when I am in difficulty, I can paddle, but the course seems clear for the present, and we must put two days' ride between us and Joe Pourrier, before we again take it easy."

It is never difficult to sleep after fatigue, when sleep is due, and the nerves are well braced, so each rolled up like a bale in his blanket and robe, the two inactive partners were lost to the cares and toils of the hour.

Chapter Sixty
Down the Missouri—parting—former acquaintances—pleasant traveling—Pourrier turns up

It is needless to relate how morn came, and how strange appearances ever kept up the belief of pursuit, how hard and exciting was the short hunt taken only in the peninsula of a bend, and how anxious the calculation of when it might be safe to make our store of meat for the lower part of the voyage, which is through a country deserted by game, and where the wretched Indians on the banks are driven to thieving by famine, we passed through all these difficulties, and arrived at Cabane's trading house at Council Bluffs[1], where fresh supplies of eatables, and a feeling of security from the danger of pursuit, was balanced by watching for snags, and the other dangers of the ever-shifting course, and ever renewed obstructions which are occasioned by the fall of the lofty timber encumbering the ground under which the water eats its course, engulfing whole groves, which I have seen at once fall in all their pride of leaf and disappear, causing still another eddy and another change. But the forest was alive with birds and bees, the whip-poor-will chaunted his constant and well known note, the kingfisher skimmed along the margin of the more tranquil pools, and the red bird and the whole family of woodpeckers presented their glowing plumage strangely mirrored in the muddy flood. All this was again new, but it was a sad thought, the want of the

---

1. Cabane's trading house at Council Bluffs: An ally of prominent French fur traders in St. Louis and a successful businessman, Jean Pierre Cabanne (1773-1841) worked in the Council Bluffs region from 1819 to 1833, when he was removed from his position for his involvement in the LeClerc affair, which nearly resulted in the loss of the American Fur Company's license to trade. The trading house was eight miles below the Council Bluffs. See Ray H. Mattison, *John Pierre Cabanne, Sr.* in Hafen, *The Mountain Men and the Fur Trade*, II, 69-73.

great bison, that never ceasing resource of the hunter, which is found in the richer countries above, so that peopled as was the forest, redundant of fruit and varied life, it wore to the mind of the hunter of the plains, the aspect of a melancholy solitude, which an occasional steam boat only rendered the more irksome.

We were at the mouth of the Kanzas, and there that partnership which had existed between Jim and myself was for the present to end, though he considering me migratory, looked upon our parting as of but a season, but the goodhearted fellow told me always to reckon upon him if he was in the country. We had settled the small account between us, which had not been completely paid.

John was easily recompensed, for service from which he himself derived the greatest relief, and we parted, I to take my way down to the Independence landing with the aid of an Indian who undertook the short voyage on the understanding, that he was to have the skiff to bring back some goods.

It was the morning when I parted with my true and useful friend Jim, by afternoon I had again set out on my waterway, and toward four o'clock I had arrived at the landing of Independence.

My load of clothes was light, an obliging waggoner hauled my baggage to the town where he was bound, disdaining thanks, and Sam Owens, ever accommodating, again lent me a horse, and I returned to the hospitable roof of the former owner of the mule.

The sisters were alone when I arrived, and welcomed me with unostentatious kindness, and the first question was, if I had not found I had been cheated by Heald.

I told them pretty nearly my adventures till I got fairly under way, and asked about old Brent.

"Oh," said the youngest, "he is the heartiest old man here abouts, and he talks always about you and his boy, as if you held almost the same place in his thoughts, he heard news of his son last year, but you must go and see him."

Here the ringing laugh of brother Dick broke in, and I had to sustain a torrent of questions, and to be grateful for most overflowing goodwill.

I was to get a horse and a small sack at Lexington, not caring to return four or five miles for my worn-out old wardrobe.

Next morning, wringing the hand of my host, and kissing the blooming cheeks of his sisters, I launched forth again in the lightest marching order for Lexington.[i]

The ripe peaches loaded the trees of the orchards on either side the road, and altogether it was one of the most beautiful rides of the west, cultivation had not been carried to the extent of denuding the enclosures of trees, and the green sward and the stubble were partially shaded by the spreading plane, the elm and the oak. I had remarked the rich fruit-bearing trees on either side, whenever near a habitation, and the liberal license for the wayfarer to eat his fill, but I had not yet learned that amid this abundance of fruit, in which he had indulged to satiety, the Phillipson of the year before, so young and full of life, had fallen a victim to his love of those luxuries of which he had been so long deprived, inducing a cholera which proved fatal, and his remains lie there under the shade of the forest, a lesson how little is respected by our common enemy, beauty or youth, with its seemingly unquenchable fire.[ii] I rode on, little tempted by the peach, the apricot, and the melon, which everywhere hung ready to my hand, or encumbered the path.

At Lexington, I found it was better to get upon a boat, and go down by water, I had to leave but one message for the brother of Kit Carson on the way, opposite Arrow Rock, and this was easily undertaken by Auld's people at their universal store, as mountain news circulates with a kindly feeling of exactness from mouth to mouth, to relieve the anxious thoughts of relatives and friends. I passed again the groves near Owen's Ferry[2], where I had spent some time amongst a colony of worthy Germans, where the virgin forest had rang with the yudle and the songs of father land, which in another generation there will be unknown.

The old Baron Martel is long at rest, his brave Charles was killed in Texas, and Henry has, I believe, settled in that country, and Gustave was doing well in New Orleans, but there is no Daniel Boon on the Phemasage nearby, and the groves of the Missouri no longer echoed to the bugle or the hunting song of the gallant boys whom I had remembered two years before.

The grains of autumn were spread about in profusion, the solace and the reward of he who had cultivated, as well the traveler who passed through the land.

The time was not come for the gathering of Indian corn, its forests of stalks, loaded with cobs, were yet uncut, the flocks of wild fowl had not left the north—the crane waiting the last moment when he could light and be unseen in the field of maize. The flights of prairie cock had not yet quitted the plains to seek more redundant food than the seeds of grass, which were there his natural resource. The wild goose still remained to furnish in Rupert's land those quills which balance the accounts of nations, and are used for signing treaties to settle, as also to raise the convulsions of war. The pigeon, migrating in millions, had not yet appeared to overload and crush primeval groves at evening rest, and of that tribe the brilliant wood-duck alone tenanted the slues and tributaries whose entrances were visibly still and clear from the river's

---

2. The groves near Owen's Ferry: Samuel Owens operated a ferry at Independence, Missouri. Matt Field described it in 1839: *There are two landing places for boats, where ferries are also stationed to cross the river. These ferries are open flat boats, worked by two negroes with long paddles, but Col. Owen, proprietor of the lower landing, is about having a steamboat built for his ferry* (*Matt Field on the Santa Fe Trail,* ed. John E. Sunder, Norman, Oklahoma 1960, pp. 62-63).

course, the stream ran, however unceasingly on, though we outstripped its speed while in the safety of an open channel or in the light of day.

The second evening we were at St. Charle's[3], where some of the passengers took to the road, which though anything but good, in dry weather is passable. The time for deciding was not very long, and I determined to remain on board to the end of my journey.

The boat was just putting off, when a horseman came down the steep road on the north side of the river, he seemed to be known, as a few words in French procured several ready hands to take charge of the jaded animal he had ridden, to one of whom he threw the bridle. The plank up which he sprung was already veering, from the motion of the boat, and was hauling inboard, and upon it the eager passenger.

I was a little astern, observing the crowd of persons who had assembled to witness the departure of the boat, Janisse amongst the rest, who hollowed, "What takes you off in such a hurry, Joe, anything wrong with Fontinelle?"

This was addressed to the newly acquired passenger, who, turning round, shook his head in negative, and I discovered that it was Pourrier. I had been already so plagued by the haunting of one person, that I had little disgust to bestow on any one else who might so far think it worthwhile to lend me cause for such a feeling, and I turned to the new arrival.

"Well, you were on the upper waters, rather, when I saw you last."

"Yes, and so was you," said Joe, with a French accent.

"Has anything gone wrong at the fort," I asked.

"Only a few letters to carry, to catch a market, the robes are coming and the beaver, a little slower," he added, apparently satisfied with his own exertions.

"Is that the same horse?"

"No, nor his cousin, by a long way off," said Joe, with a chuckle.

We were under way, and I was interested in the junction we were soon to reach of the two great rivers. There is, however, little remarkable in the scenery, or in anything else, than the color of the waters, there is a strong contrast, however, in the character of the current—the Mississippi, almost clear, receives in her course the turbid and impatient stream which bore us along, and generally controuls with her calm influence, the character of the whole, which henceforth assumes her name.

The sun was setting red in the west when we passed Bloody Island[4] on our right hand. It has been the scene of several fights, but so entirely divested of romance, that when this spot, with its willows, shall be washed away, its memory will only be known as the scene of fatal strife. There is no song to

---

3. St. Charle's: Originally called San Carlos del Misuri, St. Charles was founded in 1769 about forty miles up the Missouri from St. Louis.
4. Bloody Island: An island in the Mississippi near St. Louis where gentlemen frequently dueled.

record, or no romance to inspire it, and the ruddy rays beamed upon the spot which bore the name with a glow as evanescent as the crimson blood which had so often dyed its sands.

The landing was, as it probably is still, on a rocky slope, and the hour was such as to render the search for lodging the most pressing affair of the moment. The City Hotel, newly brushed up, was still the chief house of entertainment, and I had a desire, which I was able to gratify, to sleep in the same room I had occupied when last there, and to which I had retired to grieve over the sad news I had received before setting out a year and a half before.

Chapter Sixty-One
An appointment—intrigue—a stranger—
Eastern cities—at sea

I had but one letter to St. Louis, it was to a merchant's house of New Orleans, Valdez and Co., who had a branch there. Next morning it was not difficult to make out the office and store-house on the Levee. I found the principal himself, he was smoking his cigar in a sort of recess, before which was a cabinet of pigeon-holes full of letters, and a small rod with a red curtain above.

I was not admitted into this species of sanctum, but I could see that my letter was read deliberately, and Signor Valdez rising, said to me in good French, "I shall have the honor of calling upon you at *three*, when I will give you what means you require to go on. In the meantime, as you have some account due on the other company, here is some money, and you had better, in settling, say nothing of your credit here." He put some twenty pieces of gold in a rouleau into my hand. "Will these suffice?" he added.

"Yes, perfectly."

"At the City."

And we parted, with a strange brevity as well a confidence, for I gave no receipt.

I strolled about the town—evidently it was on the increase—trade, and building, and emigration were at work to subdue the desert.

I found that three o'clock was the hour for the hotel dinner, but I remained in the ante-room, though not quite understanding why an appointment had been made at an hour when it was known the St. Louis world dined. The savoury odours entered as the hungry diners went out, and I, a martyr to the appointment, waiting the expected arrival. Instead of Signor Valdez, however, one of his clerks made his appearance at the outer door, and by a sign made me understand that he had something to say, which it was also evident he wished should be said without. So I took up my hat—new at Council Bluffs)—and followed him as he passed from the door, toward a newly-planned market-house. There I perceived my correspondent, pacing back and forward, and the messenger disappeared.

"I have thought this the best mode of meeting, as well as place," he began. "The letter indicated that there was some mystery hanging over your affairs, and that you were watched. Have you paid the American company?"

"No, not yet, but I have the amount in my pocket. With what beaver I gave in the mountains, there is exactly seventy-one dollars due as a balance."

"Well, write a note to say that you expect they will be paid in a day or two, at all events, before a boat starts you expect to be in funds. Now give me that sum out of the money you have got, I will pay the amount tomorrow. Get your capote, and put a couple of shirts and pairs of stockings in the pockets, sling it over your shoulders like a cloak, and come down to the wharf about half an hour before sunset. Or stay, leave your coat, and buy what you want on your way to the landing. The coat will pay your bill, but I will see that there is no difficulty there. Get your dinner as best you can, and be punctual."

Behind the market-house on the landing he turned round one of the pillars, and I returned with goodwill toward the wrecks of the feast, out of which I was to extract my meal.

At the appointed place I met my friend, and we walked a little way up to where there was a crowd gathered.

"You see that ferry-boat above," said Signor Valdez, "it crosses you over to where the stage will be ready in an hour's time. I would go with you, but we had best separate, as I have been told by my friend and yours to avoid anything which might give a trace to your agents or means. You have your letters safe?"

"Yes," I answered, feeling for the parafleche pocketbook which contained them.

"Then here is your ticket for the mail-stage—stop the stage, your place is kept by my clerk, whom you saw—to Cincinnati, after that you take boat for Wheeling or Pittsburg, as it suits, there, as you know, land to Philadelphia and New York. You may as well change your name to Jones when you get on board an Ohio steamer, and further I will only say, for the sake of those who take an interest in you, and who have a right to expect I should do so too, keep prudently to the letter of instructions, which I am told you have, and so farewell—let us have no leave-taking. Should you come again here, or where I may happen to be, depend upon me for any aid you may require, and be assured, at all events, I shall be glad to see you."

This was said standing at arm's length, and calmly, as if in a conversation of the most ordinary nature, and then turning round, he addressed someone near, and I penetrating the crowd, sauntered up toward the ferry-boat, it was just pushing off, but I had time still to preserve the air of absence of hurry which I had assumed.

I asked a negro woman at the opposite landing when the stage started?

She said, "In about an hour."

She was tranquilly waiting to return to the western shore, to the land of slavery again[i], and I passed up the bank on to the level on which had been built some miserable log-houses as a temporary store and shelter, besides the stables of the horses necessary for such journeys as might be undertaken on the diverging routes which there presented themselves.

I sat down under the only tree standing near, a little off the road, and delivered myself up to musings of various kinds, which were suddenly interrupted by the gallop of a horse, which was coming, as it appeared, right upon me, a halter-rope was trailing from the headstall, and he was evidently roused by some wild and sudden fear, which though more uncommon among his species in the new world, from their better education and natural temper, is still of occasional occurrence.

I was knocked over and stunned in trying to stop the animal, but I kept the hold I had seized of his trail rope.

My senses were not quite restored, and the captured fugitive was still snorting by, when a plainly dressed middle-aged man came up, and asked, as I still lay leaning on my elbow, if I was hurt.

"Not a great deal," I answered, but I did not feel very confident of being able to back my words by an effort to rise.

He then looked at his horse. "A mile or two extra will take that out of you in an hour. Where are you going, stranger?"

I said, without hesitation, "To Cincinnati."

"Then I can take you a lift for a bit, as that is my road."

We led the young animal back to the shade, where the vehicle to which he had been attached was reposing, he was put to, and I was invited to enter the sort of cab without a head which was to contain us. It had possibly never been washed since it appeared in the State, except by rain or the fording of streams, and of course had no color. My companion observed my scrutiny.

"If you mean it wants a coat of varnish, the day is gone by, and there will be some other invention before I meddle with it. Jump in."

It was anything but an uneasy carriage, though we swung about at a considerable scope. The horse was reminded of his eagerness to return, and stepped out, a wheel now and then getting into a soft hole or on to a stump, jerking us up sky-high.

My conductor was evidently proud of the pace at which we went, which was hard upon nine miles an hour, over a road where an old countryman, he said, would hardly have ventured an unloaded cart, and we soon arrived at one of those streams, half bridged, where, as I was told, the last assortment of newspapers was generally thrown overboard from the over-loaded mail in bad weather, approaching St. Louis, similar sacrifices having already been made at other crossings, where the dammed up waters neither ran nor read.

The spot where the stage was to change horses was now in sight, and I was dropped with as little ceremony as I had been taken up, and the cab was turned out of the road into the forest, to take a short cut, with as little hesitation as there might have been to enter the broadest street in Cincinnati.

I sat down on a log to watch this operation. The squirrels were busy overhead, and the eternal woodpecker, the red bird in his full plumage, was every where about, and the whip-poor-will was to be heard repeating his song, to be taken up again as far as the ear could distinguish the sound.

I was interrupted in my musings by the stage, it was empty. One way or other I got to Wheeling, and thence to New York, in somewhat more than a fortnight after leaving St. Louis.

It is difficult to account for the eagerness I felt to get back to England, having no definite object beyond the chance of finding something left to me by my father. However, I pushed on. A liner sailed in the evening of my arrival, and I stepped on board without preparation, or hesitation, or consultation, except with the waiter, who probably had inadvertently told me of her going, not having any interest in detaining me, this class not in the United States being paid by guests at hotels, either for what they do or what they let alone.

A voyage across the Atlantic is something the same now as it was then, in a sailing ship, except that the living is not of that luxurious order at present in these packets, nor is there the same choice of wines.

The wind was much to the northward, and we were consequently driven into the longer degrees, and the passage was tedious. However, in a day or two over a month we were off Cape Clear, and got an easy run up the St. George's Channel into the Mersey.

Part Four

Part Four

Chapter Sixty-Two
A letter from Rose

I was once more in what has been called Merry England, and once again took up my abode at the Waterloo Hotel, of Liverpool, and at liberty to read a letter written by my friend—for such he had shown himself—of Hell's-gate.

My sack had been deposited in a bedroom, such as inn bedrooms in the model country generally are when only charged two shillings, it had no fireplace, and partook of all the sounds of the passage and the two chambers adjoining, from none of which it was separated but by a slight partition.

I took down my letter to the coffee-room, where there was a good fire, and nothing but mastication to disturb my reading. The envelope, docketed *not to be opened until the arrival at Liverpool*, contained a letter written in the same hand, one addressed to Signor Conchas, London, and one directed to myself, in a hand rather Italian in character, but something tremulously traced.

It was this letter I first opened, it was from Rose, and was as follows:

DEAR NED,

From the first moment I saw you on the Platte I loved you, there is not time for more doubtful phrases, and the distance between us makes the avowal less embarrassing.

I was early, as you know, brought into the hunting plains, by the necessity of my father leaving Mexico, where he had taken refuge from Spain for some political cause. This necessity was caused by a duel, in which his opponent was killed, and the judge not sufficiently propitiated.

However, at the age of twelve I was put upon a horse like a boy, and rode with my mother who was a half-breed, to hunt, in the first part of our emigration. She was famous for her knowledge among the neighboring tribes, and had some considerable influence, and great Indian wealth.

I had learned to read and write, with a knowledge of French and music, before the circumstance I have mentioned occasioned our leaving the Mexican territory, where we had known David.

From the day when we first set foot on the Prairies, I became devoted to that hunting in which my mother excelled and delighted. She died a short year after, no one knew of what, but she suffered of some terrible disease— probably a poisonous bite—most excruciatingly, and then yielded—it was on the waters of the Arkansas. Since, I have become still more dear to my father, by whose indulgence I have followed up my passion for hunting till the last events, causing the illness and eternal grief in which you left me.

I had seen enough to judge and know, when we met again at the first great rendezvous, your regard for me was not of the nature of that love I bore to you. David had informed me that he believed you were the victim of some conspiracy, and I at once abandoned all idea of our fates being united. The love you had toward me as a brother was a dear remembrance, it also served to delude me from calling it by any other name. Had you, however, had no other prospects, we might have lived together, but you could never have understood the jealous pang a woman feels who thinks her affection is without adequate return.

The ardent devotion of the Swiss, and in the desire to save your life, when perhaps I should not have survived had I been unsuccessful, made me at once decide to give that promise from which there is no return. As far as the history of events goes, you know the rest.

I have reason to believe that my father has heard, by last rendezvous, that he may safely re-appear in Mexico. My mind and habits are forever changed, and perhaps I may retire, if he can spare me, to a life of seclusion, which appears the best refuge, however, in this I must make no hasty resolve.

I am thankful that, through the intercession of our blessed Lady and my patron Santa Rosalie, my mind is sufficiently calmed to assure you of all the affection I am capable of feeling on earth, and which desires only now that you should rely upon it ever in the hour of need, and this, if you will promise it, I shall consider my chief enjoyment, and I am even disinterested enough further to hope that you may never need my aid, but believe me, this last prayer has been made at a sacrifice of selfish enjoyment, which you can never appreciate.

There is but one thing I can fairly ask of you, and that is, to let us have news, through Signor Conchas, from time to time.

Now, farewell—and good night too, for I shall sleep sound after this.

Your truly affectionate sister,
ROSA.

Chapter Sixty-Three
Inquiries into the past—a fire, and foul play?

The letter from David was long, and minute in its directions. I was advised to seek out my father's servants, and by them to learn if he left anything, before I should implicate myself in any research beyond. That failing, I might try the schoolmasters with whom I had been placed, and as a last resource, my temptress at Wimbleton, and the madhouse, if I could find it out.

All this was well enough, upon the principle that the best mode of finding one thing is to look for another. I had funds sufficient for the Cheshire part of my undertaking.

There was nothing to keep me in Liverpool, and I left it for my father's former abode, without any emotion of hope, or even of local affection.

The high brick wall of the garden flanked the entrance to the grounds, the gate was as usual shut, and being solid and high, left nothing to be gathered of what was the internal state of things. There was a November fog—I am sorry to have to record this less common circumstance than is generally believed—so that I could not detect smoke from the chimneys, which were to be seen from the road through the branches of some leafless elms. I rung, however, at the porter's lodge, after a pause, the wicket was slightly opened, and I was asked what I wanted by a severe-looking woman in black. She was a stranger.

"Where is Dickson?" I asked, somewhat disappointed.

"He is no longer here, but gone to Chelsea."

"Who lives at the house?"

"No one at present."

"I then asked for the butler, he was gone—Tom was gone, a person from Liverpool was in charge of the house, the garden was let."

No trace remained—for I continued my inquiries in spite of the terse replies and rigid look of the portress—of any of the servants of my father, and the little opening vouchsafed for this repulsive communication was gradually narrowing toward its close, and finally shut, as it appeared from considering the subject exhausted.

I have since been thankful that I had not been brought up to feel acute filial affections, and to be sensitive on such subjects, but there was a great shock at the absolute baulk I experienced as to information.

The Shuttle public house, with its skittle-ground, was close by, and I had time to go there, where I might be able to gain further intelligence. The house, into which once or twice I had formerly entered, to see a game or to talk to the landlord, was close by, and I found its owner sitting in his accustomed place, and shuffling his feet back and forward upon the sanded floor, as was his habit, sending up and around the strongest vapour of tobacco, which by any ordinary effort could be drawn from a new and clear-going pipe charged with the most powerful pigtail.

"My. Eddard, shur-ly!" said the worthy host, as he rose and held out a fat red hand, in token of my former favor in his eyes. "Sit down, sir, you will be warmer by the fire, it is but chilly without." And he looked distrustfully through the lozenge-shaped panes. "There has been a change in these parts, but we never thought to see you again. The news came you were drowned on the Po—Pon—I can't make out the river, but there it was in the papers, chapter, and verse, as the clerk says, and the old gentleman never looked fresh after. Yes, it has been a quiet neighborhood, and all these things came like a blight upon us. But what will you have, sir, we publicans don't encourage dry talk more than is necessary, so I just want to show some little hospitality. Becky! A little warm beer from the old tap in the corner."

This order, with a certain significant intonation, was addressed to someone in an adjoining room.

I here put some questions as to who occupied the house of my father.

"Well, no one exactly, but a sort of half charwoman, half housekeeper, since the fire."

I interrupted, "What fire?"

"Ah, you would not learn much of the burning of a few rooms over the sea, where they say fires is of no moment, and all the town is up and down two or three times in a season. But just before your father's death—and we heard it did a good deal toward it too—the wing with the study, and all the papers in it was burnt, and as I heard, a heap of property in bonds and different ways, for the servants being most all out, nothing was saved but a few chairs and a half dozen of pictures, which some of the maids thought most valuable, but they soon ceased to try for anything, and ran screaming about, and we neighbors flocked in time enough to stop the stone passage up with turf, but the roof had fallen in, and it was all up with the wing. And the old gentleman gave us but small thanks, further than that we had acted neighbor-like. As for his part, he set no value on what was left—he never slept there again. The servants were discharged, and the next news we heard was, that he had died in London. There was no will, and everything is in Chancery."

"But who was his lawyer?" I asked.

"Well, he might be said to have no lawyer. I heard of a director of a railway awaiting upon him, indeed, he came here, and told me himself that he had been to the Squire Warren, about leave to go through a piece of his land, and in the debate the director asked who was the Squire's lawyer, who laughed in his face, and said he had none, but paid as he went for every job, having as few as might be."

A couple of pots of spiced beer here made their appearance, carried by a strong, healthy, black-eyed damsel, whose arms were red enough to have supplied the heat from which smoked the jugs in her hands.

"But you are come, I hope, to claim your own, Master Ned?" (so they were accustomed to call me here.)

"Yes. But where is Grimes the butler, and Tom?"

"Tom, poor fellow, went to Liverpool, to go to America, as to Mr. Grimes, he was sent off, had he and the housekeeper been minding their business, nothing would have happened. It was much believed, and I hold strong to the opinion myself, as to the fire, that it was to cover a robbery, as the plate was taken—that is, nothing was found melted in the ruins, and it was an orderly kept house, as you know, and the silver things were all in the stone closet of the butler's room."

We were discussing the beer, and conversing of past times, when I began to recollect that I had not been following the disinterested and kind advice contained in my letter, which enjoined caution, most especially near my father's, and where I had been at school, but being known, and having so far conversed openly, I thought it best to tell Townley that I must look for evidence about the fire, and see what property was left, and that I should be glad if he could learn anything, and let me know by a letter, directed *Post-office, Liverpool*, but that I must rely upon his secresy, as I had no one else to trust, and I feared had some enemy interested to conceal what property I might claim.

"Yes, I scarce know how to account for these newspaper stories, it looks like some job. But I'll try and get the paper, and you shall see."

The paper, however, was not to be found.

"They were axing who you be," said the host, at his return from the search, "but I told them you were some friend of Grimes." He lay his finger to the side of his nose, and closing one eye.

"Don't mind me, I can take care of myself," he added, meaning, of course, that he could take care of a vast deal more.

We shook hands, and I told him I was more refreshed by his beer than by anything I had tasted since I had left home.

He asked me no question about my travels, knowing perfectly that America was a country full of niggers and quakers.

Chapter Sixty-Four
A journey—a search—new friends

I got back to Knutsford, and determined to start the next day for London. The conveyance of travelers, limited as they were in number, compared to the tide which flows now, was confined to certain mails and stagecoaches—the former having the privilege of color and lightness, the latter room and popularity. Into one of this last descriptions I got inserted, fitting into the fat sides of two elderly ladies, who were to flank me, a Scotch divine, with a nephew, upon whom he lavished the flattest conjectures and stalest jokes, in a tongue which easily protected any copyright he might have wished to claim, were opposite, with a drab-colored mercantile traveler, composing those who were to be jolted, mix legs, eat and sleep together during the journey to town.

My own part of the mixing legs was not to be complained of, as I had only the poor nephew, with his spindle shanks and obsequious habits to deal with. The uncle and his opposite neighbor, however, appeared to have difficulties it was impossible to accommodate, and whether the insertion of one of the Reverend's dirty shoes and gaiters between the fat stumpy ankles of his vis-a-vis was too much or too little, or what objection there might be, I could not learn, but the lady puffed and hinted across me, while the Doctor, apparently suffering from his cramped position, blew his nose, and muttered, and thus I left them, only fearing to rest my head on the soft, round shoulders on either side, and fell into the sound sleep that a rough life had for some time habituated me to in almost any situation.

Morning came long before anything of daylight, with growling at divers questions and intruded lanterns, by which the night-gear of my fellow-coachmates was revealed—the divine in a red worsted cap, his nephew in a snuffy pocket handkerchief, borrowed for the occasion, the ladies looking rigidly correct, with fronts and caps turned all to one side, the traveler, par excellence, alone having retreated within a cap of the most velvety softness of fur, and having taken the entire limbs of his opposite neighbor, with all their voluminous flounces, between his, slept with comprehensive security, entirely ignoring all difficulties which might embarrass the less experienced or less recondite.

As I dared not have a leaning to either side, I had no variety of posture, but between the original position or butting forward against the sharp nose of my neighbor opposite, who dreading first his learned uncle, and next the gentleman who appeared to be so grandly dressed and so much at home, had only the same back and forward liberty, but both shrinking from such a contact, repressed all forward motions, and arrived at the hour of dawn with red, though not bloody noses, if not jolly, at least good friends—hot water and muffins, and blue milk, all smoking, as also did the fire—were a relief from cramped positions and chilly damp.

One of the fat ladies made tea, with the air of one who dispensed this blessing in a situation quite different from that she had been accustomed to, appealing to her double—though each was worthy to be called a double—in her own behalf, with a humble and charitable look, as she smelt the tea, and then gave a certain quantity of that questionable leaf up to the public wants.

The divine intruded his cup upon the infusion, making some remark about the fleeting time, and broke the spell, during which such unutterable things had been looked between the sylphs. The tea was poured over the doctor's thumb, the pourer's eyes being turned up in agony, and the brew was thenceforth forever sacrificed, to become worse every generation, until it should cease to afford any color to its name.

The traveler merely put a small glass of brandy into his cup, the nephew nearly choked in admiration, and asked if he was not a lord, the cautious priest, however, shook his head mysteriously and plunged his snuffy fingers into the muffin plate.

The sudden flourish of a horn sounded to us like a trumpet coming before its time, and we were all arrested in our choicest mouthfuls, except the traveler, who calmly prepared for another cup, the eyes of the nephew still feeding upon his smallest acts, and his majestic calm, with hungry wonder.

We were all seated in the now thoroughly chilled coach, when this individual came deliberately in, unhurried and un-pushed as we had been to retake our seats, and we started with a little jerk, a couple of slight screams, and a demand from the Reverend if there was any imminent danger.

"None in the least, keep yourself quite easy," broke in the traveler, who seemed to dread a public thanksgiving. The nephew, who probably best knew from what we were relieved, looked, as he had the best right to do, the most thankful.

The glass was so dimmed, we might have been crossing the Red Sea for aught I knew. Looks of sublime suffering beamed from my two flanks, and shot across my face, in utter disregard of my existence, as the top-heavy vehicle heaved lazily from side to side.

Save in that fatal journey of Pharaoh, the details of which are not given fully, there is no record how ordinary traveling was conducted, even by the great, in very remote ages, and men are now fast forgetting the joys and sufferings of a true blue or a green and gold stagecoach of 1834, much more of its parent, which never dreamed more than the horses of individual or dynastic death. So that I may some day be excused for chronicling these slower sufferings at a Tunbridge or a Wandsford in England stopping, in comparison with the evanescent meals and bye-law politenesses of the present more rapid journey, where the wants of nature themselves are subject to express regulations.

However, notwithstanding a road more greasy than ever had been traveled before to one side wheels, and lumpy in frosted ruts to the others upon which the sun had not shone, and sometimes both sides suffering for a while of what, at others, only one had to complain, we made out but half an hour behind our time to rumble along Oxford Street about dusk.

I thought I had better keep to that unobtrusive neighborhood which my father frequented, fully confident I should be recognized by no one, only changing from the New Hummums to the Old, in the corner of the square, and going one story higher to sleep. With these important alterations, I betook myself to a bed only not damp because of the housemaid's asseverations to the contrary, which being a matter of opinion, might have been confirmed by oath.

It was near the end of December—I might have said Christmas, had I felt in that vein, for it was the twenty-second—a late dark breakfast in-doors, a yellow haze, and falling soot, without a *Times*, a *Herald*, and a *Sun*, a waiter in rusty black, with questionably white stockings and pale face, greeted my arrival in the coffee-room, a sign that there were but few others there to absorb attention or spell the morning prints.

I found something about cock-pits, and an abuse of Spanish bull-fights, which interested me, as now did everything related to that country. There was no name of any one I personally knew in the whole paper, as far as I could find. The muffin was gone, an egg followed, which in no way encouraged a desire for another.

The direction of my letter was simply *Signor Conchas, London*, but I remembered sufficiently that an intelligent waiter can give any information you may require, either through himself or some other means, and at once asked where such a person was to be found. A conjecture that the name began with a *C*, was uncontradicted, and he returned from behind a small wooden pen with a thick volume, open at *CON*. I soon ran my eye down the column—there was no such name.

"He is no resident, or has no established house," broke in the waiter, "but if there is such a person, and as you say, a Spaniard, he must be known to his Consul. I recommend you to ask there."

This appeared the only thing to do, and I set out over slippery pavements, to feel my way to Northumberland Street, Strand, happily not far off.

The Consul was a timid-looking little sallow man, but he knew Signor Conchas. His house, for he was a merchant, was Munos and Co., Leadenhall Street, and his residence was in Lincoln's Inn Fields.

"You might call first at his dwelling, as it is nearest."

This seemed to be no very decided step, but one always in the right direction, and I left, with every courteous leave-taking, short of shaking hands, which it was possible for me to get up on the emergency.

A cab was to be my carriage, and its driver was to find his own way. The fog thickened, and I shut up the glasses, the horse slipped, but the humane society were out of sight, and he was whipped up, and at last I was delivered at the front of a large old house in this square, which notwithstanding its legal name, is one of the most agreeable looking open spaces in London.

I offered two shillings to the driver—I was much abused, and four were demanded. Happily, the law is reasonable on this point, if on this alone, in the matters appertaining to everyday life, and the cab takes up at its own responsibility, having, on a dispute of fare, only the right of summons. After obtaining an address, I offered half-a-crown, and then proffered my name and place of abode, this was refused, and it was not till the door had been opened, and I was told to wait, that I got rid of my vehicle, the man of straw thinking, probably, that it was a dangerous locality, and that eighteen-pence might be bid too high for, amid so many chambers, and at a great green door where the owner was evidently at home. He took the money, and in return gave me back my card, which was not of any walley to him, who was obliged to take little more than half what was clearly his due—he did not say fare—in that thick fog.

The white cotton legs of the servant, who superintended this discussion, began to shiver, short as it was before the door could be closed upon the chilly atmosphere.

I had said I bore a letter, which was now produced, with a fresh card, unindorsed by a coachman's thumb. The legs vanished behind a scarlet cloth door, which with a spring shut out the second edition of the outward air, and shut in the third. In a few moments I was invited to pass this barrier by another servant, who said the first must have thought I was following, and here I found myself in a dark and spacious hall, from which commenced a broad flight of steps with quaint oak banisters.

I was looking up, as we naturally do, toward the light, which came sparingly through a window on the first landing, when a side door opened, and I was invited to enter by the servant who had last appeared.

The room was plainly furnished and large, having, by a table in the middle, the appearance of a dining room. The opening of another door stopped my survey, and fixed my attention upon a small-sized dark man, who entered. He said he was glad to see me, and that he was perfectly at my command, motioning toward the doorway through which he had just appeared.

The room led to was a comfortably fitted up study—maps hanging on the walls, and the lower shelf of a large table stored with what appeared to be books of reference.

"You have not, I hope, been long in town," said my new acquaintance. "We shall have plenty of time for business after, and perhaps you would dine here at seven. I am now just going out to keep an appointment, and I shall have great pleasure in introducing you to Miss Conchas."

I said I should be very glad, and then rose to take my leave.

"I have been very lucky in being so late, else I should have missed you. I shall now, having secured a meeting, have time to read my friend's letter before I see you again—and it is a long one. I will drop you at the first coach-stand," he said, as he pointed to me to enter his brougham, which was at the door.

"This is not Andalusian," he observed, looking at the rails, which could hardly be seen on the opposite side of the carriage-way, and we drove off, I knew not whither, my companion asking many questions about my journey and about his distant countryman and his daughter.

At last, we came to a place where the carriage stopped, I let myself out, called a sort of machine which rumbled along streets and stood on stands, just before the time of Hansard, and started for the hotel, thinking that the brougham I had just quitted was a species of vehicle which could not have been invented by the noble lord in his capacity of Chancellor, from all I remembered to have heard of the court, or to have experienced in my pugilistic encounters at school.

The thick atmosphere and the lamps had been long combating for mastery before it was time to start for dinner, the transport was to be by contract, which the waiter made the porter pre-pay, and I was taken to Lincoln's Inn Fields nearly about the proper hour.

I found the house not over-lighted, that is, neither the entrance hall nor the staircase, perhaps in honor of the fog. I remarked the latter as being better and more commodious than any one I had seen in London, among the fine houses I had been in during my previous visit.

One servant remained below, the other, on a soft carpet, noiselessly showed the way. There was no one in the room into which I was ushered, and the door shut, a couple of candles were on a table, and a fire, from which there was heat without blaze, glowed silently in the grate, which was deep and capacious.

I was looking round, to note what other signs might give an indication toward the nature of the family I was about to meet, when the quiet door admitted the host.

"I have had you brought here in case I should not have been in time to present you myself to my family. My eldest daughter, since my wife's death, takes charge of the house, she has one married sister, whom you will see some other day, and one almost a girl, who is our great pet, and dines only at table when we are a family party, and I begin by asking you to send to say you hope you may be considered one of ourselves, and I promise you will be a favorite of the favorite."

I felt the kind and true hospitality of his words, and followed, as he went out of a door in a corner concealed by a heavy velvet curtain. The room into which it led was large and lofty, scarcely sufficiently lighted by four pairs of candles, which burned on different tables, and on the chimney piece, there were several pictures, landscapes, which hung on the walls, which were wainscot painted over with sea-green, and the moldings profusely gilt. There was no one in this room as we entered, and the bell was rung by my conductor.

"We hope my daughters will both soon be ready, as it is past the hour, and I have had no luncheon," said the master of the house to an elderly sedate-looking servant out of livery, who entered.

"They will only have been waiting for our summons," said the father with evident pleasure.

And, in confirmation of his words, there was but the smallest time to have delivered a message, before the door again opened, and a dark and handsome young lady entered, leading or rather holding back a girl of twelve or thirteen, the young creature was apparently restrained by her graver sister from the outburst of pleasure which beamed in a most expressive countenance. I was presented as a friend of the house, and then the young thing bounded into her father's arms, and I was left to make the best of my introduction to her sister, who spoke English perfectly.

"Papa," she said, "you will have to wait, though not for us, and I hope not long, Sir Charles Wentworth sent to say he wished to see you, and if you were alone would come to dinner. I told his nephew, who brought the message, that it was my full belief you were, and he will be as nearly punctual as he thinks it would be correct to be."

"He is in the main a good person, and honest merchant, full of English traditions—not the least liberal, save where it suits him," said the Spaniard, addressing himself to me. "And dreams, as far as a mind not imaginative permits, of being someday Lord Mayor."

It was not long before the subject of our conversation appeared. He came in grey hair, blue coat, bright buttons, rosy face, as if he felt he was diffusing happiness with a gentle fuss.

I was duly introduced when he had given some account of Lady Wentworth having lost her way, with both the footmen and the coachman, who had been all their lives in London, and might have been born in a December fog—and dinner was announced.

The father desired his eldest daughter to take me down, as the knight and he would follow with the young Christina.

The two elders had their talk in a sort of enigmatical language, which piqued the curiosity of their companion. I heard her silvery voice asking for explanations as we glided down the carpeted stair.

There was nothing particular about the room, lighted now more than in the morning's obscurity, a couple of full-length portraits, one—apparently the older)—of a man in a court dress, the other in that of a cavalry officer, both well done, were the only paintings in the room, there was no over-display of plate, some I observed was old, and almost of a Moorish-looking pattern, three servants and a page waited—two in a leaden grey with crimson. Altogether, the whole thing was different from any other house I had seen, as were the people.

The Alderman did most of the eating, and fully his share of talking. The venison smoked on the sideboard, and the city guest said it was better to have it up fresh, and keep it till ready, than have to get up a fashion of eating it putrid, from the long journey buried in a carrier's cart.

Our host congratulated him upon a liberality of principles which it would have been dangerous to express near the Mansion House a few years ago—and the knight returned to the weather. This had been the second thick fog within the month, and he told us anecdotes of persons meeting in a shock, who had each arrived from opposite corners of the earth to butt against each other in Lothbury, he wound up by saying that both fogs had been very bad, and that London was lucky they had not come on the same day.

This was evidently the joke of the feast, and having been got rid of, the alderman felt at liberty to apply himself to the pleasures of the table.

I found my fair neighbor did not go much out, occasionally to the Westend, where there were a few families in which she was intimate.

Before taking leave, I made an appointment to meet the Signor next day, to talk over my own affairs, and committed myself again to the cab which waited my appearance—there being but one cab, one passenger, visible upon the scene at once that night, single houses and solitary lamps guided our way, and again the Hummums showed its un-demonstrative welcome in the green door ever ready to open, ever ready to close.

Some Cambridge under-graduates, and a decent-looking rector or two, looked from their mahogany boxes, I lit my candle and retired.

Chapter Sixty-Five
Mr. Searle, solicitor—investigations & revelations—a letter from Rose

In a house of Golden Square, two days afterward, in a room which served as a place of waiting for me, though evidently a family dining room, I sat looking at a round concave looking glass, which reflected what little was to be seen in that dullest and deadest of squares. The fog was gone, but the dark December was not wholesomely bright or cold. I awaited a summons from Mr. Searle, to whom I had sent in the letter of introduction which had been the result of my promised interview with the Signor Conchas.

This lawyer had been described to me as a solicitor of all works, if such a term could be used, a man of general connection and knowledge, having a considerable practice in police cases, as well as those of the Old Bailey and New Courts, but such a man was not to be had at a moment's notice, till you got to his private hours, so, ignorant as well as impatient, I had to wait.

At last a sort of clerk put an end to a suspense I in no way understood, and I was shown into a room not over furnished, a man in black sat at a table writing, while he finished perhaps a sentence, I had time to remark that his hair was iron-grey, his brows black, and his features regular, a pair of spectacles concealed the color of what his whole appearance indicated as being most earnest eyes, he pointed to one of two seats as he sat, and hardly looking from his paper, the door had closed as I obeyed his gesture, and then he turned his chair toward me, pushing into a pigeon hole on his table the paper upon which he had been employed. His look was that of one who was accustomed to read in the human countenance, and understood what he read. I let him examine mine, not over pleased at my observer's manner.

"I have read the letter of Mr. Conchas, which leaves me to gather whatever little you can tell of your case from yourself. I have got rid of all the pressing business just now in hand, and am ready to hear you." He broke the cake of coal on the grate, and produced a blaze. "You must be cold, you have come from a warmer latitude lately," he added, finding I hesitated. "When did you leave the United States?"

I told him.

"Then you have been away two years. Your father, Mr. Warren, lived?"

"In Cheshire," I answered, "near Knutsford."

"A family place?" he enquired.

"No! I had no reason to suppose so, he was however so silent on all such matters, that it might have been so."

I then gave the best account I could of my young recollections, and of my visit to London, then of the confinement in the madhouse, and journey to America, and the irksome persecution I had experienced from some unknown enemy.

My interrogator took notes down from what I said occasionally, like one who was accustomed to remark the salient points.

"You say you were not born near Knutsford, but in some northern county, do you know where?"

"No!"

"Well, we must find that out. All the papers lost at the fire, and no account of property whatsoever?"

"None, as far as I know."

"Land?"

"Probably, but I know absolutely nothing of my father's occupations or possessions, but there was a considerable extent of land always considered his."

"Well, we can come to know of that, you heard a nephew claims as heir-at-law—a sister's son—against a cousin, who as tenant in tail, puts in a counter claim. We must first make out your register of birth, and then you come in place of both—curious history—no other relations?"

"Yes, he called the late Lord Fernwold his cousin."

"Yes, that is the name, only spelt De Warenne. Let me see what Debret says. 'Present lord succeeded only this year, cousin to the late lord, who obtained a marquisate to go to his next heir.' But it was Adelbert, who died young, whom you knew? I know a curious Mr. Wilson, a lawyer at Knutsford, he can be put upon the scent of your birthplace, as also in regard to the property. In the meantime, it can do no harm to be Mr. Jones, and to keep out of the way, come here when you have anything to say, there ought to be some news for you in eight days."

I was taking my leave somewhat disheartened by the dismissal, and the more so, as I could in no way have expected a better, when the lawyer added, not unkindly, "It would be useless to say, that I took a strong newborn interest in your affairs, but I see in the case, there must be something beyond the common routine, and it suits me, as I have a real liking for all that is intricate and difficult in this way, so depend upon me, as an honest man, who will do his best, and as also an amateur—the latter word pronounced like a Parisian— at the Old Hummums, you say, good morning."

And I let myself out into a small ante-room, not by the door by which I had entered, it was empty, and another door let me into the passage, from whence the issue into the wide, and to me naked world, was now ready, as it had been to many before.

Ten days had passed, during which I had paid frequent visits at Lincoln's Inn Fields, where always the same friendly welcome came like a solace to my forlorn state, but these visits came only at dinnertime and in the evening, the gloomy day was to be passed in wandering about, or in making notes, which have served for amusement as well as to enable me to recollect such points as might be of use in tracing my claims upon any position in what is called the world. I had come to dinner, as I often did, upon one of those general invitations, in this case bearing every mark of being sincere. Signor Conchas was alone and motioned to me to come and sit down by him.

"I have just seen Mr. Searle, there is no proof of any marriage of your father, and he never lived in any of the northern counties, he brought you to his house in Cheshire when very young, no one knew anything of your mother in those parts, and he was, as well as yourself, in deep mourning. His abode had been Lisbon in earlier life, and he was reputed rich, fond of gambling in the funds, and taking shares in ventures of other houses, when they suited his fancy, but having no commercial establishment of his own. We can, however, write to Lisbon for an account of his life there. But Mr. Searle suggests sending to St. Louis, to try and find out who it has been who has thought it worthwhile to persecute and dodge you."

This was the same substance, and nearly the words of the first news I had from Mr. Searle.

Time kept on its course, a season that is more than a year elapsed, my tormentor had turned out to be a certain Jonas Robinson, he had left St. Louis about a month after me. Lloyd's house had furnished him with a New York credit. Lloyd knew nothing of him else, either personally or by business. Lisbon ignored my father's married state. The heir at law had got possession of certain personal property belonging to my father, his land being of a yearly value of upward of four thousand pounds, must be taken into another category than a sum of money, and was being melted toward the support of that hungry or rapacious horde, the ministers of British justice. There have been few who have had to complain of wrong decisions, but it is hard to bear the suspense and delay, the useless technicalities and expensive forms which are conjured up to surround the investigation of a case which can pay, and which are necessarily laid aside when there is but the fifty pounds of a poor peasant to come upon, perhaps his all, and more important in proportion than the fifty thousand to a Mr. Coutts.

But reader—if such a being ever should exist—forgive this digression, it comes from one who paid in money, furnished by the more than charity, the munificence of my noble minded friend, Diego of the west.

I had spoken of refusing this aid, and determined to obtain some employment by which I could earn my own subsistence, everywhere there were advertisements, and everywhere disappointments. I however had hopes of a recommendation to go abroad, though I waited to receive the answer I expected to a letter, in which, after expressing as imperfectly as truthfully my sense of gratitude and desire to be able to shew some return, I hoped I could be of some use in some of the many interests my benefactor had, I was now glad to hear, recovered in his native country.

At last, the answer came, it was sent to me from the Signor's house in the city, it was a March morning, just as I was about to go out, I took up the letter to my bedroom and locked the door. My manner, I suppose disturbed, perhaps in the eyes of the housemaid was wild, I knocked over a chair by accident, and then threw myself with some emphasis upon an old sofa, which creaked under the shock, the letter made me groan aloud, and a door was suddenly opened from another room, and the perturbed maid rushed in, happily not having had time to bring a coroner and jury to view the body, which lay upon the crimson lining of a dressing gown, a paper cutter raised above the head, and the fatal letter of which it had burst the seal, still open in the hand, the face pale as wont. The intruder, come to a pretty mature age, though not ugly, had acquired a perfect knowledge in her career of how to conduct herself on all occasions, a slight scream, and then the inanimate beholder of the bloody scene sunk into a easy chair, the arm screening the eyes, which were not closed, this appeared to be a proper state of swoon, and tender apprehension, should the worst appearances not be borne out, and were anything the matter, gave a little time for reflection on the horrid crime, brought on by despair, a sin more especially to be eschewed, also from the suggestion of practical wisdom to be able to look about her, was not inapplicable. My voice, almost angry in its tone at this unaccountable scene, determined the part to be taken, and after a moment, the tender-hearted maid expressed her thanks that nothing had happened to me, as she had really believed I was all bloody.

I fear I was too much taken by surprise to treat the intrusion as good-naturedly as I ought, and only muttered something about a letter which interested me very much, and I was anxious to read in quiet, the poor spinster gathered herself up, and I felt a reproach of conscience as she left the room.

The first words of Rose's letter were, *you could not be surprised, after my* last, to see this dated from a cotivent, and only thus far had I read on first opening it, I was overwhelmed to think that I had been the cause of what I could not but consider as an immolation, the free, the beautiful Rose, who might have queened among the ancient Amazons, to be shut up to mumble Latin prayers, and never feel again the air of the mountain side, or the bound of the fleet and favorite courser on the plain. I cannot describe the shock I suffered from this, though long dreaded, suddenly announced news, and lay wanting nerve to read further, however, with a little exertion, I again raised the paper to my eyes, resolved now to know the whole, as I believed I already knew the worst of its contents.

But my single minded and beloved parent, it went on, *has put matters in such a light before me, that I feel I cannot yield to my griefs, and refuse to be useful where I know I may be so, and where he gives me the means, I have consented, with more cheerfulness than I expected, to accompany him to Cuba, and thence to Spain, and we may meet before this long year is closed, for it creeps but wearily. Now make no plan, till we can confer together but watch as if in the prairies. I am a woman, though you have known me as a boy, and I advise your getting to know some woman relation of your father's, you will find news and sympathy, if they are to be had, best in our sex. The attempt—it must be more, for you cannot fail—to get into some circle where you were formerly known, must obtain you some knowledge of family connections, and most people of birth, I believe, have a talent or a turn for genealogy. I have written by this post to your friend, Signor Conchas, and you may, by playing the part I ask you, of a gay young man of London, for a short time, be the means of making me feel, should I have so much influence, that I am still useful, and ought to have still in the world some affection and active part. I hope I know you well, Ned, and as I give up a scheme of promised peace for a voyage to Europe, in the faith of your not refusing my wishes and my aid, you will require all the intermediate time to harden your heart sufficiently to refuse and consign me to an oblivion more atoning perhaps, but more painful than death.*

Thus wrote Rose. I had gathered that her father's fortunes were on the rise before, and that some attention was required to manage their great value, and the diversified sources from which they sprung.

Chapter Sixty-Six
Changes—Society—Isabel!

They had news of the same date in Lincoln's Inn Fields.

It is needless to say, I at once yielded to a wish from Rose, which circumstances had made an obligation.

My change of quarters was managed by Mr. Searle, who got me a small apartment, consisting of two public rooms, a bedroom, and dressing room, with accommodation for servants, at thirty-five shillings a week. They were in Holies Street, so not very much out of the way, and I was installed Mr. Jones, with an Irish servant, who appeared at one door of my dining room, as I entered by the other, I had gone to Mr. Searle's with my luggage, and thus arrived after dining with him at a place in Oxford Street, where we got a good and cheap repast, his own house being at or near St. John's Wood.

Soon after dinner, a coach brought my worldly wealth from the office, and I parted with my lawyer, and drove to the future abode.

It is needless to relate the gradual steps of launching into west-end life, the hire of a cab and a tiger by the month, with an extra horse for night work, and in all this, I was most passive, but when a stall at the opera was proposed, I at once rebelled, and the measure was given up.

Signor Conchas had every means of getting me into a good set, and from this, I was expected to pervade through the sphere around, and it opportunely happened, that it was most convenient for him that I should often be found in his circle, where his daughter could have a devoted brother at her service.

I may here state, that they were persons of family in their own country, and received with every distinction wherever they were known.

It was near Easter, and the heavier part of society had moved up to town, it was only the desperate visits of those who came up for a specified time, and specific objects, which were deferred till after the English holy week, some had left town to be out of the way of its solemnities, others had come up to be enraptured by the thrilling discourses of favorite preachers, but I cannot say that the houses I visited were much subject to these tastes, and nothing was to be remarked, but the quieter tone of the parties, and the greater prevalence of foreigners. At last Parliament was to meet, and some additional interest instilled into the daily prints.

The blossom of a plum-tree was to be seen over a garden fence, and the daylight was sensibly increased, the London sparrow was busy making nests, pluming himself that he is not a pheasant, and that he really enjoys a degree of liberty few living creatures, with the same number of legs can boast of, even in this favored land. The leaves expanded, and my visiting list increased as April wore on, and I cannot say I had met with anything worthy of recording. There was a certain mystery about me which seemed to take, being unknown, and here upon family business, which, of course, was not proclaimed. A few months, and I should be of age.

There was a grand party to be given at the French Embassy, the King and Queen were expected, and of course the persons to be invited were selected by favor, as well as with some care. I had cultivated every opportunity of learning Spanish, and was already intimate with Signor Munos, who was a relation of my friend of St. Louis, who had written to him about me in answer to some enquiry. I often accompanied the Signora Conchas to the embassy, and at her father's request, the minister asked for me an invitation to Hertford House. My dressy inclinations were something wounded, at having to appear in the same guise as a club waiter, except that I was allowed the latitude of tight pantaloons, instead of shorts, but I envied the sentinel at a palace door, as I anticipated appearing in my uncourtly suit, in a radiance of uniforms military and diplomatic. The hour had come for the fete, I had dined in Lincoln's Inn Fields, and the well-appointed coach of the Signor conveyed us to the end of a long line of carriages, which had not the entry, that is, in cases of no separate entrance, the privilege of breaking the line, at last, it was our turn to set down, and the operation was performed with that precise celerity which exemplifies the just valuation of time on these occasions. The beautiful feet of the Spanish girl barely reached the carpeted ground where we, who had jumped out first to receive her, already stood, when the carriage started with a jerk, as one of the servants finished shutting its door. State porters and exotics lined the inner hall and staircase, whilst something like a bustle below, perhaps the arrival of royalty, made us hurry up. The rooms were so nearly filled, that the reception of majesty would be anything, but in naked apartments without any other precaution than the selection of the guests, a quarter of an hour after, produced the royal couple.

The King possessing, in an eminent degree, a certain dignity of manner, with extraordinary simplicity and frankness, nodded as he proceeded up the line which formed itself to let the august party pass. I was near the Spanish Minister at the time, and saw the affable manner in which he was recognised, they passed on to an inner drawing room, where the Queen took her seat, and the rest of the world passed on to their several amusements.

I cannot say there was anything very gay in such a party, but there was a room set apart for dancing. I was soon left alone with Signor Conchas, and at last, delivered up to my own thoughts and observations, by his sitting down with some friends in a corner, apparently occupied in an interesting discussion.

The house was to me historical, and I was wending my way toward the small room where the Regent used to sit in conversation with the good, as well as agreeable Marchioness, while the lookers-on were squeezed into pancakes at the sacred door.

In passing to search for this cabinet, now occupied by card tables, I saw one of the convives I had met at Fernwold's nearly three years before, he looked hard, and then put out his hand, he was an Austrian, there was no refusing his kindly recognition.

"We have lost our poor friend, and I have never seen you since," he said, almost in a tone of inquiry.

"We both went abroad about the same day," I answered. "And poor Fernwold never returned."

"Then we have all three been out of the way, though I asked you where you had been, with the air of a resident in London, and have not been back from Constantinople but a couple of months. Where do you hang out, as they term it?"

He was putting his own address into my hand, as he spoke.

I had liked him much for his gay humour and winning manners, and therefore yielded myself up to his advances with a good grace, determining to explain myself to him, as to my change of name and position the first opportunity.

He was not early, he said, in answer to my enquiry, and as I had no card, merely named 23, Holies Street as my abode, and promised to call upon him in Duchess Street, not far off, before one next day.

"Before two," he rejoined, as we separated. "I am a hired servant to the Emperor, and must be in the office at that hour."

His Majesty had rather a taste for banquets, and liked to make a speech, but his stay at a party, such as this, was seldom much prolonged, I did not dance, but sauntered about observing, and when I could, getting pointed out to me the great notables, the Duke, amongst the rest, who somewhat bent, looked the head of all veterans, even in his plain attire, for he was not in military uniform, but wore that of Windsor, in which he appeared like a deified Chelsea Pensioner.

It was a curious scene, the *in* and the *ex* meeting, the minister absent and the minister present, Dudley and Palmerston, and the exclusive Greys, were all there, the toothless old premier, who though bearing himself like a person of station, had the air of one who overvalued himself, less than he undervalued others. Lord John looked over worked, or over trained, and the only person, except the Sovereign, who seemed to bear his office naturally, was the Chamberlain, who appeared unoppressed by its cares, and if he did not invite dead duchesses to court, like one of his successors, he not having one of his own, went through his list the more easily with the living.

"Ned, my boy, how are you," said a well-remembered voice, as a hand was laid upon my shoulder from behind, it was Harry Smith, in a blue uniform, profusely embroidered, the diplomatic dress of the United States. "I am glued tight to my boss," he whispered, "but I will come and see you early tomorrow—where?"

"No. 23, Holies Street, before eleven." And he was gone.

There had been some stir, and it was evident that some royal movement was about to be perpetrated. I stood a little away from the door of the room, inspired by the presence of their majesties, and perceived the Signora Conchas taking leave of the Countess Munos, and beckoning to me. I was by her side in a moment, just as my German friend approached also, but too late.

"I should have thought to have tired you of me in the last quadrille." the Signora said as she acknowledged his salute, in which appeared some disappointment.

We passed on in search of the Signor, when a certain bustle announced the departure, as the Queen came slowly through the doorway speaking to someone, whose head was turned rather away from our view, being between us and Her Majesty.

But my companion, who felt me tremble, said, "are you then so affected by the sight, what would you be by the touch."

I tried to rally, but could not take my eyes from that fair neck, and those rich tresses. I had seen enough, it was Isabel, it was the doubt made me tremble, for I now felt recovered, firm, and almost vengeful. They had come out of the inner room together, Queen Adelaide and Isabel, and separating immediately after I had recognised the latter.

For a second, she stood waiting to get back, against the tide, it was at this moment she turned her head, and our eyes met. I cannot tell what the feelings were, but I found them overpowering, she became deadly pale. Happily she seemed known to the Signora, who instantly rushed to her support, and I really believe, prevented her falling.

"Do take her arm," she said to me. "She seems so faint."

My arm was taken, instead of my taking hers, and owing to the appearance of real illness, room was made on a sofa near, and an old lady bustled through the crowd, and made up to her to know what had happened, and if she was ready to go home.

At this juncture, a fattish looking youth came up, and announced that the carriages were near, and would be up by the time they could be in the entrance hall.

"Take my cousin, Lord Albric," said the elder dame. "I shall get down well enough."

"No!" said Isabel. "Take care of the countess, I shall trouble Mr. Edward to continue his help a little longer, as he has already been so obliging—we will follow."

Signor Conchas had come up, and his daughter stood bewildered, leaning on his arm, as we moved toward the door.

"I am married, and must trust to you, that our former meetings shall be unknown. You cannot unmarry me, but may make me miserable."

"Never!" was all I could utter.

"I will find a way to see you, you shall at least know how I have come to act the part I have done."

We were at the foot of the stairs, sundry servants rushed back and forward, two in long overcoats awaited with the wrappings necessary for going into the cold, flambeaus glared as well as gas through the glass door, which shut the outer from the inner hall. A departure had taken place, and a voice proclaimed the Marchioness of Connemara's carriage, the old lady appeared not ill-pleased to have the attendance of an assiduous young man.

She turned about, before getting up the steps of the coach, and said to me, "Thank you, Mr. —, I should have known you too, from the likeness." But Isabel hurried her on, complaining of cold, and she scrambled up what would now be described as almost a staircase. A slight pressure of the arm was all I received as thanks or farewell. The young lord sprung in after them, the door was shut, and the coach, glittering in armorial bearings drove off, the tall footmen making it look lowly beneath their protecting shade.

I ran up again to get warmed, and to recover my presence of mind, at this strange meeting.

Was Isabel the Marchioness or the old lady, whom I vaguely remembered to have seen before. I found Count Riris lounging about, though the party was in full activity, dancing revived with every energy since Queen Adelaide left, the Count seemed anxious to have a talk, I had little to do, and indulged him.

"That was a handsome person you were with tonight," he began.

"Yes," I answered, rather absently.

"But you came with her, I think."

"Oh, if you mean Signora Conchas, I agree with you, and am now looking about to find her."

Purposely, I believe, he led me the wrong way in our search, and got out of me all I knew about the position of the family, at last we came upon the Signor, who said his daughter was dancing, I introduced the Count, who was known to the Spanish Minister I found, and left them, I had need to be alone.

All my first violent passion was re-awakened, and Isabel was, I found, a married woman. I felt absolutely giddy, all that took place since this meeting, had been instinctively done, I had never been what is called rational since, and was now awaking as if from a trance, but there were no two such Marchionesses, if there were two such women as Isabella, and there could be no difficulty in finding her out, this occurred to me near the door, and I made my way forth, like one getting out of a burning house, the cool breath of night blew about my hair as I threaded my way through the small enclosure in front of the ungainly pile. I walked home, had I then waiting a dozen carriages at command, it would have been on foot I should have gone away. I ran against few people, there were not many to be met.

For two days, my eyes ached in the streets in fruitless search, and I rode like a madman round the park, but in vain. The third found me, a little more composed, in Lincoln's Inn.

The Signor had not come in, and indeed I was early on purpose to gain any information I could, as to the recognition of the night of the fete. Isabel, as I conjectured, was slightly known to the Signora, and we produced Dodd. The Marchioness of Connemara had been married about a year, to a husband of about sixty, she was the only child of the Marquis of Gillsland, thus far all appeared clear. Her father not long succeeded to his title, the Signora understood lived abroad. They were people of great wealth, and high position in society, a real old Irish family, not made of upstarts, and lit their beacons over the best part of a western county, when there was subject for family rejoicing. They were high in favor, the more so, as offices about court befitting their rank had been offered and declined, it was said, with a view of not impeding the benefit such patronage might produce where it was more required.

I mentioned our acquaintance as one of almost childhood, so slight also, that I did not know more than her first name, nor did she know more I believed of me.

"It seemed a curious meeting for two persons so little acquainted."

"It must have seemed so to indifferent spectators," I answered, somewhat embarrassed.

"Ah, then there was something of love in it."

My countenance, which could not in this belie me, told the hopeless passion. There was a pause, the generous girl had no idea of extracting a painful secret, and was somewhat ashamed of having pressed her questions, and the entrance of the Signor put an end to the conversation.

Next morning's Post announced the departure of the Marquis and Marchioness of Connemara for Paris.

Chapter Sixty-Seven
A sailor?—reveries—an impulsive act

On my way home from Manchester Square, I had been too much disturbed by what had passed, to observe particularly a person considerably muffled up, dressed in the pea-jacket and hat of a sailor, who once or twice passed me, and then turned to have a look by a lamp, he was alone, and not concealing himself, besides inferiority of size, there was nothing to make me apprehend an attack, and I had but sufficiently noted the circumstance to remember it as curious, when I saw the same figure disappear round the corner of the square as I returned home three nights afterward.

Next morning, however, on opening the window to consult the cloudy sky about going out on foot, I saw a street sweeper in conversation with a person similarly dressed, who went away as soon as he saw me look out, it was then, as his back was turned, that I observed his walk was not the usual roll of a sailor, but he had a short quick step, more like that of a person carrying a message.

The day had not so bad an appearance as the morning at first threatened, the trees budded in the park at Cumberland gate, and I stretched my way across the sward, where the cows were picking up what grass they could find amongst the blue cartridge papers which were thickly strewed over that open part, divided between their rights and those of the foot-guards. The various short cuts were characteristic, they were dusty paths in dry, and greasy cavities in wet weather, but I disdained such lines, and made for the recruit-house of the guards and thence the bridge of the Serpentine. It was the first exercise I had taken in such a rural fashion, for there was no apparent restraint, and I might have dreamed that I was on some of the prairies, between the woody tributaries of the Kanzas or the Missouri, were it not for the ominous looks of an occasional policeman to remind me of the wants of civilisation, the perplexed recruit was looking unnatural by reiterated command, and I myself heard a corporal recommending a swain, who hitherto had been probably accustomed to follow a plough with four horses, carrying a hundred weight of clay stuck to his boots, to perform some evolution with a celerity and precision, which he compared to *lightning going through a gooseberry bush*. From the recruit-house to the magazine, following the regular path, I overtook two persons in earnest conversation, who stopped as I turned down toward the Serpentine. There was a slight ripple on the water, and several fishermen watched their floats, the ends of whose rods were stuck in the shore, the waterfowl were chasing each other about, and here and there hanging over the bank the bud of a horse-chesnut looked ready to burst. For the time, there was no voice, or even vision of authority to intervene between the spectator and the scene, or the actor and the part he chose to play. It was but a corner, and there were but few people about, and I thought of those far distant waters, wherein thousands fish came to take the most clumsy baits, though clear as crystal their own element, and bright the sun at high noon, and not a breath of air lower than the current which carried an occasional white streak across the sky, high above the jagged tops which towered around.

The rifle, the bow and the lance, were at the foot of the gigantic pine on the shore, and the courser browsed on the thick short turf which was nourished by spray, when the wild tempest found its ways opened through the hollows of the hills. I remembered once to have heard its voice, by those dark waters, in the dead of night. The camp was sheltered below a crag of overhanging granite, and the influence of the gale scarce came near, but between the clouds at short intervals, as the hurricane carried them broken across the sky, came a mocking light of the moon, which showed round the headland formed by the wing of the protecting mass a stream of scud, which defaced the crested waves, it was a wild night. The whole lake appeared driving past the point, rushing to the plains—a strange scene to wake upon from the calm of sleep, and the memory of the placid day.

I do not know how I came to let my thoughts wander back and dwell upon that storm, as I leaned against the paling which enclosed a few bushes, by the dry arch of the bridge, people had not come out to ride or drive, and the examples of well-sustained patience and perfect abstraction in such a place had prompted, I suppose, the remembrance of the last similar occupation in which I myself had been engaged.

I was interrupted in my reverie by the coming of two persons, who laid themselves down on the bank just by, they were the same I had seen before me on the path from the magazine, except that they were half showily half shabbily dressed. There was nothing to remark about them. The one dark and come to maturity, the other young and fair.

"She must surely be here so fine a day," said the younger, as they sat down, and then came a long conversation, pretty much composed of slang and enigmatical allusions.

It was astounding to myself how often, and with what zest, I recurred to my two seasons of wandering in the Wild West, and I was still dreamingly indulging in its most minute memories, with eyes fixed on a motionless float, which was not however to be looked down by the united gaze of its owner and myself, when the older of the two persons before alluded to rose up, impatiently saying,

"I'm blasted if I wait any longer, what does she care whether we hang about or not? I rather think Mr. Deacon has a taste for high-flyers, but it won't pay me."

"The belle is gone out of town, Ben owned as much," he added to some remark of his companion, in an undertone.

"But what cause could Ben have, to be anything but straight about her?" said the younger.

"May be he is getting soft, like a certain Mr. Deacon."

A curl of the handsome lip, and a look of scorn, indicated the opinion of this youth as to any pretensions but his own.

"Well," said the other, "I know one thing, this is no go."

He was already on his legs, and moving off, the other seemed but reluctantly to follow, and as they went, in their conversation, I heard the words swell, blowen, and Ben, but not the nature of their relations to the subject of discussion.

The birds were in full song, and the rooks, in the gardens, I entered their shade, it was a change of scene, the ear was soothed by the rural choruses, and but for the model southdowns, there might have breathed a fresh odour of spring, the way I took was toward Rotten Row, and several persons on horseback, and some carriages had appeared on the side of the water. I stood for a moment, looking toward the fine old elms, with their black trunks, which dotted the sloping shore, leaning against one of the trees bordering the green walk, a horse had become restive, or his rider had got into some discussion with him, by which he had nearly been unseated, and had already gathered about him that numerous class, the spectators of all gratis exhibitions. The two persons whose conversation I had remarked near the bridge were amongst the rest, and I observed Mr. Deacon, as he had been called, slap a bye-stander on the back as he came up, who turned somewhat abruptly away, but not before I had remarked something in his features, which I thought I ought to recognise, the glance was but momentary, the rider had been thrown, the horse was taking his own way down the side of the water, and his owner, rather than his master with a bruised hip and chafed temper, was about to proceed toward some region of cabs, amid many offers of every kind of aid, short of pecuniary, from the dull sincerity of the pensioner of sixty, to the ready-witted gamin often, whose course of literary studies had not yet been decided upon, but is a subject of parliamentary debate.

I walked on, those who had so suddenly gathered, as unaccountably dispersed, and as the turf of Kensington is fat and greasy, I thought I too might as well ride, could I get my horse. I had but to fix my eye upon a pale face and light limbs, on getting out of the wicket, and wish, they were immediately put under my entire command. I scrawled two words of an order for my horse, signed my initials, gave a shilling, indicated Rotten Row as the rendezvous, and my messenger set off in a businesslike trot, rather to be characterised by promise of endurance, than flashing speed, I watched the start after the little paper had been put within the lining of a cap, and its bearer never turned his head, nor seemed to intend to do so, till he got to Holies Street.

The second day after this found me at Mr. Searle's, the visits I paid to him were periodical and pretty regular, he seemed interested, and had got wind of a number of curious stories, but nothing to throw light upon our search. The prime agent, as was supposed, in the burning at my father's was known to be gone to America, the police thought there was some chance of finding something out, as the subordinates might be found implicated in some other crime.

I had not mentioned Isabel's marriage, and I resolved at any sacrifice not to bring her into trouble.

I was musing about this, when Mr. Searle, whose eye had been fixed upon me, said suddenly, "You have something to tell me?"

I then recollected the object of my coming. "Yes, the day before yesterday I had taken a ride toward Highgate, and seeing there was a bye-way between high hedges, I turned into it, sometimes finding it broad and margined with green, at others narrow and bad, at one of the broad parts there was a waggon tilt, and a smouldering fire, an old woman and some children sat in the entrance. I scarcely looked at them, and was passing on at a walk, when a man rushed past me, he said some words which I did not understand, and then made a rush at my horse's bridle, which he got hold of, attempting to throw me off by the leg, and in fact so overbalanced me, as to make it a choice between a fall and a jump down. Happily, I was able to convert it into the latter. I was swinging my heavy whip about me as the crone came up to aid my assailant, whom I seized with a grasp which was not of encouraging gentleness. He then made an attempt to get at a pistol, the handle of which I saw as his coat was torn open in the struggle.

"'I want your horse and must have him,' he said, through his shut teeth.

"We were near the bank, the woman caught hold of the horse, who was frightened, and as much as she could manage, we slipped into the ditch, my antagonist pinned against the bank. At this moment a little girl crept through the hedge near, and gave some alarm, the woman groaned and looked wildly distracted, between the desire to help and the necessity of retaining hold of the bridle. The man was mastered, and I was considering what was next to be done, and whether the help that might first arrive would be for him or me, when I perceived a dull despair had settled on his features, not harsh or bad in themselves, nor wearing the stamp of anything but a certain reckless impudence, now subdued into a sadness which was almost pitiable. Our eyes met, there was no fierceness in the shrunken pupils under those dark lids.

"'What did you want with my horse?' I asked.

"'The beaks are upon me, and a horse would save me.'

"The little girl again said something, and he continued, 'They are stopped three fields off, but will be here, and you will see me swing for it for want of a nag. May you never know what I feel now—but it is bitter.'

"There was no tear, but a withered hopelessness in his eye, which I could not stand.

"'Oh, give him the beast, it will be brought back. An old grandmother would not care to lie at such a pinch. Oh, good gentleman, do not kill my boy! He has no father! Oh, bless you! I see you will do it.'

"I looked round—a hideous hag had become changed by the enthusiasm of real prayer. I loosed my hold, and for the first time the youth trembled, but collecting his ideas, as I pointed to the horse, he looked at his attire. I threw off my overcoat, which he put on, his hat already being of the flexible order of wide-awakes.

"'Where is he to be sent?'

"I told him.

"'He shall be with you tomorrow, before twelve.'

"He was in his seat and off, at a rate to leave pursuit at fault by anything but telegraph.

"The old woman seized my hand. 'A blessing come upon you.' She gasped, as a single tear stole down her withered cheek. 'I shall never see him again—you have beheld our parting—a blessing on you forever! It is no light thing given from the heart-strings—nor,' she added, solemnly, 'would have been a curse. Come some time soon, for I must remain to keep them haunting about here, come kindly, for he gave his last look to you, and I feel I get it back from the glance of your eye.'

"A slight movement of the little girl, almost imperceptible—and the look of a hag—the attitude of a beggar—the demand for charity—took place on the weird woman, the soul had shrunk away from those squalid features. Two detectives, as I afterward learned they were, had been in pursuit from a neighboring public house, where a certain person they expected to take was to pass, one of them looked hard at me, the other at the old woman, who denied stoutly that she had been begging, while the children came and stared in seeming innocent surprise at the newcomers. The officer who took a survey of me did not omit to look at my feet—they were mudded in the ditch, as if from a long walk. I asked the nearest way to Strawberry Hill, and was answered by a question, had I seen anyone pass lately?

"I said, 'A man on horseback.'

"'Which way did you come?'

"'How should I tell, who have but just been asking where I am,' I said laughing.

"'Which way did the man on horseback go? Was he going fast?' again inquired the other.

"I pointed to the direction opposite to that by which they came.

"'His horse had not a hair turned, as far as I could see, he ought not to have been in a hurry, or he would not have turned back.'

"They had seen the hoof marks of the horse.

"The men seemed not satisfied, and I could perceive eyed me askance. I took off my glove, there was no ring on my fingers, and my hand was tender-skinned and white, the nails, of which I took the most particular care, were trimmed as if to be taken as a model, and as I selected a shilling with some deliberation, not wishing to give too much, I saw the look of one of the detectives withdrawn from scrutinizing it, turn with a negative shake toward his companion. I gave the shilling to the little girl, who appeared to have been acting scout, and who immediately ran off with it, as if to conceal it from the exacting hands of the beldame, who moved off toward the fire, muttering incoherently, but never looking back. I was now civilly enough asked if I wanted to go to Primrose Hill, and turned toward the road up which the police had made their appearance. I had some difficulty in avoiding the questions of my companions—I was out to take a long stretch, and somewhat lost. At last we came to a turn where the land joined the road which took up toward the northeast, and down toward the Swiss Cottage, when just upon it, one of the officers faced about abruptly, and said, 'Perhaps, sir, your evidence may be wanted to trace a runaway, please let us have your address.'

"I pulled out my card-case and gave my name without hesitation. They turned up, and I passed down toward Regent's Park."

"Well, that is an adventure, they cannot put you upon oath before the man is taken, and only wanted to know whether you were an accomplice, as soon as they find you to be Mr. Jones, of Holies Street, you will drop from their recollection as naturally as the leaf from the tree in autumn."

Mr. Searle seemed to think he had roamed far into the world of imagination for this metaphor, and soon recalling himself, added, taking off his spectacles and looking fixedly, "This was not what brought you here, I see there is something behind."

I was silent.

"My young friend, you may have hesitations about imparting information affecting others, a physician must know the nature of the case to make a cure. Now, I will just say one word on this head. A lawyer in criminal cases receives confidential communications, which he may be bound not to disclose, for instance, a prisoner could be best defended by a man who knew if he was really guilty. But here I have only further to assure you that you may relate any suspicions of complicity that may have occurred to you, without my going an inch forward in our investigation unsanctioned, and as to gossip, it is absolutely not in my way at all." Mr. Searle turned and stirred the fire.

I immediately saw that I should be deprived of the ardour and interest he took in the inquiry if I withheld anything which really so strongly bore upon the case.

I then told him of my discovery at Hertford House.

He had resumed his spectacles, and took up a new Peerage, he cast his eye lightly over the Connemara notice.

"Yes, Isabel, daughter of the Marquis of Gillsland, second Marquis survived his brother. Well, I might try and trace the lady's connection with your kidnapping, that may be all-natural enough, though a bad and illegal means of getting you out of what a father might have considered a ruinous connection. But we can gain nothing by bringing home the fact of her complicity, and probably she does not know who were employed. But we must look closer to see who could be interested in the burning of the house, as there was not property enough taken, unless in bank notes—a thing I have learned to be quite improbable, from your father's habit of giving cheques for every account she paid. I say there was not plate enough, and that the butler knew, to divide, and the risk was great. Now, unless we can get at the papers, we do not begin to know what we would be at. If I should hear anything before this day week, I will let you know."

I saw his brain was at work, and left him.

Chapter Sixty-Eight
The gipsy woman—a romantic tale—of Bernard—the Lyceum

My horse had been returned safe at the time appointed, by a respectable-looking rosy farming man, as my groom described him, with many thanks, he did not seem the least the worse of his exertions. A man had also come to ask whether I lived there, and went away immediately, and this was all that occurred as the consequence of my adventure, which however I had not forgotten, nor a certain desire to learn if my aid had indeed saved the ill-starred youth from being taken.

Accordingly, I set off again to visit the old gipsy woman. She was sitting, or rather crouching, in the ditch where had been my struggle with her grandson, a small fire had been lit on the opposite brink, where she had held the horse, and near by had been removed the bows of the waggon, with all the household gear, in which consisted her domestic wealth, her hands were supporting her head—her elbows on her knees, she never looked up, and the two least children were putting dry willow twigs into the scanty fire, to hear them crack as they burned, but the vidette of the former day again crept through the hedge, and again made the ancient dame awake. She looked up, it was no gradual recognition, but I at once appeared never to have been absent from her thoughts.

I had alighted, holding my horse by one of the reins, which drew out into a long leading cord, the girl brought out a bit of goat-skin, and laid it down beside the fire, and I sat down, some trouble had been taken to clear a lower part of the ditch, which dried the bottom where we sat, and in which a few small green branches had been placed.

"I knew you would come," said the old woman, with a brightened eye and a faint flush in her wan cheek.

"Yes," I answered, "I came back as soon as I thought it would be safe, to know if your boy had got off."

A signal from the old woman again sent the vidette to the side from which any one would approach by the way I had previously taken.

"They never come the same way," she muttered. "Yes, Tom is safe, I hope, and may the lord send that you never want a true heart and ready hand at hour of need."

"But you scarcely talk like a..." I hesitated for a word.

"Gipsy," said the old woman. "No, I was not born among them. I was the natural daughter of a great lord, who died before I was born, and I believe had promised and intended to marry my mother, but one obstacle and another came, put in the way by his family, and he died—it was whispered by foul means. My mother went crazed, and spoke wildly, and also died—and in a madhouse—two years after. The family thought right to take me up, and make a show of great love for the poor orphan of a dear brother, and I had an expensive education. But it is a long story."

I begged of her to proceed, and she saw I was in earnest, as her eyes never ceased to gaze upon mine.

"I was wild, and flighty, and romantic, no pains were taken to give me any other than a show of being accomplished, and I overheard people who were visiting at the great house, and whom I occasionally met, talking of the noble generosity of the family. This aroused a curiosity, which the first serious quarrel with my instructress most cruelly satisfied. I became from that time different in my feelings to all the world, and began to consider every one as an enemy, and nothing did I love at the age of twelve but to steal into the great hall, where, amongst the pictures of his armoured fathers, I could gaze upon that of mine.

"Thus become easier to manage, I was the more neglected, and read romances, dreaming away my life, until upon some occasion, when I had caused some trouble or disappointment to the person who had the charge of me, I heard the word *beggar* applied in a sort of soliloquy. This was a view I had never yet taken of my own position, I had always what clothes I required —and they were showy too—and ten shillings a month pocket money, mostly given away in not the best directed charities.

"I was thus awakened to my own situation, the family coming to see me with a sort of parade, and asking, with every appearance of interest, about my progress, or sending for me, when I was brought and allowed to sit on a seat set apart, and talked to with the height of condescension.

"At last, at eighteen, I fell in love. Did you ever hear of the song of Johnny Faa? it is Scotch, I believe. But my alms-giving brought me to know a gipsy mother—she read my fortune, I was to marry for love, and to be loved dearly, and so I was." The eye again dimmed. "But I was to be poor. A boy, my own age, was her son, he was a beautiful brown youth, who was blithe and merry, and carolled and gambolled like a child, strong as a bull, and gentle and true, but he was all to me, and I need not try to make you know how he was everything to love.

"I would not take anything from that proud house but a few changes of linen, I was too wildly happy to think of wants, and my Harry was ready to take me on any terms—I must do him that justice, who is long in his grave. That was his son's son you saved, and I never saw my poor Harry much older.

"My poor Tom was not weak, but he was but a child to Harry, and a jolly-looking pretty boy as you can find in a summer's day's ride, but my poor husband would have so out-shone him with one look, that the child would have looked stale. And his father, too, my own poor son, I never took much thought for him.

"These are his sister's children, they were all dead to me, when at twenty-two my Harry was hung for stealing a horse. I never much distressed myself, nor thought of anything else after, till my poor Tom went the same way for a half sheep, and his mother, before she died, brought me the boy, and some love woke up again in me and grew.

"Our people helped me, and I did some little in fortune-telling, but the law came upon me, and I got into trouble—two months for vagrancy, a month for fortune-telling, under pretence of extracting money by fraud—and I got separated from the rest of the people, only at last finding my daughter and little Tom, and we have led various kinds of lives, but I have got so broken—for I am not sixty—that I have not been able to do much to keep above water.

"We were in Lancashire, and there I got a little help from one of the nephews of my father, the son of a younger brother, but he is now dead, and I have no friend, and was obliged to let the poor boy go out to see what he could do, and I scarce know into what trouble he has got. But there are some bloods that won't stand work, and his and all of them were in that the same.

"I will be on the path through the wood near Dulwich," she said, hurriedly, as a word or two in a young voice of some ballad, announced something before the young creature herself appeared.

A quick motion of the hand, pointing to the way I had come, made me see that the wish for my departure was urgent. I was in my saddle in a minute, and off, turning up the hill to the left, away from town, never turning my head.

On my return I found Harry Smith, waiting for me.

"Well, Ned, I have been hunting about for you quite hungrily. You surely did not come till yesterday, or I should have heard. But why change your name, is anything turned up to make it worthwhile?"

"No, but I am hunting sly."

"Well, it may be as sure as running.[i] But how do you get on?"

I told him generally that we were at fault, and hardly knew where to begin.

He immediately said, "Find out the back track of that rascal Bernard—he is the man. But I don't think he was fully trusted himself."

"It is hopeless," I answered. "He was recommended to the school by a poor curate, long dead, and he had other testimonials as being an orphan rescued from Catholicity, there the thing ends, and I really believe such documents are given back on quitting, and from the inquiries I made, probably were given back."

"But he was not precisely an orphan," rejoined Harry, "as he told me his mother was in a convent in England."

"That might be probable, as there was a mystery about his birth I never could make out."

After some general conversation, we went to Brunet's in Leicester Square, and had our dinner, preparatory to going to the Lyceum. Of course I had not a word to say in defence of London hotels, compared with those of New York and New Orleans, and the specimen of French and Italian we found left us rather proud of our own countries in comparison.

The Lyceum was in its first period, that is, full price, and there were many more benches in the pit than people, and the piece went on mincingly—a genteel sort of comedy, eked out with occasionally an excruciating song. We were in the centre of the fourth row from the music, and the performance seemed to be addressed to us, and to claim our attention. Happily the hour for half-price at last arrived, and an infusion of spirit was evinced in everything, from the shrill pipe of a fattish heroine to the thunder of the big drum, and the curtain fell upon the sublime sentiments of the denouement, amid an uproar of applause.

A pantomime succeeded, really amusing, but between the acts, two persons who were immediately in front, in deep council, had attracted Harry's attention by the slang with which they interlarded their conversation, and which he remarked to me as a specimen of English.

I explained how this sort of language was used, and by whom, though owning that no language in the civilised world was spoken with such universal purity as English by born Americans, there being no provincialisms, but only what we were now hearing, slang terms, used for special things and by choice.

During these remarks I heard with some surprise the name of *Ben* used, and upon looking close, perceived that one of the two persons was the elder of those I had seen at the Magazine in the Park some days before, the other a stranger.

"Yes, he has got something new to raise the steam, someone has come whom they have gone to Fulham to get shot of." I heard, but it appeared they were to get let go ahead, and a counter-mine sprung, at least so I understood, from the stray words which came to my ears, but the sudden turn of the head of the one I had not seen before, discovered that I was intently listening. An act finished at this moment, and they left without looking round.

I remarked to Harry that they were after no good. He laughed, and said he had seen many such come out to New Orleans to cool themselves.

Harry was a good deal occupied, and rather liked the gay doings to which he had access, and where his frank manner and handsome person found his ready favor, but we agreed to meet occasionally, and he was to be ready should I require his aid.

Chapter Sixty-Nine
A daring robbery—deep in the plot—
nunneries—an old woman's despair

The next day was Sunday, so I could not see Mr. Searle, and I went with my German friend Reus to Lincoln's Inn. They were just at luncheon, and were afterward going out to drive in Regent's Park, and we agreed to follow them to the Zoological Gardens, and then return to dinner.

When we left in the evening I found that I had hardly, during the whole time we had been with them, exchanged a word with Mademoiselle Conchas, and I could not help remarking this to her as we parted, she colored a little, and I could see had been sufficiently occupied by the Count.

But the news of Rosa's being daily expected in England, accompanied by an aunt, was what chiefly interested me, and in my turn I was silent and abstracted during our way home, of course this was put down to some other cause by my companion—so selfish are we in our interpretations of each other's conduct.

On reaching Golden Square I was admitted at once, and Mr. Searle, as he finished a letter put a morning paper into my hands, pointing to the report of a daring robbery.

> DARING ROBBERY. *We have to record a most daring robbery, committed on Thursday last in the neighborhood of Vauxhall Bridge. Near some ground laid out for building, there has been made use of by the workmen a sort of path, leading obliquely from the road toward the river under a high fence, which for a short space overshadows it. One of the workmen returning from his dinner, perceived a man running off in an opposite direction as he came in sight, and almost immediately turned a corner, upon advancing a few steps, he came upon*

an old man lying in the water in a ditch at the side of the path, whom he immediately set about relieving. A constable coming up, he mentioned the circumstance, and he set off in pursuit of the fugitive. The poor old gentleman was speechless, had a bad cut on the head, and his waistcoat-pockets turned inside out. He was removed to a neighboring public house, and we hear is in a very precarious state. It appears that he had been to a lawyer who usually draws his dividends. The constable followed the supposed robber by the description of his dress, he had taken a cab, and the original constable having found two detectives, set them on the track, they were thrown out several times, and renewed the chase, until at last alighting, and getting through an entry near Regent's Canal, they were obliged to do the same, and the pursuit was continued on foot, until all trace was lost near Primrose Hill. What is remarkable in the case is, that the robber appeared to have no accomplices, and not much knowledge of London. He wore a drab-colored shooting coat and black wide-awake.

"You see," said Mr. Searle, "how we help the culprit and embarrass justice, to furnish some interest to our morning journals, however that man may come back, and he may be caught again, if he does not become wiser. But now for your own affairs. I have made out that there had been a project of marriage between your father's nephew, who may be his heir, and it is believed will become so, and this same Isabel De Warenne, this was broken off, but I am still looking out for the agents. If we could get the papers, that is all we want, but she would not have appeared so agitated, nor would she have made her husband leave town for a trifle, and she might be sure you were not going to make a blow-up for nothing. No, no, should we never make it out, depend upon it there is something deep in the plot, and heavy in the stake, or my experience of such people goes for nothing."

I then mentioned what Harry Smith had told me about Bernard's having a mother in England.

"Ah!" said the lawyer, with some interest, "but how to get at her? We require delicate handling—but they are ruthless against apostates—we will see, I will think of that. Come again the day after tomorrow."

"Yes, but I have another little incident." And I mentioned that the name of *Ben* had been used on two different occasions. That was the name of the intelligent tiger who used to accompany me on my rides to Wimbledon, and who in fact proposed them. I then related the conversations, and described the men, my auditor looking earnest, and taking down what I said.

"I think we have come to a knowledge of the reasons of your kidnapping, but that will little serve, unless we get at the papers taken from your father."

I was going, and had my hand on the lock of the door, when he added, "Do you know any Catholics?"

"Yes, of course the Conchas are Catholics, and I believe my Irish servant is also. Why?"

"Because you might try and learn something of the different nunneries in England. If it is true that there is such a person as Bernard's mother, she ought to be found—they are not so numerous. Try your own servant first."

Michael was as usual at home, and laid a note on the table. I told him to shut the door.

"Do you know anything of the nunneries near London, for I believe there are two or three?"

Michael smiled.

"I'm no lady-killer, so they have no fear of anything in that way."

"But they admit no male whatever in these places."

"You mistake altogether what I mean. Do you know whereabouts such places are, or do you know any one who could give me any information?"

"Faith I do not."

"The fact is," I rejoined, "that a young man died in Amerca, who, if he owned anything, must have left it to his mother, who is in one of these."

"Well, to be sure, the priest should know Father Deleyney."

I saw that the most remote prospect of gain was, by Michael, held a sufficient inducement to open an acquaintance with the Father, and an appointment was to be proposed for the next evening.

This done, I ordered my horse, to proceed to Dulwich, and riding slowly down Regent Street, I perceived a showy-looking equipage standing by the pavement, and two ladies, attended by two huge footmen, were just starting in a sort of procession up the street, the elder, immediately on seeing me, beckoned, and I was at her side, one of the servants holding my horse.

"I want you, Mr. Thingame for a hundred yards, you are so like the family, I seem to have known you all your life, poor dear Adelbert, I liked him best of all, though he did not take much trouble. It is very odd I should have forgotten your name."

"Jones," I interposed.

"Ah, well, but I dreamed you were a relation, you are so like the family. Now we are near, and can drop our attendant. I want a lady's dressing case, and if we go in parade, it will ruin me. What do you think, I inherited all poor dear Adelbert's ready money, it has made me very rich, but I'd rather not have had it, I honestly assure you—these tiresome marriages. Here I am actually shopping, and going in like Mrs. Tomkyns, to make a bargain. Keep out of sight," she added, to the footman, who hid himself behind a lamppost with a demure grin.

Lady Davenport—for I now remembered her name—got into the shop, and seating herself, contrived in a twinkling to have the floor covered with open dressing cases for both sexes. Sitting like a shepherdess amongst a flock of sheep, she said she could not see them sitting on a level, and as they were really beautiful, the old lady was delighted, and the shopmen knelt to pass the glittering array the more clearly in view, altering their positions and expatiating on their merits.

"Dora, come and sit by me. I cannot afford another box—sixty pounds, well, get it into the carriage and let us go—they are much too pretty."

And we issued into the street.

"That will do, take it to the coach."

"Certainly, Ma'am, shall we call a coach?"

"No, no—we are close by," said her ladyship, now more reassured upon finding herself fairly out of temptation's way.

A sort of indistinct signal with the parasol was seen over the heads of the passers-by, and the coach, in all its bravery of gilding, and hammercloth, and foaming horses, moved majestically to meet us, while my horse humbly followed.

"Now we will have to see the box safe on the front seat, and Mr. Thingame mounted, before we get in, otherwise we should lose one of the servants while he was holding the stirrup, and all that, so let us see you up, and come to dinner at eight."

So I leaped upon my horse without the aid of the stirrup.

Her ladyship was charmed, but said there was no hurry, and got in, telling Dorothea that I was very active, and the glorious equipage and the well-appointed horse parted company.

I was anxious to see the old woman, and assure her that if her grandson came back in any other coat than a drab, he would be quite safe.

The ride was very agreeable, and fresh spring welcomed me in every guise as I proceeded, but most agreeably in that balmy air which had gathered the odours of all the flowers, which decked in their varied hues the sunny meadows and shady lanes of Norwood.

I got a man of ticketed honesty to walk about my horse near the college, while I went up through the wood to get upon the height, where I expected to find the old lady. I was busy peering into some opens in the coppice, and looking for the smoke which her small fire would send up, when I saw at my heels the little scout, who passed on with the kindly smile, rather of an affectionate little sister then the sordid expression to be acquired by her usual habits, she stopped to look for violets, and to gather primroses and cowslips, carolling in young sounding notes of touching sweetness, some stanzas of the Scotch ballad, which her grandmother loved to hear through the bushy brake, as if from some young spirit. The child told me this, she never sang in sight, but near and never very long, nor had she ever been spoken to, but her mother had done it, and it made granny quiet, and her eyes look kind, so when her mother died she did it. She had been at the college and had sold some flowers to an old gentleman, and got a sixpence from a lady who drew her picture, she held out her treasure, amounting to ninepence, to be counted up, as there was a fourpenny piece, she was puzzled.

"Why don't you ask me about Tom," at last I said.

"Hush," she answered seriously, "granny told me best never say the name, for fear of michief."

We were arrived, and my guide stopping pointed forward, and again the sweet young notes sang plaintively, came with a sad wild charm that went to the heart.

I still had the little treasure in my hand, and its little pink cotton rag to be rolled up in. The grandmother was before me in a few steps, seated in a recess, and throwing a few little sticks into the fire, over which hung a little tin pan, she was rocking herself back and forward as she sat, the effect of the song was in her eye, for it was serene as well as sad. She pointed to a grass mat, seemingly newly completed.

"I do not know how to get it sold, I don't think his sister can carry it."

I said, "He may be here himself, as soon as you can get him word, for they have never seen his face, he was only followed by the drab coat, there is not a bit of proof, but you and me and the children."

The old woman turned deadly pale as I spoke, and leaned forward, as if to save herself from falling over.

"Oh!" she muttered, "this is hardest of all, he may be on the broad sea, how shall 1 ever know, and all for no need. Oh! Come again to morrow, and bring some bright gold, perhaps I can find some who may get on his track, to lose my own boy and his son, and his, who might he saved. You shall be paid back. I have never asked a groat from this Earl or the last, and I could have said words, which would have made them poor enough. Yes, the old man would have known all, had I liked to tell, and now the day is come when I am to be paid, for I want the money, come tomorrow, perhaps you haven't it?"

"Yes, I have."

"Oh, Tiney, where are you?"

She had recovered herself, and the languid blood had rushed back on her wan cheek, the child crept up to where she sat, and put her ear to the mouth which was bent toward her, and after listening to a few earnest words, disappeared amongst the bushes behind.

"Perhaps I shall not need your gold, but do not let me be at the mercy of their hard hearts, be early, I shall watch awake all night. Oh, let me but have my poor boy's grandson at my forelorn fire." She sunk her head upon her knees, and pointed to the path.

I laid the little calico with its contents down by her side, and went.

The ride to town was not long, I was too anxious about the poor old woman's almost despairing measures for getting back her boy, to reflect that he had probably caused the death of the old gentleman whom he had robbed.

Chapter Seventy
Rose—Isabel at dinner

I had none of that morbid thirst for justice, which inspires the great part of the English public, and the appeal of even a robber in his need, was too strong for public duty. I was not long of getting over the gravelled roads, but took it more easily over the greasy pavement of London, there were several notes, one from Signor Conchas, announcing the arrival of Rose. She was at the Burlington Hotel, and her aunt, the Countess de Matagios was, with a priest, her only companion. I dressed sooner than I need have done, and drove first to the hotel, I learned they were all at home, and my name was required. I told the waiter to announce a friend from America, sent by M. Conchas, and received soon after an invitation to go up.

Rose came to the door of the room to meet me, and gave me her cheek to kiss, saying, "I knew it must be you." Continuing in her dear calm tones, "Oh, Ned, it almost brings me back to the world, look up, and tell me that you are happy."

At this moment I caught sight of the grinning Navahoe, seated in a corner with her eternal embroidery, and an answering smile was yet in my eyes, when they turned upon Rose.

"I see you have not forgotten poor Maria. You see she has chosen a fine sounding baptismal name."

"Yes, I see she is faithful still, but how is your father?"

"Oh, he is sadly tired playing the grandee, he has a thousand messages, and I believe, loves you as well as I do."

She then sent the Navahoe for the Countess.

"The poor Indian," she said, "had complained much of being made to eat so much grass, for she has no other word for vegetables, and cannot get over the degredation of being so often treated like a Chochoco."

I found my companion of the mountains, as I thought grown, and something paler, she wore a body and skirt of black velvet, a straw colored collar turning down over the neck, which was open in front, but buttoned up to the throat, the petticoat was of a dark brown, the hair gathered off the brow, upon which it naturally came thick and low, was confined by a narrow black velvet band, and fell waving in rich profusion to her shoulders.

"You are stupid, I think, Ned, you do nothing but stare."

"Would you have me rave? I cannot talk reasonably of the delight I have in gazing on you, it seems as if but yesterday we were on the plains."

"Oh! Forbear that, let it be but a memory untold, you know not what it costs me to think of those days."

The Countess here made her appearance, stately, large eyed and grave, she said, she would have known me at once, so often had I been described, she seemed pleased to hear the few words of Spanish I spoke. We were however interrupted again by the Indian abigail, who laughed outright at the Countess having known me from description, when she herself did not recognise me at first in black coat and tights.

It was now necessary to explain that I was on my way to dine with an old lady, but that I would call when it might suit next day.

"We have something to do in the way of visits, and perhaps dress," said Rose.

"Oh, do not change a particle of that."

"No, I do not mean, but cloaks and carriage things."

"Well, you will be in about two?"

"Yes, good night." I made my best bow to the Countess, and ran downstairs.

It was not far to St. James's Square, and I almost thought myself too late. I found the fat cousin, Lord Albric Finch, Lady Dorothea, his sister and the Lady of the house, sitting upon someone's absence.

"You have not brought the Marchioness with you, we thought you had gone after her," said the hostess, as I made my excuses, fearing I had been too late.

"No, we are waiting for Isabel, who did you say was come?"

I told her two Spanish ladies, one the daughter, the other sister of a grandee of Spain, full of Mexican wealth, high blood, and the deepest romance.

"What, aunt and niece both," said the Countess, restored to good humor by a thundering peal at the hall door. "How I hate street doors, I wish Cubitt would build houses with court-yards, paved with wood."

I was just beginning to remember who I was about to meet, when the door, opened in both its folds by a dignified looking groom of the chambers, gave admission to the beautiful Marchioness.

"I have run all the way upstairs, and had it been dark, you would have seen the fiery path of our horses over the stones," said the young creature, in that coaxing manner, which became her so well.

"That is, if you had been a little later, but I will take your word for it," said the old lady, patting her guest's one cheek, and kissing the other.

"I hope she has made her peace, and told the truth," said an Irish voice at the door.

I was looking for a pair, but how could I find any body I could pair off with on even terms. I had a learned Lord ready, who was to dine with the Royal society, I refused him flat, bowing to the Countess, on the score of stupidity. Then one engaged to an agricultural Duke, worse still. At last there came a youngster, who was to dine with my Lady Connemara. I told him he had mistaken the day, but that I would pair with him as a consolation, and the Marquis offered his arm to the Countess to follow Lord Albric and his wife who had set out. We did not dine in the dining room, but in a sort of anteroom to the suite of drawing rooms, the acting host seemed to grow fat from taking things easy, he knew nothing of that useful, as well as sublime art gastronomy, and instead of being able to appeal to the orders of the day, when a change was to be desired, or a halt helped in the conversation, he seemed to look at the flourishing document beside him with a respectful detestation, at last the Marquis called it an epitaph, his wife remarked in an undertone, that was an after dinner joke.

Lady Connemara was next to me, and when ever the hostess ceased addressing me questions about the new Spaniards or the Americans, she conversed in that easy way about trifles and passing events, which shewed a desire to talk, and a manner of confident affection, which she let me discover in various little ways, though hardly did she ever look as if she was addressing me more than her other neighbor.

At last, Lady Davenport begged me to describe Rose, and I did so with what in society would be termed enthusiasm. Her beautiful long eyes and waving hair, her noble and unembarrassed carriage, her courage, and withal feminine grace. I felt I had astonished my neighbor on the right, who opened her eyes, and turned to the left to see if Isabel had thought me equally wild. Her lustrous eyes were fixed upon me in dark earnestness, when her good-natured husband said, "I like a warm heart, my boy, and I hope she deserves all your praise."

"She deserves that I should admire and love her, she saved my life," I said, somewhat sheepishly. "But you will judge for yourself, she is to be presented the day after tomorrow."

The young Lord looked puzzled, the Marchioness talked rapidly, and Lady

Davenport wondered what sort of dress a Spanish belle would wear, as she had never seen but elderly minister's wives, they discussed the plans for the evening, and the ladies got up to leave the three lords of the creation to discuss a few glasses of wine in hebdomadal stupidity.

The Marquis was a great hunter, and at once attacked me on my western campaign. I was not sorry to be able to explain to a certain degree, how sisterly kind Rose had been, and how unhappy the loss of her child and husband, that I believed she intended to become a votary of religion, wherever she could do so and be of use, and her father could spare her. I was in hopes of all this being repeated.

The Marquis seemed to like my stories, and told me he would call on me, he said this as we were going toward the drawing room.

"That fellow has no more feeling than my glove, but there is no harm in him for all that, he does well enough for the old lady to talk at." And he gave me a dig in the side in the warmth of confidence.

I was called to the side of Lady Davenport.

"Now was not this the prettiest dressing case of its kind we saw? Isabel wants to persuade me that it is masculine looking, fancy how easy it is to call names masculine looking, when there is no soap-brush, and no razor nor tweezers. She says it ought to have had buhl cupids, and hearts, and darts, and lyres, and laurel. Isabel, there you are talking to your husband, as eagerly as if he wanted a separation."

"Pray Dora, is there a comet going on?"

Lady Dorothea gravely asked her brother, who said,

"Certainly."

"Well," said the Marquis, "let me have a look at the box, nobody has so much taste as me."

"Well said, and true," broke in the Countess.

The new critic set the dressing case question at rest by unqualified admiration, with the serious counsel that it should be a profound secret, or all the young couples in town would run wild in similar cases. A few people came in, and there was some gossip. There had been a dinner at Buckingham House, and his Majesty had made a speech, and there was much nodding and whispering, meantime I had sat down near the Marchioness.

"I must see you some day, and have some serious talk with you, if the Marquis calls upon you tomorrow or next day, on Saturday you may return his visit. If you come at three o'clock, we may have a walk in the gardens, for it is a beautiful villa we have near Esher. Remember!" she added, as some persons drew near.

They were all interested by some report, which notwithstanding Lord Melbourne's injunction, had vaguely got abroad, and even the Marquis looked serious, and said, it must be altogether incorrect. The time was waning, and it became necessary to think of home. A light running carriage with two fast horses were to take them to where they should be sung to sleep by the nightingale, and awakened by the thrush.

"They have announced the carriage, Isabel."

They slipped out of the room as if for an elopement.

The old lady told me to come often, in an undertone, she liked to see me, and I too took my leave. But there was no use hurrying. I was too late for the priest.

Michael looked as if he expected I had met with some accident, to have forgotten an appointment with a priest he could hardly conceive, as in all his irregularities and want of memory, which were of considerable amount, I do not suppose such a neglect as this had yet burthened his conscience.

"I fear Father Delayney will think me very remiss, but I have been detained by the arrival of a Spanish lady, a stranger in London, to whom I owe more than my life, and could not help it, she is a good Catholic too."

At this last observation, Michael's eyes sparkled, and he said, "Perhaps the father may be known to them, or may be of use."

I said, "Very probably, and that I would write a note before I went to bed, which Michael might take or send in the morning, that I would be at his house in the cab by half-past one to take him with me, if it would be more convenient than his calling here."

I then ordered my horse at eight, and jumped into bed, and without suffering a single memory or thought, began to repeat numbers by rota, until sleep banished the power of this simple unimaginative recapitulation.

Chapter Seventy-One
Old Maud—Father Delayney—Rose—Mr. Searle

Shortly after ten next morning, I was by the side of the little fire, not unagreeable in its small lively crackling, and overhung by that blackened pan which seemed forever in use, the resource and the stand-by of the widow and what remained of her brood.

She was seated, and her look was calm, "I have not been long back, I saw my cousin Lord, he was not the brother I knew best, but a year younger, I told him neither nephew nor brother would have had a penny, had I told his uncle of things I knew."

"He said, 'That concerned them, not him.'"

"I said, 'T was rightfully his cousin, and but for some mumbling words, would have been in a different place.'"

"'Is that all?' he inquired."

"I said, 'Yes, and enough, for all I want of you', and I told him a few pounds would enable me to get back my grandson, who was the support of my old age.

"He said, 'There is no end to these sort of claims, once admitted.'"

"I told him I was as proud as himself, and only asked what I thought he ought to be glad to give. He turned away and shook his head, and I turned too, but he called after me, *Maud*—for he remembered my name well, though he pretended to doubt my being the person, or indeed that there had ever been such a one.

"'I may be able to do something for you, if you come here in a few days.'"

"I said, 'Will you be still here?'"

"He said, 'Yes.'"

"'Well,' I said, 'I will thank you kindly when it comes.'
"I knew he was up to some mischief.
"'And will you really wait?' I said.
"'No! I will move in an hour on my road to Boxhill.'
"'And have you any one you can trust to?'
"'I trust as little as I can, but I have a lock of my boy's hair, he gave it to me with his own hand, and it was beautiful, that hand which had never done any hard work but handling a cudgel, he was not allowed scissors to cut it himself, nor could he well, in his heavy irons, but a jailor, for they liked him, though they dreaded him too, did it for him, he gave it to me to keep as a token, I put it in my bosom, and I never remember more than the sad hazel eyes that looked so loving, but had lost their blitheness, mine were dry, I was burning with fever, and they took me away, it was weeks before I knew anything, and then I was widowed, but I had ever known the knot of hair, and they tamed me when I was wildest, I heard, by threatening to take it away. Many a mat I worked, and many a fortune I told to get a locket in which to put the hair, just as he tied it, for it was his own knot that is on it still, but I was wasting with grief, and losing what was now of no value, my youth and my beauty's pride, but the locket was made, and I put the hair in it myself and saw it fastened, and it has never been from my neck since. It is a fearful thing to me, but I must run the risk, but I believe the poor fellow is honest, and he is only to show this, and tell my poor Tom to come back, that I forgive him if he brings it with him, besides, a word or two which he could only hear from me, and will make him believe in the message.'

"She held out her hand and received the small purse, in which were ten sovereigns, and put it in her bosom.

"'It is far to Boxhill, but when I send for you, it will be to pay you your gold again I hope, and bless you for what you have done, something tells me when I look at you, that I shall be able to do you a good turn, now I am awaiting for my messenger, and he need not see you, so farewell till I can send you some good news."

She gathered her cloak round her as she spoke, and as I retook the path by which I came, I saw her disappear in a different direction.

I had now to ride back to be home in time, in case Father Delayney should go there in preference to my fetching him from his own apartments. I arrived about half-past twelve, and found my man already in Holies Street, he had probably been discoursing with my servant about the chance of a conversion, but accosted me with that ease, which shewed a man of the world. He was tall, slightly corpulent, and rosy.

He said, "You see from my appearance that a walk would do me good, and I have the day to myself, as there is a friend who will attend to any sick calls in my absence, and I came early, that we may not be hurried, so as to have any serious conversation rattling over the stones."

"Oh, I ought to apologize for troubling you on such a matter, as it does not appear directly to bear upon my own interests, but there died a young man in America, who left, I believe, no family except a mother, who has taken the vows in some convent in England, and whatever property he may have left ought to belong to her, and my object is to try and find out this mother, the youth would have been five-and-twenty had he been now alive, and his mother about forty-two or forty-three."

"Well, sir, I must see first that there is nothing to tempt the nun to think with reluctance on her vow, next I must find out where she is, and consider what is the best way, discovering whether there is anything worth enquiring after, and then I will let you know."

We drove to the Burlington Hotel and found the carriage of the Spanish ladies just leaving, so that they had but just returned from their morning drive.

Father Delayney spoke Spanish, so I thought he would be the more useful to the strangers. I begged the Father to remain a moment in the ante-room, till I mentioned his having come to offer his services. Rose seemed much pleased at the thought, and the poor Spaniard was inexpressibly delighted, so that the easy manners and benevolent look of the reverend gentleman, met the most welcome reception, the Countess, who was very regular in her attendance of church, was delighted that she could find a chapel close by in Warwick Street, and that of her own embassy in Spanish Place, and we turned over the Irish priest to become the guide of his brother ecclesiastic. Rose and I in the meantime getting into a corner, in order that I might explain to her how we were involved about Bernard's parentage, and how necessary it appeared for me to learn who he was, and how he had been singled out and worked upon to be my persecutor, and from whence he got the funds.

I found her a good deal shocked at a recurrence to the name, but she said, "You have offered to give this all up if it pains me, it does pain me, but it would pain me more, did I think I stood in the way of your research, so you must refer Father Delayney to me, and I think I can satisfy him that it is a becoming duty in a nun to do good to all, and in every way."

"Then I had better leave you to manage it your own way, shall I come back this evening, for I have a quantity of adventures to tell you?"

"Oh, surely, come back about eight if you can, as we are early, I have seen the Signora Conchas, you are a great favorite there, but come at eight." I slipped out of the room, leaving the cab, if the two priests thought themselves capable of its navigation, quite at their service.

Walking to see Harry, to whom I related what I had done about Bernard's mother.

"I am thinking, it would be best not to ask to see Rose, as you say she is not quite seared of those sad wounds of the Popoagee."

"That is a kindly thought, but I will find out, as she must have a regard for you, and would otherwise be right glad."

He made me stay dinner, which he had served in his own room in Park Street from a coffee house, and we had two sofas with a table between us, and though we sat up to dinner, it was with cross legs on the seat, and then a dressing gown and a segar. I however thought it best to put on an evening dress, as the Countess looked as if she would like such little attentions to rule. I was, however, not too late, and found Rose seated at a table, on which were quantities of pieces of vellum, she was cutting these into a certain size, preparatory to their being written upon, and ruling them lightly, so as to guide and terminate the lines.

"You see my work, when there is light, is writing a missal in black letter, and illuminating it, I can shew you tomorrow copies from Gotto and Fra Anjelica, but at night I can do little except cut out."

The Navahoe here shewed me a piece of tapestry-looking blanket which she was working, and which she was justly proud of, she approved highly of the colors of worsted in England, and faithful to her early habits, had procured a flower piece of the most gaudy brilliancy she could find to pull to pieces to compose a pattern of her own invention, turning an immense group of dahlias into prisms angular, obtuse and acute, squares and circles, and sections of circle, with the ready variety of a kaleidoscope, and without pattern or mark.

While I was looking at this, Rose said, "I have shown the good priest you brought us, that he might benefit the community of the poor nun, by letting some knowledge be obtained of her whereabouts, but you must forgive me for having acceded to a stipulation he made, that I myself should be the agent in carrying on this search, and that no one else should know where the monastery, nor what the assumed name of the nun, and that under this assurance he would make every research in his power, and her being a foreigner, narrowed the extent and difficulty of the undertaking."

We passed the remainder of the evening in an account of the castle, and its dependant town in Andalusia, where her father had been born, and the noble mules, which looked down with contempt upon the Spanish horse, and excited the respect even of the Navahoe. We agreed that it would be a sad blow to the Countess a London chapel, after Seville and Toledo, and I felt glad, feeling that I could make these two forlorn women happier by the sympathy of affection in that cold London, which is death to any foreigner, who has not a title to be feted, and who does not give himself up to society.

I had explained that there was no capital in the world more open to a name or a celebrity, and where there is more kindness shown to any one with such pretensions, but that quiet intimacy was a labor of years.

Rose had informed me, that her father had made her promise to enter a little into the London world, and to be presented at Court, but that for some little time she hoped this might be put off. She warned me not to talk of their inquiries about Bernard's mother, and I left them anxiously expecting the Countess, who had gone to the Spanish Embassy.

Next day produced a summons from Mr. Searle, and from him I learned that the butler of my father who had left after the fire, had gone to America, and there all trace ceased, that some papers had been discovered in his house, which had been secreted in the wall behind the sliding panel of a press, but they were of no value, being only a lease of his house, granted by my father, and some memorandums, which appeared to have been written on a piece of paper which had been used to wrap up the other document, they consisted of jottings, apparently of transactions specifying certain quantities of tallow, corn, wine, cotton, and hides, at stated prices, also certain mercantile houses, and the word *St. Martins*, and then a date-month and year defaced—*St. Martin's-day*.

"This seems of no use, but as a specimen of your father's hand. The lease was dated 1822, and had expired, being only for ten years, so the persons now in possession gave it up without difficulty to Townley, the keeper of the Shuttle, who had declared that he valued highly any document in the old Squire's hand. I have some agents at work, and there are some hopes of a trace as to the arson, but as I promised, I have not pushed on in anyway so as to force matters into premature disclosure, but I can see no harm in finding out who were the agents in this affair, and probably some documents may be found by giving up a criminal prosecution. But it requires someone to be trusted to go with the officer, and perhaps the best person would be yourself. I do not know when it may be, but if you choose I can let you know."

I at once assented, partly from interest in such a research, and partly to prevent anything being brought out about Isabel.

"Well," said Mr. Searle, "I think, early next week, we can start on a track, and you shall have timely notice."

Chapter Seventy-Two
Isabel tells—and asks—a proof of confidence

It was Saturday, the day appointed for my visit to the villa. There were plenty of coaches down to Guildford, and one dropped me not far from where the villa was situated.

I learned that there was a beautiful garden, and that both the Marquis and Marchioness were very fond of flowers. The grounds were surrounded by a high park paling, and a quantity of black-looking fir and other evergreens threw a gloomy shade over the approach, and contrasted strongly with the tender greens of the deciduous trees. After winding for half a mile, the road came upon the gravel space in front of the house.

A servant had brought out an Italian greyhound to have a little exercise, and he was gambolling about.

I asked if the Marquis was at home, and was told he had gone to town.

I inquired if it would be possible to see the garden, the man said the orders were, not when there was any one of the family about, and the Marchioness has just gone out.

I immediately begged that my card might be taken to the Marchioness, and I would await the answer.

The man disappeared through a side door, saying he would be back in a minute, and presently there came out a grave-looking servant, out of livery, who said the Marchioness had mentioned that I might go into the flower-garden, if I wished, should neither herself or the Marquis be in the way, he opened the door as he spoke, and I entered a passage which, without passing through the main building, led into a sort of open cloister, which was screened by a thicket through which the passage led, this arcade was the communication between the villa and a wing, which though old-fashioned, was, in fact, a conservatory. The flower-garden was embosomed in wood, aided in its height by the rising of the ground around it, in the shape of a horseshoe, for the greatest part, and bounded at the open end by a piece of water, and the wild heath and woods of Claremont beyond.

This garden was entirely devoted to flowers, and of course merely showed the forms of the different beds, and their promises of spring in various stages, the plants put under shelter during winter had reappeared in their rows or groups of terra-cotta, and some activity had been shown to meet the efforts of nature in every variety—but no hand was visible—the feathered tribe and myself seemed the sole living occupants of the space.

I passed downward over the smooth turf toward the water, where various kinds of wild fowl were employed in hatching, while others swam about, all this was peaceful and beautiful, and the clear water was dimpled with the movements of tame carp, a few pheasants also walked about, as if they expected to be fed. Altogether, had I been less troubled about the promised interview I could have enjoyed the scene—not an air stirred a leaf, and the afternoon sun shone warm in the sheltered spot.

I sat down on the steps of a ruined portico, most of whose columns were cut off before their prime, and spoke the language of dilapidation with the air of as much truth as any others, whether at Corinth or in Windsor Park, and the seat was near the odour of violets, which grew under its shaded side. The strange cry of the coot, the song of the thrush, and the pheasant's scream, with the lulling cooing of the wood-pigeon, formed a rural convocation of considerable extent.

I was giving way to the calm influence of this scene, and beginning to forget what I was about, when I saw two bright plumaged pheasants rush across before me, as if attracted by some promise of food, and following their course with my eye, perceived Isabel at the other extremity of the steps, looking amused at the start with which I announced having seen her.

"You had forgotten mighty London, and everything in it, and might have remained till dark in that trance. Pray, did you believe yourself among the ruins of Carthage," said that mocking voice, which, whatever tone it assumed, thrilled to my heart of hearts.

"No," I answered. "But I have had one object, and one thought, so constant in my breast, that when I was cooed just now into a musing mood, I felt as if I was gone on a distant voyage, from which your appearing called me suddenly back. How beautiful and calm all this is," I added, as she did not speak.

"Calm!" she said, looking at me with an almost fierce wonder in her dark grey eye.

I was taken aback, and muttered something.

"Yes, I forgot," she said, and shook the heavy hair from off her temples.

"You have come from town, and there are no cockatoos here, so it is comparatively calm. But you did not look for me diligently, or you would have seen where I was, and there are not many hours to lose. Let us move about. I really believed you were dead. It is a long story mine: My mother long gone, and never known—a father who idolized me—no wonder then he obtained a power far greater than parental authority. But I wander into my own history, instead of explaining anything of yours, suffice it to say, my father had mixed himself up with yours, in a desire to prevent you coming to form an attachment, which both parents—at all events mine—believed to be most untoward, and I was prevailed upon to play a part, and also to conceal a knowledge of the fact. I consented, and you had seen me from the nursery garden, and then at the common. All this was begun in mere wantonness, as well as to oblige my father. It was continued—"

Here she paused, but rallying herself with a proud look. "Because I began to take an interest in you myself, and when that interest ripened to a warmer feeling, I determined to save you, and by that means see whether you had really a love for another. I thought you had escaped the plan of seizure—heard you had followed your fair one beyond seas—and saw the account of your having been blown up in a steamer on the Potomac. I remained partly cured of my young liking for you by pride. Various changes took place, and for more than a year I never saw my father, who had gone to the West Indies, and thence to Brazil. I got letters pretty regularly from him through a mercantile house which took charge of them, and to whom they were directed. Before my father's return he had succeeded to the marquisate of his brother, who had obtained the reversion to him to be included in the patent. I know nothing of our family history. My father asked me if I had any objection to marry. I asked to what sort of a man?

"'An elderly man,' he answered, 'of the best Irish blood and old Marquisate, but one of the best of good and honorable people, and should my affairs carry me abroad, or should the attacks of apoplexy, by which I have been warned, take me away from you altogether, you have husband, father, brother, all in one, all my property going only to heirs male, you would be but slenderly off should anything occur, and I do not conceal that it would be a consolation and comfort to me I cannot describe, to see you settled, and so well settled in life.'

"Of course I have divested my account of the tender expressions he used, and which I knew were true. 'Nay,' he added, upon seeing me hesitate. 'I will not weigh for a second my happiness against yours. You have loved someone else?' And he fixed eyes upon me which, however they were wont to beam upon me the softest expression of love, seemed at this moment to read my inmost thoughts. Fearful of an extorted confession, I declared myself free from any such feelings, and ready, if I found nothing disagreeable in my proposed husband, to entertain the thought. I found my lover elderly, to be sure, but light-hearted, and elegant in his manners—altogether, what is called an accomplished man—and, to cut the matter short, we were married, and he has more than confirmed all the hopes of making a happy union—he is loyal, trusting, generous, and good-tempered. Now, had you been bad-hearted enough to publish the little conspiracy in which I took part, or should you be so, you see you would make me perhaps appear in a bad light to one whom I would not for the world make unhappy. So I have begged of you to come, that we might have this explanation."

She had spoken rapidly and we were moving about, as if talking of the place, to all appearance. I was confused by this new light thrown on the Wimbledon affair, and could only express my surprise, also adding that I hardly knew any young person of the other sex, except Miranda, and that there never had been any love passages between us, that I had not escaped, as she thought, but had been taken to a madhouse—let out on a promise to go quietly away—and had obeyed my father's letter to that effect, not having had any other motive for going abroad but obedience to his commands.

There was now a pause I saw the cheek flush red, and then pale—a slight tremor of a nosegay of violets betrayed, with a faltering step, an emotion Isabel in vain tried to conceal, but sitting down on one of those china seats which presented itself for once usefully, she said, "Go—go away a little distance, and look for some lily of the valley. I shall be composed in a minute—this scene has been too much for me."

I saw she was anxious, and moved off a few paces, as if on a search, almost needing as much as my companion to collect my thoughts. But a signal brought me again to her side as she arose.

"Dear Edward," she said, "I know you will not give me useless pain. I fear my father has been led by some cause unknown to me, to take some strange part in regard to you, and happily I have not told him of having seen you. Do put me also out of dread of your taking any step against him, unless in self-defense—remember how we have both been deceived, he may have been so also."

I assured her I would never let any consideration induce me to call her father to any account, even could I prove anything against him.

"I knew you would do what was right about myself, or I never could have left you a day without the promise, but this is generous about my father and I shall watch that you do not suffer by it. Now, perhaps, we have been here unaccountably long, so let me show you the way out."

We were moving toward the angle of the garden which came on the right-hand side of the front, it was a wing of similar shape as the conservatory, and the windows opened upon steps leading to the shaved turf.

"That is my own more particular sitting-room, and it opens from my dressing room. Do you see this key-hole cover—it is pushed aside, and this key opens the door, the usual entrance is by the middle window, this is never opened but by myself or his Lordship, and indeed, I do not know, as I have never used it, why he gave me this key, except to show me how entirely free I am. Now listen—perhaps I may require to see you, and that you may not be seen—not by my husband, mind, but by others, it may be at night. If such summons reaches you, do not hesitate, but come here straight, I shall show you the way." She strode on with increased speed, through a thicket of box and yew, by a small path green and slippery with a sort of velveteen moss, which after a few windings joined one better kept, and apparently more used, this took an almost straight course, beneath pine-trees, toward the outer enclosure, and here again there was another key to use.

"Now remember," she said, suddenly turning upon me those eyes, always expressive, but now lambent with excitement, "I am giving you a proof of confidence, which however nothing but your extreme peril could justify me in letting you use. Here is the other key, when you are summoned, come, unlock the window, and enter—there will be a curtain drawn. If I am not there, wait, there is no fear of any one, but try and be as punctual as you can, should I send—which God forbid should be necessary—but I am sure to see you soon. I forgot my husband had taken a liking to you, and you may have to be here a day or two on a visit."

A smile, almost as of yore, passed over her features, but shone not in her eyes, she shut the door almost with precipitation, on hearing voices on the public road—the key she had flung at my feet—and I was to find my way to London in a state of still greater perplexity than before.

Chapter Seventy-Three
Complications—messages—Sister Magdalene

Easily getting a seat, I gave myself up to a reverie, which had hardly ended, when I was let out somewhere near Vauxhall.

I had ordered a beefsteak at home, in the expectation of needing some quiet after an interview with Isabel. How little did she need being raised in my estimation. I would have excused almost crime in her, so much I loved her, but to find that, although believing herself played with in her dearest affections and slighted for another, she had been ready to forego the reprisal put in her power, and what was more, the means of preventing a rival's success, was a high-mindedness for which I was quite unprepared.

I was finishing my solitary meal, when Mr. Searle sent up to know if I could see him. I knew there must be something of importance to bring him to me in this way.

"My dear Mr. Jones," he began, "I make no apology for intruding on your quiet, but I sent an hour ago to beg you to step round to the office, and as my time was free, I have run here instead of waiting for you. A proclamation has appeared in the *Gazette*, offering a free pardon to any one of the persons who were concerned in setting fire to the house of the late Edward Neville Warren, Esq., in the neighborhood of Knutsford, upon giving such evidence as would bring his accomplices to be convicted. What do you think of that? There is someone moving in the matter besides us."

"I suppose one of the nearest heirs," I said, "but we may get at the papers should it come to any trial."

"Yes, but it is quite clear that you, of all others, must keep out of the way, and by rights you would be best out of town, though not far. As soon as any one is taken up I will offer myself agent to defend—and we will see. Now I do not say that it is necessary, absolutely, for you to be away, but keep as much out of the way of any of your father's friends as you can."

I explained that I did not wish to leave Holies Street at present, till some reason should appear for it.

"My opinion is," said Mr. Searle, gravely, "that some party or parties have got a suspicion that we are mining, and that this proclamation and trial is to be a counter-mine—else we are altogether out. You must give up coming to my office, a penny-post letter, or one sent by a common porter, will keep you warned of when I may be expected, and if you are out, or busy, an answer by a porter will be the best way of your communicating."

I was soon ready to go to Burlington Street, and Rose seemed anxious to know what had taken place at Pine Lodge, the name of the Marquis's villa. I had never told of my love for Isabel, but with that quick perception in such matters which women possess, I saw she had a guess, which of course she tried to hide.

She was going the evening after next, Monday, to the Spanish Embassy, Sunday, she hoped to be able to get through by means of the illumination and the Conchas, and had written to offer herself for the early part of the evening, a servant brought in the answer as she was speaking. They hoped the Countess and Rose would come to dinner, so I offered to go with them, and the evening passed with a little conversation and a little music.

A fortnight had elapsed, and we were in the blithe month of May. I had led a life almost blank, and began to think that an universal lethargy had taken possession of every one in whose movements I was much interested—it was a Saturday.

Upon getting into my breakfast room in the morning, after a rather late party of the previous night, I found on my table a newspaper, a prettily-folded note, another from Golden Square, and a dirty post letter.

I opened first the Golden Square missive—the trial was to be next assizes, they had apprehended two persons for arson and robbery at my father's, and Mr. Searle was off to Chester.

The letter was, I suppose, from the old woman, now of Boxhill, and read—

T—— is come back. Blessing be upon you! I want to see you, we are not hard to find.

It was written possibly by herself, for though a trembling, it was not a bad hand, and evidently female.

The last I took up, I had left after the others, as probably an invitation, and I opened it without interest.

Something has occurred which renders it necessary we should meet. I shall await you tomorrow at nine.

I was then to go again to Pine Lodge, and be again alone with its mistress. Twice I had been down during the last ten days, to visit the good Marquis, who though a man of sixty, had all the vivacity and fire of youth, and I had on the last occasion learned that Lord GiIsland was still abroad.

I was now going down—though for no bad purpose—in the secresy of a stolen visit, clandestinely to have an interview with the wife of a confiding host, my intentions were pure—so I was sure were hers, but at what a risk was such a meeting to be held, and if discovered, could it be cleared of suspicion? But go I must.

While I was musing on the chances of detection, and the dread of evil arising to one whom I in vain tried not to love with engrossing ardour, the door was quietly opened by Michael, and in walked Father Delayney.

"I have come to you first, because you are probably earliest. I found the search was the most difficult matter, and as I had undertaken it and had funds supplied, I was bound not to spare trouble. I found, at last, there was a Sister Magdalene in a convent near York, who answered to the description of the person of whom we were in search, but upon my presenting myself to make some inquiries, I found that of all others she was the least accessible to any worldly considerations, that a handsome sum was paid annually for her support, and that there was nothing like a disposition to communicate further. This was disheartening, but I persevered. I gave snuff to the old porteress, till my coming was looked for by her, and I got a pair of spectacles for the Confessor, which made him see what he never could make out before, and the Abbess herself promised me an interview. This was my great object. I thought I could paint accounts of rosaries, relics, and missals, and hint at an organ, in short, I saw my way, could I once be listened to. Success generally crowns good temper and perseverance, always remember that," said the kind-hearted priest. "I was at last told the Superior would see me, and I was ushered into the parlour. She was an old Flemish dame, fattish, and with coarse features.

"'You have been very anxious about communicating something to Sister Magdalen,' she began, hardly looking at me.

"'I was so, but am now no longer so,' I answered.

"She looked up in some surprise. 'You have changed your purpose then?'

"'No, but I had no expectation of being honored by an interview with the Abbess, now that I have it in my power, my business will be much more satisfactorily laid before her.'

"The cold grey eyes again fell modestly upon the beads which she held in her hand.

"'The fact is, I have a friend, she is a beautiful worker in illuminations, by the bye, who holds some property—not a great fortune, it is true—which she conscientiously believes belonged to her husband, who died in America, and all she wants is, that I, or any Catholic clergyman you may choose to appoint, should be made acquainted with the statement of Sister Magdalen, to be able to verify that we believe that whoever she appoints ought to receive this sum.'

"'It is a subject which requires consideration. You are aware that a living husband could force his wife, against her vows, into a court of justice, and perhaps oblige her to return to her home.'

"'That is the reason I have been so glad to see the Superior herself, who can consider the matter calmly, and no one knows anything but myself of this visit. Perhaps I may say, that the sum would be small in most hands, but laid out with judgment, might conduce to the comfort as well as assist the piety of the Sisterhood.'

"'Perhaps you can call again tomorrow,' said the Abbess, rising. She was already impatient to have the matter put to the test.

"I officiated at vespers in the chapel, and afterward had a chat with the porteress, who hardly knew the name of the king, believing George to be the proper name of all English monarchs. Next morning, after daily mass, I was summoned to the parlour.

"'There is no danger as to the law about husbands, they are both dead, but I really forget what she said, perhaps she would come and tell you herself.' And she rang a small bell, someone knocked, and the Abbess went to the door and said something, presently another summons, and she then opened the door, bringing in Sister Magdalen.

"'The Sister will perhaps explain such particulars as she thinks may be of use in clearing up the birth of her son.'

"'I had two—of which?' asked a sweet voice in a foreign accent.

"'I really am at a loss, but of one who died in America?'

"'Ah! that must have been Bernard, my eldest, he would have been more than twenty-five now, my other poor boy never saw his father and scarcely his mother, he died young, that child's death, in heretic hands, is my greatest grief, let no good Catholic ever marry a Protestant of this country. My child, oh! what I have suffered for that sin.' A signal from the Abbess made the poor Sister retire.

"She had been a person of fine appearance, as far as could be discovered through her disfiguring garb.

"'Yes, the poor Sister has never, she thinks, sufficiently atoned for that false step, she was from the time she committed it, a wife without a husband, and became a mother without a child, but I think it was of the first marriage you wished to know. Are you satisfied?'

"'It only wants names, which are so easily forgotten, that I have not been able to remember about which I was to enquire, if I was furnished with a memorandum of the names, the answer could be sent, if one of them tallied, at once. And would you also say where you would have the sum lodged?'

"'Yes, certainly, that is but reasonable.'

"And she left the room, bringing back in a couple of minutes a paper, upon which was written the address of a banker at Leeds, into whose hands the money was to be paid to the credit of the Abbess. Beneath was written Baron Warulf, Mr. Edward Nevil, and nothing more, and here is the paper, and the worthy Priest shewed me the document, adding, 'I have not been to the Donna Rosalie as yet.'

"I thanked him for his friendly search.

"You see I had to write down Bernard," and there was in his hand the name written across the end of the paper.

Then Bernard was accounted for, but not his connection with me. I put the facts down on paper, as far as I had been told, but I did not state who or what the mother of Bernard was, nor where to be found, and sent the note to Golden Square.

Chapter Seventy-Four
A secret rendezvous—a surprise

I was now to leave town for Esher, and loiter about till the period named for the meeting. I must here hurry to that scene, which had so much to do with my future fate, I found the door without meeting any one, and entered the dark walk, and had proceeded some distance, when some person, probably a watcher, crossed my path, I stopped near the windows and sprung my repeater, it wanted more than a quarter of nine, and I waited, at last it was nine, and I opened the window and went into the room, there was a light, but so screened, as to prevent distinguishing persons, my eye, unaccustomed to such obscurity, could scarcely make anything out, but I sat down in a shaded part near the window, awaiting Isabel, I will not say without a beating heart. It was not long before a door at the other end opened, and I felt that some of those mysterious sensations awakened, which communicate by the eye, as well as by the touch. I rose, but did not move from my position, so favorable for retreat.

"Do not fear, the door-window shuts with a spring, and is not to be opened outside without a key, what a wind has sprung up." We heard the blast through the trees. "I am obliged to you for coming, you know my father thinks he is not safe from a prosecution about the Wimbledon affair, and some of his people have told him—for he is but just arrived in town—that you are here, and you have no idea what a state it has put him in. I did not say you visited us, it would have made him wild, and so I have begged you to come, that we may be able to lay some plan for your keeping out of the way, or re-assuring him of not taking any steps. I never closed my eyes last night, and upon you now rests the saving his reputation and mine, upon giving your word of secrecy, as to the past, something may be done, but I doubt even that."

"O, Isabel," I said, much moved, "can you doubt how far I would go, even in self-injury to save you a pang, you whom I have ever loved since the first time I saw you."

"Pray listen, I did not seek for protestations, the Spanish Rosalie ought to have every affection of your heart."

"Yes, but hear me too but once, do you remember, when I told you the other day, that she had sent her craven husband to save my life, when I was on the steps of that ladder I never once thought of her, and the mind which in a supreme moment of agony, points true its strongest impressions reverted to the last time we were together."

She interrupted, "Well, dear Ned, I believe you, but this is worse than foolishness to recur to such thoughts. Oh, let them be forever banished, you would not give me pain for my father or my good and noble husband, do not lead me to give pain to myself." She pressed her hand tight to her side. "You will promise to go out of the way for ten days, till after the Derby, which is next week by the bye. Now promise, I cannot tell what, but I dread everything, my father has appeared different to what he has ever been, and I dread evil as much for you, as agony for myself. If I may not be able to get him out of England again, without something happening between you, he absolutely looked demoniac. Will you promise?"

"Yes, anything you desire, is more than a law to me," I said, with a despairing heart.

"Nay, I will just tell you once and forever, you do not sorrow alone, one thing and another has brought the avowal from my inner heart, and therefore, let such conversations, and all such intercourse as might lead to such, end between us, that we may be able to meet as the truest of true friends in the open day. Now let us say farewell, but let there not be a scene. I shall sit down on this sofa and ring, as soon as you shut the door, but lay the key of the inner door there, on the table, leave the other in the lock inside, it will shut with pulling to."

She was deadly pale, and I hurried to leave her, that she might ring and get that aid I dared not offer.

A loud and cold wind was blowing. I saw lights moving through the joinings of the shutters, and I fled, a disappointed, but not an unhappy man. The door opened, I shut it again with the key inside, I got to town by dog-cart and post-chaise together, a little after midnight.

Next day was Sunday, and therefore I had to go early to see Rose, and appointed my horse to come to meet me at Spanish Place. My wardrobe for a ten days' absence was not difficult to put up, and I selected Guildford as my first halt, my luggage was left at the Burlington, and Michael, who was too well meaning to be always cautious, I left on board wages till my return. Rose appeared more serious than I had ever seen her, she was kneeling when I came into the church, and occupied in earnest prayer, but on seeing me, held out her hand with that expression of pleasure, which though tinged with melancholy, was ever my greeting. I waited till the service was over, and then we went out together and walked toward Oxford Street, I told her that I had been ordered out of town, and begged she would take any opportunity of getting acquainted with Isabel which might offer, and let me know the opinion she formed of her, as well as any news of her father's movements. The carriage was following, and we got in, and drove to the hotel, I parted with Rose at the foot of the stairs, and desired a cab to be called, with a view of going to Piccadilly to await the starting of a coach.

A waiter at this moment said, there was a gentleman wished to see me in one of the parlours adjoining the lobby. What was my surprise to find Lord Connemara, he had not his usual cheery look, and his air though not unfriendly, had something of constraint in it, waiting till the door was shut, he placed a chair by the window, where there already was another, to which he pointed courteously enough, in a way to invite me to sit down, and then placed himself in the one by my side.

Muttering that it was always best to come at once to the point, he said, "Mr. Jones, I was present at your meeting with my wife last night."

I started with an expression of surprise which was too evident to my companion to be passed over.

"Your surprise shews me you think you have been betrayed, it is not so, I was there by accident, I saw someone loitering about, and went into the Marchioness's room to watch, before I had been long there, the window was opened, and you entered and sat down, looking anxiously at the door, I was mystified and confounded, and before making up my mind what course to adopt, Lady Connemara came in, I was in one respect at once set at rest, I ought at first to have told you by your demeanour the one to the other, but I learned what has deeply pained me, however, that cannot be helped, there is no one to blame—but that villain of a father—God forgive me, but I must be a little calm. My poor wife was much moved, and had a slight fit of faintness, they had rushed in—her people—and I joined, as if brought in by the noise, after her recovery a little, she looked me full in the face, my eye fell under hers."

"'I see you are aware of the meeting I have had,' she said, calmly.

"'Yes, I was present,' I answered.

"'Then all the purpose of it is lost, and you will be the avenger, instead of Ned. I mean Mr. Jones.'

"'No, I will be as considerate with you as he was, but we must set off for Ireland forthwith.'

"'That is well, but some means must be taken to keep that poor young man out of further harm.'

"'Will you trust that to me?' I asked. She pressed my hand, and for the first time burst into tears.

"'Here I am, my dear, with a good heart and ready hand for you, but not a plan in life.' And the worthy man looked ingenuously kind, and almost pitying at me."

Just at this moment I happened to turn my eyes toward the window, and saw Michael pacing up and down in some anxiety, I asked leave to open the window to tell him to go as I did not want him, when the Marquis asked if that was not an Irishman.

I said, "yes," as I opened the window, but I found that my companion was the object of attraction, as he made a profound bow to his Lordship.

"Ah, my friend Mic O'Rurk, is he your servant," he added, turning briskly to me.

"Yes," I said.

"Then tell him to speak to me at the door."

I had no need, for Mic was there, the Marquis went out and had a few minutes' conversation with him, and then came back.

"I never have any idea, as they call it, but look about, and am sure to find one. Now listen, that fellow is good and true, though I would not answer for his discretion, he, however during my absence, is to watch about and find what that man—I will not trust myself to call names—is about, and when he leaves Wimbledon Villa. I find Mic's priest is known to you, write him a note and beg him to send any information Mic may communicate to him for me by letter to you, without telling Mic where you are. Mic knows the connection, and is charmed to be a family confidant, his intructions are only to watch his movements, and report. Now Mr. Jones, you see it is best we should be far apart, my dear and good wife is well pleased to enter upon the duties of an Irish proprietress, and she is anything but Orange, so she will have her hands full, and to spare. I'll give her carte blanche."

I said I could not but reverence and admire the Marchioness, and that he must himself have the satisfaction of feeling that his own conduct had been noble.

He interrupted me, "But all this has not passed on my part without a pang, and that is that here we, mutually esteeming each other, as I hope we do, should have to say farewell." He held out his hand, I felt with no misgiving, and he left the room.

Chapter Seventy-Five
Tom's tale—honesty—meeting a dandy

I was recalled to a recollection of myself, by some common place question of a waiter. I had now nothing to do but write a note to Father Delayney, stating that any news Mic might give him of Lord Gillsland, he might send to me at Guildford, till I informed him I had changed my quarters. This I dispatched by Mic, whom by a signal I had kept in waiting, and then I got into the cab with my portmanteau, and was carried off and deposited at the White Horse Cellars, from whence I was safely lodged in a coach for Guildford. The day after, I mounted a hack to ride to Boxhill, it was a pretty long way, but in one of the most beautiful parts of England. There is nothing more strange than the commons and bits of waste and open woodlands, found so near the corrupt and monstrous London, the cool-fresh green, the odour of the box, and the various flowers which it overshadows, there are many roads through this shrub grove. I went previously, however, to put up my horse at an inn by the river in the bottom, and then climbed up to the top, as the letter said, there was but little difficulty in finding the old woman's whereabouts. I had not proceeded far in my most agreeable search by fragrant and fresh paths, when I saw the sparkling eyes of the little scout, like gems shining among the foliage, as soon as she found she was discovered, she came out laughing, and bounded on before, there was something went to my heart in the artless confidence and joy she shewed, till the plaintive air succeeded, but she still tripped on through the obstructed ways, till a turn as of wont, brought us right upon the eternal kettle, if not the eternal fire.

The eyes of the crone brightened at my approach, the songstress as usual disappeared, and while I sat and asked questions about how things were going on, I perceived the legs of a man protrude from the second shanty, for there were now two, and presently the rich black locks of my former antagonist were shaken outside its profile, and he sprung to his feet with a bound, as if to renew the struggle we had had at our last meeting, his white teeth and brown skin, smiling mouth, and glistening eyes, the slight but sinewy limbs and the well-formed hands which he held out to me, were all cheering in their welcome, and pleasant to see.

"The horse was none the worse?" he said, enquiringly.

"Not the slightest, he had been in good hands."

"I have been late out last night, so am something dim just taken out."

I asked an account of his escape, he said it was easy enough, as he was not in any bad books that road, but at Liverpool I had a find, there lay before me on the street a pocketbook, which I took up, and under the arches of the Exchange opened it inside my overcoat, the name of the owner and address was there, then several bills to bearer, they were for thousands, besides bank notes, it was too great a concern, and I bethought myself I would be sure to get into trouble, I then thought I might burn all but one bank note, and get it changed before it could be known there had been a loss, but I thought that would not be fair, and I resolved to give the book and all it held back to the owner. I walked fast for fear of changing, and just as I came to the street, and was looking for the number, I saw a man come running out of a counting-house with such a face, as I never saw in any shanty of ours, nor in any green lane frequented by our people, even when hunted for their lives, and curious, it was a Mr. Jones, and that partly made me think to do right out of gratefulness.

"Well," I said, "where is Mr. Jones's office, he scarcely heeded me, but was passing on in a haggard stare, I stopped him however.

"And he said, 'What do you want? There it is, let me go.'

"'No,' I said, 'I want to see Mr. Samuel Jones.'

"'Well, but I cannot see you now,' and he struggled to shake me off.

"'Nay, I won't keep you long.'

"'Well, what is it?'

"'I must go into the office. You say you are Jones.'

"'But I want to know—'

"He seemed distracted, but I got him into the house. 'Is this *Mr. S. Jones*?' I said, to the clerks, astonished at my almost pulling in the principal partner into his own office.

"'I believe the man is mad or worse,' he said.

"'No,' I answered, 'I wish to know if Mr. Jones has lost anything today?'

"The poor man bounded at me, as if he wanted to swallow me up, and then put his back against the door, I laughed out, and the clerks themselves seemed amused at the desperation of the chief of the band. 'Do you know what is in it?'

"'I knew what was in it,' said the trembling merchant.

"'That is the same thing,' I said stoutly, feeling I was strong. 'There's the lot.'

"'Well,' said a respectable-looking man, coming out from behind the counter, 'Sit you down, young man, it is better that everything should be clear, so count what you have got, Mr. Jones, and unless the book has passed through other hands, before it was found by you, Sir'—looking at me—'I am satisfied it is all right.'

"The merchant counted with desperate eagerness, three bills, three cheques, and ten fifty-pound notes.

"'All right,' he said, almost convulsively, 'and the time not up neither,' and he rushed out of the office with the pocketbook inside his waistcoat.

"The elderly person who had before interposed, again spoke to me.

"'If you are not very busy, will you call here tomorrow, it would be an advantage to us to know how we might best show our sense of your promptness in returning our property, as any delay would have been very hurtful to our credit just now.'

"I said I should be glad to call, if he liked, about one o'clock, so took my leave. It was on going down to the docks after this, that I saw a person who eyed me pretty close, and who I soon found to be in search of me, Ben is not a bad fellow, so he did not try to get anything out me, but merely said, 'I've a word for you, Tom, from the old woman, and a token.' He showed me the locket, which I took, and told me that I should be welcome back. I knew old granny to be no fool, so I told him I would put back next evening, but I must tell you that when I went back to the Jones's office, the old gentleman was out of his fluster, and they said they wished to know what would do me most service in the way of a remembrance. I said, if they would give me a letter, naming what had happened, it might some time be of use. One of the clerks soon gave me this, and the principal gave me a little parcel with a twenty, and six five-pound notes.

"I was about to say something, when Tom added, 'But wait, Sir, till I show you this!' There was a newspaper in his hand, and I read—

> "*The solicitor of the old gentleman who was robbed and knocked down into a ditch near Vauxhall Bridge, some time since, received a twenty pound note in a letter, left at his office by a person, who immediately disappeared, stating that it was intended to repay the money which had been taken by the person who robbed him, believing himself in desperate need, but who had since found the means of refunding him, and stating his regret that for the occurrence.*

"Now, unless it be for poultry or game, in a very small way, no man in England has a word to say against me." And he tossed his hat high in the air. "There's the Derby the day after tomorrow, I may let your honor in for something worth having, if I get the news I look for. Now if you'll only come round on your nag quietly, and look about you a little on the outside of the course near the rails, between the Red House and the starting-post behind the hill, I will see you, and your book will be no worse of it, but my time's up now, so good day.' And he was off, taking under his arm, what appeared to be a new smock-frock, which, however, he tied up in a red handkerchief.

———

"Here is your gold back," said the grandmother, holding out a purse, "I got it, but hardly given. I said I had need, and they might let me have as much, if all was known, I saw this last word had its effect, and I got it, and there it is."

I hesitated about receiving back the money.

"Nay, take it, perhaps I may need as much again, though God forbid, and then it will be safer in your hands than in mine, for I am best when kept pretty bare."

I took the purse, which was not that which I had given.

"That is one I made myself, it was meant for one who was kind and good to me, though only a boy, but I never had a chance to give it, but keep it in memory of him, as if he had given it to me, it doesn't matter now, as I am about withered up, there have been but few who have cared for me, I make the most of what there are." She checked herself suddenly, as if dreading to say too much. "We will let you know when we move. It is no fun to the like of you," she added, "to come and see the crone, but it would be gladness to me to see you now and again, will you come?"

I readily promised, when I was within reach to come, and we parted as usual, with the short escort of the little vidette, and I carolled along picking up flowers, and enjoying the flight of the birds down the opens, laden with stores for their young, and the flurry of the rabbits, which occasionally shot across the path.

As I turned the last corner before getting to the verge of the cover, I came upon a good-looking well-dressed man, who was picking his way over the damp grass.

"I fear it is very slimy walking, greasy and damp I mean," he said, touching his hat somewhat condescendingly. "There has been some wet weather lately, and the sun does not get in so easy through the box to dry the roads like those outside. I think I must turn, pray can you tell me the shortest and best way to the inn? my boots are thin, you see."

They were indeed both thin and well shaped, he then examined a glove, which had been stained green by some incautious handling of a branch, I was thus shown his gloves and boots, he then pulled off the offending gauntlet, his fingers were well ringed, but rather square at the ends, there was a diamond shone upon one, and there was a seal ring on another, but not engraved. A watch was then produced and consulted, first by the ear to see whether it still went, and then by the eye, which dwelt upon it with satisfaction. I was then looked at, to see the effect of all this personal equipment, or to observe whether I had any chance in a competition.

"I think all the ways are pretty nearly alike," I observed, in answer to his question. "But perhaps the least slippery is the best." A slide down the hill seemed to be a poser, and my new acquaintance actually gave out an odour of musk at the idea, he took off his hat and wiped his brow, flushed and heated by the dread of such a descent.

I ran down to show that by taking the bushes and rougher parts, there was but little fear of the slide, which I have since witnessed in Greenwich Park, and which I suppose he held as the type of all rash descents. He seemed to dread being left alone, for he made desperate attempts to keep near, falling however at the first open space, and staining his fawn-colored pantaloons in a way which his frock-coat immediately concealed, with its proper regard for the parts usually under its protection.

"I suppose we are at the same inn," said my new acquaintance. "I wonder what my lady will say to me, I'm in regular mess."

I was not prepossessed much by the manners of this man, he spoke French, too, and elaborated its pronunciation like a popular deputy—the whole seemed a show-off. He talked of dinner—I would perhaps honor him. His card, in black letter, bore the name of *Mr. Albert Dacre*. I was just going to make some excuse, when the air of *Jonny Faa* was sung, not far up the bank behind, and I saw the eager eyes almost bursting with meaning, and a slight motion of the head pointing upward.

I knew this must be a summons, and that no light matter would have caused it to be made. Making the excuse of having left something above, I hastily remounted the hill, the little girl busying herself in picking up flowers.

"I will be down again immediately," I said to the astonished dandy, and doubled the strides to put it out of his power to follow, having, at the top, the satisfaction to see that he had not attempted to do so.

I had not proceeded far into the covert when I met Tom full in the face, he sidled into the thicket as soon as he saw me.

"So you know that man you have been with?" he said.

"No, not in the least."

"Well, he is one of those mean prigs who filch and cozen to get their tin—swindling, picking pockets, and doing dirty jobs for pay, that man will, for hire, swear to anything, and there are so many it would ruin to be put in the papers. What name did he give you?"

I told him.

"Ah, his real one is Jack Coalman. However, I'll bet he's up to no good. Give him the widest berth you can. I came back for something I had left, and the little one told me, so I sent her to fetch you back, he knows me, or I'd a come myself, and it is best such a cove did not guess we were anyway acquainted, or he would be sure to work something out of it. I cannot help you, so keep clear. Say you are going to Epsom, he is a little too well known to come there, and put out the other way, come up here first, and I can stop long enough to show you the way to a lane which will take you down toward the Aldboro road to Guildford. I'll wait where the foot path comes up, you can ride it easy."

I turned at once, and went back to the inn stables to get my horse, asking the way to Epsom. I mounted and left, without seeing Mr. Dacre, giving a message, however, to the ostler, to say I would call when I returned.

Tom was waiting.

"The little crittur can show you as well as I, and by rights I should have been a good way off before this. Look well to yourself, you have someone who wants to get you into trouble—it was a dead set, I'm sure, he turned the moment he found you, but I think the Epsom dodge will throw him out."

He then put off at a swinging rate in another direction, and I dived under the bushes to follow the obscure paths of my small conductress.

My horse was fresh, and walked free after the tripping figure, whom he seemed to recognize as his leader. After twenty minutes we were in a dell, which sloped and narrowed to a lane, over which hung thick hedges of thorn, holly, hazel, and yew, she said, "Now you can go alone, ask for Aldboro."

I would have offered her something, but she said, "If they knew it—but I won't, anyway." And she ran off, with something between a leer and a frown, which I read that something else than money might be accepted, but she was through the hedge before I could frame any such proposal, and I trotted on, wondering for what purpose Mr. Dacre honored me with his acquaintance.

Arrived at Guildford, I returned my horse to the livery stable, paid my bill, and taking a porter from the coach-office, took away my trunk. Depositing it in the bar, though booking myself to town, I took a seat in a down coach to Godalming, just as the other started the opposite way.

In driving down the street, I saw Mr. Dacre, who had just arrived, going up and entering the office I had just left. There had been several persons waiting, but my name was down for town in the books, the while I was safely dragged down the steep, ill-paved street of Guildford.

Chapter Seventy-Six
Schemes—cells—thoughts of love—
Tom's news

I had been so annoyed by the circumstance of becoming again the victim of active persecution, that I had taken no notice of a letter put into my hands on my return to the inn, it was from Father Delayney, simply inclosing one from Mr. Searle, upon which *haste*, had been written under the direction. The letter was a summons to Chester.

> *I cannot get on, it ran. Without asking you questions, which it would be impossible to answer so clearly in writing. We have summoned Lord Gilsland, at a venture, for the defence, but nothing can be traced as advantageous to him in your father's robbery, or the loss of his papers. However, as both these prisoners had seen him in conversation with the prosecutor, whom they declare knows nothing of the matter, we must try and get something out of him.*

———

Next morning I set out for Oxford, where I got, by sundry ways and means, before very late that night, there was no difficulty in getting to Chester the next.

I inquired, as directed, for Mr. Searle, at the Mitre Inn. He was busy writing.

"You have been a little later than I expected," he said, looking at me through those bluish spectacles steadily.

"Yes, I was at Guildford. I went down to be out of the way of Lady

Connemara's father. I cannot make out what he has against me, but he has sent someone on my track, and I was not sharp enough to get out of London without his knowing where I went, but I think I shook him off at Guildford. But what have you got at in the matter of the fire?"

"What sort of person was set to watch you, and how did you know? When you have told your adventures, I will tell mine." And my auditor drew a piece of paper and dipped his pen in the ink. "Day before yesterday, you said?"

"Yes."

"Tom is not of much use, he is but on the outskirts of crime. Ah! you say John Coalman—he has many aliases, I know the name, we can get at him. From what I recollect of the description of the people you have mentioned, as being in the theatre and in the park, I think one, at least, is a prisoner here on this very charge, and the other is the King's evidence. They are none of them much known as housebreakers—indeed, not at all—only as poachers, and persons who got money in any sneaking way. The prosecutor in the case is the nephew and heir-at-law, he was in the house at the time, and he had laid the informations as soon as he heard of the confession of Blackburn, who is also in custody. Now, would you know the persons you mentioned before?"

"Yes, certainly."

"Well, we will see them tomorrow, that is, I will get you to where you can see them."

A letter was brought in at this moment, the eyes of the solicitor were hardly fixed upon it, when he let it drop, and seemed buried in thought.

"Well, I cannot make this out," he said at last. Having again cast his eyes on the letter:

> It is believed, upon good authority, that the Mr. Sykes, nephew to the late Mr. Warren, of the manor near Knutsford, will withdraw from the prosecution for arson, and forfeit his recognizances. If so, there can be no trial this assizes, unless there comes another prosecutor, and you have time for such arrangements, which I suspect will not be the case.

"I fear here is a dead lock. You are not known here, are you?"

"No, I should think not."

"Well, tomorrow you shall see the men, and then be off. Lord Gillsland fears facing an examination in Court."

We parted for the night, and next morning were admitted into the prison. Mr. Searle seemed to have the ear of the governor, for we had a person appointed to take us to a certain room, from whence, through Venetian blinds, we could see distinctly any one in the yard.

The two prisoners were soon introduced, and after waiting till I had seen the younger and fairer of the two I saw together in the park, who had been called Deacon, and the other who was one of the two who were talking of Ben in the theatre, they passed on into another door, and presently I saw the elder companion of Mr. Deacon, who came out alone, and being told it was a mistake—that he was not wanted—returned by the door from which he had come out.

Mr. Searle said, "You know all these faces?"

I said, "Yes."

"I thought so. Now for Ben, you know no Ben?"

I shook my head. "There was a bow-legged tiger of Lord Fernwold's, called Benjamin, it was he who took me to Wimbledon, I remember."

"Pest upon it, here we get upon that Lord we must hold sacred. Was your father's name Edward?"

"Yes."

"What age?"

"Upward of sixty."

"We can find out, by letter from the priest, what age the second husband was. Now I will see my clients that were to have been, and you can return to Guildford."

He knocked at the door, which was opened, and I was shown along the dreary corridors, with its iron wickets, that dead white, with the black doors and iron work, and all the cold security of watchful eyes and silence, the smallest clank of a key against another ringing along the echoing passages. Those guards, too—stolid, calm, well fed, and imperturbable. There was no warmth of temperament within these cold walls. Monks are to be found wasted in conflict with evil passions, who might pray against temptation and withstand it, living wrecks of spiritual strife, but here the calm sleek cheek showed a spirit ungalled by any consciousness of weakness—a nervous system without mercy or compassion, as the fish of the great subterranean caverns are without sight, the eye never having been developed.

I lingered in this loathsome place. Bright and pure innocence would rebel against yielding to melancholy in a deep dark cell and iron fetters, and courage rises to meet its fate when tortured, with however frowning a front, but here there was something to damp all hope, a sort of calm calculated security pervading every object around, that made the mind feel distrust in itself, its own knowledge of events, and even its own innocence.

Such was the impression this dreadful place made upon me, and I got out into the street to hurry out of Chester, as if the cold cell, the clank of keys, and the heavy clinking of a closing grating were pursuing me along the way.

At Guildford I found a letter, announcing the sudden departure of the Marquis. Mr. Dacre had not been back, and I resolved to change my abode to Godalming, and wait the issue of events for a few days, till Mr. Searle should confirm the news of the coast being clear.

It was the Saturday of the Derby week. Next morning the universal calm of a provincial town was almost too touching, and I was left to those busy memories and that forbidden love, which I scarcely could wish were to find but hopeless. Getting up early, I wandered out among the green meadows, covered with cowslip, and lay down by the bank of a gentle brook, listening to those bells which called forth the population to their devotions—the maiden, in her hurriedly tied bow of fresh ribbons, peony cheeks, and dimpling mouth—the rustic swain, in the clean smock-frock and tight laced boots, there were many such passed in eager haste, not to be too late to be able to sit by those they liked to be near, others, who went already paired, and whose fear of hearing a few words less or more seemed scarcely to overbalance the content of being together. There was the universal pocket handkerchief of the fair sex, folded, rolled, and squeezed, according to the anxieties of the owner—in all cases the index of her state of mind.

My own thoughts were not in tone for rustic happiness nor calm methodical devotion, so I turned from the path others took, and loitered musingly on. Finding a green lane, I followed it, barely knowing I was going from the sun, for it beamed warm upon my back, the ringing had ceased, all but the sheep-bells were still, and they came but at intervals, as if by stealth.

I noted not the time, I had been thinking what I was to do, and how long I was to lead the idle life of a dependent upon the bounty of the generous Spaniard, a crowded mass of schemes and anxieties were coming upon me, which were difficult to separate, but there was still one thought which insensibly assumed the mastery. I was chiefly thinking of the stormy coast of western Ireland, and of the wind waving those rich tresses—remembered so well—upon its shores. How could I waft myself to see and be unseen, to hear her tones, and watch for a thoughtful look beneath those long eyelashes, listen for the smallest sigh, and dream it was caused by the absence of one it was forbidden to love. At this moment I heard a low, but jolly voice, trolling the words of some well known ditty close by, and looking up, found my friend Tom standing right before me.

"Do you know," he said, "had you been a whale and I Jonas, I could a been far down your throat by this time, and you never the wiser."

"Well, I don't think I should have been much the wiser, as you say."

There was something kindly in the deep grey eye, which looked fully and confidently in mine, it was a strange colored eye, for I had, till seeing it in this strong light, always thought it black.

"Well, you had that fellow, Coalman, after you, I set Tiney on your track as soon as I saw him, but she has told me since she saw you were not going to be taken in by his blarney—she is pretty sharp, Tiney."

I laughed, for I had just felt disgusted at his calling his wife *my lady*, and asked why he called the intelligent little vidette Tiney?

"She is so little, you wouldn't believe she is near fourteen."

"Yes, but has she no name?"

"I don't believe there has been much christening in the family," said my companion, laughing.

"Well, I thought you had talked of Jonas, and had read the Bible."

"I talked of Jonas, any one who has heard the story may talk of it, without reading the Bible. But did you see anything more of Coalman?"

"No, I avoided him, and took a place to London, then turned and came here instead."

I saw that it was known, from the silent look he gave me, that I had been away, at last he looked up, shaking back the thick clustering locks which had fallen over his brow.

"Mammy wants to know if you have been at Chester."

I hesitated, but not long, they could have no wish to do me wrong. "Yes, I have been at Chester."

"And about the trial for burning near Knutsford?"

"Quite right, but how did you know?"

"Oh, the old one knows a heap—she'll tell you some day—but she is not ready yet. She sent me to see after you, and say she is going to Wimbledon tomorrow, that is, we set out, for we haven't a light four-horse coach to go in."

"Well, goodbye, till we meet at Wimbledon, you'll be down soon."

"I'll perhaps first turn a penny on a cob I picked up from an old gentleman in a passion, because he started, tumbled, and flung him off, then put out. The old fellow saw me laughing. I offered to go after the nag, if he was inclined for another trial.

"'No,' he said. He'd never get on his back again, and he would sell him to the first dealer he came across.

"'Well, what will you give to get a hold of him first?' I said. 'For I'd like a job.'

"'Perhaps you'd take job and pony both?' said the old fellow.

"'Yes, if the figure be not too high.'

"'Well, I declare, if brass would pay for a serviceable beast, you'd have ere a one in the county.'

"'Well, brass if you like, or yellow gold, we won't quarrel about names.'

"The bargain was struck at last, after I produced some coin, and after a great deal of chaffing I was just going off, telling him he was much too hard-fisted, and too sharp-tongued for me. I had not heard so much slang at the Derby. I called him a *brick* and an *out-and-outer*, at last he called me back, and I got the beast for eleven sovereigns. It is honestly worth five-and-twenty, and I believe there was a bushel of beans inside him at the time, and fat enough to set up a candle shop, so I'll just sober him down a little, and he will make my fortune, for I'll give him on trial, and tell where he came from, with a certificate—*Parted with for skittishness and ingratitude, no other vice—John Sparks, justice of the peace.* You see it is all regular."

"But where is he?" I said.

"Oh, he's forthcoming fast enough, but he is not of your kind, or you would have him under you now, and no mistake. No, no, have a little patience, if I've luck, you'll have something out of me yet will carry you with hounds."

The good-hearted fellow now took leave, and I turned to my quarters, perfumed by the baked meats which paraded the streets between services, and obstructed by the solemn well-dressed crowd, which had been emptied out of the different temples in which they had worshipped.

Chapter Seventy-Seven
In society—a painful memory—court news— to former haunts—vivid memories— mysterious doings

Lady Davenport just drove off as I came to the door, a message, however, was left, begging me to dine in St. James's Square, to meet some friends. I thought this must mean to meet Rose. I had to send a note to thank Father Delayney, and tell him of my return.

Mike, who never learned anything he could help, found out nothing of Lord Gilsland, and I went to dinner as much to learn what was going on as to partake of a repast. I was the first arrival, but as they had been some time returned from a drive, the ladies were fussing about among certain exotics which, like the milch cows at Brighton, were kept in health in their everlasting confinement, by being eternally kept clean. I learned on my arrival, that Lord Albric had been sent for that very day to smoke at a favorite plant, which had been threatened with some insects, and he had in consequence been emancipated from attendance at dinner.

"I knew you would come if you arrived from Epsom, as you could not be engaged by note, as my message was to be delivered on your getting out of the carriage. Well, she is a noble creature, your Spaniard, and the greatest success at the drawing room—amber satin and black, and the great black veil, looped up with such diamonds in the hair, which was plaited round the brow in a black massive crown, she was a noble-looking creature. The Minister's wife treated her with the utmost deference—in short, it was quite pleasing to see such a triumph."

Here the good-natured hostess was called from the praise of the absent to the pleasure of receiving its object present before us—Signor Conchas and his daughter, and Baron Reus, were announced. Immediately after, I was told to take in the Countess and act host, Lady Davenport sent Mademoiselle Conchas with the Baron, and Lady Dorothea with the Signor, taking Rose's arm under hers, she said she would be her chaperone.

I talked cookery to the placid Countess, and we had a sort of general skirmish about the art, then a little discussion on hunting, and then music and bull-fights were introduced, and the large eyes of the Countess flashed with sudden animation, but the guitar and fandango seemed more generally popular, we were all so mixed up, for her ladyship ordered away a huge mass of antique plate, filled with fruit and flowers, from the centre of the table, that we might see each other, so that there was little but general conversation.

The Countess was in high good humour, as was Lady Davenport, everything was magnificent, and the dessert service was gilt and of ancient Italian sculpture, much of it Cellini, the servants were in state liveries, and the whole affair conducted so free from fuss, as to be the true type of one of those good establishments in England which are unrivalled any where else. It seemed to please the Spanish ladies, particularly the stately decorum of the service and the perfect calm.

I let Rose know of Lady Connemara's departure. She had a letter from her father, he was most anxious to come to England to see her. Political opinions were very dangerous things to have, and he only waited to find someone in whom he could trust to set his affairs in order, to leave Spain, and be with her once more.

We had a little guitar music, Rose sang, as also the Baron—he had not much voice, but a good knowledge of music. I know not how the instrument got into my hands, or why I struck a few notes, but Lady Dorothea begged me to go on, and I sung the same Spanish air I had sung on the Susquadee. I had hardly finished, when the Countess and Rose took their leave.

I handed the latter downstairs, and felt her hand tremble slightly as she said, "Ned, spare me ever these things which touch the sores of memory, that can never heal."

"Pardon me, dearest Rose," was all I could say, as I put her into the carriage.

On returning upstairs, I found Lady Davenport in the highest spirits. She made me come and sit by her, and told me I put her so in mind of poor Fernwold.

"Ah, it was a sad loss, his death, no one promised so well, of all the young men in town—but his mother's malady. No one ought to marry into a consumption, it is a sin to have creatures of children, to be taken away in their prime—they put everything in confusion. I am the only one of the family who survived of the same branch."

The good old lady made me promise to write to her before leaving town, and announce my return—Dora telling me to be sure to come often, as it did her aunt so much good, and put her into such excellent humour.

Mr. Searle returned to town. The prosecution had failed—the prosecutor had not appeared, the King's evidence, who only acknowledged having been accessory after the fact, could not speak to several important points, his evidence was defective, and it was thought useless to go into any further investigation. Some papers had been inclosed to Mr. Sykes, which detailed certain funds and mortgages, and where they were to be found, also declaring the prisoners accused innocent. There was no name signed, but the writer stated that the things were given up because they were of no use to the writer.

I have not a sufficiently accurate recollection of the explanation given by Mr. Searle, but the trial was not to take place, and the three persons were liberated whom I had seen in confinement at Chester, so this phase of our researches was at an end.

Rose was most anxious that I should go to Cadiz to meet her father, and let him get out of Spain before his enemies should be able again to get him compromised. I was almost glad to have something actively to employ me, and consented.

I was to sail in a week by a packet to Malta, which would touch at Cadiz or Gilbraltar. Mr. Searle even approved, and I had only the duty of getting down to Wimbledon, to muse over the scene of meeting and of parting on my first acquaintance with Isabel.

My cab-horse was fresh and strong, I thought he might be put to this use, and leave me the more free in my visit. I had a wish, too, that it should be at the same time of night, and the same state of moon, the same birds to sing, the same tinkling sheep-bells, and fresh perfumes, which three years before had greeted me on my evening way.

I took my tiger inside at Knightsbridge, and my horse took me down at a swinging trot without seeming to think it an exertion.

I drew up at the same inn I stopped at before, the cherry cheeks were gone, but in their place a face little less rosy, but of mature age, a female boniface, stout, good humored, and methodical. I ordered dinner, lamb cutlets it was impossible to avoid, veal of course in all country inns, and bacon, for I was obliged to take cognizance of all and each, and to hear before hand that new potatoes were watery, and bacon very fat, lamb cutlets not being large moreover, but the veal very nice, the table being wiped clean at the bare mention of such dainties, groaned under the sturdy hand more than tables do as far as my experience goes, under the most gorgeous repast. At half-past six the feast was to be spread. I walked out, the same road led upon the common near an angle, and there was the same gorse and briars, among which the little companion of Isabel had fallen, and now I remembered it, I had never thought of asking who she was then, nor in my latter interviews, so much had I been engrossed by one object.

It was not long after five, the day sufficiently hot for the season, had subsided into a most agreeable evening temperature. There were the same flowers, the same hawthorns, and horse-chesnuts. I wandered on looking for opens into lanes, nooks, or bends, in which to find my friend the gipsy widow, the little brown canvass was not in sight, but I thought I could recognize Tom with a smock-frock, but no clodhopper's gait, who sauntered near an adjoining fence, as this figure turned the corner, which now hid him from me, I made straight for the spot, knowing that were it the gipsy, the fire was not far off. I was not mistaken, Tom and his grandmother were there, and for the first time I saw something like cooking, there were two young ducks split up, laid upon a light gridiron, and some thin slices of bacon hissing and frizzling above them, with small chips of onion over all, which last shed around a most inviting odour.

"You're just in time, sir, for a little bite, there's enough for mammy and you, I can forage about."

The old woman looked up kindly, "I doubt if you would relish a dinner in the open air, and cooked by such a crone," she said.

"And no plates," said Tom, laughing.

"Oh," I interposed, "I've eaten many a dinner, and the happiest too of my life, where the blue Heaven was alone above us, and not a house within a summer's ride."

The old woman looked fixedly at me. "And you so young, that was far away perhaps, where they say our people are to be found."

"No! I have heard of them too, far east, among the Tartars and in Russia, but I did not find any of them where I went among the great mountains and plains of Western America."

She simply said, "Ah!" As if her momentary interest had died away, and resumed her attention to the gridiron.

"Tiney" broke in Tom, "has been off looking after some baddish sort of fellows, but now you are here, I'll call her in." He went off a little way, and gave two kind of half whistles, and then a more lengthened one.

I sat down and asked, "How things were going on?" She brightened up again.

"Tom is a sort of horse dealer, and likes it, a good luck has been upon us ever since we set eyes on you, my poor child would give his heart's blood for you, so don't fear to trust him."

"I have come to tell you that I am going abroad, and to ask if can I do anything for you before I go."

She continued her cares for the fire, and all it bore, for some little time before she answered, "No, Sir, no, you have done all already, better think what we can do for you or yours, while you are far off. You have someone you love, a mother, a brother, or sister."

She tried on the one after the other degree of relationship, and seeing ever but a blank where she looked for assent.

"Well, you've no kin, but you love someone or some place, or some animal, if it is but an old horse or dog, if you love him he shall be looked after."

"My horses are all hired, dogs I have none, nor kith nor kin. There was a bright and good lady I have long loved." I here described the villa near Esher, and the Marchioness. "She is gone to Ireland, but bye and bye she may come back, if she returns, tell her you are ready to do any behests she has, for the sake of her absent brother."

She looked at me, and shook her head. "It will take more than one winding sheet to put things straight there," she said slowly and oracularly. "But I will mind to let her know, and also to note how it goes with her and hers, but will you eat a bit at the gipsy's fire?" she broke in.

"Have you a glass of water or beer," I said.

"Yes, Tom brought us two bottles of ale t' other day, he said it came from Dorchester, and to be kept snug, till perhaps you'd have a pot sometime." She looked round, Tom was standing behind her with the promised beer, it was famous stout stuff, and I cried out for water to Tiney, who just appeared from the mouth of the very lane I had reason to remember so well. She laughed as she brought me a little water which she had never seen poured into beer before.

"What's come of those coves you were a taking care of?" asked Tom.

"Oh, they're gone straight away down the lane, and then across by the foot path."

I observed the grandmother never spoke to either of the children, but they understood all she wanted of them by signs.

"The cob had been sold at twenty-two pounds, and I am to go," said Tom. "To Eaton Place in a month," he added, "to get a present, if he answers, he's worth the money I got to a butcher's boy."

I found my time was up. Tom would see me as far as the inn, poor fellow, his eyes dimmed when I told him I was going to leave. A sudden thought came upon me, I told him to call at the Burlington, and tell Rose I had sent him. I wrote down the name on the back of one of my cards, and then I gave my hand to the poor lad, saying, "You could have come with me, but we should have had no one to take care of the old woman."

"Well, that's kindly said, and just right for the sore place, but you won't be long away?"

"I hope not, mind you have a good horse for me when I come back." He wrung my hand and turned away, there was no merry song nor bound over intervening bushes, and he never turned his head back.

I cannot say I felt disposed to be merry, so my meal passed off with some extorted encomiums on the cooking, which with the expected reversion of nearly a pint of sherry, put my Hebe in constant good humor, and I was allowed to smoke a clay pipe to comfort me for being so lonely till eight, when I had calculated it would be so dusky as to inspire my visit with that air of romance, which was to give it its chief value. An unusual calm was the characteristic of the more than twilight, for clouds had dimmed the sun's going down, which though not drawing to rain, gave an earlier gloom than might have been expected from the hour, it was such an air as precedes, as I have heard, the earthquake, or as I have sometimes observed before thunder or tempest.

After looking toward the stable, where a light shewed some care was being taken of mine or some other horse, I sauntered on toward the common, and turned to the right into the dark lane of former times, but I could not remember particular spots in it, and returned to the little island of turf among the furze, it was a little overgrown, but not much. I threw myself down on the fresh green grass, I could have liked to sleep there and dream. I had even laid down my head upon that spot where that beautiful foot had rested, the whole world was shut out, and I curled up in that small spot, which, did it now contain what once had been there, was all the world to me. The same prickles which had torn her stocking before, I felt on my cheek now, it was easy to make a dream, and I was busy with the cherished materials, when I heard footsteps approaching on the road, there was no occasion to start up, I lay still, merely raising my head as they approached, for I made out two men, they came nearer, and I thought I knew the two again, whom I had seen at Chester accused of arson. I was almost sure of the one, younger and lighter haired, their looks however were turned suspiciously behind, and they passed on. I could distinguish no sound when they quitted the road for a narrow path, one went on before the other, and they turned, after a moment's pause at its mouth, into the lane I had just left. For some time I remained unaccountably disturbed by the passing of these persons. I did not feel any personal fear for two men, I had an iron headed whip handle in my hand, my musing mood had however given way to something for the time less contemplative. I was already advanced some paces toward the narrow road, when I again reflected that I had come here to recall memories of the past, in scenes where lasting impressions, and an unaccountable event had occurred to me, why was I to indulge in dodging others in vague curiosity. I slackened my pace, and again the image of her I loved but too well, took its place in my imagination, thus sauntering on, I got to the turn which led to the house in which the dripping figure I had once supported to that garden door, had then lived.

I went up to that doorway, all was closed and silent, and to me sad. I could see no lights at any windows visible over the wall, and turned back to follow the course I had taken on the last memorable night I had visited these scenes. There was no nightingale to be heard, but an owl hooted, and I thought was answered, had I been in the war ground of those red men, who used the howl and the croak in place of the whistle or other sign of communication of the whites, I should have taken the voice of that gloomy bird rather as a warning of some foul play, then as I did an indefinite omen of evil, a little further, and the song of the nightingale came distinctly from a neighboring grove, but as I thought thrilling and pathetic. I wished to shake off this moody sensibility, yet it hung like a cloud about me, I heard a rook, possibly disturbed in its cares for its young, it seemed to me in my present humour to bode evil, like the failing raven in his night croak,[i] but I invited the vision of her who was absent to come in between me and these dark thoughts. Had she been here, how lately? and with whom had she staid in her former abode? I had got to the stile over which we had passed together, and found the spot where we had together sat down, when I declared how truly I loved, in that mad young ardour it is so difficult to disbelieve. There I sat down, and remembered how true had been those fevered words when she held my hand on in doubt, when I would have thrown back with it, the thick tresses which shaded her eyes, and that when I had pressed my lips to that pale cheek, I had felt the moisture of a tear. The moon too shone out, and as then shone not on this spot which was in dark shadow, I had lain here for nearly an hour, though the air of night was dead and dank below, there was a carry in the upper sky, and clouds careered wildly far above.

I remarked this as I looked up at a sudden light, and I perceived two figures coming silently, with lengthened stride across the field, striking into the path close by where I lay, and near where there was a small pond, they threw something into the water and washed their hands, but never spoke. I felt my flesh creep as they got up and wiped them on the grass. Moonlight gives a dead pallor to the skin, by daylight red or brown. I thought by the moment's glance I had of one of these faces, that it was uneathly pale, and they went on along the narrow way without a sound or sign.

It was unaccountable what strange influence so oppressed me, but I felt uneasy and almost nervous, a nightingale sung loud and clear, but not cheerily to me, the fragrant flowers shed their odours by the way, but I was depressed, a weight was at my heart. Those memories I came there to woo came not to make me linger, I was soon on the border of the common, two figures stood darkly some little distance before, and near the road. I felt my blood again curdle, it was not personal apprehension, for I did not shift my whip in my hand in a way to let its armed head tell. No, it was a superstitious creeping of every fibre, but while I advanced the figures had probably fallen down for concealment amongst the furze, as they had disappeared. There are few who have not felt moments of fear, for which it would be difficult to account, I quickened my pace as I passed the spot where these dark shadows had vanished, and met no one on my further way.

The horse was ready to put to, a draught of ale and I was also ready, it happened that I met no one till I got over the river, the head of the cab was down, and the tiger snug and asleep by my side, the horse stepped out worthy of the good cheer with which his visit had no doubt been received, it was twelve o'clock when I got to Knightsbridge, but no change of scene for the moment cheered me up from that depression I felt ever since seeing the two silent figures come and wash in the pool.

Chapter Seventy-Eight
His evil genius—leave-taking—a storm at sea
—Don Diego

Next day, I was to go to Falmouth by steamer, to be picked up by the packet for Gibraltar. I told Rose of poor Tom, and she promised to see him, as also his mother, she gave me letters to her father from several persons, and instructions to get him away from Spain, in case of any accident discovering his too liberal views.

"You may say to him that I am not well, that I have never been much separated from him, and never so far, that I am pining and anxious, which is not favorable for my health, and that I could not have sent you, and you may I hope and," she said, with a faint smile. "Neither would you have left me, but for the urgency of getting him back to calm me."

I was full of grief, and also shame, why could I not return such noble affection?

"The going we have already discussed, it will do you good, in ten days there will be a courier by land, and you shall have a letter waiting for you at the post-office at Cadiz, and another sent under cover to my father."

I kissed her on either cheek.

"I'll write to Ireland, and do all I can to soothe the Marchioness, at all events, she shall have all the friendship I have left to bestow. Have you any directions to leave me about your own affairs?"

"No, we are come to a standstill, some vigilance may possibly discover by accident what seems quite hopeless at present."

"Have you seen nothing of your evil genius again?"

"No, I have seen him three times," I answered, musingly, for the thought brought back the different times, so different the scenes, and how exciting the last.

"You will see him no more," she said, with a serious air, and after a pause.

"Perhaps I may be wrecked," I observed, willing to infuse something less of graveness into our conversation.

"No, it is not that, something tells me I shall see you again, so farewell. Write—I shall so look for a letter, and pray for your preservation."

She left me calm, to all outward seeming, and I went downstairs, shocked to think that, lightly as she talked, I might have observed some marks of wasting and illness in her I had known strong almost as myself, and to whom illness had been unknown.

I had one other visit to pay besides that to Signor Conchas, which was to the kind old Lady Davenport, and thither I drove, early as it was.

I sent up my card.

My lady would see me, and I mounted the steps, perfumed by flowers, which no air disturbed rudely, nor hardly any sound. A humming-bird flew about, and carried some message of sweets, there was also a canary or two, who seemed indifferent to our passing, for there was but one quiet servant, with well trimmed fair hair. Lady Davenport told me she hated powder and whiskers in servants, so she had them all fair-haired, to look clean.

My fair-haired guide then showed me through a glass door, to where the rooms opened into the small green-house, where the open windows let in the breeze from Hyde Park ways, but the birds could not be trusted with that liberty, which is easier defined as applied to them, than to ourselves. There was a book or two busy, having its leaves turned over by the zephyr, and on the whole, the plants and rooms adjoining them appeared to be enjoying their morning airing.

I was shown into another room by another scout.

"Has anything happened to you, or to me? It would be better to me—I am old," said the kind old lady, as she held out her hand. "Dora, dear, will you write and ask if Monday will do for Mrs. Poyntz, but be very civil, you know."

Dora left the room.

"Well now, something has happened?"

"Yes, I am just starting for Cadiz."

"What! That place of Moors, and robbers, and gipsies, and priests, and sherry, in the south of Spain! Cannot you get robbed, or fall in love, or have your fortune told, or do penance, without going there, and at the beginning of the season too—you're not in debt?"

I laughed, though deeply touched by her earnestness. "No, it is on business with Don Diego, the father of Rose. I go, and I hope to be soon back."

"Well, I never sent anyone away from me whom I liked," said the old lady, innocently. "But, perhaps, you are bound to go, if they want you."

"So far, I ought to do whatever they wish, as I owe so much to them." I reddened at the thought of the obligations I was entangled into.

"Well, I see—yes, go, if you do them any service, it would be bad-hearted not, but remember to come to me straight when you come back. My poor dear Adelbert liked you, and so do I. Jones!—strange name—never mind, I jumble things so, but I shall not forget you. Now, do you want to go away?" She rung the bell. "Goodbye, take care of yourself, and come back safe. Too gay to marry yet. Send Lady Dorothea—to a servant. Now, goodbye again, or I shall forget."

So I took my departure as Lady Dora came in at another. I saw them shuffling amongst piles of note-paper as I took a stolen look in my retreat, wondering at the earnestness of the old lady's apparent interest in me at one moment, and my abrupt dismissal at the next.

I left Michael under the care of Father Delayney, recommending his paying a visit to his native place until my return, and from Lincoln's Inn Fields went straight on board my Falmouth steamer.

A voyage from London along the south coast of England, is not one necessarily of any interest, and there was no incident connected with it worthy of record.

The packet arrived at Falmouth two days after us, and in a few hours again heaved anchor. There was a slight northeast breeze, but a long heavy swell set in from the southwest, all sail was set, and we made some considerable way, and the breeze held during all the night, toward morning it freshened, and we were, in twenty-four hours, nearly two hundred miles on our way, when certain signs occasioned an anxious look in our weather-beaten captain.

It was past noon, he had made his observation, and came up on deck, the first and second mates were also there.

"Glass fallen!" I heard fall from the old man.

The mate looked uneasily upward.

"We had best be ready for it chopping, it will never hold at this, nor last, with such a glass."

The mate said nothing, but walked forward, looking at the haulyards as he went. I saw some of the crew of the watch speak to him and look up. The wind had slackened, and the vessel pitched heavily.

"You may handle those studdingsails at once, Mr. Jennings," said the captain, looking uneasily to the northwest, where already with a glass you could discern a white cresting on the waves.

He walked forward himself, and presently the other watch was called, and were running up the shrouds to take in top gallants and royals, those aloft were soon after seen stretching on the main and fore-yards, reefing their heavy and flapping topsails, the mizen still drew a little.

I followed the captain down to look at the chart, he had marked one position about 170 miles from the Land's End. He had a biscuit and a glass of weak brandy-and-water, his usual lunch, and we returned on deck, the sails had been double-reefed and trimmed, and the ship was on a wind. There was a cloud still to the northwest, from whence came the breeze, but the swell had increased, and was still right ahead, and we could see a wild white cloud flying from the southwest, far above the height of that from which we got our present breeze.

Most of the passengers were sick, and the deadlights were battened to, the table fitted with those ominous ridges, which the most inveterate lover of the sea must loathe, in the darkened cabin. There is something no one can like in the preparation for a storm, besides an uneasy anxiety as to how it is to come, but little change occurred till bedtime, and I fell asleep, rocked by no gentle hand.

I was awoke by a crash, as if the vessel had struck, but she for the moment rode steady, as if quivering on the crest of a wave, for I had rushed up the companion stair, then she bent down her bows, as if to dive forever, and another sea made us again stagger and washed the deck from stem to stern. We were heading southwest, and the captain ordered the course to be changed to northwest, as there was a cross sea, and that was the least heavy which came from that quarter.

During my short stay at the head of the stairs—for I was soon sent back, and the companion closed—I could see that the upper spars had been taken down entirely, and the top-gallant-masts lowered—all looked dreary enough. I got into my berth again, but the creaking of bulkheads and increased motion prevented my falling asleep.

Morning broke—it was a terrible sight—we were upon a fore-staysail and spencer—dark and thick. The wind came in a gale from the southwest, there was nothing to cheer the eye.

She was a gallant ship, and not loaded beyond her powers of buoyancy, but we had rather been beaten back in the night, and were labouring in that terrible sea off the chops of the channel.

It was a drear miserable day, and night came on—an anxious captain and restless crew, the lead was kept going constantly, and her head nearly west—but she must be drifting.

I looked on the melancholy stunted masts, as they creaked back and forward, and thought what would be the fate of a ship, good even as the Dart, on a lea-shore, and how surely we would be off one by the morrow, if things were not changed, the terrible howl of the gale through the cordage, the sullen sky, and labouring hull, were sad things for contemplation. What would I have given for freedom then—that is, sea-room for the gallant ship.

"Go down and turn in, Mr. Jones, take rest when you can, we cannot tell how soon all hands may be needed." And the old sailor closed the door of the stairs upon me as he spoke.

I turned in, and strange to say, fell asleep. It was late in the following morning when I awoke, the motion of the vessel was not much decreased, but was more regular, and the light acquired through the door from the cabin was somewhat brighter. I pulled on a pair of trowsers, slipped on a pea-jacket, and got up the stairs.

There was a partially cleared sky, and the wind from the north, we were upon our course with a topsail breeze, re-fitting was going on with energy, and the second mate, who was on deck, reported the glass risen, and the ship making eight knots.

This storm was the only incident of the voyage, and I mention it because of what it did to others, on whom my thoughts had dwelt as it roared around.

It was a ten days' voyage the Dart made to Gibraltar, and some days elapsed before I found my way to Cadiz.

Don Diego, who had hired a fine house, put me up easily, and I was to have horses and everything I wanted. It was my first care to make him aware of Rose not being well, and her great desire to see him, added to the anxiety she felt lest those who would have to make restitution of usurped property, could in some way again involve her father.

I asked to be at once made aware of what his difficulties were, and was delighted to find it was not a legal matter but merely one of honest reckoning, and care not to grant receipts but as they appeared to cover sums actually paid.

"My revenues remain, and are restored, but without distrusting Government, I should be quite as contented to have all arrears and sums due paid over to some merchant, who could make them safe in another country, and this is the chief way in which you can help me."

Such was the drift of the conversation we had on this subject, and he promised to give me such powers as would enable me to do all this, and then sail the first opportunity for London.

Chapter Seventy-Nine
A murder—Father Delayney's mission—a double loss?

It was a few days after the father's departure that I heard from the daughter, there were two letters, both long, and one dated soon after my departure, to which by priority of course my attention was first directed, that if, in case any narrative should me made, I should find things recorded in their order. There was little but ordinary news, though a style of sisterly affection made them come in the most agreeable shape. She had written to Ireland, seen Tom, and regularly received visits from Father Delayney.

The second letter—dated ten days after the first—I shall give, as far as I remember it, exactly:

> You will have to contrast the tranquil gossip of my first letter with this, charged with terrible events, which must deeply interest you.
>
> You had not been gone but three or four days, when the newspapers announced a terrible murder near Wimbledon. A body had been found in a field, about a mile from the common, of a man, apparently a gentleman. The body was lying in a ditch, on its back, the pockets empty, the head much bruised, close by a pool of blood, marks of a struggle on the edge of a footpath near were visible, and then tracks, which were distinct on a mole-hill in the paddock, seemed to have gone across the grass, to cut off an angle, to where they fell into another path near the corner of the field, in which there was a pond. Here the trace of feet was distinct in the clay, two persons had stood close to the edge of the water, and floating on the opposite side, under the hedge, was a bludgeon newly cut, which at one end had been partially peeled

by blows against something hard, and slightly discolored. It was not ascertained who the murdered man had been, but on a close examination of the stick found in the water little doubt remained as to its having been used in the attack, as sundry hairs were attached to it under part of the bark. The hat found near the body was of Paris manufacture.

Inspector Vickery has gone down to make further search, in which the parish authorities are also deeply engaged.

The day after this, appeared another paragraph.

It has been ascertained that the body of the person found near Wimbledon (mentioned in our Tuesday's paper), was that of the Marquis of Gilsland. He had been abroad, and had only come back the day before the murder. It is ascertained that he walked out in the evening, and never returned—as expected by his servants—to his villa, which is close to the spot where the body was found.

This startling news was immediately communicated to Lady Connemara. At my request—for I did not like to write—the good Father Delayney started by the Holyhead mail, to prepare the daughter for this terrible shock. He had a favorable voyage to Dublin, but just after landing there came on one of those terrible storms which so try the hearts of those who love upon the wild sea. The mail in which he traveled was nearly blown over, trees strewed the way with their branches, and sometimes their trunks stopped for a time his further progress. So wrote the worthy man.

We had it here in London, blowing slates and chimneys about the streets. Good Lady Davenport wrote to say she trusted you were not gone. But I must give you the reverend Father's own words.

I got, one way or other, to the post-town near Duncryn Castle, there, as the weather had in some degree moderated, I asked for a gig or car to take me forward the three or four miles which remained of my journey, but except the landlord, an old ostler, and some women, no one was left at the Connemara Arms, the coast was strewed with wrecks, and all the boys were away down to the shore, even women seemed gone, a few remaining only with that melancholy wail, which though not so distinct as the howl on the way to the grave, is not the less a sign that the hand of death has stricken.

I asked an old woman if she had heard of anybody's loss.

"How can I miss—how can I miss. I had three generations of my own out, and many near friends beside, some must come in cold, with slimy weeds to cover them, when their own mothers would not know them, and unshriven. O-hone!—o-hone!"

I found there was nothing for it but a walk, the road lay over uneven ground first, and then got into the valley, through which a river ran toward the woods, now visible, of the more immediate Castle demesne, everything appeared neglected, and still the wind, though come round to the northeast, was high and cold. I pressed on.

I have not time to describe that from a sort of promontory, at the outer end of which was perched the old castle, was on either hand to be seen the beach stretching far and white with the roaring breakers, and on one side, where the eye could more immediately reach from the approach, it was visibly crowded with that lawless set, the wreckers of the coast. But my object was to reach the ear of the Marquis, and prevent the sudden breaking of my mournful tidings to his orphan lady, and I passed on, gates stood half open, and the deserted state of the neighboring town and country seemed repeated here.

The door of entrance stood thrown back, and only within it appeared one of red cloth, which I made bold to push open. I was in the old hall, where on one side on a sort of settle, sat an old man in a sort of French grey coat with a faded crimson collar, he looked absorbed and dim, but started as he saw me dressed in black, for I had thrown my overcoat on to a table.

I asked for the Marquis.

The old man looked bewildered. "And it is I should be asking your reverence," he at last stammered, "sure we know nothing here, the say was dark, he may be to the fore after all, an' beat'n out."

You may conceive my consternation—it was my turn to be taken aback. "And the Marchioness?" I hazarded, almost trembling with apprehension.

The old man shook his head, and I really felt overpowered.

"She is just the same, down yonder, in the little chapel under the cliff, before the altar, she has been there ever since the messengers came back from the coast behind the island, where the schooner might have sheltered, but there was nothing there, and the day was clear, and many a glass on the heights, but not a rag or a standing mast was to be seen."

This was the substance of what the old porter had to tell, he had been, man and boy, upward of fifty years about the castle, and had never seen such a storm.

I asked the way to the chapel.

"Oh, you will see the first little path to the right—it is well beaten, which the others are not any longer, it was but built for the servants and the workpeople, for, poor man, he was a kind-hearted free-handed gentleman, now that he is gone, and that's the truth." And the old servant crossed himself reverently.

I felt that what I had to tell might well be told nigh that holy place, and followed down the winding road, which, turning round an angle of the rock, brought me upon the smaller entrance-door.

The Marchioness was on her knees before the tabernacle containing the

The Marchioness was on her knees before the tabernacle containing the blessed Sacrament, with its lamp burning before it, the light had almost been excluded, as I afterward learned, by the closing of the shutters against the tempest, and the little church looked sad and gloomy. I knelt down beside her, to pray for those who were gone as well as for they who still lived to enjoy mercy.

Something probably struck her as if I had some news, and she got up. I followed her out, and up that rugged path, which however was the main road to the chapel. It is needless to relate how I introduced myself and apologized for intruding at such a time.

She turned her eyes almost sternly on me, "Sir, you would not do so had you not cause."

I said something about resignation.

"You, a stranger, would not come to preach resignation to one who makes, I hope, no unseemly repining."

"Have you received, madam, any news from England?"

"Not of note. But why? for you must be aware I have a terrible dispensation to bear up against, they try to feed me with false hope."

She paused, my eyes were turned to the earth, I knew not how to break the additional loss. She moved a step or two. "From whence have you come?" she said, abruptly turning.

I answered simply, "From London."

There was a quick keen flash from her eye, and she started as if electrified at the word—the calm settled grief of before was gone, and I stood before an imperious woman. "Who sent you?" she said, in a voice desperately calm.

I told her.

She moved forward a step or two. "Give me your aid, good Father, I am tried beyond my strength." And she took, or rather caught at my arm. I found her ready to faint, and seated her on a bit of turf amongst the rocks, happily her maid had been also in the chapel, and was following at a short distance, and I was glad to be enabled to leave someone with her till I should have got assistance from the castle. Suffice it to say, the Marchioness was carried in an armchair to her own room, scarcely conscious, and put to bed. I gave special directions that no letters were to be delivered to her, indeed, as all were undercover to his lordship, this was so far unnecessary.

It was late in the afternoon, twelve hours of moderate wind from the northeast had partially smoothed the sea and cleared the horizon. Far to the west, and as far as could be seen for the other headlands, the best telescopes had swept the sea, there was still nothing to be discovered, and no doubt seemed to remain that the unfortunate schooner had gone down, which had borne the ill-fated lord and some of his most trusty followers out upon a cruize three days before.

I sat in a dreary sort of library, for there were but few shelves and few *worm-eaten folios upon them, a door gently opened, and a maid gave me a message from her mistress that she would be glad to see me.*

I found her stretched, dressed, on her bed, and a light covering thrown over her feet, there was some wildness in her eye and a hectic on her cheek.

"I fear I have been very weak, as I have not even heard what your sad errand is, though beforehand I know it is of death." She looked eagerly at me.

"Can you bear the news of a loss almost as near to your heart as the one we dread to have happened here?"

She covered her face.

I tried to say something in consolation for the double loss of father and husband, saying, that perhaps it was merciful that she was spared from watching a long and suffering sickness.

"What!" she said. "My Father?" She looked bewildered.

"Yes."

"And where, and how? So sudden. I heard from him from Calais but ere yesterday."

I felt I had stepped on too far, it was, however, impossible to retreat. "He was killed near Wimbledon."

"God have mercy!" But again she sprung to a sitting posture, and grasped my hand. "And who did this deed?" she said, wildly.

"There is no trace, but robbery seems to have been the object, and there appears to have been two persons. I had special charges from Mr. Jones to do everything the Donna told me, so, when she sent for me, I could not hesitate, she pointed to a letter she was writing to him, and said, 'Had he been in England, it would have been him I should have sent, but he is on the Bay of Biscay.'"

She sunk back on her bed, and to own the truth, I was glad to steal out of the room. I met the priest on my way back—it was a vast relief, he came to say that some part of the schooner had been found a little to the northward, washed ashore within some bad reefs.

I explained all that was known about the murder to the good old man, who promised to deal as tenderly and consolingly as he could.

Thus ran the excellent Father Delayney's letter, and in due time he returns, after paying some visits on the way, but he hints that there is some terrible dread about the murderers in the mind of Lady Connemara, which he cannot comprehend, but in other respects she was wonderfully calm.

I have written to say to the worthy priest, that I trust he will have an opportunity of telling her, if it would not be disagreeable to be intruded upon at such a moment, I should offer any services a sister in such a case might propose, and one of the same faith.

I think it right to mention this, that you may know there is always one friend who thinks of your wishes as you are doing of hers.

A few messages to her father, and assurances of her interest in all that was connected with me.

Chapter Eighty
A fight—a good Samaritan—police inquiries

About the middle of May, 1836, on a dark night, soon after eleven, a man passed down the broadway of Whitechapel, just before reaching the turnpike, which, unlike its vis-a-vis of Hyde Park Corner still reminds the Essex yeoman that though he has good roads to travel upon, he has to pay well for them, and without a voice in their administration. After passing downward a little way, he turned and retraced his steps, it was evident he was waiting for someone, by the anxious looks he gave to one or two persons, whose figures came to light as they passed under the rays of a lamp, he kept the side of the street farthest from the river, and his attention was fixed on the other. At last, the figure of a man appeared under a lamppost, who stopped to examine something in his hand by its light, and then turned into a street leading off the road on the same side.

He whom we have described as appearing on the watch, followed quickly the steps of the other, who was to be recognized by a whitish handkerchief or wrapper round his neck, visible behind over the coat collar, and under a small cap, which he had on his head, the follower gained rapidly upon the followed for the first little space until the other perceived someone after him, and without running, very much, quickened his pace, first toward a solitary open space, where some boarding had been put up in an abortive attempt to build, and left to hide the failure, proceeding to the left, then to the right, and then to the left again. The houses were mean and dark looking, and the lamps dim and rare, not a soul was about, and the chase continued in reality, though at a walk, at last the man upon whom the follower had now considerably gained, crossed from the left to the right-hand side of the street, and said something to two men who stood in a doorway, the person in pursuit had crossed also, and was passing on intent on the movements of the one before, when he was almost tripped up by one of these two, and struck on the head by the other, stumbling forward a few paces, he had barely recovered himself, when he was again attacked, one throwing his arms round his neck, and the other attempting to rifle his pockets, in this struggle, one hand of the single man had got free, and with this he flung one adversary over to the other side of the street, while the other, who had grappled with him was still endeavouring to retain his hold, at this juncture, when to all appearance he was about to be disposed of like his companion, a knife blade gleamed in his hand a moment, and then was buried in the side of his antagonist. They had both come against a door, which not being securely fastened gave way, the wounded man falling down a small flight of steps within, while the other having let go his hold of his victim, saved himself against the door post from following his descent. Just at this moment a low whistle and some words were spoken in German by the confederate from the other side, and each disappeared quietly on his own side into neighboring doorways, two men at this moment made their appearance from the same end of the street, by which had come the first two, and strange to say, one of these had a white handkerchief tied over his neckcloth, and an angle hanging over his collar behind, they walked quietly on and turned again to the left at the end of the street, apparently disappointed. The one of these was a policeman, and the other, as he passed the house into which the wounded man had fallen, looked up at the windows, but said nothing.

"This is the end of Buckley Street," said the policeman, as they turned.

The floor of the low room which now contained the wounded man, was covered so with dirt, that it might have been of any material, and a considerable sprinkling of blood, mixed so well with its dark color and clammy coating, as almost to prove itself no foreign agent to its composition. This room opened from the passage, from which it was but slenderly divided, two persons stood with an ill-fed light, behind them the third occupant lay on the floor.

"You are certain they passed," said a female voice.

"As sure as that I see that body before me, and he looked up at the window as I looked down, they will be lurking near."

At this moment, the wounded man, who had lain almost insensible, breathed hard, and both the others started, one was a sleek good-looking man about five and twenty, all his features handsome except his eye, which was rather poor than ill-shaped, lacking only that steadiness and strength of expression, which is almost necessary to masculine beauty. The other person was a woman of fifty in appearance, rather stout than otherwise, and possessing features not bad in themselves, though of an expression which it was difficult to behold without distrust, she was much bloated, and apart, her sinister look bore strongly the traces to be left by a life of debauchery. For a few seconds they talked together in an undertone.

"I know it is he," at last said the man, in a confident tone.

His companion, who appeared to possess the stronger intellect, as well as a command over the other, looked fixedly on the floor, as if in consideration, and then turning to the other said, "He must be got to bed and examined, if he is too badly hurt, we will report it tonight, if not, we may make a better thing of it by tending him till he is well." This was said rapidly, and with a foreign accent.

And they both set about raising the head of the patient, who looking wildly round, asked where he was.

"I told you he would soon be better," muttered the woman.

They united their efforts to the returning strength of the young man, and he was placed upon a sort of rude couch, which seemed to be used as the temporary resting place of people, or clothes as was found most convenient. The squalid appearance of the woman, and the shabby looking finery of the man, together with the dirty discomfort of the den, all seemed to create rather wonder than any other feeling in the new inmate.

"I have been wounded by some rascal," said the latter, recovering himself, and examining his waistcoat, covered with blood, as he lay.

"I think you may say that," said the woman. "And how is your head?"

"Oh! I feel a sort of singing in it. Have you a drop of water to give me?"

"I hope so, but if not, there is beer," said the woman. "But let us see your side, John, see for something to wet his lips." And she set about opening the buttons, but it was not till the jug of water had come, and till their united efforts had enabled them to get off the coat, which they would not hear of cutting, that the shirt could be pulled up, and the nature of the wound discovered, the knife had not penetrated deep, but had glanced the ribs, partially slitting open the gash. The woman, to whom such wounds seemed to be familiar, put her hands on the inner part, and compressed it tight, while a bit of sticking plaster was put over it, and then moving her hands along the lips of the open, held them together as a similar application was placed over them by the hands of the assistant, till the whole was packed up tight in the blood.

"Keep quiet, and you will be all right, but you have another hurt." She added, "Let me have the lamp nearer." Her obedient attendant brought forward the lamp.

"The other I am not aware of," said the young man, "but you have been most expert in closing the cut, and most—" Here he was interrupted.

"No thanks, good Sir, but how did you get this mark?"

"Oh, if it is that you mean, it is natural, at least I have always had it since I can remember."

"Oh, then we have no business to meddle with whole skin, but it looked so red."

She was eyeing her patient attentively with her keen grey eyes, but perceiving her male companion's attention had been attracted, continued, "I don't think he has any fever, perhaps a little warm beer would give a good sleep."

The name of beer brought probably his own wants on that score to the notice of the man who had been called John, and he went to a nail upon which hung a key, and with a tin pitcher left the room.

"Do you think you could sleep?" said the female, in a tone which she seemed to wish to make as kind as a harsh German accent would allow.

"Yes, I feel rather heavy, and would be glad to have a little quiet."

"Well, could you come upstairs?"

"Yes, I think I could."

"Don't move quickly."

She took up the lamp, and the two proceeded up the filthy old stair, which was at the end of the passage, and getting on the landing above, two doors presented themselves, one directly over the passage below, opening into a room which probably ran along the whole front. The woman made a sign, as if to enjoin as little noise as possible, and put the key into another door, probably of a room looking to the back, this room contained two beds, various articles of finery for the male and female form, and a fireplace, in which burned the remains of a well heaped fire. Motioning the stranger, whose coat was thrown mantlewise over his shoulders, to take a seat, his conductress at once proceeded to put a pair of sheets upon the smaller bed, from which various articles had previously to be removed. Presently the bearer of the jug of beer made his appearance, he never seemed to question the acts of his female associate, but looked with some surprise at her proceedings.

"Are we to warm it?" he said, approaching a cupboard, from which he took some sugar and spices.

There was a saucepan standing on the hearth ready for duty, and a single poke woke up the caked and dull red of the fire into a brisk blaze.

"Now you carry these things down," said the mistress, pointing to the other bed.

The chair upon which the stranger sat, had its back to this last piece of furniture, so had he been inclined to object to the evident displacement of the garniture of the family couch, he had no idea it was taking place. The beer smoked, and the landlady recommended her patient getting to bed, and taking the potion after lying down.

This it was not difficult to arrange, as the woman went out of the room, however, she turned back and said, "Do not open the door to any one." Then added, "It is best to let me lock you up—should you want anything, knock three times with this stick on the floor." And she put a bludgeon with a loaded head on the chair at the bedside, and left the room, carefully locking the door, and taking off her shoes to make the less noise in going down, she bore in her hand the remains of the ale, and seemed in deep thought and almost trouble as she went.

The other, whom we have heard called John, was below putting the last touches to the bed substituted for the one above. They both sat down, and a long conversation ensued, the result of which was, that the wounded man was to be as well treated as possible, but each seemed to have some reserve about him, they only united in thinking it more for their interest to create a favorable impression, than do further injury.

Shortly after dawn, two or three ruffian looking Germans, apparently of the order of students, came downstairs from the front room, grumbling at finding all the other doors closed against them, unfastened that of the house and sallied into the street.

It was nine o'clock before the sleeping invalid was brought to a sense of his situation, and a recollection of the strange adventure of the night.

The sun shone bright, as a Whitechapel sun could shine through the more than dingy lozenges of the casement, everything seemed to look strange and suspicious, but the life preserver remained in its place, and the bludgeon and a pair of pistols. He had lain awake but a short time, when the door was softly opened, and the woman of the night before appeared with as Dorcas a look as her features could assume, not improved by the light of day. The dry yellow locks which had been somewhat disordered the night before, were decorously confined within the borders of a muslin cap, and an air of care about her appearance had taken place of the former disarray in her dress as well as looks.

"You feel the better for the sleep, I see," said she. "But perhaps you might as well lie still, and on the other side, to let the thing join kindly, moving is all that can do you harm now. How is your head?"

"Oh, if I cough it hurts me still a little, but when quiet there is no pain."

"Well, you see it gives the best advice, do you want to send for anything?"

The stranger seemed to deliberate. "No, hardly just yet, when do you think I can move?"

"You had best be quiet all day at least—let me see how the side is?" She seemed satisfied with the appearances of the bandages. "I will bring you some tea and a newspaper, you can have any book you like to send for."

"We will see after breakfast," said the invalid.

She left the room, examining the adjoining apartment with a practised and piercing eye. The three beds which occupied the one side of this room were empty, horse-rug-looking bed clothes were tossed about in disorder, and hung over their sides, a table stood in the middle of the room on which lay pipes, dirty glasses, some music books, and an empty beer jug. The survey of the mistress of the house, for so she seemed, did not result in any discovery worthy of interest, and the door was re-shut.

On her arrival below, her husband, for as such she had described him, in offering his assistance to get anything for their guest, observed that he need not be more seen than was necessary.

The other upbraiding him for the dirty scrapes he got into, which made him fear to show his face.

A little wrangling took place, and the man went out, but dressed like a German student, instead of the more slovenly guise of the night before, he had not been out long, when he returned rather hurriedly, double-barred the street-door, and told his helpmate there had been some enquiries by the police, and that they might expect a visit.

"Well, get out of the way, if you do not want to be seen," she said, "and leave me to manage."

He left the house as quickly as he had entered it, the woman mounting the stair at the same moment.

"They are inquiring about the people who attacked you last night, will you be able to give any information?"

"Scarcely," said the young man, looking up, "but thanks to your door giving way first, and to your kind care afterward, it is hardly worthwhile."

"Just as you like, they are mostly foreigners about here—musicians."

"I do not think," said the other, "that there could have been anything but a mistake, or a street robbery intended, as I am not many hours returned from a foreign country."

"Well, if you do not know who it was attacked you, nothing can be done, but get up some trouble in the neighborhood, so I will keep the door fast."

She descended the stair and drew the bolts, a knocking came soon after and then a conversation was held from a front window of the next house, the result of which was, the persons who came to make inquiries departed without gaining any information.

Chapter Eighty-One
Report to Mr. Searle—Mr. Edward Warren—a bloodhound—the quarry found

Three days after that upon which we left the wounded man in Whitechapel, about eleven in the forenoon a hackney carriage stopped at the door of Mr. Searle's, in Golden Square, and a young man got out, who was at once admitted. His right arm was in a sling, and he was rather pale, the door of the family parlour into which he was shown was hardly shut, when it re-opened to admit the worthy lawyer, with whom the reader is already acquainted.

"What has been the matter? I have been full of alarm that something had occurred, and I fear you have got into some difficulty," said he, with unusual excitement of manner.

"I had better tell the whole night's adventure succinctly," said the other smiling, and narrating what the reader already knows.

"You followed a man dressed as I told you, and was attacked when close behind him?"

"Yes."

"The people of the house you would know again, and the house?"

"No, the woman told me it might get them into trouble with their neighbors, if I gave any information as to the house, so I let her blindfold me till I got out of the street, when I left last night, I have never seen the man but on the first night, and all that is to me most curious in the matter is, that I almost thought his face not unknown."

"Well, Wilson the detective is here, whom you should have followed, but by tomorrow I shall know more, I hope you do not feel hurt much."

"No, if I keep quiet, all is right, but the place feels stiff and sore when I move."

"Well, it will not hurt you to go and see Lady Davenport, the Conchas are not in town, I believe they are gone to Paris, I will send to you tomorrow." With this the visitor was dismissed—that is left to find his way out as best he could—by the lawyer, who had quitted the business which had previously occupied him, to come and see him.

Shortly after, a servant ascended the quiet stair of Lady Davenport's house, in St. James's Square, there were plants as when last we visited that stately mansion, midway the servant stopped and said, with a sort of half-smile, as if he pitied a man who did not know his own name, "Mr. Jones, I believe."

"No, Mr. Edward Warren." The man was silenced, if not convinced, and went on.

"I know my Lady will see you, Sir," he had previously observed, "as she often asks about you."

The visitor was left in an ante-room, between the conservatory and the breakfast parlour, there was some little delay, and the same servant with sedate complacency opened the door, saying, "Her Ladyship would see Mr. Warren."

"Now I really think you are Mr. Warren, rather than Mr. Jones, myself," said the kind Countess. "But how are you so pale, and bandaged up? Tell me what is happened."

"I am only returned a few days from Spain, and had occasion to go to an out of the way part of London, to look for some person with whom I had some business, and was attacked by two men, I fell against the door—happily not securely barred—of some good Samaritan. I had a flesh wound, but was much stunned by the fall into the passage down several steps."

"Well, I see you are not quite recovered, so send your cab away, and stay quietly here, if we go out, we can leave you all the last resources of Chapman, or you might come with us, but better remain quiet."

My carriage was sent off, and I had to tell all my history as far as I knew it, omitting of course anything in which Isabel was concerned.

"Well," said the kind old lady, "I always felt as if you were a Warren, did I not, Dora?"

"Yes, aunt, indeed you did, and I think you were right," said the good-natured Lady Dorothea. "But have you heard anything of the Donna Rosa? You know her father has gone to Mexico."

"No, I have heard nothing."

"She is down in Cumberland or Westmoreland, as their residence is on the borders of one or t'other, at Gilsland Place. You know Lady Connemara has inherited all her father's great estates, sad business, he was my cousin, odd, mysterious man, murdered strolling about the fields near his villa, no one knew he was in England, he was always flying about as if haunted."

"They have found out the murderers," hazarded the visitor.

"No! No one knows anything of the matter, there was a gipsy about the common, but he could account for passing his time for two or three nights after the servants last saw their master."

This was all the information her Ladyship possessed on the subject, nor did it appear much to interest her.

There was a great family dinner, and the invalid was sent home in a coach, the blazonry of which so bewildered an Irish servant at the Burlington, that he for some time believed his master had been privately elected Lord Mayor.

It was about the beginning of June, an early spring had pushed forth leaf and flower in the wild dells of Gilsland, where primeval oaks, and gigantic beech in all the gradations of youth, vigor, and decay, mingled together their shadows over the clear brook. The spotted deer and the wild cattle roamed over the never turned sward of the bold swells, or crouched in the thick beds of fern which were but now beginning to form a covert. The heron and the rook had each their branchy domain, but secure in centuries of protection, disdained the noisy fears which agitate the winged tribe in more ordinary situations. Roads traversed the great space of wild moor and pasture, which was called the park, in all directions, but it was remarkable, always in straight lines, sometimes crossing, but never following the valleys, which were generally heavily timbered. An occasional scream from a pheasant or a peacock, or the bray of a donkey, the murmur of a stream, or the deep tone of a clock, followed each other curiously in breaking a spell-like silence which reigned on the hill as in the dell.

There is a period of the day, generally a little after one in the afternoon, when wild animals go to water, this time had not arrived, and the heights were in various places studded with small herds of deer in repose, who heeded little the passing of ordinary persons along the roads. At the moment, however, we refer to, there came along the ridge on which ran the road, a conical forehead, and deep set eye, shewed him to be of the race called bloodhound, he was rather what might be termed leggy and loosely made, it is a race nearly extinct, but perhaps is the most perfect in its organs of smell, or some other perception for following a track though cold, of any animal known to man. The dog was leading, and though occasionally the cord was tightened as he pressed on, he appeared to be accustomed to guide another, rather than pursue himself, his head was down, the eye haggard, perhaps with age, and the stern carried high. The man who followed was little less distinct in his outward characteristics, he appeared about fifty, from the weather-beaten texture of his skin, and the deepening wrinkles of the brow, his hair was of a curly iron-grey, thick and coming to a point low on the forehead, he was a tall man, strongly built, with something of a stoop in his shoulders. He wore a short smock-frock, had leathers and leggings down to meet a pair of those iron garnished lace boots, in which an English keeper's feet and ankles appear to be laced up forever. The man, who carried a short gun, followed the dog along the grassy edge of the road, which as the ridge turned, cut straight down into a valley filled with timber, the shade under these ancient trees was deep, and the way here took a bend under a rock to obtain a shallow crossing of the stream when in flood, and a better ascent on the opposite bank. The shadows became deepened into gloom, compared with the bright glare without, the hound held on his way, followed by the man, they had got to where the foad, keeping on a shelf of rock along the side of the brook, was much narrowed for a short distance, and here the dog began to give signs of impatience, and the man found himself right in front of a person who already stood as if to bar his way. The dog gave one dash, as if to seize upon the stranger, but was pulled back by a powerful hand, the beast, however, had ascertained that was not the object of his pursuit, and strained to follow along the edge of the rock, where he seemed to have recovered his trail.

The old man looked up and stopped, there stood before him a tall youth, his head bare, and carrying a small switch in his hand, as if he had just dismounted. His brow was not lofty but broad, and over it clustered waving hair of light brown, his brows were thick and darker than his hair, as also were his eyelashes, his eyes deep hazel, were long and almond-shaped, there was something of sternness in the brow, and softness in the eye, the mouth was large, but curved into a habitual smile where it entered the cheek, the chin was well developed and strong, the limbs appeared to be powerful, and the whole attitude seemed natural, calm, and commanding.

"I have been looking for a way to the house," he said. "Perhaps you can put me upon one without much trouble."

The old man, who had been gazing at his questioner with a stupid stare, quite unlike his habitual expression, said, "Your Lordship can't go wrong, if you keep that path anything like a woodsman, though it is something blind, it is an old keeper's road, and leads straight to the back of the place."

"Thank you, but I am not a Lord," said the other gravely, and with a slight though courteous bow, turned to take the way pointed out.

The keeper still looked after him, pulled along by the hound, whose deep note told of impatience at the increased restraint.

There were some large stones, which, without being quite regularly placed, served to enable the foot passenger to get dryly over the shrunken current, on the opposite side of which the road mounted straight out of the wood on to a bare down, across this, which was of considerable extent, the way ran straight and open, till it entered amongst some dwarf thorns, and a few stunted oak, reedy pools, and patches of heath, they passed through all this without turning aside or stopping.

"Well," said the man, as he stretched out in good earnest, "he's made a sheer cut of it."

They were now near a line of tall beech, which ran across the road, where also on a nearer approach was a gate and an old lodge, there ran the wall, partly covered with ivy under these trees, which had perhaps once been planted to screen it from view, the gate was simple, and but a bar or two higher than an ordinary farm gate, and beside it was a wicket capable of letting pass a horse, which was open, they went through this without hesitation, and were now on a turnpike road, but the country through which it passed, was a sort of waste, a few enclosures of stone formed here and there a field, but much of the surface had been broken by quarries and thickets, so that wherever they intervened, they were avoided by the fences, and left uninclosed. Large flocks of geese seemed to have the chief profit of these abandoned portions of ground.

The hound made some doubles about the road, crossed and then came back to the narrow skirt of shrubs and heath, which ran between it and the park wall, the beeches within threw some spreading branches over the fence, and trees of a younger growth had here and there sprung up without, on a footpath in the grass, at the edge of this, the bloodhound again found the track, and went on as staunchly as before.

It was not more than three hundred yards from the gate, that a thicker and higher growth of trees completely concealed the wall, leaving a mossy carpet under their shade, a screen of thorn and briar surrounding for the most part the outer edge, it was here the hound found he had come close upon his quarry, straining and bounding against his master's hold, the tightening of the collar checking the deep note of his bay. The keeper, however, now seized him by the throat, and spoke to him to restrain his eagerness, they were opposite an open in the bushes, a small waggon tilt was there, and a lean-to against the park wall, an old gipsy woman was sitting with her back against a tree, and her face turned away, a young man sat facing her in the wide and low fork of another.

"That will be a Nevil, perhaps, Ralph," said the old woman. "I knew the voice of his hound, though I haven't been here for forty years."

"Then, Mistress, you never saw the dog, that's sure enough. But, young man, will you please to come over here and give Wanderer this crust." And he took from the greasy bag a crust of crisped toast saturated with melted butter. "It will show him all is right, and make friends, for he has brought me here straight on your track."

The youth laughed a merry laugh, and came as he was bid. The hound took the reward of his success greedily, and snuffed the limbs of the man upon whom, a minute before, or under different circumstances, he would have flown with fury. The keeper all the time was curiously examining the old woman.

"Ah, you will look long before you read much in me."

"But I would like just to know how you came to know me without looking."

"I heard the voice of the dog, the same as of old. And why should not Ralph, the son of Ralph, be the man?"

The keeper hardly appeared satisfied. "And is this your son?"

"He is my grandson. But what of him, and why do you dog his steps," said the old woman, uneasily.

"For no harm, good mother, he has never been off the path, and I never wish harm to those who don't meddle with me. But I had almost forgot—it must be you was down at the place to see the Spanish Lady Rose?"

The youth nodded an assent.

"She did not know where to send after you, as there are many roads lead through the grove, so my lady sent for me as I passed the house, to ask if I had seen such a one, as she wanted him back particularly. I said I had seen no one, but being told the young man crossed the lawn, I was not long of putting Wanderer on him—and here we are. You haven't cut a twig nor stopped the whole way, and it is nigh about three miles, and there are not many such likely sort of lads could say as much, as I could have killed a rabbit or two and a fawn myself, as I came along, with a stick." And he smiled good-naturedly, as he wiped his shaggy, honest, bull-looking head.

"Well, Mr. Ralph—if that is your name—I will tell you one thing—that is, I go at her bidding, and another, that the lady of the place and the Lady Rose are the friends of one I would give my warm blood to serve. So, were I inclined, which I am not, to do any business in the poaching line, your ground is as safe as your own hearth-stone from harm by me, on the word of a true man." He took up a short sort of quarter-staff. "Is there any near cut?"

"Yes, when you get to the first brook, where it runs under the red cliff, you will take to the left through the underwood, there is a sort of track, something blind sometimes, but such as I reckon you could make out with half an eye, it goes straight to the old place."

A few bounds took the active youth out of immediate sight, and Ralph sat down upon the bough formerly occupied by the youth just gone away, whom the reader has no doubt recognized as Tom.

A conversation by side-wind, as it might be called, now took place, begun by the old woman, who inquired about old Ralph, who was dead, about the old Earl, and about his grandson, who had succeeded him. Of the last two lords, no one at the place knew anything, as they had never been in the north.

For this information, Ralph got but little in return. The woman had been a fortune-teller, had got into trouble forty years ago, and never came back. He was told he had no son, that there was one favorite daughter, whom she would like to see.

Ralph at last took his leave, something impressed with respect for the strange knowledge the old gipsy seemed to possess.

Chapter Eighty-Two
A portentous interview

We must, however, go backward to the hour of half-past ten, and introduce the reader to an apartment in the place. It was a lofty square room, with heavy cornices, and a rich stuccoed roof, some pictures of favorite horses, quaintly done, hung on the dark wainscoted walls, it was furnished with tarnished gilt chairs, their bottoms and backs of arras. The principal feature of this room, however, consisted in a large window, which opened like a door upon a flight of steps, which conducted to a succession of terraces with balustrades, rows of huge yews between the one and the other obscured the view, except where the steps, led from different levels, the lowest of which, quay-like, ran for a quarter of a mile along the stream in the bottom, which being dammed up, wore the appearance of a broad canal. The opposite bank here confined the view, a mass of forest circling round, so as at no point from the house on that side, or from the garden, to leave an open. Certain implements of drawing, various wrappers and parasols laid upon a table, the room contained but one person, who had just been left by a servant, who said her ladyship would pass presently as she went out.

The person who waited was a woman, she was perfectly well dressed, and sat down as if intending to feel herself at her ease, but putting to rights certain curls which appeared too dark for the light eyes and eyebrows they clustered over—a glance at the mirror seemed not unsatisfactory, but this person was not so tranquil as she seemed to desire.

It was not, however, many minutes before the door from an adjoining gallery opened, and a lady in deep mourning entered. Her hair was entirely confined within a plain widow's cap, but was in such quantities as to threaten to protrude, swelling out the cap, plaited though it was round the head, the eyes were strangely lustrous, and the brows finely marked, the skin was pale—that is, had no ruddiness or pink, though their want did not appear to arise in any degree from ill-health, the lips were full, and sweet in expression, her stature was tall for a woman, and her figure perfectly well proportioned. Just after her, passed a slim page, who took from a table some of the wrappings lying on it, to aid in putting them on.

The lady of the house—for such she could not fail to appear, young as she was—turned, however, to the servant, and told him to wait in the gallery, adding a request to be seated, to the inquiry if the person waiting had not said she wished to see Lady Connemara on important business.

"It is quite correct, my lady," began the stranger. "My business is of importance, and I have come all the way from London to ask your advice how I am to act."

An almost imperceptible smile played on Lady Connemara's lips, as she said, "You could hardly have supposed that the advice of one so inexperienced could much benefit you."

"It is from none other I could ask it so well, however," said the other, "as it most concerns you."

This was said in a tone something less deferential than that in which the conversation on her part had been commenced.

"Well, I am perfectly willing to hear you, and to give any advice I can," resumed the Marchioness.

"I have made a discovery lately which may take away all your property, my lady."

The eyes of the Marchioness became intent, which appeared to be a sign wrongly interpreted by the other.

"Yes," she added, "every acre, if the affair is not properly managed. No one knows of this but myself and your ladyship, and I have come to learn what I ought to do, here under the roof-tree of your house."

"If what you guess proves correct, it is no longer my roof," said the lady, gravely, "but I cannot be expected to take such an account seriously, unless I am made acquainted with some details."

"Well, that is reasonable. I was maid to a lady of north Italy, she had married a Swiss Baron, they had a son. The Baron was engaged in some communication with Malta, and afterward went to Lisbon—it was on political business, before the campaign of 1813, he died on his arrival at Lisbon of an accident on board a ship during a storm something fell on his head, as I heard —however, he died soon after our reaching Lisbon.

"My mistress was very beautiful.

"About six months after this—for we were obliged to stay, not having the means of getting back—the Baroness got acquainted with a young Englishman, who had come out for his health and to recover his spirits, for he had lost his wife some months before. He was fond of music, and so was the Baroness, and it was in that way they first met. I understood that, though he suffered much from the loss of an excellent lady, there had been no passionate love between them, and it was soon apparent that he was much struck with my mistress.

"Things went on in this way for some little time. He was very handsome, and most agreeable and accomplished. The short and long of it was, they were married secretly at Santarem, and in course of time it was resolved to go to England, where Mr. Warren thought he might be able to reconcile his father to his having married a foreigner and a Catholic, the young Baron was three years old at this time.

"Mr. Warren contracted a chest complaint, it was gaining on him fast since his return to his own country. His father had heard that he had a mistress with him, but what was worse, he was duly informed she was a Catholic. I heard he was wild upon this subject, as he had thirty-two English churches in his gift. However, distress of mind helped on disease of body, and the son burst a blood vessel, and was carried off suddenly at his father's house.

"There had been a cousin of his, with whom he was a great favorite, though an elderly man and a bachelor, a most kind-hearted gentleman, he had come from one of his visits to Lisbon before us, but had heard of our arrival and the circumstances of the case, and wrote simply to say he might with confidence be applied to, should it be found necessary. I heard Mr. Warren say so to his wife, it seemed as if he knew what was coming, for he never saw her again, it was near the time she was to become a mother. I learned of his death by some of the people about, but concealed it, making different excuses, as he had before been absent for a month, and the poor lady suspected nothing, for to the last her husband had been beautiful in his complexion, and those eyes so bright, that she loved to look upon, but I saw that melancholy warning in them which never fails in those doomed to an early death.

"However, little as she understood English, she had overheard a conversation which made her anxious about the long silence as well as absence of her husband, more than a week had passed without a letter from him. I saw some fear had disturbed her, and attempted to account for everything, but people who have an affection for any one, when they begin to tell them lies, even with the best intention, never do it well or naturally, and my consolations made matters worse.

"In the night the poor lady, a second time a widow, was seized with the pains of child-birth, and before morning she was delivered of a son. A good priest wrote to the cousin of my late master to tell what had happened, four days after he arrived, and the child was christened, but his birth was also registered in St. Martin's parish. There were several plans about nursing, and an

Irish woman was got, but Mr. Warren was not satisfied with her, and got someone else.

"The child's mother—my poor mistress—cared for nothing after she heard of her husband's death, the oldest boy she could not bear to see, and the infant was purposely kept out of her way. At last the child was settled with a gardener's wife near Dulwich, and I afterward heard, died. Another relative of her last husband took charge of the eldest boy, whom I have. since seen once or twice, and my poor mistress was anxious to go into a convent, and in the end she left me to shift for myself, as she had herself been forced to do, and for twenty-one years I have fought my way as best I could.

"Now, to bring this long story to a close, I have merely to add, that I have reason to believe the child of my mistress by her second husband is alive, and if so, is your uncle—in short, is the heir after your father. But I thought it best to keep all as dark as possible, but I cannot say I know the rights of it myself."

The Marchioness sat silently watching the countenance of the woman, in which hardness and cupidity seemed to be predominant expressions.

"I was not aware of my father having any brother, or of his father having been twice married."

"Of that I cannot tell, but if you wish to keep the property, that young man must never make any claim."

"Well, but I know it is now mine, and no such loose tale would take it from me, nor do I know who you mean."

"Why, to be sure, the grandson of the old gentleman, who hated Catholics, his father never told me his real name, but I was not to be blinded so easily. But he is gone—I have no friend left." Here a cambric pocket handkerchief was pulled forth to attest to her sorrowful state.

"The best advice I can give you," said the Marchioness, "is to go to the convent and see your former mistress, if you have forgotten the address, I have a foreign friend here who probably knows it, as I have heard her speak of such a person. She may believe in the accuracy of your account of her son being alive, and it may be right enough, but it does not prove who he is, or take from me what is my own. So I shall wish you good day, thanking you for the intention of being serviceable to me in this matter."

Chapter Eighty-Three
Matters of birth and family

The lady of the house rose, and touching a small bell on the table, the page reappeared from the gallery, and at the signal, showed the visitor out by the door by which she had entered, and near which waited the servant who had let her in.

"Is the Lady Rosa in the green drawing room?" she asked the page, as she re-entered.

The page *believed*—but his mistress passed quickly through the end of the gallery into the first door.

"My dearest Rose," she said, "I have been so afraid of acting wrong. There has been a Swiss woman here, who was the maid of the nun of York, she has got some strange version of a story—but she says she can get me turned out of house and land. She has herself seen the true heir. I did not press her, but there must be something very near the truth in her belief, or she would not have come from town to tell me, though evidently with the expectation of getting something for the news. So I have sent her off to the monastery."

"And who is this woman?" asked Rose.

"Well, just think how foolish I have been, I never asked, nor have I any idea."

"Oh, we can easily get to know that by means of Tom, who could scour the country, so strong is his steed at present."

"But he has been gone himself these two hours."

"Yes, but we can send after him, he will not be far, for his grandmother is come."

At this moment, they saw, from the window, Ralph walking across from the house to the bridge, having been to know, as was his wont, if there were any orders.

He was asked, from the window, if he knew where Tom was.

Ralph did not know who such a person was, by name.

"Oh, you might have seen him about, and it was only this morning he was here, and went off by the east road."

"Well, my lady, I can soon let you know, if he is at the place, or near the park." And he touched his hat.

"That is, you can send him here when you find him," the Marchioness called after him.

Another time was the hat doffed, and the sturdy keeper held on his way.

The green plush coat exchanged for a smock-frock, and the old hound taken out on the leash, and we found him but shortly after following the trail on the road to the red cliff.

Something more than an hour after, Rose was walking on the lowest terrace along the banks of the canal, she was alone, and appeared occupied, if not sad, and there was a change in her appearance since the last year—the cheek was less round, and the eye more open, and appearing larger and brighter, her step, which had never been the pigeon-gait of the ordinary squaw, had that marked time of the Indian of the other sex, which is characterized by dwelling long on the step, as well as considerable length of stride. She had taken two or three turns, and at last, sat down on the balustrade, seeming to watch the fish, which being accustomed to be fed, gathered about the place where any one stopped. There was an earthen jar of grains near, she took a ladle-full, and seemed amused by the struggles of the crowd below, various kinds of ducks came from under branches and behind reeds, to join the scramble, and a couple of portly swans were forcing their way with indignant impetus from the other end.

But there was a tread on the smooth gravel, and it was the assured step of a man. A slight hectic colored the wan cheek of the Mexican Donna, but she did not at once look round, and when she did, her composure was returned.

She held out both her hands. "I knew it was you, as I heard the footfall."

They were seated together—the fish and the fowls forgotten.

"All your father's debts which could be collected, and which amount to a large sum, have been sent to America or to England, and his revenues in Spain are well arranged for transmission where he may choose. I have already written, but we may as well write again, as the English post is as sure as the Spanish at least, he nor you need have no more hesitation nor fear about the safety of these monies. I only tell you this, that you may join in the satisfaction I feel at the first trust and business transaction I have been engaged in having been satisfactorily finished."

"But I never doubted it would."

"I did though. You look pale, Rose."

"And why should I not, mewed up in a house, or walking in a shady grove, as they do in this country of care?"

An inexpressible sigh showed how true the words.

"And you do not ask for that fine creature who is the lady of all the hills and dales you see, and of that stately mansion, who would not have been so long of asking about you, did she know I had just seen you."

"She would do no such thing," said a voice close by. "I have been watching Mr. Edward stealing upon you, after getting over the old garden wall like a squirrel, and he could hardly ask for me, after such a trespass, but our poor traps and spring guns are rusty from want of use, or we might have had wounds to dress, lint, and laudanum, and sentiment."

It was with a bright color the Marchioness spoke, and quick. Our friend Edward seized the not unwilling hand. The keen eye of their companion had, however, discovered someone, who seemed to be coming toward the wall at the end of the terrace.

"Isabel, dear, there is Tom, do speak to him, and get what you want done, before he sees Ned, or he will be useless for the rest of the day, we will get into the next walk, while you see him."

The Marchioness seemed almost glad to get a little away, and her interview with Tom appeared to go on with fluency from the wall to the park, the two others sat on the middle steps, which led from one gradation to another, down the middle of the garden, before them rose the bank of the river, high in itself, and covered with lofty timber. Trees grouped above trees, to a great height, the flights of steps and quaint vases on either side, the vista opening but a small portion behind of the extended front of the ancient looking house. But the looks of Edward and the Spanish Lady were fixed on the dark wood in front, the occasional note of the thrush was heard there, and the coo of the wild pigeon, but that bit of forest was dead, like the leafy masses of Poussin, it was to those two no living grove, neither spoke, but the deep dark eyes of Rose turned upon those of her companion, and forbade the words that were upon his lips.

"Dearest brother, we have not been idle while you have been away, and though we have not as yet a knowledge of your father, there is but little doubt that your mother is still alive, and she was by another father the mother of a half brother, whom I shall never name again."

The Marchioness here appeared below. "That dear gipsy is gone our errand like an arrow. Did you see the grandam?" she inquired of Ned.

"No!" he answered, "nor did I know she was here."

"She is near the moor gate, on the south of the park, some distance west of the great gate, I know you would like to see the old lady, so you shall be free till dinner time, here is a pass key, no more trespassing."

The two ladies mounted the steps which led to the fretted iron work gate of the upper terrace, and thence into the parterre of flower beds and box-bordered walks of inlaid pavement, which the ingenuity of some Dutch gardener had laid out under the windows of that whole front.

There was an entrance through a private door in the wall, which divided these more private grounds from the park, when the family was at home this gate was never locked, but shut with a bolt, to be opened outside by a concealed spring not usually known, as it was a door by which neither gardeners nor work-people ever entered. The two ladies were on their way to the steps leading to the garden window as it was called, when they saw a figure seated near this private door upon the pedestal of a vase, it was that of an old woman, with a skin browned by exposure, notwithstanding the sort of Nice hat, which shadowed her from the sun, her elbows were on her knees, and her two hands each supporting a cheek, her dark eyes intently fixed upon the Marchioness, on whose near approach she addressed.

"Stop, lady, a moment on your way, and let me look upon you, I am no beggar, as you might deem, but one who was bred near your own kin, and after many a year, I have come back to look upon the old place, its lady, and perhaps its lord."

There was something impressive and picturesque in the words, and attitude of the speaker, her head still bent down on one hand, but the other stretched out with the knuckles uppermost to stay the progress of those she addressed.

The Marchioness looked not unkindly on this strange personage, before saying, "And who are you, and how came you in this garden?"

"I am she, who but for that fatal stroke of illness, which took away a father I never saw, should have been in the Hall in a gilded chair, and you—but no, you would in all truth have been the lady, but of another home."

The Marchioness looked in pity to her companion, saying in an undertone, "She is mad."

"I came in just now by that gate, forty years ago I did the same, they have never changed the spring."

"Well, then can we be of any use?"

"No, no, Ralph even did not know me, and he is about the oldest of your people. But I have come now, that I have named the name, because that Ralph said he had met his lord by the Red Cliff, it was even a place of note for the Lords of Gilsland, they say. Ralph is no slight maiden to be scared, but he said as sure as he stood there to tell it, that he met his young Lord, that is, the father of the late Earl Adelbert, who asked the way to the place, he was unearthly pale, but it was he, if your Ladyship asks, you will find the old keeper has been to know if any mishap has befallen his lady." And in fact, as she spoke, the page, who seemed to be the more especial attendant, came to ask if her Ladyship had any further orders for the keeper. "You still want to know why I am here," continued the hag. "I would have been glad to see the old place once more, and I would have been rejoiced to see its bright lady, but what brought me here with the step and the longing of youth, was to see him again. I have seen his father, a child in the arms of my own boy, he loved to pull his curly hair with his little hands, and I have seen my poor Tom, my own boy's grandson in his arms as a child in a death struggle, and the runners near, I sat and saw all that, and then the deliverance. To me, that head, which poor Nevil thought was of one dead, is the gladdest the widow's eye has ever looked upon for many a year. I thought to come quick, but he has been, and is gone. Lady," she said, solemnly, "you had not the heart to drive him hence. I know it all now, I knew there had been a marriage and a son, for I was near, and I told your father so, but it was no affair of mine then, he always said it could not be, and that I was a poor crazy thing and should go to Bedlam."

The Marchioness's countenance changed to ashy white, and she took the arm of Rose to totter away.

"Lady, stop a little moment, and stop alone, I have but few words to say, but they are good."

Rose whispered, "Stay dearest, if you can, she means you well, I do believe." The Marchioness lingered, but with a downcast look.

"Lady, I wished in no way to hurt you, my lips have been shut but to yourself, and there is one I wot of, whom I love as if he were my own, though I miss him here, and he would not ruffle the lightest thought you have for a golden crown, instead of an Earl's cap, I shall never say a word, whatever betide, so let the memory of the dead rest, now tell him to come and see me, there is luck in the good wishes of those that look upon you with an eye of love." She turned as she spoke, and left the garden.

Chapter Eighty-Four
Edward Warren's letter—the evil genius

Letter from Edward Warren to Harry Bromley Smyth.

Dear Harry,

Had I hosts of relatives, you would still be the dear friend to whom I should write, as to one who would understand my thoughts, and respond my feelings, but I am still unowned as a relative by all the world, but that bond which unites shipmates and the wild comrades of the west, exists in its strongest tie between us, and I shall feel unspeakable relief in imparting my thoughts and anxieties as they gush. The two ladies—for I am installed at the Place of Gilsland—have taken charge of my affairs in my absence and M. Conchas, so that Mr. Searle treated me in London, except letting me in for an adventure in Whitechapel, as if I had no need to know the progress of my affairs, and I feel satisfied that if anything is to be made out for me, the necessary investigation cannot go on under better auspices. This is a great house, long galleries, courts, and endless suites of rooms, so that though under the same roof, I am at a long walk's distance from where Lady Connemara and her friend are lodged, we meet to walk, and to drive over the grounds. Rose cannot be got to ride, she says she should fall off riding on a side-saddle, she has, however never I hear been in the stable, where there are nearly thirty horses of different kinds. It is a subject she cannot bear to speak upon, the remembrance of the past still preys upon her spirits, but the strangest news I have heard is, that I am believed to be the brother, by the same mother, to Bernard, by degrees I put things together to corroborate this, my being sent to the school where he was a teacher, my unaccountable sympathy for him, the having had him sent after me, all tend to make me believe this strange first discovery they had made. But though all seems to point to my turning out an independent person of honorable birth, I am not leading so happy a life as you might suppose, though in daily intercourse with our dear brave Rose, and one for whom love would be a word much too weak to express my feeling. The numerous servants are all in black, the house is furnished in a heavy antique style, certain sober and reverend neighbors come to dinner occasionally, and an Earldom and his wife, of George the Second's creation. They are people of wealth and good family, but they—I have heard—have always knocked under at Gilsland, and they actually appeared as if paying a sort of homage, his Lordship never spoke, and his Countess echoed whatever she heard, so that had they not really both been good people, she might have been what is called sold in every sentence. Rose looks stately, and her dress is so much more becoming than any one's else, that the squires' wives are puzzled to know who she is, there is a very fair private band, and the whole establishment is that of a family who could live within themselves. The deer and the wild cattle are attractive at first, but you cannot help seeing that they are there by the will of an owner, who derives pleasure from seeing them. The trees are grand in girth and height, not one too many in a grove, there are birds on their boughs, and they are there by their own consent, but it is as in a sanctuary, and you do not feel as if you could kill anything in this great domain—even had you need, without violating a law of hospitality and trust.

You remember what is called the buckeye in the west, there is no fruit yet, but the trees are many, and the deer stand, with the large brown eye which gives color to the name, gazing at you from near their shade in a sort of security, I know I could not betray.

Mi-lady rather queens it over me, and I think it makes things go on more decently, as I should not perhaps otherwise be able to control myself. I believe, however, scandal, which is to be found strong and pungent in the country, as well as in town, makes me the lover of Rose, as we are most together.

I finished my letter last night, and when breakfast was ended this morning, was about to retire to a small study to seal and direct it, when Rose let me understand by a look, that she wished to speak to me. I was enabled to make the Indian sign of good, which means of course assent.

She followed me, and said, I wish to show you a picture of the late Marquis, which arrived yesterday, it is in Isabel's dressing room at present, and as she has gone out, I thought it a good chance, as I particularly want you to see it.'

She then led the way through a long corridor, which had been added inside the quadrangle, and at its end we passed through the room of the lady's maid, which seemed like a guard-room to the apartments of the

Marchioness, and her guest beyond, for here the corridor had terminated, and the rooms opened into one another filling up the breadth of the building.

I was amused at this intrenchment behind a maid, as a defence. The two rooms were stately and old-fashioned—Rose's first, then the sleeping-room of Isabel, and beyond, a large square room, hung with yellow silk, there was piano, and harp, and guitar music strewed about, a table covered with the most exquisite objects of vertu, with a half open drawer, which seemed to come out to be written upon, opposite mirrors reflected and multiplied Venetian chandeliers of the varied hues of the opal, a small white Roman dog, with long hair and the head of a fox, leapt from his well-padded basket at our entry—he was the guardian of the room for the present.

I was admiring the painted ceilings, and rich Louis XIV. hangings and furniture, when Rose touched my arm, and pointed to a sofa, upon which, as I got a little further toward the light that fell across it, I discovered a picture, it was oval, in a rich frame. Still the light was unfavorable, and Rose pulled down the blind of the nearest window, my head was turned as she did so, and upon looking again I could scarcely believe my eyes—but that dreadful face was before me—that head which had followed me like a fate from Fernwold's supper to the distant Popagee—there it was—the stern searching eye, as if still hungering for vengeance. The portrait was strongly drawn—faithful to a fault—and the eyes had the expression of fixing themselves upon the beholder.

"I thought it would be a surprise to you," said Rose, "and I was anxious you should have seen this picture before Isabel might invite you here to look at some drawings she has made, which she talked of doing only yesterday. Now, when you see this face again—which I myself have never forgotten—it will be without any visible emotion."

I cannot settle to write further, so unhinged am I by this last discovery.

Yours,
E.W.

Chapter Eighty-Five
Come to reason—on trial for murder

It was in a small inn, in the western part of Yorkshire, in a village on one of the great roads, that a couple of persons sat over the remains of tea. There seemed to be but little comfort in their thoughts, and few words passed between them. A female waiter entered at the moment we describe.

"What coaches, tomorrow, for town, and when?" said the male—for the room was occupied by a male and female—with an air of some little pretension.

"Two in the morning, at six and eight, and two in the evening, at five and seven. There is a young gentleman has just arrived on horseback, who wishes to see you, sir, if your name be Dacre."

"A young gentleman, you say?" said Mr. Dacre, in some surprise.

"Why, perhaps you would call him a young man, but he is good-looking and well-spoken—so I call him a gentleman, till I know better," answered the damsel, with a toss of her head.

"Oh—Ah, that is another story," said the elegant Mr. Dacre. "We are partikley engaged just now, and only stopping because we were too late to get on." He looked at the sour expression on his partner's face, who broke in—

"Speak for your own share, John, I am no ways busy myself."

"Well, as you like, my dear. Let the young man then come in," he added, graciously, to the waiting maid.

It was not long before the door again opened, giving entrance to a youth, a little above the middle height, slimly made, but not wanting a certain appearance of muscle in his limbs and length in his arms, he appeared little over the age of boyhood, to look only at his head, the chin being beardless, long, thick, and glossy raven hair, clustering on his brow, fell over his ears, there was a certain air of daring in the countenance, though the features were, except the eyes, small and regular, these were large and dark, and usually shaded by thick and long lashes.

Mr. Dacre rose as this youth made his appearance, and got between him and his female companion, putting his finger significantly on his lips, and pointing with his thumb backward toward his amiable partner.

"Sir," said the youth, "I will not disturb you long. I only came with a message from Father Reeves, of M——, he found I was going your way, and might overtake you. The lady you wished to see has consented—should it be convenient for you to return—to the interview you asked for."

"But how do we know that it is we you have been sent to, or that you have been sent at all?" broke in the lady.

"How should I have known your name, madam, or where to find you, or what good would it do me, who deal in horses, to meddle uncalled in the matter? I was asked to give the message, if you understand it, my part is done, and I wish you good night." Saluting with a carelessly rustic bow and scrape of the foot, the speaker withdrew.

"Well," said the dame, exultingly, "I knew they would come to reason, where there is money in the case, all the world are to be comeat, if you take the right way."

It was about two months afterward that the Assize was held at York, and we invite the reader into a small, inconvenient, box-shaped, square courtroom, where sat the Judge of the criminal or Crown side. There was nothing of the majesty of law to be discovered, a ravenous love of the excitement of horrors seemed to have drawn as many spectators as could be squeezed into the small galleries destined for the public.

A trial was in progress, several counsel were crowded together, while the examination of a witness was being made on the part of the prosecution. The trial was for murder, with highway robbery upon two old people, husband and wife, the wife, now in the witness-box for examination, had just stated that her husband had resisted, and made several attempts to cry out, she having during the time been almost choaked, to prevent her calling for aid, fell down into a ditch, and the man who had held her, then as she supposed, struck her husband on the head while he grappled with his companion, for, on coming to her senses, and raising her head, she saw no one but her husband, who was groaning on the ground close by. They lay in this state till a carrier, happening to pass, took them home in his cart, their house not being far off. The husband died of the injuries he had received the following day, and he had not spoken collectedly after the attack. The old woman knew nothing more than that they were struck by two men from behind, as they went along a road toward their home, they had not long entered the lane, which was lonely, they had walked from M——, the market-town, distant from the spot where they were robbed, about two miles, they left M—— about a quarter to seven—probably took three quarters of an hour to walk the distance. Neither knew the appearance of the men's faces nor their dress.

The examination of this witness seemed of little importance, and a group of solicitors and counsel were occupying themselves with some other affair of livelier interest.

The two men who stood in the dock charged with this crime, were both young, one dark and somewhat sinister-looking, the other slighter and younger, with fair hair, and not an unpleasing expression of face. They both maintained an attentive and decent demeanour, but a close observer might detect, occasionally, a certain tightening of the hold the latter had of the dock-combing in front of him.

Meanwhile, another witness was called, but at this juncture one of the officers of the Court handed a letter to one of the group before mentioned, who looking at the direction, said, "Here, Mr. Searle, I trust we shall occupy you with this, instead of spoiling my sport."

Our friend of the blue spectacles, for it was he, received the missive like one who was never in a hurry, yet never delayed unnecessarily to do what was to be done. He opened it, and sat down to read its contents, but it was evident, after the few first minutes, that there was something in it which unusually awakened his interest—his brow contracted, and the envelope was crushed in the hand which held it, and his look became fixed on the paper, as if in earnest thought, in this way he sat for ten minutes, and then rose and joined the group, who were still laughing at some story in which they seemed interested, he then turned and seated himself beside the counsel for the prisoners.

Meanwhile, the evidence of a labourer, making up a gap in the fence of the lane, not far from its junction with the high-road, spoke to the passing of the old couple, and soon after of two men, of whom he did not take particular notice, they were strangers. No one else passed for half an hour. He could not recognize the two men, they might have been three hundred yards—the breadth of a field—behind the old people, passed down the road half an hour afterward with a bundle of sticks he had delayed his leaving the field to collect, and only met a man on horseback—a stranger—said, *good night*, but received no answer. Heard of the murder next morning, and recognized the body.

The next witness was a lad of fourteen, who having spent a half-holiday at home, about four miles from M——, where he was at school, was returning at night, he met some labourers between half-past seven and eight, but saw no strangers—no one on horseback, he knew the persons he met—there were three, they had all smock-frocks on, two were old men, and one a lad of sixteen, they lived in the same village with his father after meeting them, he is certain he saw no one else. Has since seen the place where the old people lay, they might have been there, as it was dark as he passed, and he might not have been on that side of the lane, the hedges are high, and make it darker there than in an open or wide road.

A tollkeeper, near where the lane leaves the high-road, observed two men, but could not say whether they followed the old people, or even went into the lane, but he remembers having seen two persons, strangers, going at a loitering pace, he mentioned the circumstance when he heard of the robbery.

And now a certain bustle in the Court, and at the bar, evinced that a witness of some importance in the trial was to be called, and the galleries, and even the Bench and Counsel looked toward the corner where the evidence was to be given. After a moment's pause and a slight bustle, a man appeared in the witness-box, by some means, as if he had been raised up from a trap door underneath, he was dressed like a fop, was about twenty-five years old, was very good-looking, though he wanted the air of a well-bred man. He faced toward the Bench with a smiling air of confidence, as if he was doing or about to do, something in which he expected its protection.

The Counsel for the Crown, after this man was sworn—a ceremony which seemed to be treated still more lightly by the witness than even by the flippant officer of the Court who administered the oath—addressed the following questions:

"Your name is Adolphus Dacre?" and was answered in the affirmative.

"You were in the neighborhood of M—— on the evening of the murder of the old man Rushworth?"

"Yes."

"Go on."

"I was passing through M—— on business and took a ride out on the evening of the murder it was near eight o'clock, and the evening was cloudy. I turned up a lane, and had proceeded about a mile and a half, when I met two men coming from an opposite direction."

"Would you know them again?"

"Yes."

"Can you recognize them in Court?"

"Yes, certainly, they are at the bar."

"You met no other persons?"

"No."

"And you continued in the lane some way?"

"Yes, I went on to a turning, and then through a gate, across a field, through another, and got into a road I did not know, which led me a long way about. Did not see the two men again, they had each a stout stick in his hand."

"Did you speak to them?"

"I hardly remember, but perhaps I said *Good evening*. I was shy of them in a lonely place at night."

"You may stand down."

"Stop a little," said a counsel, rising carelessly, and looking about for some papers, the tone of voice was bland, and his manner gentle and almost timid.

Mr. Searle, who was seated with his back to the witness, looked up a moment as the young lawyer spoke and then resumed reading his letter.

"You had been some days at M——?"

"Yes, three or four before this occurrence."

"The night was cloudy, it appears, to others, how came you to see so distinctly?"

"A slight degree of apprehension made me more observant."

"Well, for a man who had not known these persons before, and now only seeing their heads, you seem very confident. Pray look attentively, it is no light matter, and your evidence is most important—so consider whether there may not be a doubt on your mind."

"I can have no doubt," answered the witness, "though had the direction of his eyes been closely watched, his look fell upon the front of the dock below where the prisoners were to be seen."

The Counsel threw down his brief, saying, as if he felt it was useless, "You did not know the prisoners before?"

"No, of course I did not."

"You may stand down."

The leading Counsel for the prisoners was at this moment in animated conversation with Mr. Searle, and the Judge asked if there was any more evidence on their part.

A stick had been found thrust into the hedge a few steps from where the old man had fallen, it had been light-colored, but was stained as if with blood in some parts. The person who found it was an old woman, and it was the morning after the robbery, a constable took the stick from her, when he heard where it had been found. There was a stain of blood at the handle, and also near the end. There was nothing remarkable, this witness said, in the appearance of the prisoners when they were apprehended, money was found upon the younger prisoner—a five-pound note and four sovereigns. The landlord said they had complained of having no means of paying their bill.

The landlord was called. He said it was the elder prisoner who wished to have credit for a short time, they had been eight days at M——.

It was on the younger prisoner the money was found. The note was quite clean, and though a five-pound note had been taken, and some gold, the old woman could not tell the number of the note, nor the quantity of gold.

An earnest conversation was here held between Mr. Searle and the senior

Counsel, who unwillingly, as it seemed, informed the Court he had no more evidence.

Both the prisoners showed evident agitation at this moment, and beads of perspiration burst out on the pale brow of the darker-looking of the two, when the clear tones of the Judge arrested their attention, as he began to sum up.

"The prisoners had been out, and in the immediate neighborhood of the spot where the wound had been given, which next morning produced death. He must remind the jury of the gravity of the charge—it was most wanton murder, unmitigated by passion, by resistance, of these two old and weakly persons, or by any other circumstance which could soften the character of the crime.

"The question was whether the circumstantial evidence was sufficient to bring clearly home to them this appalling crime. They were out that night, two persons had been seen by two different parties near, and one witness swore to two persons following, within the breadth of a field, the old persons who had gone along the lane. There was but one witness who identified the prisoners, and the other evidence, though seeing the two persons previously, and consequently when lighter declined to swear to them, or to describe their dress. It is true the first of these saw them some thirteen yards off, but it was more than half an hour before the witness Dacre had met them. His lordship owned that witness had not left a very favorable impression upon his mind, from the manner of his evidence.

"Now came the evidence of a youth, who had met no one on the road, which was only a part corroboration of that witness who had seen the two men go along the lane, as it might have been possible for many persons to have gone from the adjoining fields into the lane, and then have retired from it by the same way.

"There was one point something remarkable, which, in his mind, threw a doubt upon the evidene of Dacre as to accuracy, or exculpated the prisoners, to all appearance—and that was, he swore to their having had each a stick when he met them, and that must have been immediately after the murderous attack. The prisoners, it was true, gave no good account of themselves, but it was the duty of the jury to decide upon the evidence, and it was his duty to tell them that it was incomplete, as there was nothing proved which put facts in such a position as not to leave it quite possible that other parties might have done this deed."

The jury seemed to be unwilling to decide, and retired.

The Counsel approached the dock and said a few words to the prisoners, who looked in the last state of irritable suspense, and they sat down.

In a quarter of an hour the Jury returned a verdict of *Not guilty*, and another trial was commenced upon the return of the Judge, who for a few minutes had left the bench.

Just as Mr. Searle was leaving the inclosed space set apart for counsel, he observed to the senior, with whom he appeared to have had the discussion, "You see how useless it would have been to have damaged this Dacre, we shall have him some other day."

The other looked after him as he went, shrugged his shoulders, only uttering "An epicure!" as he left the Court.

That evening the two persons we have just seen tried left the Castle, and the same night there also left its precincts a young man, of pale and sodden complexion and diminutive stature, carrying, like the others, a small packet of clothes—and the gloomy portals shut for the night.

Chapter Eighty-Six
Travelers—met at an inn—mysterious literary business

Three days after, on a not, much frequented road to the westward of Harrowgate, which passes here over some desolate heath, where strange rocks worn by time and tempest stand remnants of a range, or isolated masses, deprived of the soil which might once have been level with their heads, and long since washed away, leaving them in bare and fantastic nakedness, these crags, as they are called, have been marked by the wonder of the peasant, and the curiosity of the traveler. But the day of which we speak brought neither along that lonely road—the storm—a cold rain, almost sleet drifting white against the dreary heather and darkened sky, beat across the rugged path, but behind one of those, whose form projected at the top, an overhanging ledge, sat two men, their conversation was earnest, without being loud, the drops fell unheeded at their feet from the projecting shelter of the ledge above, the cold drifted past their refuge without notice—there could be no listener to windward of that block, and were there, what words could reach him against that rushing blast? Yet their heads were brought close together, but there was no brotherly love in these eyes, and no kindliness in these tones, their brows are not knit, but they hang heavy over these eyes, which watch but never meet.

The darker of the two at last seeming to yield to the reasons or the willfulness of his companion, said, "Well, let us take that chance first, since you will have it, but we must get out of these wolds, I can't stand such places, I never was used to them." The clouds were breaking as he spoke, and he got up, "We'll get to the highway, not far off if our bearings have been right, there must be some chance of a cast, I should think, where do we make for?"

"Kendal," was the reply.

They had each a bundle, not of great bulk, which they secured under their great coats as they stood up, as if awaiting the expected clearing of the weather, slowly the clouds rolled away, as if to answer to their wish, and they cut across the heath by a sheep path, toward the northwest. Some four hours elapsed, however, before they neared the town of Skipton, and the evening closing in with indications of wet, they seemed to have made up their minds by the looks they gave at the different houses on its outskirts that this was to be their halting place. There was a public house called the Rose, perhaps only to be contemplated as distinguished from the thistle, being, though somewhat bleached, a red rose within the boundaries of York.

A man about thirty, by his dress a dealer in horses, or a patron of such as were, stood at the door, and on a stone seat under a sort of porch, sat a figure, whose dress, the reverse of that of the other in form, was more calculated to conceal than to indicate to what caste he belonged, his pantaloons of black cloth had been turned up to preserve them from the effects of a muddy walk, of which the lace boots beneath gave ample evidence, the coat was rusty black, and the neckcloth of faded yellow, showed itself under a white knitted comforter, which had been untied, there was a small bundle and a square packet, enclosed in an oilskin cover, lying beside him, on his head was one of those hats which seem to have been set apart for evangelical persons, and was worn on the back of the head, so as to cover little of the forehead, and in no way protect the eyes, but giving the wearer an aspect of self-sufficiency, more akin to ignorance than impudence or conceit.

The host stood leaning at the door post, "But if I have monies worth, and instructive reading to add, the balance you think would be in my favor," finished the Yorkshireman.

At this juncture, the two men we have described on the heath, passing them, entered the sanded parlour, whose door stood ready open beyond the entrance, its little boxes of sawdust, its bowl full of pipes on the chimneypiece, garnished by their long diverging stems with some popularly painted jugs on which William and Henry were represented with superabundant neckcloth, and most correct deportment. There was also a few colored prints, and a painting, evidently by a British artist, vividly representing the great bunch of grapes being brought back by the messengers sent to reconnoitre the Holy Land, deserving more particular attention, as the painter, knowing his own power, and feeling a dread of giving way to his talent for representing action, had hit upon the only expedient he could think of for keeping the figures within bounds, by placing the bearers back to back.

There was no cheerful blaze on the hearth, the times were gone when the homely kitchen welcomed with its warmth and its stores the weary wayfarer, light blue and pink shreds of paper filled the closed-up grate, which might have held some ounces of burning coals, had they been specially ordered, the tables and chairs were of deal, and seemed to be intended for scrubbing rather than any other use, on which the sins of some red-elbowed maid were daily expiated in an atmosphere of exhausted tobacco smoke and confined air.

A female, who from the interest she took in asking what the travelers required, might be considered the mistress, though older than the apparent host, had entered, and waited an answer or an order, looking attentively at the two men's dress, in which she apparently found nothing to dislike.

The question, could they be put up, was answered in the affirmative, a certain supply of food at a certain expense was stipulated for, and added the landlady, should this gentleman remain also, I can let you have a fire into the bargain.

The eyes of all were thus turned upon the person who was to be the means of introducing genial warmth amongst them at small expence.

No words escaped him, and there was no kindling intelligence in his eye, but he took a seat, and turning his leaden orbs upon the square packet on his knee. "Little could be done," he said, "tonight to benefit others, and remunerate ourselves, so I will stay to partake in the comfort this good lady has promised."

Slices of cold bacon with bread, formed the repast of the two travelers, and the example was followed, not without some compunction, by the bearer of the black packet, who had removed his hat to a peg, and smoothed down his wet-looking straight hair over his forehead, and with a painful expression, offered up a short prayer, as might be supposed from the motion of his lips.

Three jugs of ale loomed soon after upon the table through the fumes of tobacco, and as the smoke increased, something like conversation was carried on between the smokers, till an allusion to trade brought out the hawker of religious books, in a modest avowal of serving the holy cause, and obtaining for himself a small remuneration.

"We merely cover the expence of paper, printing, and distributing, their inestimable contents are quite gratis."

"I shouldn't wonder," said the younger companion.

"Oh! I have got amusing books too—The Lyrics of the Lark, Live long Love, which I only sell when the others are repulsed. Now look here, The Harvest of Instruction, Bowers of Heavenly Love, Hannah the Reprobate, and Hannah the Elect, Lawrence Lackgrace. I could sit under a hedge, if I had time and fair weather, and improve upon such reading all day, but business first, you know and there are many thirsty souls who wait but to read these, to be refreshed and restored, I must therefore press on."

All this was said as if the chief desire was to distribute tracts, but that other wants literary might be alleviated from the same source.

"All these are twopence, Pilgrim's Progress, a shilling, the Profane Poetry, sixpence, it is better got up."

"And what are these?"

"Oh! they are gloomy, to awaken remorse, edifying ends of murderers, tragic histories, and these are a bundle of Proclamations, about some south country affair."

The packet tied together, turned up as he spoke, and the heading of *One hundred pounds reward* looked large on its face.

"These," continued the hawker, "I only carry and put up, or cause to be put up somewhere in the north, where I understood there were some gipsies who saw something, or might get the money if they could find the men to swear to, but I don't know the rights of the story. I have also in this little parcel a sample of each kind—in case of wet I can open this under a doorway—it behoves to be methodical, traveling in my way of business-it would hold letters besides, I'll sell you the lot cheap, I have not done sixpence worth of good since breakfast." There was a sideling glance passed from the elder toward his light-haired companion, who, without looking up, shuffled his feet on the floor.

"I shouldn't mind trying how cheap you could give it to one like me, who didn't much want it."

"Ah! I am glad you did not say you did not much need them, we all." Looking up, and half-closing his eyes, he said, "More than need them, sinful as we are, our poor souls, if not stifled, are crying out for such food, there are three Samaritan tracts, and a sweet sounding paraphrase and holy song, and I will give you the oilskin cover which would keep them dry if you swam the Red Sea, they shall be but eight-pence. I wouldn't give the oilcloth for the money, but that you may read as you go along, if you would but take the Pilgrim too, your's *would* be a progress, my friends."

The dark traveler paid the money from a leathern bag, and not without some contempt, pushed back that celebrated Murray of religious allegory which had been tendered. "Come, come, we've been customers enough, it's only for goodwill we've taken the others, we're not literary much, we may foregather again."

"Yes, if you go north, perhaps we shall."

The pedlar eyed him askance, as he felt the consistency of the oilskin.

"Nay, you can hold it up to the light, that is the best test, and need not fear to carry it in your hand in rain, it is warranted practically useful." But thinking this too exclusively worldly, he added, "As also the tracts."

It was not long after that certain stretchings out of the limbs on the part of the two companions, denoted symptoms of readiness for bed, and presently they were shown to a double-bedded room, clean, but scantily furnished. Their bundle was laid upon a chair, and the two sat down on the bed. He of the fair hair, who may be recognized as Mr. Deacon, undid the knots, and produced from among three or four shirts and pairs of stockings a small paper parcel carefully sealed, the two men looked at the seals, of which the impression remained perfect, and then wrapped the parcel in the oilskin, carefully tying it up with the red tape which before had served for the tracts.

"That was a blessed old thing never to break a seal, nor peach while we were away, the old lady was of the uneducated order though well to do."

"Yes, it might turn out good, but I'll tell you one thing, there must be no more country rambling," said the other. "I have given in to you long enough, it is my turn now, if I don't make it out, you may have another try."

"Well, what is your plan?" said Deacon. "There is no one that knows the value of these papers, unless it be the one who should not, you think, have them. Now you have gained that point, well, there remains but that rascal Coalman, who could give the tin, no he's not up to such matters, and I know a plan to put the wide sea between us and risk. Will you let me have fair play?"

"Yes."

"It is a bargain, let's put our faces toward Whitechapel by early dawn."

The bundle was placed at the back of the bed against the wall, the bed itself being in an alcove, they were to sleep together the bundle beyond both, the door was locked, the conversation had been in a whisper, side by side they sat, the arm of the darker man was round the neck of Deacon, and their heads were close together, and the candle was put upon the same chair on which had rested the packet, and when both were laid down was blown out.

Before sunrise, the vendor of tracts was roused by the sound of steps descending the wooden stair which led past the small dormitory he occupied, he had to await the rising of the reading world to commence that sale, which was to form part of his daily mission, he came down, and had an early cup of warm tea, he seldom, he said, drank beer, even at night, but he was in no hurry, asked no questions, and abstained perhaps with difficulty from reading any of the edifying treasures he bore about him.

It was not till after this miserable tea, and less than watered milk, with its modicum of moist sugar had been disposed of and paid for, with the other accommodation, as he called it, though he did not distinctly imply on which side it had lain, that he seemed to remember that he had a letter to write, and asked for the means, the sour landlady was all in all, and perhaps hesitated a moment to keep in the fire for a penny, but possibly some idea of her guest's memory being awakened to the claims of a supposed waiting maid, and the opportune possibility of want of change, operated in favor of a stationary movement. The paper came forth, the epistle was written and sealed, a sixpence was given with a distracted air toward the paper and was as abstractedly received, and the peddler moved to the door and went out, as if still meditating upon what he had done, or the good he might do on the day which opened before him.

We will, however, follow the two persons who had been his fellow lodgers. It was about a week after their leaving Skipton, we find them in a narrow court, not far from the filthy marketplace of Whitechapel, they had been making inquiries of a ragged little girl, but were now standing looking about, as if at a loss to find their way, as she seemed inclined only to impart such information as would involve a necessity of requiring more, she had loitered nearly out of sight, but on a signal and a penny being shown, at once started forward and proceeded toward a few steps, at the bottom of which was a door, it had no lock, and opened at her touch, showing a muddy passage.

"First door on the right, after you get out," said the child, with that clearness which is brought out by the love of gain so early taught to every scale of intellect and every civilized condition.

They entered the passage, lighted by the opening at the other end, and the door they had been directed to was easily found.

There was a small book-stand at the window beside it, which however was shut, but on these persons stopping, the entrance was immediately opened, and an old man, with a faded green forage-cap, a dirty dressing gown and slippers, appeared, as if filling up the space against inroad, or ready to transact any business in books, in the safety of which he seemed to place complete confidence.

"Mr. Alter, I think, from Switzerland, the Rucio, as Teddy told me?" said the darker of the two.

"Ah! You are from Teddy?"

"Yes. You know that letter you did."

"My goot friend, come in, it is not right to talk of poor Teddy's affairs in the street." And the door was widened to give entrance to these men.

"Now, what can I do for you?"

"Not much, but it must be done cheap—that is, if it answers, there will be more, you know we must be honorable, because you could blow."

"But it is a letter, then?" said the old man.

"It is to copy some old papers—three—not long ones, but the paper must be rusty, as also the ink faint, like the original. It will take you three hours, perhaps—it is now ten, we must stay by you, you know. Have you time? It is now or never."

"My dear, you frighten an old man for no use. If it is a small matter, better not, as I should keep an appointment at twelve, which may be better for me."

"If you do it well—and you can do it—it will not be better."

"How much certain?"

"Five shillings."

"And if it passes? For I see it has to pass."

"A half-sovereign—fifteen shillings."

"Poor pay for three hours' work."

"But the value is ours, the time and the writing only yours. Decide, we have no time to spare—it is hit or miss."

For all answer the old man took from a shelf an ink-horn, and made some marks on a piece of paper. "That looks like old color," he said, "but I can make it match. Let us see."

The oilskin was produced, and its contents, there were five papers—two were letters, of the three others, two were large, and contained what appeared attested certificates, the other was smaller, and was only a memorandum.

The old copier looked at the size, and then ran his hand over a pile of books, till he came to one from which he took a loose fly-leaf, something brown and soiled, and arranged himself to write upon it. The round Italian-looking hand was laid out before him, and he desired not to be interrupted.

"You need not begin, I tell you, if you do not know you can finish, our time is counted out to us like change, so go on or not, accordingly", and the speaker —for but one had spoken—set himself to charging and lighting his pipe.

The room was low, and of moderate extent, a sort of postless bed, serving apparently as a seat or table, or both, stood in one corner, the table upon which the writing was now going on was near the window, but the chair on which the old man sat was placed across it, the light on his left, and the seat close to the wall, so that no one could see over his shoulder, books, boxes of papers, some old and not very solid shelves finished the furnishing of the room, and a coke fire burned sullenly in a very small grate, there was a sort of order in everything, but dust seemed to be the guardian of all, as it told every finger-mark distinctly, and there were but few.

"I could tell what the old one had been about yesterday, and the day before, if I had an object, you see his mark of both days," said the dark visitor to the fair.

"Don't talk," said the old scribe, "a mistake, and I have to begin again."

He looked up—the dirty little girl was passing, he knocked and beckoned her. "Tell her," he said, "to bring me a cup of coffee from the stand—*hot*," he added, as if he would have employed a similie, and then he continued his task.

"Look here, now I have got through one. Does it come near the same fabric?" he asked, with a leer.

The imitation was evidently surprising to those who saw the original with the copy. But the copier was again at work, and when about half through the next, the dirty little girl appeared with the coffee at the window, it was taken in by Mr. Deacon, and placed within reach, the document was finished, and a teaspoonful of this hot liquid was put into the ink before commencing anew, at last certain marks were made with a pin point wetted with it, as if to imitate flea spots, the three pieces were then folded and re-folded, as if they had been made to suit two different sized packets, and then the old artist got up, and looking into a box which held many bundles of papers tied together, selected one with a yellow and brown silk cord, these he re-tied with red tape, and transferred the old-fashioned silk cord to the three now antique-looking documents.

The little girl here looked in at the window, and was told to wait—the copies were about being put up in paper, and the originals consigned to the impenetrable oilskin. The miser-looking fabricator looked keenly, as if he almost dreaded not being paid, but the money was produced.

"You'd make a fortune over-hand, on such terms, you are as limber of the fingers as a young lady."

Here a five-shilling piece was tendered and accepted with an ill-disguised avidity.

"And where shall we meet to have the rest—I know they'll pass?"

"Why here, if you like, at six this evening."

The door was already open, Alter, however, seemed to think this too like a go-by, he said, hesitatingly, "You'll know the book-stand, you know it will be of no use to shirk, I can copy papers, and state I have done so in the public prints."

"Curse the public prints," said the darker, as the two men went into the passage and disappeared.

"I will go to the detective," muttered the old man to himself, "he shall spoil the sale, the rascals would never come back."

He was already busy with his stall, intending to shut up to pursue his revenge, but a sudden thought arrested his haste—he appeared to hesitate, and at last, quietly restored what he had moved, to its former place, and sat himself down to await some fresh job, as his customers generally consisted of Swiss or Italians, who resided near, and came to his residence for advice or assistance.

Chapter Eighty-Seven
Maneuvers—headed to sea—apprehended

It was about two o'clock, the sooty sheep of St. James's Park browsed busily on the greasy turf, which was hurdled off—a sort of purgatory to the Sussex downs—near the high elms which border the strange-shaped piece of water which, of villa size and design, forms an aquatic communication between the parade of the Palace of Buckingham and that of the Regent's Mortar at the Horse Guards, the trees alluded to are on the southern side, and at their roots are seats for the weary or contemplative or the bountiful, who are busy feeding both fish and fowl. The nursery-maid, who teaches the child of England that everything that is agreeable is wrong, and that all his tiney pleasures must be forbidden, in order to have their zest. Here also is found the soldier, who would be purely ornamental, were he not redolent of pipe-clay, and the quiet quid-nunc, who is the victim of all.

These are sometimes the dramatis personae of that rural shore, but on the present occasion, the gentle Coalman alone looked apprehensively at the dark clouds, and then at the blackened leaves above him, dropping his eye in pity upon his lavender-colored pantaloons, while our acquaintances of the court in Whitechapel were walking rapidly along the devious path which causes the tourist of the Park to lose sight occasionally of the element of England's glory, to rush again upon it in the ecstacy of a newborn view. They were in conversation with a serjeant of the East India Company's artillery, with whom they parted upon arriving in sight of Mr. Coalman.

"There is nothing like the open air," said Mr. Deacon, on observing the anything but open countenance of the swell. "Have you a witness in the trunk of that tree, that you stick so close to it, let us be moving, we can talk as we walk."

Mr. Coalman, who did not seem to relish being seen with his present companions, nor the confident tone in which he had been addressed, joined them in moving toward Storey's Gate.

About three quarters of an hour previous to the present moment, a young man, dressed in black, wearing a high white hat, passed down one of those narrow streets leading toward the Haymarket, and from thence crossed into Cockspur Street, and turning sharp to the right, was making his way into the Park, when, just at Berkley House, he was accosted by a man who seemed to have been watching his coming.

"My name is Trueman, the detective," he said, simply, "and we need be as little seen together as you like, follow your own course, I'll be at hand." And Trueman passed on, as if he had been neglecting Northumberland House, and was about to make up for lost time.

The other continued his course, looking superciliously at the tranquil cows drawn up to belie surreptitious milk in the abstract, or to prove that some of it only may be from a Tees water source.

Mr. Bankes walked on with the air of a man who could pay his way and was confident in his own powers, Mr. Bankes loitered, and enjoyed the scene, the nursery-maids and children were with the ducks, and the benevolent public in full occupation, he read the names of the trees, and admired the mazy windings of the walks—but he also watched the meeting we have described, and threw himself on the damp grass, regardless of its filth, as the two men approached with Mr. Coalman, who appeared too eager to have made a good bargain, and too well satisfied with his acquisition to wish longer to enjoy the society of those from whom he had obtained it, and was now hurrying toward the wicket leading out of the Horse Guards, while the others made their way toward Storey's Gate, and thence over Westminster Bridge.

Nearly opposite Astley's they entered a trunk-maker's shop and purchased a portmanteau, which being hoisted upon the back of an errand-boy or apprentice, who required outdoor exercise, they continued their way.

It was a little beyond the trunk-maker's that Bankes was attracted by the appearance of a book-stall, which stopped his course, and just as the two intended travelers, with their trunk, appeared at his back, Mr. Trueman stepped up and asked, with the air of one bent on a capture, "What are you up to here, Mr. Thompson? You may as well come along with me at once, as I expect to have a warrant before very long."

Bankes's astonishment was unfeigned, as probably Mr. Trueman intended it should be, and he did not attempt to speak.

The portmanteau-carrier and its owners stopped.

"Well, just as you like, I know you are getting off to New York, but I shall be at Blackwall, perhaps, to see you, so, goodbye at present."

"You are mistaken for once in your practice, Mr. Trueman," said Mr. Bankes. "You will have no more hold over me tonight than you have now. I'd be glad if you touched me." And he faced round in quiet impenetrable composure.

"What, you threaten?" said the officer, touching him lightly with a cane.

"Well," said Bankes, "I take these men to witness." He turned round toward Deacon and his companion.

"Whew!" whistled Trueman. "I'd like to see you show yourself in a Court. Do you think I don't know you? Good day, for the present." He turned upon his heel.

Mr. Bankes, with an air of triumph, accompanied the trunk party a little way, and remarked, previous to disappearing down a narrow street to the left, "I'd better make myself scarce. I've had the best of this bout, but it might not be so next time."

"I thought," said the dark companion, to Mr. Deacon, "that fellow was up to mischief—those saints are all alike." And they pursued their way, stealing a glance behind them occasionally.

Entering at last, a hackney carriage, they were driven to Broad Street where, in the office of an American shipping company, they secured two second-class places in a packet which was to sail that evening's tide from the Thames, touching at Portsmouth.

———

It was about eight o'clock, when a light Portsmouth coach was passing gaily along one of these graveled streets in the neighborhood of Vauxhall, into which the coachman loved to deviate in preference to even a more direct paved street. There was not the usual overloading of the top, owing to its character of *light* and the pace they were bound to maintain, but there were some larking middies, and a passenger or two for Guildford, besides Mr. Bankes and another, bound for the Bald Eagle, a fine 500 ton ship, carrying passengers and a general cargo to New York.

The wind was high and cold, and Mr. Bankes wrapped himself up and chose a place accordingly, with his back to the horses, as it was from the southwest. Certain defenses against cold had so accumulated round his neck, and encroached so much upon his face, that he would have been quite unrecognizable—a broad-brimmed hat crowning the metamorphosis. He had a middy in close converse, from whom he extracted a full account of coming ashore from Spithead, and sometimes landing on the beach near Southsea Castle, to save a cruise. He objected to swearing, but signified he thought grog a commendable beverage in cold weather taken in moderation. On the whole, he was easily persuaded in his greenness, and adapted himself to the humours of these youths, who promised to take charge of him when they got to their journey's end, and open the way to all the pleasures the place could afford.

On these bright prospects sleep came, not to cloud, but to seal in dreams what it required the imagination of youth awake to believe.

The morning, in its chills, its hot ales and spices, and at last its dismal breakfast, came, finding them within an easy distance, which was accomplished about ten o'clock. Landport was the gate by which they entered, Mr. Bankes receiving constant instructions as to the place and its ways as they drove down High Street, where they stopped at the Fountain.

Much was told him of the former glories of this great port, but to Mr. Bankes, who expected to meet the yard-arm of a three-decker elbowing out of a cross street, the appearance of this eminently common-looking English town was anything but imposing. He got his trunk, which was all his baggage, down from the roof, and guarded and guided by the three youths, he found himself rapidly passing the drawbridge of the gate, which leads to that point to which all the hopes of the way had tended.

The time these young gentlemen had to spare was industriously employed in the consumption of all kinds of shell-fish, different admixtures of brandy, and gin, and several young ladies were introduced to Mr. Bankes, in order that they might have a small sop, and make a promise not further to tempt or disturb his peace. He was also shown some two or three steady boatmen, who could undertake to set him on board the Bald Eagle, whenever she arrived, blew it any gale of wind but from the northwest. "And then," they remarked, "it was probable she would not be there."

But the time of the middies was up, they promised to reform their ways, and read a list of works their host recommended to them on his paying the bill. It was blowing fresh from the west, but a boat was returning to the ship—the best friends must part, and Mr. Bankes was left on the unromantic beach between the Quebec and the saluting battery, as the tide was too low for the landing-piers, and these future admirals had been obliged to embark from the shingle.

There is no specific account of how this gentleman spent his time during the day, or the next, but it may be inferred that he was on the outlook for the other passengers of the Eagle, who might be induced to get on board at Spithead, for he was seen in one of the remoter streets of Southsea, on the second evening, with two men, who might be recognized as the same who were with him at the time Mr. Trueman accosted him near Astley's the day before.

Mr. Bankes appeared somewhat hazy, and was confidential in his manner. He had been asked what he was accused of.

"I am but a pedlar—nothing handsome, but it wasn't true, all the same," said he, with an expression of almost waggishness, which appeared to please his auditors.

"We may as well see about a boat, it will be evening before she can be down. I've been here before," said the darker man, now rigged out as a sailor.

"Let us draw lots who goes," said Deacon.

The three agreed, and the lot fell upon Bankes.

"Well, errors excepted, as the banker's accounts say, I'll do my best. You say—two-oared boat—quite enough—the tide favorable to go down—wind southeast—about dusk, opposite the landmark on the beach."

"But you'll be back yourself?" interposed Deacon, his pale and something worn countenance overshadowed by a momentary distrust.

"How should I get my baggage else?" answered Bankes, innocently.

There was no answer, and he moved off in the direction of Landport.

"This wind will do," continued Deacon, looking anxiously up to the light clouds, which were drifting across the dark heavens.

"It must do," was the answer, "didn't you see the blue Peter up?"

They were proceeding toward, and soon entered, the Gunner public house, where they had lodged the night before.

"He's a sly rascal, that, had he been bred in town, he would have topped most of his calling."

"We are the better of him at present, however," added his companion.

They sat down. It was above an hour that their messenger was gone, and the shadows were deepening, and with them the gloom and a certain restlessness in the two men. They spoke with an air of confidence in the ship, of which they had heard good accounts, but as if in so doing they were fortifying themselves against some inward fear. There were but few persons about, and none in the house—which was principally a military one—but themselves. The suppressed agitation of these men became painful, and they swallowed glass after glass of brandy.

At last, the latch of the outer door opened, and Bankes asked the rheumatic landlord in the bar if he had kept the ship for him, and then entered in his methodical way. He had acquired a piece of old crape for his hat, and stated that a boat would be ready, opposite the signal-post on the Southsea beach, in half an hour.

"And it may be a quarter's walk across," said one of his hearers.

The charge was paid by each, without inquiry, contributing a third—they were all eager to be off. The baggage was two trunks, so exactly similar, that Banks, the more methodical, had his address on a card ready to attach with a string.

They left the house, but before getting to the opening, now the road to the Five Cricketers, Deacon discovered he had left a pea-jacket, and ran back for it. There was a squall on, and some rain, which beat up from the southeast, so the other two waited for him at the corner, looking anxiously at the stormy-looking sky.

When their companion rejoined them, there was still time for a pause to let the shower pass over. As they stood, an old man had come up with a basket of apples, he seemed to dread turning the corner, and stood shivering behind the group already there.

Thus passed about three or four minutes in silence, when a slight appearance of light between the clouds gave token of a favorable change, and a cracked but hollow voice uttered, *Pippins and wannuts*, just at the ear of the darker emigrant, who started and turned round, as did also his companion. The speaker had his wrinkled face turned up to Heaven, he was very old, and his eyes looked unusually dim in that leaden twilight.

"Let us be gone out of this, or we'll never get to the beach," said Bankes, and they took up the trunks, one in the middle, the others on the flanks, and proceeded abreast along the road.

Bankes, who thought he discovered some appearance of contempt upon the countenance of Deacon, remarked, "I thought you would laugh at me for being startled, but one didn't expect an old phantasma to start up and speak so near." And he looked behind him with that glance of dread, which is not much mended by an endeavor at concealment.

His companions appeared to exchange some look, they passed the most inland beacon, and here the shingle retarded their progress, but they fought on, not a word was said, the rain had ceased, but the wind was high and cold, a ridge of gravel, thrown up by the storms, rose between them and the sea, but they heard it breaking hoarsely on the other side, a vigorous exertion brought them to the top, where they expected, at least one of them expected to have found the surf too high for embarking, but the sound had been harsh and hollow, though the sea was but little rough near shore, but there was no boat. The three men set down the trunks, the other two looked at each other, then at Bankes, but there was a real anxiety and dismay upon the countenance of their companion, who, if his faculties had not been overpowered by his own apprehension, must have shrunk from the appalling look of the darker man, who was near him, not a word was said. Bankes of the three was furthest from the harbour, and the nearest of the two turned from him, as if to consult and meet the pale look of desperation of the other.

They all stood, and out of the three, it would have been difficult to say which shewed the most utter discomfiture, at last, Bankes said, "Well, they are villains, I wouldn't care for the money, but here where there's no other boat to be had." His companions maintained an ominous silence, "But there are more ships on the sea than the Eagle," added Bankes, rallying and trying to resume his ordinary composure.

"I half believe that you are afraid of the sound of the sea," said the man nearest him. "And are glad at this cursed balk."

"It must be gladness of a queer sort, I feel if it is so," said Bankes, with a bitter smile.

A Coast Guard came upon the party rather abruptly, "What's this dunnage?" he said, pointing to the trunks with his stick.

"Well, its baggage, waiting to get aboard of the Bald Eagle."

"Yes, landed from that boat."

"What boat? I wish there was a boat."

The coast guard eyed them sharply, pointed a little higher than opposite, and moved on.

The eyes of the three in the meantime were strained in the direction indicated, where the dark hats of two men were first to be noticed, then the outline of a white boat, she was almost run ashore before becoming plainly visible, and already a man had jumped out, and was coming toward them, before they had quite recovered their energies.

"I don't think you have over more than enough time," said a rough-looking sailor. "And I wouldn't have taken such a chance for the money, were it not for Mr. Merry, so get aboard cleverly, and let's be off."

The trunks were already being handed through the low wave that broke on the beach, and the live stock got in with a little wetting, and the boat was turned across toward the Spithead, near which lay the ship, at clearer intervals visible, and to be distinguished through the intervals of the squalls, by her sails being loosened.

No one spoke, the men at the oars seemed to think there would be a loss in a breath uttered, but there was a little breeze, and the mast was stepped, and a lug-sail shaken out, with an alacrity, which showed them in earnest, the little barque heeled over and skimmed the waters as if she really was bent on a cruise.

"Now we might just be squaring accounts, and that will save time when we are under the ship's side," said the man who had come ashore for them.

Bankes gave three five-shilling pieces, the tide favored them, and the wind, though sometimes there was more of it than was wanted, the boatmen looked as if they wished the matter over, as they would have a run against tide to return, the passengers sat quiet, each watchful, and all anxious and pale.

"Luff," said one of the boatmen, who was sitting forward, "or you'll be foul of that boat."

The sheet was hauled in, and the tiller put down, the ship was close under their lea bow. There appeared several boats by her side, and the usual bustle of departure caused lights to be moving on board, and the hails of leave-taking, and the orders of the captain, mingled indistinctly from her deck, they had neared, and already was Bankes, haggard and anxious, on his unsteady legs, when the skiff which had been on their lea joined in upon them, almost jamming his hand, which rested on the starboard gunwale, he turned as he staggered from the loss of its support.

"You said we should not meet in the river so you see I have brought this young lady down here, so perhaps you will not disappoint her." The vendor of tracts had sunk again on a thwart.

"Now, no nonsense, I wish to do the thing decently. Boatmen be easy, you know me, Superintendent Trueman! I wish to give as little trouble as possible, hand Mr. Bankes over."

Bankes looked imploringly helpless.

"Come along, don't be downcast yet, the law presumes every man innocent till he gets through their hands, the law is werry presumptuous," said the officer.

His intended prisoner asked to be allowed to bring his trunk.

"Certainly, it will not be in the way, bear-a-hand, but keep clear of the others until I'm off," said the officer. "There, in with it, that's the direction, *passenger* and all, it will do for next time. I should much like to see these gentlemen's faces, I'm sure they must regret to lose you, sir," said Mr. Trueman, as the boat set off on her return to port.

The wind freshened, and it blew heavy from the southeast, the boat, in which little conversation was held, scudded before it, though against the now turned tide.

The ship had weighed immediately after Deacon and his companion got on board.

Chapter Eighty-Eight
Gilsland Park—summoned by Rose—vows—
the last rite—a farewell

It was spring again, and the unusual mildness of the season had rendered May almost what it used to be of yore, in regard to flowers, though there were not the merry faces of which we read, to meet on the village green round the May-pole, nor the rustic sports, nor the gala dresses, labor, engrossing labour, in its sordid garb, held on its sway, holyday was only in the hedge flower and the garden plot, while the lords of the creation plodded on in diurnal toil.

With slight variations of place, to find cleaner pasture for the sturdy mule, which carried along the covered cart, Tom's grandmother was still under the shelter of Gilsland Park wall, though it was not in a grove of firs the tilt was pitched, amongst which the openings of the beech buds shewed their pale green in contrast with the somber shadow of the pines. Tom himself, a little filled out and improved, had just returned from a journey, and was seated upon a log of wood, a wind fall, which had been hauled in to be cut up for burning. There was a shade of sadness on his face.

"Mother," he said, "I think she would be glad to see you, she has a leaning for our dark people, and frets because he is not yet come, I can't make it out, if they don't both love him." And the youth raised his eyes to read in the old woman's countenance some clue to the opinion her superior wisdom must have enabled her to form.

"Yes," said the crone, "he is under the finger of God, he is as yet little advanced in what is called good luck, but woe betide the hand that touches him, or the heart that wishes him evil. Have they not all gone to an evil end? That Marquis that did him wrong, the other that but stood in his way, that foster-brother and the two murderers perished in wild madness and starvation, reviling each other, and blaspheming, till they were cast off the raft, where other misery was unregarded on the great sea, but I'll go down, there may be comfort in seeing the love I bear him, and in homely truth."

Her grandson, who occasionally heard her speak in this strain, when the recollections of former instruction came upon her in exciting moments, considered these ebullitions oracular.

Tiney, not taller, but more old-fashioned, here silently put the better cloak of the old woman upon the roof of the abode.

She moved toward it, muttering to herself, "Yes, they can hang quick enough my poor boy for a leg of mutton, his son for a broken-kneed horse, but him to get his own, where there is plenty to go in fees and expenses, though the right be as clear as day at noon, it will take years of waste and writing, but he need care little, or it would break his heart, as many a one has been broken before."

She left the grove, and following the road, came to the gate we have before mentioned, as leading into the park.

The house at Gilsland had much changed in its habits of late, it was more than a month since Rose had burst a blood vessel, and she had been almost constantly confined ever since, there were no visitors, and the empty suites of rooms looked more gloomy than their wont, the great court was closed up to prevent noise, and no one came near the other entrances, but a restless looking doctor of a neighboring town, who was charged to fulfill the prescriptions of a London medical man of the first celebrity.

Rose had been moved to a room with windows to the garden, where she loved to look out upon the opening blossoms. Where she saw the Marchioness go out, and looked for her return, where the thrush and the ring-dove made themselves heard in the hanging grove beyond the water, and sometimes the voice of Tiney, when the weather was warm and the window open, was heard in those notes of childhood, which when used with feeling are so sad and sweet. The little creature watched for a bright sun to see the dark lady, by stealing toward the window among the flowers, and behind the balustrades, the little girl believed she saw in her one of her own race, as she lay with her long raven tresses falling over the pillow of her couch.

This day, the Marchioness had gone out as usual to please the invalid. The doctor was fidgeting in one of the anti-rooms to the Donna's chamber, the friend was not far, and every minute there was expected news of Edward Warren, who had been sent for.

Rose, sometime before, had broken a blood vessel, and was now suffering, besides debility, from a palpitation of the heart, within a few days she had become very anxious to see her friend and companion of the Prairies, whose presence had been at first interdicted, as likely to cause too much emotion, but this it had been found necessary to remove, and the answer to a summons to Gilsland was hourly expected.

The old gipsy sat on a low stool, heedless of all the splendor around her, and watching the suppressed anxiety of Rose, who was stretched on a sofa near the window, where flowers had been brought from hot-houses and conservatories, to yield their bright colors and grateful perfumes.

"You think he may be here by horseback, taking a shortcut, but it seems no shortcut to me—and you say he is the rightful lord," said Rose, with difficulty.

"He will be here—I have been reckoning up—at two o'clock, if he rides the last stage, he may arrive soon after one, but then..."

"What then?" said Rose, with a slight hectic on her sallow cheek.

"There are accidents to those who travel fast over bad roads."

But the thoughts of the invalid were already far away.

"I asked you if he is still recognized as of this house, did I not?"

"It matters but little, though there is not a person of age, to have seen any of his race in five parishes around the place, who would not take him for the young lord his father, who never came to the earldom."

"And you think the Lady of Gilsland would love him and cherish him as he should be loved by a wife?"

"If there is truth in anything I have seen to judge of, she will love him better as a wife, than she likes to own now, even to her own heart. I've heard of juries, in such a case, a jury of blind men to hear his word would make him a Warren of Gilsland, look at the pictures," she added. But the thoughts of the Spanish Lady were again wandering, when the notes of Tiney, as usual, when anyone approached, gave their plaintive warning, a little distance from the window, the old woman started and listened, the air was sweet, it was that song she loved best, and which the little girl held too sacred to be caroled, except on momentous occasions.

Rose, who had sunk into abstraction for the last five minutes, here asked what hour it was, for she could not, from where she lay, conveniently see the clock on the mantel-piece, she was told it was a little after twelve.

"Something tells me he will ride, and steal softly in, and before long."

"He cannot be far away just now," said the old woman.

"They are all so timid, they will stop him."

"No, nothing will stop him!" said the voice of him she sought to see, and the flowers gave way, and his head, to her more beautiful than the day, appeared between the foliage.

"It would never do, dearest Rose, to enter the place by a window," he said, "but now that I have seen you, I shall be round by the door in less time than you can think."

The old gipsy half rose at seeing the change this appearance made on the dark complexion of the sick lady. That pale sallow, with a tinge of gold in it, had left in a moment her skin, and in its place came a deadly leaden blue. She pressed her hand on her heart a moment, and her lips moved, as if repeating a prayer.

The tapestry of the doorway was pushed aside, and her companion of the Platte knelt at the sofa side, and buried his face in the ermine-lined cloak on which she lay.

The old woman, with instinctive delicacy, rose to go, but was beckoned back by the hand of the invalid.

"Where is Isabel?" she said, and the Marchioness was called by the voice of Tiney.

"My prayers and the intercessions of the blessed Virgin have been heard. This last earthly comfort has been allowed me. I never thought to live," she said, "to be glad my dear father was away, but I am thankful he is spared this parting. Isabel, dear, come here, and kneel by Edward's side. My voice much fails me—I will not keep you long. You will be a good wife to my dear brother when I am gone—promise—and take his hand."

Isabel, with convulsive sobs, tried to speak, and took the hand that was stretched toward her.

"Nay, do not speak, 'tis I who have least time. You remember, Ned, that night of my boy's death, I never told you, but love of gold was the affection of my husband. He never cared more for me than as the means of coming by Deigo's wealth, and his craven heart allowed him to suffocate my babe to save his own mean and worthless life. Say they what they will, a child belongs to his mother by nature. I fevered and maddened—they called it a milk-fever—but I had sufficient reason to direct my vengeance upon the proper victim—he died a coward. When I went to confession, I tried to justify my act—but in vain, my penance was to withdraw from the sacred communion for a year, and never, in case I had loved another—which might have been an unacknowledged motive—to marry him. But I am spared much of my suffering. Is the good Father near, Isabel?"

"Yes."

"I feel I am in extreme need. I did not think to die on a velvet couch, while others were careering in the sun. Ned, you remember when my favorite horse ran, others seemed to stand still. And how true the arrow is—it is a silent and eating death, but the tomahawk is violent and vengeful.

"Do you remember on the banks of—"

Here she was interrupted by the entrance of the meek Priest, with the tapers borne before him, and the sacred Chrism.

There was a silence of the tomb, the two that had knelt near rose, and moved to kneel further off, the old gipsy gazed ghastly on the lights, the kneeling assistants, the clasped hands, and dying look of her who was to receive the last rite of religion, and involuntarily also dropped upon her knees, but when Lady Connemara bared the feet of the patient for the office, they were already cold and feelingless.

The good Father hardly restrained his emotions—the others wept, the eyes had been shut, and the long lashes were marked in shadow on the cheek, now somewhat less dead in its color—they were opened in an expression of holy calm—a revived look seemed imbued into her features.

"Now, dearest," she said slowly, "let me be alone, and leave that little bell within reach. I may sleep, for I feel better."

Her look was earnestly marked upon each as they went out of the room, but dwelt last on Edward, as the curtain closed. Then—for there were two young and affectionate eyes which wonderingly watched through the flowers—she closed her eyes, as if to sleep, and drew a part of her mantle over her face.

Nearly an hour had elapsed, and no bell tinkled in the chamber of sickness, however slightly—for anxious ears watched—and there might be hopes, so revivifying had been the effect of the last Sacrament, and the apparently calm sleep they could observe by peeping through the opening of the arras.

"She has never moved," said Isabel to Edward.

The Doctor overheard her words, and shook his head. They both started.

The gipsy woman, who unperceived still lingered near, here remarked, "There are many such who wish to die unseen."

———

It was some days after, and the body of Rose had been embalmed and laid in the vault of the family. The Marchioness was waiting to bid adieu of her now accepted lover who was leaving the place for London. The two walked together over the lawn, toward a short cut by which Edward was to arrive, where a post-chaise awaited to take him to the nearest coaching point on the Carlisle road.

"You will write often, then, as I have need to hear from you. This end has been so sudden, of Rose's, she was so noble, and so free from all the nonsense of our ways, and yet so delicate and minute in all she did. It might have been needless to have said anything about the restriction from marriage, owing to her rash vengeance, but she thought I had a scruple as to having deprived her of a union she had done so much to deserve. I was set right in that, and I have learned, from a study Of her conduct, how much more lofty the female character is, when divested of its artificial helplessness, and I feel that I should have as much pleasure in attending to your horse, or gathering wood for our fire, where it would be necessary, as I should find it agreeable to join you in a duo, or cull you a nosegay of exotics. Now I have made my speech, I am not going to undo it by silly complaints at our now parting, but truthfully to say, dearest Ned, that I shall long for your return, so, now, farewell."

He would have spoken, but contending emotions choked his utterance. Isabel, however, cut the parting short, by kissing him with the air of a matron, and turning away.

He, who well knew her ways, ventured not a step after her, but pursued his road.

Chapter Eighty-Nine
Communications

Letter from E. Warren to Harry Smith.

Dearest Harry,

I cannot say I hasten to write to you of the death of our dear Rose. The noble spirit is gone from us. The agitations occasioned by her child's death, and consequent scenes and illness, had affected, as I learn, her circulation, and she died of a heart complaint which ended in the rupture of a vessel. She is gone, and I scarcely know how to describe her end. I am deeply melancholy from the double loss, as I have been obliged to come to town to learn my own precise position, as far as I can, which seems to be as difficult as ever. But I inclose you two letters, one of which may show you what I have to expect in the way of the legal recognition of the rights of birth I claim, and the other will remind you of my good kind aunt, as she allows me to call her.

Many thanks for your important information. Ben is a youth of some sense, he is not to be damaged by his father's acts, and he now sees there is no more to be made of the dead, and does not care to do evil for evil's sake.

We have got the documents, which would be conclusive to any one but a lawyer, who would gain by delay. My marriage, however happily does not await the legal decision of my claims of birth.

Extract of a Letter from Lady Dorothea to E. Warren, Esq.

We have had my aunt's solicitor made a Baronet (Sir Francis Rider), she came and told us in great triumph, that he had been to announce the event. He is a sort of favorite with her, but with no one else in the house, and Albric is always abusing him, so the news was received with sufficient indifference, and my aunt said, possibly to awake some interest, "Poor man, he had one of his eyes much bloodshot."

Still no answer.

"He must have met with some accident," persisted my aunt.

"Or, rubbed it with his bloody hand," said my brother, as he left the room.

Albric had been in some disgrace previously, having been employed to find a picture, from the collection at Willersly Manor, on a sacred subject, and present it to the Reverend Earl of Handlebury, who had been importuning her ladyship for a subscription to a church-building society, she, never giving money, thought of this plan to appease her zealous friends. Albric had bethought him to write to the land-steward in Suffolk, instead of going down himself, and it turns out the letter produced the painting of a steeple-chase, to the great astonishment and scandal of the pious lord. So, the whole family have moved down to make a proper selection, to repair our credit at Exeter Hall.

But A. has only the luck to get out of one scrape into another, for he addressed the very pretty landlady of the Black Swan at Bury as Leda. My aunt looking reproof, he was beginning to ask what she could know of the story.

When we retired to our bedrooms soon after Lady D. sent for me, she was under the hands, of her maid, sitting in an armchair, with a night-cap on, equal to a Lord Chief Justice's wig, her countenance was mild and serene, and alarmed me much more than would have done an appearance of anger —she had evidently made up her mind to some great resolution.

"I always like," she said, "to have explanations, and say outright what I have to say. It appears to me that your brother, who has a perfect right even to have a bad opinion of lawyers, made a very serious attack against my attorney, Sir Francis Rider. Now I have thought the thing over, and Sir Francis is not a Criminal Judge, so there could be no allegory (I think that is the proper word), now, as there was no allegory, he must have meant to make a specific charge, so I have made up my mind to demand to know what he meant by the sanguinary allusion, and as I thought, my dear, you would listen more patiently than anyone else to my reasons for desiring to bring this matter— here she was puzzled for a word—to light, I thought it best to speak to you, that you might prepare your brother to—"

Here my poor aunt came to a dead stop, she looked dignified and determined, while I was quite unable to offer more than acquiescence to her remarks, which seemed to have assumed such a magisterial form as really to alarm me, and I went off straight to A.'s room, impressed with the solemnity of the scene, and almost adopting the inquiring spirit which appeared so reasonably exerted.

He was seated at the fire, reading something of Dickens's, as he said, 'to learn what was doing among the lower orders.'

"What has kept you up, Dora? you look portentious! Pray don't, consider I am going to bed with a lively imagination and a decided talent for dreaming —a Spartan talent, from its weight, I fear, so spare me, if you can."

"You will sleep the sounder, dear brother, if you unburthen your mind, or confess an error," I said, something sententiously.

"Unburthening my mind is easy," he answered, "at this moment, if the confession of an error could do it. The only difficulty which could arise would be in the selection."

Seeing he would have the best of it if I let him go on, I was obliged at once to tax him with the accusation he had made against Sir F. He looked at me in some alarm.

"What does my aunt think of it?"

I repeated her exordium as near as I could.

"Well," he said, "I hope I may laugh at it, but you are dangerous people, by my faith—both my aunt and you—for an ingenuous youth to be planted beside. You will find the explanation of the bloody hand, upon the shield of Ulster."

I hardly yet understood, but perceived we had made ourselves ridiculous, and retired.

Extract of a Letter from Mr. Searle to E. Warren, Esq.

Perhaps it is well that the Marchioness does not know that the murderers of her father are traced back to the deed itself, and that the hand of the Almighty has avenged it. From what instructions I have already received, it is evident we ought not to attempt to connect the fire, the loss of the documents so strangely recovered, and the persecutions and dangers to which you have personally been subjected, to the person who was to profit by your loss. You will therefore see that the case to be brought forward in your behalf will be, though complete in documents, disjointed in facts, I am empowered by Mr. H. Smith's letter to state, that the papers were saved from the fire by Ben the groom's father, and given to him, that he, knowing the Marquis to be the possessor of the titles and estates, gave them to him at the spot where he was murdered, and received a sum of money to take him to America, that the murder took place, we can infer, in the expectation of the sum promised for the documents being still on the person of the Marquis, but as we cannot produce evidence to shew from whence these papers came, our story must be incomplete. I am in some hopes, however, from the detective officer's letter, that some trace may be found of the late Mr. Warren's butler having given certain hints as to their being saved from the fire before he went abroad.

He says, 'there is some reason to think, that the butler of the late Mr. Warren, has said something to his sister regarding the documents we have found, but she is very tender of her words, fearing the consequences to her brother, as also dreading to bring odium on her family. Mr. Bankes has taken the matter in hand, he has an astonishing natural capacity, when he exchanged trunks in the boat, I did not perceive him do it, and when he came into my custody, and was out of reach of the ship, I could not help thinking him a prisoner, as did my daughter, who was with me. The whole plan was admirable, I think they would not have gone, were it not for the dread of that rascal Coalman, when the papers should be found to be copies."

If we can trace these documents into the hands of one of the servants after the house was burnt, it will in part prove a connecting chain, but we are barred from shewing how you were kidnapped, and induced to go abroad. In the clearest case that could be framed, the different Courts through which it had to pass, must create delay, and raise difficulties and doubts, but when you add to this high rank and vast possessions, the cause will adhere to the Bench with a tenacity proportioned to its importance, however, I trust ultimately we may succeed, and you may depend upon my best exertions.

Letter from E. Warren to Harry Smith continues.

Having given these extracts, you will be able to see how I stand as to my claims of birth, and that they will be much strengthened by your kind and friendly communication. I forgive Ben everything, for stipulating that Isabel and her father's name should not be sullied in public court, our marriage she wishes to take place before the suit is raised.

You will not receive this in time, before starting again for the west, to read my good wishes for your summer's campaign, but my spirit shall be with you. Much as I should have wished—no duties elsewhere intervening—to have again roamed on the hunting grounds of the Indian Arab, I feel I could not have mastered the memories of that brief and happy space upon the waters of the Platte, where she who is departed was my rival in woodcraft, my admiration, and my friend, I could not behold the Butte of Laramy, or the thirsty plains at its base, over which we rode, or its clear streams, and groves in which we reposed, without an aching heart, such as I trust you will never feel. On that scene the blytheness of youth would be gone, and the spirit of the hunter tamed, and you would have to mourn, rather than rejoice, at my reappearance on the western wilds.

A Look at Book Six:
Journal of a Mountain Man

A first-hand account of one of America's most joyful explorers.

As a member of Jedediah Smith's first mountain man brigade, James Clyman was there when the South Pass was discovered, opening the inter-mountain West to fur trappers. Traversing the American West, he experienced a host of events in the untamed 1800's frontier.

From encountering the Donner Party to sewing Jim Bridger's ear back on after a grizzly bear attack, and walking six hundred miles to Fort Atkinson, Clyman journeyed twice to the Pacific before settling in Napa Valley. There, he raised a family and began sharing legendary tales of the mountain men.

Told with vivid description and using Clyman's historic journal entries, Win Blevins brings to life a bygone era of adventure and danger in this colorful memoir.

AVAILABLE DECEMBER 2024

About the Author

Win Blevins was an award-winning author best known for his fiction and nonfiction books of Western lore and Native American leaders, lifestyle, and spirituality. He was the recipient of a lifetime achievement award from the Western Writers of America, and a member of the Western Writers Hall of Fame; a three-time winner of Wordcraft Circle Native Writers and Storytellers Book of the Year; two-time winner of a Spur Award for Best Novel of the West; and was nominated for a Pulitzer for his novel about Crazy Horse, *Stone Song*.

Blevins, whose own origins were a mix of Cherokee, Welsh-Irish, and African American, published his first novel in 1973. That book, *Give Your Heart to the Hawks, a Tribute to the Mountain Man*, is still in print fifty years later and recently returned to the *New York Times* bestseller list.

Over his long career, Blevins wrote nearly forty books, including the historical fiction Rendezvous series, a dozen screenplays, and numerous magazine articles. His *Dictionary of the American West* is held in 750 libraries.

Born in Little Rock, Arkansas, on October 21, 1938, Blevins was an honors graduate of Columbia University—where he earned a master's degree—and the Music Conservatory of the University of Southern California. He began his writing career as a music and drama critic for the *Los Angeles Times* and became the principal entertainment editor for the *The Los Angeles Herald Examiner*. During that time, he hung out with the likes of Sam Peckinpah and Strother Martin, and began diving into the lives of Mountain Men and Native Americans of the West.

He also served as the Gaylord Family Visiting Professor of Professional Writing at the University of Oklahoma. For fifteen years, he was a book editor for Macmillan Publishing and TOR/Forge Books.

Win loved and felt a deep connection with nature. He climbed mountains on four continents and was a boatman-guide on the Snake River. Once caught in a freak blizzard while climbing, he took shelter inside a tree for more than twenty-four hours. His feet were frozen, but he refused to have them amputated. Almost twenty years after that event, he climbed the Himalayas—despite an awkward gait.

Native Spirituality suited him. He was pierced during a Lakota ceremony and was a pipe carrier. He went on twelve vision quests and felt the pull of the red road.

Win spent the last twenty years of his life, living quietly in the Southwest among the Navajo. His passions grew with time. In the center was his wife Meredith, their children, and many grandchildren. Classical music, baseball, roaming red rock mesas, and rafting were great loves, and he considered himself blessed to create new stories about the West. He was also proud to call himself a member of the world's oldest profession—storytelling.

Notes

Chapter 1

i. Nathaniel Wyeth, who having first penetrated by land to Fort Vancouver, and founded Fort Hall, sent a fine ship round to the Columbia River under an excellent commander, Captain Lambert, to take back a cargo of pickled salmon, but notwithstanding all the ability and energy of those engaged in this speculation, it did not pay.

ii. The messenger had received oral instructions, in case of the letter he bore being lost or destroyed. This is mentioned as an example of the difference which had taken place in point of safety in this route, as well as the distinctness of the trail.

iii. To cut it up and dry it, so as that it should keep, and be a portable supply.

iv. A light fusil, used generally in running bison.

v. Son of a Canadian and half-bred Cree mother, born on the Siscatchnan of the northwest territory.

vi. We had been robbed of all our clothes but those we had on, by the Crows, during the previous autumn, and were obliged to take off our shirts and wash them, to keep ourselves clean, hanging them up to dry at night by the fire while we lay in bed.

  Editor's note: The incident described took place on September 5, 1833, when Stewart was left in charge of the camp while Thomas Fitzpatrick visited a nearby Crow village. During Fitzpatrick's absence some Crows overawed Stewart and his men and stole their goods. See Bernard DeVoto, Across the Wide Missouri, Boston, 1947, p. 125, and Davenport and Porter, Scotsman in Buckskin, p. 71.

vii. The "Turn out!" repeated twice.

viii. Even at that period, there were many reports of the precious metal having been found to the westward of the upper waters of the Platte, amongst others by Milton Soublette, but more especially on the desert region on the left bank of Green River, where it passes through many days' journey of precipitous cliff, which renders access to the river impossible, from the adjoining country being a canon of many hundred feet of perpendicular height of rock.

  Editor's note: Milton Green Sublette (1801-1837), the second youngest of the Sublette brothers, was called by a contemporary journalist the "Thunderbolt of the Rockies." Going west perhaps as early as 1822, Milton participated in several celebrated incidents, including the Battle of Pierre's Hole and the amputation of Thomas "Peg-Leg" Smith's foot. A tough and determined man, well-liked by his peers, Milton died early from what may have been bone cancer. See Doyce B. Nunis, Jr., "Milton Green Sublette," in Hafen, Mountain Men, IV, 331-49.

ix. A name given promiscuously to brooks and smaller rivers.

x. From the Spanish "canon."

xi. A mutilation, found not unfrequently, and caused by accident, when the animal is young.

xii. I had the two best horses within a thousand miles, a large bore Manton rifle, and health.

Chapter 3

i. This incident is faithfully taken from a real occurrence many years ago, and the speech was made by the Earl of at a Silver Hell, in Bury Street.

Chapter 7

i. The plane tree (platanus is called in the United States sycamore). The tree mentioned in the New Testament, and translated sycamore, must be the platanus, as what is usually called sycamore in England, is not found in Turkey or Palestine, the Americans have retained the proper English name for the tree, if the word in the New Testament is correct.
ii. Anona Assiminier, in French.
iii. Gumbo is a stringy soup made of some peculiar vegetables, and sometimes of sassafras.
iv. A man need take no pledge, could he depend upon himself.
v. This anecdote is founded on fact, as also the subsequent history of the German's adventures and death.

Chapter 11

i. Name given to the panther in the United States.

Chapter 12

i. Common name for the Kanzas tribe.

Chapter 13

i. The mountain name for a small piece of Bison skin, dressed with the hair on, used as a saddle blanket.

Chapter 14

i. Term used in the mountains for stalking the bison.

Chapter 16

i. A small narrow piece of buckskin, used in the same way as narrow tape or coarse thread, and generally pulled from a fringe, when needed for mending or tying anything.

Chapter 17

i. Penses Cuvus of the Indians.
ii. Mountain term for a deep and steep sided rocky ravine, taken from the Spanish.
iii. To fort, means with the trappers, build oneself a fort for safety.
iv. Captain Stewart, who had first brought up an ounce balled rifle in 1833, that season went to rendezvous with Campbell's party, and there was more meat killed by that rifle in his hands, and in those of that wonderful hunter, Antonio Clement, than by any other gun in the camp, and not by one third so much lead used as by those who had rifles forty or fifty to the pound, which was the usual bore, for seasons after, the first double rifle and fowling piece was brought up by the same person on a later excursion.

   Editor's note: It is believed that all of these guns were made by Joseph Manton at London. In Stewart's footnote read "four" in place of "for" seasons later, that is, 1837. Joseph Manton (1766-1835) was one of the finest London gunsmiths in the early nineteenth century. He devised an elevating rib sight in 1806, and experimented with various percussion lock and ignition systems between 1816 and 1820. See Macdonald Hastings, English Sporting Guns and Accessories, London and Sydney, 1969, pp. 12, 13, 46, 47.

Chapter 19

i. The timbers of a boat tied together with bark, and bull hides, sewed with sinews, stretched over it.

   Editor's note: Commonly framed with willow poles, bullboats had seams caulked with a mixture of ashes and tallow, and required frequent maintenance. The Indian form was a small, circular affair using one hide, but the fur companies made larger ones, at times even fashioning an envelope for a wagon box out of bull hides. See Ross, The West of Alfred Jacob Miller, plates 8, 123, 180. Chittenden says the size of the trappers' bull boats "was commonly about twelve by thirty feet and twenty inches deep" (Chittenden, Fur Trade, I: 35). See also Chittenden's fine description in History of Early Steamboat Navigation on the Missouri River, New York, 1903, pp. 96-102. In 1843 Matt Field transcribed a story told to him by Stewart of an 1833 event, which Stewart incorporated into Edward Warren, p ? 106. See Field, Prairie and Mountain Sketches, p. 89.

ii. To make medicine, means charm or occult power among the Indians, and is used in that sense by the mountain men.

iii. Term used to signify the person who hires the services of another.

Chapter 21

i. Mountain expression for party, or lot of people, company, and collection.

Chapter 22

i. An instance of this occurred not far from the present scene. On the great slope of one of the Black Hills, several streams with wooded banks track their way to the medicine bow, which receives their tributes, the expanse is laid out panorama-like, and of great extent. Jim Bridger's camp were early afoot, and someone spied out a grisly bear, not yet returned to his lair, root digging about a mile off, halfway up the side of a hanging covert. The cry was no sooner raised, than every disposable hand was off, one hunter, better mounted than the rest, made for the opposite side of the stream, and did not pull up until at its head, where there was a bushy thicket, there he awaited the bear, while the whole course below rung with the challenges of the eager troop. It was not long before the bear was heard by the solitary hunter—who was a greenhorn—he then got a sight of him through the bushes, put up his rifle, which snapped, it was a Manton which never missed fire, there was not even a cap on it, it had been washed the night before and never reloaded. The bear heard the snap, but saw nothing, and hesitating to face an unseen foe turned back, the hunter jumped down to load, the pursuers were coming on, and the ball was home, when the horse broke away from the slight hold and bounded off, the bear was again tearing up through the bushes. A cap was yet to be adjusted, the animal was within ten feet, when he received the ball in the cheek, which ranged through the whole length of the body, as he was mounting an acclivity, he rolled back into the bushes, tearing them up with his teeth, and roaring. The field came up, and knowing what was the matter, each took a hasty aim. Twelve men fired, only one hit, and that was a cook, John D'Villié, who claimed the shot, as he alone was loaded with slugs, but he also claimed the bear, and the hunter let him take the pattes as a trophy, amid the cheers of the rest, upon whom he considered he had gained a victory, and he never was told that the bear was in his death agony before he fired.

   Editor's note: Since the greenhorn carried a Manton rifle, it is likely that he was Stewart himself.

ii. Over the shaft of the Indian arrow, small grooves are irregularly traced, not very deep, and resembling veins, which are made it is said, to allow the wound to bleed while the arrow is still working deep into the flesh.

Chapter 24

i. The term woodsman is applied to all who live the life of the hunter in an uncultivated country. The term possibly takes its origin from the fact of the great mass of wasteland of any richness, as a harbor for wild animals, being covered with timber.

Chapter 26

i. Frayed—an old term in venery for cleaned.—See Bloom's "Sports and Pastimes."
ii. The terms of venery for the round-horned deer of Europe, that is, the red deer, are hart for the full grown master-deer, stag for the male not yet come to his complete growth, and hind and calf for the female and young.

Chapter 27

i. This is to a certain degree taken from fact. John Gray stabbed Milton Sublette in the back, in a similar scene got up on purpose, the blow happily was not fatal.

   Editor's note: Evidently Grey did stab Sublette, after some insult Sublette offered to Grey's daughter.

Chapter 28

i. The elevation of the plain at the base of the Mountains of the Winds, is about eight thousand feet.
ii. From the little knowledge the author has of the diamond in its brute state, he has no doubt that these regions abound in precious stones.
iii. I remember, on one occasion, we roused a bear from a thicket, some dozen of us riding before camp, on the Platte. Dr. Whitman, afterward killed, with all his family, by the Cayusses of the *Nezperce* tribe, near Walla-Walla, a most excellent man, a curious divine, for he sometimes preached, and a most bold operator, for he without hesitation let out water from the chest with a penknife, or cut out an arrow-head with a butcher's knife, which had been for years wandering about Jim Bridger's back and hip, which I have in my pocket while I write, was with the party behind. The dogs brought the bear to a sort of bay, there was no honor to be gained by killing him with a quiet shot, so Fitzpatrick proposed to let him be kept there, until someone went back a quarter of a mile and brought up the greenhorns—the doctor among the number. We were all stationed at different points, knowing the bear would break bay on the arrival of the crowd, the dogs were fresh and furious, the bear made charges, and each was ready if he should break by on his post. In the middle of all this, we heard the amateurs of the camp, but the doctor never deficient in courage or zeal—-so often kindly and laudably directed among us—had outstripped his companions on a fat new horse, we were looking for the effect of his assemblage of matadors in the arena, as we waited their coming, when the doctor's horse caught the wind of the bear just before he entered the circle. We were credibly informed afterward that the doctor and his steed had a furious conflict for a moment, among the bushes, but all we of the hunt know of our own knowledge was. The doctor, though a large and powerful man, came upon the stage describing a parbolum over the intervening shrubs. The bear roared and charged—the doctor gathered himself up, and ran—the bear passed me, almost lifeless with laughter, untouched, and the doctor never saw him, nor any other, till the day of his death.
iv. No one in America would think of tying a horse to a post, or to the trunk of a tree, or a bar, a branch above his head, with the power to move round below, is perhaps the best. To leave a horse loose on the plain, you have to let down the rein over his head with something to trail after it, sufficient to be trodden on, and thus check his movements. To teach a horse,

use a powerful bit, and if he once moves and receives a severe check, he will never attempt it again.

Chapter 29

i. Name given to a booth or gypsey-tent.
ii. Ucre is an American game, said to have been brought from Holland.
iii. Medicine box is the small horn or hollowed piece of wood corked like a bottle, containing a matter secreted in the beaver, with which he anoints his fur, to render it impervious to wet, it has a strong odor, and is generally rubbed on a small stick, which is stuck in the water bank, in such a position, that the beaver coming to examine it, gets his feet into the trap, which is set underwater close opposite.
iv. Captain Walker.

Editor's note: Joseph Reddeford Walker (1798-1872) was born in Tennessee, and his family moved to the Missouri frontier in 1819. Joe soon entered the fur trade, and was also active in the early Santa Fe trade. He signed on with Captain Bonneville in 1831 and led a brigade to California the next year, an exploration described in Irving's Captain Bonneville.

Chapter 30

i. There is also the bye-play of those who back the caster, especially if he is an adept, and this sometimes supersedes the necessity of his backing himself.
ii. In a trial for seduction of a daughter on the part of a father, in asking damages in an English court of justice, he founds upon the loss he sustains in the labor of his child, so among the Indians of the Rocky Mountains, a father, or the nearest of kin acting as guardian, requires, when the young squaw is married, a compensation for the loss, which, if he is rich and well disposed toward her, he makes the less, provided the husband to whom she is sold settles handsomely upon her in the way of horses and other property, so as to render her independent, in case of death or a separation.
iii. I was with Campbell's camp, we had moved to the spot but a day or two before, and George Holmes, a young mountaineer, had aided me in constructing a bower of birch and willow, over which to throw a blanket in case of rain, and in which to contain our couch, the leaves were fresh and fragrant, and the little abode had its open end upon the brink of the river rushing past clear and swift over its pebbly bed. I had no news to read, and no letters, but the recollections of a former home were not obliterated, nor of country, and I loved to sit in the shade, and let my memory wander over bye-gone years, when tired of a visit to the Snake Camp, or the now frequent jollities of the wild free trappers, who came dropping in from distant and unknown haunts, where they had perilled their lives for the ephemeral joys and riot of the few days of jubilee. The best looking of the young squaws of the neighboring camp, came over in groups to wonder at the riches of the white man, as well as to tempt him to dispense them, and many happy matrimonial connections were formed by means of a dower of glittering beads and scarlet cloth.

On an evening of one of these days, I had for some cause, which appeared to me at the time sufficiently reasonable, begged of my friend Holmes to take his blanket, and make himself a welcome in some other hut, as I wished to have our shanty for the night at my own disposal, he consented, but as I afterward found he had laid himself down on the ground to sleep by a brake of fragrant rose bushes close by. I thought, afterward, there was some reluctance in his manner and that I could read some little expression of disappointment in his eye, his temperament was gay and reckless, or I might not have remarked this shade, but he removed his blanket and a small piece of skin, but left his saddle, the usual pillow of the wanderer. The night came, and deepened on toward the middle watch, when I was roused by confused sounds, shouts, and the discharge of firearms, as well as the deep roar of a bull, such as he emits in terror or in rage. There could be no Indian attack, and I still hestitated about getting up, when there came a sharp cry close to the bower and in a voice I well knew, and no longer hesitating, belted a blanket round me and rushed out. Poor Holmes was seated on the ground, the side of his head and his ear bleeding and torn, a mad wolf was ravaging the camp. We did not get her, she had other lives to sacrifice elsewhere. Poor Holmes changed from that hour, instead of alertness and joy, melancholy and despondency grew upon him day by day, and though I stood beside him in another night, when we were but a small party in the hands of the Crow Indians, and when neither of us thought to see another sun, I felt I was linked in a death struggle with one, who whatever he might do to help a friend, considered his own fate as sealed. That day at noon, he had quarrelled with the camp leader for calling him "Beauty," a nickname by which he was known, from his blithe and sunny smile. Next day the eye was wan, and the smile was gone. In November, a melancholy and wasted form set out with Dr. Harrison, the son of the General, and Major Harris, in search of the stone which is believed to be the talisman for the cure of hydrophobia, and his bones were left, we could never learn exactly where, on the branch of some stream, and the bough of some tree, where I would have willingly made a pilgrimage to render the last tribute of regret, and contrast the living memory with the dead remains. There never has quitted my breast a reproachful remorse for the part I played him on that sad night.

Chapter 31

i. Herd of horses.

Chapter 32

i. There were many sailors who had been over half the world, as well as many Sandwich Islanders (Kanockers) hired as camp keepers.
ii. Lent by Jem Bridger, who had received them in a present brought from Europe expressly for him.

   Editor's note: The armor was a facsimile of that of the English Life Guards, brought to rendezvous for Bridger by Stewart. Alfred Jacob Miller made a painting of Bridger wearing the armor (see Ross, The West of Alfred Jacob' Miller, plate 159, and DeVoto, Across the Wide Missouri, plate LXXV). In Victor's The River of the West (p. 238), Joe Meek describes himself "arrayed in a suit of armor belonging to Captain Stuart [sic]."

iii. Mark Head had come early in the spring of life to the mountains, and was considered one of the most successful beaver hunters of the West, though rather under the usual scale of intellect, he had contrived to get through difficulties and dangers, such as had checked or baffled men who considered themselves as possessing more intelligence and experience than himself. It was in the spring of 1834, I was with Jem Bridger and one of the bravest and most dashing hunters of the day, Captain Lee, of the U.S.A., in a range of mountains whose western slopes give birth to the waters of California, and near the city of Taos. We had in camp a young Ioway Indian, who had been brought up in a French village near St. Louis, and had hired as a camp follower to the company of which Jem Bridger was chief. This youth, whose name was Marshall, had become so lazy and disobedient, that Bridger and Fitzpatrick had discharged him, and he was—without an animal—obliged to follow the camp on foot. I took compassion on him and hired him, giving him traps and a mule to ride, but having found that he was perfectly unwilling to do anything, had recourse to frequent lectures, and at last threatened to turn him adrift also. Seeing that his love of idleness, inherent in all Indians, was likely to bring him again into trouble, he determined to abscond, and one night went off with a favorite rifle, my best running horse—Otholoho—and another, this was announced to me at the turn out, and I got up, scarcely believing in such ingratitude. The rifle was a serious loss, a most accurate-shooting gun, the horse, which was the swiftest in the West, beat the Snake nation, and would, had there not been unfair play on the part of the man who took charge of him the night before the race, have beaten all the horses of the whites. I was in great trouble, and rushed out of my lodge, the greatest part of the camp were assembled to examine the pickets, no rope had been cut, and the rifle had been taken from beside the fire, and Marshall was missing, there was therefore no doubt in the group of who was the thief, and I exclaimed in my wrath, for they laughed a little at my having thought to get any good out of such a scamp, "I'd give five hundred dollars for his scalp."

After breakfast, upon reflection we saw that, not knowing the country, he would probably miss his way, and not be out of reach, I organized two or three parties to go in search of him, cautioning them, however, that he was armed with bow and arrow as well as a rifle, both of which would be dangerous in the hands of a cunning and desperate man. The result proved how much I was mistaken in this Indian from first to last. Mark Head and a Spaniard found him not far off, unable to resist the desire of killing a bison on the fastest horse in the plains, after having dropped two bulls with his arrows, he had dismounted to take the meat of one, while thus engaged, these two came upon him unperceived, and accosting him, asked "What he was about?" "He was," he stated, "sent out for meat by the Captain, but thought perhaps the meat of the other bull was better, and would ride over to it to see." His drift was evident, the Spaniard hung back, Mark thought there might be some technical difficulty about the reward if he did not bring the scalp, or he was afraid of the Spaniard joining the other, Marshall was putting the cord to rights as he was about to mount, when Mark shot him dead under the horse's neck. In the evening, between us and the sun, the loiterers of the camp saw two men leading two horses making their way toward camp, and on a rifle was displayed the scalp of the horse-thief. This was a little more than I looked for, and I tore the bloody trophy from the gun and flung it away. The horse returned to my hands, but I never afterward crossed his back—he was a year after taken by the Blackfeet, and beat everything in their country.

Editor's note: Mark Head (1815?-1847) was a specimen of the devil-may-care mountain man. Born in Virginia andraisedin Missouri, Headwas in the mountains by 1832, trapping for William Sublette, and soon was a companion of Carson, Bridger, Meek and other notables. Stewart here details Head's most famous escapade, also told by Alfred Jacob Miller (Ross, The West of Alfred Jacob Miller, note to plate 159). Headwas apparently legendary by the age of about twenty-two, for in 1837 Miller painted a watercolor of an old trapper telling a "Mark Head story" (Ross, The West of Alfred Jacob Miller, plate 135). He is also described by Matt Fieldin 1843 (Prairie and Mountain Sketches, p. 146,152-155), and by Ruxton in 1847 (Ruxton of the Rockies, LeRoy R. Hafen, ed., Norman, Oklahoma, 1950, pp. 219-221). Head was one of about a dozen trappers killed along with Territorial Governor Charles Bent in the Taos Rebellion of January 1847. See Harvey L. Carter, "Mark Head," in Hafen, The Mountain Men and the Fur Trade, I: 287-293, Peters, Life and Adventures of Kit Carson, pp. 95-96, and Brown, Three Years in the Rocky Mountains, pp. 13-15. The Captain Lee of the U.S.A. mentioned by Stewart was a fur trader of Virginia stock who became a Mexican citizen. Appointed sheriff of Taos in December 1846, he died with Mark Head and the other trappers a month later in the Taos Rebellion. See David J. Weber, "Stephen Louis Lee," in Hafen, Mountain Men and the Fur Trade, III: 181-187.

Chapter 33

i. It is thus, that the time and difficulty of using a ramrod in the course is avoided.

Chapter 34

i. There is the regular grey or grisly bear, of almost an uniform color, and also a bear of the same family, who has an appearance as if a dirty white blanket had been thrown over him, and the chocolate bear, which, as far as my experience goes, is the largest, and is similar to one found in Norway and Sweden. I have seen one of these haul a large bison bull out of a crevice at least eight feet deep, and lay him out to cool. I have never heard of this animal devouring a man while warm, and in regard to game, they invariably lay the dead animal out on as nice a spot as they can find near, to keep for a future repast.

Chapter 35

i. On the Big Horn river, I was roused from sleep by a cry in camp that a bull Campbell was taking with some cows down to the Yellow stone, and who had been bitten by the mad wolf at rendezvous, was gone mad, and spreading confusion all around. I got suddenly up, and took the blanket, which had covered a bundle of twigs serving for a pillow, to throw round me, as I ran toward the quarter where his roaring and attacking the horses caused a general rush. The bundle was turned over in my hurry, an enormous rattlesnake had been coiled beneath, and I afterward remembered being once disturbed soon after lying down, by what I thought was a mouse, moving about under my head. The snake, I believe, did not pay for his warm bed.

Editor's note: Stewart probably is referring to the Western rattlesnake, Crotalus viridis. The story about Campbell's bull and the mad wolf is corroborated by Charles Larpenteur and commented on by Bernard DeVoto. See Larpenteur, Forty Years a Fur Trader, pp. 36-37 (including note 3), and DeVoto, Across the Wide Missouri, p. 105. Larpenteur saw this incident, and wrote that he could have shot the wolf but "was hindered by Captain Stward [sic] which was officer of the guard at the time."

ii. These adventures with rattlesnakes happened to the author.

Chapter 36

i. There is much morally to blunt the finer feelings in these countries, where life is held so cheap, but it is a fact easily to be authenticated, that feeding solely on the beef of the bison has the effect of hardening the nerves, and rendering an ordinarily humane disposition absolutely cruel, or at least indifferent to the pain of others. I think Bruerinus somewhere points at the flesh of the ox as having this effect on the human temperament. I quote from the "Anatomy of Melancholy."

Chapter 38

i. The death of Reece really took place by the hand of a man he had threatened, in the way described. The object of Reece's mad love was this man's wife, thinking, if it was reported to him that he had sworn on the Bible to destroy him the first opportunity, he would believe him in earnest and let her go. He met with his death from the husband on one of the small streams which run into Snake River, near Fort Hall, waylaying him on one of his visits. There was a court of inquiry, or something of the sort, but the threats had been so notorious, that the act was universally considered justifiable, and Reece himself, in dying, declared that he had nothing to say against the hand by which he fell.

Editor's note: This footnote of Stewart's sheds light on an obscure tale mentioned in few sources. William Marshall Anderson wrote that on July 8, 1834, "I was offered a fee of $150.00 to defend a man accused of murder before a self constituted court-I rode down to the other camp to appear for him, but conscience made a coward of my client and he fled." Morgan says that the defendant "was perhaps T. S. Reese, whose name recurs in mountain annals from 1829 to 1833, then disappears, except for an ambiguous entry in the Fort Hall Account Books, which may or may not indicate that Reese was still alive in 1835." Morgan also mentions that Stewart had left the rendezvous of 1834 six days before the court time specified by Anderson. See Morgan and Harris, eds., The Rocky Mountain Journals of William Marshall Anderson, pp. 156-157.

Chapter 40

i. Both these dangers occurred to the author.

Chapter 41

i. Long Hair was the name of one of the great chiefs of the Crows, his hair was upward of eleven feet long, he was very old, but retained his influence till his death, though hardly able to walk, he was miserably poor, but had the means of bestowing riches upon others, and his had all been expended in furnishing arms and horses to an army of braves, who enforced his authority when he thought it right to interfere.

Editor's note: Long Hair was principal chief of the Mountain Crows, and was variously reported as between seventy and eighty years old around 1833. Estimates of the length of his hair ranged from ten feet (Maximilian, 1833) all the way to thirty-six feet (Denig, 1856), with a consensus at something over eleven feet. Long Hair died about 1845. See the brief biography of him in Morgan and Harris, eds., The Rocky Mountain Journals of William Marshall Anderson, pp. 334-337.

Chapter 42

i. A root resembling that of the tulip, I never saw it in flower. The Indians dry it, and it is a not disagreeable sweetish root of gummy substance, and is the vegetable the Nez Perce tribe of Indians depend upon for at least half their support. Poor Dr. Whitman took possession of one of the rich kammas plains, near Walla-Walla, the grande ronde, which was the original cause with the destruction of a race course, which led ultimately to his being killed by the Kai-ouses.

ii. Crow name for the nation.

Chapter 43

i. A gigantic American, who some years previous, had belonged to a hunting party, and they were encamped on a small feeder of the Popoagee, he was an overbearing man, trusting to great personal strength, to give him a right to bully or plague, as his humour might tend. One of his companions had been on this occasion the victim, and was driven to such a state of rage, that he took up a pistol, and struck his tormentor over the head, as it happened, the dog-head of the weapon entered the brain. In passing in 1833, I found the jawbone taken from the grave, probably by wolves. It was of great size, and the spot has been marked from the incident.

Editor's note: This account adds to a typically brief note by Jedediah Smith that reads "1828. Bray was killed by a blow from the hand of Mr. Tullock" (Dale L. Morgan, Jedediah Smith and the Opening of the West, Indianapolis, 1953, p. 343). Samuel Tullock was associated with Kenneth McKenzie, the ramrod of American Fur Company in the mountains, at least from 1828, and was the Fort Cass partisan who accepted furs stolen by the Crows from the Fitzpatrick-Stewart party of 1833. See Hafen, The Mountain Men and the Fur Trade, I: 140.

Chapter 44

i. Spirituous liquors are expressly forbidden by United States law in the Indian country.

Editor's note: A series of federal laws restricting the use of alcohol in the Indian trade was enacted between 1790 and 1832, but these laws were more honored in the breach than the observance. In 1832 a new act categorically prohibited alcohol in the trade. Although again not enforced strenuously, this law provided Nathaniel J. Wyeth with the means of spoiling Kenneth McKenzie's distillery operation at Fort Union in 1833.

ii. On the Columbia, fish is dried in the sun, and the wind raising the sand, it is almost incrustated by it, and the inhabitant of the river banks who feed upon it when they cannot afford the flesh of the dog, have teeth at the age of maturity ground down to stumps.

iii. This vast green basin is of such extent and depth, that with the naked eye, you cannot discern a herd of bison in the bottom, one of the three most distant branches of the Missouri rises at its head, called, I was told by General Clark, the Wisdom Fork.

Editor's note: This is the Big Hole Basin in present Beaverhead County, Montana, near Gibbonsville. The Wisdom Fork is the Big Hole River, which joins with the Beaverhead River to make the Jefferson Fork, one of the three forks of the Missouri River. "A party of the North West" probably refers to a brigade of the North West Company, a British fur rival of the Hudson's Bay Company merged into HBC in 1821.

iv. Cayack, a name given to a bison bull, by the mountain men.

Editor's note: This word, of French or Spanish derivation, is found in the literature in a variety of spellings. See McDermott, A Glossary of Mississippi Valley French: 1673-1850, pp. 45-46.

Chapter 47

i. Traders.

ii. I have a drawing in water-colors, made by the Little Chief of the Snakes, it is a hieroglyphic, he did it to show that the art of drawing was not to copy life, but to represent it in a way not to be mistaken. He had his own theory, and maintained it against an artist, who had made a likeness of himself, which could not be surpassed, if equalled for truth. The objection to which on his part, and which gave rise to the discussion was, that it was too like, which he considered a vulgar and familiar species of art, such as he said, could be made by his looking glass.

Chapter 48

i. This is transferred, almost word for word, from the French translation of the only song of which I could find out the meaning among these tribes as it was given to me by a Metif of the Cree nation. I have rendered it into the doggerel of the text, as being a specimen of what their other songs might be, and the attempt at versification has been adopted in reference to the still more terse and abrupt style in which it would have been to be given in prose.

Chapter 49

i. Mark of an axe to point out a road.

ii. Brent brow is an expression which I remember in the old Scottish ballad, *John Anderson my Joe*, and some apology may be due for using a word not perhaps generally understood.

Chapter 51

i. The Presbyterian and some other Protestant sects, do not pray for the dead, there is no heathen nation which has not some such rite, which I have ever heard of. In regard to the intercession of saints, these either are purified spirits in Heaven or not, if there are not, there is but little harm done, if there are, surely a purified spirit is preferable as an intercessor to the prayers of a congregation, made up of the most mixed, and perhaps impure ingredients, and which is constantly asked for by the living Protestant, on occasions of illness or distress.

Chapter 52

i. The loudness and agony of supplication having efficacy, is not a belief confined to Presbyterian ranters, or the Covenanters of Scotland, it is to be found in all religions, according to the temperament of their professors.

ii. In all cases where the word Frenchman or French trader are used, the Americans of French descent inhabiting the States of Louisiana, Indiana, and Missouri, are meant, or coming from Canada.

Chapter 54

i. These blankets are elaborately worked in different colors by these Mexican Indians, and are very much esteemed and of high value in the mountain region.

Chapter 60

i. John Auld told me when I met him in 1839—40, in the Mediterranean, that he had first been attracted to that part of the Missouri as a honey merchant and collector of wax, he then bought such peltries as were to be had from wandering hunters, and established the first stores at Lexington and Independence, far outstripping Daniel Boon in penetrating toward the west, and rendering himself wealthy, while he at the same time was most useful and beneficent to the first frontier settlers.

ii. The father was a Polish Jew, an agreeable old man, who had an old wooden house on a square plot, call in St. Louis an island, that is, a square space surrounded by streets, he had a large poultry yard, and very much lived upon eggs, either in kind, or converted into money. He had a small barrel which he carried under his arm once in two days to a brewery to get replenished with small beer, and his abode contained an assortment of old pictures, and other objects, either of use or vertu, but was never swept, save when a plume of ostrich feathers was called upon to clean anything for exhibition to a rare hunter of the old and curious in these parts. He was most kind and hospitable to the extent of those commodities in which he indulged, his family consisted of Philippe, the belle of the mountains, the darker and more serious, but no less handsome Louis and Miranda, the two last, the most extraordinry pianists I ever heard. The old man never saw his Philippe again, from the day he left for the west. Louis accompanied the author to the rendezvous of 1836, and was drowned in Lewis's Fork, and Miranda married a most accomplished violinist, and lies in an early grave, leaving a son now ten years old, who I hope may inherit the talents and attractions of his parents.

Chapter 61

i. Illinois is a free, Missouri a slave State. Perhaps the ladies of Sutherland House may be surprised to hear that, in many cases, families from slave States have taken their negro servants all over the Union, to be preached at, and attempts made to seduce them in every direction, remaining attached to the families to whom they felt they belonged.

Chapter 68

i. "Hunting sly," means stealing upon game, "running," dashing openly after it.

Chapter 77

i. In the Rocky Mountains, it is universally believed that the raven's note after the fall of night is the forerunner of death, or severe disaster. I have to confirm this myself by experience, on every occasion where that croak was heard where I have been. An old Canadian, who had been more than half his life a homeless hunter in the forest and the prairie, told me he had never known this sign of evil fail, and always made up his mind when he heard it, that he or someone with him was "in for something" when it occurred.

Bibliography

Alter, J. Cecil. *Jim Bridger.* Norman, Oklahoma, 1962.

Barry, Louise. *The Beginnings of the West: Annals of the Kansas Gateway to the American West: 1540-1854.* Topeka, Kansas, 1972.

Berry, Don. *A Majority of Scoundrels: An Informal History of the Rocky Mountain Fur Company.* New York, 1961.

Brown, David L. *Three Years in the Rocky Mountains.* New York, 1950.

Chittenden, Hiram Martin. *History of the American Fur Trade of the Far West.* Two volumes. Stanford, California, 1954.

Chittenden. *History of Early Steamboat Navigation on the Missouri River.* Two volumes. New York, 1903.

Cuthbertson, Stuart, and John C. Ewers. *A Preliminary Bibliography on the American Fur Trade.* St. Louis, 1939.

Davenport, Odessa, and Mae Reed Porter. *Scotsman in Buckskin: Sir William Drummond Stewart and the Rocky Mountain Fur Trade.* New York, 1963.

DeVoto, Bernard. *Across the Wide Missouri.* Boston, 1947.

Favor, Alpheus H. *Old Bill Williams, Mountain Man.* Norman, Oklahoma, 1962.

Ferris, Warren Angus. *Life in the Rocky Mountain,* ed. LeRoy R. Hafen, Denver, 1983.

Field, Matt. *Matt Field on the Santa Fe Trail,* ed. John E. Sunder. Norman, Oklahoma, 1960.

Field. *Prairie and Mountain Sketches,* ed. Kate L. Gregg and John Francis McDermott. Norman, Oklahoma, 1959.

Flint, Timothy. *The Shoshone Valley.* Two volumes. Cincinnati, 1830.

Garrard, Lewis Hector. *Wah-To-Yah and the Taos Trail.* Norman, Oklahoma, 1955.

Gowans, Fred R. *Rocky Mountain Rendezvous: A History of the Fur Trade Rendezvous 1825-1840.* Provo, Utah, 1975.

Hafen, LeRoy R., ed. *The Mountain Men and the Fur Trade of the Far West.* Ten volumes. Glendale, California, 1965-1972.

Hastings, Macdonald. *English Sporting Guns and Accessories.* London and Sydney, 1969. Hodge, Frederick Webb, ed. *Handbook of American Indians North of Mexico.* Washington, D.C., 1907.

Irving, Washington. *The Adventures of Captain Bonneville, U.S.A., in the Rocky Mountains and the Far West,* ed. Edgeley W. Todd. Norman, Oklahoma, 1961.

Jackson, Donald, and Mary Lee Spence, eds. *The Expedition of John Charles Frémont.* Urbana, Illinois, 1970.

Johansen, Dorothy O., ed. *Robert Newell's Memoranda.* Portland, Oregon. 1959.

Kennedy, William Clark. *Persimmon Hill: A Narrative of Old St. Louis and the Far West.* Norman, Oklahoma, 1948.

Kurz, Rudolph Friederich. *The Journal of Rudolph Friederick Kurz,* ed. J. N. B. Hewitt. Washington, D.C., 1937.

Lamar, Howard O., ed. *The Reader's Encyclopedia of the American West.* New York, 1977.

Larpenteur, Charles. *Forty Years a Fur Trader on the Upper Missouri: The Personal Narrative of Charles Larpenteur,* ed. Elliott Coues. New York, 1898.

Luttig, John C. *Journal of a Fur Trading Expedition, 1812-1813,* ed. Stella M. Drumm. New York, 1964.

McDermott, John Francis. *A Glossary of Mississippi Valley French: 1673-1850.* St. Louis, 1941.

McHugh, Tom. *The Time of the Buffalo.* New York, 1972. Magoffin, Susan Shelby. *Down the Santa Fe Trail and into Mexico: The Diary of Susan Shelby Magoffin, 1846-1847,* ed. Stella M. Drumm. New Haven, Connecticut, 1926.

Morgan, Dale L. *Jedediah Smith and the Opening of the West*. Indianapolis, 1953. Morgan, ed. *The Overland Diary of James Avery Pritchard from Kentucky to California in 1849*. Denver, 1959.

Morgan, ed. *The West of William H. Ashley*. Denver, 1964. Morgan and Eleanor Towles Harris, eds. *The Rocky Mountain Journals of William Marshall Anderson: The West in 1834*. San Marino, California, 1967.

Museum of the Fur Trade Quarterly, "Guitars for the Mountains," by the "Engages," p. 14-15, Volume 19, Number 4 (Winter, 1983).

Nasatir, Abraham P., ed. *Before Lewis and Clark: Documents, Illustrating the History of the Missouri: 1785-1804*. St. Louis, 1952.

Nash, Roderick. *Wilderness and the American Mind*. New Haven, Connecticut, 1973.

Parker, Samuel. *Journal of an Exploring Tour beyond the Rocky Mountains...in the Years 1835, '36, and '37*. Ithaca, New York, 1842.

Peters, DeWitt Clinton. *The Life and Adventures of Kit Carson: the Nestor of the Rocky Mountains*. New York, 1859.

Quaife, Milo Milton, ed. *Kit Carson's Autobiography*. Chicago, 1935.

Ross, Marvin C. *The West of Alfred Jacob Miller*. Revised edition. Norman, Oklahoma, 1968.

Russell, Osborne. *Journal of a Trapper*, ed. Aubrey L. Haines. Portland, Oregon, 1955.

Ruxton, George Frederick. *Life in the Far West*, ed. LeRoy R. Hafen. Norman, Oklahoma, 1951.

Smith, Henry Nash. *Virgin Land: The American West as Symbol and Myth*. Cambridge, Massachusetts, 1970.

Sprague, Marshall. *A Gallery of Dudes*. Boston, 1967.

[Stewart, William Drummond.] *Altowan: Or, Incidents of Life and Adventure in the Rocky Mountains. By an Amateur Traveler*, ed. J. Watson Webb. New York, 1846.

Swanton, John R. *Indian Tribes of North America*. Washington, D.C., 1952.

Taylor, Hugh A., ed. *Braves and Buffalo: Plains Indian Life in 1837*, illus. Alfred Jacob Miller. Toronto, 1973.

Thomas, Davis and Karin Ronnefeldt. *People of the First Man: Life among the Plains Indians in Their Final Days of Glory*. New York, 1976.

Thwaites, Reuben Gold, ed. *Original Journals of the Lewis and Clark Expedition: 1804-1806*. Eight volumes. New York, 1904.

Tobie, Harvey Elmer. *No Man Like Joe: The Life and Times of Joseph L. Meek*. Portland, Oregon, 1949.

Townsend, John Kirk. *Narrative of a Journey across the Rocky Mountains to the Columbia River*, in Reuben G. Thwaites, ed., *Early Western Travels, 1748-1846*. Cleveland, 1904.

Tyler, Ron, ed. *Alfred Jacob Miller: Artist on the Oregon Trail*. Fort Worth, 1982.

Victor, Frances Fuller. *The River of the West: The Adventures of Joe Meek*, ed. Winfred Blevins and Lee Nash. Two volumes. Missoula, Montana, 1983 and 1985.

Wagner, Henry R. and Charles L. Camp. *The Plains and Rockies: A Critical Bibliography of Exploration, Adventure and Travel in the American West, 1800-1865*, revised and enlarged by Robert H. Becker. San Francisco, 1982.

Wilhelm, Paul. *Travels in North America, 1822/1824*, ed. Savoie Lottinville. Norman, Oklahoma, 1973.

www.ingramcontent.com/pod-product-compliance
Lightning Source LLC
Chambersburg PA
CBHW011954150426
43198CB00020B/2927